Mastering

Modern World History

MACMILLAN MASTER SERIES

Accounting
Advanced English Language
Advanced Pure Mathematics
Arabic
Banking
Basic Management
Biology
British Politics
Business Administration
Business Communication
Business Law
C Programming
C++ Programming
Catering Theory
Chemistry
COBOL Programming
Communication
Databases
Economic and Social History
Economics
Electrical Engineering
Electronic and Electrical Calculations
Electronics
English as a Foreign Language
English Grammar
English Language
English Literature
French
French 2
German
German 2

Global Information Systems
Human Biology
Internet
Italian
Italian 2
Java
Manufacturing
Marketing
Mathematics
Mathematics for Electrical and
   Electronic Engineering
Microsoft Office
Modern British History
Modern European History
Modern World History
Pascal and Delphi Programming
Philosophy
Photography
Physics
Psychology
Science
Shakespeare
Social Welfare
Sociology
Spanish
Spanish 2
Statistics
Study Skills
Visual Basic
World Religions

Macmillan Master Series
Series Standing Order ISBN 0–333–69343–4
(outside North America only)

You can receive future titles in this series as they are published by placing a standing order.
Please contact your bookseller or, in case of difficulty, write to us at the address below with
your name and address, the title of the series and the ISBN quoted above.

Customer Services Department, Macmillan Distribution Ltd
Houndmills, Basingstoke, Hampshire RG21 6XS, England

Mastering

Modern World History

Third Edition

Norman Lowe

Foreword by Keith Foreman

MACMILLAN

First edition 1982
Reprinted 6 times
Second edition 1988
Reprinted 9 times
Third edition 1997

Published by
MACMILLAN PRESS LTD
Houndmills, Basingstoke, Hampshire RG21 6XS
and London
Companies and representatives
throughout the world

ISBN 0–333–68523–7

A catalogue record for this book is available
from the British Library.

This book is printed on paper suitable for recycling and
made from fully managed and sustained forest sources.

10   9   8   7   6   5   4   3   2
06   05   04   03   02   01   00   99   98

Printed and bound in Great Britain
by Biddles Ltd
Guildford and King's Lynn

Contents

List of figures

List of maps

List of tables

List of illustrations

Acknowledgements

The author and publishers would like to thank the following for permission to reproduce copyright material: The Guardian for the extract from an article on Chernobyl, *The Guardian*, 13.4.96; Hodder and Stoughton Educational for a table from John Laver, *Russia 1914–41*, 1991, p. 30; Institute of Contemporary British History for Tables 1–6 from Frank McDonough, 'Why Appeasement?', *Modern History Review*, April 1994; Macmillan Press Ltd for Figs 19.1, 19.2 from D. Harkness, *The Post-War World*, 1974, pp. 231, 232; John Murray (Publishers) Ltd for Figs 6.1, 10.1 from J. Watson, *Success in Modern World History Since 1945*, 1989, pp. 3, 150.

The following new photograph sources are acknowledged: Associated Press, 8.2, p. 153, 18.3, p. 367, 22.6, p. 478; Camera Press, 16.3, p. 333, 17.3, p. 353, 18.2, p. 361, 18.4, p. 365, 20.2, p. 405, 20.3, p. 407, 23.1, p. 489; Hulton Getty Picture Collection, 1.3, p. 13, 10.2, p. 190, 10.3, p. 191, 10.5, p. 203, 11.2, p. 231, 13.3, p. 280, 15.4, 312, 17.2, p. 353; International Planned Parenthood Assoc., 24.3, p. 506; Magnum (Thomas Hopner), 23.3, p. 497; Mansell Collection, 2.4, p. 34, 6.6, p. 114; Oxfam, 23.2, p. 493; Peter Newark's Western Americana, 19.1, p. 379, 19.3, p. 386, 19.5, p. 393, 19.6, p. 397; Popperfoto, 6.4, p. 110, 7.1, p. 124, 8.3, p. 159, 10.4, p. 194, 11.4, p. 236, 20.4, p. 410, 21.2, p. 438, 21.3, p. 438, 22.3, p. 473, 22.5, p. 474; Suddeutscher Verlag, 6.3, p. 110, 7.2, p. 133, 7.3, p. 135, 17.1, p. 347; Topham/Picture Point Collection, 7.5, p. 139, 22.1, p. 458, 22.2, p. 460; Ullstein Bilderdeinst, 1.2, p. 11; UN Information Services, 9.1, p. 165.

Every effort has been made to trace all the copyright-holders, but if any have been inadvertently overlooked, the author and publishers will be pleased to make the necessary arrangement at the earliest opportunity.

Foreword

I am pleased to write this foreword to Norman Lowe's *Modern World History*. It is a valuable addition to the growing list of books which cover this complex century, and to my mind it has a number of advantages. Mr Lowe's approach has been to cover the major topics of world history in a clear and concise style, following a consistent pattern in each chapter. After a general introduction, themes are developed in more detail with headings, key words and phrases underlined. Students will find the system of cross referencing easy to follow, while the problem-solving approach will be of considerable benefit to those taking examinations. Controversial issues are highlighted and discussed with refreshing clarity and fairness, admitting the fallibility of human judgement.

Mr Lowe's style is economical yet avoids the sterility of note form. It is lively and comprehensible, with major terms and concepts carefully explained. The text is supported by relevant maps and by sample examination questions including those involving stimulus material which are fast becoming a feature of the 'new' history. The bibliography will be of particular benefit to those who wish to develop themes in greater depth.

I believe that *Modern World History* will provide an excellent basic text for examinations at 16+ in schools and colleges, and will also be a first-class introduction for higher level study. Students taking General and Liberal Studies and the general reader will find its approach comprehensive and well signposted. Although it is written with the examination candidate in mind it is not narrowly conceived, dealing as it does with some of the topics of world history frequently omitted in other basic texts. One particular merit is its treatment of the post-1945 period to which ten chapters are devoted. Events of the very recent past, including, for instance, developments in Latin America, the crisis in Poland, the Russian occupation of Afghanistan and the policies of the Carter Administration are included.

As a teacher and examiner of modern world history over many years I can recommend this book. It has long been needed to fill a gap in the available literature.

KEITH FOREMAN
Warden
The Village College
Comberton
Cambridge

Preface to the third edition

Eight years have passed since I put the finishing touches to the Second Edition of this book, and much has happened during that time. Many important developments have taken place in world history – the collapse of communism in eastern Europe, the survival of communism in China, the end of white minority rule in South Africa, the Gulf War, more progress towards an Israeli–Palestinian peace, and many terrible civil wars – in Rwanda and Yugoslavia, to name but two examples. This new edition covers all these developments, and more besides. I have taken the opportunity of adding new material to all the chapters, taking account of the latest research and thinking, and I have grouped all the chapters on war and international relations together, and the chapters on communism together, and so on, in place of the chronological order of the first two editions. Rather than trying to deal with the internal affairs of as many countries as possible, I have aimed to take a more general 'world' view, covering:

- major conflicts and international relations;
- internal affairs of the major powers – USA, Russia/USSR and China;
- Europe as an entity – the European Community and communist unity in eastern Europe;
- important topics and events with an international significance, such as the rise and fall of fascism and communism, decolonization, and some typical problems in Africa;
- serious global problems like poverty and the North–South divide, pollution and population growth (in two new chapters, 23 and 24).

Inevitably though, given the sheer immensity of the history which has happened since 1900, I have had to be selective, and topics which some people may think important do not appear.

As before, the book aims to provide GCSE students with the basic core information which they will need: **it meets all the requirements of the revised, post-Dearing, Modern World History courses**. The questions have been rewritten yet again, with lots of new sources, to bring them into line with the most recent types of GCSE question. Attainment targets being tested and marks to be awarded are indicated. The larger format has allowed the inclusion of many more maps and illustrations. I hope also that the book will continue to serve as an introduction to the study of twentieth-century history for Advanced Level and first-year university students, and that it will be useful for the general reader who wants to find out how the world at the end of the twentieth century got into its present state. I hope too that general readers who have no intention of wasting their time answering the questions will nevertheless find the source material enlightening and stimulating.

I am grateful once again to my friends Glyn Jones of Bede College, Billingham, who read the new material and made many helpful suggestions, and Mark Bateman, Head of History at Nelson and Colne College, who helped me to compile the up-to-date further reading list and also to Suzannah Tipple of Macmillan Press for her encouragement, help and advice. I must thank my wife, Jane, who gave me invaluable help with maps, diagrams and illustrations, and who carefully read the entire typescript, smoothing out the roughest edges of my English style. Whatever errors and faults remain are entirely my own.

NORMAN LOWE

PART I

War and international relations

The world in 1914: outbreak of the First World War

1.1 Prologue

Under cover of darkness late on the night of 5 August 1914, five columns of German assault troops, which had entered Belgium two days earlier, were converging on the town of Liège, expecting little resistance. To their surprise they were halted by determined fire from the town's outlying forts. This was a setback for the Germans: control of Liège was essential before they could proceed with their main operation against France. They were forced to resort to siege tactics, using heavy howitzers. These fired shells up into the air and they plunged from a height of 12 000 feet to shatter the armour-plating of the forts. Strong though they were, these Belgian forts were not equipped to withstand such a battering for long; on 13 August the first one surrendered and three days later Liège was under German control. This was the first major engagement of the First World War, that horrifying conflict of monumental proportions which was to mark the beginnng of a new era in European and world history.

1.2 The world in 1914

(a) *Europe still dominated the rest of the world in 1914*

Most of the decisions which shaped the fate of the world were taken in the capitals of Europe. Germany was the leading power in Europe both militarily and economically. She had overtaken Britain in the production of pig-iron and steel, though not quite in coal, while France, Belgium, Italy and Austria–Hungary (known as the Habsburg Empire) were well behind. Russian industry was expanding rapidly but had been so backward to begin with that she could not seriously challenge Germany and Britain. But it was outside Europe that the most spectacular industrial progress had been made over the previous forty years. In 1914 the USA produced more coal, pig-iron and steel than either Germany or Britain and now ranked as a world power. Japan too had modernized rapidly and was a power to be reckoned with after her defeat of Russia in the Russo-Japanese War of 1904–5.

(b) *The political systems of these world powers varied widely*

The USA, Britain and France had *democratic forms of government*. This means that they each had a parliament consisting of representatives elected by the people, and these parliaments had an important say in running the country. Some systems were not as democratic as they seemed: Germany had an elected lower house of parliament (Reichstag), but real power lay with the Chancellor (a sort of Prime Minister) and the Kaiser (emperor). Italy was a monarchy with an elected parliament, but the franchise (right to vote) was limited to wealthy people. Japan had an elected lower house, but here too the franchise was restricted, and the emperor and the privy council held most of the power. The governments in Russia and Austria–Hungary were very different from the democracy of the west. The tsar (emperor) of Russia and the emperor of Austria (who was also king of Hungary) were *autocratic rulers*. This means that although parliaments existed, they could only advise the rulers; if they felt like it, the rulers could ignore the parliaments and do exactly as they wished.

(c) *Imperial expansion after 1880*

The European powers had taken part in a great burst of imperialist expansion in the years after 1880. *Imperialism* is the building up of an empire by seizing territory overseas. Most of Africa was taken over by the European states in what became known as the Scramble for Africa; the idea behind it was mainly to get control of new markets and new sources of raw materials. There was also intervention in the crumbling Chinese empire; the European powers, the USA and Japan all at different times forced the helpless Chinese to grant trading concessions. Exasperation with the incompetence of their government caused the Chinese to overthrow the ancient Manchu dynasty and set up a republic (1911).

(d) *Europe had divided itself into two alliance systems*

The Triple Alliance
Germany
Austria–Hungary
Italy

The Triple Entente
Britain
France
Russia

In addition, Japan and Britain had signed an alliance in 1902. Friction between the two main groups (sometimes called 'the armed camps') had brought Europe to the verge of war several times since 1900 (Map 1.1).

(e) *Causes of friction*

There were many causes of friction which threatened to upset the peace of Europe:

- naval rivalry between Britain and Germany;
- French resentment at the loss of Alsace–Lorraine to Germany at the end of the Franco-Prussian War (1871);
- the Germans accused Britain, Russia and France of trying to 'encircle' them;
- the Russians were suspicious of Austrian ambitions in the Balkans;
- Serbian *nationalism* (the desire to free your nation from control by people of another nationality) was probably the most dangerous cause of friction. Serbia had ambitions of uniting all Serbs and Croats, many of whom lived inside the Habsburg Empire, into a South Slav kingdom (Yugoslavia). This would involve taking certain areas from Austria–Hungary, and threatened to cause the collapse of the ramshackle

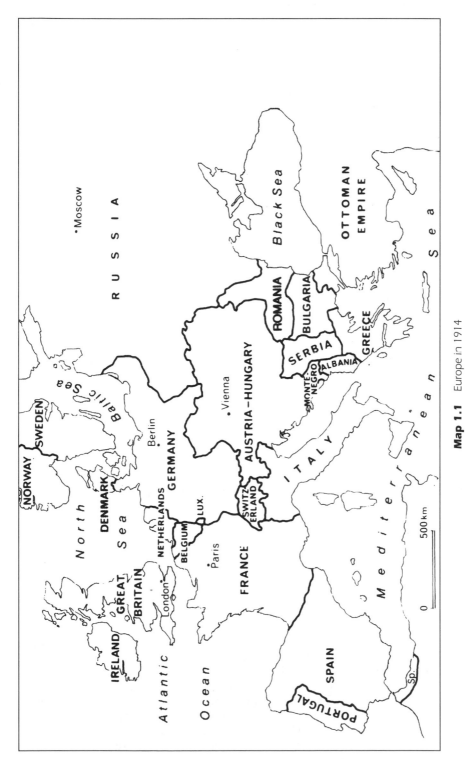

Map 1.1 Europe in 1914

Source: Harriet Ward, *World Powers in the Twentieth Century* (Heinemann, 1978) p. xvi

Map 1.2   Peoples of the Habsburg Empire

Source: Neil DeMarco, *The World This Century* (Bell & Hyman) p. 28

Habsburg Empire which contained people of many different nationalities (Map 1.2). There were Germans, Hungarians, Magyars, Czechs, Slovaks, Italians, Poles, Romanians and Slovenes, as well as Serbs and Croats. If the Serbs and Croats left the fold, many of the others would demand their independence as well, and the Habsburg Empire would break up. Consequently many Austrians were keen for what they called a 'preventive war' to destroy Serbia before she became strong enough to destroy Austria–Hungary.

Arising from all these resentments and tensions came a series of events which culminated in the outbreak of war in late July 1914.

1.3   Events leading up to the outbreak of war

(a) *The Moroccan Crisis (1905–6)*

This was an attempt by the Germans to test the recently signed Anglo-French 'Entente Cordiale' (1904) with its understanding that France would recognize Britain's position in Egypt in return for British approval of a possible French takeover of Morocco; this was one of the few remaining areas of Africa not controlled by a European power. The Germans announced that they would assist the Sultan of Morocco to maintain his country's independence, and demanded an international conference to discuss its future. A conference was duly held at Algeciras in southern Spain (January 1906). The British believed that if the Germans had their way, it would be an important step on the road to German diplomatic domination. The Germans did not take the 'Entente Cordiale' seriously because there was a long history of hostility between Britain and France. But to the amazement of the Germans, Britain, Russia, Italy and Spain supported the French demand to control the Moroccan bank and police. This was a serious diplomatic defeat for Germany, which realized that the new line-up of Britain and France was a force to be reckoned with, especially as the crisis was soon followed by Anglo-French 'military conversations'.

Time chart of main events

Europe divides into two armed camps:

1882	Triple Alliance of Germany, Austria–Hungary and Italy
1894	France and Russia sign alliance
1904	Britain and France sign 'Entente Cordiale' (friendly 'getting-together')
1907	Britain and Russia sign agreement

Other important events

1897	Admiral Tirpitz's Navy Law – Germany intends to build up fleet
1902	Britain and Japan sign alliance
1904–5	Russo-Japanese War, won by Japan
1905–6	Moroccan Crisis
1906	Britain builds first 'Dreadnought' battleship
1908	Bosnia Crisis
1911	Agadir Crisis
1912	First Balkan War
1913	Second Balkan War
1914	28 June	Archduke Franz Ferdinand assassinated in Sarajevo
	28 July	Austria–Hungary declares war on Serbia
	29 July	Russia orders general mobilization of troops
	1 August	Germany declares war on Russia
	3 August	Germany declares war on France
	4 August	Britain enters war
	6 August	Austria–Hungary declares war on Russia

(b) *The British agreement with Russia (1907)*

This was seen by the Germans as another hostile move. In fact it was a logical step given that in 1894 Russia had signed an alliance with France, Britain's partner in the 'Entente Cordiale'. For years the British had viewed Russia as a major threat to their interests in the Far East and India, but recently the situation had changed. Russia's defeat by Japan (1904–5) had weakened her considerably, and she no longer seemed so much of a threat. The Russians were keen to end the long-standing rivalry and anxious to attract British investment for their industrial modernization programme. The agreement therefore settled their remaining differences. It was not a military alliance and not necessarily an anti-German move, but the Germans saw it as confirmation of their fears that Britain, France and Russia were planning to 'encircle' them.

(c) *The Bosnia Crisis (1908)*

This heightened the tension. The Austrians, taking advantage of a revolution in

Turkey, annexed (took over) the Turkish province of Bosnia. This was a deliberate blow at the neighbouring state of Serbia, which had also been hoping to take Bosnia because it contained about 3 million Serbs among its mixed population of Serbs, Croats and Muslims. The Serbs appealed for help to their fellow Slavs, the Russians, who called for a European conference, expecting French and British support. When it became clear that Germany would support Austria in the event of war, the French drew back, unwilling to become involved in a war in the Balkans. The British, anxious to avoid a breach with Germany, did no more than protest to Austria–Hungary. The Russians, still smarting from their defeat by Japan, dared not risk another war without the support of their allies. There was to be no help for Serbia; no conference took place, and Austria kept Bosnia. It was a triumph for the Austro-German alliance, *but it had unfortunate results*:

● Serbia remained bitterly hostile to Austria, and it was this quarrel which led to the outbreak of war; and
● the Russians were determined to avoid any further humiliation and embarked on a massive military build-up. They intended to be prepared if Serbia should ever appeal for help again.

(d) *The Agadir Crisis (1911)*

This crisis was a further development in the Morocco situation. French troops occupied Fez, the Moroccan capital, to put down a rebellion against the Sultan. It looked as if the French were about to annexe Morocco. The Germans sent a gunboat, the *Panther*, to the Moroccan port of Agadir, hoping to pressurize the French into giving Germany compensation, perhaps the French Congo. The British were worried in case the Germans acquired Agadir, which could be used as a naval base from which to threaten Britain's trade routes. In order to strengthen French resistance, Lloyd George (Britain's Chancellor of the Exchequer) used a speech which he was due to make at the Lord Mayor of London's banquet at the Mansion House, to warn the Germans off. He said that Britain would not stand by and be taken advantage of 'where her interests were vitally affected'. The French stood firm, making no major concessions, and eventually the German gunboat was removed. The Germans agreed to recognize the French protectorate (the right to 'protect' the country from foreign intervention) over Morocco in return for two strips of territory in the French Congo. This was seen as a triumph for the Entente powers, but in Germany public opinion became intensely anti-British, especially as the British were drawing slowly ahead in the 'naval race'. At the end of 1911 they had built eight of the new and more powerful 'Dreadnought' type battleships, compared with Germany's four.

(e) *The First Balkan War (1912)*

This war began when Serbia, Greece, Montenegro and Bulgaria (calling themselves the Balkan League) attacked Turkey, capturing most of her remaining territory in Europe. Together with the German government, Sir Edward Grey, the British Foreign Secretary, arranged a peace conference in London. He was anxious to avoid the conflict spreading, and also to demonstrate that Britain and Germany could still work together. The resulting settlement divided up the former Turkish lands among the Balkan states. However, the Serbs were not happy with their gains: they wanted Albania, which would give them an outlet to the sea, but the Austrians, with German and British support, insisted that Albania should become an independent state. This was a deliberate Austrian move to prevent Serbia becoming more powerful.

Map 1.3 The Balkans in 1913 showing changes of territory from the Balkan wars (1912–13)

(f) *The Second Balkan War (1913)*

The Second Balkan War began because the Bulgarians were dissatisfied with the peace settlement. They were hoping for Macedonia, but most of it was given to Serbia. Bulgaria therefore attacked Serbia, but their plan misfired when Greece, Romania and Turkey rallied to support Serbia. The Bulgarians were defeated and, by the Treaty of Bucharest (1913), they forfeited most of their gains from the first war. It seemed that Anglo-German influence had prevented an escalation of the war by restraining the Austrians, who were itching to support Bulgaria and attack Serbia. In reality though, *the consequences of the Balkan Wars were serious*:

- Serbia had been strengthened and was determined to stir up trouble among the Serbs and Croats living inside Austria–Hungary;
- the Austrians were equally determined to put an end to Serbia's ambitions;
- the Germans took Grey's willingness to co-operate as a sign that Britain was prepared to be detached from France and Russia.

(g) *The assassination of the Austrian Archduke Franz Ferdinand*

This event, which took place in Sarajevo on 28 June 1914, was what sparked off the war (Illus. 1.1). The Archduke, nephew and heir to the Emperor Franz Josef, was paying an official visit to Sarajevo, the Bosnian capital, when he and his wife were shot dead by a Serb terrorist, Gavrilo Princip (Illus. 1.2). The Austrians blamed the Serb government and sent a stiff ultimatum. The Serbs accepted most of the points in it, but the Austrians, with the promise of German support, were determined to use the incident as an excuse for war. On 28 July Austria–Hungary declared war on Serbia. The Russians, anxious not to let the Serbs down again, ordered a general mobilization (29 July). The German government demanded that this should be cancelled (31 July), and when the Russians failed to comply, Germany declared war on Russia (1 August) and on France (3 August). When German troops entered Belgium on their way to invade France, Britain (who in 1839 had promised to defend Belgian neutrality) demanded their withdrawal. When this demand was ignored, Britain entered the war (4 August). Austria–Hungary declared war on Russia on 6 August. Other countries joined later.

The war was to have profound effects on the future of the world. Germany was soon to be displaced, for a time at least, from her mastery of Europe, and Europe never quite regained its dominant position in the world.

Illus. 1.1 Archduke Franz Ferdinand and his wife, shortly before their assassination in Sarajevo

Illus. 1.2   Arrest of Gavrilo Princip moments after shooting Franz Ferdinand and his wife

1.4   What caused the war, and who was to blame?

It is difficult to analyse why the assassination in Sarajevo developed into a world war, and even now historians cannot agree. Some blame Austria for being the first aggressor by declaring war on Serbia; some blame the Russians because they were the first to order full mobilization; some blame Germany for supporting Austria, and others blame Britain for not making it clear that she would definitely support France. The theory is that if the Germans had known this, they would not have declared war on France, and the fighting could have been restricted to eastern Europe.

The point which is beyond dispute is that the quarrel between Austria–Hungary and Serbia sparked off the outbreak of war. The quarrel had become increasingly more explosive since 1908, and the Austrians seized on the assassination as the excuse for a preventive war with Serbia. They genuinely felt that if Serb and Slav nationalist ambitions for a state of Yugoslavia were achieved, it would cause the collapse of the Habsburg Empire; Serbia must be curbed. In fairness, they probably hoped the war would remain localized like the Balkan Wars. The Austro-Serb quarrel explains the outbreak of the war, but not why it became a world war. *Here are some of the reasons which have been suggested for the escalation of the war.*

(a)   *The alliance system or 'armed camps' made war inevitable*

American diplomat and historian George Kennan believed that once the 1894 alliance had been signed between France and Russia, the fate of Europe was sealed. As suspicions mounted between the two groups, Russia and Germany got themselves into situations which they could not get out of without suffering further humiliation; war was the only way out. However, many historians think this explanation is not convincing; there had been many crises since 1904, and none of them had led to a major war. In fact, *there was nothing binding about these alliances.* France had not supported Russia when she protested at the Austrian annexation of Bosnia; Austria took no interest in Germany's unsuccessful attempts to prevent France from taking over Morocco (Morocco and Agadir Crises, 1906 and 1911); Germany had restrained Austria from attacking Serbia during the Second Balkan War. Italy, though a member of the Triple Alliance, was on good terms with France and Britain, and entered the war *against* Germany in 1915. No power actually declared war because of an alliance treaty.

(b) *Colonial rivalry in Africa and the Far East*

Again, this theory is not convincing: although there had certainly been disputes, they had always been sorted out without war. In early July 1914 Anglo-German relations were good: an agreement favourable to Germany had just been reached over a possible partition of Portuguese colonies in Africa. However, there was one side-effect of colonial rivalry which did cause dangerous friction – this was naval rivalry.

(c) *The naval race between Britain and Germany*

Starting with Admiral Tirpitz's Navy Law of 1897, the growth of the German fleet probably did not worry the British too much at first because they had an enormous lead. The introduction of the powerful British 'Dreadnought' battleship in 1906 changed all this because it made all other battleships obsolete. This meant that the Germans could begin building 'Dreadnoughts' on equal terms with Britain. The resulting naval race was the main bone of contention between the two right up to 1914. According to Winston Churchill though, in the spring and summer of 1914 naval rivalry had ceased to be a cause of friction, because 'it was certain that we [Britain] could not be overtaken as far as capital ships were concerned'.

(d) *Economic rivalry*

It has been argued that the desire for economic mastery of the world caused German businessmen and capitalists to want war with Britain, who still owned about half the world's tonnage of merchant ships in 1914. Marxist historians support this theory because *it puts the blame for the war on the capitalist system.* Opponents of the theory point out that Germany was already well on the way to economic victory; one leading German industrialist remarked in 1913: 'Give us three or four more years of peace and Germany will be the unchallenged economic master of Europe'.

(e) *Russia made war more likely by backing Serbia*

This probably made Serbia more reckless in her anti-Austrian policy than she might otherwise have been. Russia was the first to order a general mobilization, which provoked Germany to mobilize. The Russians were worried about the situation in the Balkans, where both Bulgaria and Turkey were under German influence. This would enable Germany and Austria to control the Dardanelles, the outlet from the Black Sea and the main Russian trade route, and Russian trade could be strangled (this happened to some extent during the war). Thus Russia felt threatened, and once Austria declared war on Serbia, saw it as a struggle for survival. The Russians must also have felt that their prestige as leader of the Slavs would suffer if they failed to support Serbia. Possibly the government saw the war as a good idea to divert attention away from domestic problems. Perhaps the blame lies more with the Austrians: though they must have hoped for Russian neutrality, they ought to have realized how difficult it would be for Russia to stay neutral in the circumstances.

(f) *German backing for Austria was crucially important*

It is significant that in 1913 Germany restrained the Austrians from declaring war on Serbia, but in 1914 egged them on; the Kaiser sent them a telegram urging them to attack Serbia and promising German help without any conditions attached. This was like giving the Austrians a blank cheque to do whatever they wanted. The important question is: *why did German policy towards Austria–Hungary change?* This question has caused great controversy among historians, and three different answers have been suggested:

1   After the war, when the Germans had been defeated, the Versailles Treaty imposed a harsh peace settlement on Germany. The victorious powers felt the need to justify this by putting all the blame for the war on Germany (see Section 2.8). At the time, most non-German historians went along with this, though German historians were naturally not happy with this interpretation. After a few years, opinion began to move away from blaming solely Germany and accepted that other powers should take some of the blame. Then in 1961 a German historian, Fritz Fischer, caused a sensation by suggesting that Germany should, after all, take most of the blame, because they risked a major war by sending the 'blank cheque' to Austria–Hungary. He claimed that Germany deliberately planned for, and provoked war with Russia, Britain and France in order to make Germany the dominant power in the world, both economically and politically, and also as a way of dealing with domestic tensions. In the elections of 1912, the German Socialist Party (SPD) won over a third of the seats in the Reichstag (lower house of parliament), making it the largest single party. Then in January 1914 the Reichstag passed a vote of no confidence in the Chancellor, Bethmann-Hollweg, but he remained in office because the Kaiser had the final say. Obviously a major clash was on the way between the Reichstag, which wanted more power, and the Kaiser and Chancellor, who were determined to resist change. A victorious war seemed a good way of keeping people's minds off the political problems, and keeping power in the hands of the Kaiser and aristocracy.

Illus. 1.3   Kaiser Wilhelm II and General von Moltke

Fischer based his theory partly on evidence from the diary of Admiral von Müller, who wrote about a 'war council' held on 8 December 1912; at this meeting, Moltke (the German Commander-in-Chief) said 'war the sooner the better'. Another piece of evidence was a note by von Jagow, who was German Foreign Minister in 1914 (see question 3, Sources B and C, at the end of the chapter). Fischer's claims made him unpopular with West German historians, and another German, H.W. Koch, dismissed his theory, pointing out that nothing came of the 'war council'. However, historians in Communist East Germany supported Fischer because his theory laid the blame on the capitalist system which they opposed.

2   Other historians argue that Germany wanted war because she felt encircled and threatened by British naval power and by the massive Russian military expansion. The German generals decided that a 'preventive' war, *a war for survival*, was necessary, and that it must take place before the end of 1914. They believed that after 1914 Russia would be too strong.

3   Some historians reject both answers 1 and 2 and suggest that Germany did not want a major war at all; the Kaiser Wilhelm II and Chancellor Bethmann-Hollweg believed a strong line in support of Austria would *frighten the Russians into remaining neutral* – a tragic miscalculation, if true.

(g) *The mobilization plans of the great powers*

These accelerated the tempo of events and reduced almost to nil the time available for negotiation. The German *Schlieffen Plan*, first approved in 1905 and modified by Moltke (Illus. 1.3) in 1911, assumed that France would automatically join Russia; the bulk of German forces were to be sent by train to the Belgian frontier, and through Belgium to attack France, which would be knocked out in six weeks. German forces would then be switched rapidly across to face Russia, whose mobilization was expected to be slow. Once Moltke knew that Russia had ordered a general mobilization, he demanded immediate German mobilization so that the plan could be put into operation as soon as possible. However, Russian mobilization did not necessarily mean war – their troops could be halted at the frontiers; unfortunately the Schlieffen Plan, which depended on the rapid capture of Liège in Belgium, involved the first aggressive act outside the Balkans when German troops entered Belgium on 4 August. Almost at the last minute the Kaiser and Bethmann tried to avoid war and urged the Austrians to negotiate with Serbia (30 July), which perhaps supports point 3 above. Wilhelm suggested a partial mobilization against Russia only, instead of the full plan; he hoped that Britain would remain neutral if Germany refrained from attacking France. But Moltke, scared of being left at the post by the Russians and French, insisted on the full Schlieffen Plan; he said there was no time to change all the railway timetables to send the troop trains to Russia instead of to Belgium. It looks as though *the generals had taken over control of affairs from the politicians*. It also suggests that a British announcement on 31 July of her intention to support France would have made no difference to Germany: it was the Schlieffen Plan or nothing, even though Germany at that point had no specific quarrel with France.

(h) *A 'tragedy of miscalculation'*

Another interpretation was put forward by Australian historian L.C.F. Turner. Maybe the Germans did not deliberately provoke war; it was caused by 'a tragedy of miscalculation'. Most of the leading rulers and politicians seemed to be incompetent and made bad mistakes:

● the Austrians miscalculated by thinking that Russia would not support Serbia;

- Germany made a crucial mistake by promising to support Austria with no conditions attached; therefore the Germans were certainly guilty, as were the Austrians, because they risked a major war;
- politicians in Russia and Germany miscalculated by assuming that mobilization would not necessarily mean war; and
- generals, especially Moltke, miscalculated by sticking rigidly to their plans in the belief that this would bring a quick and decisive victory.

No wonder Bethmann, when asked how it all began, raised his arms to heaven and replied: 'Oh – if I only knew!'

In conclusion, it has to be said that at the present time, the majority of historians, including many Germans, accept Fritz Fischer's theory as the most convincing one: that the outbreak of war was deliberately provoked by Germany's leaders.

Questions

1   Section 1.4 has described a number of possible causes which have been suggested for the First World War.

   (a)   Which of these causes do you think were:

   - long-term causes?
   - short-term causes?

Illus. 1.4   Hitler celebrates the outbreak of the First World War
This fascinating picture shows Hitler in the crowd which heard the declaration of war in Munich on 2 August 1914

- political causes?
- military causes?
- economic causes?
- nationalistic causes?   1.4b–5b

(b) What links can you find between the various causes?   1.4b–7b

(c) Place the causes in a list with the ones you think most important at the top and the least important at the bottom. Explain why you have chosen this order.   1.6b–9b

(d) Why do you think there has been so much disagreement among historians about the causes of the First World War?   2.6–8

2   *Who was to blame for the First World War?* Study Sources A–F and then answer the questions which follow.

Source A

Note to the Cabinet from the Prime Minister, Lord Salisbury, in May 1901

The British government cannot undertake to declare war, for any purpose, unless it is a purpose of which the people of this country would approve ... I do not see how we could invite nations to rely upon our help in a struggle which must be formidable, where we have no means whatever of knowing what may be the attitude of our people in circumstances which cannot be foreseen.

Source B

An extract from an interview with Kaiser Wilhelm II, in the Daily Telegraph, *28 October 1908*

You English are like mad bulls; you see red everywhere! What on earth has come over you, that you should heap on us such suspicion? What can I do more? I have always stood forth as the friend of England.

Source C

From a speech made in the German Reichstag, November 1911, at the end of the Agadir Crisis

Now we know where our enemy stands. Like a flash of lightning in the night, these events have shown the German people where its enemy is. ... When the hour of decision comes we are prepared for sacrifices, both of blood and of treasure.

Source: M. Balfour, *The Kaiser* (Cresset, 1964)

Source D

Lenin in 1911

A war with Austria would be a splendid thing for the revolution. But the chances are small that Franz Josef and Nicholas will give us such a treat.

Source: E.H. Carr, *The Bolshevik Revolution* (Macmillan, 1951, vol. I)

The cartoon 'A Chain of Friendship' (Figure 1.1) published in an American newspaper, the Brooklyn Eagle, July 1914. Britain is at the end of the line (right)

Source F

Telegram from Tsar Nicholas II of Russia to George V of England, 2 August 1914

Ever since the presentation of the Austrian ultimatum at Belgrade, Russia has devoted all her efforts to some peaceful solution of the questions raised by Austria's actions. The effect of this action would have been to upset the balance of power in the Balkans which is of such vital interest to my Empire. Every proposal put forward was rejected by Germany and Austria.

(a) Explain briefly how the situation shown in Source E had arisen during the twenty years before 1914.　　　　　　　1.4b–7b, 4c–7c　4 marks

(b) According to Source F, why was the Tsar so worried about 'Austria's actions'?　　　　　　　　　　　　　　　1.6c–7c　2 marks

(c) Using information from Sources B and C, describe Germany's attitude towards Britain.　　　　　　　　　　　1.6c–8c　4 marks

(d) From the evidence of Sources A and E, how did the British attitude to war change between 1901 and 1914?　　　1.4a, 6c–7c, 3.4　3 marks

(e) Using the Sources and Sections 1.3 and 1.4, explain why this change took place.　　　　　　　　　　　　1.4b, 7b, 9a, 3.4　5 marks

(f) 'Nobody really wanted war in 1914'. How useful are these sources in helping you to decide whether this statement is true or not?　1.6c–8c, 3.4–6　6 marks

(g) How reliable do you think each of these sources is for historians trying to decide who was to blame for the war?　　　　3.7–8　6 marks

Total 30 marks

3　*Germany and the origins of the First World War* – study the sources A–E below and then answer the questions which follow.

A lecture given in October 1913 by an Englishman, J.A. Cramb, who had lived in Germany for many years

The German answer to all our talk about the limitation of armaments is: Germany shall increase to the utmost of her power irrespective of any proposals made to her by England or by Russia or by any other State upon this earth ... I have lived among Germans and I have been impressed by the splendour of that movement which through the centuries has brought Germany to her position today. But with the best will in the world I can see no solution to the present collision of ideals but a tragic one. England desires peace and will never make war on Germany. But how can the youth in Germany, that nation great in war, accept the world-predominance of England? The outcome is certain and speedy. It is war.

Source B

The diary of Admiral von Muller, head of the Kaiser's naval cabinet, 8 December 1912 (meeting with the Kaiser and top military and naval personnel)

General von Moltke [Chief of German General Staff] said: I believe war is unavoidable; war the sooner the better. But we ought to do more through the press to prepare the popularity of a war against Russia. The Kaiser supported this. Tirpitz [Naval Minister] said that the navy would prefer to see the postponement of the great fight for one and a half years. Moltke says the navy would not be ready even then and the army would get into an increasingly unfavourable position, for the enemies were arming more strongly than we. That was the end of the conference; the result amounted to almost nothing.

Source C

Report of a conversation held in May or June 1914, written from memory by Gottlieb von Jagow, after Germany's defeat in the war. *In 1914 Jagow was the German Foreign Secretary.*

On 20 May and 3 June 1914 our Majesties gave lunches in honour of the birthdays of the Emperor of Russia and the King of England. On one of these occasions – I cannot remember which – Moltke said he would like to discuss some matters with me. In his opinion there was no alternative to making preventive war in order to defeat the enemy while we still had a chance of victory. I replied that I was not prepared to cause a preventive war and I pointed out that the Kaiser, who wanted to preserve peace, would always try to avoid war and would only agree to fight if our enemies forced war upon us. After my rejection, Moltke did not insist further. When war did break out, unexpectedly and not desired by us, Moltke was very nervous and obviously suffering from strong depression.

Source: Sources A, B and C are quoted in J.C.G. Röhl, *From Bismarck to Hitler*, Longman, 1970, extracts

Naval statistics

Table 2.1 Relative strengths of Germany and Britain in battleships and Dreadnoughts, 1907–11

| Year | Battleships | | | | Dreadnoughts | | | |
| | Less than 15 yrs | | Under construction | | Completed | | Under construction | |
	GB	G	GB	G	GB	G	GB	G
1907	47	21	5	8	1	0	3	4
1908	40	21	8	9	1	0	6	7
1909	43	22	6	10	2	0	6	10
1910	45	23	9	8	5	2	9	8
1911	43	24	10	9	8	4	10	9

Table 2.2 Fleet sizes, 4 August 1914 (Figures in brackets indicate ships under construction)

	Germany	Great Britain
Battleships	33 (+7)	55 (+11)
Battlecruisers	3 (+3)	7 (+3)
Cruisers	9	51
Light cruisers etc	45 (+4)	77 (+9)
Destroyers	123 (+9)	191 (+38)
Torpedo ships	80	137 (+1)
Submarines	23 (+15)	64 (+22)
Dreadnoughts	13	20

Source: R. Wolfson, *Years of Change* (Arnold, 1978)

A British cartoon (Figure 1.2) from Punch, *12 August 1914*

BRAVO, BELGIUM!

(a) How does Source A show that the writer had mixed feelings about Germany?

1.6c   4 marks

(b) Why do you think he had these mixed views about Germany?

1.7c–8c   2 marks

(c) Does the cartoon in Source E give a good impression of Britain's attitude towards Germany? Explain your answer.   1.4c–9c   4 marks

(d) In what ways and to what extent does Source D support Moltke's statement in Source B that 'the enemies were arming more strongly than we'.

3.3–4   5 marks

(e) Using the sources and the information in Section 1.4, explain why there has been so much disagreement among historians about how far Germany was to blame for the First World War.   2.4–10, 3.5–10   10 marks

Total: 25 marks

2 The First World War and its aftermath

Summary of events

The two opposing sides in the war were:

The Allies or Entente Powers

Britain
France
Russia (left December 1917)
Italy (entered May 1915)
Serbia
Belgium
Romania (entered August 1916)
USA (entered April 1917)

The Central Powers

Germany
Austria–Hungary
Turkey (entered November 1914)
Bulgaria (entered October 1915)

The war turned out to be quite different from what most people had anticipated. It was widely expected to be a short, decisive affair, like other recent European wars; this is why Moltke was so worried about being left at the post when it came to mobilization. However, the Schlieffen Plan failed to achieve the rapid defeat of France. Although the Germans penetrated deeply, Paris did not fall, and *stalemate quickly developed on the western front*, with all hope of a short war gone. Both sides dug themselves in and spent the next four years attacking and defending lines of trenches.

   In eastern Europe there was more movement, with early Russian successes against the Austrians, who constantly had to be helped out by the Germans, causing friction between the two allies. But by December 1917 the Germans had captured Poland (Russian territory) and forced the defeated Russians out of the war. Britain, suffering heavy losses of merchant ships through submarine attacks, and France, whose armies were paralysed by mutiny, seemed on the verge of defeat. Gradually the tide turned; the Allies, helped by the entry of the USA in April 1917, wore down the Germans, whose last despairing attempt at a decisive breakthrough in France failed in the spring of 1918. The success of the British navy in blockading German ports and defeating the submarine threat by defending convoys of merchant ships, was also telling on the

Germans. By the late summer of 1918 they were nearing exhaustion. *An armistice (ceasefire) was signed on 11 November 1918*, though Germany itself had hardly been invaded. A controversial peace settlement was signed at Versailles the following year.

2.1 1914

(a) *The western front*

On the western front the Schlieffen Plan was held up by unexpectedly strong Belgian resistance; it took the Germans over two weeks to capture Brussels, the Belgian capital. This was an important delay because it gave the British time to organize themselves, and left the Channel ports free, enabling the British Expeditionary Force to land. Instead of sweeping round in a wide arc, capturing the Channel ports and approaching Paris from the west (as the Schlieffen Plan intended), the Germans found themselves making straight for Paris, just east of the city. They penetrated to within twenty miles of Paris and the French government withdrew to Bordeaux; but the nearer they got to Paris, the more the German impetus slowed up. There were problems in keeping the armies supplies with food and ammunition, and the troops became exhausted by the long marches in the August heat. In September the faltering Germans were attacked by the French under Joffre in the *Battle of the Marne* (see Map 2.1); they were driven back to the River Aisne, where they were able to dig trenches. *This battle was vitally important; some historians call it one of the most decisive battles in modern history*:

● it ruined the Schlieffen Plan once and for all: France would not be knocked out in six weeks, and all hopes of a short war were dashed;

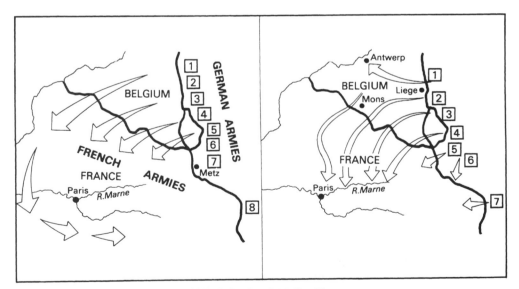

Map 2.1   The Schlieffen Plan

The Schlieffen Plan intended that the German right wing would move swiftly through Belgium to the coast, capture the Channel ports, and then sweep round in a wide arc to the west and south of Paris, almost surrounding the French armies. In practice, the Plan failed to work out. The Germans were held up by strong Belgian resistance; they failed to capture the Channel ports, failed to outflank the French armies, and were halted at the First Battle of the Marne.

- the Germans would have to face full-scale war on two fronts, which they had never intended;
- the war of movement was over – the trench lines eventually stretched from the Alps to the Channel coast (see Map 2.2); and
- there was time for the British navy to bring its crippling blockade to bear on Germany's ports.

The other important event of 1914 was that though the Germans took Antwerp, the British Expeditionary Force held grimly on to Ypres; this probably saved the other Channel ports so that more British troops could be landed and kept supplied.

(b) *The eastern front*

On the eastern front the Russians, having mobilized more quickly than the Germans expected, made the mistake of invading both Austria and Germany at the same time. Though they were successful against Austria, occupying the province of Galicia, the Germans brought Hindenburg out of retirement and defeated the Russians twice, at *Tannenburg* (August) and *the Masurian Lakes* (September), driving them out of Germany. *These battles were important*: the Russians lost vast amounts of equipment and ammunition which had taken them years to build up. Although they had six and a quarter million men mobilized by the end of 1914, a third of them were without rifles. The Russians never recovered from this setback, whereas German self-confidence was boosted. When Turkey entered the war, the outlook for Russia was bleak, since Turkey could cut her main supply and trade route through the Dardanelles. One bright spot for the Allies was that the Serbs drove out an Austrian invasion in fine style at the end of 1914, and Austrian morale was at rock bottom.

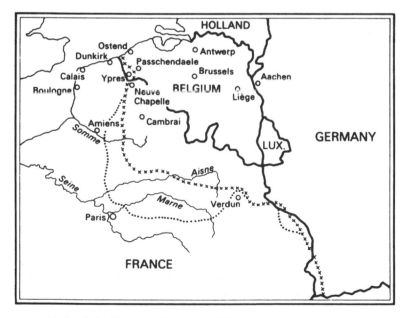

······· Limit of the German advance in 1914

×××××× The trench line for most of the war

Map 2.2   The Western Front

Map 2.3 Europe at War

2.2 1915

(a) *The west*

In the west the stalemate continued, though several attempts were made to break the trench line. The British tried at Neuve Chapelle and Loos, the French in Champagne; the Germans attacked again at Ypres. These, like all attacks on the western front until 1918, failed. *The difficulties of trench warfare were always the same*:

- there was barbed wire in no man's land between the two lines of opposing trenches which the attacking side tried to clear away by a massive artillery bombardment – but this removed any chance of a quick surprise attack, since the enemy always had plenty of warning;
- reconnaissance aircraft and observation balloons could spot concentrations of troops on the roads leading up to the trenches;
- trenches were difficult to capture because the increased fire-power provided by magazine rifles and machine-guns made frontal attacks suicidal and meant that cavalry were useless;
- even when a trench line was breached, advance was difficult because the ground had been churned up by the artillery barrage and there was more deadly machine-gun fire to contend with;
- any ground won was difficult to defend, since it usually formed what was called a

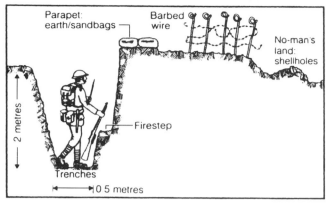

Figure 2.1   Trench cross-section

Source: Barry Bates, *The First World War* (Blackwell), p. 14

salient – a bulge in the trench line. The sides, or flanks of these salients were vulnerable to attack, and troops could be surrounded and cut off; and

● at Ypres the Germans used poison gas, but when the wind changed direction it was blown back towards their own lines and they suffered more casualties than the Allies, especially when the Allies released some gas of their own.

(b) *The east*

In the east, Russia's fortunes were mixed: they had further successes against Austria, but they met defeat whenever they clashed with the Germans, who captured Warsaw and the whole of Poland. The Turkish blockade of the Dardanelles was beginning to hamper the Russians, who were already running short of arms and ammunition. It was partly to clear the Dardanelles and open up the vital supply line to Russia via the Black Sea that the *Gallipoli Campaign* was launched. This was an idea strongly pressed by Winston Churchill (First Lord of the Admiralty) to escape from the deadlock in the

Illus. 2.1   British soldiers blinded by poison gas

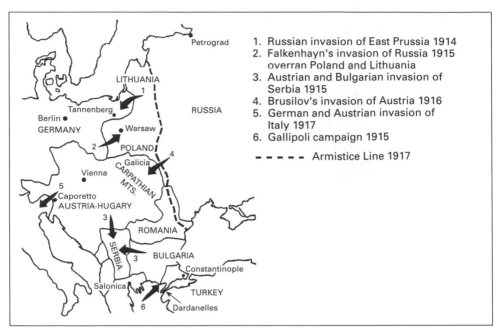

Map 2.4 War on the Eastern, Italian and Balkan Fronts

1. Russian invasion of East Prussia 1914
2. Falkenhayn's invasion of Russia 1915 overran Poland and Lithuania
3. Austrian and Bulgarian invasion of Serbia 1915
4. Brusilov's invasion of Austria 1916
5. German and Austrian invasion of Italy 1917
6. Gallipoli campaign 1915

– – – – – Armistice Line 1917

west by eliminating the Turks. They were thought to be the weakest of the Central Powers because of their unstable government. Success against Turkey would enable help to be sent to Russia and might also bring Bulgaria, Greece and Romania into the war on the Allied side. It would then be possible to attack Austria from the south.

The campaign was a total failure; the first attempt, in March, an Anglo-French naval attack through the Dardanelles to capture Constantinople, failed when the ships ran into a series of mines. This ruined the surprise element, so that when the British attempted landings at the tip of the Gallipoli peninsula, the Turks had strengthened their defences and no advance could be made (April). Further landings by Australian and New Zealand troops (Anzacs) in April and by British troops in August were equally useless, and positions could only be held with great difficulty. In December the entire force was withdrawn. *The consequences were serious:* besides being a blow to Allied morale, it turned out to be the last chance of helping Russia via the Black Sea. It probably made Bulgaria decide to join the Central Powers. A Franco-British force landed at Salonika in neutral Greece to try to relieve Serbia, but it was too late. When Bulgaria entered the war in October, Serbia was quickly overrun by Bulgarians and Germans. The year 1915 was therefore not a good one for the Allies; even a British army sent to protect Anglo-Persian oil interests against a possible Turkish attack became bogged down in Mesopotamia as it approached Baghdad; it was beseiged by Turks at Kut-el-Amara from December 1915 until March 1916, when it was forced to surrender.

(c) *In May Italy declared war on Austria–Hungary*

Italy hoped to seize Austria's Italian-speaking provinces as well as territory along the eastern shore of the Adriatic Sea. *A secret treaty was signed in London* in which the Allies promised Italy Trentino, the south Tyrol, Istria, Trieste, part of Dalmatia, Adalia, some islands in the Aegean Sea, and a protectorate over Albania. The Allies hoped that by keeping thousands of Austrian troops occupied, the Italians would relieve pressure on the Russians. But the Italians made little headway and their efforts made no difference to the eventual Russian defeat.

2.3 1916

(a) *The western front*

On the western front, 1916 is remembered for two terrible battles, *Verdun* and *the Somme.*

1   *Verdun* was an important French fortress town against which the Germans under Falkenhayn launched a massive attack (February). They hoped to draw all the best French troops to its defence, destroy them and then carry out a final offensive to win the war. But the French under Pétain defended stubbornly, and in June the Germans had to abandon the attack. The French lost heavily (about 315 000 men) as the Germans intended, but so did the Germans, with over 280 000 dead, and nothing to show for it.

2   *The Battle of the Somme* was a series of attacks, mainly by the British, beginning on 1 July and lasting through to November. The aim was to relieve pressure on the French at Verdun, take over more of the trench line as the French army weakened, and keep the Germans fully committed, so that they would be unable to risk sending reinforcements to the eastern front against Russia. At the end of it all, the Allies had made only limited advances varying between a few hundred yards and seven miles, along a thirty-mile front. *The real importance of the battle was the blow to German morale*, as they realized that Britain (where conscription was introduced for the first time in May) was a military power to be reckoned with. Losses on both sides, killed or wounded, were appalling (Germans 650 000; British 418 000; French 194 000) and Haig (British Commander-in-Chief) came under severe criticism for persisting with suicidal frontal attacks (see Question 1, Source C, at the end of the chapter). Hindenburg himself admitted in his Memoirs that the Germans could not have survived many more campaigns like Verdun and the Somme. The Somme also contributed to the fall of the British Prime Minister, Asquith, who resigned in 1916 after criticism of British tactics mounted.

(b) *David Lloyd George became Prime Minister*

His contribution to the Allied war effort and the defeat of the Central Powers was invaluable. His methods were dynamic and decisive; as Minister of Munitions since May 1915, he had already improved the supply of shells and machine-guns, encouraged the development of new weapons (the Stokes light mortar and the tank), which Kitchener (Minister of War) had turned down, and taken control of mines, factories and railways so that the war effort could be properly centralized. As Prime Minister during 1917, he set up a small *war cabinet*, so that quick decisions could be taken. He brought shipping and agriculture under government control and introduced the Ministry of National Service to organize the mobilization of men into the army. He also played an important part in the adoption of the convoy system (see Section 2.4(e)).

(c) *In the east*

In June the Russians under Brusilov attacked the Austrians, in response to a plea from Britain and France for some action to divert German attention away from Verdun. They managed to break the front and advanced 100 miles, taking 400 000 prisoners and large amounts of equipment. The Austrians were demoralized, but the strain was exhausting the Russians as well. The Romanians invaded Austria (August), but the Germans swiftly came to the rescue, occupied the whole of Romania and seized her wheat and oil supplies – not a happy end to 1916 for the Allies.

> (a) Make a list of differences which you have noticed in the Chapter so far between what happened on the western front and what happened on the eastern front.   1.5c
> (b) What were the reasons for these differences?
>
> 1. 4b–7b

2.4 The war at sea

The general public in Germany and Britain expected a series of naval battles between the rival Dreadnought fleets, something like the Battle of Trafalgar (1805). But both sides were cautious and dared not risk any action which might result in the loss of their main fleets. The British Admiral Jellicoe was particularly cautious; Churchill said he 'was the only man on either side who could have lost the war in an afternoon'. Nor were the Germans anxious for a confrontation, because they had only 16 of the latest Dreadnoughts against 27 British.

(a) *The Allies aimed to use their navies in three ways*

- to blockade the Central Powers, preventing goods from entering or leaving, slowly starving them out;
- to keep trade routes open between Britain, her empire and the rest of the world, so that the Allies themselves would not starve; and
- to transport British troops to the continent and keep them supplied via the Channel ports.

The British were successful in carrying out these aims; they went into action against German units stationed abroad, and at the *Battle of the Falkland Islands*, destroyed one of the main German squadrons. By the end of 1914 nearly all German armed surface ships had been destroyed, apart from their main fleet (which did not venture out of the Heligoland Bight) and the squadron blockading the Baltic to cut off supplies to Russia. In 1915 the navy was involved in the *Gallipoli Campaign* (see Section 2.2(b)).

(b) *The Allied blockade caused problems*

Britain was trying to prevent the Germans from using the neutral Scandinavian and Dutch ports to break the blockade; this involved *stopping and searching all neutral ships* and confiscating any goods suspected of being intended for enemy hands. The USA objected strongly to this, being anxious to continue trading with both sides.

(c) *The Germans retaliated with mines and submarine attacks*

This seemed to be their only alternative, since their surface vessels had either been destroyed or were blockaded in port. At first they respected neutral shipping and passenger liners, but it was soon clear that the German U-boat blockade was not effective. This was partly because they had insufficient U-boats and partly because there were problems of identification: the British tried to fool the Germans by flying neutral flags and by using passenger liners to transport arms and ammunition. In April 1915 the British liner *Lusitania* was sunk by a torpedo attack. In fact the *Lusitania* was armed and carrying vast quantities of arms and ammunition, as the Germans knew; hence their claim that the sinking was not just an act of barbarism against defenceless civilians. *This had important consequences:* out of almost 2000 dead, 128 were Americans. President Wilson therefore found that the USA would have to take sides to protect her trade. Whereas the British blockade did not interfere with the safety of passengers and crews, German tactics certainly did. For the time being, however, American protests caused Bethmann to tone down the submarine campaign, making it even less effective.

(d) *The Battle of Jutland (31 May 1916)*

This was the main event of 1916; it was the only time the main battle-fleets emerged and engaged each other; the result was indecisive. The German Admiral von Scheer tried to lure part of the British fleet out from its base so that that section could be destroyed by the numerically superior Germans. However, more British ships came out than he had anticipated, and after the two fleets had shelled each other on and off for several hours, the Germans decided to retire to base, firing torpedoes as they went. On balance, the Germans could claim that they had won the battle, since they lost only 11 ships to Britain's 14. The real importance of the battle lay in the fact that *the Germans had failed to destroy British sea power*: the German High Seas Fleet stayed in Kiel for the rest of the war, leaving Britain's control of the surface complete. In desperation at the food shortages caused by the British blockade, they embarked on 'unrestricted' submarine warfare, and this was to have fatal results for them.

(e) *'Unrestricted' submarine warfare (started January 1917)*

As the Germans had been concentrating on the production of U-boats since the Battle of Jutland, this campaign was extremely effective. They attempted to sink all enemy and neutral merchant ships in the Atlantic; although they knew that this was likely to bring the USA into the war, they hoped that *Britain and France would be starved into surrender*, before the Americans could make any vital contribution. They almost did it: the peak of German success came in April 1917, when 430 ships were lost; Britain was down to about six weeks' corn supply, and although the USA came into the war in April, it was bound to be several months before their help became effective. However, the situation was saved by Lloyd George, who insisted that the Admiralty adopt the convoy system. A convoy was a large number of merchant ships sailing together, so that they could be protected by escorting warships. This drastically reduced losses and meant that the German gamble had failed. *The submarine campaign was important because it brought the USA into the war.* The British navy therefore, helped by the Americans, played a vitally important role in the defeat of the Central Powers; by the middle of 1918 it had achieved its three aims.

Illus. 2.2   Troops crossing the sea of mud at Passchendaele, 1917

2.5   1917

(a) *In the west*

1917 was a year of Allied failure. A massive French attack under Nivelle in Champagne achieved nothing except mutiny in the French army, which was successfully sorted out by Pétain. From June to November the British fought the *Third Battle of Ypres*, usually remembered as *Passchendaele*, in appallingly muddy conditions; British casualties were again enormous – 324 000 compared with 200 000 Germans – for an advance of only four miles (Illus. 2.2).

More significant was *the Battle of Cambrai, which demonstrated that tanks, used properly, might break the deadlock of trench warfare*. 381 massed British tanks made a great breach in the German line, but lack of reserves prevented the success from being followed up. However, the lesson had been observed, and *Cambrai became the model for the successful Allied attacks of 1918*. Meanwhile the Italians were heavily defeated by Germans and Austrians at Caporetto (October) and retreated in disorder. This rather unexpectedly proved to be an important turning point. Italian morale revived, perhaps because they were faced with having to defend their homeland against the hated Austrians. The defeat also led to the setting up of an *Allied Supreme War Council*. The new French premier, Clemenceau, a great war leader in the same mould as Lloyd George, rallied the wilting French.

(b) *On the eastern front*

Disaster struck the Allies when *Russia withdrew from the war*. Continuous defeat by the Germans, lack of arms and supplies, problems of transport and communications, and utterly incompetent leadership, caused two revolutions (see Section 15.2), and the Bolsheviks (later known as Communists), who took over power in November, were willing to make peace. Thus in 1918 the entire weight of German forces could be thrown against the west; without the USA, the Allies would have been hard pressed. Encouragement was provided by the British capture of Baghdad and Jerusalem from the Turks, giving them control of vast oil supplies.

(c) *The entry of the USA (April)*

This was caused partly by the German U-boat campaign, and also by the discovery that Germany was trying to persuade Mexico to declare war on the USA, promising her Texas, New Mexico and Arizona in return. The Americans had hesitated about siding with the autocratic Russian government, but the overthrow of the tsar in the March revolution removed this obstacle. *The USA made an important contribution to the Allied victory*, supplying Britain and France with food, merchant ships and credit, though actual military help came slowly. By the end of 1917 only one American division had been in action, but by mid-1918 over half a million men were involved. Most important was the psychological boost which the American potential in resources of men and materials gave the Allies and the corresponding blow it gave to German morale.

> The previous sections have described a number of battles and their consequences; these included the Battles of the Marne (1914), Tannenburg and the Masurian Lakes (1914), the Somme (1916), Jutland (1916), Passchendaele (1917) and Cambrai (1917).
>
> • Which of these battles do you think had the most important consequences?
> • Explain why you think some had less important consequences than others.   1.4b–6b

2.6 The Central Powers defeated

(a) *The German spring offensive 1918*

This was launched by Ludendorff in a last desperate attempt to win the war before too many US troops arrived, and before discontent in Germany led to revolution. It almost came off: throwing in all the extra troops released from the east, the Germans broke through on the Somme (March), and by the end of May were only 40 miles from Paris; the Allies seemed to be falling apart. However, under the overall command of the French Marshal Foch, they managed to hold on as the German advance lost momentum and created an awkward bulge.

(b) *An Allied counter-offensive began (8 August)*

This was near Amiens, with hundreds of tanks attacking in short sharp jabs at several

Illus. 2.3 Tanks were the only way to break the stalemate produced by trenches and machineguns

different points instead of on a narrow front (Illus. 2.3). This forced the Germans to withdraw their entire line and avoided forming a salient. Slowly but surely the Germans were forced back, until by the end of September the Allies had broken through the Hindenburg Line. Though Germany itself had not yet been invaded, Ludendorff was now convinced that it would be defeated in the spring of 1919. He insisted that the German government ask President Wilson of the USA for an armistice (ceasefire) (3 October). He hoped to get less severe terms based on Wilson's 14 Points (see Section 2.7(a)). By asking for peace in 1918 he would save Germany from invasion and preserve the army's discipline and reputation. Fighting continued for another five weeks while negotiations went on, but eventually *an armistice was signed on 11 November.*

(c) *Why did the Central Powers lose the war?*

The reasons can be briefly summarized.

1   Once the Schlieffen Plan had failed, removing all hope of a quick German victory, it was bound to be a strain for them, *facing war on two fronts.*
2   *Allied sea power was decisive*, enforcing the deadly blockade which caused desperate food shortages and crippled exports, while keeping Allied armies fully supplied.
3   The German submarine campaign failed in the face of *convoys* protected by British, American and Japanese destroyers; the campaign itself was a mistake because it brought the USA into the war.
4   The entry of the USA brought *vast new resources* to the Allies.
5   Allied political leaders at the critical time – Lloyd George and Clemenceau – were probably more competent than those of the Central Powers. The unity of command under Foch probably helped, while Haig learned lessons from the 1917 experiences about the effective use of tanks and the avoidance of salients.
6   The continuous strain of heavy losses told on the Germans – they lost their best troops in the 1918 offensive and the new troops were young and inexperienced. An epidemic of deadly Spanish flu did not help the situation, and morale was low as they retreated.

7   Germany was badly let down by her allies and was constantly having to help out
the Austrians and Bulgarians. The defeat of Bulgaria by the British (from
Salonika) and Serbs (29 September 1918) was the final straw for many German
soldiers, who could see no chance of victory now. When Austria was defeated by
Italy at Vittorio–Veneto and Turkey surrendered (both in October), the end was
near.

The combination of military defeat and dire food shortages produced a great war
weariness, leading to mutiny in the navy, destruction of morale in the army and revolution at home.

> (a) Looking back over this chapter so far, make a list of the
>   main changes which took place during the war in the
>   military tactics of the Allies on the western front.
>
> (b) Explain whether each change was good for the Allies or
>   not.   1.4a–6a
>
> (c) Section 2.6(c) looked at reasons for Germany's defeat.
>   Pick out which you think were the **two** most important
>   reasons for their defeat, and explain why you have
>   chosen these two.   1.4b–7b

2.7 The problems of making a peace settlement

(a) *War aims*

When the war started none of the participants had any specific ideas about *what they
hoped to achieve*, except that Germany and Austria wanted to preserve the Habsburg
Empire, and thought this required them to destroy Serbia. As the war progressed,
some of the governments involved, perhaps to encourage their troops by giving them
some clear objectives to fight for, began to list their war aims:

1 *Britain:* Lloyd George mentioned (January 1918) the defence of democracy and
    the righting of the injustice done to France in 1871 when she lost Alsace and
    Lorraine to Germany. Other points were the restoration of Belgium and Serbia, an
    independent Poland, democratic self-government for the nationalities of
    Austria–Hungary, self-determination for the German colonies and an international
    organization to prevent war.
2 *USA – Woodrow Wilson's famous 14 Points (January 1918) were:*

    (1)   abolition of secret diplomacy;
    (2)   free navigation at sea for all nations in war and peace;
    (3)   removal of economic barriers between states;
    (4)   all-round reduction of armaments;
    (5)   impartial adjustment of colonial claims in the interests of the populations
           concerned;
    (6)   evacuation of Russian territory;
    (7)   restoration of Belgium;
    (8)   liberation of France and restoration of Alsace and Lorraine;
    (9)   readjustment of Italian frontiers along the lines of nationality;

(10) self-government for the peoples of Austria–Hungary;
(11) Romania, Serbia and Montenegro to be evacuated and Serbia given access to the sea;
(12) self-government for the non-Turkish peoples of the Turkish Empire and permanent opening of the Dardanelles;
(13) an independent Poland with secure access to the sea;
(14) a general association of nations to preserve peace.

These points achieved publicity when the Germans later claimed that they had expected the peace terms to be based on them and that, since this was not the case, they had been cheated.

(b) *Differing Allied views about how to treat the defeated powers*

When the peace conference met (January 1919), it was soon obvious that a settlement would be difficult:

1 *France* (represented by Clemenceau) wanted a harsh peace to ruin Germany economically and militarily so that she could never again threaten French frontiers.
2 *Britain* (Lloyd George) was in favour of a less severe settlement, enabling Germany to recover quickly so that she could resume her role as a major customer for British goods. However, Lloyd George had just won an election with slogans such as 'Hang the Kaiser', and talk of getting from Germany 'everything that you can squeeze out of a lemon and a bit more'. The British public therefore expected a harsh peace settlement.
3 *USA* (Woodrow Wilson) was in favour of a lenient peace, though Wilson had been disappointed when the Germans ignored his 14 Points and imposed the harsh *Treaty of Brest-Litovsk* on Russia (see Section 15.3(b)). He wanted a just peace: although he had to accept British and French demands for *reparations* (compensation for damages) and *German disarmament*, he was able to limit reparations to losses caused to civilians and their property, instead of 'the whole cost of the war'. Wilson was also in favour of *self-determination*: nations should be freed from foreign rule and given *democratic governments of their own choice*.

Illus. 2.4 The three leaders at Versailles: (left to right) Clemenceau, Wilson and Lloyd George

By June 1919 the conference had come up with *the Treaty of Versailles for Germany*, followed by other treaties dealing with Germany's former allies. The Treaty of Versailles in particular was one of the most controversial settlements ever signed, and it was criticized even in the Allied countries on the grounds that it was too hard on the Germans, who were bound to object so violently that *another war was inevitable*, sooner or later. In addition, many of the terms, such as reparations and disarmament, proved *impossible to carry out*.

2.8 The Treaty of Versailles with Germany

(a) *The terms*

1 *Germany had to lose territory in Europe:*

- Alsace–Lorraine to France
- Eupen, Moresnet and Malmédy to Belgium
- North Schleswig to Denmark (after a plebiscite, i.e. a vote)
- West Prussia and Posen to Poland – though Danzig (the main port of West Prussia) was to be a free city under League of Nations administration, because its population was wholly German
- Memel was given to Lithuania
- the Saar was to be administered by the League of Nations for 15 years, after which the population would be allowed to vote on whether it should belong to France or Germany. In the meantime France was to have the use of its coalmines
- Estonia, Latvia and Lithuania, which had been handed over to Germany by Russia at Brest-Litovsk, were taken away from Germany and set up as independent states. This was an example of *self-determination* being carried into practice
- Union between Germany and Austria was forbidden.

2 *Germany's African colonies were taken away* and became 'mandates' under League of Nations supervision: this meant that various member states of the League 'looked after' them.

3 *German armaments were strictly limited*, to a maximum of 100 000 troops and no conscription (compulsory military service); no tanks, armoured cars, military aircraft or submarines, and only six battleships. The Rhineland was to be permanently demilitarized. This meant that German troops were not allowed in the area.

4 *The War Guilt clause* fixed the blame for the outbreak of the war solely on Germany and her allies.

5 *Germany was to pay reparations* for damage done to the Allies; the actual amount was not decided at Versailles, but it was announced later (1921), after much argument and haggling, as £6600 million.

6 *A League of Nations* was set up; its aims and organization were set out in the *League Covenant* (*see* Chapter 3).

The Germans had little choice but to sign the treaty, though they objected strongly. The signing ceremony took place in the Hall of Mirrors at Versailles, where the German Empire had been proclaimed less than 50 years earlier.

(b) Why did the Germans object, and how far were their objections justified?

1 It was a dictated peace

The Germans were not allowed into the discussions at Versailles; they were simply presented with the terms and told to sign. Although they were allowed to criticize it in writing, all their criticisms were ignored except one (see point 3 below). Some historians feel that the Germans were justified in objecting, that it would have been reasonable to allow them to join in the discussions. This might have led to a toning down of some of the harsher terms. It would certainly have deprived the Germans of the argument much used by Hitler, that because the peace was a 'diktat', it should not be morally binding. On the other hand, it is possible to argue that the Germans could scarcely have expected any better treatment after the harsh way they had dealt with the Russians at Brest-Litovsk – also a 'diktat' (see Section 15.3(b)).

2 Many provisions were not based on the 14 points

The Germans claimed that they had been promised terms based on Wilson's 14 Points, that many of the provisions were not based on the 14 Points, and were therefore a swindle. This is probably not a valid objection: the14 Points had never been accepted as official by any of the states involved, and the Germans themselves had ignored them in January 1918, when there still seemed a chance of outright German victory. By November, German tactics (Brest-Litovsk, destruction of mines, factories and public buildings during their retreat through France and Belgium) had hardened the Allied attitude and led Wilson to add two further points: Germany should pay for the damage to civilian population and property and should be reduced to 'virtual impotence'; in other words, Germany should be disarmed. The Germans were aware of this when they accepted the armistice, and, in fact, most of the terms did comply with the 14 Points and the additions.

There were also objections on specific points:

3 Loss of territory in Europe

This included Alsace–Lorraine and especially West Prussia, which gave Poland access to the sea. However, both were mentioned in the 14 Points. Originally Upper Silesia, an industrial region with a mixed population of Poles and Germans, was to be given to Poland, but this was the one concession made to the German written objections: after a vote among the population, Germany was allowed to keep about two-thirds of the area. In fact most of the German losses could be justified on grounds of nationality (Map 2.5).

4 The loss of Germany's African colonies

The Germans probably had more grounds for objection to the loss of their African colonies, which was hardly an 'impartial adjustment'. The mandate system allowed Britain to take over German East Africa (Tanganyika, now part of Tanzania) and parts of Togoland and the Cameroons, France to take most of Togoland and the Cameroons, and South Africa to acquire German South West Africa (now known as Namibia); but this was really a device by which the Allies seized the colonies without actually admitting that they were being annexed (Map 2.6).

Territory lost by Germany

Former territory of tsarist Russia

Austria–Hungary until 1918

Curzon Line – proposed by Britain (Dec.1919) as Poland's eastern frontier. Russian territory east of the line was seized by Poland in 1920

Map 2.5 European frontiers after the First World War and the Peace Treaties

5   The disarmament clauses were deeply resented

The Germans claimed that 100 000 troops were not enough to keep law and order at a time of political unrest. Perhaps the German objection was justified to some extent,

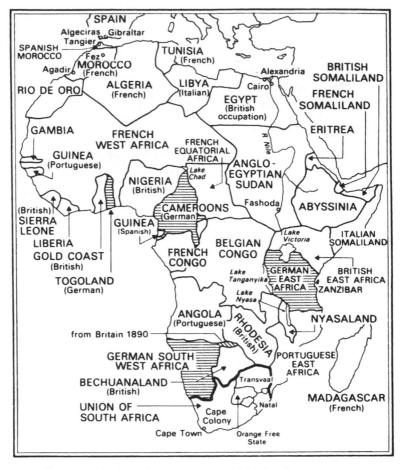

=== German colonies taken away as mandates by the
=== Versailles Treaty, 1919

Map 2.6 *Africa and the Peace Treaties*

though the French desire for a weak Germany was understandable. The Germans became more aggrieved later, as it became clear that none of the other powers intended to disarm, even though Wilson's Point 4 mentioned 'all-round reduction of armaments'. However, disarmament was impossible to enforce fully, because the Germans were determined to exploit every loophole.

6   The 'War Guilt' clause (Article 231)

The Germans objected to being saddled with the entire blame for the outbreak of war. There are some grounds for objection here, because although later research seems to indicate Germany's guilt, it was hardly possible to arrive at that conclusion in the space of six weeks during 1919, which is what the Special Commission on War Responsibility did. However, the Allies wanted the Germans to admit responsibility so that they would be liable to pay reparations.

7 Reparations

Reparations were the final humiliation for the Germans. Though there could be little valid objection to the general principle of reparations, many historians now agree that the actual amount decided on was far too high at £6600 million. Some people thought so at the time, including J.M. Keynes, who was an economic adviser to the British delegation at the conference. He urged the Allies to take £2000 million, which he said was a more reasonable amount which Germany would be able to afford. The figure of £6600 million enabled the Germans to protest that it was impossible to pay, and they soon began to default (fail to pay) on their annual instalments.This caused resentment among the Allies, who were relying on German cash to help them pay their own war debts to the USA. There was international tension when France tried to force the Germans to pay (see Section 4.2(c)). Eventually the Allies admitted their mistake and reduced the amount to £2000 million (*Young Plan, 1929*), but not before reparations had proved disastrous, both economically and politically.

The Germans clearly did have some grounds for complaint, but it is worth pointing out that the treaty could have been even more harsh. If Clemenceau had had his way, the Rhineland would have become an independent state, and France would have annexed the Saar. However, Germany was still the strongest power in Europe economically, so that the unwise thing about the settlement was that it annoyed the Germans, but did not leave them too weak to retaliate.

2.9 The peace treaties with Austria–Hungary

When Austria was on the verge of defeat in the war, *the Habsburg Empire disintegrated* as the various nationalities declared themselves independent. Austria and Hungary separated and declared themselves republics. Many important decisions therefore had already been taken before the peace conference met. However, the situation was chaotic, and the task of the conference was *to formalize and recognize what had taken place*.

(a) *The Treaty of St Germain (1919), dealing with Austria*

By this treaty Austria lost:

- Bohemia and Moravia (wealthy industrial provinces with a population of 10 million) to the new state of Czechoslovakia;
- Dalmatia, Bosnia and Herzegovina to Serbia, which, with Montenegro, now became known as Yugoslavia;
- Bukovina to Romania;
- Galicia to the reconstituted state of Poland;
- the south Tyrol (as far as the Brenner Pass), Trentino, Istria and Trieste to Italy.

(b) *The Treaty of Trianon (1920), dealing with Hungary*

This was not signed until 1920 because of political uncertainties in Budapest (the capital); the Communists led by Bela Kun seized power and were then overthrown.

- Slovakia and Ruthenia were given to Czechoslovakia;
- Croatia and Slovenia to Yugoslavia; and

- Transylvania and the Banat of Temesvar to Romania. Both treaties contained the League of Nations Covenant.

These settlements may seem harsh, but it has to be remembered that much of it had already happened; on the whole they did keep to the spirit of self-determination. More people were placed under governments of their own nationality than ever before in Europe, though they were not always as democratic as Wilson would have liked (especially in Hungary and Poland). There were some deviations from the pattern though – for example, three million Germans (in the Sudetenland) now found themselves in Czechoslovakia, and the Treaty of Versailles had placed a million Germans in Poland. The Allies justified these on the grounds that the new states needed them in order to be economically viable. It was unfortunate that both these instances gave Hitler an excuse to begin territorial demands on these countries.

The treaties left both Austria and Hungary with serious economic problems

Austria was a small republic, its population reduced from 22 million to 6.5 million; most of its industrial wealth had been lost to Czechoslovakia and Poland. Vienna, once the capital of the huge Habsburg Empire, was left high and dry, surrounded by farming land which could hardly support it. Not surprisingly, Austria was soon facing a severe economic crisis and was constantly having to be helped out by loans from the League of Nations.

Hungary was just as badly affected, her population reduced from 21 million to 7.5 million, and some of her richest corn land lost to Romania. Matters were further complicated when all the new states quickly introduced tariffs (import and export duties). These hampered the flow of trade through the whole Danube area and made the industrial recovery of Austria particularly difficult. In fact there was an excellent economic case to support a union between Austria and Germany.

2.10 The settlement with Turkey and Bulgaria

(a) *The Treaty of Sèvres (1920), dealing with Turkey*

Turkey was to lose Eastern Thrace, many Aegean islands and Smyrna to Greece; Adalia and Rhodes to Italy; the Straits (the exit from the Black Sea) were to be permanently open; Syria became a French mandate, and Palestine, Iraq and Transjordan British mandates. However, the loss of so much territory to Greece, especially Smyrna on the Turkish mainland, outraged Turkish national feeling (self-determination was being ignored in this case). Led by Mustafa Kemal, they rejected the treaty and chased the Greeks out of Smyrna. The Italians and French withdrew their occupying forces from the Straits area, leaving only British troops at Chanak. Eventually a compromise was reached and the settlement was revised by the *Treaty of Lausanne (1923)*, by which Turkey regained Eastern Thrace including Constantinople, and Smyrna (see Map 2.7). Turkey was therefore the first state to challenge the Paris settlement successfully. One legacy of the Treaty of Sèvres which was to cause problems later was the situation in the mandates. These were peopled largely by Arabs who had been hoping for independence as a reward after their brave struggle, led by an English officer, T.E. Lawrence (Lawrence of Arabia), against the Turks. Nor were the Arabs happy about the talk of establishing a Jewish 'national home' in Palestine (see Section 11.2(a)).

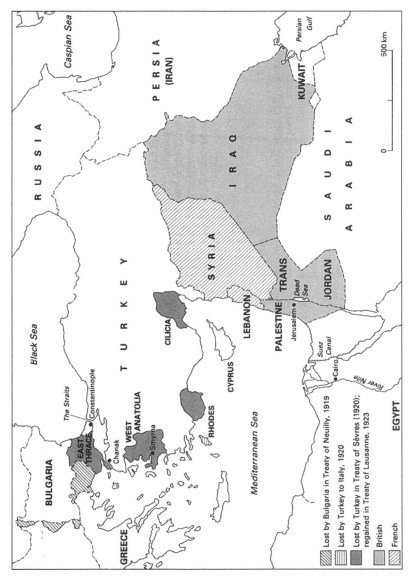

Map 2.7 The treatment of Turkey by the Treaty of Sèvres, and of Bulgaria by the Treaty of Neuilly

(b) *The Treaty of Neuilly (1919), dealing with Bulgaria*

Bulgaria lost territory to Greece, depriving her of her Aegean coastline, and also to Yugoslavia and Romania. She could claim, with some justification, that at least a million Bulgars were under foreign governments as a result of the Treaty of Neuilly.

2.11 Verdict on the peace settlement

In conclusion, it has to be said that this collection of peace treaties *was not a conspicuous success*. It had the unfortunate effect of dividing Europe into the states which wanted to revise the settlement (Germany being the main one), and those which wanted to preserve it.

On the whole the latter turned out to be only lukewarm in their support. The USA failed to ratify the settlement (see Section 4.4) and never joined the League of Nations. This in turn left France completely disenchanted with the whole thing because the Anglo-American guarantee of her frontiers given in the agreement would not now apply. Italy felt cheated because she had not received all the territory promised her in 1915, and Russia was ignored, because the powers did not want to negotiate with its Bolshevik government. Germany, on the other hand, was only temporarily weakened and was soon strong enough to cause trouble.

All this tended to sabotage the settlement from the beginning, and it became increasingly difficult to apply the terms fully. But it is easy to criticize after the event; Gilbert White, an American delegate at the conference, put it well when he remarked that, given the intricacy of the problems involved, 'it is not surprising that they made a bad peace: what is surprising is that they managed to make peace at all'.

Questions

1 *Trench warfare and the Battle of the Somme (1916)* – study Sources A–D below and Sections 2.2 and 2.3 and then answer the questions which follow.

Source A

A modern historian's view

Strategically, the battle of the Somme was an unredeemed defeat. . . . The Somme set the picture by which future generations saw the First World War: brave helpless soldiers; blundering obstinate generals; nothing achieved. After the Somme men decided the war would go on for ever.

Source: A.J.P. Taylor, *The First World War* (Penguin, 1963)

British soldiers manning a captured German trench on the Somme (Illus. 2.5)

Source C

The first day of the Somme – a German view.

The men in the dugouts waited ready, belts full of hand-grenades around them, gripping their rifles ... it was of vital importance to lose not a second in taking up position in the open to meet the British infantry which would advance immediately behind the artillery barrage.

At 7.30 a.m. the hurricane of shells ceased.... Our men at once clambered up the steep shafts leading from the dugouts to daylight and ran ... to the nearest craters. The machine-guns were pulled out of the dugouts and hurriedly placed in position.... As soon as the men were in position, a series of lines were seen moving forward from the British trenches. The first line appeared without end to right and left. It was quickly followed by a second, then a third and fourth ... 'Get ready' was passed along our front from crater to crater.... A few minutes later, when the leading British line was within a hundred yards, the rattle of machinegun and rifle broke out along the whole line of shell holes. Whole sections seemed to fall ... the advance rapidly crumbled under the hail of shells and bullets. All along the line men could be seen throwing up their arms and collapsing, never to move again. Badly wounded rolled about in their agony.

Source: quoted in A.H. Farrar-Hockley, *The Somme* (Pan/Severn House, 1976)

Extracts from two poems written by soldiers serving in the British army

(i)
If I should die, think only this of me:
That there's some corner of a foreign field
That is for ever England. There shall be
In that rich earth a richer dust concealed;
A dust whom England bore, shaped, made aware,
Gave, once, her flowers to love, her ways to roam,
A body of England's, breathing English air,
Washed by the rivers, blest by suns of home.

Rupert Brooke

(ii)
What passing-bells for those who die as cattle?
Only the monstrous anger of the guns.
Only the stuttering rifles' rapid rattle
Can patter out their hasty orisons.
No mockeries for them from prayers or bells,
Nor any voice of mourning save the choirs,
The shrill, demented choirs of wailing shells;
And bugles calling for them from sad shires.

Wilfred Owen

[*orisons = prayers*]

(a) How do you know that the soldiers shown in Source B are British?

1.4c   2 marks

(b) Source B shows British soldiers manning a German trench captured during the battle of the Somme. Does this prove that the author of Source A was wrong in his judgement, or is there some other explanation? Give full reasons for your answer. 2.4–6, 2.9; 3.4   4 marks

(c) Sources D(i) and D(ii) were written by soldiers who served in the British army. One of the soldiers died in 1915. Using all the sources and the information in the chapter to help you decide, which poem do you think was most likely to have been written by the soldier who died in 1915? Explain your answer fully. 1.4a–6a; 1.4c–7c; 3.4   5 marks

(d) How reliable do you think the following sources of evidence would be if you wanted to use them to help you write a report about life in the trenches on the western front?

(i)   poems written by soldiers who were there (as in Source D);
(ii) photographs (as in Source B);
(iii) accounts given by soldiers on the front line (as in Source C)?

3.5–9   9 marks

Total: 20 marks

[*based on a Midland Examining Group question*]

2   *The Versailles Settlement* – study Sources A–E below and then answer the questions which follow. You may also use information from Sections 2.8–11.

Part of a speech made by President Woodrow Wilson to the US Congress on 8 January 1918, in which he outlined his 14 Points for the establishment of future peace.

The programme of the world's peace, therefore, is our programme; the only possible programme, as we see it, is this:...
Four. Adequate guarantees given and taken that national armaments will be reduced to the lowest point consistent with domestic safety. [for the other 13 points, see Section 2.7(a)].

Source B

Extracts from the Treaty of Versailles

Clause 160: The German army ... must not exceed one hundred thousand men, including officers ... The army shall be devoted exclusively to the maintenance of order within the territory and to the control of the frontiers ...

Clause 231: Germany accepts the responsibility of Germany and her allies for causing all the loss and damage to which the Allied governments have been subjected as a consequence of the war imposed upon them by the aggression of Germany and her allies [War Guilt Clause].

Sources: Sources A and B are taken from J.H.Bettey, *English Historical Documents* (Routledge & Kegan Paul, 1967)

Source C

From a speech by a German MP in parliament, 1919

The criminal madness of this peace [the Versailles Treaty] will drain Germany's national life-blood. It is a shameless blow in the face of common-sense. It is inflicting the deepest wounds on us Germans as our world lies in wreckage about us.

Source: quoted in J.W. Hiden, *The Weimar Republic* (Longman, 1974, adapted)

Source D

Information from a modern historian

In Germany there was a tremendous outcry. But already in 1919, among the military and the more thoughtful politicians, it was realized that the sources of Germany's strength would recover and her industries revive. As memories of the war receded, opportunities would arise to modify or get round the restrictions imposed on Germany.... The conditions for a stable peace had not been laid in 1920.

Source: J.A.S. Grenville, *History of the World in the Twentieth Century* (Collins, 1994, adapted)

The view of another British historian

The Treaty of Versailles was not excessively harsh on Germany, either territorially or economically. It deprived her of about 13 and a half per cent of her territory (including Alsace–Lorraine), about 13 per cent of her economic productivity and about 7 million of her inhabitants – just over 10 per cent of her population – as well as her colonies and large merchant vessels. However, the German people were expecting victory and not defeat. It was the acknowledgement of defeat as much as the treaty terms themselves, which they found so hard to accept.

Source: Ruth Henig, *Versailles and After* (Methuen,1984)

(a) 'It is inflicting the deepest wounds on us Germans'.
Does the evidence in Sources B, D and E support this statement by the
German MP in Source C? Explain your answer.   1.4c–5c; 3.4   7 marks

(b) Why do you think Sources C, D and E present such different views?
2.4–8   6 marks

(c) 'The conditions for a stable peace had not been laid in 1920', according to the
writer of Source D.
How useful are these sources in explaining why this statement can be seen
as a fair criticism of the Versailles Settlement?   3.5–8   12 marks

Total 25 marks

3 | The League of Nations

Summary of events

The League of Nations formally came into existence on 10 January 1920, the same day that the Versailles Treaty came into operation. With headquarters in Geneva in Switzerland, one of its main aims was to settle international disputes before they got out of hand, and so prevent war from ever breaking out again. After some initial teething troubles, the League seemed to be functioning successfully during the 1920s; it solved a number of minor international disputes, as well as achieving valuable economic and social work; for instance, it helped thousands of refugees and former prisoners of war to find their way home again. In 1930 supporters of the League felt optimistic about its future; the South African statesman, Jan Smuts, was moved to remark that 'we are witnessing one of the great miracles of history'.

However, during the 1930s the authority of the League was challenged several times, first by the Japanese invasion of Manchuria (1931) and later by the Italian attack on Abyssinia (1935). Both aggressors ignored the League's orders to withdraw, and for a variety of reasons it proved impossible to force them to comply. After 1935, respect for the League declined as its weaknesses became more apparent. During Germany's disputes with Czechoslovakia and Poland which led on to the Second World War, the League was not even consulted, and it was unable to exert the slightest influence to prevent the outbreak of war. After December 1939 it did not meet again, and it was dissolved in 1946 – a complete failure, at least as far as preventing war was concerned.

3.1 What were the origins of the League?

The League is often spoken of as being the brainchild of the American President Woodrow Wilson. Although Wilson was certainly a great supporter of the idea of an international organization for peace, the League was the result of a coming together of similar suggestions, made during the First World War, by a number of world statesmen. Lord Robert Cecil of Britain, Jan Smuts of South Africa and Léon Bourgeois of France put forward detailed schemes as to how such an organization might be set up. Lloyd George referred to it as one of Britain's war aims, and Wilson included it as the last of his 14 Points (see Section 2.7(a)). Wilson's great contribution was to insist that the League Covenant (the list of rules by which the League was to operate), which had been drawn up by an international committee including Cecil, Smuts, and Bourgeois, as well as Wilson himself, should be included in each of the separate peace treaties. This ensured that the League actually came into existence instead of merely remaining a topic for discussion.

The League had two main aims

- To maintain peace through collective security: if one state attacked another, the member states of the League would act together, collectively, to restrain the aggressor, either by economic or by military sanctions;
- to encourage international co-operation, in order to solve economic and social problems.

3.2 How was the League organized?

There were forty-two member states at the beginning and fifty-five by 1926 when Germany was admitted. Its main organs were as follows.

(a) *The General Assembly*

This met annually and contained representatives of all the member states, each of which had one vote. Its function was to decide general policy. It could, for example, propose a revision of peace treaties, and it handled the finances of the League. Any decisions taken had to be unanimous.

(b) *The Council*

This was a much smaller body which met more often, at least three time a year, and contained four permanent members – Britain, France, Italy and Japan. The USA was to have been a permanent member but decided not to join the League. There were four other members elected by the Assembly for periods of three years. The number of non-permanent members had increased to nine by 1926. It was the Council's task to deal with specific political disputes as they arose; again, decisions had to be unanimous.

(c) *The Permanent Court of International Justice*

This was based at the Hague in Holland and consisted of fifteen judges of different nationalities; it dealt with legal disputes between states, as opposed to political ones.

(d) *The Secretariat*

This looked after all the paperwork, preparing agendas, and writing resolutions and reports for carrying out the decisions of the League.

(e) *Commissions and committees*

There were a number of these, to deal with specific problems, some of which had arisen from the First World War. The main commissions were those which handled the mandates, military affairs, minority groups and disarmament. There were committees for international labour, health, economic and financial organization, child welfare, drug problems and women's rights.

Peacekeeping

In its function of peacekeeping, it was expected that the League would operate as follows: all disputes threatening war would be submitted to the League, and any member which resorted to war, thus breaking the Covenant, *would face collective action by the rest*. The Council would recommend 'what effective military, naval or air force the members should contribute to the armed forces'.

3.3 The successes of the League

(a) *It would be unfair to dismiss the League as a total failure*

Many of the committees and commissions achieved valuable results and much was done to foster international co-operation. One of the most successful was the *International Labour Organization (ILO)* under its French socialist director, Albert Thomas. Its purpose was to improve conditions of labour all over the world by persuading governments to:

- fix a maximum working day and week;
- specify adequate minimum wages;
- introduce sickness and unemployment benefit;
- introduce old age pensions.

It collected and published a vast amount of information, and many governments were prevailed upon to take action.

The *Refugee Organization* led by Fridtjof Nansen, the Norwegian explorer, solved the problem of thousands of former prisoners of war marooned in Russia at the end of the war; about half a million were returned home. After 1933, valuable help was given to thousands of people fleeing from the Nazi persecution in Germany.

The *Health Organization* did good work in investigating the causes of epidemics, and it was especially successful in combating a typhus epidemic in Russia, which at one time seemed likely to spread accross Europe. The *Mandates Commission* supervised the government of the territories taken from Germany and Turkey, while yet another commission was responsible for administering the Saar. It did this very efficiently, and concluded by organizing the 1935 plebiscite in which a large majority voted for the Saar to be returned to Germany.

Not all were successful, however; the *Disarmament Commission* made no progress in the near impossible task of persuading member states to reduce armaments, even though they had all promised to do so when they agreed to the Covenant.

(b) *Political disputes resolved*

Several political disputes were referred to the League in the early 1920s. *In all but two cases the League's decisions were accepted*. For example:

- in the quarrel between Finland and Sweden over *the Aaland Islands*, the verdict went in favour of Finland (1920).
- Over the rival claims of Germany and Poland to the important industrial area of *Upper Silesia*, the League decided that it should be partitioned (divided) between the two (1921).
- When *the Greeks invaded Bulgaria*, after some shooting incidents on the frontier, the League swiftly intervened: Greek troops were withdrawn and damages paid to Bulgaria.

- When *Turkey claimed the province of Mosul*, part of the British mandated territory of Iraq, the League decided in favour of Iraq.
- Further afield, in South America, squabbles were settled between *Peru and Colombia* and between *Bolivia and Paraguay*.

It is significant, however, that none of these disputes seriously threatened world peace, and none of the decisions went against a major state, which might have challenged the League's verdict. In fact, during this same period, *the League found itself twice over-ruled by the Conference of Ambassadors based in Paris*, which had been set up to deal with problems arising out of the Versailles treaties. There were first the rival claims of Poland and Lithuania to Vilna (1920), followed by the *Corfu Incident (1923)*; this was a quarrel between Mussolini's Italy and Greece. The League made no response to these acts of defiance, and this was not a promising sign.

3.4 Why did the League fail to preserve peace?

At the time of the Corfu Incident in 1923 (see (d) below), many people wondered what would happen if a powerful state were to challenge the League on a matter of major importance, for example, by invading an innocent country. How effective would the League be then? Unfortunately several such challenges occurred during the 1930s, and on every occasion the League was found wanting.

(a) *It was too closely linked with the Versailles Treaties*

This initial disadvantage made it seem like an organization specially for the benefit of the victorious powers. In addition it had to defend a peace settlement which was far from perfect. Some of its provisions were bound to cause trouble – for example, the disappointment of Italy and the inclusion of Germans in Czechoslovakia and Poland.

(b) *It was rejected by the USA*

The League was dealt a serious blow in March 1920 when the United States Senate rejected both the Versailles Settlement and the League. The reasons behind their decision were varied (see Section 4.4). The absence of the USA meant that the League was deprived of a powerful member whose presence would have been of great psychological and financial benefit.

(c) *Other important powers were not involved*

- Germany was not allowed to join until 1926; and
- the USSR only became a member in 1934 (when Germany left).

So for the first few years of its existence the League was deprived of three of the world's most important powers.

(d) *The Conference of Ambassadors in Paris was an embarrassment*

It was only intended to function until the League machinery was up and running, but it lingered on, and on several occasions, it took precedence over the League.

- In 1920 the League supported Lithuania in her claim to Vilna, which had just been

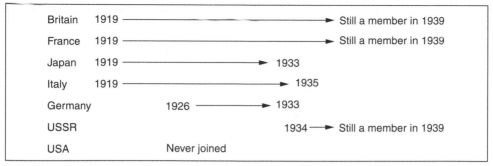

Figure 3.1 Great power membership of the League of Nations

seized from her by the Poles; but when the Conference of Ambassadors insisted on awarding Vilna to Poland, the League allowed it to go ahead.

● A later example was the *Corfu Incident (1923)*: this arose from a boundary dispute between Greece and Albania, in which three Italian officials working on the boundary commission were killed. Mussolini blamed the Greeks, demanded huge compensation and bombarded and occupied the Greek island of Corfu. Greece appealed to the League, but *Mussolini refused to recognize its competence to deal with the problem.* He threatened to withdraw Italy from the League, whereupon the Ambassadors ordered Greece to pay the full amount demanded.

At this early stage, however, supporters of the League dismissed these incidents as teething troubles.

(e) *There were serious weaknesses in the Covenant*

These made it difficult to ensure that decisive action was taken against any aggressor. It was difficult to get unanimous decisions; the League had no military force of its own, and though Article 16 expected member states to supply troops if necessary, a resolution was passed in 1923 that each member would decide for itself whether or not to fight in a crisis. This clearly made nonsense of the idea of collective security. Several attempts were made to strengthen the Covenant, but these failed because a unanimous vote was needed to change it, and this was never achieved.

The most notable attempt was made in 1924 by the British Labour Prime Minister, Ramsay MacDonald, a great supporter of the League. He introduced a resolution known as the *Geneva Protocol*. This pledged members to accept arbitration and help any victim of unprovoked aggression. With supreme irony, the Conservative government which followed Macdonald informed the League that they could not agree to the Protocol; they were reluctant to commit Britain and the Empire to the defence of all the 1919 frontiers. A resolution proposed by one British government was thus rejected by the next British government, and the League was left, as its critics remarked, still 'lacking teeth'.

(f) *It was very much a French/British affair*

The continued absence of the USA and the USSR, plus the hostility of Italy, made the League very much a French/British affair. But as their rejection of the Geneva Protocol showed, the British Conservatives were never very enthusiastic about the League. They preferred to sign the *Locarno Treaties (1925)* outside the League instead of conducting negotiations within it (see Section 4.1(e)).

> None of these weaknesses necessarily doomed the League to failure, however, provided all the members were prepared to refrain from aggression and accept League decisions. Between 1925 and 1930 events ran fairly smoothly.

(g) *The world economic crisis began in 1929*

This contributed to the League's decline. It brought unemployment and falling living standards to most countries, and caused extreme right-wing governments to come to power in Japan and Germany; together with Mussolini, they refused to keep to the rules and took a series of actions which revealed the League's weaknesses (points (h)–(j)).

(h) *The Japanese invasion of Manchuria (1931)*

In 1931 Japanese troops invaded the Chinese territory of Manchuria (see Section 5.1); China appealed to the League, which condemned Japan and ordered her troops to be withdrawn. When Japan refused, the League appointed a commission under Lord Lytton which decided (1932) that there were faults on both sides and suggested that Manchuria should be governed by the League. However, Japan rejected this and withdrew from the League (March 1933). The question of economic sanctions, let alone military ones, was never even raised, because Britain and France had serious economic problems. They were reluctant to apply a trade boycott of Japan in case it led to war, which they were ill-equipped to win, especially without American help. Japan had successfully defied the League, and its prestige was damaged, though not yet fatally.

(i) *The failure of the World Disarmament Conference (1932–3)*

This met under the auspices of the League, and its failure was a grave disappointment. The Germans asked for equality of armaments with France, but when the French demanded that this should be postponed for at least eight years, Hitler was able to use the French attitude as an excuse to withdraw Germany from the conference and later from the League.

(j) *The Italian invasion of Abyssinia (October 1935)*

This was the most serious blow (see Section 5.2(b)). The League condemned Italy and introduced economic sanctions; however, this did not include exports of oil, coal and steel to Italy. So half-hearted were the sanctions, that Italy was able to complete the conquest of Abyssinia without too much inconvenience (May 1936). A few weeks later sanctions were abandoned, and *Mussolini had successfully flouted the League*. Again Britain and France must share the blame for the League's failure. Their motive was the desire not to antagonize Mussolini too much, so as to keep him as an ally against the real danger – Germany. But the results were disastrous:

- Mussolini was annoyed by the sanctions anyway, and began to draw closer to Hitler;
- small states lost all faith in the League; and

- Hitler was encouraged to break the Versailles treaty.

After 1935, therefore, the League was never taken seriously again.

> The real explanation for the failure of the League was simple: when aggressive states such as Japan, Italy and Germany defied it, the League members, especially France and Britain, were not prepared to support it, either by decisive economic measures or by military action. *The League was only as strong as the determination of its leading members to stand up to aggression* – unfortunately, determination of that sort was sadly lacking during the 1930s.

Questions

1 (a) Using the information in the chapter, make two lists:

   (i)   ways in which the League of Nations can be said to have helped progress in international relations;

   (ii) ways in which the League did not help progress in international relations.

   Do you think your results suggest that the League was a complete waste of time?   1.4a–6a

(b) Section 3.4 has suggested some reasons why the League failed to preserve peace. Which of them were:

   (i)   long-term causes of its failure;

   (ii) short-term causes?   1.5b

(c) Show how the various causes were inter-linked.   1.7b

(d) Which do you think were the two most important causes of this failure? Explain your answer fully.   1.6b–8a

2 *The League and its problems* – study Sources A–E below, and then answer the questions which follow.

Source A

The Covenant of the League of Nations, signed 1919

In order to promote international co-operation and to achieve peace and security, by the acceptance of obligations not to resort to war, and by the firm observance of international law . . ., and by the maintenance of justice and a scrupulous respect for all treaty obligations, the member states agree to this Covenant of the League of Nations.

   Article 16 – Should any member of the League resort to war in disregard of its covenants, it shall be deemed to have committed an act of war against all other members of the League, which hereby undertake immediately to subject it to the severance [cutting off] of trade or financial relations. . . . It shall be the duty of the Council in such case to recommend to the several governments what effective military, naval or air force the members of the League shall contribute to the armed forces to be used to protect the covenants of the League.

Source: quoted in J.H. Bettey, *English Historical Documents* (Routledge & Kegan Paul, 1967, adapted extracts)

British cartoon of 1931 (Figure 3.2). The figure on the right using the 'face-saving outfit' represents Britain.

Source C

Speech by Maxim Litvinov, Soviet Foreign Affairs Minister, to the League at Geneva, 1934

The policy of non-resistance to evil and bartering with aggressors, which the opponents of sanctions propose to us, can have no other result than further strengthening the forces of aggression. And the moment might really arrive when their power has grown to such an extent that the League, or what remains of it, will be in no condition to cope with them, even if it wants to.... With the slightest attempt at aggression, collective action, as mentioned in Article 16, must be brought into effect ... against the aggressor, but decisively, resolutely and without any wavering.

Source: quoted in G. Martel (ed.), *The Origins of the Second World War Reconsidered* (Unwin Hyman, 1986, adapted extracts)

Source D

Speech by Sir Samuel Hoare, British Foreign Secretary, to the League at Geneva, 11 September 1935

I do not suppose that in the history of the Assembly there was ever a more difficult moment for a speech. When the world is stirred to excitement over the Abyssinian controversy, I will begin by re-affirming the support for the League by the government that I represent and the interest of the British people in collective security. On behalf of the government of the United Kingdom, I can say that they will be second to none in their intention to fulfil within the measure of their capacity, the obligations which the Covenant lays upon them. The League stands, and my country stands with it, for the collective maintenance of the Covenant, especially to all acts of unprovoked aggression.

Source: quoted in J.H. Bettey, *English Historical Documents* (Routledge & Kegan Paul, 1967, extracts)

Extracts from two speeches by Winston Churchill, then a back-bench Conservative MP

(i) in the House of Commons, February 1933
I do not think the League of Nations would be well advised to have a quarrel with Japan.... I hope we shall try in England to understand a little the position of Japan ... on the one side they see the dark menace of Soviet Russia; on the other, the chaos of China, four or five provinces of which are now being tortured under Communist rule.

(ii) in the House of Commons, 22 October 1935
We must not become a sort of bell-wether to lead opinion in Europe against Italy's Abyssinian designs ... we are not strong enough to be the lawgiver and the spokesman of the world. I regard this episode as a very small matter compared to the [German] dangers I have just described ... no one can keep up the pretence that Abyssinia is a fit, worthy and equal member of a League of civilized nations.

Source: quoted in R. Rhodes James, *Churchill: A Study in Failure* (Weidenfeld & Nicolson, 1970)

An American view

The American people deluded themselves that because the League sat in far-off Geneva and we had no official association with it, it did not concern us. Without our political support, the League was predominantly a British bulwark, and it could not make its sanctions against Italy effective in the Abyssinian crisis. It took a second World War with its terrible cost, to bring the United States into the United Nations. If a nation can sit in sackcloth and ashes, the United States should do so for its selfish rejection of the League.

Source: Harry Hansen, *The Forgotten Men of Versailles*

(a) (i) What points is the cartoonist in Source B trying to make? Use Section 3.4(h) and Source E to help you decide.   4 marks
    (ii) Which of the participants in the Manchuria crisis do you think the cartoonist most sympathises with? Explain your answer.   2 marks
    (iii) How well do you think the cartoonist gets his message across?
                                                        1.4c–7c 2 marks
(b) Read again carefully what Sir Samuel Hoare said (Source D) about Britain's attitude towards the Abyssinia crisis. Does the information in Section 3.4(j) and in Source E(ii) mean that Hoare was lying, or is there some other explanation?   1.6c–9b 7 marks
(c) How useful is each of these Sources A to F for explaining why the League of Nations failed to preserve the peace?   3.4–9 15 marks

Total: 30 marks

4 International relations 1919–33

Summary of events

International relations between the two world wars fall into two distinct phases, with the division at January 1933, the fateful month in which Adolf Hitler came to power in Germany. Before that, there seemed reasonable hope that world peace could be maintained, in spite of the failure of the League of Nations to curb Japanese aggression in Manchuria. Once Hitler was firmly in control, there was little chance of preventing a war of some sort, either limited or full-scale, depending on one's interpretation of Hitler's intentions (see Section 5.3). The first phase can be divided roughly into three:

- 1919–23
- 1924–9
- 1930–3.

(a) *1919 to 1923*

In the aftermath of the First World War, relations were disturbed by problems arising from the peace settlement, while the newborn League of Nations struggled to sort things out.

- Both Turkey and Italy were dissatisfied with their treatment; Turkey was prepared to defy the settlement (see Section 2.10). The Italians, soon to come under the rule of Mussolini (1922), showed their resentment first by the seizure of Fiume, which had been awarded to Yugoslavia, and then in the Corfu Incident; later Italian aggression was turned against Abyssinia (1935).
- The problem of German reparations and whether or not she could afford to pay, caused strained relations between Britain and France, because of their different attitudes towards German recovery.
- An attempt by Lloyd George to reconcile France and Germany at the 1922 Genoa Conference failed miserably.
- Relations deteriorated still further in 1923 when French troops occupied the Ruhr (an important German industrial region) in an attempt to seize in goods what the Germans were refusing to pay in cash. This succeeded only in bringing about the collapse of the German currency.
- Meanwhile the USA, while choosing to remain politically isolated, exercised considerable economic influence on Europe by, among other things, insisting on full payment of European war debts.

- Russia, now under Bolshevik (Communist) rule, was viewed with suspicion by the western countries, several of which, along with Japan, intervened against the Bolsheviks in the civil war which ravaged Russia during 1918–20.

(b) *1924 to 1929*

There was a general improvement in the international atmosphere caused partly by changes in political leadership. In France Edouard Herriot and Aristide Briand, in Germany Gustav Stresemann, and in Britain James Ramsay MacDonald, came to power, and all were keen to improve relations. The result was the *Dawes Plan*, worked out in 1924 with American help, which eased the situation regarding German reparations. 1925 saw the signing of the *Locarno Treaties* which guaranteed the frontiers in western Europe fixed at Versailles; this seemed to remove French suspicions of German intentions. Germany was allowed to join the League in 1926 and two years later, 65 nations signed the *Kellogg–Briand Pact* renouncing war. The 1929 *Young Plan* reduced German reparations to a more manageable figure; all seemed set fair for a peaceful future.

(c) *1930 to 1933*

Towards the end of 1929 the world began to run into economic difficulties, which helped to cause a deterioration in international relations. It was partly for economic reasons that Japanese troops invaded Manchuria in 1931; mass unemployment in Germany was important in enabling Hitler to come to power. In this unpromising climate, the World Disarmament Conference met (1932) only to break up in failure when the German delegates walked out (1933). With such a complex period, it will be best to treat the various themes separately.

4.1 What attempts were made to improve international relations, and how successful were they?

(a) *The League of Nations*

The League played an important role, settling a number of international disputes and problems (see Chapter 3). However, its authority tended to be weakened by the fact that many states seemed to prefer signing agreements independently of the League, which suggests that they were not exactly brimming with confidence at the League's prospects.

(b) *The Washington Conferences (1921–2)*

These tried to improve relations between the USA and Japan. The USA was increasingly suspicious of growing Japanese power in the Far East, and of Japanese influence in China, especially bearing in mind that during the First World War, Japan had seized Kiaochow and all the German islands in the Pacific.

- To prevent a naval building race, it was agreed that the Japanese navy would be limited to three-fifths of the size of the American and British navies.
- Japan agreed to withdraw from Kiaochow and the Shantung province of China, which she had occupied since 1914.

- In return she was allowed to keep the former German Pacific islands as mandates.
- The western powers promised not to build any more naval bases within striking distance of Japan.
- The USA, Japan, Britain and France agreed to guarantee the neutrality of China and to respect each other's possessions in the Far East.

At the time, the agreements were regarded as a great success, and relations between the powers involved improved. In reality, however, Japan was left supreme in the Far East, possessor of the world's third largest navy, which she could concentrate in the Pacific. On the other hand, the navies of Britain and the USA, though larger, were spread more widely. This was to have unfortunate consequences for China in the 1930s when the USA refused to become involved in checking Japanese aggression.

(c) *The Genoa Conference (1922)*

This was the brainchild of the British Prime Minister, Lloyd George. He hoped it would solve the pressing problems of Franco-German hostility (the Germans were threatening to stop paying reparations), European war debts to the USA, and the need to resume proper diplomatic relations with Soviet Russia. Unfortunately the conference failed: the French refused all compromise and insisted on full reparations payments; the Americans refused even to attend, and the Russians and Germans withdrew and signed a mutual agreement at Rapallo. When, the following year, the Germans refused to pay the amount due, French troops occupied the Ruhr, and deadlock quickly developed when the Germans responded with passive resistance.

(d) *The Dawes Plan*

Worked out at a conference in London in 1924, this was an attempt to break this deadlock. The three newcomers to international politics, MacDonald, Herriot and Stresemann, were eager for reconciliation; the Americans were persuaded to take part, and the conference was chaired for part of the time by the American representative, General Dawes. No reduction was made in the total amount Germany was expected to pay, but it was agreed that she should pay annually *only what she could reasonably afford until she became more prosperous*. A foreign loan of 800 million gold marks, mostly from the USA, was to be made to Germany. France, now assured of at least some reparations from Germany, *agreed to withdraw her troops from the Ruhr*. The plan was successful: the German economy began to recover on the basis of the American loans, and international tensions gradually relaxed, preparing the way for the next agreements.

(e) *The Locarno Treaties (1925)*

These were a number of different agreements involving Germany, France, Britain, Italy, Belgium, Poland and Czechoslovakia. The most important one was that *Germany, France and Belgium promised to respect their joint frontiers*; if one of the three broke the agreement, Britain and Italy would assist the state which was being attacked. Germany signed agreements with Poland and Czechoslovakia providing for arbitration over possible disputes, but Germany would not guarantee her frontiers with Poland and Czechoslovakia. It was also agreed that France would help Poland and Czechoslovakia if Germany attacked them.

The agreements were greeted with wild enthusiasm all over Europe, and the reconciliation between France and Germany was referred to as the 'Locarno honeymoon'.

Later, historians were not so enthusiastic about Locarno; there was one glaring omission from the agreements – no guarantees were given by Germany or Britain about *Germany's eastern frontiers with Poland and Czechoslovakia*, the very areas where trouble was most likely to arise. By ignoring this problem, Britain gave the impression that she might not act if Germany attacked Poland or Czechoslovakia. For the time being though, as the world enjoyed a period of great economic prosperity, such uneasy thoughts were pushed into the background and Germany was allowed to enter the League in 1926. Stresemann and Briand (French Foreign Minister 1925–32) met regularly and had friendly discussions; often Austen Chamberlain (British Foreign Minister 1924–9) joined them. This 'Locarno spirit' culminated in the next piece of paper signing.

(f) *The Kellogg–Briand Pact (1928)*

This was originally Briand's idea: he proposed that France and the USA should sign a pact renouncing war. Frank B. Kellogg (American Secretary of State) proposed that the whole world should be involved; eventually 65 states signed, agreeing *to renounce war as an instrument of national policy*. This sounded impressive but was completely useless because no mention was made of sanctions against any state which broke its pledge. Japan signed the Pact, but this did not prevent her from waging war against China only three years later.

(g) *The Young Plan (1929)*

This aimed to settle the remaining problem of reparations – the Dawes Plan had left the total amount payable uncertain. In the improved atmosphere, the French were willing to compromise, and a committee chaired by an American banker, Owen Young, decided to reduce reparations from £6600 million to £2000 million, to be paid on a graded scale over the next 59 years. This was the figure that Keynes had urged at Versailles, and its acceptance ten years later was an admission of error by the Allies.

The plan was welcomed in Germany, but before there was time to put it into operation, a series of events following in rapid succession destroyed the fragile harmony of Locarno: the death of Stresemann (October 1929) removed one of the outstanding 'men of Locarno'; the Wall Street Crash in the same month soon developed into the great depression, and by 1932 there were over six million unemployed in Germany. Hope was kept alive by the *Lausanne Conference (1932)* at which Britain and France released Germany from most of the remaining reparations payments. However, in January 1933 Hitler became German Chancellor, and after that, international tension mounted.

(h) *The World Disarmament Conference (1932–3)*

This met in Geneva to try and work out a formula for scaling down armaments; all League members had undertaken to reduce armaments when they accepted the Covenant. In fact Germany was the only state to disarm, as Stresemann regularly pointed out; but the rest shrank from being the first to start the ball rolling. If no progress could be made during the Locarno honeymoon, there was little chance in the disturbed atmosphere of the 1930s. The French, alarmed by the rapid increase in support for the Nazis in Germany, refused either to disarm or to allow Germany equality of armaments with them. Hitler, knowing that Britain and Italy sympathized with Germany, withdrew from the conference (October 1933) which was dead from that moment. A week later Germany also withdrew from the League.

In retrospect, it can be seen that the statesmen of the world had only limited success in improving international relations. Even the 'Locarno spirit' proved an illusion, because so much depended on economic prosperity. When this evaporated, all the old hostilities and suspicions surfaced again, and authoritarian regimes came to power, which were prepared to risk aggression.

4.2 How did France try to deal with the problem of Germany between 1919 and 1933?

As soon as the First World War ended, the French, after all they had suffered in two German invasions in less than 50 years, wanted to make sure that the Germans never again violated the sacred soil of France; this remained the major concern of French foreign policy throughout the inter-war years. At different times, depending on who was in charge of foreign affairs, the French tried different methods of dealing with the problem:

- trying to keep Germany economically and militarily weak;
- signing alliances with other states to isolate Germany and working for a strong League of Nations; and
- extending the hand of reconciliation and friendship.

In the end, they all failed.

(a) *Trying to keep Germany weak*

1 Insistence on a harsh settlement

At the Paris peace conference the French premier, Clemenceau, insisted on a harsh settlement:

- in order to strengthen French security, the German army was to number no more than 100 000 men and there were to be severe limitations on armaments (see Section 2.8(a));
- the German Rhineland was to be de-militarized to a distance of 50 kilometres east of the river; and
- France was to have the use of the Saar for 15 years.

Britain and the USA promised to help France if Germany attacked again. Although many French people were disappointed (Foch wanted France to be given the whole of the German Rhineland west of the river, but they were only allowed to occupy it for 15 years), it looked at first as though security was guaranteed.

Unfortunately French satisfaction was short-lived: the Americans were afraid that membership of the League might involve them in another war, and so they rejected the entire peace settlement (March 1920) and abandoned their guarantees of assistance; the British used this as an excuse to cancel their promises, and the French understandably felt betrayed.

2 Clemenceau demanded that the Germans should pay reparations

The figure for reparations (money to help repair damages) was fixed in 1921 at £6600 million. It was thought that the strain of paying this would keep Germany economically weak for the next 66 years – the period over which reparations were to be paid in annual instalments – and consequently another German attack on France would be less likely. However, financial troubles in Germany soon caused the government to fall behind with its payments. The French, who needed the cash from reparations to balance their budget and pay their own debts to the USA, became desperate.

3 Attempts to force the Germans to pay

The next Prime Minister, the anti-German Raymond Poincaré, decided that drastic methods were needed to force the Germans to pay and to weaken their powers of revival. *In January 1923 French and Belgian troops occupied the Ruhr* (the important German industrial area which includes the cities of Essen and Dusseldorf). The Germans replied with passive resistance, strikes and sabotage. A number of nasty incidents between troops and civilians resulted in the deaths of over a hundred people.

Although the French managed to seize goods worth about £40 million, the whole episode caused galloping inflation and the collapse of the German mark, which by November 1923 was completely valueless. It also revealed the basic difference between the French and British attitudes towards Germany: while France adopted a hard line and wanted Germany completely crippled, Britain now saw moderation and reconciliation as the best security; she believed that an economically healthy Germany would be good for the stability of Europe (as well as for British exports). Consequently Britain strongly disapproved of the Ruhr occupation and sympathized with Germany.

(b) *A network of alliances and a strong League*

At the same time *the French tried to increase their security by building up a network of alliances*, first with Poland (1921) and later with Czechoslovakia (1924), Romania (1926) and Yugoslavia (1927). This network, known as the 'Little Entente', though impressive on paper, did not amount to much because the states involved were comparatively weak. What the French needed was a renewal of the old alliance with Russia which had served them well during the First World War; but this seemed out of the question now that Russia had become communist.

The French worked for a strong League of Nations, with the victorious powers acting as a military police force compelling aggressive powers to behave themselves. However, in the end it was the much more vague Wilson version of the League that was adopted. French disappointment was bitter when Britain took the lead in rejecting the Geneva Protocol which might have strengthened the League (see Section 3.4(e)). Clearly there was no point in expecting much guarantee of security from that direction.

(c) *Compromise and reconciliation*

By the summer of 1924, when the failure of Poincaré's Ruhr occupation was obvious, the new premier, Herriot, was *prepared to accept a compromise solution* to the reparations problem; this led to the Dawes Plan (see Section 4.1).

During the Briand era (he was Foreign Minister in 11 successive governments between 1925 and 1932), *the French approach to the German problem was one of reconciliation*. Briand persevered with great skill to build up genuinely good relations with Germany, as well as to improve relations with Britain and strengthen the League (Illus.

Illus. 4.1 Briand and Stresemann, the Foreign Ministers of France and Germany

4.1). Fortunately Stresemann, who was in charge of German foreign policy from November 1923 until 1929, believed that the best way to foster German recovery was by co-operation with Britain and France. The result was the Locarno Treaties, the Kellogg–Briand Pact, the Young Plan and the cancellation of most of the remaining reparations payments (see section 4.1).

There is some debate among historians about how genuine this apparent reconciliation between France and Germany really was. A.J.P. Taylor suggested that though Briand and Stresemann were sincere, 'they did not carry their peoples with them'; nationalist feeling in the two countries was so strong that both men were limited in the concessions they could offer. The fact that Stresemann was secretly determined to get the frontier with Poland re-drawn to Germany's advantage (see Source B in question 2 at the end of the chapter) would have caused friction later, since Poland was France's ally. He was equally determined to work for union with Austria and a revision of the Versailles terms.

(d) *A tougher attitude towards Germany*

The death of Stresemann, the world economic crisis and the growth of support in Germany for the Nazis, alarmed the French, and made them adopt a tougher attitude towards Germany. When in 1931 the Germans proposed an Austro-German customs union to ease the economic crisis, the French insisted that the matter be referred to the International Court of Justice at the Hague, on the grounds that it was a violation of the Versailles Treaty. Though a customs union made economic sense, the court ruled against it, and the plan was dropped. At the World Disarmament Conference (1932–3) relations worsened (see Section 4.1), and when Hitler took Germany out of the Conference and the League, all Briand's work was ruined. The German problem was as far from being solved as ever.

4.3 How did relations between the USSR and Britain, Germany and France develop between 1919 and 1933?

For the first three years after the Bolsheviks came to power (November 1917), relations between the new government and the western countries deteriorated to the point of open war. This was mainly because the Bolsheviks tried to spread the revolution further, especially in Germany. As early as December 1917, they began to pour floods of propaganda into Germany in an attempt to turn the masses against their capitalist masters. After the Russian defeat in the First World War, Karl Radck, one of the Bolshevik leaders, went secretly to Berlin to plan the revolution, while other agents did the same in Austria and Hungary. It was hoped that world-wide revolution would follow.

This sort of behaviour did not endear the communists to the governments of Britain, France, USA, Czechoslovakia and Japan. These states tried rather half-heartedly to destroy the Bolsheviks by intervening in the Russian civil war to help the other side (known as the Whites) (see Section 15.3(c)). The Russians were not invited to the Versailles conference in 1919. By the middle of 1920, however, circumstances were gradually changing: the countries which had interfered in Russia had admitted failure and withdrawn their troops; communist revolutions in Germany and Hungary had failed; and Russia was too exhausted by the civil war to think about stirring up any more revolutions for the time being. The way was open for communications to be re-established.

(a) *The USSR and Britain*

Relations blew hot and cold according to which government was in power in Britain. The two Labour governments (1924 and 1929–31) were much more sympathetic to Russia than the others.

1   After the failure to overthrow the communists, Lloyd George (British Prime Minister 1916–22) was prepared for reconciliation. This corresponded with Lenin's desire for improved relations with the west so that Russia could attract foreign trade and capital. The result was *an Anglo-Russian trade treaty (March 1921)* which was important for Russia, not only commercially, but also because Britain was one of the first states to acknowledge the existence of the Bolshevik government; it was to lead to similar agreements with other countries and to full political recognition.

    The new rapprochement (drawing together) was soon shaken, however, when at the Genoa conference (1922), *Lloyd George suggested that the Bolsheviks should pay war debts* incurred by the tsarist regime. The Russians were offended; they left the conference and signed the separate *Treaty of Rapallo with the Germans* (see below). This alarmed Britain and France, who could see no good coming from what Lloyd George called 'this fierce friendship'.

2   Relations improved briefly in 1924 when MacDonald and the new Labour government gave *full diplomatic recognition to the communists*. A new trade treaty was signed and a British loan to Russia was proposed. However, this was unpopular with British Conservatives and Liberals, who soon brought MacDonald's government down.

3   *Under the Conservatives (1924–9) relations with Russia worsened.* British Conservatives had no love for the communists, and there was evidence that Russian propaganda was encouraging the Indian demands for independence. Police raided the British Communist Party headquarters in London (1925) and the

premises of Arcos, a Soviet trading organization based in London (1927), and claimed to have found evidence of Russians plotting with British communists to overthrow the system. The government expelled the mission and broke off diplomatic relations with the Russians, who replied by arresting some British residents in Moscow.

4   *Matters took a turn for the better in 1929* when Labour, encouraged by the new pro-western Foreign Minister, Maxim Litvinov, resumed diplomatic relations with Russia and signed another trade agreement the following year. But the improvement was only short-lived.

5   The Conservative-dominated National government which came to power in 1931, *cancelled the trade agreement (1932)*, and in retaliation the Russians arrested four Metropolitan-Vickers engineers working in Moscow. They were tried and given sentences ranging from two to three years for 'spying and wrecking'. However, when Britain placed an embargo on imports from Russia, Stalin released them (June 1933). By this time Stalin was becoming nervous about the possible threat from Hitler, and was therefore prepared to take pains to improve relations with Britain.

(b) *The USSR and Germany*

The USSR's relations with Germany were more consistent and more friendly than with Britain. This was because the Germans saw advantages to be gained from exploiting friendship with the USSR, and because the Bolsheviks were anxious to have stable relations with at least one capitalist power.

1   *A trade treaty was signed (May 1921)* followed by the granting of Soviet trade and mineral concessions to some German industrialists.

2   *The Rapallo Treaty, signed on Easter Sunday 1922* after both Germany and Russia had withdrawn from the Genoa conference, was an important step forward.
   - Full diplomatic relations were resumed and reparations claims between the two states cancelled.
   - Both could look forward to advantages from the new friendship: they could co-operate to keep Poland weak, which was in both their interests.
   - The USSR had Germany as a buffer against any future attack from the west.
   - The Germans were allowed to build factories in Russia for the manufacture of aeroplanes and ammunition, enabling them to get round the Versailles disarmament terms.
   - German officers trained in Russia in the use of the new forbidden weapons.

3   *The Treaty of Berlin (1926)* renewed the Rapallo agreement for a further five years; it was understood that Germany would remain neutral if the USSR were attacked by another power, and neither would use economic sanctions against the other.

4   *About 1930 relations began to cool* as some Russians expressed concern at the growing power of Germany; the German attempt to form a customs union with Austria in 1931 was taken as an ominous sign of increasing German nationalism. Russian concern changed to alarm at the growth of the Nazi party, which was strongly anti-communist. Though Stalin and Litvinov tried to continue the friendship with Germany, they also began approaches to Poland, France and Britain. In January 1934 Hitler abruptly ended Germany's special relationship with the soviets by signing a non-aggression pact with Poland (see Section 5.5(b)).

(c) *The USSR and France*

The Bolshevik takeover in 1917 was a serious blow for France because Russia had been an important ally whom she relied on to keep Germany in check. Now her former ally was calling for revolution in all capitalist states, and could only be regarded as a menace to be destroyed as soon as possible. The French sent troops to help the anti-Bolsheviks (Whites) in the civil war, and it was because of French insistence that the Bolsheviks were not invited to Versailles. The French also intervened in the war between Russia and Poland in 1920; troops commanded by General Weygand helped to drive back a Russian advance on Warsaw (the Polish capital), and afterwards the French government claimed to have stemmed the westward spread of Bolshevism. The subsequent alliance between France and Poland (1921) seemed to be directed as much against Russia as against Germany.

Relations improved in 1924 when the moderate Herriot government resumed diplomatic relations. But the French were never very enthusiastic, especially as the French Communist Party was under orders from Moscow not to co-operate with other left wing parties. Not until the early 1930s did the rise of the German Nazis cause a change of heart on both sides.

4.4 United States foreign policy 1919–33

The USA had been deeply involved in the First World War, and when hostilities ceased, she seemed likely to play an important role in world affairs. President Woodrow Wilson was a crucial figure at the peace conference; his great dream was the League of Nations, through which the USA would maintain world peace. However, the American people, tired of war and suspicious of Europe, rejected Wilson and his League of Nations. From 1921 until early 1933 the USA was ruled by Republican governments which believed in a policy of *isolation*: she never joined the League and she tried to avoid political disputes with other states and the signing of treaties. Some historians still blame the failure of the League on the absence of the USA. In spite of this desire for isolation, the Americans found it impossible to avoid some involvement in world affairs, because of overseas trade, investment and the thorny problem of European war debts and reparations.

1   During the prosperous years of the 1920s, Americans tried to *increase trade and profits by investment abroad*, in Europe, Canada, and in Central and South America. It was inevitable therefore, that the USA should take an interest in what was happening in these areas. There was, for example, a serious dispute with Mexico which was threatening to seize American-owned oil wells; a compromise solution was eventually reached.

2   *The Washington Conferences (1921–2)* were called by President Harding because of concern at Japanese power in the Far East (see Section 4.1(b)).

3   *Allied war debts to the USA caused much ill-feeling.*   During the war the American government had organized loans to Britain and her allies amounting to almost 12 billion dollars at 5 per cent interest. The Europeans hoped that the Americans would cancel the debts, since the USA had done well out of the war (by taking over former European markets), but both Harding and Coolidge insisted that repayments be made in full. The Allies claimed that their ability to pay depended on whether Germany paid her reparations to them, but the Americans would not admit that there was any connection between the two. Eventually Britain was the first to agree to pay the full amount, over 62 years at the reduced

interest rate of 3.3 per cent. Other states followed, the USA allowing much lower interest rates depending on the poverty of the country concerned; Italy got away with 0.4 per cent, but this caused strong objections from Britain.

4   *Faced with the German financial crisis of 1923, the Americans had to change their attitude* and admit the connection between reparations and war debts. They agreed to take part in the Dawes and Young Plans (1924 and 1929) which enabled the Germans to pay reparations. However, this caused the ludicrous situation in which America lent money to Germany so that she could pay reparations to France, Britain and Belgium, and they in turn could pay their war debts to the USA. The whole set-up, together with American insistence on keeping high tariffs, was a contributory cause of the world economic crisis (see Section 19.4), with all its far-reaching consequences.

5   *The Kellogg–Briand Pact (1928)* was another notable, though useless, American foray into world affairs.

6   *Relations with Britain were uneasy*, not only because of war debts, but because the Conservatives resented the limitations on British naval expansion imposed by the earlier Washington agreement. MacDonald, anxious to improve relations, organized a conference in London in 1930. It was attended also by the Japanese, and the three states reaffirmed the 5:5:3 ratio in cruisers, destroyers and submarines agreed at Washington. This was successful in re-establishing friendship between Britain and the USA, but the Japanese soon exceeded their limits.

7   *The USA returned to a policy of strict isolation* when the Japanese invaded Manchuria in 1931. Although President Hoover condemned the Japanese action, he refused to join in economic sanctions or to make any move which might lead to war with Japan. Consequently Britain and France felt unable to act and the League was shown to be helpless. Throughout the 1930s, though acts of aggression increased, the Americans remained determined not to be drawn into a conflict.

Questions

1   (a)   Using information from the chapter, explain briefly how and why different people had different ideas about, and attitudes to, the following problems or situations:

(i)   the problem of German reparations;
(ii)   Communist rule in the USSR;
(iii)   Allied war debts to the USA.   1.4c–8c

(b)   Explain how the changes brought about by the following could be seen as helping progress in international affairs in some ways, but not in others:

(i)   the Washington Conferences, 1921–2;
(ii)   the Rapallo Treaty, 1922;
(iii)   the Locarno Treaties, 1925.   1.4a–7a

2   *German foreign policy during the 1920s* – study Sources A–F below, and then answer the questions which follow.

___ **Source A** _____

Memorandum by General von Seeckt, Head of the German Army (Reichswehr), September 1922

Poland's existence is intolerable, incompatible with the survival of Germany. It must disappear. For Russia, Poland is even more intolerable than for us; no Russian can allow Poland to exist. Russia and Germany within the frontiers of

1914 should be the basis of reaching an understanding between the two. . . We aim at two things: first a strengthening of Russia in the economic and political, and thus also in the military field, and so indirectly a strengthening of ourselves, by strengthening a possible ally of the future. We further desire a direct strengthening of ourselves by helping to create in Russia an armaments industry which in case of need will serve us.

Source: quoted in F.L. Carsten, *The Reichswehr and Politics, 1918–1933* (Oxford, 1966, adapted)

Source B

Letter from Gustav Stresemann to the former German Crown Prince, September 1925

In my opinion there are three great tasks which confront German foreign policy in the immediate future –
In the first place the solution of the reparations question in a way acceptable to Germany, and the assurance of peace.
Secondly the protection of Germans abroad, those 10 to 12 million of our kindred who now live under a foreign yoke in foreign lands.
The third is the readjustment of our eastern frontiers; the recovery of Danzig, the Polish corridor, and a correction of the frontier in Upper Silesia.
Hence the Locarno Pact which guarantees us peace and makes England, as well as Italy, guarantors of our western frontiers.
I would utter a warning against any ideas of flirting with Bolshevism; we cannot involve ourselves in an alliance with Russia though an understanding is possible on another basis. When the Russians are in Berlin, the red flag will at once be flown from the castle, and in Russia, where they hope for a world revolution, there will be much joy at the spread of Bolshevism as far as the Elbe. The most important thing for German policy is the liberation of German soil from any occupying force. On that account German policy must be one of finesse and avoidance of great decisions.

Source: E. Sutton, *Gustav Stresemann, His Diaries, Letters and Papers* (Macmillan, 1935, adapted)

Source C

Announcement by Chancellor Wilhelm Marx (Catholic Centre Party) to the Reichstag, February 1927

The foreign policy which the Reich government has pursued unceasingly and unflinchingly since the end of the war and which ultimately led to the London Dawes Agreement, to the treaties of Locarno and to entry into the League of Nations, is characterized by a rejection of the notion of revenge. Its purpose is rather the achievement of a mutual understanding.

Source D

A German historian, Fritz Ernst, writes about his education

In our high school in Stuttgart, as, indeed, in most of the secondary schools in Germany after 1918, a noticeable right-wing tendency prevailed, which most of our teachers followed, at least those who spoke to us about politics. We believed that it was the stab in the back alone that had prevented a German victory. We were convinced that one could only be patriotic on the rightist side. . . We did not know what the actual situation of the war had been in 1918; we were taught to hate the French and the British and to despise the Americans.

(a) What different ideas about German foreign policy can you find in Sources A to E?   1.4c–6c   10 marks
(b) What reasons can you suggest for these differences?   1.7c–8c   5 marks
(c) In what ways (apart from being a cartoon) is Source F different from the other sources?   1. 4c–8c   3 marks
(d) How useful are these sources for explaining why the prospects for peace were not as good as they might have seemed in 1925?   3.4–7   12 marks
Total: 30 marks

5 International relations 1933-9

Summary of events

This short period is of crucial importance in world history because it culminated in the Second World War. Economic problems caused the Locarno spirit to fade away, and the new rule seemed to be: every country for itself. Affairs were dominated by the three aggressive powers – Japan, Italy and Germany; their extreme nationalism led them to commit so many acts of violence and breaches of international agreements that in the end, the world was plunged into total war.

Japan became the first major aggressor with her successful invasion of Manchuria, (1931); both Hitler and Mussolini took note of the failure of the League of Nations to curb Japanese aggression. Hitler, by far the most subtle of the three, began cautiously by announcing the reintroduction of conscription (March 1935). This breach of Versailles caused Britain, France and Italy to draw together briefly in suspicion of Germany. At a meeting held in Stresa (on Lake Maggiore in N. Italy), they condemned Hitler's action, and soon afterwards (May) the French, obviously worried, signed a treaty of mutual assistance with the USSR.

However, the *Stresa Front*, as it was called, was only short-lived· it was broken in June 1935 when the British, without consulting France and Italy, signed the *Anglo-German Naval Agreement*; this allowed the Germans to build submarines – another breach of Versailles. This astonishing move by Britain disgusted France and Italy and destroyed any trust which had existed between the three of them. Mussolini, encouraged by Japanese and German successes, now followed suit with his successful invasion of Abyssinia (October 1935), which met only half-hearted resistance from the League and from Britain and France.

March 1936 saw Hitler sending troops into the Rhineland, which had been demilitarized by the Versailles treaty; Britain and France again protested but took no action to expel the Germans. An understanding then followed (October 1936) between Germany and Italy, Mussolini having decided to throw in his lot with Hitler; it was known as the *Rome–Berlin Axis*. The following month Hitler signed the *Anti-Comintern Pact* with Japan. (The Comintern or Communist International was an organization set up in 1919 by Lenin with the aim of starting communist parties in other countries to work for revolution.) During the summer of 1936 the Spanish Civil War broke out; it quickly developed an international significance when both Hitler and Mussolini, flexing their military muscles, sent help to Franco, while the republicans received Soviet help (see Section 14.3(c)). Predictably, Britain and France refused to intervene and by 1939 Franco was victorious.

In 1937 the Japanese took full advantage of Europe's preoccupation with events in Spain to embark on a full-scale invasion of northern China. The resulting Sino-Japanese War eventually became part of the Second World War.

By this time it was clear that the League of Nations, working through collective security, was totally ineffective. Consequently Hitler, now sure that the Italians would not object, carried out his most ambitious project to date – the annexation of Austria (known as the *Anschluss*, March 1938). Next he turned his attentions to Czechoslovakia and demanded the *Sudetenland*, an area containing 3 million Germans, adjoining the frontier with Germany. When the Czechs refused Hitler's demands, the British Prime Minister, Neville Chamberlain, anxious to avoid war at all costs, took up Hitler's invitation to a conference at Munich (September 1938), at which it was agreed that Germany should have the Sudetenland, but no more of Czechoslovakia. War seemed to have been averted. But the following March, Hitler broke this agreement and sent German troops to occupy Prague, the Czech capital. At this Chamberlain decided that Hitler had gone too far and must be stopped. When the Poles rejected Hitler's demand for Danzig, Britain and France promised to help Poland if the Germans attacked. Hitler did not take these British and French threats seriously, and grew tired of waiting for Poland to negotiate. After signing *a non-aggression pact with the USSR* (August 1939), the Germans invaded Poland on 1 September. Britain and France accordingly declared war on Germany.

5.1 Relations between Japan and China

(a) *The Japanese invasion of Manchuria in 1931*

The *motives* behind this were mixed (see Section 14.1(b)). They felt it was essential to keep control of the province because it was a valuable trade outlet. China seemed to be growing stronger under the rule of Chiang Kai-shek, and the Japanese feared this might result in their being excluded from Manchuria. In fact, it is possible to present a good defence of Japanese actions; this is what Sir John Simon, the British Foreign Minister, did at the League of Nations. Japan had been involved in the province since the 1890s, and was given Port Arthur and a privileged position in South Manchuria as a result of the Russo-Japanese War (1904–5). Since then, the Japanese had invested millions of pounds in Manchuria in the development of industry and railways. By 1931 they controlled the South Manchurian Railway and the banking system; they felt they could not stand by and see themselves gradually squeezed out of such a valuable province with a population of 30 million, especially when the Japanese themselves were suffering economic hardship because of the Great Depression. The Japanese announced that they had turned Manchuria into the independent state of Manchukuo under Pu Yi, the last of the Chinese emperors. This fooled nobody, but still, no action was taken against them. The next Japanese move, however, could not be justified, and could only be described as flagrant aggression.

(b) *The Japanese advance, 1933*

In 1933 the Japanese began to advance *from Manchuria into the rest of north-eastern China* (see Map 5.1), to which they had no claim whatsoever. By 1935 a large area of China as far as Peking had fallen under Japanese political and commercial control (see Map 5.1), while the Chinese themselves were torn by a civil war between Chiang Kai-shek's Kuomintang government and the communists led by Mao Tse-tung (see Section 17.3).

Map 5.1 Japanese Expansion 1931–42

Source: Martin Gilbert, *Recent History Atlas* (Weidenfeld & Nicolson, 1977) p. 52

(c) *Further invasions, 1937–8*

After signing the *Anti-Comintern Pact with Germany (1936)*, the Japanese army seized the excuse provided by an incident beteween Chinese and Japanese troops in Peking to begin an invasion of other parts of China (July 1937). Although the Prime Minister, Prince Konoye, was against such massive intervention, he had to give way to the wishes of General Sugiyama, the War Minister.

By the autumn of 1938 the Japanese had captured the cities of *Shanghai, Nanking* (Chiang Kai-shek's capital) and *Hankow*, committing terrible atrocities against Chinese civilians. However, complete victory eluded the Japanese: Chiang had reached an understanding with his communist enemies that they would both co-operate against the invaders. A new capital was established well inland at Chungking, and spirited Chinese resistance was mounted with help from the Russians.

Japanese troops landed in the south of China and quickly captured Canton, but Chiang still refused to surrender or accept Japanese terms.

> Meanwhile the League of Nations had again condemned Japanese aggression but was powerless to act, since Japan was no longer a member and refused to attend a conference about the situation in China. Britain and France were too busy coping with Hitler to take much notice of China, and the USSR did not want full-scale war with Japan. The USA, the only power capable of effectively resisting Japan, was still bent on isolation. Thus, on the eve of the Second World War, the Japanese controlled most of eastern China (though outside the cities their hold was shaky) while Chiang held out in the centre and west.

5.2 Mussolini's foreign policy

In the early days of Mussolini's regime, Italian foreign policy seemed rather confused: Mussolini knew what he wanted, which was 'to make Italy great, respected and feared', but he was not sure how to achieve this, apart from agitating for a revision of the 1919 peace settlement in Italy's favour. At first he seemed to think an adventurous foreign policy was his best line of action, hence the *Corfu Incident* (see Section 3.4(d)) and the *occupation of Fiume in 1923*. By an agreement signed at Rapallo in 1920, Fiume was to be a 'free city', used jointly by Italy and Yugoslavia; after Italian troops moved in, Yugoslavia agreed that it should belong to Italy. After these early successes, Mussolini became more cautious, perhaps alarmed by Italy's isolation at the time of Corfu. After 1923 his policy falls roughly into two phases:

- 1923–34
- after 1934.

(a) *1923–34*

At this stage Mussolini's policy was determined by rivalry with the French in the Mediterranean and the Balkans, where Italian relations with Yugoslavia, France's ally, were usually strained. Another consideration was the Italian fear that the weak state of Austria along her north-eastern frontier, might fall too much under the influence of Germany; Mussolini was worried about a possible German threat via the Brenner Pass. He tried to deal with both problems mainly by diplomatic means.

1   *He attended the Locarno Conference (1925)* but was disappointed when the agreements signed did not guarantee the Italian frontier with Austria.

2   *He was friendly towards Greece, Hungary, and especially Albania*, the southern
    neighbour and rival of Yugoslavia. Economic and defence agreements were
    signed, with the result that Albania was virtually controlled by Italy, which now
    had a strong position around the Adriatic Sea.
3   *He cultivated good relations with Britain:* he supported her demand that Turkey
    should hand over Mosul province to Iraq and in return, the British gave Italy a
    small part of Somaliland.
4   Italy became the first state after Britain to *recognize the USSR*; a non-aggression
    pact was signed between Italy and the USSR in September 1933.
5   *He tried to bolster up Austria against the threat from Nazi Germany* by supporting
    the anti-Nazi government of Chancellor Dollfuss, and by signing trade agreements
    with Austria and Hungary. When Dollfuss was murdered by the Austrian Nazis
    (July 1934), Mussolini sent three Italian divisions to the frontier in case the
    Germans invaded Austria; the Nazis immediately called off their attempt to seize
    power in Austria. This decisive anti-German stand improved relations between
    Italy and France. However, though he was now highly respected abroad, Mussolini
    was getting impatient; his successes were not spectacular enough.

(b) *After 1934*

Mussolini gradually drifted from extreme suspicion of Hitler's designs on Austria to
grudging admiration of Hitler's achievements and a desire to imitate him. After their
first meeting (June 1934) Mussolini described Hitler contemptuously as 'that mad little
clown', but he later came to believe that there was more to be gained from friendship
with Germany than with Britain and France. The more he fell under Hitler's influence,
the more aggressive he became. His changing attitude is illustrated by events.

1   When Hitler announced the re-introduction of conscription (March 1935),
    *Mussolini joined the British and French in condemning the German action and
    guaranteeing Austria* (the Stresa Front, April 1935). Both British and French
    carefully avoided mentioning the Abyssinian crisis which was already brewing;
    Mussolini took this to mean that they would turn a blind eye to an Italian attack on
    Abyssinia, regarding it as a bit of old-fashioned colonial expansion. The Anglo-
    German Naval Agreement signed in June (see Section 5.3(b)(6)) convinced
    Mussolini of British cynicism and self-interest.
2   *The invasion of Abyssinia (Ethiopia)* was the great turning point in Mussolini's
    career. Italian involvement in the country, the only remaining independent state
    left in Africa, went back to 1896, when an Italian attempt to colonize it had ended
    in ignominious defeat at Adowa. *Mussolini's motives for the 1935 attack were:*

    ● Italy's existing colonies in East Africa (Eritrea and Somaliland) were not very
      rewarding, and his attempts (by a treaty of 'friendship' signed in 1928) to
      reduce Abyssinia to the position of Albania had failed. The Emperor of
      Abyssinia, Haile Selassie, had done all he could to avoid falling under Italian
      economic domination;
    ● Italy was suffering from the Depression, and a victorious war would divert
      attention from internal troubles and provide a new market for Italian
      exports;
    ● it would please the nationalists and colonialists, avenge the defeat of 1896 and
      boost Mussolini's sagging popularity.

The Italian victory over the ill-equipped and unprepared Ethiopians was a
foregone conclusion, though they made heavy weather of it. *Its real importance was*

Map 5.2 The position of Abyssinia and the territories of Britain, France and Italy

Source: Nichol and Lang, *Work Out Modern World History* (Macmillan, 1990) p. 47

that it demonstrated the ineffectiveness of collective security. The League condemned Italy as an aggressor and applied economic sanctions; but these were useless because they did not include banning sales of oil and coal to Italy, even though the resulting oil shortage would have seriously hampered the Italian war effort. The League's prestige suffered a further blow when it emerged that the British Foreign Secretary, Sir Samuel Hoare, had made a secret deal with Laval, the French Prime Minister (December 1935) to hand over a large section of Abyssinia to Italy; this was more than the Italians had managed to capture at that point. Public opinion in Britain was so outraged that the idea was dropped.

Reasons for this weak stand against Italy were that Britain and France were militarily and economically unprepared for war and were anxious to avoid any action (such as oil sanctions) which might provoke Mussolini into declaring war on them. They were also hoping to revive the Stresa Front and use Italy as an ally against the real threat to European peace – Germany; so their aim was to appease Mussolini.

Unfortunately the results were disastrous:

• the League and the idea of collective security were discredited.

- Mussolini was annoyed by the sanctions anyway, and began to be drawn towards friendship with Hitler, who had not criticized the invasion and had not applied sanctions. In return Mussolini dropped his objections to a German takeover of Austria.
- Hitler took advantage of the general preoccupation with Abyssinia to send troops into the Rhineland.

3   When the Spanish Civil War broke out in 1936, *Mussolini sent extensive help to Franco*, hoping to establish a third fascist state in Europe and to get naval bases in Spain from which he could threaten France. His excuse was that he wanted to prevent the spread of communism.

4   An understanding known as the *Rome–Berlin Axis* was reached with Hitler. Mussolini said that the Axis was a line drawn between Rome and Berlin, around which 'all European states that desire peace can revolve'. In 1937 Italy joined the *Anti-Comintern Pact* with Germany and Japan, in which all three pledged themselves to stand side by side against Bolshevism. This reversal of Mussolini's previous policy and his friendship with Germany were not universally popular in Italy, and disillusionment with Mussolini began to spread.

5   *His popularity revived temporarily with his part in the Munich agreement of September 1938* (see Section 5.5) which seemed to have secured peace. But Mussolini failed to draw the right conclusions from his people's relief (that most of them did not want another war) and committed a further act of aggression ...

6   *In April 1939 Italian troops suddenly occupied Albania*, meeting very little resistance. This was a pointless operation, since Albania was already under Italian economic control, but Mussolini wanted a triumph to imitate Hitler's recent occupation of Czechoslovakia.

7   Carried away by his successes, Mussolini signed a full alliance with Germany, the *Pact of Steel* (May 1939), in which Italy promised full military support if war came. Mussolini was committing Italy to deeper and deeper involvement with Germany, which in the end would ruin him.

5.3 What were Hitler's aims in foreign policy and how successful had he been by the end of 1938?

(a) *Hitler aimed to make Germany into a great power again*

He hoped to achieve this by:

- destroying the hated Versailles settlement;
- building up the army;
- recovering lost territory such as the Saar and the Polish Corridor;
- bringing all Germans inside the Reich; this would involve annexing Austria and taking territory from Czechoslovakia and Poland, both of which had large German minorities as a result of the peace settlement.

There is some disagreement about what, if anything, Hitler intended beyond these aims. Most historians believe that annexing Austria and parts of Czechoslovakia and Poland was only a beginning, and that Hitler planned to follow it up by seizing the rest of Czechoslovakia and Poland, and then conquering and occupying Russia as far east as the Ural Mountains. This would give the Germans what he called *Lebensraum* (living space) which would provide food for the German people and an area in which the ess German population could settle and colonize. An additional advantage was that ommunism would be destroyed. The next stage would be to get colonies in Africa and naval bases in and around the Atlantic. Not all historians agree about these further aims; A.J.P. Taylor, for example, claimed that Hitler never intended a major war, and at most was prepared only for a limited war against Poland.

(b) *A series of successes*

Whatever the truth about his long-term intentions, Hitler began his foreign policy with a series of brilliant successes (one of the main reasons for his popularity in Germany). By the end of 1938 almost every one of the first set of aims had been achieved, without war and with the approval of Britain. Only the Germans in Poland remained to be brought within the *Reich*. Unfortunately it was when he failed to achieve this by peaceful means that Hitler took the fateful decision to invade Poland.

1 Given that Germany was still militarily weak in 1933, *Hitler had to move cautiously at first.* He withdrew Germany from the World Disarmament Conference and from the League of Nations, on the grounds that France would not agree to Germany having equality of armaments. At the same time he insisted that Germany was willing to disarm if other states would do the same, and that he wanted only peace. This was one of his favourite techniques: to act boldly while at the same time soothing his opponents with the sort of conciliatory speeches he knew they wanted to hear.

2 *Next Hitler signed a ten-year non-aggression pact with the Poles (January 1934),* who were showing alarm in case the Germans tried to take back the Polish corridor. This was something of a triumph for Hitler: Britain took it as further evidence of his peaceful intentions; it ruined the Little Entente (see Section 4.2(b)), which depended very much on Poland; and it guaranteed Polish neutrality whenever Germany decided to move against Austria and Czechoslovakia. On the other hand, it improved relations between France and Russia, who were both worried by the apparent threat from Nazi Germany.

3 July 1934 saw Hitler suffer a setback to his ambitions of an *Anschluss* (union) between Germany and Austria. The Austrian Nazis, encouraged by Hitler, staged a revolt and murdered the Chancellor, Engelbert Dollfuss, who had been supported by Mussolini. However, when Mussolini moved Italian troops to the Austrian frontier and warned the Germans off, the revolt collapsed. Hitler, taken aback, had to accept that Germany was not yet strong enough to force the issue, and he denied responsibility for the actions of the Austrian Nazis.

4 *The Saar was returned to Germany (January 1935)* after a plebiscite resulting in a 90 per cent vote in favour. Though the vote had been provided for in the peace settlement, Nazi propaganda made the most of the success. Hitler announced that now all causes of grievance between France and Germany had been removed.

5 Hitler's first successful breach of Versailles came in March 1935 when he announced *the reintroduction of conscription*. His excuse was that Britain had just announced air force increases and France had extended conscription from 12 to 18 months (their justification was German rearmament). Much to their alarm, Hitler told his startled generals and the rest of the world that he would build up his peacetime army to 36 divisions (about 600 000 men). The generals need not have worried: although the Stresa Front condemned this violation of Versailles, no action was taken; the League was helpless, and the Front collapsed anyway as a result of Hitler's next success . . .

6 Shrewdly realizing how frail the Stresa Front was, Hitler detached Britain by

offering to limit the German navy to 35 per cent of the strength of the British navy. Britain eagerly accepted, signing the *Anglo-German Naval Agreement (June 1935)*; British thinking seems to have been that since the Germans were already breaking Versailles by building a fleet, it would be as well to have it limited. Without consulting her two allies, Britain had condoned German re-armament, which went ahead with gathering momentum. By the end of 1938 the army stood at 51 divisions (about 800 000 men) plus reserves, there were 21 large naval vessels (battleships, cruisers and destroyers), many more under construction, and 47 U-boats. A large air force of over 5000 aircraft had been built up.

7   Encouraged by his successes, Hitler took the calculated risk of *sending troops into the demilitarized zone of the Rhineland (March 1936)*, a breach of both Versailles and Locarno. Though the troops had orders to withdraw at the first sign of French opposition, no resistance was offered, except the usual protests. At the same time, well aware of the mood of pacifism among his opponents, Hitler soothed them by offering a peace treaty to last for 25 years.

8   Later in 1936 Hitler consolidated Germany' position by reaching an understanding with Mussolini (*the Rome–Berlin Axis*) and by signing *the Anti-Comintern Pact with Japan* (also joined by Italy in 1937). Germans and Italians gained military experience helping Franco to victory in the Spanish Civil War. One of the most notorious exploits in this war was the bombing of the defenceless Basque market town of Guernica by the German Condor Legion.

9   *The Anschluss with Austria (March 1938)* was Hitler's greatest success to date. Matters came to a head when the Austrian Nazis staged huge demonstrations in Vienna, Graz and Linz, which Chancellor Schuschnigg's government could not control. Realising that this could be the prelude to a German invasion, Schuschnigg announced a plebiscite about whether or not Austria should remain independent. Hitler decided to act before voting took place, in case the vote went against union; German troops moved in and Austria became part of the Third Reich. It was a triumph for Germany: it revealed the weakness of Britain and France, who again only protested. It showed the value of the new German understanding with Italy, and it dealt a severe blow to Czechoslovakia, which could now be attacked from the south as well as from the west and north (see Map 5.3). All was ready for the beginning of Hitler's campaign to get the German-speaking Sudetenland, a campaign which ended in triumph at the Munich Conference in September 1938.

> Before examining the events of Munich and after, it will be a good idea to pause and consider why it was that Hitler was allowed to get away with all these violations of the Versailles settlement. The reason can be summed up in one word – *appeasement*.

5.4 Appeasement

(a) *What is meant by the term 'appeasement'?*

Appeasement was the policy followed by the British and later by the French, of *avoiding war with aggressive powers such as Japan, Italy and Germany*, by giving way to their demands, provided they were not too unreasonable.

Map 5.3 Hitler's gains before the Second World War

There were **two distinct phases** of appeasement:

1 *From the mid-1920s until 1937* there was a vague feeling that war must be avoided at all cost, and Britain and sometimes France drifted along, accepting the various acts of aggression and breaches of Versailles (Manchuria, Abyssinia, German re-armament, the Rhineland reoccupation).
2 When Neville Chamberlain became British Prime Minister in May 1937, he gave appeasement new drive; he believed in taking the initiative – he would find out what Hitler wanted and show him that reasonable claims could be met *by negotiation rather than by force*.

The beginnings of appeasement can be seen in British policy during the 1920s with the Dawes and Young Plans which tried to conciliate the Germans, and also with the Locarno Treaties and their vital omission – Britain did not agree to guarantee Germany's eastern frontiers, which even Stresemann, the 'good German', said must be revised. When Austen Chamberlain, the British Foreign Minister (and Neville's half-brother) remarked at the time of Locarno that no British government would ever risk the bones of a single British grenadier in defence of the Polish Corridor, it seemed to the Germans that Britain had turned her back on eastern Europe. Appeasement reached its climax at Munich, where Britain and France were so determined to avoid war with Germany that they made Hitler a present of the Sudetenland, and so set in motion the destruction of Czechoslovakia. Even with such big concessions as this, appeasement failed.

(b) *How could such a policy be justified?*

At the time appeasement was being followed, there seemed lots of very good reasons in its favour, and the appeasers (who included MacDonald, Baldwin, Simon and Hoare as well as Neville Chamberlain) were convinced that their policy was right.

1 *It was thought essential to avoid war*, which was likely to be even more devastating than ever before, as the horrors of the Spanish Civil War demonstrated. The great

fear was the bombing of defenceless cities. Britain, still in the throes of the economic crisis, could not afford vast rearmament and the crippling expenses of a major war. British governments seemed to be supported by *a strongly pacifist public opinion*: in February 1933 the Oxford Union voted that it would not fight for King and Country, and Baldwin and his National Government won a huge election victory in November 1935 shortly after he had declared: 'I give you my word of honour that there will be no great armaments'.

2 *Many felt that Germany and Italy had genuine grievances.* Italy had been cheated at Versailles and Germany had been treated too harshly. Therefore the British should show them sympathy – as far as the Germans were concerned, they should try to revise the most hated clauses of Versailles. This would remove the need for German aggression and lead to Anglo-German friendship.

3 Since the League of Nations seemed to be helpless, *Chamberlain believed that the only way to settle disputes was by personal contact between leaders.* In this way, he thought, he would be able to control and civilize Hitler, and Mussolini into the bargain, and bring them to respect international law.

4 *Economic co-operation between Britain and Germany would be good for both.* If Britain helped the German economy to recover, Germany's internal violence would die down.

5 *Fear of communist Russia* was great, especially among British Conservatives. Many of them believed that the communist threat was greater than the danger from Hitler. Some British politicians were willing to ignore the unpleasant features of Nazism in the hope that Hitler's Germany would be a buffer against communist expansion westwards. In fact many admired Hitler's drive and his achievements.

6 Underlying all these feelings was the belief that Britain ought not to take any military action in case it led to *a full-scale war for which Britain was totally unprepared.* British military chiefs told Chamberlain that Britain was not strong enough to fight a war against more than one country at the same time. The USA was still in favour of isolation and France was weak and divided. Chamberlain speeded up British rearmament so that 'nobody should treat her with anything but respect'. (see Source F in Question 2 at the end of this chapter). The longer appeasement lasted, the stronger Britain would become, and the more this would deter aggression, or so Chamberlain hoped.

(c) *What part did it play in international affairs, 1933–9?*

Appeasement had a profound effect on the way international relations developed. Although it might have worked with some German governments, with Hitler it was doomed to failure. Many historians believe that it convinced Hitler of the complacency and weakness of Britain and France to such an extent that he was willing to risk attacking Poland, thereby starting the Second World War.

It is important to emphasize that appeasement was mainly a British policy, with which the French did not always agree. Poincaré stood up to the Germans (see Section 4.2(d)), and although Briand was in favour of conciliation, even he drew the line at the proposed Austro-German customs union in 1931. Louis Barthou, Foreign Minister for a few months in 1934, believed in firmness towards Hitler and aimed to build up a strong anti-German group which would include Italy and the USSR. This is why he pressed for Russia's entry into the League of Nations which took place in September 1934. He told the British that France 'refused to legalize German re-armament' contrary to the Versailles treaties. Unfortunately Barthou was assassinated in October 1934, along with King Alexander of Yugoslavia, who was on a state visit to France. They were both shot by Croat terrorists shortly after the king had arrived in Marseilles.

Barthou's successor, Pierre Laval, signed an alliance with Russia in May 1935, though it was a weak affair – there was no provision in it for military co-operation, since Laval distrusted the communists. He pinned his main hopes on friendship with Mussolini, but these were dashed by the failure of the Hoare–Laval Pact (see Section 5.2(b)). After this the French were so deeply split between left and right that no decisive foreign policy seemed possible; since the right admired Hitler, the French fell in behind the British.

Six examples of appeasement at work were:

1   *No action was taken to check the obvious German rearmament.* Lord Lothian, a Liberal, had a revealing comment to make about this, after visiting Hitler in January 1935: 'I am convinced that Hitler does not want war ... what the Germans are after is a strong army which will enable them to deal with Russia'.

2   *The Anglo-German Naval Agreement* condoning German naval rearmament was signed without any consultation with France and Italy. This broke the Stresa Front, gravely shook French confidence in Britain, and encouraged Laval to look for understandings with Mussolini and Hitler.

3   There was only *half-hearted British action against the Italian invasion of Abyssinia.*

4   Although disturbed at the German re-occupation of the Rhineland (March 1936) *the French did not mobilize their troops.* They were deeply divided, and ultra cautious, and they received no backing from the British, who were impressed by Hitler's offer of a 25-year peace. In fact, Lord Londonderry (a Conservative and Secretary of State for Air from 1931–5) was reported to have sent Hitler a telegram congratulating him on his success. Lord Lothian remarked that German troops had merely entered their own 'back garden'.

5   *Neither Britain nor France intervened in the Spanish Civil War*, though Germany and Italy sent decisive help to Franco. Britain tried to entice Mussolini to remove his troops by officially recognizing Italian possession of Abyssinia (April 1938); however, Mussolini failed to keep his side of the bargain.

6   Though both Britain and France protested strongly at the *Anschluss* between Germany and Austria (March 1938), many in Britain saw it as *the natural union of one German group to another.* But Britain's lack of action encouraged Hitler to make demands on Czechoslovakia, which produced Chamberlain's supreme act of appeasement and Hitler's greatest triumph to date – Munich.

5.5 Munich to the outbreak of war: September 1938 to September 1939

This fateful year saw Hitler waging two pressure campaigns: the first against Czechoslovakia, the second against Poland.

(a) *Czechoslovakia*

It seems likely that Hitler had decided to destroy Czechoslovakia as part of his *Lebensraum* (living space) policy, and because he hated the Czechs for their democracy, as well as for the fact that their state had been set up by the hated Versailles settlement.

1 The propaganda campaign in the Sudetenland

Hitler's excuse for the opening propaganda campaign was that 3.5 million Sudeten Germans, under their leader Konrad Henlein, were being discriminated against by the Czech government. It is true that unemployment was higher among Germans, but apart from that, they were probably not being seriously inconvenienced. The Nazis organized huge protest demonstrations in the Sudetenland, and clashes occurred between Czechs and Germans. The Czech President, Benes, feared that Hitler was stirring up the disturbances so that German troops could march in 'to restore order'. Chamberlain and Daladier, the French Prime Minister, were afraid that if this happened, war would break out. They were determined to go to almost any lengths to avoid war, and they put tremendous pressure on the Czechs to make concessions to Hitler. Chamberlain flew to Germany twice to confer with Hitler, but no progress could be made.

2 The Munich Conference, 1938

When it seemed that war was inevitable, Hitler invited Chamberlain and Daladier to a four-power conference which met in Munich (29 September 1938) (Illus. 5.1). Here a plan produced by Mussolini (but actually written by the German Foreign Office) was accepted. The Sudetenland was to be handed over to Germany immediately, but Germany, along with the other three powers, guaranteed the rest of Czechoslovakia. Neither the Czechs nor the Russians were invited to the conference. The Czechs were told that if they resisted the Munich decision, they would receive no help from Britain or France, even though France had guaranteed the Czech frontiers at Locarno. When Chamberlain arrived back in Britain, he was given a rapturous welcome by the public,

Illus. 5.1   Chamberlain and Hitler at Munich, September 1938

who thought war had been averted. Chamberlain himself remarked: 'I believe it is peace for our time'.

However, not everybody was so enthusiastic: Churchill called Munich 'a total and unmitigated defeat' (see Source B in question 2 at the end of the chapter); Duff Cooper, the First Lord of the Admiralty, resigned from the Cabinet, saying that Hitler could not be trusted to keep the agreement. They were right.

3 German troops occupy the rest of Czechoslovakia, March 1939

As a result of the Munich Agreement, Czechoslovakia was crippled by the loss of 70 per cent of her heavy industry and almost all her fortifications to Germany. Slovakia began to demand semi-independence, and it looked as if the country was about to fall apart. Hitler pressurized the Czech President, Hacha, into requesting German help 'to restore order'. Consequently in March 1939 German troops occupied the rest of Czechoslovakia. Britain and France protested but as usual took no action. Chamberlain said the guarantee of Czech frontiers given at Munich did not apply, because technically the country had not been invaded – German troops had entered by invitation.

However, the German action caused a great rush of criticism: for the first time even the appeasers were unable to justify what Hitler had done – he had broken his promise and seized non-German territory. Even Chamberlain felt this was going too far, and his attitude hardened.

Illus. 5.2 Enthusiastic crowds greet Hitler on his first visit to the ceded Sudetenland

(b) *Poland*

After taking over the Lithuanian port of Memel (which was admittedly peopled largely by Germans), Hitler turned his attentions to Poland.

1 Hitler demands the return of Danzig

The Germans resented the loss of Danzig and the Polish Corridor at Versailles, and now that Czechoslovakia was safely out of the way, Polish neutrality was no longer necessary. In April 1939 Hitler demanded *the return of Danzig and a road and railway across the corridor, linking East Prussia with the rest of Germany*. This demand was, in fact, not unreasonable, since Danzig was mainly German-speaking; but coming so soon after the seizure of Czechoslovakia, the Poles were convinced, probably rightly, that the German demands were only the preliminary to an invasion. Already fortified by a British promise of help 'in the event of any action which clearly threatened Polish independence', the Foreign Minister, Colonel Beck, rejected the German demands and refused to attend a conference; no doubt he was afraid of another Munich. British pressure on the Poles to surrender Danzig was to no avail.

2 Full-scale invasion

The only way the British promise of help to Poland could be made effective was through an alliance with Russia. But the British were so slow and hesitant in their negotiations for an alliance, that Hitler got in first and signed *a non-aggression pact with the USSR*. It was also agreed *to divide Poland up between Germany and the USSR* (24 August). Hitler was convinced now that with Russia neutral, Britain and France would not risk intervention; when the British ratified their guarantee to Poland, Hitler took it as a bluff. When the Poles still refused to negotiate, a full-scale German invasion began early on 1 September.

Chamberlain had still not completely thrown off appeasement and suggested that if German troops were withdrawn, a conference could be held – there was no response from the Germans. Only when pressure mounted in parliament and in the country did Chamberlain send an ultimatum to Germany. When this expired at 11 a.m. on 3 September, Britain was at war with Germany. Soon afterwards, France also declared war.

5.6 Why did war break out? Who or what was to blame?

The debate is still going on about who or what was responsible for the Second World War.

- *The Versailles Treaties* have been blamed for filling the Germans with bitterness and the desire for revenge.
- *The League of Nations* and the idea of collective security have been criticized because they failed to secure general disarmament and to control potential aggressors.
- *The world economic crisis* has been mentioned (see Section 19.4(c)), since without it, Hitler would probably never have come to power.

While these factors no doubt helped to create the sort of tensions which might well lead to a war, something more was needed. It is worth remembering also that by the end of 1938 most of Germany's grievances had been removed: reparations were largely cancelled, the disarmament clauses had been ignored, the Rhineland was remilitarized, Austria and Germany were united, and 3.5 million Germans had been brought into the Reich from Czechoslovakia. Germany was a great power again. So what went wrong?

(a) Was Hitler to blame?

During and immediately after the war there was general agreement outside Germany that Hitler was to blame. By attacking Poland on all fronts instead of merely occupying Danzig and the corridor, Hitler showed that he intended not just to get back the Germans lost at Versailles, but to destroy Poland. Martin Gilbert argues that his motive was to remove the stigma of defeat in the First World War; 'for the only antidote to defeat in one war is victory in the next'. Hugh Trevor-Roper and many other historians believe that Hitler intended a major war right from the beginning. They argue that he hated communism and wanted to destroy Russia and control it permanently; this could be achieved only by a major war. The destruction of Poland was an essential preliminary to the invasion of Russia. The German non-aggression pact with Russia was simply a way of lulling Russian suspicions and keeping her neutral until Poland had been dealt with.

Evidence for this theory is taken from statements in Hitler's book *Mein Kampf* (My Struggle) and from the Hossbach Memorandum, a summary made by Hitler's adjutant, Colonel Hossbach, of a meeting held in November 1937, at which Hitler explained his plans to his generals. Another important source of evidence is Hitler's *Secret Book* which he finished around 1928 but never published.

If this theory is correct, appeasement cannot be blamed as a cause of war, except that it made things easier for Hitler. Hitler had his plans, his 'blueprint' for action, and this meant that war was inevitable sooner or later. Germans, on the whole, were happy with this interpretation too. If Hitler was to blame, and Hitler and the Nazis could be viewed as a kind of grotesque accident, a temporary 'blip' in German history, that meant that the German people were largely free from blame.

However, it seems certain that Hitler had no intention of starting a *world war*. He believed that Poland and Russia were weak and would be swiftly knocked out by lightning strikes (*Blitzkrieg*).

(b) Were the appeasers to blame?

Other historians claim that appeasement was equally to blame. They argue that *Britain and France should have taken a firm line* with Hitler before Germany had become too strong: an Anglo-French attack on western Germany in 1936 at the time of the Rhineland occupation would have taught Hitler a lesson and might have toppled him from power. By giving way to him, the appeasers increased his prestige at home. As Alan Bullock writes, 'success and the absence of resistance tempted Hitler to reach out further, to take bigger risks'. He may not have had definite plans for war, but after the surrender at Munich, he was so convinced that Britain and France would remain passive again, that he decided to gamble on war with Poland.

Chamberlain has also been criticized for choosing *the wrong issue over which to make a stand* against Hitler. It is argued that German claims for Danzig and routes across the corridor were more reasonable than her demands for the Sudetenland (which contained almost a million non-Germans). Poland was difficult for Britain and France to defend and was militarily much weaker than Czechoslovakia. Chamberlain therefore should have made his stand at Munich and backed the Czechs.

Chamberlain's defenders claim that his main motive at Munich was *to give Britain time to rearm* for an eventual fight against Hitler. But his critics point out that if he had genuinely intended to curb Hitler, it would have been better for Britain to have fought alongside Czechoslovakia, which was militarily and industrially strong and had excellent fortifications.

(c) *Did Hitler intend a major war?*

A.J.P. Taylor, in his book *Origins of the Second World War* (1961), came up with the most controversial theory about the outbreak of the war. He believed that *Hitler did not intend to cause a major war, and expected at the most, a short war with Poland.* According to Taylor, Hitler's aims were similar to those of previous German rulers – Wilhelm II and Stresemann; only his methods were more ruthless. Hitler was a brilliant opportunist taking advantage of the mistakes of the appeasers and of events such as the crisis in Czechoslovakia in February 1939. Taylor thought the German occupation of the rest of Czechoslovakia in March 1939 was not the result of a sinister long-term plan: 'it was the unforeseen by-product of events in Slovakia' (the Slovak demand for more independence from the Prague government). Whereas Chamberlain miscalculated when he thought he could make Hitler respectable and civilized, Hitler misread the minds of Chamberlain and the British. How could Hitler foresee that the British and French would be so inconsistent as to support Poland (where his claim to land was more reasonable) after giving way to him over Czechoslovakia (where his case was much less valid)?

Thus for Taylor, Hitler was lured into the war almost by accident, after the Poles had called his bluff. Many people in Britain were outraged at Taylor because they thought he was trying to 'whitewash' Hitler. But Taylor was not defending Hitler; just the opposite in fact – Hitler was still to blame, and so were the German people, for being aggressive.

> Hitler was the creation of German history and of the German present. He would have counted for nothing without the support and cooperation of the German people ... Many hundred thousand Germans carried out his evil orders without qualm or question.

(d) *Did the USSR make war inevitable?*

The USSR has been accused of making war inevitable by signing the non-aggression pact with Germany. It is argued that she ought to have allied with the west

> What conclusion are we to reach? Today, 35 years after Taylor published his famous book, very few historians accept his theory that Hitler had no long-term plans for war. Some recent writers believe that Taylor ignored a lot of evidence which did not fit in with his own theory. Hitler *was* largely responsible for the war. It is perhaps appropriate to allow a recent German historian, Eberhard Jäckel, the final word:
>
> > Hitler's ultimate goal was the establishment of a greater Germany than had ever existed before in history. The way to this greater Germany was a war of conquest fought mainly at the expense of Soviet Russia ... where the German nation was to gain living space for generations to come. (Quoted in Martel, pp. 134–7, see Further Reading List.)

and with Poland, thus frightening Hitler into keeping the peace. On the other hand, the British were most reluctant to ally with the Russians. Like the Poles, Chamberlain distrusted them (because they were communists), and he thought they were militarily weak. Russian historians justify the pact on the grounds that it gave the USSR time to prepare its defences against a possible German attack.

Questions

1 (a) Using the information from the chapter, make a brief list of the causes which have been suggested for the outbreak of the Second World War. Put the ones you consider most important at the top, and the least important at the bottom.
1.4b–6b

   (b) Why has there been disagreement among historians about how far Hitler was to blame for the war? 2.4–9

2 *The Munich Agreement 1938* – study Sources A–F below and then answer the questions which follow.

Source A

Speech in the House of Commons by Neville Chamberlain on the Munich Agreement, 3 October 1938

Ever since I assumed my present office my main purpose has been to work for the peace of Europe and for the removal of those suspicions which have so long poisoned the air. The path which leads to appeasement is long and bristles with obstacles. The question of Czechoslovakia is the latest and perhaps the most dangerous. Now that we have got past it, I feel that it may be possible to make further progress along the road to sanity ... I am too much of a realist to believe that we are going to achieve our paradise in a day. We have only laid the foundations of peace. The superstructure is not even begun. For a long period now we have been engaged in this country in a great programme of rearmament. Let no one think that because we have signed this agreement we can afford to relax our efforts in regard to that programme.

Source B

Speech in the House of Commons by Winston Churchill on the Munich Agreement, 5 October 1938

If I do not begin this afternoon by paying the usual tributes to the Prime Minister for his handling of this crisis, it is certainly not from any lack of personal regard. But I will say the most unpopular thing, namely that we have sustained a total and unmitigated defeat, and that France has suffered even more than we have. ... I believe the Czechs, left to themselves, would have been able to make better terms than they have got – they could hardly have worse. I think that in future the Czechoslovak state cannot be maintained as a separate entity. You will find that in a period of time which may be measured by years, but may be measured only by months, Czechoslovakia will be engulfed in the Nazi regime. But our loyal brave people should know the truth: that there has been gross neglect and deficiency in our defences; that we have suffered a defeat without a war.

Sources: Sources A and B are quoted in J.H. Bettey (ed.), *English Historical Documents* (Routledge & Kegan Paul, 1967, adapted extracts)

Source C

Remarks by Hitler about Munich

That damned Chamberlain has spoiled my parade into Prague (October 1938). I had not thought it possible that Czechoslovakia would be served up to me by her friends (January 1939).

We should have started the war in 1938. That was our last chance to keep it localized. But they yielded to us everywhere. Like cowards they gave in to all our demands. That actually made it difficult to seize the initiative for hostilities. We missed a unique opportunity at Munich (February 1945).

Source: Quoted in J.C. Fest, *Hitler* (Weidenfeld & Nicolson, 1974)

Source D

Russian cartoon about Munich: Chamberlain and Daladier act as traffic policemen; the sign-post reads 'Left – Western Europe, Right – USSR' (Figure 5.1).

Source E

Article by a Russian historian, A.O. Chubaryan

To the Soviet Union, the Munich Agreement constituted a direct threat. In the first place by conquering the Sudeten region and soon after the whole of Czechoslovakia, the German armies drew near to the very frontiers of the USSR.

Secondly Munich showed that Britain and France preferred an agreement with the aggressor to the formation of an alliance against him. After Munich the Soviet Union was directly confronted with the danger of isolation, of being left to face German fascism on its own, and with the prospect of an alliance between Britain, France, Italy and Germany.

Source: *History of the 20th Century* (Purnell-BPC Publishing, 1969, adapted extract)

Source F

Military statistics

Table 5.1 Aircraft production of the Great Powers (1932–9)

	1932	1933	1934	1935	1936	1937	1938	1939
Fr.	600	600	600	785	890	743	1 382	3 163
GB	445	633	740	1 140	1 877	2 153	2 827	7 941
Ger.	36	368	1 968	3 183	5 112	5 606	5 235	8 295
Italy	500	500	750	1 000	1 500	1 500	1 850	2 000
USSR	2 595	2 595	2 595	3 578	3 578	3 578	7 500	10 382
Jap.	691	766	688	952	1 181	1 511	3 201	4 467
USA	593	466	437	459	1 141	949	1 800	2 195

Table 5.2 Army divisions committed to European war

	Jan. 1938	Aug. 1939
Germany	81	130
Italy	73	73
France	63	86
USSR	125	125
Czechoslovakia	34	0
Poland	40	40
Great Britain	2	4*

Note: *This was the size of force immediately available in September 1939, although Britain was committed to sending a further 39 divisions when they had completed military training.

Table 5.3 Percentage of Gross National Product devoted to defence

	Great Britain	Germany
1935	3.3	7.4
1936	4.2	12.4
1937	5.6	11.8
1938	8.1	16.6
1939	21.4	23.0
1940	51.7	38.0

Table 5.4 Size and distribution of British army (1938)

Home Defence	107 000
British India and Burma army	55 000
Indian army	190 000
Middle East	21 000
Far East	12 000
West Indies	2 000
Total	*387 000*

Table 5.5 The size of the German army (1939)

Home Defence	730 000
Trained Conscripts	2 970 000
Total	*3 700 000*

Table 5.6 Naval strength of the Great Powers (1939)

	Battleships	Aircraft carriers	Submarines
Great Britain	15	6	57
Germany	5	0	65
France	7	1	78
Italy	4	0	104
Japan	9	5	60
USSR	3	0	18
USA	15	5	87

Source: Frank McDonough, 'Why Appeasement?' in *Modern History Review*, April 1994

(a) How far do you think Sources A, B and F support or contradict each other?

1.4c–9b   9 marks

(b) Why do you think Hitler in Source C seems to be displeased with the outcome of the Munich Conference?

1.6c–9b   4 marks

(c) How well do you think the cartoonist in Source D gets his message across? Use Source E to help you.

1.7c, 3.4   4 marks

(d) (i) How useful

(ii) How reliable do you think each of these sources is for the historian trying to explain why the Munich Agreement failed to secure a lasting peace?

1.4b–9a, 3.4–8   18 marks

Total: 35 marks

3   *The Nazi–Soviet Pact, August 1939* – study sources A–E below and then answer the questions which follow.

Source A

Cartoon from the Evening Standard, *1939 (Figure 5.2)*

Source B

From 'The Soviet–German Treaty', an article published in 1969

The treaty with Germany was a step the USSR was forced to take in the difficult situation which had come about in the summer of 1939. The Soviet government did not deceive itself regarding Hitler's aims. It understood that the treaty would not bring the USSR lasting peace but only a more or less lengthy breathing-space. When it signed the treaty with Germany the Soviet government undertook the task of using the time thus gained to carry through the political and military measures needed in order to ensure the country's security and strengthen its capacity for defence.

Source C

From 'Directing Hitler Westwards', an article published in 1969

The Soviet authorites knew that Hitler was preparing to attack the West if he could not frighten them off – and he expected the signing of the Nazi–Soviet Pact to do this. Yet no serious evidence has been produced to show that British policy was directed to attempting to procure a German attack on the Soviet Union. If the Soviet leadership believed this to be the aim of British policy, they would appear to have been influenced by a major misjudgement.

The real defence of Soviet policy in 1939 is that the British were casting them in a role which, if it succeeded in restraining Hitler, would be to the credit of Great Britain, whereas if it failed, the Soviet Union would have to bear the burden of fighting on land. Great Britain had no forces available for a major land offensive in Europe and the French saw no point in abandoning their fortifications.

Source D

From The Brutal Courtship, *by David Floyd, published in 1969*

In reply to a question about the military situation in western Europe in the spring of 1940, Stalin said with a smile:

'Daladier's government in France and Chamberlain's government in Britain don't want to get seriously involved in a war with Hitler. They are still hoping to push Hitler into a war with the Soviet Union'.

In March 1941 the Russian military asked Stalin to agree to the call-up of reserves for re-training. Stalin refused on the grounds that 'it might provide the Germans with an excuse for provoking war'. At this time German reconnaissance planes were making daily flights over Soviet territory and providing the Germans with detailed pictures of the Russian defences. Stalin issued strict orders that the planes were not to be fired on.

In the period 1939–41, Russian industry was not put on to a war footing: many types of new weapons, tanks, and aircraft, which had already been tested and were superior to their German equivalents, were not put into production; some proven weapons, such as the 44-mm. anti-tank gun, were actually withdrawn from service; the reorganization of armoured units was not carried through; troop training was still on a peacetime basis.

Sources: Sources B, C and D are from *History of the 20th Century* (Purnell-BPC Publishing, 1969)

A more recent view from a British historian, Alan Bullock

Hitler's objective was not to avoid war; he believed war was essential if he was to re-arm the German people psychologically for the conquest of empire.The key was to isolate those Powers which opposed him and defeat them one at a time in a series of single campaigns. The diplomatic coup of the Nazi–Soviet Pact, relieving him of any threat of Soviet intervention in case of war . . . gave Hitler a free hand in defeating first the Poles, then the French. The destruction of Poland was followed by the defeat of France and the eviction of Britain from the continent. Hitler never wanted a war with the British, whom he admired for their success in creating an empire; all he asked was that they should not interfere in Europe. When they refused and the defeat of the German Air Force in the Battle of Britain convinced him that invasion would be a risky gamble, he decided to ignore them and go ahead with his real objective from the beginning, the attack on Russia. While Hitler became more and more impatient with the Nazi–Soviet Pact, Stalin did all in his power to prolong it. He persisted in believing that Hitler would not attack before 1942–43, and that the Western Powers were trying to trick him into provoking Hitler by counter-measures . . . On the night of 21–22 June 1941, 3 200 000 German troops broke across the frontiers, driving to the outskirts of Leningrad and Moscow, capturing three million prisoners, most of whom were so badly treated by the Germans that they died. This was the price of Stalin's obstinacy.

Source. Allan Bullock, 'Personality in History: Hitler and Stalin', in *Modern History Review*, November 1993

(a) Sources A, B and C come from either British or Russian documents. Which of the Sources are more likely to be British and which are more likely to be Russian? Give reasons for your answer.   1.6c–7c   6 marks

(b) 'Russia should not have made the pact with Germany in 1939'. Using the sources, explain how far you agree with this opinion.   1.4b–6b   5 marks

(c) After this pact had been signed, the German leader said, 'now I have the world in my pocket'. What do you think he meant by this?   1.4c–7c   3 marks

(d) Does the evidence in Source D and E support the views expressed in B? Give reasons for you answer.   1.4b–5b, 1.4c–7c   6 marks

(e) Choose *one* of these sources and comment on its reliability for the historian.   3.7–8   5 marks

Total: 25 marks

[*Based, with permission, on a Northern Examining Association question*]

The Second World War 1939–45

Summary of events

Unlike the 1914–18 war, the Second World War was a war of rapid movement and was a much more complex affair, with major campaigns taking place in the Pacific and the Far East, in North Africa and deep in the heart of Russia, as well as in central and western Europe and the Atlantic. *The war falls into four fairly clearly defined phases:*

1 **Opening moves: September 1939 to December 1940** By the end of September the Germans and Russians had occupied Poland. After a five-month pause (known as the 'phoney war') the Germans occupied Denmark and Norway (April 1940). In May attacks were made on Holland, Belgium and France, who were soon defeated, leaving Britain alone to face the dictators (Mussolini had declared war in June, just before the fall of France). Hitler's attempt to bomb Britain into submission was thwarted in the *Battle of Britain* (July to September 1940), but Mussolini's armies invaded Egypt and Greece.

2 **The Axis offensive widens: 1941 to summer 1942** The war now began to develop into a world-wide conflict. First Hitler, confident of a quick victory over Britain, launched an invasion of Russia (June 1941), breaking the non-aggression pact signed less than two years earlier. Then the Japenese forced the USA into the war by attacking the American naval base at Pearl Harbor (December 1941), and they followed this up by occupying territories such as the Philippines, Malaya, Singapore and Burma, scattered over a wide area. At this stage of the war there seemed to be no way of stopping the Germans and Japanese, though the Italians were less successful.

3 **The offensives held in check: summer 1942 to summer 1943** This phase of the war saw three important battles in which Axis forces were defeated. In June 1942 the Americans drove off a Japanese attack on *Midway Island*, inflicting heavy losses. In October the Germans under Rommel, advancing towards Egypt, were halted at *El Alamein* and later driven out of North Africa. The third battle was in Russia, where by September 1942, the Germans had penetrated as far as *Stalingrad*. Here the Russians put up such fierce resistance that the following February the German army was surrounded and forced to surrender. Meanwhile the war in the air continued with both sides bombing enemy cities, while at sea, as in the First World War, the British and Americans gradually got the better of the German submarine menace.

4 **The Axis powers defeated: July 1943 to August 1945** The enormous power and resources of the USA and the USSR, combined with an all-out effort from Britain

and her empire, slowly but surely wore the Axis powers down. Italy was eliminated first, and this was followed by an Anglo-American invasion of Normandy (June 1944) which liberated France, Belgium and Holland. Later, Allied troops crossed the Rhine and captured Cologne. In the east, the Russians drove the Germans out and advanced on Berlin via Poland. *Germany surrendered in May 1945 and Japan in August, after the Americans had dropped an atomic bomb on Hiroshima and one on Nagasaki.*

6.1 Opening moves: September 1939 to December 1940

(a) *Poland defeated*

The Poles were defeated swiftly because of the German *Blitzkrieg* (lightning war) which they were ill-equipped to deal with. It consisted of rapid thrusts by motorised divisions and tanks (*Panzers*) supported by air power. The *Luftwaffe* (the German air force) put the Polish railway system out of action and destroyed the Polish air force. Polish resistance was heroic but hopeless: they had no motorized divisions and they tried to stop advancing German tanks by massed cavalry charges. Britain and France did little to help their ally directly because French mobilization procedure was slow and out-of-date, and it was difficult to transport sufficient troops to Poland to be effective. When the Russians invaded eastern Poland, resistance collapsed. *On 29 September Poland was divided up between Germany and the USSR* (as agreed in the pact of August 1939).

(b) *The 'phoney war'*

Very little happened in the west for the next five months. In the east the Russians took over Estonia, Latvia and Lithuania and invaded Finland (November 1939), forcing her to hand over frontier territories which would enable the Russians to defend themselves better against any attack from the west. Meanwhile the French and Germans manned their respective defences – the *Maginot* and *Siegfried* Lines. Hitler seems to have hoped that the pause would weaken the resolve of Britain and France and encourage them to negotiate peace. This lack of action pleased Hitler's generals, who were not convinced that the German army was strong enough to attack in the west. It was the American press which described this period as the 'phoney war'.

(c) *Denmark and Norway invaded, April 1940*

Hitler's troops occupied Denmark and landed at the main Norwegian ports in April 1940, rudely shattering the apparent calm of the 'phoney war'. Control of Norway was important for the Germans because Narvik was the main outlet for Swedish iron ore, which was vital for the German armaments industry. The British were interfering with this trade by mining Norwegian coastal waters, and the Germans were afraid that they might try to take over some of Norway's ports, which they were in fact planning to do. Admiral Raeder, the German navy chief, realized that the fjords would be excellent naval bases from which to attack Britain's trans-Atlantic supply lines. When a British destroyer chased the German vessel *Altmark* into a Norwegian fjord and rescued the 300 British prisoner aboard, Hitler decided it was time to act. On 9 April the Germans landed at Oslo, Kristiansand, Stavanger, Bergen and Trondheim; although British and

French troops arrived a few days later, they were unable to dislodge the Germans, who were already well established. After a temporary success at Narvik, all allied troops were withdrawn by early June because of the growing threat to France itself. *The Germans were successful* because the Norwegians had been taken by surprise and their troops were not even mobilized; local Nazis under their leader, Vidkun Quisling, gave the invaders every assistance. The British had no air support, whereas the German air force constantly harrassed the allies.

This Norwegian campaign had important results:

- Germany was assured of her bases and her iron ore supplies, but had lost three cruisers and ten destroyers. This made the German navy less effective at Dunkirk than it might have been (see (d) below).
- It showed the incompetence of Chamberlain's government. He was forced to resign and *Winston Churchill became British Prime Minister*. Although there has been criticism of Churchill's mistakes, there is no doubt that he supplied what was needed at the time – drive, a sense of urgency, and the ability to make his coalition cabinet work well together.

(d) *Hitler attacks Holland, Belgium and France*

The attacks on Holland, Belgium and France were launched simultaneously on 10 May, and again *Blitzkrieg* methods brought swift victories (see Map 6.1). The Dutch, shaken by the bombing of Rotterdam which killed almost a thousand people, surrendered after only four days. Belgium held out longer, but her surrender at the end of May left the British and French troops in Belgium perilously exposed as German motorized divisions swept across northern France; only Dunkirk remained in Allied hands. The British navy played the vital role in evacuating over 338 000 troops, two-thirds of them British, from Dunkirk between 27 May and 4 June. This was a remarkable achievement in the face of constant *Luftwaffe* attacks on the beaches. It would perhaps have been impossible if Hitler had not ordered the German advance towards Dunkirk to halt (24 May), probably because the marshy terrain and numerous canals were unsuitable for tanks.

The events at Dunkirk were important: a third of a million Allied troops were rescued to fight again, and Churchill used it for propaganda purposes to boost British morale with the 'Dunkirk spirit'. In fact it was a serious blow for the Allies: the troops at Dunkirk had lost all their arms and equipment, so that it became impossible for Britain to help France.

The Germans now swept southwards: *Paris was captured on 14 June and France surrendered on 22 June.* At Hitler's insistence the armistice (ceasefire) was signed at Compiègne in the same railway coach which had been used for the 1918 armistice. The Germans occupied northern France and the Atlantic coast, giving then valuable submarine bases, and the French army was demobilized. Unoccupied France was allowed its own government under Marshall Pétain, but it had no real independence and collaborated with the Germans. Britain's position was now very precarious. Lord Halifax, the Foreign Secretary, allowed secret enquiries to be made via Washington about what German peace terms would be; even Churchill thought about the possibility of a negotiated peace.

(e) *Why was France defeated so quickly?*

1   *The French were psychologically not prepared for war, and were bitterly divided between right and left.* The right was fascist in sympathy, admired Hitler's

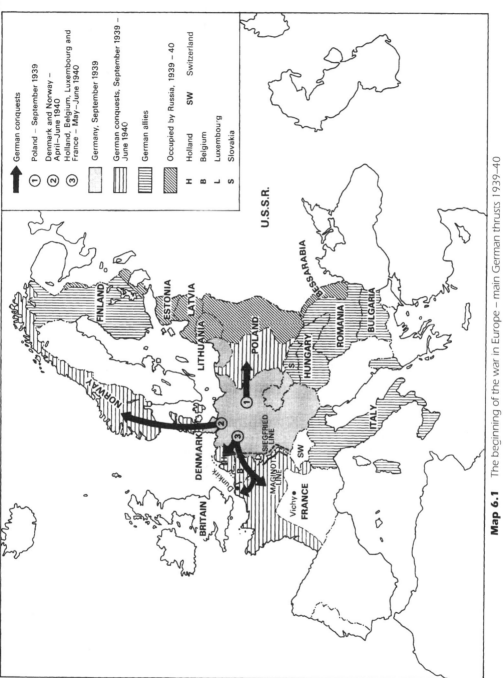

Map 6.1 The beginning of the war in Europe – main German thrusts 1939–40

Source: D. Heater, *Our World This Century* (Oxford, 1992) p. 73

German conquests

→ German conquests

① Poland – September 1939

② Denmark and Norway –
April–June 1940

③ Holland, Belgium, Luxembourg and
France – May–June 1940

Germany, September 1939

German conquests, September 1939 –
June 1940

German allies

Occupied by Russia, 1939 – 40   **SW** Switzerland

H Holland
B Belgium
L Luxembou'g
S Slovakia

achievements in Germany and wanted an agreement with him. The communists, following the non-aggression pact between Germany and the USSR, were also against the war. The long period of inaction during the 'phoney war' allowed time for a peace party to develop on the right, headed by Laval. He argued that there was no point in continuing the war now that the Poles, whom they were supposed to be helping, had been defeated.

2   *There were serious military weaknesses:*

- France had to face the full weight of an undivided German offensive, whereas in 1914 half the German forces had been directed against Russia.
- The French High Command was content to sit behind the *Maginot Line*, a line of defences stretching from the Swiss to the Belgian frontiers. Unfortunately the Maginot Line did not continue along the frontier between France and Belgium, partly because that might have offended the Belgians, and because Pétain believed that the Ardennes would be a strong enough barrier, but this was exactly where the Germans broke through.
- France had as many tanks and armoured vehicles as Germany, but instead of being concentrated in completely mechanized armoured divisions (like the Germans), allowing greater speed, they were split up with a certain number to an infantry division. This slowed them to the speed of marching soldiers (infantry).
- The German divisions were supported by combat planes, another area neglected by the French.

3   *The French generals made fatal mistakes.*

- No attempt was made to help Poland by attacking Germany in the west in September 1939, which might have had a good chance of success.
- No troops were moved from the Maginot Line forts (most of which were completely inactive) to help block the German breakthrough on the River Meuse (13 May 1940).
- There was poor communication between army and air force, so that air defence to drive German bombers off usually failed to arrive.

4   *Military defeats gave the defeatist right the chance to come out into the open and pressurise the government to accept a ceasefire.* When even the 84-year old Pétain, the hero of Verdun in 1916, urged peace, Prime Minister Reynaud resigned and Pétain became Prime Minister.

(f) *The Battle of Britain (12 August to 30 September 1940)*

This was fought in the air, when Goering's *Luftwaffe* tried to destroy the RAF *as a preliminary to the invasion of Britain*. The Germans bombed harbours, radar stations, aerodromes and munitions factories; in September they began to bomb London, in retaliation, they claimed, for a British raid on Berlin. The RAF inflicted heavy losses on the *Luftwaffe* (1389 German planes were lost as against 792 British); when it became clear that British air power was far from being destroyed, Hitler called off the invasion.

Reasons for the British success were:

- their chain of new radar stations gave plenty of warning of approaching German attackers;
- the German bombers were poorly armed – though the British fighters (Spitfires and Hurricanes) were not significantly better than the German Messerschmitts, the Germans were hampered by limited range; they could only carry enough fuel to enable them to stay in the air about 90 minutes; and

- the switch to bombing London was a mistake because it relieved pressure on the airfields at the critical moment.

The Battle of Britain was probably the first major turning point of the war: for the first time the Germans had been checked and so they were not invincible. Britain was able to remain in the struggle, thus facing Hitler (who was about to attack Russia) with *the fatal situation of war on two fronts.* As Churchill remarked when he paid tribute to the British fighter pilots: 'Never in the field of human conflict was so much owed by so many to so few'.

(g) *Mussolini invades Egypt, September 1940*

Not wanting to be outdone by Hitler, Mussolini sent an army from the Italian colony of Libya which penetrated about 60 miles into Egypt (September 1940), while another Italian army invaded Greece from Albania (October). However, the British soon drove the Italians out of Egypt, pushed them back far into Libya and defeated them at Bedafomm, capturing 130 000 prisoners and 400 tanks. They seemed poised to take the whole of Libya. British naval aircraft sank half the Italian fleet in harbour at Taranto and occupied Crete. The Greeks forced the Italians back and invaded Albania. Mussolini was beginning to be an embarrassment to Hitler.

6.2 The Axis offensive widens: 1941 to the summer of 1942

(a) *North Africa and Greece*

Hitler's first moves in 1941 were to help out his faltering ally. In February he sent Erwin Rommel and the Afrika Korps to Tripoli, and together with the Italians, they drove the British out of Libya. After much advancing and retreating, by June 1942 the Germans were in Egypt approaching El Alamein, only 70 miles from Alexandria (see Map 6.2).

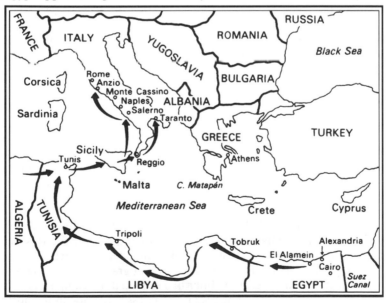

➤ Allied advances and offensives 1942–4

Map 6.2 North Africa and the Mediterranean

In April 1941 Hitler's forces invaded Greece, the day after 60 000 British, Australian and New Zealand troops had arrived to help the Greeks. The Germans soon captured Athens, forcing the British to withdraw, and after bombing Crete, they launched a parachute invasion of the island; again the British were forced to evacuate (May 1941).

The campaign in Greece had important effects:

- it was depressing for the Allies, who lost about 36 000 men.
- Many of the troops had been removed from North Africa, thus weakening British forces there just when they needed to be at their most effective against Rommel.
- More important in the long run was that Hitler's involvement in Greece and Yugoslavia (which the Germans invaded at the same time as Greece) may well have delayed his attack on Russia. This was originally planned for 15 May and was delayed for five weeks. If the invasion had taken place in May, the Germans might well have captured Moscow before the winter set in.

(b) *The German invasion of Russia (Operation Barbarossa) began on 22 June 1941*

1 *Hitler's motives seem to have been mixed:*
   - fear that the Russians might attack Germany while she was still occupied in the west;
   - hope that the Japanese would attack Russia in the Far East;
   - the more powerful Japan became, the less chance there was of the USA entering the war (or so Hitler thought).
   - But above all there was his hatred of communism and his desire for *Lebensraum* (living space).

   According to historian Alan Bullock, 'Hitler invaded Russia for the simple and sufficient reason that he had always meant to establish the foundations of his thousand-year *Reich* by the annexation of the territory lying between the Vistula and the Urals'. It has sometimes been suggested that the attack on Russia was Hitler's greatest mistake, but in fact, as Hugh Trevor-Roper pointed out, 'to Hitler the Russian campaign was not a luxury: it was the be-all and end-all of Nazism; it could not be delayed. It was now or never'.

2 *The attack was three-pronged:*
   - in the north towards Leningrad,
   - in the centre towards Moscow, and
   - in the south through the Ukraine.

   It was *Blitzkrieg* on an enormous scale involving close on 3.5 million men, and 3550 tanks supported by 5000 aircraft. Important cities such as Riga, Smolensk and Kiev were captured (see Map 6.3). The Russians had been caught off their guard, still re-equipping their army and air force (see Question 2 at the end of the chapter), and their generals, thanks to Stalin's purges, were inexperienced (see Section 16.3(b)).

   However, the Germans failed to capture Leningrad and Moscow. They were severely hampered by the heavy rains of October which turned the Russian roads into mud, and by the severe frosts of November and December when in some places the temperature fell to minus 38 degrees centigrade. The Germans had inadequate winter clothing because Hitler had expected the campaigns to be over before winter. Even in the spring of 1942 no progress was made in the north and centre as Hitler decided to concentrate on a major drive south-eastwards towards the Caucasus to sieze the oil-fields.

---- Line of the German advance in December 1941

········ German line in November 1942

Map 6.3 The Russian Front

(c) *The USA enters the war, December 1941*

The USA was brought into the war by the *Japanese attack on Pearl Harbor* (their naval base in the Hawaiian Islands) on 7 December 1941 (Illus. 6.1). Until then, the Americans, still intent on isolation, had remained neutral, though after *the Lend-Lease Act (April 1941)*, they had provided Britain with massive financial aid.

1 Japan's motives for the attack were tied up with her economic situation

The government believed they would soon run short of raw materials and they cast longing eyes towards territories such as Britain's *Malaya* and *Burma*, which had rubber, oil and tin, and towards the *Dutch East Indies*, also rich in oil. Since both Britain and Holland were in no fit state to defend their possessions, the Japanese prepared to attack, though they would probably have preferred to avoid war with the USA. However, relations between the two states deteriorated steadily. The Americans assisted the Chinese, who were still at war with Japan; when the Japanese persuaded Vichy France to allow them to occupy French Indo-China (where they set up military bases), President Roosevelt demanded their withdrawal and placed *an embargo on oil supplies to Japan* (26 July 1941). Long negotiations followed, in which the Japanese tried to persuade the Americans to lift the embargo. But stalemate was reached when the Americans insisted on a

Illus. 6.1   Pearl Harbor, 7 December 1941. US warships lie in ruins after the Japanese air attack

Japanese withdrawal both from Indo-China and from China itself. *When the aggressive General Tojo became Prime Minister (16 October), war seemed inevitable* (see Question 1, Sources A–C at the end of the chapter).

2   The attack was brilliantly organized by Admiral Yamamoto

There was no declaration of war: 353 Japanese planes arrived undetected at Pearl Harbor, and in two hours, destroyed 350 aircraft and five battleships. 3700 men were killed or seriously injured. Roosevelt called 7 December 'a date which will live in infamy'.

Pearl Harbor had important results:

- it gave the Japanese control of the Pacific, and by May 1942 they had captured Malaya, Singapore, Hong Kong, and Burma (all part of the British empire), the Dutch East Indies, the Philippines, and two American possessions, Guam and Wake Island (see Map 6.4)
- it caused Hitler to declare war on the USA.

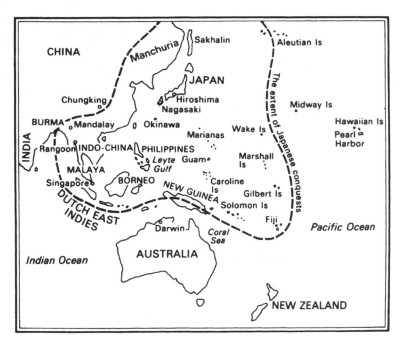

Map 6.4 The War in the Pacific

> *This was perhaps Hitler's most serious mistake:* he need not at this stage have committed himself to war with the USA, in which case the Americans might well have concentrated on the Pacific war. As it was, Germany was now faced with the immense potential of the USA. This meant that with the vast resources of the USSR and the British Commonwealth as well, the longer the war lasted, the less chance there was of an Axis victory. It was essential for them to deliver swift knock-out blows before the American contribution became effective.

(d) *Brutal behaviour by Germans and Japanese*

The behaviour of both Germans and Japanese in their conquered territories was ruthless and brutal. The Nazis treated the peoples of eastern Europe as sub-humans, fit only to be slaves of the German master-race. Jews were even lower – they were to be exterminated. As American journalist and historian William Shirer put it:

> Nazi degradation sank to a level seldom experienced by man in all his time on earth. Millions of decent, innocent men and women were driven into forced labour, millions were tortured in the concentration camps, and millions more still (including nearly six million Jews) were massacred in cold blood or deliberately starved to death and their remains burned.

This was both immoral and senseless behaviour: in the Baltic states and the Ukraine the Soviet government was so unpopular that decent treatment would have turned the people into allies of the Germans.

The Japanese treated their prisoners of war and the Asian peoples badly. Again this was ill-advised: many of the Asians, like those in Indo-China, welcomed the Japanese, who were thought to be freeing them from European control. The Japanese hoped to organize their new territories into a great economic empire known as a *Greater East Asia Co-prosperity Sphere*, which would be defended by sea and air power. However, harsh treatment by the Japanese soon turned the Asians against rule from Tokyo, and determined resistance movements began, usually with communist involvement.

6.3 The offensives held in check: summer 1942 to summer 1943

In three separate areas of fighting, Axis forces were defeated and began to lose ground:

- Midway Island
- El Alamein
- Stalingrad.

(a) *Midway Island, June 1942*

At Midway Island in the Pacific (June 1942) the Americans beat off a powerful Japanese attack, which included five aircraft carriers, nearly 400 aircraft, 17 large war-ships and an invasion force of 5000 troops. The Americans, with only three carriers and 233 planes, destroyed four of the Japanese carriers and about 330 planes.

There were several reasons for the American victory against heavier odds:

- they had broken the Japanese radio code and knew exactly when and where the attack was to be launched;
- the Japanese were over-confident and made two fatal mistakes:
  —they split their forces, thus allowing the Americans to concentrate on the main carrier force;
  —they attacked with aircraft from all four carriers simultaneously, so that when they were all rearming, the entire fleet was extremely vulnerable.

At this stage the Americans launched a counter-attack by dive-bombers which swooped unexpectedly from 19 000 feet, sinking two of the carriers and all their planes.

Midway proved to be a crucial turning-point in the battle for the Pacific: the loss of their carriers and strike planes seriously weakened the Japanese, and from then on the Americans maintained their lead in carriers and aircraft, especially dive-bombers. Although the Japanese had far more battleships and cruisers, they were mostly ineffective: the only way that war could be waged successfully in the vast expanses of the Pacific was by air power operating from carriers. Gradually the Americans under General MacArthur began to recover the Pacific Islands, beginning in August 1942 with landings in the Solomon Islands. The struggle was long and bitter and continued through 1943 and 1944 by a process known as 'island hopping'.

(b) *El Alamein, October 1942*

At El Alamein in Egypt Rommel's Afrika Korps were driven back by Montgomery's Eighth Army. This great battle was the culmination of several engagements fought in the El Alamein area: first the Axis advance was temporarily checked (July); when Rommel tried to break through he was halted again at Alam Halfa (September); finally, seven weeks later in the October battle, he was chased out of Egypt for good by the British and New Zealanders.

The Allies were successful partly because during the seven-week pause massive reinforcements had arrived, so that the Germans and Italians were heavily outnumbered – 80 000 men and 540 tanks against 230 000 troops and 1440 tanks. In addition, Allied air power was vital, constantly attacking the Axis forces and sinking their supply ships crossing the Mediterranean, so that by October there were serious shortages of food, fuel oil and ammunition. At the same time the air force was strong enough to protect the Eighth Army's own supply routes. Montgomery's skilful preparations probably clinched the issue, though he has been criticized for being over-cautious, and for allowing Rommel and half his forces to escape into Libya.

However, there is no doubt that *the El Alamein victory was another turning-point in the war:*

- it prevented Egypt and the Suez Canal from falling into German hands;
- it ended the possibility of a link-up between the Axis forces in the Middle East and those in the Ukraine; and more than that,
- it led on to the complete expulsion of Axis forces from North Africa. It encouraged landings of British troops in the French territories of Morocco and Algeria to threaten the Germans and Italians from the west, while the Eighth Army closed in on them from Libya. Trapped in Tunisia, 275 000 Germans and Italians were forced to surrender (May 1943), and the Allies were well-placed for an invasion of Italy.

The desert war had been a serious drain on German resources which could have been used in Russia where they were badly needed.

(c) *Stalingrad*

At Stalingrad the southern prong of the German invasion of Russia, which had penetrated deeply through the Crimea, capturing *Rostov*, was finally checked. *The Germans had reached Stalingrad at the end of August 1942*, but though they more or less destroyed the city, the Russians refused to surrender. In November they counterattacked ferociously, trapping the Germans, whose supply lines were dangerously extended, in a large pincer movement. With his retreat cut off, the German commander, von Paulus, had no reasonable alternative but to *surrender with about 100 000 men (2 February 1943)*.

If Stalingrad had fallen, the supply route for Russia's oil from the Caucasus would have been cut off, and the Germans had hoped to advance up the River Don to attack Moscow from the south-east. This plan had to be abandoned; but more than this was at stake – *the defeat was a catastrophe for the Germans:* it shattered the myth that they were invincible and boosted Russian morale. They followed up with more counterattacks, forcing the Germans to abandon the siege of Leningrad and to retreat from their position west of Moscow. It was now only a matter of time before the Germans, heavily outnumbered and short of tanks and guns, were driven out of Russia.

6.4 What part was played by Allied naval forces?

The previous section showed how the combination of sea and air power was the key to success in the Pacific war and how, after the initial shock at Pearl Harbor, the Americans were able to build up that superiority in both departments which was to lead to the eventual defeat of Japan. At the same time the British navy, as in the First World War, had a vital role to play: this included protecting merchant ships bringing food supplies, sinking German submarines and surface raiders, blockading Germany, and transporting and supplying Allied troops fighting in North Africa and later in Italy. At first success was mixed, mainly because the British failed to understand the importance of air support in naval operations and had few aircraft carriers. Thus they suffered defeats in Norway and Crete where the Germans had strong air superiority. In addition the Germans had lots of naval bases in Norway, Denmark, France and Italy. In spite of this the British had some successes:

1 *Aircraft from the carrier* Illustrious *sank half the Italian fleet at Taranto (November 1940).* The following March five more warships were destroyed off Cape Matapan.
2 *The threat from surface raiders was removed* by the sinking of the *Bismarck*, Germany's only battleship at the time (May 1941).
3 *The navy destroyed the German invasion transports* on their way to Crete (May 1941) though they could not prevent the landing of parachute troops.
4 *They provided escorts for convoys carrying supplies to help the Russians.* These sailed via the Arctic to Murmansk in the far north of Russia. Beginning in September 1941, the first 12 convoys arrived without incident, but then the Germans began to attack them, until convoy 17 lost 23 ships out of 36 (June 1942). After this disaster Arctic convoys were not resumed until November 1943, when stronger escorts could be spared. Altogether 40 convoys sailed: 720 out of a total of 811 merchant ships arrived safely, with valuable cargo for the Russians; this included 5000 tanks, 7000 aircraft and thousands of tons of canned meat.
5 *Their most important contribution was their victory in the Battle of the Atlantic.* See below.
6 *Sea and air power together made possible the great invasion of France in June 1944* (see below Section 6.6(b)).

The Battle of the Atlantic

This was the struggle against German U-boats attempting to deprive Britain of food and raw materials. At the beginning of 1942 the Germans had 90 U-boats in operation and 250 being built. In the first six months of that year the Allies lost over 4 million tons of merchant shipping and destroyed only 21 U-boats. Losses reached a peak of 108 ships in March 1943, almost two-thirds of which were in convoy. However, after that the number of sinkings began to fall, while the U-boat losses increased. By July 1943 the Allies could produce ships at a faster rate than the U-boats could sink them, and the situation was under control.

The reasons for the Allied success were:

- more air protection was provided for convoys by long-range Liberators;
- both escorts and aircraft improved with experience;
- the British introduced the new centimetric radar sets which were small enough to be fitted into aircraft; these enabled submarines to be detected in poor visibility and at night.

The victory was just as important as Midway, El Alamein and Stalingrad: Britain could not have continued to sustain the losses of March 1943 and remain in the war.

6.5 What contribution did air power make to the defeat of the Axis?

1   *The first significant achievement was in the Battle of Britain (1940)* when the RAF beat off the *Luftwaffe* attacks, causing Hitler to abandon his invasion plans (see Section 6.1(f)).

2   *In conjunction with the British navy, aircraft played a varied role:*
   - the successful attacks on the Italian fleet at Taranto and Cape Matapan;
   - the sinking of the German battleship *Tirpitz* by heavy bombers in Norway (November 1943);
   - the protection of convoys in the Atlantic; and
   - anti-submarine operations.

   In fact in May 1943 Admiral Doenitz, the German navy chief, complained to Hitler that since the introduction of the new radar devices, more U-boats were being destroyed by aircraft than by naval vessels.

3   *The American air force together with the navy played a vital part in winning the Pacific War against the Japanese:*
   - dive-bombers operating from aircraft carriers won the *Battle of Midway Island in June 1942* (see Section 6.3(a));
   - later, in the 'island hopping' campaign, attacks by heavy bombers prepared the way for landings by marines, for example at the Mariana Islands (1944) and the Philippines (1945);
   - American transport planes kept up the vital flow of supplies to the Allies during the campaign to recapture Burma.

4   *The RAF took part in specific campaigns which would have been hopeless without them:* for example, during the war in the desert, operating from bases in Egypt and Palestine, they constantly bombed Rommel's supply ships in the Mediterranean and his armies on land.

5   *British and Americans later flew in parachute troops to aid the landings in Sicily (July 1943) and Normandy (June 1944), and provided air protection for the invading armies.* (However, a similar operation at Arnhem in Holland in September 1944 was a failure.)

Allied bombing of German and Japanese cities

This was the most controversial action by the Allied air forces. The Germans had bombed London and other important British cities and ports during 1940 and 1941, but these raids dwindled during the German attack on Russia which required all the *Luftwaffe*'s strength. The British and Americans retaliated with what they called a 'strategic air offensive' – this involved massive attacks on military and industrial targets in order to hamper the German war effort. *The Ruhr, Cologne, Hamburg and Berlin all suffered badly.* Sometimes raids seem to have been carried out to undermine civilian morale, as when about 50 000 people were killed during a single night raid on *Dresden (February 1945).*

   Early in 1945 the Americans launched a series of devastating raids on Japan from bases in the Mariana Islands. In a single raid on *Tokyo* (March), 80 000 people were killed and a quarter of the city destroyed.

There has been argument about how effective the bombing was in hastening the Axis defeat, beyond merely causing inconvenience. Critics also point to the heavy losses suffered by air-crews – over 158 000 Allied airmen were killed in Europe alone. Others argue that this type of bombing, which caused the deaths of so many innocent civilians (as opposed to bombings which targeted industrial areas, railways and bridges) was morally wrong. Estimates of German civilian deaths from Allied bombing vary between 600 000 and a million; German raids on Britain killed over 60 000 civilians.

The conclusion now seems to be that the campaign against Germany was not effective until the autumn of 1944. German industrial production continued to increase until as late as July 1944. After that, thanks to the increasing accuracy of the raids and the use of the new Mustang fighter escorts which could outmanoeuvre all the German fighters, synthetic oil production fell rapidly, causing acute fuel shortages. In October the vital Krupp armament factories at Essen were put out of action permanently, and the war effort ground to a halt in 1945. By June 1945 the Japanese had been reduced to the same state.

In the end, therefore, after much wasted effort early on, *the Allied strategic air offensive was one of the decisive reasons for the Axis defeat*: besides strangling fuel and armaments production and destroying railway communications, it caused the diversion of many aircraft from the eastern front, thus helping the Russian advance into Germany.

6.6 The Axis powers defeated: July 1943 to August 1945

(a) *The fall of Italy*

This was the first stage in the Axis collapse. British and American troops landed in *Sicily* from the sea and air (10 July 1943) and quickly captured the whole island. This caused the *downfall of Mussolini*, who was dismissed by the king. Allied troops crossed to Salerno, Reggio and Taranto on the mainland and captured *Naples* (October 1943).

Marshall Badoglio, Mussolini's successor, signed an armistice and *brought Italy on to the Allied side*. However, the Germans, determined to hold on to Italy, rushed troops through the Brenner Pass to occupy Rome and the north. The Allies landed a force at *Anzio*, 30 miles south of Rome (January 1944), but bitter fighting followed before *Monte Cassino* (May) and *Rome* (June) were captured. Milan in the north was not taken until April 1945. The campaign could have been finished much earlier if the Allies had been less cautious in the early stages, and if the Americans had not insisted on keeping many divisions back for the invasion of France.

Nevertheless the elimination of Italy did contribute towards the final Allied victory:

● Italy provided air bases for bombing the Germans in Central Europe and the Balkans, and
● German troops were kept occupied when they were needed to resist the Russians.

(b) *Operation Overlord, 6 June 1944*

Operation Overlord – the invasion of France (also known as the Second Front) – began on 'D-Day', 6 June 1944. It was felt that the time was ripe now that Italy had been eliminated, the U-boats brought under control and Allied air superiority achieved. The

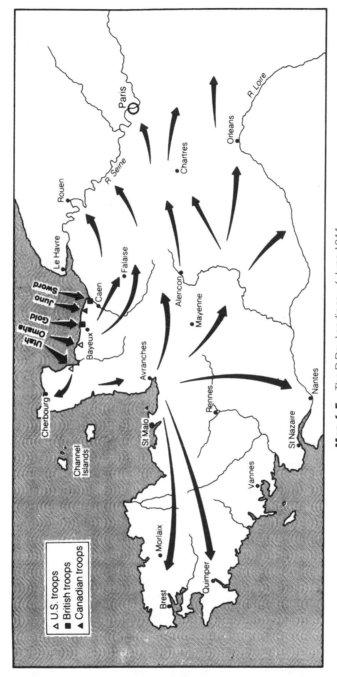

Map 6.5 The D-Day Landings – 6 June 1944

Source: C.K. Macdonald, *The Second World War* (Basil Blackwell, 1984) p. 39

Illus. 6.2 D-Day, 6 June 1944: US assault troops landing in Normandy

Russians had been urging the Allies to start this Second Front ever since 1941, to relieve pressure on them. The landings took place from sea and air on a 60-mile stretch of Normandy beaches (code-named Utah, Omaha, Gold, Juno and Sword) *between Cherbourg and Le Havre* (Illus. 6.2). There was strong German resistance, but at the end of the first week 326 000 thousand men with tanks and heavy lorries had landed safely.

It was a remarkable operation: it made use of prefabricated 'Mulberry' harbours which were towed across from Britain and positioned close to the Normandy coast, mainly at Arromanches (Gold beach), and of PLUTO – pipelines under the ocean – carrying motor fuel. Eventually over 3 million Allied troops were landed. Within a few weeks most of northern France was liberated (*Paris on 25 August*), putting out of action the sites from which the German V1 and V2 rocket missiles had been launched with devastating effects on south-eastern Britain. In Belgium, *Brussels and Antwerp were liberated in September.*

(c) *The assault on Germany*

The assault on Germany itself followed, but the end was delayed by desperate German resistance and by disagreements between the Americans and British. Montgomery wanted a rapid thrust to reach Berlin before the Russians, but the American General Eisenhower favoured a cautious advance along a broad front. The *British failure at*

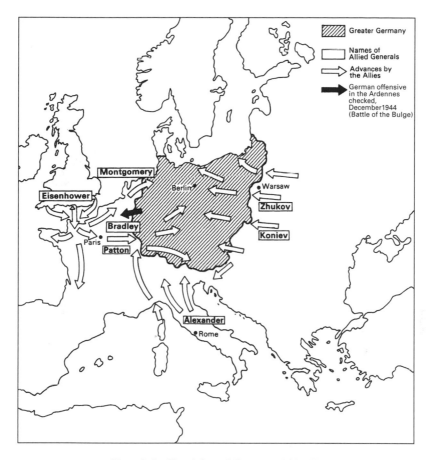

Map 6.6 The defeat of Germany, 1944–5

Source: D. Heater, *Our World This Century* (Oxford, 1992) p. 90

Arnhem in Holland (September 1944) seemed to support Eisenhower's view, though in fact the Arnhem operation (an attempt by parachute troops to cross the Rhine and out-flank the German Siegfried Line) might have worked if the troops had landed nearer the two Rhine bridges.

Consequently Eisenhower had his way and Allied troops were dispersed over a 600-mile front, with *unfortunate results*:

● Hitler was able to launch an offensive through the weakly defended Ardennes towards Antwerp;
● the Germans broke through the American lines and advanced 60 miles, causing a huge bulge in the front line (December 1944).

Determined British and American action stemmed the advance and pushed the Germans back to their original position. But the *Battle of the Bulge*, as it became known, was important because Hitler had risked everything on the attack and had lost 250 000 men and 600 tanks, which at this stage could not be replaced. Early in 1945 Germany was being invaded on both fronts, from east and west. The British still wanted to push ahead and take Berlin before the Russians, but supreme commander

Illus. 6.3 Victorious Russian troops on top of the Reichstag building in Berlin

Illus. 6.4 Nagasaki a month after the atomic bomb was dropped

Eisenhower refused to be hurried, and Berlin fell to Stalin's forces in April (Illus. 6.3). *Hitler committed suicide and Germany surrendered.*

(d) *The defeat of Japan*

On 6 August 1945 *the Americans dropped an atomic bomb on Hiroshima, killing perhaps as many as 84 000 people and leaving thousands more slowly dying of radiation poisoning.* Three days later they dropped one on *Nagasaki* which killed perhaps another 40 000; after this the Japanese government surrendered (Illus. 6.4).

The dropping of these bombs was one of the most controversial actions of the entire war. President Truman's justification was that he was saving American lives, since the war might otherwise drag on for another year. Many historians believe that the bombings were not necessary, since the Japanese had already put out peace feelers in July via Russia. One suggestion is that the real reason for the bombings was to end the fighting swiftly before the Russians (who had promised to enter the war against Japan) gained too much Japanese territory which would entitle them to share the occupation of Japan (see Question 1, Sources D–F at the end of this chapter).

6.7 Why did the Axis powers lose the war?

The reasons can be summarized briefly:

* shortage of raw materials;
* the Allies learned from their failures;
* the Axis powers took on too much;
* the combined resources of the USA, USSR and British empire;
* tactical mistakes by the Axis powers.

(a) *Shortage of raw materials*

Both Italy and Japan had to import supplies, and even Germany was short of rubber, cotton, nickel and, after mid-1944, oil. These shortages need not have been fatal, but success depended on a swift end to the war, which certainly seemed likely at first, thanks to the speed and efficiency of the German *Blitzkrieg*. However, the survival of Britain in 1940 was important because it kept the western front alive until the USA entered the war.

(b) *The Allies soon learned from their early failures*

By 1942 they knew how to check *Blitzkrieg* attacks and appreciated the importance of air support and aircraft carriers. Consequently they built up an air and naval superiority which won the battles of the Atlantic and the Pacific and slowly starved their enemies of supplies.

(c) *The Axis powers simply took on too much*

Hitler did not seem to understand that war against Britain would involve her empire as well, and that his troops were bound to be too thinly spread – on the Russian front, on both sides of the Mediterranean, and on the western coastline of France. Japan made the same mistake: as military historian Liddell-Hart put it, 'they became stretched out far beyond their basic capacity for holding their gains. For Japan was a small island state with limited industrial power'. In Germany's case, Mussolini was partly to blame: his incompetence was a constant drain on Hitler's resources.

(d) *The combined resources of the USA, USSR and the British empire*

These were so great that the longer the war lasted, the less chance the Axis had of victory. The Russians rapidly moved their industry east of the Ural Mountains and so were able to continue production even though the Germans had occupied vast areas in the west. By 1945 they had four times as many tanks as the Germans and could put twice as many men in the field. When the American war machine reached peak production it could turn out over 70 000 tanks and 120 000 aircraft a year, which the Germans and Japanese could not match.

(e) *Serious tactical mistakes*

● The Japanese failed to learn the lesson about the importance of aircraft carriers, and concentrated too much on producing battleships.
● Hitler failed to provide for a winter campaign in Russia and became obsessed with the idea that the Germans must not retreat; this led to many disasters in Russia, especially Stalingrad, and left his troops badly exposed in Normandy (1944).
● Perhaps most serious of all was Hitler's decision to concentrate on producing V-rockets when he could have been developing jet aircraft; these might well have restored German air superiority and prevented the devastating bomb attacks of 1944 and 1945.

Illus. 6.5 The devastation of war. Women salvage their belongings after an air raid on London

6.8 What were the effects of the war?

(a) *Enormous destruction*

There was enormous destruction of lives, homes, industries and communications in Europe and Asia (Illus. 6.4, 6.5 and 6.6).

Almost 40 million people were killed: well over half of them were Russians, six million were Poles, four million Germans, two million Chinese and two million Japanese. Britain and the USA got off comparatively lightly (see Figure 6.1).

Another 21 million people had been uprooted from their homes: some had been taken to Germany to work as slave labourers, some had been put into concentration camps, and some had been forced to flee from invading armies. The victorious powers were left with the problem of how to repatriate them (arrange for them to return home).

Large parts of Germany, especially her industrial areas and many major cities, lay in ruins. Much of western Russia had been completely devastated, and some 25 million people were homeless. France had suffered badly too: taking into account the destruction of housing, factories, railways, mines and livestock, almost 50 per cent of total French wealth had been lost. In Italy where damage was very serious in the south, the figure was over 30 per cent. Japan suffered heavy damage and a high death toll from bombings.

Though the cost was high, it did mean that the world had been rid of Nazism which had been responsible for terrible atrocities. The most notorious was **the Holocaust** – *the deliberate murder in extermination camps of over 5 million Jews and hundreds of thousands of non-Jews*, mainly in Poland and Russia (Illus. 6.6).

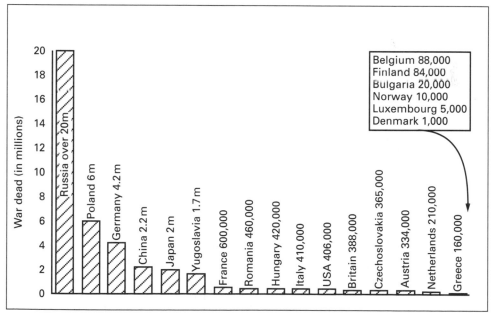

Figure 6.1 War dead

Source: based on statistics in Jack B. Watson, *Success in Modern World History Since 1945* (John Murray, 1989) p. 3

Illus. 6.6 Bodies at the Belsen concentration camp

(b) *There was no all-inclusive peace settlement*

This was not like the end of the First World War when an all-inclusive settlement was negotiated at Versailles. This was mainly because the distrust which had re-emerged between the USSR and the west in the final months of the war made agreement on many points impossible.

However, a number of separate treaties were signed:

- *Italy* lost her African colonies and gave up her claims to Albania and Abyssinia (Ethiopia);
- *The USSR* took the eastern section of Czechoslovakia, the Petsamo district and the area round Lake Ladoga from Finland, and held on to Latvia, Lithuania and Estonia, which they had occupied in 1939;
- *Romania* recovered northern Transylvania, which the Hungarians had occupied during the war;
- *Trieste*, claimed by both Italy and Yugoslavia, was declared a free territory protected by the United Nations Organization;
- Later, at San Francisco (1951) *Japan* agreed to surrender all territory acquired during the previous ninety years, which included a complete withdrawal from China.

However, *the Russians refused to agree to any settlement over Germany and Austria*, except that they should be occupied by Allied troops and that East Prussia should be divided between Russia and Poland.

(c) *The war stimulated important social changes*

Apart from the population movements during the war, once hostilities were over, many millions of people were forced to move from their homes. The worst cases were probably in the areas taken from Germany by Russia and Poland, and in the German-speaking areas in Hungary, Romania and Czechoslovakia. About 10 million Germans were forced to leave and make their way to West Germany so that no future German government would be able to claim those territories. In some countries, especially the USSR and Germany, extensive urban redevelopment took place as ruined cities had to

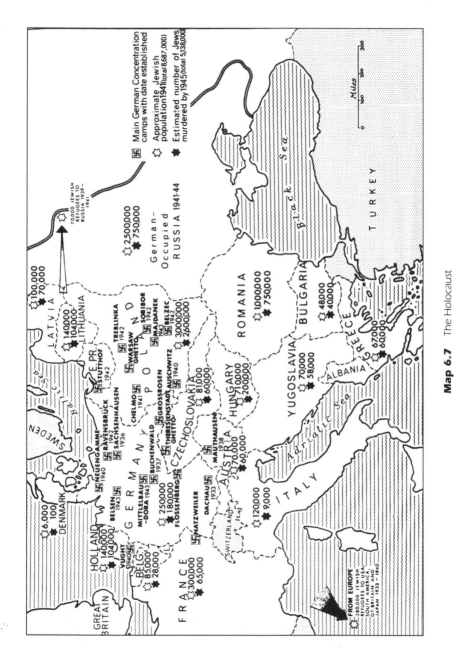

Map 6.7 The Holocaust

Source: M. Gilbert, *Recent History Atlas* (Weidenfeld & Nicolson), 1977 p. 86

be rebuilt. In Britain the war stimulated, among other things, the *Beveridge Report (1942)*, a plan for introducing a Welfare State.

(d) *The war caused the production of nuclear weapons*

The first ever use of these weapons, on Hiroshima and Nagasaki, demonstrated their horrifying powers of destruction. The world was left under the threat of a nuclear war which might well have destroyed the entire planet. Some people argue that this acted as a deterrent, making both sides in the Cold War so frightened of the consequences that they were deterred or discouraged from fighting each other.

(e) *Europe's domination of the rest of the world ended*

The four western European states which had played a leading role in world affairs for most of the first half of the twentieth century, were now much weaker than before. Germany was devastated and divided, France and Italy were on the verge of bankruptcy; and although Britain seemed strong and victorious with her empire intact, the cost of the war had been ruinous. The USA had helped to keep Britain going during the war by sending supplies, but these had to be paid for later. As soon as the war was over, the new US President Truman abruptly stopped all further help, leaving Britain in a sorry state: she had overseas debts of over £3000 million, many of her foreign investments had been sold off, and her ability to export goods had been much reduced. She was forced to ask for another loan from the USA which was given at a high rate of interest; the country was therefore closely and uncomfortably dependent on the USA.

(f) *Emergence of the super-powers*

The USA and the USSR emerged as the two most powerful nations in the world, and they were no longer as isolated as they had been before the war. The USA had suffered relatively little from the war and had enjoyed great prosperity from supplying the other allies with war materials and food. The Americans had the world's largest navy and air-force and they controlled the atomic bomb. The USSR, though severely weakened, still had the largest army in the world. Both countries were highly suspicious of each other's intentions now that the common enemies, Germany and Japan, had been defeated. *The rivalry of these two super-powers in the Cold War was the most important feature of international relations for almost half a century after 1945*, and was a constant threat to world peace (see next chapter).

(g) *Decolonization*

The war encouraged the movement towards decolonization. The defeats inflicted on Britain, Holland and France by Japan, and the Japanese occupation of their territories – Malaya, Singapore and Burma (British), French Indo-China and the Dutch East Indies – destroyed the tradition of European superiority and invincibility. It could hardly be expected that, having fought to get rid of the Japanese, the Asian peoples would willingly return to European rule. Gradually they achieved full independence, though not without a struggle in many cases. This in turn intensified demands for independence among the peoples of Africa and the Middle East, and in the 1960s the result was a large array of new states (see Chapters 21–22).

The leaders of many of these newly emerging nations met in conference at Algiers in 1973 and made it clear that they regarded themselves as a *Third World*. By this they meant that *they wished to remain neutral or non-aligned* in the struggle between the other two worlds – communism and capitalism. Usually poor and under-developed industrially, the new nations were often intensely suspicious of the motives of both communism and capitalism, and they resented their own economic dependence on the world's wealthy powers.

(h) *The United Nations Organization (UNO)*

This emerged as the successor to the League of Nations. Its main aim was to try to maintain world peace, and on the whole it has been more successful than its unfortunate predecessor (see Chapter 9).

Questions

1 *Japan and the USA during the Second World War* – study Sources A–G below and then answer the questions which follow

---

Source A

By the summer of 1941 opinion in Japan had veered round to the view that Japan should strike south. There lay the vastly rich resources of oil, tin, rubber and other valuables. This was the area of colonies: British, Dutch, French and American. If it seized them, Japan could hope for three results: it would make itself free from the economic pressure of the western countries which had the nerve to threaten it with economic sanctions in order to control Japanese expansion; it would make China ask for peace; and it would build up a great Japanese empire overseas, to be called 'The Greater East Asia Co-Prosperity Sphere' . . . The Japanese people responded to this policy; quite sincerely, they saw themselves, in opposing western activity in Asia, as fighting a battle against imperialism . . . In December 1940 the American government, disturbed by the increasing warlike tone of Japan, placed a ban on the sales of scrap iron and war materials to Japan. This action was an attempt to halt Japan's military activity against China. In July 1941, when the Japanese extended their political control of Indo-China from the north to the south, Roosevelt responded firmly – he froze Japanese assets and announced a ban on Japanese trade in oil and steel.

Source. P. Calvocoressi and G. Wint, *Total War* (Allen Lane/Penguin, 1972, adapted extracts)

Source B

By Howard Zinn, an American historian

Pearl Harbor was presented to the American public as a sudden, shocking, immoral act. Immoral it was, like any bombing, but not really sudden or shocking to the American government . . . In initiating economic sanctions against Japan, the USA undertook actions that were widely recognized in Washington as carrying grave risks of war . . . One of the judges in the Tokyo War Crimes Trial after World War II, disagreed with the general verdict against Japanese officials and argued that the USA had clearly provoked the war with Japan and expected Japan to act. The records show that a White House Conference two weeks before Pearl Harbor anticipated a war and discussed how it should be justified. A State Department Memorandum, a year before Pearl Harbor, did not talk of the independence of China or the principle of self-determination [as reasons for American action].

Source: Howard Zinn, *A People's History of the United States* (Longman, 1980, adapted extracts)

Remarks of President Truman.

If this bomb explodes, as I think it will, I'll have a hammer on those boys [the Russians] . . . Force is the only thing the Russians understand.

Source: quoted in D.S. Clemens, *Yalta* (Oxford University Press, 1970)

(a) (i) 'Pearl Harbor was presented to the American public as a sudden, shocking, immoral act' according to Source B. Using evidence from Sources A, B and C, why do you think the American government acted in this way?   1.4c–7c   5 marks

   (ii) Do these three sources prove that the American government was deliberately giving a wrong impression?   2.4–10, 3.4   6 marks

(b) Using Sources D to G, make a list of possible motives behind the dropping of the atomic bombs on Japan. Put the ones you think most important at the top, and the least important at the bottom.   1.4b–9a, 4c–9b   7 marks

(c) According to Source D, the government said that the atomic bombs had been dropped to end the war quickly. How far do you think Sources D, E, F and G prove that the American government was lying?

                                   2.4–10, 3.4–10   12 marks

Total: 30 marks

2   *The German attack on the USSR, 22 June 1941* – study Sources A–D below and then answer the questions which follow.

Source A

Report sent to Stalin by a Russian spy working in Japan, 2 May 1941

Hitler has resolved to begin war and destroy the USSR in order to utilize the European part of the Union as a raw materials and grain base. The critical term for the possible beginning of war . . . completion of the spring sowing. The decision regarding the start of the war will be taken by Hitler in May.

Source B

Announcement by Tass, *the Soviet News Agency, 13 June 1941*

In view of the persistent rumours, responsible circles in Moscow have thought it necessary to state that they are a clumsy propaganda manoeuvre of the forces arrayed against the Soviet Union and Germany which are interested in the spread and intensification of the war. In the opinion of Soviet circles the rumours of the intention of Germany to break the Non-Aggression Pact and to launch an attack against the Soviet Union are completely without foundation. The recent movement of German troops to the eastern part of Germany must be explained by other motives which have no connection with Soviet–German relations. As a result, all the rumours according to which the Soviet Union is preparing for a war with Germany are false and provocative.

Source C

Extract from the diary of General Halder, Hitler's Chief of Staff, 23 June 1941

The offensive of our forces caught the enemy with tactical surprise. Evidence of the complete unexpectedness for the enemy of our attack is the fact that units were captured quite unawares in their barracks, aircraft stood on the airdromes secured by tarpaulins, and forward units, attacked by our troops, asked their commanders what they should do.

Source D

Extracts from a work by an American writer

In the view of Admiral Kuznetsov, Stalin unquestionably expected war with Hitler. Stalin regarded the Nazi–Soviet Pact as a time-gaining stop-gap, but the time-span proved shorter than he anticipated. His chief mistake was in underestimating the period he had available for preparation. 'The suspiciousness of Stalin towards England and America made matters worse', concluded Kuznetsov. 'He doubted all evidence about Hitler's activities which he received from the English and the Americans and simply threw it on one side' . . . On 6 June he approved a plan for the shift-over of Soviet industry to war production; this timetable called for the completion of the plan by the end of 1942 . . . When the Soviet commander at Kiev ordered some of his troops to occupy sections of the frontier fortifications which had not yet been completed, he received the following order telegraphed from Moscow: 'Your action may quickly provoke the Germans to armed clash with serious consequences. You are ordered to reverse it immediately'.

(a) Using Source A and Section 6.2(b), make a list of reasons why the Germans invaded the USSR. Point out the different types of motive: political, economic and military, and mention any links you can find between the various causes.

　　　　　　　　　　　　　　　　　　　　　　　　　1.4b–7b　10 marks

(b) How far do Sources B, C and D disagree with each other about whether or not Stalin expected war with Germany?　　　1.4c–8c, 3.4　10 marks

(c) (i) How reliable　　　　　　　　　　　　　　　　　　　8 marks

　　(ii) How useful is each of these sources for the historian investigating the German attack on the USSR?　　　　　　　　　　8 marks

　　(iii) Explain which one of the sources you think is most useful as evidence for Stalin's attitudes in June 1941?　　　　3.4–8　4 marks

Total: 40 marks

7 The Cold War: problems of international relations after the Second World War

Summary of events

Towards the end of the war, the harmony which had existed between the USSR, the USA and the British empire began to wear thin and all the old suspicions came to the fore again. Relations between Soviet Russia and the West soon became so difficult that, although no actual fighting took place directly between the two opposing camps, the decade after 1945 saw the first phase of what became known as *the Cold War*. This continued, in spite of several 'thaws', until the collapse of communism in eastern Europe in 1989–91. What happened was that instead of allowing their mutual hostility to express itself in open fighting, *the rival powers attacked each other with propaganda and economic measures, and with a general policy of non-co-operation.*

Both super-powers, the USA and the USSR, gathered allies around them: between 1945 and 1948 the USSR drew into its orbit most of the states of eastern Europe, as communist governments came to power in Poland, Hungary, Romania, Bulgaria, Yugoslavia, Albania, Czechoslovakia and East Germany (1949). A communist government was established in North Korea (1948) and the communist bloc seemed to be further strengthened in 1949 when Mao Zedong (Mao Tse-tung) was at last victorious in the long-drawn-out civil war in China (see Section 17.4). On the other hand the USA hastened the recovery of Japan and fostered her as an ally, and worked closely with Britain and fourteen other European countries, as well as with Turkey, providing them with vast economic aid in order to build up an anti-communist bloc.

Whatever one bloc suggested or did was viewed by the other as having ulterior and aggressive motives. There was a long wrangle, for example, over where the frontier between Poland and Germany should be, and no permanent settlement could be agreed on for Germany and Austria.

Then in the mid-1950s, after the death of Stalin (1953), the new Russian leaders began to talk about 'peaceful co-existence', and the icy atmosphere between the two blocs began to thaw. It was agreed to remove all occupying troops from Austria (1955); however, relations did not improve enough to allow agreement on Germany, and tensions mounted again over Vietnam and the Cuban missiles crisis (1962).

7.1 What caused the Cold War?

(a) *Differences of principle*

The basic cause of conflict lay in the differences of principle between the communist states and the capitalist or liberal-democratic states:

- *the communist system* of organizing the state and society was based on the ideas of Karl Marx; he believed that the wealth of a country should be collectively owned and shared by everybody. The economy should be centrally planned and the interests and well-being of the working classes safeguarded by state social policies;
- *the capitalist system* on the other hand, operates on the basis of private ownership of a country's wealth. The driving forces behind capitalism are private enterprise in the pursuit of making profits, and the preservation of the power of private wealth.

Ever since the world's first communist government was set up in Russia (USSR) in 1917 (see Section 15.2(d)), the governments of most capitalist states viewed it with mistrust and were afraid of communism spreading to their countries. This would mean the end of the private ownership of wealth, as well as the loss of political power by the wealthy classes. When civil war broke out in Russia in 1918, several capitalist states – the USA, Britain, France and Japan – sent troops to Russia to help the anti-communist forces. The communists won the war, but Joseph Stalin, who became Russian leader in 1929, was convinced that there would be another attempt by the capitalist powers to destroy communism in Russia. The German invasion of Russia in 1941 proved him right. The need for self-preservation against Germany and Japan caused the USSR, the USA and Britain to forget their differences and work together, but as soon as the defeat of Germany was clearly only a matter of time, both sides, and especially Stalin, began to plan for the post-war period.

(b) *Stalin's foreign policies contributed to the tensions*

His aim was to take advantage of the military situation to strengthen Russian influence in Europe. As the Nazi armies collapsed, he tried to occupy as much German territory as he could, and to acquire as much land as he could get away with from countries such as Finland, Poland and Romania. In this he was highly successful, but the west was alarmed at what they took to be Soviet aggression; they believed that he was committed to spreading communism over as much of the globe as possible.

(c) *US and British politicians were hostile to the Soviet government*

During the war the USA under President Roosevelt sent war materials of all kinds to Russia under a system known as 'Lend-Lease', and Roosevelt was inclined to trust Stalin. But after Roosevelt died in April 1945, his successor, Harry S. Truman, was more suspicious, and he toughened his attitude towards the communists. Some historians believe that Truman's main motive for dropping the atomic bombs on Japan was not simply to defeat Japan, which was ready to surrender anyway, but to show Stalin what might happen to Russia if he dared to go too far.

Stalin suspected that the USA and Britain were still keen to destroy communism; he felt that their delay in launching the invasion of France, the Second Front (which did not take place until June 1944) was deliberately calculated to keep most of the pressure on the Russians and bring them to the point of exhaustion. Nor did they tell Stalin about the existence of the atomic bomb until shortly before its use on Japan, and they rejected his request that Russia should share in the occupation of Japan. *Above all, the west had the atomic bomb and the USSR did not.*

So which side was to blame?

During the 1950s, most Western historians, such as the American George Kennan, blamed Stalin, arguing that his motives were sinister, and that he intended to spread communism as widely as possible through Europe and Asia, thus destroying capitalism. The formation of NATO (see next Section 7.2(i)) and the American entry into the Korean War in 1950 (see Section 8.1) were the West's self-defence against communist aggression.

On the other hand, Soviet historians, and during the 1960s and early 1970s some American historians, argued that *the Cold War ought not to be blamed on Stalin and the Russians*. Their theory was that Russia had suffered enormous losses during the war, and therefore it was only to be expected that Stalin would try to make sure that neighbouring states were friendly, given Russia's weakness in 1945. They believe that Stalin's motives were purely defensive and that there was no real threat to the west from the USSR. Some Americans claim that the USA should have been more understanding and should not have challenged the idea of a Soviet 'sphere of influence' in eastern Europe. The actions of American politicians, especially Truman, provoked Russian hostility unnecessarily. This is known among historians as the '*revisionist*' view.

The main reason behind this new view was that during the late 1960s many people in the USA became critical of American foreign policy, especially American involvement in the Vietnam War (see Section 8.3). This caused some historians to reconsider the American attitude towards communism in general; they felt that US governments had become obsessed with hostility towards communist states and they were ready to take a more sympathetic view of the difficulties Stalin had found himself in at the end of the Second World War.

Later a third view – known as the '*post-revisionist*' *interpretation* – was put forward by some American historians, and this became popular in the 1980s. They had the benefit of being able to look at lots of new documents and visit archives which had not been open to earlier historians. The new evidence suggested that the situation at the end of the war was far more complicated than earlier historians had realized; this led them to take a middle view, arguing that *both sides should take some blame for the Cold War*. They believe that American economic policies such as Marshall Aid (see next Section 7.2(e)) were deliberately designed to increase US political influence in Europe. However, they also believe that although Stalin had no long-term plans to spread communism, he was an opportunist who would take advantage of any weakness in the west to expand Soviet influence. With their entrenched positions and deep suspicions of each other, the USA and the USSR created an atmosphere in which every international act could be interpreted in two ways. What was claimed as necessary for self-defence by one side was taken by the other as evidence of aggressive intent, as the events described in the next section show. But at least open war was avoided because the Americans were reluctant to use the atomic bomb again unless attacked directly, while the Russians dared not risk such an attack. (See Question 2 at the end of this chapter for extracts from the different western interpretations.)

7.2 How did the Cold War develop between 1945 and 1953?

(a) *The Yalta Conference (February 1945)*

This was held in Russia (in the Crimea) and was attended by the three Allied leaders, Stalin, Roosevelt and Churchill, so that they could plan what was to happen when the

Illus. 7.1   Churchill, Roosevelt and Stalin at Yalta, February 1945

war ended (Illus. 7.1). *At the time it seemed to be a success, agreement being reached on several points:*

- a new organization – to be called *the United Nations* – should be set up to replace the failed League of Nations;
- *Germany was to be divided into zones* – Russian, American and British (a French zone was included later) – while Berlin (which happened to be in the middle of the Russian zone) would also be split into corresponding zones. Similar arrangements were to be made for Austria;
- *free elections* would be allowed in the states of eastern Europe;
- *Stalin promised to join the war against Japan* on condition that Russia received the whole of Sakhalin Island and some territory in Manchuria.

However, there were ominous *signs of trouble over what was to be done with Poland.* When the Russian armies swept through Poland, driving the Germans back, they had set up a communist government in Lublin, even though there was already a Polish government-in-exile in London. It was agreed at Yalta that some members (non-communist) of the London-based government should be allowed to join the Lublin government, while in return, Russia would be allowed to keep a strip of eastern Poland which she had annexed in 1939. However, Roosevelt and Churchill were not happy about Stalin's demands that Poland should be given all German territory east of the rivers Oder and Neisse; no agreement was reached on this point.

(b) *The Potsdam Conference (July 1945)*

This revealed a distinct cooling-off in relations. The three leaders at the beginning of the conference were Stalin, Truman and Churchill, but Churchill was replaced by *Clement Attlee*, the new British Labour Prime Minister, after Labour's election victory.
   The war with Germany was over, but no agreement was reached about her long-term

future – the big questions were: whether or when the four zones would be allowed to join together to form a united country again. She was to be disarmed, the Nazi party disbanded and its leaders tried as war criminals. It was agreed that the Germans should pay something towards repairing the damage they had caused during the war. Most of these payments (known as reparations) were to go to the USSR, which was to be allowed to take non-food goods from their own zone and from the other zones as well, provided the Russians sent food supplies to the western zones of Germany in return.

///// Land taken by Poland from Germany: territory east of the *Oder–Neisse* Line and part of East Prussia

≡≡≡ Land acquired by the USSR during the war

Occupation zones in Germany and Austria:
1 Russian   3 French
2 British   4 American

Map 7.1   Europe after 1945

It was over Poland that the main disagreement occurred. Truman and Churchill were annoyed because Germany east of the Oder–Neisse Line had been occupied by Russian troops and was being run by the pro-communist Polish government which expelled some 5 million Germans living in the area; this had not been agreed to at Yalta (see Map 7.1).

Truman did not inform Stalin about the exact nature of the atomic bomb though Churchill was told about it. A few days after the conference closed the two atomic bombs were dropped on Japan and the war ended quickly on 10 August without the need for Russian help (though the Russians declared war on Japan on 8 August and invaded Manchuria). They annexed south Sakhalin as agreed at Yalta, but they were allowed no part in the occupation of Japan.

(c) *Communism established in Eastern Europe*

The establishment of communist governments in eastern Europe caused alarm in the west. In the months following Potsdam, the Russians systematically interfered in the countries of eastern Europe to set up pro-communist governments. This happened in Poland, Hungary, Bulgaria, Albania and Romania. In some cases their opponents were imprisoned or murdered; in Hungary for example, the Russians allowed free elections; but although the communists won less than 20 per cent of the votes, they saw to it that a majority of the cabinet were communists. Stalin frightened the west further by a widely reported speech in February 1946 in which he said that communism and capitalism could never live peacefully together, and that future wars were inevitable until the final victory of communism was achieved.

Churchill responded to all this in a speech of his own at Fulton, Missouri (USA) in March 1946, in which he repeated a phrase he had used earlier: 'From Stettin in the Baltic to Trieste in the Adriatic, *an iron curtain has descended across the continent*' (see Map 7.2). Claiming that the Russians were bent on 'indefinite expansion of their power and doctrines', he called for *a western alliance* which would stand firm against the communist threat. The speech helped to widen the rift between east and west; Stalin was able to denounce Churchill as a 'warmonger', while over a hundred British Labour MPs signed a motion criticizing the Conservative leader.

(d) *The Russians continued to tighten their grip on eastern Europe*

By the end of 1947 every state in that area with the exception of Czechoslovakia had a fully communist government. Elections were rigged, non-communist members of coalition governments were expelled, many were arrested and executed, and eventually all other political parties were dissolved. All this took place under the watchful eyes of secret police and Russian troops. In addition Stalin treated the Russian zone of Germany as if it were Russian territory, allowing only the communist party and draining it of vital resources.

Only Yugoslavia did not fit the pattern: here the communist government of Marshal Tito had been legally elected in 1945. Tito had won the election because of his immense prestige as leader of the anti-German resistance; it was Tito's forces, not the Russians, who had liberated Yugoslavia from German occupation, and Tito resented Stalin's attempts to interfere.

The west was profoundly irritated by Russia's attitude, which disregarded Stalin's promise of free elections made at Yalta. And yet they ought not to have been surprised at what was happening: even Churchill had agreed with Stalin in 1944 that much of eastern Europe should be a Russian sphere of influence. Stalin could argue that friendly governments in neighbouring states were necessary for self-defence, that these

Legend:
- Iron Curtain, 1949
- Germany, 1945
- Zones of occupation, Germany and Austria
  - American
  - British
  - French
  - Russian
- Russian satellites with dates of complete Communist control
- Communist but expelled from the Cominform
- Lands taken from Germany

Map 7.2   Central and Eastern Europe during the Cold War

Source: D. Heater, *Our World This Century* (Oxford, 1992) p. 129

states had never had democratic governments anyway, and that communism would bring much-needed progress to backward countries. It was Stalin's methods of gaining control which upset the west, and they gave rise to the next major developments.

(e) *The Truman Doctrine and the Marshall Plan*

1 The Truman Doctrine

This sprang from events in Greece where communists were trying to overthrow the monarchy. British troops, who had helped liberate Greece from the Germans in 1944, had restored the monarchy, but they were now feeling the strain of supporting it against the communists, who were receiving help from Albania, Bulgaria and Yugoslavia. Ernest Bevin, the British Foreign Minister, appealed to the USA and Truman announced (March 1947) that the USA 'would support free peoples who are resisting subjugation by armed minorities or by outside pressures'. Greece immediately received massive amounts of arms and other supplies, and by 1949 the communists were defeated. Turkey, which also seemed under threat, received aid worth about 60 million dollars. The Truman Doctrine made it clear that the USA had no intention of returning to isolation as she had after the First World War; *she was committed to a policy of containing communism*, not just in Europe, but throughout the world, including Korea and Vietnam.

2 The Marshall Plan

Announced in June 1947, this was an economic extension of the Truman Doctrine. American Secretary of State George Marshall produced his *European Recovery Programme (ERP)*, which offered economic and financial help wherever it was needed. 'Our policy', he declared, 'is directed not against any country or doctrine, but against hunger, poverty, desperation and chaos'. One of its aims was to promote the economic recovery of Europe, thus ensuring markets for American exports; but *its main aim was probably political*: communism was less likely to gain control in a prosperous Western Europe. By September, sixteen nations (Britain, France, Italy, Belgium, Luxembourg, Netherlands, Portugal, Austria, Greece, Turkey, Iceland, Norway, Sweden, Denmark, Switzerland and the western zones of Germany) had drawn up a joint plan for using American aid. During the next four years over 13 000 million dollars of Marshall Aid flowed into Western Europe, fostering the recovery of agriculture and industry, which in many countries were in chaos because of war devastation.

The Russians were well aware that there was more to Marshall Aid than pure benevolence. Although in theory aid was available for Eastern Europe, Russian Foreign Minister Molotov denounced the whole idea as 'dollar imperialism'. He saw it as a blatant American device for gaining control of Western Europe, and worse still, for interfering in Eastern Europe which Stalin considered to be Russia's sphere of influence. The USSR rejected the offer, and neither her satellite states nor Czechoslovakia, which was showing interest, were allowed to take advantage of it. *The 'iron curtain' seemed a reality*, and the next development only served to strengthen it.

(f) *The Cominform*

This was the communist response. Set up by Stalin in September 1947, this was an organization to draw together the various European communist parties. All the satellite states were members, and the French and Italian communist parties were represented. Stalin's aim was to tighten his grip on the satellites: to be communist was not enough –

it must be Russian-style communism. Eastern Europe was to be industrialized, collectivized and centralized; states were expected to trade primarily with Cominform members, and all contacts with non-communist countries were discouraged. When Yugoslavia objected, she was expelled from the Cominform (1948) though she remained communist. In 1949 the *Molotov Plan* was introduced, offering Russian aid to the satellites. Another organization known as *Comecon (Council of Mutual Economic Assistance)* was set up to co-ordinate their economic policies.

(g) *The communist takeover of Czechoslovakia (February 1948)*

This came as a great blow to the Western bloc, because it was the only remaining democratic state in Eastern Europe. There was a coalition government of communists and other left-wing parties which had been freely elected in 1946. The communists had won 38 per cent of the votes and 114 seats in the 300 seat parliament, and they held a third of the cabinet posts. The Prime Minister, Klement Gottwald, was a communist; President Benes and the Foreign Minister, Jan Masaryk, were not; they hoped that Czechoslovakia with its highly developed industries, would *remain as a bridge between east and west.*

However, a crisis arose early in 1948. Elections were due in May, and all the signs were that the communists would lose ground; they were blamed for the Czech rejection of Marshall Aid which might have eased the continuing food shortages. The communists decided to act before the elections; already in control of the unions and the police, they seized power in an armed coup. All non-communist ministers with the exception of Benes and Masaryk resigned. A few days later Masaryk's body was found under the windows of his offices. His death was officially described as suicide. However, when the archives were opened after the collapse of communism in 1989, documents were found which proved beyond doubt that he had been murdered. The elections were held in May but there was only a single list of candidates – all communists. Benes resigned and Gottwald became president.

The western powers and the UN protested but felt unable to take any action because they could not prove Russian involvement – the coup was purely an internal affair. However, there can be little doubt that Stalin, disapproving of Czech connections with the west and of their interest in Marshall Aid, had prodded the Czech communists into action. Nor was it just coincidence that several of the Russian divisions occupying Austria were moved up to the Czech frontier. The bridge between east and west was gone; *the 'iron curtain' was complete.*

(h) *The Berlin blockade and airlift (June 1948–May 1949)*

This brought the Cold War to its first climax. The crisis arose out of *disagreements over the treatment of Germany:*

1   At the end of the war, as agreed at Yalta and Potsdam, *Germany and Berlin were each divided into four zones.* While the three western powers did their best to organize the economic and political recovery of their zones, Stalin, determined to make Germany pay for all the damage inflicted on Russia, treated his zone as a satellite, *draining its resources away to Russia.*

2   *Early in 1948 the three Western zones were merged to form a single economic unit,* whose prosperity, thanks to Marshall Aid, was in marked contrast to the poverty of the Russian zone. The west wanted all four zones to be re-united and given self-government as soon as possible; but Stalin had decided that it would be safer for Russia if he kept the Russian zone separate, with its own communist, pro-Russian

government. The prospect of the three Western zones re-uniting was alarming enough to Stalin, because he knew they would be part of the Western bloc.

3   *When in June 1948 the West introduced a new currency and ended price controls in their zone and in West Berlin.* The Russians decided that the situation in Berlin had become impossible; already irritated by this island of capitalism a hundred miles inside the communist zone, they felt it impossible to have two different currencies in the same city, and they were embarrassed by the contrast betweeen the prosperity of West Berlin and the poverty of the surrounding area.

The Russian reponse was immediate: *all road, rail and canal links between West Berlin and West Germany were closed*; their aim was to force the west to withdraw from West Berlin by reducing it to starvation point. The Western powers, convinced that a retreat would be the prelude to a Russian attack on West Germany, were determined to hold on. They decided to fly supplies in, rightly judging that the Russians would not risk shooting down the transport planes. Truman had thoughtfully sent a fleet of B 29 bombers to be positioned on British airfields. Over the next ten months 2 million tons of supplies were airlifted to the blockaded city in a remarkable operation which kept the 2.5 million West Berliners fed and warm right through the winter. In May 1949 the Russians admitted failure by lifting the blockade.

The affair had important results:

● the outcome gave a great psychological boost to the Western powers, though it brought relations with Russia to their worst ever;
● it caused the Western powers to co-ordinate their defences by the formation of NATO;
● it meant that, since no compromise was possible, Germany was doomed to remain divided for the foreseeable future.

(i)   NATO formed

The formation of the North Atlantic Treaty Organization (NATO) took place in *April 1949*. The Berlin blockade showed the West's military unreadiness and frightened them into making definite preparations. Already in March 1948 Britain, France, Holland, Belgium and Luxembourg had signed the *Brussels Defence Treaty* promising military collaboration in case of war. Now they were joined by the USA, Canada, Portugal, Denmark, Eire, Italy and Norway. All signed the *North Atlantic Treaty*, agreeing to regard an attack on any one of them as an attack on them all, and placing their defence forces under a joint NATO command organization which would co-ordinate the defence of the west. *This was a highly significant development:* the Americans had abandoned their traditional policy of 'no entangling alliances' and for the first time had pledged themselves in advance to military action. Predictably Stalin took it as a challenge, and tensions remained high.

(j)   *The two Germanies*

Since there was no prospect of the Russians allowing a united Germany, the western powers went ahead alone and set up *the German Federal Republic, known as West Germany (August 1949)*. Elections were held and Konrad Adenauer became the first Chancellor. The Russians replied by setting up their zone as *the German Democratic Republic, or East Germany (October 1949)*. Germany remained divided until the collapse of communism in East Germany (November–December 1989) made it possible early in 1990 to re-unite the two states into a single Germany (see Section 10.7(e)).

(k) More nuclear weapons

When it became known in September 1949 that the USSR had successfully exploded an atomic bomb, an arms race began to develop. Truman responded by giving the go-ahead for the USA to produce *a hydrogen bomb* many times more powerful than the atomic bomb. His defence advisers produced a secret document known as NSC-68 (April 1950) which shows that they had come to regard the Russians as fanatics who would stop at nothing to spread communism all over the world. They suggested that expenditure on armaments should be more than tripled in an attempt to defeat communism.

It was not only the Russians who alarmed the Americans: *a communist government was proclaimed in China (October 1949)* after the communist leader Mao Zedong had defeated Chiang Kai-shek, the nationalist leader, who had been supported by the USA and who was now forced to flee to the island of Taiwan (Formosa). When *the USSR and communist China signed a treaty of alliance in February 1950*, American fears of an advancing tide of communism seemed about to be realized.

It was in this atmosphere of American anxiety that the Cold War spotlight now shifted to *Korea*, where, in June 1950, troops from communist North Korea invaded non-communist South Korea (see Section 8.1).

7.3 To what extent was there a thaw after 1953?

There is no doubt that in some ways East–West relations did begin to improve during 1953, though there were still areas of disagreement and the thaw was not a consistent development.

(a) Reasons for the thaw

1 The death of Stalin

The death of Stalin was probably the starting point of the thaw, because it brought to the forefront new Russian leaders – Malenkov, Bulganin and Khrushchev – who wanted to improve relations with the USA. Their reasons were possibly connected with the fact that by August 1953 the Russians as well as the Americans had developed a hydrogen bomb: the two sides were now so finely balanced that international tensions had to be relaxed if nuclear war was to be avoided.

Nikita Khrushchev explained the new policy in a famous speech (February 1956) in which he criticized Stalin and said that 'peaceful co-existence' with the west was not only possible but essential: 'there are only two ways – either peaceful co-existence or the most destructive war in history. There is no third way'. This did not mean that Khrushchev had given up the idea of a communist-dominated world; this would still come, but it would be achieved when the Western powers recognized the superiority of the Soviet economic system, not when they were defeated in war. In the same way, he hoped to win neutral states over to communism by lavish economic aid.

2 McCarthy discredited

Anti-communist feelings in the USA, which had been stirred up by Senator Joseph McCarthy, began to moderate when McCarthy was discredited in 1954. It had gradually become clear that McCarthy himself was something of a fanatic, and when he began to accuse leading generals of having communist sympathies, he had gone too far. The Senate condemned him by a large majority and he foolishly attacked the new Republican President Eisenhower for supporting the Senate. Soon afterwards Eisenhower announced that the American people wanted to be friendly with the Soviet people.

(b) *How did the thaw show itself?*

1 The first signs

- The signing of the peace agreement at Panmunjom ended the Korean War (July 1953) (see Section 8.1(c))
- and the end of the war in Indo-China in 1954 (see Section 8.3(c–e)) were the first signs.

2 The Russians made important concessions in 1955

- They agreed to give up their military bases in Finland.
- They lifted their veto on the admission of sixteen new member states to the UN.
- The quarrel with Yugoslavia was healed when Khrushchev paid a visit to Tito.
- The Cominform was abandoned, suggesting more freedom for the satellite states.

3 The signing of the Austrian State Treaty (May 1955)

This was most important. At the end of the war in 1945 Austria was divided into four zones of occupation, with the capital, Vienna, in the Russian zone. Unlike Germany, she was allowed her own government because she was viewed not as a defeated enemy but as a state liberated from the Nazis. The Austrian government had only limited powers, and the problem was similar to the one in Germany: whereas the three Western occupying powers organized the recovery of their zones, the Russians insisted on squeezing reparations, mainly in the form of food supplies, from theirs. No permanent settlement seemed likely, but early in 1955 the Russians were persuaded, mainly by the Austrian government, to be more co-operative. They were also afraid of a merger between West Germany and western Austria.

As a result of the agreement, all occupying troops were withdrawn and Austria became independent with her 1937 frontiers. She was not to unite with Germany, her armed forces were strictly limited, and she was to remain neutral in any dispute between east and west. This meant that she could not join either NATO or the European Economic Community. One point the Austrians were unhappy about was the loss of the German-speaking area of the South Tyrol which Italy was allowed to keep.

(c) *The thaw was only partial*

Khrushchev's policy was a curious mixture which western leaders often found difficult to understand. While making the conciliatory moves described above, he was quick to respond to anything which seemed to be a threat to the east, and he had no intention of relaxing Russia's grip on the satellite states. The Hungarians discovered this to their cost in 1956 when *a rising in Budapest against the communist government was ruthlessly crushed by Russian tanks* (see Sections 9.3(e) and 10.6(d)). Sometimes he seemed to be prepared to see how far he could push the Americans before they stood up to him:

- *The Warsaw Pact (1955)* was signed between Russia and her satellite states shortly after West Germany was admitted to NATO. The Pact was a mutual defence agreement which the west took as a gesture against West Germany's membership of NATO.
- *The Russians continued to build up their nuclear armaments* (see next section).
- *The situation in Berlin caused more tension* (see below).
- Most provocative of all was when *Khrushchev installed Soviet missiles in Cuba*, less than a hundred miles from the American coast (1962).

The situation in Berlin

In 1958, perhaps encouraged by the USSR's apparent lead in some areas of the nuclear arms race, Khrushchev announced that the USSR no longer recognized the rights of the western powers in West Berlin. When the Americans made it clear that they would resist any attempt to push them out, Khrushchev did not press the point.

In 1960 it was Khrushchev's turn to feel aggrieved when an American U-2 spy plane was shot down over a thousand miles inside Russia. President Eisenhower declined to apologize, defending America's right to make reconnaissance flights, and the affair ruined the summit conference which was about to begin in Paris (Illus. 7.2).

Illus. 7.2 Nikita Khrushchev gets excited at the Paris Conference in 1960 as he protests to the Americans about the U-2 incident

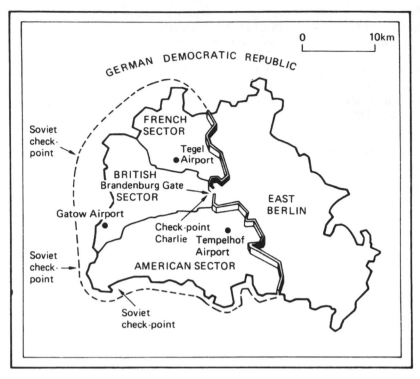

Map 7.3 Berlin and the wall, 1961

In 1961 Khrushchev again suggested, this time to the new American President John F. Kennedy, that the west should withdraw from Berlin. The communists were embarrassed at the large number of refugees escaping from East Germany into West Berlin – these averaged about 200 000 a year and totalled over 3 million since 1945. When Kennedy refused, *the Berlin Wall was erected (August 1961)*, a 28-mile-long monstrosity across the entire city, effectively blocking the escape route (see Map 7.3 Illus. 7.3).

7.4 The nuclear arms race and the Cuban missile crisis (1962)

(a) *The arms race began to accelerate*

The arms race between east and west arguably began in earnest towards the end of 1949 *after the Russians had produced their own atomic bomb*. The Americans already had a big lead in bombs of this type, but the Russians were determined to catch up, even though production of nuclear weapons placed an enormous strain on their economy. When *the Americans made the much more powerful hydrogen bomb* towards the end of 1952, the Russians did the same the following year, and had soon developed a bomber with a range long enough to reach the USA.

The Americans remained well ahead in numbers of nuclear bombs and bombers, but it was the Russians who took the lead in August 1957 when they produced *a new*

Illus. 7.3 The Berlin Wall. To the right is East Berlin, to the left, West Berlin

type of weapon – the inter-continental ballistic missile (ICBM). This was a nuclear war-head carried by a rocket so powerful that it could reach the USA even when fired from inside the USSR. Not to be outdone, the Americans soon produced their version of an ICBM (known as Atlas), and before long they had many more than the Russians. The Americans also began to build nuclear missiles with a shorter range; these were known as Jupiters and Thors, and they could reach the USSR from launching sites in Europe and Turkey.

When *the Russians successfully launched the world's first earth satellite (Sputnik 1) in 1958*, the Americans again felt that they dared not be left behind; within a few months they had launched an earth satellite of their own.

(b) *The Cuban missile crisis, 1962*

Cuba became involved in the Cold War in 1959 when Fidel Castro, who had just seized power from the corrupt, American-backed dictator Batista, outraged the USA by nationalising American-owned estates and factories (see Section 8.2). As Cuba's relations with the USA worsened, those with Russia improved: in January 1961 *the USA broke off diplomatic relations with Cuba*, and the Russians increased their economic aid.

Convinced that Cuba was now a communist state in all but name, the new US President John F.Kennedy, approved a plan by a group of Batista supporters to invade Cuba from American bases in Guatemala (Central America). The American Central Intelligence Agency (CIA), a kind of secret service, was deeply involved. The small invading force of about 1400 men landed at the *Bay of Pigs* in April 1961, but the operation was so badly planned and carried out that Castro's forces and his two jet planes had no difficulty crushing it. Later the same year *Castro announced that he was now a Marxist and that Cuba was a socialist country*.

Map 7.4 The Cuban missile crisis, 1962

Khrushchev, the Soviet leader, decided to set up nuclear missile launchers in Cuba aimed at the USA, whose nearest point was less than a hundred miles from Cuba. He intended to install missiles with a range of up to 2000 miles, which meant that all the major cities of central and eastern USA such as New York, Washington, Chicago and Boston would be under threat (see Map 7.4). This was a risky decision, and there was great consternation in the USA when in October 1962, photographs taken from spy planes showed a missile base under construction. *Why did Khrushchev take such a risky decision?*

- The Russians had lost the lead in ICBMs, so this was a way of trying to seize the initiative back again from the USA.
- It would place the Americans under the same sort of threat as the Russians themselves had to put up with from American missiles based in Turkey. As Khrushchev himself put it in his memoirs, 'the Americans had surrounded our country with military bases, now they would learn what it feels like to have enemy missiles pointing at you'.
- It was a gesture of solidarity with his ally Castro, who was under constant threat from the USA; the missiles might be used against invading American troops.
- It would test the resolve of the new young American President Kennedy.
- Perhaps Khrushchev intended to use the missiles for bargaining with the west over

Illus. 7.4 The Berlin Wall. An 18-year-old East Berliner lies dying after being shot during an escape attempt (left); he is carried away by East Berlin guards (right).

removal of American missiles from Europe, or a withdrawal from Berlin by the west (Illus. 7.4).

Kennedy's military advisers urged him to launch air strikes against the bases, but he acted more cautiously. He:

- alerted American troops;
- began a blockade of Cuba to keep out the 25 Russian ships which were bringing missiles to Cuba; and
- demanded the dismantling of the missile sites and the removal of those missiles already in Cuba.

The situation was tense, and the world seemed to be on the verge of nuclear war. The Secretary-General of the UN, U Thant, appealed to both sides for restraint. Khrushchev promised to remove the missiles and dismantle the sites; in return Kennedy promised that the USA would not invade Cuba again and undertook to disarm the Jupiter missiles in Turkey (though he would not allow this to be announced publicly).

The crisis had only lasted a few days, but it was extremely tense and it had important results. Both sides could claim to have gained something, but most important was that both sides realized how easily a nuclear war could have started and how terrible the results would have been. It seemed to bring them both to their senses and produced a marked relaxation of tension. *A telephone link (the 'hot-line') was introduced between Moscow and Washington* to allow swift consultations, and in July 1963, the USSR, the

USA and Britain signed *a Nuclear Test Ban Treaty* agreeing to carry out nuclear tests only underground to avoid polluting the atmosphere any further.

Although Kennedy's handling of the crisis was highly praised at first, later historians have been more critical. It has been suggested that he ought to have called Khrushchev's bluff, attacked Cuba and overthrown Castro. On the other hand, some historians have criticized Kennedy for allowing the crisis to develop in the first place, arguing that since Soviet long-range missiles could already reach the USA from Russia itself, the missiles in Cuba did not exactly pose a new threat.

(c) *The race continued into the 1970s*

Although in public the Russians claimed the outcome of the missile crisis as a victory, in private they admitted that their main aim – to establish missile bases near the USA – had failed. Even the removal of American Thors and Jupiters from Turkey meant nothing because the Americans now had another threat – *ballistic missiles (known as Polaris and later Poseidon) which could be launched from submarines (SLBMs)* in the eastern Mediterranean.

The Russians now decided to go all-out to catch up with the American stock-pile of ICBMs and SLBMs. Their motive was not just to increase their own security: they hoped that if they could get somewhere near equality with the Americans, there would be a good chance of persuading them to limit and reduce the arms build-up. As the Americans became more deeply involved in the war in Vietnam (1961–75), they had less to spend on nuclear weapons, and slowly but surely the Russians began to catch up. By the early 1970s they had overtaken the USA and her allies in numbers of ICBMs and SLBMs. They had brought out a new weapon, *the anti-ballistic missile (ABM)*, which could destroy incoming enemy missiles before they reached their targets.

However, the Americans were ahead in other departments – they had developed an even more terrifying weapon, *the multiple independently targetable re-entry vehicle (MIRV)*; this was a missile which could carry as many as fourteen separate warheads, each one of which could be programmed to hit a different target. The Russians soon developed their version of the MIRV, known as the SS-20 (1977). These were targeted on western Europe, but were not as sophisticated as the American MIRV and carried only three warheads.

At the end of the 1970s the Americans responded by developing *Cruise missiles which were based in Europe*; the new refinement was that these missiles flew in at low altitudes and so were able to penetrate under Russian radar.

And so it went on: by this time both sides had enough of this horrifying weaponry to destroy the world many times over. The main danger was that one side or the other might be tempted to try to win a nuclear war by striking first and destroying all the other side's weapons.

(d) *Protests against nuclear weapons*

People in many countries were worried at the way the major powers continued to pile up nuclear weapons and failed to make any progress towards controlling them. Movements were set up to try to persuade governments to abolish nuclear weapons.

In Britain the *Campaign for Nuclear Disarmament (CND)*, which was started in 1958, pressurized the government to take the lead, so that Britain would be the first nation to abandon nuclear weapons; this was known as *unilateral disarmament* (disarmament by one state only). They hoped that the USA and the USSR would follow Britain's lead and scrap their nuclear weapons too. They held mass demonstrations and rallies, and every year at Easter they held a protest march from London to

Illus. 7.5 CND marchers reach Aldermaston and urge Britain, USA and USSR to stop the manufacture, testing and stock-piling of nuclear weapons (1958).

Aldermaston (where there was an atomic weapons research base) and back (Illus. 7.5). No British government dared take the risk, however. They believed that unilateral disarmament would leave Britain vulnerable to a nuclear attack from the USSR, and they would only consider abandoning their weapons as part of a general agreement by all the major powers (*multilateral disarmament*).

During the 1980s there were protest demonstrations in many European countries, including West Germany and Holland, and also in the USA. In Britain many women protested by camping around the American base at *Greenham Common* (Berkshire) where the Cruise missiles were positioned. One fear was that if the Americans ever fired any of these missiles, Britain could be almost destroyed by Russian nuclear retaliation. In the long run, perhaps the enormity of it all and the protest movements did play a part in bringing both sides to the negotiating table (see Section 8.5).

Questions

1   Section 7.4 gives information about the develpment of nuclear weapons.
    (a)   Using the information from this section, make two lists:
        (i)   of American nuclear weapons,
        (ii)   of the rival Russian nuclear weapons   1.4c–5c, 3.4
    (b)   Why did some people see these developments as progress, while others were
        horrified at them?   1.6a, 6c–9b
2   *The causes of the Cold War*   Here are some extracts from the different western
    interpretations of the causes of the Cold War (Sources A–C). Study them carefully
    and then answer the questions which follow.

George Kennan, American diplomat and historian, puts the conventional view in a telegram sent from the US embassy in Moscow to Washington in 1946

Russian rulers have always feared direct contact between the western world and their own, feared what would happen if Russians learned the truth about the outside world. They have learned to seek security only in a deadly struggle for total destruction of any rival power ... Soviet leaders picture the outside world as evil, hostile and menacing. This provides justification for the increase of Russian military power. This is only the steady advance of Russian nationalism, a centuries-old movement. But in its new guise of international communism, it is more dangerous than ever before.

Source: G.F. Kennan, *Memoirs 1950–63* (Bantam, New York, 1969)

William Appleman Williams puts the American revisionist view in 1962

The popular idea that soviet leaders emerged from the war ready to do aggressive battle against the USA is simply not borne out by the evidence. American leaders had come to believe in the theory of the open-door policy [to force their way into overseas markets in order to avoid a repitition of the depression of the 1930s]. It was the decision of the USA to use its new and awesome power in keeping with traditional open-door policy that crystallised the Cold War. Their determination to apply this policy to eastern Europe evolved at the same time as George Kennan's theory, which was that continued outside pressure could and would accelerate a collapse of the Soviet system. Most Americans agreed with Secretary of State James Byrnes, who remarked in July 1945 that the problem was not to make the world safe for democracy, but to make the world safe for the United States. It was simply assumed that the two things were the same.

Source: W.A. Williams, *The Tragedy of American Diplomacy* (Delta Books, New York, 1962)

British historian Martin McCauley puts the post-revisionist view in 1983

The Cold War was not inevitable: it became a reality because of the needs of both the Soviet Union and the United States. The USSR placed security above all other considerations, and this was not sufficiently appreciated in the United States. Washington never tried to see the problem from Moscow's point of view. Stalin had an acute awareness of Soviet economic weakness and American strength, and this led him to adopt a safety-first policy. The longer Washington delayed allowing credits to Russia, the more suspicious Moscow became that the Americans were not really interested in helping the Soviet Union. It forced Moscow to decide between security and credits. American influence might replace that of the Soviets in eastern Europe. It chose security, for its fear of hostile powers on its frontiers was greater than its desire for rapid economic recovery aided by US technology.

Source: M. McCauley, *Origins of the Cold War* (Longman, 1983)

(a) Using the information from Section 7.1 and the sources, make a list of the causes which have been suggested for the Cold War. Explain the different types of cause and how they are connected; for example, long-term, short-term, political and economic causes.   1.4b–7b

(b) How do these three interpretations of the causes of the Cold War differ?   2.5

(c) What explanations can you suggest for these differences?   2.4–9

(d) Read Section 7.2, and then try and decide which of the three interpretations you find most convincing.   1.6b, 8a, 9a; 2.4–7

3   *The beginnings of the Cold War* – study Sources A–E and then answer the questions which follow.

Source A

A British cartoon (Figure 7.1) of March 1946 showing Winston Churchill trying to peer under Joseph Stalin's 'iron curtain'

Source B

A speech by Winston Churchill at Fulton, Missouri, March 1946

From Stettin in the Baltic to Trieste in the Adriatic, an iron curtain has descended across the continent. Behind that line lie all the capitals of the ancient states of Central and Eastern Europe – Warsaw, Prague, Vienna, Budapest, Belgrade,

Bucharest and Sofia. All these lie in the Soviet sphere and all are subject to a very high and increasing measure of control from Moscow.

Source: quoted in M. Gilbert, *Winston S. Churchill* (Heinemann, 1986)

Source C

A speech by President Truman of the USA in March 1947

One way of life is based upon the will of the majority with free institutions, elected government, free elections, guarantees of individual liberty . . .

The second way of life is based upon the will of the minority forced upon the majority. It relies upon terror and repression, a controlled press and radio, fixed elections . . .

I believe that it must be the policy of the USA to support free peoples who are resisting the attempt by armed minorities or by outside pressure to control them.

Source: quoted in H.S. Truman, *Memoirs* (Hodder & Stoughton, 1955)

Source D

The Russian view put forward at a conference held in Poland, September 1947

All communist parties must take the lead in resisting the plans of American imperialist expansion and aggression in all spheres. The western camp has as its basic aim the establishment of the world domination of American imperialism and the smashing of our democracy.

Source: quoted in A. Bullock, *Hitler and Stalin* (HarperCollins, 1991)

Source E

Comments from an American historian, Howard Zinn

Truman presented the USSR as not just a rival but as an immediate threat. He established a climate of hysteria about Communism which would steeply escalate the military budget and stimulate the economy with orders for war materials. This would permit more aggressive actions abroad.

Source: Howard Zinn, *A People's History of the United States* (Longman, 1980)

(a)   Does the cartoon in Source A give a good impression of the west's attitude towards Stalin and his policies?   1.4c–9b   5 marks
(b)   In what ways does Source D seem to disagree with Sources B and C?
                                                                        1.6c, 3.4   5 marks
(c)   Do you think Source E supports Source C or Source D? Explain your answer.
                                                                        1.6c, 3.4   3 marks
(d)   How useful is Source E as evidence about the causes of the Cold War?
                                                                        1.4b, 3.5   8 marks
(e)   Take Sources B, C and D in turn and explain:
      (i)   how reliable you think each source is;
      (ii)   how useful each one is for the historian trying to discover the causes of the Cold War.   3.5–9   9 marks

Total: 30 marks

8 | The spread of communism outside Europe and its effect on international relations

Summary of events

Although the first communist state was set up in Europe (in Russia in 1917), communism was not confined to Europe; it later spread to Asia where several other communist states emerged, each with its own brand of Marxism. As early as 1921, encouraged by the Russian revolution, the Chinese Communist Party (CCP) had been formed. At first it co-operated with the Kuomintang (KMT), the party trying to govern China and to control the generals who were struggling among themselves for power. As the KMT established its control over more of China, it felt strong enough to do without the help of the communists and tried to destroy them. Civil war developed between the KMT and the CCP.

The situation became more complex when the Japanese occupied Manchuria in 1931 and invaded other parts of China in 1937. When the Second World War ended in the defeat and withdrawal of the Japanese, Chiang Kai-shek, the KMT leader, with American help, and the communists under their leader, Mao Zedong, were still fighting it out. At last *in 1949 Mao triumphed*, and Chiang and his supporters fled to the island of Taiwan (Formosa); the second major country had followed Russia into communism (see Section 17.4). In 1951 the Chinese invaded and occupied neighbouring Tibet; an uprising by the Tibetans in 1959 was crushed, and the country has remained under Chinese rule ever since.

Meanwhile *communism had also gained a hold in Korea*, which had been controlled by Japan since 1910. After the Japanese defeat in 1945, the country was divided into two zones: the north occupied by the Russians, the south by the Americans. The Russsians set up a communist government in their zone, and since no agreement could be reached on what government to have for the whole country, Korea, like Germany, remained divided into two states. *In 1950 communist North Korea invaded South Korea.* United Nations forces (mostly American) moved in to help the south, while the Chinese helped the north. After much advancing and retreating, the war ended in 1953 with South Korea still non-communist.

In *Cuba* early in 1959 Fidel Castro drove out the corrupt dictator, Batista. Although Castro was not a communist to begin with, the Americans soon turned against him, particularly in 1962 when they discovered that Russian missiles were based on the island. These were later removed after a tense Cold War crisis which brought the world to the brink of nuclear war.

In *Vietnam* a similar situation to that in Korea occurred after the Vietnamese had won their independence from France (1954): the country was divided, temporarily it was thought, into north (communist) and south (non-communist). When a rebellion broke out in the south against a corrupt government, communist North Vietnam gave military assistance to the rebels; the Americans became heavily involved, supporting the South Vietnamese government to stop the spread of communism. In 1973 the Americans withdrew from the struggle, following which the South Vietnamese forces rapidly collapsed, and the whole country became united under a communist government (1975). Before the end of the year neighbouring *Cambodia* and *Laos* had also become communist.

In *South America*, which had a tradition of right-wing military dictatorships, communism made little headway, except in Chile, where in 1970 a Marxist government was democratically elected, with Salvador Allende as President. This was an interesting but short-lived experiment, since in 1973 the government was overthrown and Allende killed.

Africa saw the establishment of governments with strong Marxist connections in *Mozambique* (1975) and *Angola* (1976), both of which had just succeeded in winning independence from Portugal. This caused more western alarm and interference (see Sections 21.6(d) and 22.6).

During the second half of the 1970s a more consistent thaw in the Cold War began, with *the period known as détente (a more permanent relaxation of tensions)*. There were several hiccups though, like the Russian invasion of Afghanistan (1979), before Mikhail Gorbachev (who became Russian leader in March 1985) made a really determined effort to end the Cold War altogether, and some arms limitations agreements were signed. Then the international situation changed dramatically: in 1989 communism began to collapse in eastern Europe; by 1991 the communist bloc had disintegrated and East and West Germany were re-united. Even the USSR split up and ceased to be communist. Although communism still remained in China, Vietnam and North Korea, the Cold War was well and truly over.

8.1 War in Korea and its effects on international relations

(a) *Background to the war*

The origins of the war lay in the fact that Korea had been under Japanese occupation since 1910; when the Japanese were defeated (August 1945), the USA and the USSR agreed to divide the country into two zones along the 38th parallel (the 38 degree north line of latitude), so that they could jointly organize the Japanese surrender and withdrawal – Russia in the north (which had a frontier with the USSR) and the Americans in the south (Map 8.1). As far as the Americans were concerned, it was not intended to be a permanent division. The United Nations wanted free elections for the whole country and the Americans agreed, believing that since their zone contained two-thirds of the population, the communist north would be outvoted. However, the unification of Korea, like that of Germany, soon became part of Cold War rivalry: no agreement could be reached, and the artificial division continued. Elections were held in the south, supervised by the UN, and the *independent Republic of Korea or South Korea* was set up with Syngman Rhee as president and its capital at Seoul (August 1948). The following month, the Russians created the *Democratic People's Republic of Korea or North Korea* under the communist government of Kim Il Sung, with its capital at Pyongyang. In 1949 Russian and American troops were withdrawn, leaving a potentially dangerous

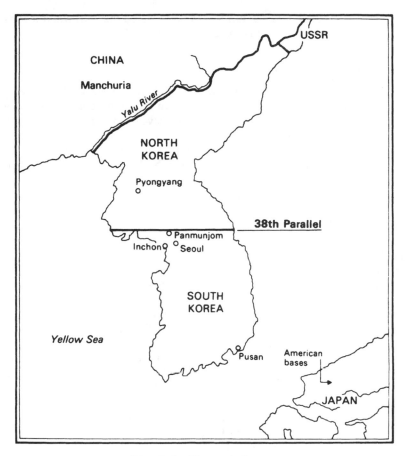

Map 8.1 The war in Korea

situation: most Koreans bitterly resented the artificial division forced on their country by outsiders, but both leaders claimed the right to rule the whole country. Without warning, North Korean troops invaded South Korea in June 1950.

(b) *Why did the North Koreans invade the South?*

Even now it is still not clear how the attack originated, or whose idea it was. *It has been suggested that:*

● it was Kim Il Sung's own idea, possibly encouraged by a statement made by Dean Acheson, the American Secretary of State, earlier in 1950. Acheson was talking about which areas around the Pacific the USA intended to defend, and for some reason he did not include Korea;

● Kim Il Sung may have been encouraged by the new Chinese communist government, which was at the same time massing troops in Fukien province facing Taiwan, as if they were about to attack Chiang Kai-shek;

● the Russians were responsible, perhaps wanting to test Truman's determination; they had supplied the North Koreans with tanks and other equipment. A communist takeover of the south would strengthen Russia's position in the Pacific and be a splendid gesture against the Americans to make up for Stalin's failure in West Berlin;

- the communists claimed that South Korea had started the war, when troops of the 'bandit traitor' Syngman Rhee had crossed the 38th parallel.

(c) *The USA takes action*

Truman was convinced that the attack was Stalin's doing; he took it as a deliberate challenge and saw it as part of a vast Russian plan to spread communism as widely as possible. American policy therefore changed decisively: instead of just economic help and promises of support, *Truman decided it was essential for the west to take a stand by supporting South Korea.* American troops in Japan were ordered to Korea even before the UN had decided what action to take. The UN Security Council called on North Korea to withdraw her troops, and when this was ignored, asked member states to send help to South Korea. This decision was reached in the absence of the Russian delegation, who were boycotting meetings in protest against the UN refusal to allow Mao's new Chinese regime to be represented, and who would certainly have vetoed such a decision. In the event, the USA and fourteen other countries (Australia, Canada, New Zealand, Nationalist China, France, Netherlands, Belgium, Colombia, Greece, Turkey, Panama, Philippines, Thailand and Britain) sent troops, though the vast majority were Americans. All forces were under the command of American *General MacArthur*.

Their arrival was just in time to prevent the whole of South Korea from being overrun by the communists. By September communist forces had captured the whole country except the south-east, around the port of Pusan. UN reinforcements poured into Pusan and on 15 September, American marines had landed at Inchon, near Seoul, 200 miles behind the communist front lines. Then followed an incredibly swift collapse of the North Korean forces: by the end of September UN troops had entered Seoul and cleared the south of communists. Instead of calling for a cease-fire now that the original UN objective had been achieved, Truman ordered an invasion of North Korea, with UN approval, aiming to unite the country and hold free elections. Chinese Foreign Minister Zhou Enlai had warned that China would resist if UN troops entered North Korea, but the warning was ignored. By the end of October UN troops had captured Pyongyang, occupied two-thirds of North Korea and reached the Yalu River, the frontier between North Korea and China (Illus. 8.1).

The Chinese government was seriously alarmed: the Americans had already placed a fleet between Taiwan and the mainland to prevent an attack on Chiang, and there seemed every chance that they would now invade Manchuria (the part of China bordering on North Korea). In November therefore, the Chinese launched a massive counter-offensive with over 300 000 troops described as 'volunteers'; by mid-January 1951 they had driven the UN troops out of North Korea, crossed the 38th parallel and captured Seoul again. MacArthur was shocked at the strength of the Chinese forces and argued that the best way to defeat communism was to attack Manchuria, with atomic bombs if necessary. However, Truman thought this would provoke a large-scale war, which the USA did not want, so *he decided to settle for merely containing communism*; MacArthur was removed from his command. In June UN troops cleared the communists out of South Korea again and fortified the frontier. Peace talks opened in Panmunjom and lasted for two years, ending in July 1953 with an agreement that the frontier should be roughly along the 38th parallel.

(d) *The results of the war were wide-ranging*

1   For Korea itself it was a disaster: the country was devastated, about four million Korean soldiers and civilians had been killed and five million people were homeless. The division seemed permanent; both states remained intensely

Illus. 8.1 US marines guard North Korean prisoners, who are stripped so that their clothes can be searched for hidden weapons

suspicious of each other and heavily armed, and there were constant ceasefire violations.

2 Truman could take some satisfaction from having contained communism and could claim that this success, plus American rearmament, dissuaded world communism from further aggression. However, many Republicans felt that the USA had lost an opportunity to destroy communism in China, and this feeling contributed towards McCarthyism (see Section 20.3).

3 The UN had exerted its authority and reversed an act of aggresssion, but the communist world denounced it as a tool of the capitalists.

4 The military performance of communist China was impressive; she had prevented the unification of Korea under American influence and was now clearly a world power. The fact that she was still not allowed a seat in the UN seemed even more unreasonable.

5 The conflict brought a new dimension to the Cold War. American relations were now permanently strained with China as well as with Russia; the familiar pattern of both sides trying to build up alliances appeared in Asia as well as Europe. China supported the Indo-Chinese communists in their struggle for independence from France, and at the same time offered friendship and aid to under-developed Third World countries in Asia, Africa and Latin America; 'peaceful co-existence' agreements were signed with India and Burma (1954).

Meanwhile the Americans tried to encircle China with bases: in 1951 defensive agreements were signed with Australia and New Zealand, and in 1954 these three states together with Britain and France set up the *South East Asia Treaty Organisation (SEATO)*. However, the USA was disappointed when only three Asian states – Pakistan, Thailand and the Philippines – joined SEATO. It was obvious that many states wanted to keep clear of the Cold War and remain uncommitted.

Relations between the USA and China were also poor because of the Taiwan situation. The communists still hoped to capture the island and destroy Chiang Kai-shek and his Nationalist party for good; but the Americans were committed to defend Chiang and wanted to keep Taiwan as a military base.

8.2 Cuba

(a) *Why did Castro come to power?*

The situation which resulted in Fidel Castro coming to power in January 1959 had built up over a number of years.

1   *There was a long-standing resentment among many Cubans at the amount of American influence in the country.* This dated back to 1898 when the USA had helped rescue Cuba from Spanish control. Although the island remained an independent republic, American troops were needed from time to time to maintain stability, and American financial aid and investment kept the Cuban economy ticking over. In fact there was some truth in the claim that *the USA controlled the Cuban economy*: American companies held controlling interests in all Cuban industries (sugar, tobacco, textiles, iron, nickel, copper, manganese, paper and rum), owned half the land, about three-fifths of the railways, all electricity production and the entire telephone system. The USA was the main market for Cuba's exports, of which sugar was by far the most important. All this explains why the American ambassador in Havana (the Cuban capital) was usually referred to as the second most important man in Cuba. The American connection need not have been resented so much if it had resulted in an efficiently run country, but this was not so.

2   Though Cuba was prosperous compared with other Latin American countries, *she was too dependent on the export of sugar, and the wealth of the country was concentrated in the hands of a few.* Unemployment was a serious problem; it varied from about 8 per cent of the labour force during the five months of the sugar harvest to over 30 per cent during the rest of the year. Yet there was no unemployment benefit, and the trade unions, dominated by workers who had all-the-year-round jobs in sugar mills, did nothing to help. The poverty of the unemployed was in stark contrast to the wealth in Havana and in the hands of corrupt government officials; consequently *social tensions were high.*

3   *No effective political system had been developed.* In 1952 Fulgencio Batista, who had been a leading politician since 1933, seized power illegally and began to rule as a dictator. He introduced no reforms, and according to historian Hugh Thomas, 'spent a lot of time dealing with his private affairs and his foreign fortunes, leaving himself too little time for affairs of state'. As well as being corrupt, his regime was also brutal.

4   Since *there was no prospect of a peaceful social revolution*, the feeling grew that violent revolution was necessary. The leading exponent of this view was Fidel Castro, a young lawyer from a middle-class background. Before he came to power, Castro was more of a liberal nationalist than a communist: he wanted to rid Cuba of Batista and corruption, and to introduce limited land reforms so that all peasants would receive some land. After an unsuccessful attempt to overthrow Batista in 1953, which earned him two years in jail, Castro began a campaign of guerrilla warfare and sabotage in the cities. The rebels soon controlled the mountainous area of the east and north and won popular support there by carrying through Castro's land reform policy.

5   *Batista's reaction played into Castro's hands.* He took savage reprisals against the guerrillas, torturing and murdering suspects. Even many of the middle classes began to support Castro as the most likely way of getting rid of a brutal dictator. Morale in Batista's poorly paid army began to crumble in the summer of 1958 after an unsuccessful attempt to destroy Castro's forces. The USA began to feel embarrassment at Batista's behaviour and cut off arms supplies; this was a serious blow to the dictator's prestige. In September a small rebel force under Che Guevara, an Argentinian supporter of Castro, gained control of the main road across the island and prepared to move on Santa Clara. On 1 January 1959 Batista fled from Cuba, and a liberal government was set up with Castro at its head.

(b) *How were Cuba's foreign relations affected?*

Cuban relations with the USA did not deteriorate immediately; Castro was thought to be, at worst, a social democrat, and so most Americans were prepared to give him a chance. Before long, however, he outraged the USA by *nationalizing American-owned estates and factories.* President Eisenhower threatened to stop importing Cuban sugar, forcing Castro to sign a trade agreement with Russia. In July 1960 when the Americans carried out their threat, the USSR promised to buy Cuba's sugar, and Castro confiscated all remaining American property. As Cuba's relations with the USA worsened, those with Russia improved: in January 1961 the USA broke off diplomatic relations with Cuba, but the Russians were already supplying economic aid. For what happened next – the Bay of Pigs invasion and the missiles crisis – see Section 7.4(b). After the missiles crisis, relations between the USA and Cuba remained cool.

The attitude of other Latin American states, most of which had right-wing governments, was one of extreme suspicion; in 1962 they expelled Cuba from the Organisation of American States (OAS), which only made her more dependent on Russia.

(c) *Castro and his problems*

Cuba was heavily dependent on the USA, and later the USSR, buying most of her sugar exports; the economy relied far too much on the sugar industry and was at the mercy of fluctuations in world sugar prices. The whole government and administration was riddled with corruption, and in addition there was serious unemployment and poverty. The new government launched itself into tackling the problems with enthusiasm and dedication. Historian David Harkness writes that during his first ten years, Castro took this poor and backward country by the scruff of the neck and shook it into new and radically different patterns of life. Agricultural land was taken over by the government and collective farms introduced; factories and businesses were nationalized; attempts were made to modernize sugar production and increase output, and to introduce new industries and reduce Cuba's dependence on sugar. Social reform included attempts to improve education, housing, health, medical facilities and communications. There was equality for black people and more rights for women. There were touring cinemas, theatres, concerts and art exhibitions. Castro himself seemed to have boundless energy; he was constantly touring the island, making speeches and urging people to greater efforts.

By the end of the 1970s the government could claim considerable success, especially in the area of social reform. All children were now receiving some education (instead of fewer than half before 1959); sanitation, hygiene and health care were much improved, unemployment and corruption reduced, and there was a greater sense of equality and stability than ever before. The government seemed to be popular with the vast majority of people. On the other hand there were some failures: the attempt to diversify industrial and agricultural output met with very little success, and so the island's economy still depended dangerously on the quality of the sugar harvest, the world price of sugar, and the willingness of the USSR and her satellites to buy up Cuba's exports. In 1980 the sugar crop was reduced by a fungus infection, while the tobacco crop was seriously affected by another fungus. This plunged the island into an economic crisis, unemployment rose again and thousands of people began to emigrate to the USA. Food rationing was introduced and the whole economy was being heavily subsidised by the USSR. By 1991 when the USSR split up and ceased to be communist, Cuba had lost its most powerful supporter, and the Castro regime was left dangerously isolated.

8.3 The wars in Vietnam, 1946–54 and 1961–75

Indo-China, which consisted of three areas, Vietnam, Laos and Cambodia, was part of the French empire in south-east Asia, and was the scene of almost non-stop conflict from the end of the Second World War. In the first phase of the conflict the peoples of these areas fought for and won their independence from the French. The second phase (1961–75) began with civil war in South Vietnam; the USA intervened to prevent the further spread of communism, but eventually had to admit failure.

(a) *1946–54*

From 1946 until 1954 the Vietnamese were fighting for independence from France. Indo-China was occupied by the Japanese during the war. Resistance to both Japanese and French was organized by the *League for Vietnamese Independence (Vietminh)*, led by the communist Ho Chi Minh, who had spent many years in Russia learning how to organize revolutions. The Vietminh, though led by communists, was an alliance of all shades of political opinion which wanted an end to foreign control. At the end of the war in 1945 Ho Chi Minh declared the whole of Vietnam independent; when it became clear that the French had no intention of allowing full independence, the Vietminh attacked them in Hanoi. This began an eight-year struggle which ended with the French being defeated at Dien Bien Phu (May 1954). The Vietminh were successful partly because they were masters of guerrilla tactics and had massive support from the Vietnamese people, and because the French, still suffering from the after-effects of the world war, failed to send enough troops. The decisive factor was probably that from 1950 the new Chinese communist government supplied the rebels with arms and equipment. The USA also became involved: seeing the struggle as part of the Cold War and the fight against communism, she supplied the French with military and economic aid; but it was not enough.

By the Geneva Agreement (1954), Laos and Cambodia were to be independent; Vietnam was temporarily divided into two states at the 17th parallel. Ho Chi Minh's government was recognized in North Vietnam. South Vietnam was to have a separate government for the time being, but elections were to be held by 1956 for the whole country, which would then become united. Ho Chi Minh was disappointed at the partition, but was confident that the communists would win the national elections. As it turned out, *the elections were never held*, and a repeat performance of the Korean situa-

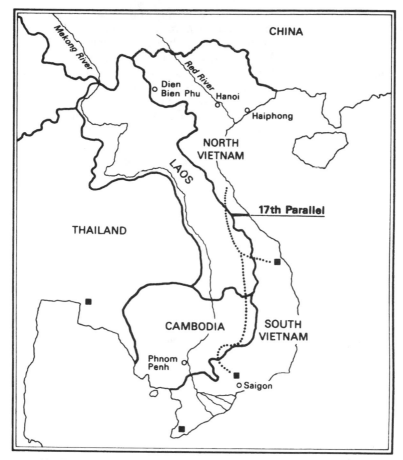

····· Ho Chi Minh Trail

■ American bases

Map 8.2 The wars in Vietnam

tion seemed likely. A civil war gradually developed in South Vietnam which eventually involved the north and the USA.

(b) *What caused the civil war in South Vietnam and why did the USA become involved?*

1 The South Vietnamese government under *President Ngo Dinh Diem* (chosen by a national referendum in 1955) refused to make preparations for the elections for the whole of Vietnam. The USA, which was backing his regime, did not press him for fear of a communist victory if the elections went ahead. *US President Eisenhower (1953–61)* was just as worried as Truman had been about the spread of communism. He seemed to become obsessed with the *'domino theory'* – if there is a line of dominoes standing on end close to each other and one is pushed over, it will knock over the next one in the line, and so on. Eisenhower thought this could be applied to countries: if one country in a region 'fell' to communism, it would quickly 'knock over' all its neighbours.

2   *Although Diem began energetically, his government soon lost popularity:* he came from a wealthy Roman Catholic family, whereas three-quarters of the population were Buddhist peasants who thought themselves discriminated against. They demanded land reform of the type carried out in China and North Vietnam. Here land had been taken away from wealthy landowners and redistributed among the poorer people; but this did not happen in South Vietnam. Diem also gained a reputation, perhaps not wholly deserved, for corruption, and he was unpopular with nationalists who thought he was too much under American influence.

3   In 1960 various opposition groups, which included many former communist members of the Vietminh, formed the *National Liberation Front (NLF)*. They demanded a democratic national coalition government which would introduce reforms and negotiate peacefully for a united Vietnam. A guerrilla campaign was started, attacking government officials and buildings; Buddhist monks had their own special brand of protest – committing suicide in public by setting fire to themselves. Diem's credibility declined further when he dismissed all criticism, however reasonable, and all opposition as communist inspired. In fact the communists were only one section of the NLF. Diem also introduced harsh security measures. He was overthrown and murdered in an army coup (1963), after which the country was ruled by a succession of generals, of whom *President Nguyen Van Thieu* lasted the longest (1967–75). The removal of Diem left the basic situation unchanged and the guerrilla war continued.

4   When it became clear that Diem could not cope with the situation, *the USA decided to increase its military presence in South Vietnam*. Under Eisenhower it had been supporting the regime since 1954 with economic aid and military advisers, and it accepted Diem's claim that communists were behind all the trouble. Having failed to defeat communism in North Korea and Cuba, the USA felt a strong stand must be made. Both Kennedy and his successor, Lyndon Johnson, were prepared to go further than just economic aid and advisers. In public the Americans said their intervention was to protect the independence of the Vietnamese people, but the real reason was to keep the country securely in the non-communist bloc.

5   The Americans were strengthened in their resolve by the knowledge that the *Vietcong* (as the guerrillas were now known) were receiving supplies, equipment and troops from North Vietnam. Ho Chi Minh believed that such aid was justified: given South Vietnam's refusal to agree to national elections, only force could unite the two halves of the country.

(c) *The phases of the war*

These correspond to successive American presidencies, each of which saw the introduction of new policies.

1   *Kennedy (1961–3)* tried to keep American involvement down to an anti-guerrilla campaign. He sent about 16 000 'advisers' plus helicopters and other equipment, and introduced the *'safe village' policy* in which local peasants were moved en masse into fortified villages, leaving the Vietcong isolated outside. This was a failure because most of the Vietcong were peasants who simply continued to operate inside the villages.

2   *Johnson (1963–9)* was not deterred by reports from American advisers in 1964 that the Vietcong and the NLF controlled about 40 per cent of South Vietnamese villages and that the peasant population seemed to support them. He assumed that the Vietcong were controlled by Ho Chi Minh and decided to bomb North

Illus. 8.2   A Vietcong suspect is executed in Saigon by police chief Nguyen Ngoc Loan, 1968

Vietnam (1965) in the hope that he would call off the campaign. Over the next seven years *a greater tonnage of bombs was dropped on North Vietnamese cities than fell on Germany during the Second World War*. In addition, over half a million American troops arrived in the south. In spite of these massive efforts, the Vietcong still managed to unleash an offensive in February 1968 which captured something like 80 per cent of all towns and villages. Although much ground was lost later, this offensive convinced many Americans of the hopelessness of the struggle. Great pressure was put on the government by public opinion in the USA to withdraw from Vietnam. Johnson had no intention of withdrawing, though he did suspend the bombing of North Vietnam in March 1968.

3   *Nixon (1969–74)* realized that a new approach was needed, since public opinion would hardly allow him to send any more American troops. Early in 1969 there were half a million Americans, 50 000 South Koreans and 750 000 South Vietnamese against 450 000 Vietcong plus perhaps 70 000 North Vietnamese. *Nixon's new idea was known as 'Vietnamization'*: the Americans would re-arm and train the South Vietnamese army to look after the defence of South Vietnam; this would allow a gradual withdrawal of American troops (in fact about half had been sent home by mid-1971). On the other hand, Nixon began the heavy bombing of North Vietnam again, and also began to bomb the *Ho Chi Minh Trail* through Laos and Cambodia along which supplies and troops came from North Vietnam.

It was all to no avail: at the end of 1972 the Vietcong controlled the entire western half of the country. By now Nixon was under pressure both at home and from world opinion to withdraw. Several factors caused a revulsion of feeling against the war:

● the terrible bombing of North Vietnam, Laos and Cambodia;

- the use of chemicals to destroy jungle foliage and of inflammable napalm jelly which burned people alive;
- the deaths of thousands of innocent civilians.

The most notorious incident took place in March 1968, when American soldiers rounded up the inhabitants of the hamlet of *My Lai*, including old people carrying young children; they were all shot and buried in mass graves; between 450 and 500 people were killed. Even Russia and China, who were helping the Vietcong, were looking for a way out. Eventually *a ceasefire was arranged for January 1973*. It was agreed that all American troops would be withdrawn from Vietnam, and both north and south would respect the frontier along the 17th parallel. However, the Vietcong continued their campaign and without the Americans, President Thieu's government in Saigon soon collapsed as his badly led armies crumbled. In April 1975 Saigon was occupied by the North Vietnamese and Vietcong. *Vietnam was at last united and free from foreign intervention – under a communist government.* In the same year communist governments were also established in Laos and Cambodia. *American policy of preventing the spread of communism in south-east Asia had ended in complete failure.*

(d) *Why did the Americans fail?*

1   The main reason was that *the Vietcong and the NLF had widespread support among ordinary people*, who had genuine grievances against an inefficient government which failed to introduce necessary reforms. When the NLF was formed in 1960 the communists were only one of several opposition groups; by ignoring the rightness of the NLF case and choosing to prop up such an obviously deficient regime in their obsession with the fight against communism, the Americans actually encouraged the spread of communism in the south.

2   *The Vietcong, like the Vietminh before them, were experts at guerrilla warfare* and were fighting on familiar territory. The Americans found them much more difficult to deal with than the conventional armies they faced in Korea. With no distinguishing uniform, guerrillas could easily merge into the local peasant population. It proved impossible to stop supplies and reinforcements moving down the Ho Chi Minh Trail.

3   *The Vietcong received important help* from North Vietnam in the way of troops, and from China and Russia who supplied arms. After 1970 the Russian contribution was vitally important and included rifles, machine-guns, long-range artillery, anti-aircraft missiles and tanks.

4   *The North Vietnamese were dedicated to eventual victory and the unification of their country.* They showed amazing resilience: in spite of appalling casualties and damage during the American bombings, they responded by evacuating city populations and rebuilding factories outside the cities.

(e) *The effects of the war were wide-reaching*

Vietnam was united but the problems of reconstruction were enormous, and the new government's policies had unpleasant aspects such as concentration camps for opponents and no freedom of speech. As well as being a blow to American prestige, their failure had a profound effect on American society; involvement in the war was seen in many circles as a terrible mistake, and this, together with the Watergate scandal which forced Nixon to resign (see Section 20.4), shook confidence in a political system which could allow such things to happen. Future American governments would have to think very carefully before committing the country so deeply in any similar situation. The war was a victory for the communist world, though both the Russians and Chinese reacted with restraint and did not boast about it to any great extent. This perhaps indicated that they wished to relax international tensions, though they now had another powerful force on their side in the Vietnamese army.

8.4 Chile under Salvador Allende 1970–3

In September 1970 Salvador Allende, a Marxist doctor of medicine from a middle-class background, won the presidential election as leader of a left-wing coalition of communists, socialists, radicals and social democrats; it called itself *Unidad Popular (UP)*. It was a narrow victory, with Allende winning 36 per cent of the votes against the 35 per cent of his nearest rival. But it was enough to make him president, the world's first Marxist leader to be voted in through a democratic election. Although it lasted only three years, Allende's government is worth looking at in some detail because it is still the only one of its kind and it shows the sort of problems likely to be faced by a Marxist government trying to function within a democratic system.

(a) *How did Allende come to be elected?*

Chile, unlike most other South American states, had a tradition of democracy. There were three main parties or groups of parties:

- the Unidad Popular on the left;
- the Christian Democrats (also left-inclined);
- the National party (a liberal/conservative coalition).

The army played little part in politics, and the democratic constitution (similar to that of the USA, except that the president could not stand for re-election immediately) was usually respected. The election of 1964 was won by Eduardo Frei, leader of the Christian Democrats, who believed in social reform. Frei began vigorously: inflation was brought down from 38 per cent to 25 per cent, the rich were made to pay their taxes instead of evading them, 360 000 new houses were built, the number of schools was more than doubled, and some limited land reform introduced: over 1200 private holdings which were being run inefficiently were confiscated and given out to landless peasants. He also took over about half the holdings in the American-owned copper mines, with suitable compensation. The American government admired his reforms and poured in lavish economic aid.

By 1967, however, the tide was beginning to turn against Frei: the left thought his land reforms too cautious and wanted full nationalization of the copper industry (Chile's most important export), whereas the right thought he had already gone too far. In 1969 there was a serious drought in which a third of the harvest was lost; large quantities of food had to be imported, causing inflation to soar again. There were strikes of copper miners demanding higher wages and several miners were killed by government troops. Allende made skilful use of this ammunition during the 1970 election campaign, pointing out that Frei's achievements fell far short of his promises. Allende's coalition had a much better campaign organization than the other parties and could get thousands of supporters out on the streets. Allende himself inspired confidence: elegant and cultured, he appeared the very opposite of the violent revolutionary. Appearances were not deceptive: he believed that communism could succeed without a violent revolution. In the 1970 election 36 per cent of the voters were in favour of trying his policies.

(b) *Allende's problems and policies*

The problems facing the new government were enormous: inflation was running at over 30 per cent, unemployment at 20 per cent, industry was stagnating, and 90 per cent of the population lived in such poverty that half the children under 15 suffered from malnutrition. Allende believed in a redistribution of income, which would enable the poor to buy more and thereby stimulate the economy. All-round wage increases of about 40 per cent were introduced and firms were not allowed to increase prices. The remainder of the copper industry, textiles and banks were nationalized, and Frei's land redistribution speeded up. The army was awarded an even bigger pay rise than anybody else to make sure of keeping its support. In foreign affairs, Allende restored diplomatic relations with Castro's Cuba, China and East Germany.

Whether Allende's policies would have succeeded in the long run is open to argument. Certainly he retained his popularity sufficiently for the UP to win 49 per cent of the votes in the 1972 local elections and to increase their seats slightly in the 1973 elections for congress. However, the Allende experiment came to an abrupt and violent end in September 1973.

(c) *Why was he overthrown?*

Criticism of the government gradually built up as Allende's policies began to cause problems.

- *Land redistribution caused a fall in agricultural production*, mainly because farmers whose land was due to be taken stopped sowing and often slaughtered their cattle (like the Russian *kulaks* during collectivization – see Section 16.2(b)). This caused food shortages and further inflation.
- Private investors were frightened off and *the government became short of funds* to carry out social reforms (housing, education and social services) as rapidly as it would have liked.
- *Copper nationalization was disappointing:* there were long strikes for higher wages, production fell, and the world price of copper fell suddenly by about 30 per cent, causing a further drop in government revenue.
- *Some communists who wanted a more drastic Castro-style approach to Chile's problems grew impatient with Allende's caution.* They refused to make allowances for the fact that he did not have a stable majority in parliament; they formed the Movement of the Revolutionary Left (MIR) which embarrassed the non-violent UP by seizing farms and evicting the owners.
- *The USA disapproved strongly of Allende's policies* and other South American governments were nervous in case the Chileans tried to export their 'revolution'.

Looming above everything else was the question of what would happen in September 1976 when the next presidential election was due. Under the constitution, Allende would not be able to stand, but no Marxist regime had ever let itself be voted out of power. *The opposition feared, perhaps with justification, that Allende was planning to change the constitution.* As things stood, any president finding his legislation blocked by congress could appeal to the nation by means of a referendum. With sufficient support Allende might be able to use the referendum device to postpone the election. It was this fear, or so they afterwards claimed, which caused the opposition groups to draw together and take action before Allende did. The right organized a massive strike and, having won the support of the army, they staged a military coup. It was organized by leading generals, who set up a military dictatorship in which *General Pinochet* came to the fore. Left-wing leaders were murdered or imprisoned; Allende himself was killed in the coup. The American Central Intelligence Agency (CIA), helped by the Brazilian government (a repressive military regime), played a vital role in the preparations for the coup, as part of its policy of preventing the spread of communism in Latin America.

The new Chilean regime soon provoked criticism from the outside world for its brutal treatment of political prisoners and its violations of human rights. However, the American government, which had reduced its economic aid while Allende was in power, stepped up its assistance again. The Pinochet regime had some economic success and by 1980 had brought the annual inflation rate down from around 1000 per cent to manageable proportions. Pinochet was in no hurry to return the country to civilian rule. He eventually allowed presidential elections in 1989 when the civilian candidate he supported was heavily defeated, winning less than 30 per cent of the votes. Pinochet allowed the winner, Christian Democrat leader Patricio Aylwin, to become president (1990), but remained Commander-in-Chief of the Armed Forces.

8.5 Détente: international relations from the 1970s to the 1990s

The word 'détente' is used to mean a permanent relaxation of tensions between east and west. The first real signs of détente could be seen in the early 1970s.

(a) *Reasons for détente*

As the nuclear arsenals built up, both sides became increasingly fearful of a catastrophic nuclear war in which there could be no real winner. Both sides were sickened by the horrors of Vietnam. In addition, countries had their own individual motives for wanting détente.

● *The USSR was finding the expense of keeping up with the Americans crippling.* It was essential to reduce defence spending so that they could devote more resources to bringing living standards up to western levels, both in the USSR and in the satellite states, all of which were suffering economic difficulties. There was unrest, especially in Poland, in the early 1970s, which threatened to destabilize the communist bloc. At the same time the Russians were on bad terms with China, and did not want to be left out when relations between China and the USA began to improve in 1971.
● *The Americans were beginning to realize that there must be a better way of coping with communism than the one which was having so little success in Vietnam.* Clearly there were limits to what their military power could achieve. Some Congressmen and Senators were even beginning to talk of a return to 'isolationism'.
● *The Chinese were anxious about their isolation*, nervous about American intentions in Vietnam (after what had happened in Korea), and not happy about their worsening relations with the USSR.
● *The nations of western Europe were worried because they would be in the front line if nuclear war broke out.* Willi Brandt, who became Chancellor of West Germany in 1969, worked for better relations with eastern Europe, a policy known as '*Ostpolitik*'.

(b) *The USSR and the USA*

They had already made progress with the 'hot-line' telephone link and the agreement to carry out only underground nuclear tests (both in 1963). An agreement signed in 1967 banned the use of nuclear weapons in outer space. The first major breakthrough came in 1972 when the two countries signed the *Strategic Arms Limitation Treaty, known as SALT 1,* which decided how many ABMs, ICBMs and SLBMs each side could have; there was no agreement about MIRVs. The agreement did not reduce the amount of armaments but *it did slow the arms race down.* Presidents Brezhnev and Nixon had three summit meetings, negotiations opened for a further treaty to be known as SALT 2, and the USA began to export wheat to Russia.

Another important step was the *Helsinki Agreement (July 1975),* in which the USA, Canada, the USSR and most European states accepted the European frontiers which had been drawn up after the Second World War (thus recognising the division of Germany). The communist countries promised to allow their peoples 'human rights', including freedom of speech and freedom to leave the country.

However, détente did not proceed without some setbacks. This was especially true in 1979 when NATO became nervous at the deployment of 150 new Russian SS-20 missiles. NATO decided to deploy over 500 Pershing and Cruise missiles in Europe by 1983 as a deterrent to a possible Russian attack on Western Europe. At the same time the US Senate decided not to accept a SALT 2 treaty which would have limited numbers of MIRVs. When the Russians invaded Afghanistan on Christmas Day 1979 and replaced the president with one more favourable to them, all the old western suspicions of Russian motives revived.

Both sides spent the first half of the 1980s building up their nuclear arsenals, and US President Reagan (1981–9) apparently gave the go-ahead for a new weapons system, the *Strategic Defence Initiative (SDI),* also known as 'Star Wars'. This was intended to use weapons based in space to destroy ballistic missiles in flight.

Détente gathered momentum again thanks to the determination of the new soviet leader, Mikhail Gorbachev (1985–91). He had summit meetings with Reagan and proposed a 15-year timetable for a 'step-by-step process for ridding the earth of nuclear weapons'. The Americans responded to some extent, though they were not prepared to go as far as Gorbachev would have liked. The result was the *INF (intermediate nuclear forces) Treaty,* formally signed by Reagan and Gorbachev in Washington in December 1987.

- All land-based intermediate range (300 to 3000 miles) nuclear weapons were to be scrapped over the next three years. This meant 436 American and 1575 Soviet warheads, and would include all Russian missiles in East Germany and Czechoslovakia, and all American Cruise and Pershing missiles based in Western Europe.
- There were strict verification provisions so that both sides could check that the weapons were actually being destroyed.

However, all this amounted at most to only 4 per cent of existing stocks of nuclear weapons, and there was still the stumbling block of Reagan's Star Wars, which he was not prepared to give up, even though it was only in the planning stage. Nor did the agreement include British and French weapons. Margaret Thatcher was determined that Britain should keep her own nuclear arsenal, and planned to develop Trident missiles, which were more sophisticated than Cruise missiles. *Nevertheless this INF Treaty was an important turning-point in the nuclear arms race, since it was the first time any weapons had been destroyed.*

By 1985 the USSR was seriously embarrassed by its involvement in Afghanistan. Although there were over 100 000 soviet troops in the country, they found it impossible to subdue the ferocious Islamic guerrillas; it was a drain on their resources and a blow to their prestige. The hostility of China, the suspicion of Islamic states all over the world, and repeated condemnations by the UN, convinced Gorbachev it was time to pull out. It was eventually agreed that the Russians would begin withdrawing their troops from Afghanistan on 1 May 1988, provided the Americans stopped sending military aid to the Afghan resistance movement.

(c) *China and the USA*

China and the USA had been extremely hostile towards each other since the Korean War and seemed likely to remain so while the Americans backed Chiang Kai-shek and the Nationalists in Taiwan, and while the Chinese backed Ho Chi Minh. However, in 1971 the Chinese unexpectedly invited an American table-tennis team to visit China. Following the success of that visit, the USA responded by calling off their veto of Chinese entry into the United Nations. *Communist China was therefore allowed to become a member of the UN in October 1971.* Presidents Nixon and Ford both paid successful visits to Peking (1972 and 1975) (Illus. 8.3).

There was still the problem of Taiwan to sour the relationship: though Chiang himself died in 1975, his supporters still occupied the island, and the communists would not be happy until it was brought under their control. Relations improved further in 1978 when Democrat President Carter decided to withdraw recognition of Nationalist China. However, this caused a row in the USA where Carter was accused of betraying his ally.

The climax of détente between China and the USA came early in 1979 when *Carter gave formal recognition of the People's Republic of China*, and ambassadors were exchanged. Good relations were maintained during the 1980s. The Chinese were anxious that détente with the USA should continue because of their conflict with Vietnam (Russia's ally) which had begun in 1979. In 1985 an agreement was signed on nuclear co-operation.

Things suddenly took turn for the worse in June 1989 when *the Chinese govern-*

Illus. 8.3 President Nixon (right) with Chinese Prime Minister Zhou Enlai, on his visit to Peking (Beijing) in 1972

ment used troops to disperse a student demonstration in Tiananmen Square, Beijing (Peking). The government was afraid that the demonstration might turn into a revolution which could overthrow Chinese communism. At least a thousand students were killed and many later executed, and this brought world-wide condemnation. Tensions rose again in 1996 when the Chinese held 'naval exercises' in the straits between the Chinese mainland and Taiwan, in protest at the Taiwanese democratic elections just about to be held.

(d) *Relations between the USSR and China*

Relations between the USSR and China deteriorated steadily after 1956. They had earlier signed a treaty of mutual assistance and friendship (1950), but later the Chinese did not approve of Khrushchev's policies, particularly his belief in 'peaceful co-existence', and his claim that it was possible to achieve communism by methods other than violent revolution. This went against the ideas of Lenin, leader of the 1917 Russian communist revolution, and so *the Chinese accused the Russians of 'revisionism'* – revising or re-interpreting the teachings of Marx and Lenin to suit their own needs. They were angry at Khrushchev's 'soft' line towards the USA. In retaliation the Russians reduced their economic aid to China.

The ideological argument was not the only source of trouble: there was also *a frontier dispute*. During the nineteenth century Russia had taken over large areas of Chinese territory north of Vladivostok and in Sinkiang province which the Chinese were now demanding back, so far without success. Now that China herself was following a 'softer' policy towards the USA, it seemed that the territorial problem was the main bone of contention. At the end of the 1970s it seemed that both Russia and China were vying for American support against each other for the leadership of world communism. To complicate matters further, Vietnam now supported Russia. When the Chinese attacked Vietnam (February 1979), relations reached rock bottom. The Chinese attack was partly in retaliation for Vietnam's invasion of Kampuchea (formerly Cambodia) (December 1978) which overthrew the Khmer Rouge government of Pol Pot, a protégé of China, and partly because of a frontier dispute. They withdrew after three weeks, having, as Beijing put it, 'taught the Vietnamese a lesson'. *In 1984 the Chinese set out their grievances against the USSR:*

- the presence of Russian troops in Afghanistan;
- Soviet backing of the Vietnamese troops in Kampuchea;
- the Soviet troop build-up along the Chinese frontiers of Mongolia and Manchuria.

Mikhail Gorbachev was determined to begin a new era in Sino-Russian relations. Five-year agreements on trade and economic co-operation were signed (July 1985) and regular contact took place between the two governments. A formal reconciliation took place in May 1989 when Gorbachev visited Beijing. Also in 1989 Vietnam withdrew its troops from Kampuchea, and so their relations with China improved.

8.6 The collapse of communism in Eastern Europe: international relations transformed

(a) *August 1988 to December 1991*

Remarkable events happened in Eastern Europe in the period August 1988 to December 1991. Communism was swept away by a rising tide of popular opposition and mass demonstrations, far more quickly than anybody could ever have imagined.

- *The process began in Poland in August 1988* when the '*Solidarity*' trade union organized huge anti-government strikes. These eventually forced the government to allow free elections, in which the communists were heavily defeated (June 1989).

Revolutionary protests rapidly spread to all the other Russian satellite states:

- *Hungary was the next to allow free elections*, in which the communists again suffered defeat.
- In *East Germany* communist leader Eric Honecker wanted to disperse the demonstrations by force, but he was overruled by his colleagues; by the end of 1989 the communist government had resigned. Soon the Berlin Wall was breached, and, most astonishing of all, *in the summer of 1990, Germany was re-united*.
- *Czechoslovakia*, *Bulgaria* and *Romania* had thrown out their communist governments by the end of 1989, and multi-party elections were held in *Yugoslavia* in 1990 and in *Albania* in the spring of 1991.
- By the end of December 1991 *the USSR* itself had split up into separate republics and Gorbachev had resigned. Communist rule in Russia was over after 74 years.

See Sections 10.7 and 16.7 for the reasons behind the collapse of communism in Eastern Europe.

(b) *How were international relations affected?*

Many people in the west thought that with the collapse of communism in Eastern Europe, the world's problems would miraculously disappear. But nothing could have been further from the truth and a range of new problems surfaced.

1 The Cold War was over

The most immediate result was that the former USSR and its allies were no longer seen by the west as the 'enemy'. In November 1990 the countries of NATO and the Warsaw Pact signed a treaty agreeing that they were 'no longer adversaries', and that none of their weapons would ever be used except in self-defence. The Cold War was over, and that was an enormous step forward. However ...

2 New conflicts soon arose

These were often caused by nationalism. During the Cold War, the USSR and the USA had kept tight control, by force if necessary, over areas where their vital interests might be affected. Now, a conflict which did not directly affect the interests of east or west would probably be left to find its own solution, bloody or otherwise. Nationalism, which had been suppressed by communism, soon re-emerged in some of the former states of the USSR and elsewhere. Sometimes disputes were settled peacefully, for example in *Czechoslovakia*, where Slovak nationalists insisted on breaking away to form a separate state of Slovakia. However, war broke out between *Azerbaijan and Armenia* (two former states of the USSR) over disputed territory. There was fighting in *Georgia* (another former Soviet republic) where the people of the north wanted to form a separate state.

Most tragic of all was *Yugoslavia*, which broke up into five separate states – Serbia (with Montenegro), Bosnia-Herzegovina, Croatia, Slovenia and Macedonia. Soon a complex civil war broke out in which Serbia tried to grab as much territory as possible from Croatia. In Bosnia, Serbs, Croats and Muslims fought each other in an attempt to set up states of their own. This increasingly bitter struggle dragged on for almost four years until a ceasefire was arranged in November 1995 (see Section 10.8(c)). So at a time when the states of Western Europe were moving into closer union with the European Community (see Section 10.5(h)), those of Eastern Europe were breaking up into even smaller national units.

3 Nuclear weapons supervision

Another fear, now that the Russians and the USA were less willing to act as 'policemen', was that *countries with what the powers considered to be unstable or irresponsible governments might use nuclear weapons* – countries like, for example, Iraq, Iran and Libya. One of the needs of the 1990s therefore, was for better international supervision and control of nuclear weapons, and also of biological and chemical weapons.

4 Economic problems

All the former communist states faced another problem – how to deal with the economic collapse and intense poverty left over from the communist *'command'* economies, and how to change to *'free-market'* economies. They needed a carefully planned and generous programme of financial help from the west. Otherwise it would be difficult to create stability in Eastern Europe. Nationalism and economic unrest could cause a right-wing backlash, especially in Russia itself, which could be just as threatening as communism was once thought to be. There was clearly cause for concern, given the large number of nuclear weapons still in existence in the region. There was the danger that Russia, desperate to raise money, might sell off some of its nuclear weapons to 'unsuitable' governments.

5 The unification of Germany created some problems

The Poles were very suspicious of a united and powerful Germany, fearing that it might try to take back the former German territory east of the rivers Oder and Neisse, given to Poland after the Second World War. Germany also found itself providing refuge for people fleeing from disturbances in other states of Europe; by October 1992 at least 16 000 refugees a month were entering Germany.This gave rise to violent protests from right-wing neo-Nazi groups who believed that Germany had problems enough of its own – especially the need to modernize the industry and amenities of the former East Germany – without admitting foreigners.

6 Relations between the western allies

The disappearance of communism affected relations between the western allies, the USA, Western Europe and Japan. They had been held together by the need to stand firm against communism, but now differences emerged over trade and the extent to which the USA and Japan were prepared to help solve the problems of Eastern Europe. For instance, during the war in Bosnia, relations between the USA and the states of Western Europe became strained when the USA refused to provide troops for the UN peacekeeping forces, leaving the burden to other member states.

Questions

1 *Castro and Allende*   Sections 8.2 and 8.4 looked at Fidel Castro in Cuba and Salvador Allende in Chile.
   (a)   Make a list of similarities and a list of differences which you have noticed about their political careers. Some of the areas you can compare are:

(i)   how and why they both came to power;   1.4b–8a
(ii) what problems faced them and what changes they introduced to deal
      with the problems;   1.4a–7a, 4c–7c
(iii) how people reacted to these changes.   1.6c–8c

(b) Why do you think Castro survived in power for so long, whereas Allende only
     lasted three years?   1.6a, 4b–7b, 4c–8c

2   *The Vietnam War 1961–75*   Read Sources A and B and then answer the questions
    which follow.

Source A

Statement by General Harkins, Head of US Operations in South Vietnam, June 1963

The NLF (National Liberation Front) guerrillas are obviously not being reinforced
or supplied systematically from North Vietnam, China, or any other place. They
depend primarily on what they can capture.

Source B

Speech by President Johnson of the USA, April 1965

North Vietnam is helping the rebels and is being helped by China, a regime which
has destroyed freedom in Tibet and which is helping the forces of violence in
nearly every continent. The contest in Vietnam is part of a world-wide pattern of
aggressive purpose. South Vietnam must remain non-communist, otherwise all of
South-East Asia will fall under communist dominance.

Sources: both are quoted in C. Bown and P.J. Mooney, *Cold War to Détente, 1945–83* (Heinemann,
1984)

(a) In what ways do these two sources contradict each other?   1.6c, 3.4   3 marks
(b) What reasons can you suggest to explain why these sources, both by
     Americans, seem to disagree?   1.7c–9b   6 marks
(c) Using the information from the sources and from Sections 8.3(a–b), explain
     the causes of the war in Vietnam. Show what types of causes were involved,
     how they were connected, and which you think were the most important.
                                                                1.5b–8a   10 marks
(d) Using the information from Sections 8.3(c–d), make a list of reasons why the
     Americans failed in their attempt to keep South Vietnam non-communist. Put
     the most important reason at the top of the list and the least important at the
     bottom.   1.6b–8a   6 marks

Total: 25 marks

The United Nations Organization

Summary of events

The United Nations Organization (UNO) officially came into existence in October 1945 after the Second World War. It was formed to replace the League of Nations, which had proved incapable of restraining aggressive dictators like Hitler and Mussolini. In setting up the UNO, the great powers tried to eliminate some of the weaknesses which had handicapped the League. *The UN Charter was drawn up in San Francisco in 1945*, and was based on proposals made at an earlier meeting between the USSR, the USA, China and Britain held at *Dumbarton Oaks* (USA) in 1944.

The aims of the UN are to:

● preserve peace and eliminate war;
● remove the causes of conflict by encouraging economic, social, educational, scientific and cultural progress throughout the world, especially in underdeveloped countries;
● safeguard the rights of all individual human beings, and the rights of peoples and nations.

In spite of the careful framing of the Charter, the UN was unable to solve many of the problems of international relations, particularly those caused by the Cold War. On the other hand it played an important role in a number of international crises by arranging cease-fires and negotiations, and by providing peacekeeping forces. Its successes in non-political work (such as care of refugees, protection of human rights, economic planning and attempts to deal with health and population problems) have been enormous.

9.1 The structure of the United Nations Organization

There are six main organs of the UN:

● the General Assembly;
● the Security Council;
● the Secretariat;
● the International Court of Justice;

- the Trusteeship Council; and
- the Economic and Social Council.

(a) *The General Assembly*

This is the meeting together of the representatives from all the member nations; each member can send up to five representatives, though there is only one vote per nation. It meets once a year, starting in September and remaining in session for about three months, but special sessions can be called in times of crisis by the members themselves or by the Security Council. Its function is to discuss and make decisions about international problems, to consider the UN budget and what amount each member should pay, to elect the Security Council members, and to supervise the work of the many other UN bodies. *Decisions do not need a unanimous vote as they did in the League*

Illus. 9.1   UN Headquarters in New York. On the right is the 39-storey Secretariat Building, in the centre the General Assembly, and in the foreground the Library

Assembly. Sometimes a simple majority is enough, though on issues which the Assembly thinks are very important, a two-thirds majority is needed. These include decisions about admitting new members or expelling existing members, and about actions to be taken to maintain peace. All speeches and debates are translated into the six official UN languages – English, French, Russian, Chinese, Spanish and Arabic.

(b) *The Security Council*

This sits in permanent session and its function is to deal with crises as they arise, by whatever action seems appropriate, and if necessary, by calling on members to take economic or military action against an aggressor. The Council began with eleven members, *five of them permanent (China, France, USA, USSR and Britain)*, and the other six elected by the General Assembly for two-year terms. In 1965 the number of non-permanent members was increased to ten. Decisions need at least nine of the fifteen members to vote in favour, but these must include all five permanent members. This means that *any one of the permanent members can veto a decision and prevent any action being taken.* In practice it has gradually been accepted that abstention by a permanent member does not count as a veto, but this has not been written into the Charter.

In order to secure some action in case of a veto by one of the permanent members, the General Assembly (at the time of the Korean War in 1950) introduced the *'Uniting for Peace' resolution*; this stated that if the Security Council's proposals were vetoed, the Assembly could meet within 24 hours and decide what action to take, even military intervention if necessary. In cases like this, a decision by the Assembly would only need a two-thirds majority. Again this new rule was not added to the Charter, and the USSR, which used the veto more often than any other member, always maintained that a Security Council veto should take precedence over a General Assembly decision. Nevertheless the Assembly acted in this way many times, ignoring Russian protests.

(c) *The Secretariat*

This is the 'office-staff' of the UN, and it consists of over 50 000 employees. They look after the administrative work, preparing minutes of meetings, translations and information. *It is headed by the Secretary-General*, who is appointed for a five-year term by the Assembly on the recommendation of the Security Council. In order to ensure some degree of impartiality, he or she is not from one of the major powers. The Secretary-General acts as the main spokesperson for the UN and is always at the forefront of international affairs, trying to sort out the world's problems. So far the post has been held by:

Trygvie Lie of Norway (1946–52)
Dag Hammarskjöld of Sweden (1952–61)
U Thant of Burma (1961–71)
Kurt Waldheim of Austria (1971–81)
Perez de Cuellar of Peru (1981–91)
Boutros Boutros-Ghali of Egypt (1991–96)
Kofi Annan of Ghana (since December 1996).

(d) *The International Court of Justice*

The International Court of Justice at the Hague (in Holland) has fifteen judges, all of different nationalities, elected for nine-year terms (five retiring every third year) by the Assembly and the Security Council jointly. It has dealt successfully with a number of disputes, including a frontier dispute between Holland and Belgium and a disagreement between Britain and Norway over fishing limits. In other cases, however, it was not so successful. In 1946, for example, Britain accused Albania of laying mines near the Greek island of Corfu, and demanded compensation from Albania for damage caused to British shipping. The Court upheld the claim and ordered Albania to pay £1 million to Britain. Albania refused to pay, claiming that the Court had no right to judge the case. Although in theory the Security Council has the power to take 'appropriate measures' to enforce the Court's decisions, it has never done so.

(e) *The Trusteeship Council*

This replaced the League of Nations Mandates Commission which had originally come into existence in 1919 to keep an eye on the territories taken away from Germany and Turkey at the end of the First World War. Some of these areas (known as *mandated territories or mandates*) had been handed over to the victorious powers, and their job was to govern the territories and prepare them for independence (see Sections 2.8 and 2.10). The Trusteeship Council did its job well and by 1970 most of the mandates had gained their independence (see Section 11.1(b) and Chapter 21).

However, *Namibia remained a problem, since South Africa refused to give the area independence*. South Africa, ruled by a government representing the white minority of the population, was unwilling to give independence to a state right on its own frontier which would be ruled by a government representing its black African majority. The UN repeatedly condemned South Africa for its attitude; in 1971 the International Court of Justice ruled that South Africa's occupation of Namibia was a breach of international law and that South Africa must withdraw immediately. South Africa ignored the UN, but as the other states of Africa gradually gained independence under black governments, it became more difficult for South Africa to maintain both its position in Namibia and its own white minority rule (see Sections 22.6(b–c) and 22.8(e)). At last in 1990 the pressure of black African nationalism and world opinion forced South Africa to release its grip on Namibia.

(f) *The Economic and Social Council (ECOSOC)*

This has twenty-seven members elected by the General Assembly, with one-third retiring each year. It organizes projects concerned with health, education and other social and economic matters. Its task is so enormous that *it has appointed four regional commissions (Europe, Latin America, Africa, Asia and the Far East)*, as well as commissions on population problems, drugs problems, human rights and the status of women. ECOSOC also co-ordinates the work of an astonishing array of other commissions and specialized agencies, around thirty in all. Among the best known are the International Labour Organization (ILO), the World Health Organization (WHO), the Food and Agriculture Organization (FAO), the United Nations Educational, Scientific and Cultural Organization (UNESCO), the United Nations Children's Fund (UNICEF) and the United Nations Relief and Works Agency (UNRWA). The scope of ECOSOC expanded in such a remarkable way that by 1980 more than 90 per cent of the UN's annual expenditure was devoted to ECOSOC activities (see Section 9.4).

9.2 How different is the United Nations from the League of Nations?

(a) *The UN has been more successful*

There are some important differences which have tended to make the UN a more successful body than the League.

- The UN spends much more time and resources on economic and social matters and its scope is much wider than that of the League. All the specialized agencies, with the exception of the International Labour Organization (founded in 1919), were set up in 1945 or later.
- The UN is committed to safeguarding individual human rights, which the League did not get involved in.
- Changes in the procedures of the General Assembly and the Security Council (especially the 'Uniting for Peace' resolution), and the increased power and prestige of the Secretary-General have enabled the UN, on occasion, to take more decisive action than the League ever achieved.
- The UN has a much wider membership and is therefore more of a genuine world organization than was the League, with all the extra prestige that this entails. Both the USA and the USSR were founder-members of the UN whereas the USA never joined the League. Between 1963 and 1968 no fewer than forty-three new members joined the UN, mainly the emerging states of Africa and Asia, and by 1985 membership had reached 159; the League never had more than 50 members. Later, many of the former member states of the USSR joined, and by 1993 the total had reached 183.

(b) *Some of the weaknesses of the League remain*

Any one of the five permanent members of the Security Council can use its power of veto to prevent decisive action being taken. Like the League, the UN has no permanent army of its own and has to use forces belonging to its member states (see Section 9.5).

9.3 How successful has the UN been as a peacekeeping organization?

Although it has had mixed success, it is probably fair to say that *the UN has been more successful than the League in its peacekeeping efforts*, especially in crises which did not directly involve the interests of the great powers, such as the civil war in the Congo (1960–4) and the dispute between Holland and Indonesia over West New Guinea.

On the other hand, it has often been just as ineffective as the League in situations – such as the Hungarian rising of 1956 and the 1968 Czech crisis – where the interests of one of the great powers (in this case the USSR) seemed to be threatened, and where the great power decided to ignore or defy the United Nations. The best way to illustrate the UN's varying degrees of success is to examine some of the major disputes in which it has been involved.

(a) *West New Guinea, 1946*

In 1946 the UN helped to arrange independence from Holland for the Dutch East Indies, which became Indonesia (see Map 21.3). However, no agreement was reached

Figure 9.1

THE UNITED NATIONS SYSTEM

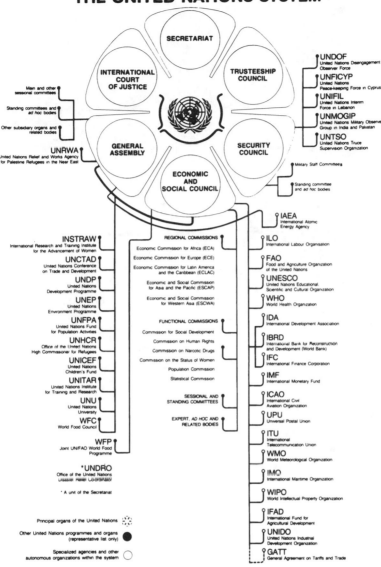

Source: UN Information Service

about the future of West New Guinea (West Irian) which was claimed by both countries. In 1961 fighting broke out; after U Thant had appealed to both sides to re-open negotiations, it was agreed (1962) that the territory should become part of Indonesia. The transfer was organized and policed by a UN force. In this case the UN played a vital role in getting negotiations off the ground, though it did not itself make the decision about West Irian's future.

Illus. 9.2   UN truce supervision in Palestine

(b) *Palestine, 1947*

The dispute between Jews and Arabs in Palestine was brought before the UN in 1947. After an investigation, the UN decided to divide Palestine, setting up the Jewish state of Israel (see Section 11.2). This was one of the UN's most controversial decisions, and it was not accepted by the majority of Arabs. The UN was unable to prevent a series of wars between Israel and various Arab states (1948–9, 1967 and 1973) though it did useful work arranging cease-fires and providing supervisory forces, while the UN Relief and Works Agency cared for the Arab refugees (Illus. 9.2).

(c) *The Korean War (1950–3)*

This was the only occasion on which the UN was able to take decisive action in a crisis directly involving the interests of one of the superpowers. When South Korea was invaded by communist North Korea in June 1950, the Security Council immediately passed a resolution condemning North Korea, and called on member states to send help to the south. However, this was possible only because of the temporary absence of the Russian delegates, who would have vetoed the resolution if they had not been boycotting Security Council meetings (since January of that year) in protest at the failure to allow communist China to join the UN. Although the Russian delegates returned smartly, it was too late for them to prevent action going ahead. Troops of sixteen countries were able to repel the invasion and preserve the frontier between the two Koreas along the 38th parallel (see Section 8.1).

Though this was claimed by the west as a great UN success, it was in fact very much an American operation – the vast majority of troops and the commander-in-chief, General MacArthur, were American, and the US government had already decided to intervene with force the day before the Security Council decision was taken. Only the absence of the Russians enabled the USA to turn it into a UN operation. This was a situation not likely to be repeated, since the USSR would take good care to be present at all future Council sessions.

The Korean War had important results for the future of the UN: one was the passing of the *'Uniting for Peace' resolution* which would permit a Security Council veto to be by-passed by a General Assembly vote. Another was the launching of *a bitter attack by the Russians on Secretary-General Trygvie-Lie* for what they considered to be his biased role in the crisis. His position soon became impossible and he eventually agreed to retire early, to be replaced by Dag Hammarskjöld.

(d) *The Suez Crisis (1956)*

This showed the UN at its best. When President Nasser of Egypt suddenly nationalized the Suez Canal, many of whose shares were owned by the British and French, both these powers protested strongly and sent troops 'to protect their interests' (see Section 11.3). At the same time the Israelis invaded Egypt from the east; the real aim of all three states was to bring down President Nasser. A Security Council resolution condemning force was vetoed by Britain and France, whereupon the General Assembly, by a majority of 64 votes to 5, condemned the invasions and called for a withdrawal of troops. In view of the weight of opinion against them, the aggressors agreed to withdraw, provided the UN ensured a reasonable settlement over the canal and kept the Arabs and Israelis from slaughtering each other. A UN force of 5000, made up of troops from ten different countries, moved in, while the British, French and Israelis went home. The prestige of the UN and of Dag Hammarskjöld, who handled the operation with considerable skill, was greatly enhanced, though American and Russian pressure was also important in bringing about a cease-fire. However, the UN was not so successful in the 1967 Arab–Israeli conflict (see Section 11.4).

(e) *The Hungarian Rising (1956)*

This took place at the same time as the Suez Crisis, and showed the UN at its most ineffective. When the Hungarians tried to exert their independence from Russian control, soviet troops entered Hungary to crush the revolt. The Hungarian government appealed to the UN, but the Russians vetoed a Security Council resolution calling for a withdrawal of their forces. The General Assembly passed the same resolution and set up a committee to investigate the problem; but the Russians refused to co-operate with the committee and no progress could be made. The contrast with Suez was striking: there, Britain and France were willing to bow to international pressure; the Russians simply ignored the UN and nothing could be done. (See question 1 at the end of this chapter.)

(f) *The Belgian Congo civil war (1960–4)*

Here the UN mounted its most complex operation to date (see Section 22.5) (except for Korea). When the Congo (known as *Zaire* since 1971) dissolved into chaos immediately after gaining independence, a UN force numbering over 20 000 at its largest, managed to restore some sort of precarious order. A special UN Congo Fund was set up to help with the recovery and development of the ravaged country. *But the financial cost was so high that the UN was brought close to bankruptcy*, especially when the USSR, France and Belgium refused to pay their contributions towards the cost of the operations, because they disapproved of the way the UN had handled the situation. The war also cost the life of Dag Hammarskjöld, who was killed in a plane crash in the Congo.

(g) *Cyprus*

Cyprus has kept the UN busy since 1964. A British colony since 1878, the island was granted independence in 1960. In 1963 civil war broke out between the Greeks, who made up about 80 per cent of the population, and the Turks. A UN peacekeeping force arrived in March 1964; an uneasy peace was restored, but it needed 3000 UN troops permanently stationed in Cyprus to prevent Greeks and Turks tearing each other apart. That was not the end of the trouble though: in 1974 the Greek Cypriots tried to unite the island with Greece. This prompted the Turkish Cypriots, helped by invading Turkish army troops, to seize the north of the island for their own territory. They went on to expel all Greeks who were unfortunate enough to be living in that area. Again UN forces achieved a cease-fire and are still policing the frontier between Greeks and Turks. However, the UN has still not been successful in finding an acceptable constitution or any other compromise, and dare not risk withdrawing its troops (See Map 21.4).

(h) *Kashmir*

In Kashmir the UN found itself in a similar situation to the one in Cyprus. After 1947, this large province, lying between India and Pakistan (see Map 21.1) was claimed by both states. Already in 1948 the UN had negotiated a cease-fire after fighting broke out. At this point the Indians were occupying the southern part of Kashmir, the Pakistanis the northern part, and for the next sixteen years the UN policed the cease-fire line between the two zones. When Pakistani troops invaded the Indian zone in 1965, a short war developed, but once again the UN successfully intervened and hostilities ceased. The original dispute still remained though, and in the 1990s there seemed little prospect of the UN or any other agency finding a permanent solution.

(i) *The Czechoslovak crisis (1968)*

This was almost a repeat performance of the Hungarian rising twelve years earlier. When the Czechs showed what Moscow considered to be too much independence, Russian and other Warsaw Pact troops were sent in to enforce obedience to the USSR. The Security Council tried to pass a motion condemning this action, but the Russians vetoed it, claiming that the Czech government had asked for their intervention. Although the Czechs denied this, there was nothing the UN could do in view of the USSR's refusal to co-operate.

(j) *Recent successes and failures*

Successes

● *The United Nations Interim Force in Lebanon (UNIFIL)* has been operating with about 7000 troops in the South Lebanon since 1978 in a frontier dispute between

Lebanese Christians (aided by the Israelis) and Palestinians. UNIFIL has had some success in maintaining relative peace in the area, but it is a constant struggle against frontier violations, assassinations, terrorism and the seizing of hostages (see Section 11.8(b)).

● *The UN was successful in bringing an end to the long drawn-out war between Iran and Iraq (1980–8).* After years of attempting to mediate, the UN at last negotiated a cease-fire, though admittedly they were helped by the fact that both sides were close to exhaustion (see Section 11.9).

● *UN action during the Gulf War of 1991 was impressive.* When Saddam Hussein of Iraq sent his troops to invade and capture the tiny, but extremely rich neighbouring state of Kuwait (August 1990), the UN Security Council warned him to withdraw or face the consequences. When he refused, a large UN force was sent to Saudi-Arabia. In a short and decisive campaign, Iraqi troops were driven out, suffering heavy losses, and Kuwait was liberated (see Section 11.10). However, critics of the UN complained that Kuwait had received help only because the west needed her oil supplies; other small nations which had no value to the west had received no help when they were invaded by larger neighbours (for example East Timor, taken over by Indonesia in 1975).

● *Problems in Cambodia (Kampuchea) dragged on for nearly twenty years, but eventually the UN was able to arrange a solution.* In 1975 the Khmer Rouge, a communist guerrilla force led by Pol Pot, seized power from the right-wing government of Prince Sihanouk. Over the next three years Pol Pot's brutal regime slaughtered about a third of the population until in 1978 a Vietnamese army invaded the country. They drove out the Khmer Rouge and set up a new government. At first the UN, prompted by the USA, condemned this action, although many people thought Vietnam had done the people of Cambodia a great service by getting rid of the cruel Pol Pot regime. But it was all part of the Cold War, which meant that any action by Vietnam, an ally of the USSR, would be condemned by the USA. The end of the Cold War enabled the UN to organize and police a solution. Vietnamese forces were withdrawn (September 1989), and after a long period of negotiations and persuasion, elections were held (June 1993), won by Prince Sihanouk's party. The result was widely accepted (though not by what was left of the Khmer Rouge, which refused to take part in the elections), and the country gradually began to settle down.

● *Mozambique, which gained independence from Portugal in 1975, was torn by civil war for many years* (see Section 21.6(d)). By 1990 the country was in ruins and both sides were exhausted. Although both sides had signed a cease-fire agreement in Rome (October 1992) at a conference organized by the Roman Catholic Church and the Italian government, it was not holding. There were many violations of the cease-fire and there was no way that elections could be held in such an atmosphere. The UN now became fully involved operating a programme of demobilizing and disarming the various armies, distributing humanitarian relief, and preparing for elections, which took place successfully in October 1994.

Failures

UN failures were in Somalia, and, some would argue, in Bosnia.

● *Somalia disintegrated into civil war in 1991* when the dictator Siad Barre was overthrown. A power struggle developed between rival supporters of Generals Aidid and Ali Mohammed; the situation was chaotic as food supplies and communications broke down and thousands of refugees were fleeing into Kenya. The Organization of African Unity (OAU) asked for UN help, and 37 000 UN troops, mainly American, arrived (December 1992) to safeguard the aid and to restore law and order by disarming the 'warlords'. However, the warlords, especially Aidid, were not prepared to be disarmed, and UN troops began to suffer casualties. The Americans withdrew their troops (March 1994), and the remaining UN troops were withdrawn in March 1995, leaving the warlords to fight it out. It was a humiliating backdown; but in fact the UN had set itself an impossible task from the beginning – to forcibly disarm two extremely powerful armies which were determined to carry on fighting each other, and to combine this with a humanitarian relief programme.

- *A similar situation developed in Bosnia* (see Section 10.8(c)). Successful UN military interventions, like Korea and the Gulf War, only happened when UN troops actively supported one side against the other.

9.4 What other work is the UN responsible for?

Although it is the UN's role as peace-keeper and international mediator which most often gets into the headlines, the majority of its work is concerned with its less spectacular aims of safeguarding human rights and encouraging economic, social, educational and cultural progress throughout the world. Figure 9.1 shows the enormous range of UN activities, and there is only space to look at a few.

(a) *The Human Rights Commission*

This works under the supervision of ECOSOC and tries to ensure that all governments treat their people in a civilized way. *A 30-point Universal Declaration of Human Rights* was adopted by the General Assembly in 1948. This means that every person, no matter what country he or she lives in, should have certain basic rights, *the most important of which are the rights to:*

- a standard of living high enough to keep him (or her) and his family in good health;
- be free from slavery, racial discrimination, arrest and imprisonment without trial, and torture;
- have a fair trial in public and to be presumed innocent until proved guilty;
- move about freely in his/her country and be able to leave the country;
- get married, have children, work, own property and vote in elections;
- have opinions and express them freely.

Later the Commission, concerned about the plight of children in many countries, produced a *Declaration of the Rights of the Child (1959). Foremost among the rights every child should be able to expect are:*

- adequate food and medical care;
- free education;
- adequate opportunity for relaxation and play (to guard against excessive child labour);
- protection from racial, religious, and any other type of discrimination.

All member governments are expected to produce a report every three years on the state of human rights in their country. However, the problem for the UN is that many states do not produce the reports and they ignore the terms of the declarations. When this happens, all the UN can do is publicize countries where the most flagrant violations of human rights take place, and hope that pressure of world opinion will influence the governments concerned. For example, the UN campaigned against *apartheid* in South Africa (see Section 22.8) and against General Pinochet's brutal treatment of political prisoners in Chile (see Section 8.4(c)).

(b) *The International Labour Organization (ILO)*

This operates from its headquarters in Geneva. *It works on the principles that:*

- every person is entitled to a job;
- there should be equal opportunities for everybody to get jobs, irrespective of race, sex or religion;
- there should be minimum standards of decent working conditions;
- workers should have the right to organize themselves into unions and other associations in order to negotiate for better conditions and pay (this is known as collective bargaining);
- there should be full social security provision for all workers (such as unemployment, health and maternity benefits).

The ILO does excellent work providing help for countries trying to improve working conditions, and it was awarded the Nobel Prize for Peace in 1969. It sends experts out to demonstrate new equipment and techniques, sets up training centres in developing countries, and runs the International Centre for Advanced Technology and Vocational Training in Turin (Italy), which provides vital high-level training for people from all over the Third World. Again though, the ILO, like the Human Rights Commission, is always faced with the problem of what to do when governments ignore the rules. For example, many governments, including those of communist countries, and of Latin American countries such as Chile, Argentina and Mexico would not allow workers to organize trades unions.

(c) *The World Health Organization (WHO)*

This is one of the UN's most successful agencies. It aims to bring the world to a point where all its peoples are not just free of disease, but are 'at a high level of health'. One of its first jobs was to tackle a cholera epidemic in Egypt in 1947 which threatened to spread through Africa and the Middle East. Quick action by a UN team soon brought the epidemic under control and it was eliminated in a few weeks. The WHO now keeps a permanent cholera vaccine bank in case of further outbreaks, and it wages a continual battle against other diseases such as malaria, tuberculosis and leprosy. The Organization provides money to train doctors, nurses and other health workers for developing countries, keeps governments informed about new drugs, and provides free contraceptive pills for women in Third World countries. One of its most striking achievements was to eliminate smallpox in the 1980s. At the same time it seemed well on the way towards eliminating malaria, but during the 1970s a new strain of malaria appeared which had developed a resistance to anti-malaria drugs. Research into new anti-malaria drugs became a WHO priority and there was much work to be done if it was to achieve its goal of 'good health for all by the year 2000'.

(d) *The Food and Agriculture Organization (FAO)*

This aims to raise living standards by encouraging improvements in agricultural production. It was reponsible for introducing new varieties of maize and rice which have a higher yield and are less susceptible to disease. FAO experts show people in poor countries how to increase food production by the use of fertilizers, new techniques and new machinery, and cash is provided to fund new projects. Its main problem is having to deal with emergencies caused by drought, floods, civil war and other disasters, when food supplies need to be rushed into a country as quickly as possible. The Organization has done an excellent job, and there is no doubt that many more people would have died from starvation and malnutrition without its work. However, there is still a long way to go: for example, FAO statistics revealed that in 1984 35 million people died from hunger, and 24 African states were heavily dependent on the UN for emergency food supplies because of drought. Critics of the FAO claim that it spends too much of its resources on food instead of helping to set up better agricultural systems in poor countries.

(e) The United Nations Educational, Scientific and Cultural Organization (UNESCO)

Operating from its headquarters in Paris, UNESCO does its best to encourage the spread of literacy; it also fosters international co-operation between scientists, scholars and artists in all fields, working on the theory that *the best way to avoid war is by educating people's minds in the pursuit of peace*. Much of its time and resources are spent setting up schools and teacher-training colleges in developing countries. Sometimes it becomes involved in one-off cultural and scientific projects. For example it organized an International Hydrological Decade (1965–75) during which it helped to finance research into the problem of world water resources. After the 1968 floods in Florence, UNESCO played an important part in repairing and restoring damaged art treasures and historic buildings. During the 1980s UNESCO came under criticism from western powers which claimed that it was becoming too politically motivated (see next Section).

(f) The United Nations Children's Emergency Fund (UNICEF)

This was founded originally in 1946 to help children left homeless by the Second World War. It dealt with this problem so efficiently that it was decided to make it a permanent agency and the word 'emergency' was dropped from its title (1953). Its new function was *to help improve the health and living standards of children all over the world, especially in poorer countries*. It works closely with the WHO, setting up health centres, training health workers, and running health education and sanitation schemes. In spite of their efforts it was still a horrifying fact that in 1983, 15 million children died under the age of five, a figure equivalent to the combined under-five population of Britain, France, Italy, Spain and West Germany. In that year UNICEF launched its 'child health revolution' campaign which was designed to reduce the child death rate by simple methods such as encouraging breast feeding (which is more hygienic than bottle-feeding) and immunizing babies against common diseases such as measles, diphtheria, polio and tetanus.

(g) The United Nations Relief and Works Agency (UNRWA)

This was set up in 1950 to deal with the problem of Arab refugees from Palestine who were forced to leave their homes when Palestine was divided up to form the new state of Israel (see Section 11.2). UNRWA did a remarkable job providing basic food, clothing, shelter and medical supplies. Later, as it became clear that the refugee camps were going to be permanent, it began to build schools, hospitals, houses and training centres to enable refugees to get jobs and make the camps self-supporting.

(h) Financial and economic agencies

1 The International Monetary Fund (IMF)

This is designed to foster co-operation between nations to encourage the growth of trade and the full development of nations' economic potential. It allows short-term loans to countries in financial difficulties, provided that their economic policies meet with the IMF's approval and that they are prepared to change policies if the IMF thinks it necessary. By the mid-1970s many Third World nations were heavily in debt (see Section 23.2), and in 1977 the IMF set up an emergency fund. However, there was a great deal of resentment among the poorer nations when the IMF Board of Governors (dominated by the rich western countries, especially the USA, which provide most of the cash) began to attach conditions to the loans. Jamaica and Tanzania, for example, were required to change their socialist policies before loans were allowed. This was seen by many as unacceptable interference in the internal affairs of member states.

2   The International Bank for Reconstruction and Development (the World Bank)

This provides loans for specific development projects, such as building dams to generate electricity, introducing new agricultural techniques and family planning campaigns. Again though, the USA, which provides the largest share of the cash for the bank, controls its decisions. When Poland and Czechoslovakia applied for loans, they were both refused because they were communist states. Both of them resigned from the Bank and from the IMF in disgust, Poland in 1950 and Czechoslovakia in 1954.

3   The General Agreement on Tariffs and Trade (GATT)

This was first signed in 1947 when member states of the UN agreed to reduce some of their tariffs (taxes on imports) in order to encourage international trade. Members continue to meet under the supervision of ECOSOC to try to keep tariffs as low as possible throughout the world.

4   The United Nations Conference on Trade and Development (UNCTAD)

UNCTAD first met in 1964 and soon became a permanent body. Its role is to encourage the development of industry in the Third World and to pressurise rich countries into buying Third World products.

9.5   Verdict on the United Nations Organization

In October 1995 the UN celebrated its fiftieth anniversary. But it was still nowhere near achieving its basic aims: the world was still full of economic and social problems and acts of aggression and wars continued. *The UN's failures were caused to some extent by weaknesses in its system.*

(a)   *The lack of a permanent UN army*

This means that it is difficult to prevail upon powerful states to accept its decisions if they choose to put self-interest first. If persuasion and pressure of world opinion fail, the UN has to rely on member nations to provide troops to enable it to enforce decisions. For example the USSR was able to ignore UN demands for the withdrawal of Russian troops from Hungary (1956) and Afghanistan (1980). UN involvement in Somalia (1992–5) and Bosnia (1992–5) showed the impossibility of the UN being able to stop a war when the warring parties were not ready to stop fighting.

(b) *When should the UN become involved?*

There is a problem about exactly when the UN should become involved during the course of a dispute. Sometimes it hangs back too long, so that the problem becomes more difficult to solve; sometimes it hesitates so long that it scarcely becomes involved at all, as happened with the war in Vietnam (see Section 8.3) and the war in Angola (see Section 22.6). This left the UN open to accusations of indecision and lack of firmness. It caused some states to put more faith in their own regional organizations such as NATO for keeping the peace, and many agreements were worked out without involving the UN; for example, the end of the Vietnam War, the Camp David peace between Israel and Egypt in 1979 (see Section 11.6), and the settlement of the Rhodesia/Zimbabwe problem in the same year (see Section 21.4(c)). At this time, critics were claiming that the UN was becoming irrelevant and was no more than an arena for propaganda speeches. Part of the problem was that the Security Council was hampered by the veto which its permanent members could use. Although the 'Uniting for Peace' resolution could offset this to some extent, the veto could still cause long delays before decisive action was taken. Anthony Parsons, for many years the UK Permanent Representative at the UN, gives two recent examples of where early action might have prevented fighting:

> If a potential aggressor knew that his forces would be met by a UN armed force, equipped and mandated to fight, this would be a powerful disincentive ... Such a force, if deployed on the Kuwait side of the Iraqi/Kuwait frontier in 1990, or on the Croatian side of the Serbia/Croatia border in 1991, might well have prevented hostilities from breaking out.

(c) *The increased membership of the UN during the 1970s*

This brought new problems. By 1970 members from the Third World (Africa and Asia) were in a clear majority. As these nations began to work more and more together, it meant that only they could be certain of having their resolutions passed, and it became increasingly difficult for both western and communist blocs to get their resolutions through the General Assembly. The western nations could no longer have things all their own way and they began to criticize the Third World bloc for being too 'political'; by this, they meant acting in a way the west disapproved of. For example, in 1974 UNESCO passed resolutions condemning 'colonialism' and 'imperialism'. In 1979 when the western bloc introduced a General Assembly motion condemning terrorism, it was defeated by the Arab states and their supporters.

Friction reached crisis point in 1983 at the UNESCO General Congress. Many western nations, including the USA, accused UNESCO of being inefficient and wasteful and of having unacceptable political aims. What brought matters to a head was a proposal by some communist states for the internal licensing of foreign journalists. According to the USA, this would lead to a situation in which member states could exercise an effective censorship of each other's media organizations. Consequently the Americans announced that they would withdraw from UNESCO on 1 January 1985, since it had became 'hostile to the basic institutions of a free society, especially a free market and a free press'. Britain and Singapore withdrew in 1986 for similar reasons.

(d) *There is a wastage of effort and resources among the agencies*

These sometimes seem to duplicate each other's work. Critics claim that the WHO and the FAO overlap too much. The FAO was criticized in 1984 for spending too much on administration and not enough on improving agricultural systems. GATT and UNC-

TAD even seem to be working against each other: GATT tries to eliminate tariffs and anything else which restricts trade, whereas UNCTAD tries to get preferential treatment for the products of Third World countries.

(e) *The UN has always been short of funds*

The vast scope of its work means that it needs incredibly large sums of money to finance its operations. It is entirely dependent on contributions from member states. Each state pays a regular annual contribution based on its general wealth and ability to pay. In addition, members pay a proportion of the cost of each peace-keeping operation, and they are also expected to contribute towards the expenses of the special agencies. *Many member states have refused to pay from time to time*, either because of financial difficulties of their own, or as a mark of disapproval of UN policies. 1986 was a bad year financially: no fewer than ninety-eight of its members owed money – chief among them being the USA, which withheld more than $100m. until the UN reformed its budgeting system and curbed its extravagance. The Americans wanted the countries which gave most to have more say in how the money was spent, but most smaller members rejected this as undemocratic. As one of Sri Lanka's delegates put it: 'in our political processes at home, the wealthy do not have more votes than the poor. We should like this to be the practice in the UN as well'.

In 1987 changes were introduced giving the main financial contributors more control over spending, and the financial situation soon improved. However, expenses soared alarmingly in the early 1990s as the UN became involved in a series of new crises, in the Middle East (Gulf War), Yugoslavia and Somalia. In August 1993 the Secretary-General, Dr Boutros-Ghali, revealed that many states were well in arrears with their payments. He warned that unless there was an immediate injection of cash from the world's rich states, all the UN's peace-keeping operations would be in jeopardy. Yet the Americans and Europeans feel that they already paid too much – the USA (with about 30 per cent), the European Community (about 35 per cent) and Japan (11 per cent) pay three-quarters of the expenses, and there is a feeling that there are many other wealthy states which could afford to contribute much more than they do.

In spite of all these criticisms, it would be wrong to write the UN off as a failure, and there can be no doubt that the world would be a far worse place without it.

• It provides a world assembly where representatives of over 180 nations can come together and talk to each other. Even the smallest nation has a chance to make itself heard in a world forum.
• Although it has not prevented wars, it has been successful in bringing some wars to an end more quickly, and has prevented further conflict. A great deal of human suffering and bloodshed have been prevented by the actions of the UN peace-keeping forces and refugee agencies.
• The UN has done valuable work investigating and publicizing human rights violations under repressive regimes like the military governments of Chile and Zaire. In this way it has slowly been able to influence governments by bringing international pressure to bear on them.
• Perhaps its most important achievement has been to stimulate international co-operation on economic, social and technical matters. Millions of people, especially in poorer countries, are better off, thanks to the work of the UN agencies. It continues to involve itself in current problems: UNESCO, the ILO and the WHO are running a joint project to help drug addicts and there has been a series of conferences on Aids.

9.6 What about the future of the UN?

Many people thought that with the end of the Cold War, most of the world's problems would disappear. In fact, this did not happen; during the 1990s there seemed to be more conflicts than ever before, and the world seemed to be less and less stable. Obviously there was still a vitally important role for the UN to play as international peace-keeper, and many people were anxious for the UN to reform and strengthen itself. Sir Edward Heath, British Prime Minister from 1970 until 1974, suggested the following reforms which he thought would make the UN more effective (in *Guardian Weekend*, 10 July 1993):

• The UN should develop a better system of intelligence to enable it to prevent conflicts breaking out, instead of waiting until things get out of control. The intelligence services of the great powers could give the UN regular information about possible trouble-spots.

• Peace-keeping operations need to be speeded up – sometimes as long as four months can elapse between the Security Council deciding to send troops, and the troops arriving on the spot. Governments could help by having specially trained units for peace-keeping services ready for rapid deployment.

• All troops need to be trained to the same high standard; in Somalia, for example, Nigerian and Pakistani troops had not been properly prepared to deal with sensitive situations. 'The creation of a core military organization, overseeing and co-ordinating the training of UN peace-keeping forces, would go a long way towards standardizing the levels of training and experience of the troops which the UN can call upon.'

• The UN could make more use of other, regional organizations such as NATO and the Arab League. For example, it could authorize the Arab League to police the frontier between Iraq and Kuwait, thus reducing the pressure on UN troops and the expense.

• The UN should monitor and restrict the flow of arms to potential trouble-spots. For example, American guns were used against American troops in Somalia; French troops in the Gulf War were fired on by French Mirage jets owned by Iraq. If the various factions had not been supplied with arms in the first place, the world would be a more stable place. 'The UN should limit the international sale of arms, through the adoption of a unified Code of Conduct for the major arms exporters'.

• The permanent membership of the Security Council should be widened. Since the end of the Cold War the UN has been dominated by the USA, Britain and France, and this has upset many Third World nations. The inclusion of other permanent members would restore harmony and ensure wider co-operation and goodwill.

As the UN moved into 1997, a new Secretary-General, Kofi Annan of Ghana, took over the helm (December 1996). His predecessor, Boutros Boutros-Ghali, had lost the support of the USA which blamed him for the UN involvement and failure in Somalia, and this cost him his chance of a second term. Better things were expected of Annan who had built up an excellent reputation over the previous few years as head of UN peacekeeping operations.

Questions

1 *The United Nations at work: Suez and Hungary 1956* In 1956 the UN tried to deal with problems in two countries which had been invaded by foreign troops: Egypt, which was invaded by Israeli, British and French troops, and Hungary, which was invaded by Russian troops. The UN was successful in getting the foreign troops to withdraw from Egypt, but if failed to get Russian troops out of Hungary.
   Study Sources A to F and then answer the questions which follow.

Map 9.1 Hungary in 1956

(New York Times)

Source B

UN General Assembly resolution, 8 November 1956

The General Assembly notes with deep concern the violent repression by the Soviet (Russian) troops of the efforts of the Hungarian people to achieve freedom and independence ... It calls upon the USSR to withdraw its forces from Hungary without any further delay. It requests that an investigation be made of the situation caused in Hungary by foreign intervention and a report given to the Security Council in the shortest possible time.

Source C

Statement by Mr Cabot Lodge, the US representative, in the General Assembly, 8 November 1956

The world has witnessed the sickening spectacle of the Hungarian people fighting for their liberty with small arms, pitchforks and bare hands against massive formations of Russian tanks.

Source D

Statement by Mr Kustnetsov, the USSR representative, in the General Assembly, 8 November 1956

This debate is an interference in the internal affairs of a sovereign state and is therefore illegal ... moreover it is a manoeuvre to direct world attention away from the imperialist aggression by France, Britain and Israel against Egypt, in which they were encouraged by the USA.

Statement by the new Hungarian government to the UN Security Council, 12 November 1956

Soviet troops are here for the purpose of restoring law and order, and at the request of the Hungarian government. We cannot permit UN observers to enter Hungary, since the situation is purely an internal affair of the Hungarian state.

Source F

Speech by Sir Anthony Eden, British Prime Minister, in the House of Commons, 9 November 1956

I welcome the setting up of a UN Emergency Force and the intentions of the Israeli government to co-operate with the UN force. As soon as it is in a position to carry out its task effectively, we are willing to hand over to it full reponsibility, and it will be possible for many of our squadrons to fly home.

Sources: Sources B to F are taken from *Keesings Contemporary Archives for 1956*

(a) How do Sources B and C and Sources D and E give different views about the Soviet (Russian) actions in Hungary?　　　　1.4c–6c, 3.4　5 marks

(b) Why do you think there is so much disagreement between Sources B and C and Sources D and E about the Russian action in Hungary?　1.7c–8c　5 marks

(c) 'The invasion of Egypt was just as much an act of aggression as the invasion of Hungary'. Do you think that Sources C, D and E support this opinion? Explain your answer fully.　　　　1.4c–8c, 2.5–6　6 marks

(d) 'Source C is a statement by the American representative at the UN; therefore it is more reliable than Source D'. Explain whether you agree or disagree with this opinion.　　　　1.6c–8c, 3.7　4 marks

(e) How useful is each one of these Sources A to F in explaining why the UN succeeded in Egypt but failed in Hungary?　　　　3.5–9　10 marks

Total: 30 marks

2　*The United Nations Organization – Success or Failure?*　Study Sources A and B and then answer the questions which follow.

Source A

The UN is an improved League of Nations. However, things did not turn out as planned. The power of veto still paralysed the UN. The five countries – USA, USSR, Britain, China and France – have used the veto to stop any resolutions with which any one of them did not agree.

Source: R.J. and J.Owen, *The United Nations and its Agencies* (Pergamon Press, 1985)

British cartoon (Figure 9.2) of 1945 comparing the United Nations with the League of Nations. The man in the cartoon is President Truman of the USA

Source: *Evening Standard.*

(a) Does the cartoon (Source B) suggest that the United Nations Organisation was likely to be more successful than the League of Nations? Explain your answer fully.   1.4c–6c, 3.3   4 marks

(b) Source A says that the UN 'is an improved League of Nations'. How did the founders of the UN try to make sure that it was different from the League? (see Sections 9.1–2).   1.4a–6a, 4c–5c   5 marks

(c) Source A tells us that 'things did not turn out as planned'. Does this mean that the cartoonist in Source B was wrong in his idea of what the UN would be like? Use information from this chapter to help you with your answer.
                                               2.4–9   5 marks

(d) Source A mentions one weakness of the UN. What other weaknesses in the way the UN is run have made its work more difficult? Give some examples. Which do you think is the most serious of its weaknesses?
                                      1.4b–7b, 4c–5c   5 marks

(e) During the 1960s, the membership of the UN increased. What consequences did this have for the UN and its work?   1.4b–5b   6 marks

Total: 25 marks

10 The two Europes, East and West, since 1945

Summary of events

At the end of the Second World War in 1945 Europe was in turmoil. Many areas, especially in Germany, Italy, Poland and the western parts of the USSR, had been devastated, and even the victorious powers, Britain and the USSR, were in serious financial difficulties because of the expense of the war. There was a huge job of reconstruction to be done, and many people thought that the best way to go about this was by a joint effort. Some even thought in terms of a united Europe, rather like the United States of America, in which the European states would come together under a federal system of government. However, Europe soon split into two over the American Marshall Plan to promote recovery in Europe (see Section 7.2(e)). The nations of Western Europe gladly made use of American aid, but the Russians refused to allow the countries of Eastern Europe to accept it, for fear that their own control over the area would be undermined. From 1947 onwards the two parts of Europe developed separately, kept apart by Joseph Stalin's 'iron curtain'.

The states of Western Europe recovered surprisingly quickly from the effects of the war, thanks to a combination of American aid, an increase in the world demand for European products, rapid technological advances and careful planning by governments. *Some moves took place towards unity, including the setting up of NATO and the Council of Europe (both in 1949), and the European Economic Community (EEC) in 1957.* In Britain enthusiasm for this type of unity developed more slowly than in other countries for fear that it would threaten British sovereignty. Britain decided not to join the EEC when it was first set up in 1957; when she changed her mind in 1961, the French vetoed her entry, and it was 1972 before it was finally agreed that she could become a member.

Meanwhile the communist states of Eastern Europe had to be content to be satellites of the USSR. *They too moved towards a sort of economic and political unity with the introduction of the Molotov Plan (1947), the formation of the Council for Mutual Economic Assistance (COMECON) in 1949 and the Warsaw Pact (1955).* Until his death in 1953 Stalin tried to make all these states as much like Russia as possible, but after 1953 they began to show more independence. Yugoslavia under Tito had already developed a more decentralized system in which the communes were an important element. Poland and Romania successfully introduced variations, but the Hungarians (1956) and the Czechs (1968) went too far and found themselves invaded by Russian troops and brought to heel. During the 1970s the states of Eastern Europe enjoyed a period of comparative prosperity, but in the 1980s they felt the effects of world depression. Dissatisfaction with the communist system began to grow; in a short period from mid-1988 until the end of 1991, communism collapsed in the USSR and all the states of Eastern Europe except Albania, where it survived for a bit longer. Germany, which had been divided into two separate states, one communist and one non-communist since soon after the war (see Section 7.2(h)), was reunified (October 1990), becoming once again the most powerful state in Europe. With the end of communism, Yugoslavia sadly disintegrated into a long civil war (1991–5).

10.1 The states of Western Europe

(a) *France*

Under the Fourth Republic (1946–58) France was politically weak, and though her industry was modernized and flourishing, agriculture seemed to be stagnating. Governments were weak because the new constitution gave the President very little power. There were five major parties and this meant that governments were coalitions which were constantly changing: in the twelve years of the Fourth Republic there were twenty-five different governments, which were mostly too weak to rule effectively. There were a number of disasters:

- French defeat in Indo-China (1954) (see Section 8.3(a));
- failure in Suez (1956) (see Section 11.3); and
- rebellion in Algeria

which brought the government down. General de Gaulle came out of retirement to lead the country (1958); he introduced a new constitution giving the President more power (which became the basis of the Fifth Republic), and gave Algeria independence. De Gaulle retired in 1969 after a wave of strikes and demonstrations protesting against, among other things, the authoritarian and undemocratic nature of the regime.

The Fifth Republic continued to provide stable government under the next two Presidents, both right-wingers – Pompidou (1969–74) and Giscard d'Estaing (1974–81). Francois Mitterrand, the socialist leader, had a long period as President, from 1981 until 1995, when Jacques Chirac of the right-wing RPR (*Rassemblement pour la République*) was elected President for the next seven years. The dominant issues in France in the 1990s were the continuing recession and unemployment, doubts about France's role in the European Community (there was only a very small majority in September 1992 in favour of the Maastricht Treaty (see Section 10. 5(h)), and uneasiness about the reunified Germany. When Chirac's new Prime Minister, Alain Juppé, began cutbacks to get the French economy into shape for the introduction of the new European currency, there were widespread protest demonstrations and strikes (December 1995).

(b) *The German Federal Republic (West Germany)*

Set up in 1949, the Federal Republic enjoyed a remarkable recovery – an 'economic miracle' – under the conservative government of Chancellor Adenauer (1949–63). (Illus. 10.1). It was achieved partly thanks to the Marshall Plan, by a high rate of investment in new plant and equipment, and by the ploughing back of profits into industry rather than distributing them as higher dividends or higher wages (which happened in Britain). Industrial recovery was so complete that by 1960 West Germany was producing 50 per cent more steel than the united Germany in 1938. All classes shared in the prosperity; pensions and children's allowances were geared to the cost of living, and ten million new dwellings were provided.

Illus. 10.1 *Chancellor Adenauer (left) with President de Gaulle, 1963*

The new constitution encouraged the trend towards a two-party system, which meant there was a better chance of strong government. The two major parties were the:

- Christian Democrats (CDU) – Adenauer's conservative party;
- Social Democrats (SPD) – a moderate socialist party;

and there was a smaller liberal party – the FDP.

Adenauer's CDU successors, Erhard (1963–6) and Kiesinger (1966–9) continued the good work, though there were some setbacks and a rise in unemployment. This caused support to swing to the SDP who stayed in power, with FDP support, for 13 years, first under Willi Brandt (1969–74) and then under Helmut Schmidt (1974–82). After the prosperous 1970s, West Germany began to suffer increasingly from the world recession. By 1982 unemployment had shot up to 2 million; when Schmidt proposed increasing spending to stimulate the economy, the more cautious FDP withdrew support and Schmidt was forced to resign (October 1982). A new right-wing coalition of the CDU and the Bavarian Christian Social Union (CSU) was formed, with FDP support, and the CDU leader, Helmut Kohl, became Chancellor. Recovery soon came – statistics for 1985 showed a healthy economic growth rate of 2.5 per cent and a big export boom. By 1988 the boom was over and unemployment rose to 2.3 million. Kohl managed to hold on to power though, and had the distinction of becoming the first Chancellor of the reunified Germany in October 1990 (see Section 10.7(e)).

Reunification brought enormous problems for Germany – the cost of modernizing the east and bringing its economy up to western standards placed a big strain on the country. Billions of Deutschemarks were poured in and the process of privatizing state industries was begun. Kohl had promised to revive the east without raising taxes and to make sure that 'nobody after unification will be worse off'. Neither of these pledges proved to be possible and the process of revival took much longer than anybody had anticipated. By 1996, with welfare costs running high and unemployment at almost 10 per cent, there were doubts as to whether even Germany could meet the requirements (a budget deficit of less than 3 per cent of GDP) of a single European currency.

(c) *Italy*

The new Republic of Italy began with a period of prosperity and stable government under de Gasperi (1946–53), but then many of the old problems of the pre-Mussolini era reappeared: with at least seven major parties ranging from communists on the left (PCI) to the Neo-Fascists (MSI) on the far right, there was a series of weak coalition governments, which failed to solve the problems of inflation and unemployment. One of the more successful politicians was the socialist *Bettino Craxi*, who was Prime Minister from 1983 to 1987; during this time both inflation and unemployment were reduced. But as Italy moved into the 1990s the basic problems were still the same.

- *there was a north–south divide* – the north with its modern, competitive industry, was relatively prosperous, while the south (Calabria, Sicily and Sardinia) was backward, with a much lower standard of living and higher unemployment.
- *The Mafia was still a powerful force*, now heavily involved in drug dealing, and it seemed to be getting stronger in the north. Two judges who had been trying Mafia cases were assassinated (1992) and it seemed as though crime was out of control.
- *Politics seemed to be riddled with corruption*, with many leading politicians under suspicion. Even highly respected leaders such as Craxi were shown to have been involved in corrupt dealings (1993), while another, Giulio Andreotti, seven times Prime Minister, was arrested and charged with working for the Mafia (1995).
- *There was a huge government debt and a weak currency.* In September 1992 Italy, along with Britain, was forced to withdraw from the Exchange Rate Mechanism and devalue the lira. Her continuing economic problems were a serious threat to Italy's hopes of joining her currency and economy to those of Germany and France later in the 1990s.

10.2 The growth of unity in Western Europe

(a) *Reasons for wanting more unity*

In every country in Western Europe there were people who wanted more unity. They had different ideas about exactly what sort of unity would be best: some simply wanted the nations to co-operate more closely; others (known as federalists) wanted to go the whole hog and have a federal system of government like the one in the USA. *The reasoning behind this thinking was:*

1   the best way for Europe to recover from the ravages of war was for all the states to work together and help each other by pooling their resources;
2   the individual states were too small and their economies too weak for them to be economically and militarily viable separately in a world now dominated by the super-powers, the USA and the USSR;
3   the more the countries of Western Europe worked together, the less chance there would be of war breaking out between them again. It was the best way for a speedy reconciliation between France and Germany;
4   joint action would enable Western Europe more effectively to resist the spread of communism from the USSR;
5   the Germans were especially keen on the idea because they thought it would help them to gain acceptance as a responsible nation more quickly than after the First World War. Then, Germany had been made to wait eight years before being allowed to join the League of Nations.

Winston Churchill was one of the strongest advocates of a united Europe. In March 1943 he spoke of the need for a Council of Europe, and in a speech in Zurich in 1946 he suggested that France and West Germany should take the lead in setting up 'a kind of United States of Europe'.

(b) First steps in co-operation

The first steps in economic, military and political co-operation were soon taken, though the federalists were bitterly disappointed that a United States of Europe had not materialized by 1950.

1 The Organization for European Economic Co-operation (OEEC)

This was set up officially in 1948, and was the first initiative towards economic unity. It began as a response to the American offer of Marshall Aid, when Ernest Bevin, the British Foreign Secretary, took the lead in organizing sixteen European nations (see Section 7.2(e)) to draw up a plan for the best use of American aid. This was known as *the European Recovery Programme (ERP)*. The committee of sixteen nations became the permanent OEEC. Its first function, successfully achieved over the next four years, was to apportion American aid among its members, after which it went on, again with great success, to encourage trade among its members by reducing restrictions. It was helped by the *United Nations General Agreement on Tariffs and Trade (GATT)* whose function was to reduce tariffs, and by the *European Payments Union (EPU)*; this encouraged trade by improving the system of payments between member states, so that each state could use its own currency. The OEEC was so successful that trade between its members doubled during the first six years. When the USA and Canada joined in 1961 it became the *Organization for Economic Co-operation and Development (OECD)*. Later Australia and Japan joined.

2 The North Atlantic Treaty Organization (NATO)

NATO was created in 1949 (see Section 7.2(i) for a list of founder-members) as a mutual defence in case of an attack on one of the member states. In most people's minds, the USSR was the most likely source of any attack. NATO was not just a European organization–it also included the USA and Canada. The Korean War (1950–3) caused the USA to press successfully for the integration of NATO forces under a centralized command; a *Supreme Headquarters Allied Powers Europe (SHAPE)* was established near Paris, and an American general, Dwight D. Eisenhower, was made Supreme Commander of all NATO forces. Until the end of 1955 NATO seemed to be developing impressively: the forces available for the defence of Western Europe had been increased fourfold, and it was claimed by some that NATO had deterred the USSR from attacking West Germany. However, problems soon arose: the French were not happy about the dominant American role; in 1966 President de Gaulle withdrew France from NATO, so that French forces and French nuclear policy would not be controlled by a foreigner. Compared with the communist Warsaw Pact, NATO was weak: with 60 divisions of troops in 1980, it fell far short of its target of 96 divisions, whereas the communist bloc could boast 102 divisions and three times as many tanks as NATO.

3 The Council of Europe

Set up in 1949, this was the first attempt at some sort of political unity. Its founder-members were Britain, Belgium, Netherlands, Luxembourg, Denmark, France, Eire, Italy, Norway and Sweden. By 1971 all the states of Western Europe (except Spain and Portugal) had joined, and so had Turkey, Malta and Cyprus, making eighteen members in all. Based at Strasbourg, it consisted of the Foreign Ministers of the member states, and an Assembly of representatives chosen by the parliaments of the states. It had no powers, however, since several states, including Britain, refused to join any organization which threatened their own sovereignty. It could debate pressing issues and make recommendations, and it achieved useful work sponsoring human rights agreements; but it was a grave disappointment to the federalists.

10.3 The early days of the European Community

Known in its early years as the *European Economic Community (EEC)* or the *Common Market*, the Community was officially set up under the terms of the *Treaty of Rome (1957)*, signed by the six founder-members – France, West Germany, Italy, Netherlands, Belgium and Luxembourg.

(a) *Stages in the evolution of the Community*

1 Benelux

In 1944 the governments of Belgium, Netherlands and Luxembourg, meeting in exile in London because their countries were occupied by the Germans, began to plan for when the war was over. They agreed to set up the *Benelux Customs Union*, in which there would be no tariffs or other customs barriers, so that trade could flow freely. The driving-force behind it was Paul-Henri Spaak, the Belgian socialist leader who was Prime Minister of Belgium from 1947 to 1949; it was put into operation in 1947.

2 The Treaty of Brussels (1948)

By this treaty Britain and France joined the three Benelux countries in pledging 'military, economic, social and cultural collaboration'. While the military collaboration eventually resulted in NATO, the next step in economic co-operation was the ECSC.

3 The European Coal and Steel Community (ECSC)

The ECSC was set up in 1951. It was the brainchild of Robert Schuman, who was France's Foreign Minister from 1948 to 1953 (Illus. 10.2). Like Spaak, he was strongly in favour of international co-operation, and he hoped that involving West Germany would improve relations between France and Germany and at the same time make European industry more efficient. *Six countries joined:*

- France
- West Germany
- Italy
- Belgium
- Netherlands and
- Luxembourg.

All duties and restrictions on trade in coal, iron and steel between the six were removed, and a High Authority was created to run the community and to organize a

Illus. 10.2 Robert Schuman

joint programme of expansion. However, *the British refused to join* because they believed it would mean handing over control of their industries to an outside authority. The ECSC was such an outstanding success, even without Britain (steel production rose by almost 50 per cent during the first five years) that *the six decided to extend it to include production of all goods*.

4 The EEC

Again it was Spaak, now Foreign Minister of Belgium, who was one of the main driving forces. The agreements setting up the full EEC were signed in Rome in 1957 and they came into operation on 1 January 1958. The six countries would gradually remove all customs duties and quotas so that there would be free competition and a common market. Tariffs would be kept against non-members, but even these were reduced. The treaty also mentioned improving living and working conditions, expanding industry, encouraging the development of the world's backward areas, safeguarding peace and liberty, and working for a closer union of European peoples. Clearly something much wider than just a common market was in the minds of some of the people involved; for example, Jean Monnet (Illus. 10.3), a French economist who was Chairman of the ECSC High Authority, set up *an action committee to work for a United States of Europe*. Like the ECSC, the EEC was soon off to a flying start; within five years it was the world's biggest exporter and biggest buyer of raw materials and was second only to the USA in steel production. *Once again, however, Britain had decided not to join.*

(b) *The machinery of the European Community*

- *The European Commission* was the body which ran the day-to-day work of the Community. Based in Brussels, it was staffed by civil servants and expert economists who took the important policy decisions. It had strong powers so that it would be able to stand up against possible criticism and opposition from the governments of the six members, though in theory its decisions had to be approved by the Council of Ministers.
- *The Council of Ministers* consisted of government representatives from each of the

Illus. 10.3 Jean Monnet

member states. Their job was to exchange information about their governments' economic policies and to try and co-ordinate them and keep them running on similar lines. There was a certain amount of friction between the Council and the Commission: the Commission often seemed reluctant to listen to the advice of the Council, and it kept pouring out masses of new rules and regulations.

● *The European Parliament*, which met at Strasbourg, consisted of 198 representatives chosen by the parliaments of the member states. They could discuss issues and make recommendations, but had no control over the Commission or the Council. In 1979 a new system of choosing the representatives was introduced. Instead of being nominated by parliaments, they were to be directly elected by the people of the Community (see Section 10.5(b)).

● *The European Court of Justice* was set up to deal with any problems which might arise out of the interpretation and operation of the Treaty of Rome. It soon became regarded as the body to which people could appeal if their government was thought to be infringing the rules of the Community.

● Also associated with the EEC was *EURATOM*, an organization in which the six nations pooled their efforts towards the development of atomic energy.

In 1967 the EEC, the ECSC and EURATOM formally merged and, dropping the word 'economic', became simply the *European Community (EC)*.

10.4 Why did the British refuse to join and change their minds later?

It was ironic that, although Churchill had been one of the strongest supporters of the idea of a unified Europe, when he became Prime Minister again in 1951, he seemed to have lost any enthusiasm he might have had for Britain's membership of it. Attlee's Labour governments (1945–51) held back from joining the ECSC, and the Conservative governments of Churchill (1951–5) and Eden (1955–7) viewed with great suspicion the activities of people like Spaak and Monnet. Britain decided not to sign the 1957 Treaty of Rome.

(a) *Reasons for Britain's refusal to join*

- Her main objection was that if Britain joined the Community *she would no longer be in complete control of her economy.* The European Commission in Brussels would be able to make vital decisions affecting Britain's internal economic affairs. Although the governments of the other six states were prepared to make this sacrifice in the interests of greater overall efficiency, the British government was not.
- *There was a problem about the British Commonwealth:* Britain had a great deal of trade with Commonwealth countries, and there were fears that her relationship with the Commonwealth would be ruined if Britain was no longer able to give preference to Commonwealth goods such as New Zealand lamb and butter. The Commonwealth, with its population of around 800 million, seemed a more promising market than the EEC, which had only 165 million.
- Britain had what was described as 'a special relationship' with the USA, which was not shared by the other states of Europe. If the British became involved too deeply in economic integration with Europe, *it might damage their special relationship with the Americans.*
- Most British politicians were deeply suspicious that *economic unity would lead to the political unity of Europe,* and that was even less appealing to the British, who were determined that British sovereignty (that is, supreme control of their own internal affairs) must be preserved.

On the other hand Britain and some of the other European states outside the EEC were worried about being excluded from selling their goods to EEC members because of the high duties on imports from outside the Community. Consequently in 1959 Britain took the lead in organizing a rival group, the *European Free Trade Association (EFTA)* (see Map 10.1). Britain, Denmark, Norway, Sweden, Switzerland, Austria and Portugal agreed gradually to abolish tariffs between themselves. Britain was prepared to join an organization like EFTA because there was no question of common economic policies and no Commission to interfere with the internal affairs of states.

(b) *Why did the British change their minds?*

Within less than four years from the signing of the Treaty of Rome, the British had changed their minds, and in 1961 Conservative Prime Minister Harold Macmillan announced that *Britain wished to join the EEC.*

- *By 1961 it was obvious that the EEC was an outstanding success* – without Britain. Since 1953 French production had risen by 75 per cent while German production had increased by almost 90 per cent.
- *Britain's economy was much less successful* – over the same period British production had risen by only about 30 per cent. The British economy seemed to be stagnating in comparison with those of the Six, and in 1960 there was a balance of payments deficit of some £270 million. This means that imports had cost Britain £270 million more than was earned from British exports. When this happens, a country has to spend some of its gold and foreign currency reserves to make up the difference.
- *Although EFTA had succeeded in increasing trade among its members, it was nothing like as successful as the EEC.*
- *The Commonwealth, in spite of its huge population, had nothing like the same*

Map 10.1 Economic unions in Europe, 1960

Source: J. Robert Wegs, *Europe Since 1945* (St Martin's Press, 1979)

purchasing power as the EEC. Macmillan now thought that there need not be a clash of interest between Britain's membership of the EEC and trade with the Commonwealth. There were signs that the EEC was prepared to make special arrangements to allow Commonwealth countries and some other former European colonies to became associate members. Britain's EFTA partners might be able to join as well.

● Another argument in favour of joining was that *once Britain was in, competition from other EEC members would stimulate British industry to greater effort and efficiency.* Macmillan also made the point that Britain could not afford to be left out if the EEC developed into a political union. He seems to have had some idea that Britain could take over the leadership and build the Community up into a strong defensive unit against the USSR, and in partnership with the USA. This may well have been Macmillan's main motive, though he could hardly give it much publicity.

Macmillan gave the job of negotiating Britain's entry into the EEC to Edward Heath, who had been an enthusiastic supporter of European unity since he first entered parliament in 1950. Talks opened in October 1961, and although there were some difficulties, it came as a shock when the French President, de Gaulle, broke off negotiations and vetoed Britain's entry (1963) (Illus. 10.4).

Illus. 10.4 President de Gaulle sees 'formidable obstacles' preventing Britain from joining the Common Market

(c) *Why did the French oppose British entry into the EEC?*

● *De Gaulle claimed that Britain had too many economic problems and would only weaken the EEC.* He also objected to any concessions being made for the Commonwealth, arguing that this would be a drain on Europe's resources. Yet the EEC had just agreed to provide economic and technical aid to France's former colonies in Africa.

● *The British believed that de Gaulle's real motive was his desire to continue dominating the Community.* If Britain came in, she would be a serious rival.

● *De Gaulle was not happy about Britain's 'American connection'*, believing that because of their close ties with the USA, Britain's membership would allow the USA to dominate European affairs. It would produce, he said, 'a colossal Atlantic grouping under American dependence and control'. He was probably annoyed that Britain, without consulting France, had just agreed to receive Polaris missiles from America. He was certainly furious with President Kennedy for not having made the same offer to France. He was determined to prove that France was a great power and had no need of American help. It was this friction between France and the USA which eventually led de Gaulle to withdraw France from NATO (1966).

● *Finally there was the problem of French agriculture:* the EEC protected its farmers with high tariffs (import duties) so that prices were much higher than in Britain. Britain's agriculture was highly efficient and subsidized to keep prices relatively low. If this continued after Britain's entry, French farmers with their smaller and less efficient farms, would be exposed to competition from Britain and perhaps from the Commonwealth, (see question 2 at the end of this chapter).

Meanwhile the EEC success story continued, without Britain. The Community's exports grew steadily, and the value of its exports was consistently higher than its imports. Britain on the other hand usually had a balance of trade deficit, and Harold Wilson's Labour government (1964–70) was forced to begin its term in office by borrowing heavily from the IMF to replenish rapidly dwindling gold reserves. This convinced Wilson that the only solution was for Britain to join the EEC, although until then the Labour party had opposed it. However, de Gaulle again vetoed the British application (1967).

(d) Britain enters the Community (1973)

Eventually, on 1 January 1973, Britain, along with Eire and Denmark, was able to enter the EEC and the Six became the Nine. *Britain's entry was made possible by two main factors:*

●   President de Gaulle had resigned in 1969 and his successor, Georges Pompidou, was more friendly towards Britain.
●   Britain's Conservative Prime Minister, Edward Heath, was in a good position to press Britain's claims strongly. He negotiated with great skill and tenacity, and it was fitting that, having been a committed European for so long, he was the Prime Minister who finally took Britain into Europe.

Public opinion in Britain was divided over whether it was a wise move to join the Community, and many people were worried about exactly how far Britain's sovereignty would be affected. The Labour party was split on the issue, and after coming to power in 1974 Wilson held a referendum. The people were asked to vote (1975) about whether or not they wanted Britain to stay in the EC; 67 per cent of those who voted expressed approval of Britain's membership. But this was not as decisive as it might seem, since only two-thirds of the electorate voted. This meant that only half the voters in Britain were convinced that membership was a good thing; the other half either did not want to stay in the Community or did not care enough either way to bother to vote.

10.5 The European Community since Britain's entry

The main developments and problems after Britain's entry in 1973. were:

(a) The Lomé Convention (1975)

From the begining the EC was criticized for being too inward-looking and self-centred, and for apparently showing no interest in using any of its wealth to help the world's poorer nations. This agreement, worked out in Lomé, the capital of Togo in West Africa, did something to offset criticism, though many critics argued that it was too little. It allowed goods produced in over forty countries in Africa and the Caribbean, mostly former European colonies, to be brought into the EEC free of duties; it also promised economic aid. Other poor Third World countries were added to the list later.

(b) *Direct elections to the European parliament (1979)*

Although it had been in existence for over twenty years by this time, the EC was still remote from ordinary people. One reason for introducing elections was to try to arouse more interest and bring ordinary people into closer contact with the affairs of the Community.

The first elections took place in June 1979, when 410 Euro-MPs were chosen. Britain, France, Italy and West Germany were allowed 81 each, Netherlands 25, Belgium 24, Denmark 16, Eire 15 and Luxembourg 6. For Britain the elections came immediately after Margaret Thatcher's victory in the UK general election (May 1979), so it was no surprise when the Conservatives swept the board in the Euro-elections as well; they won 60 out of the 81 seats, while Labour could manage only 16. The turnout was disappointing – less than a third of the British electorate were interested enough to bother going along to vote. In some other countries though, notably Italy and Belgium, the turnout was over 80 per cent. Overall in the new European parliament, the right-wing and centre parties had a comfortable majority over the left.

Elections were to be held every five years; by the time the next elections came along in 1984, Greece had joined the Community. Like Belgium, Greece was allowed 24 seats, bringing the total to 434. This time in Britain the Conservatives lost ground to Labour, winning 45 seats to Labour's 32. Overall in the European parliament the parties of the centre and right still kept a small majority. The turnout of voters in Britain was again disappointing at only 32 per cent, whereas in Belgium it was 92 per cent and in Italy and Luxembourg it was over 80 per cent. However, in these three countries it was more or less compulsory to vote. The highest turnout in a country where voting was voluntary was 57 per cent in West Germany.

(c) *The introduction of the Exchange Rate Mechanism (ERM) (1979)*

This was introduced to link the currencies of the member states in order to limit the extent to which individual currencies (Italian lira, French, Luxembourg and Belgian franc and German mark) could change in value against the currencies of other members. A state's currency could change in value depending on how well its domestic economy was performing: a strong economy usually meant a strong currency. It was hoped that linking the currencies would help to control inflation and lead eventually to a single currency for the whole of the EC. Britain decided not to take the £ sterling into the ERM; she made the mistake of joining in October 1990 when the exchange rate was relatively high.

(d) *Community membership grows*

In 1981 Greece joined, followed by Portugal and Spain in 1986, bringing the total membership to twelve and the Community population to over 320 million. (These countries had not been allowed to join earlier because their political systems were undemocratic – see Chapter 14 summary.) Their arrival caused new problems: they were among the poorer countries of Europe and their presence increased the influence within the Community of the less industrialized nations. From now on there would be increasing pressure from these countries for more action to help the less developed states and so improve the economic balance between rich and poor nations. Membership increased again in 1995 when Austria, Finland and Sweden, three relatively wealthy states, joined the Community (see Map 10.2).

Map 10.2 The Growth of the European Community

Legend:
- Original 'six' of the Common Market, 1957
- EFTA, 1959
- Countries joining the Common Market, 1973
- Countries joining the Community later (with dates)

Map labels: GREENLAND (Common Market, 1973–85), ICELAND, NORWAY, FINLAND (1995), SWEDEN (1995), IRELAND (1973), GREAT BRITAIN (1973), DENMARK (1973), NETHERLANDS, BELGIUM, LUXEMBOURG, WEST GERMANY, EAST GERMANY RE-UNITED 1990, FRANCE, SWITZERLAND, AUSTRIA (1995), PORTUGAL (1986), SPAIN (1986), ITALY, GREECE (1981)

(e) *Britain and the EC budget*

During the early years of their membership, many British people were disappointed that Britain did not seem to be gaining any obvious benefit from the EC. The Irish Republic (Eire), which joined at the same time, immediately enjoyed a surge of prosperity as her exports, mainly agricultural produce, found ready new markets in the Community. Britain on the other hand seemed to be stagnating in the 1970s, and although her exports to the Community did increase, her imports from the Community increased far more. Britain was not producing enough goods for export at the right prices. Foreign competitors could produce more cheaply and therefore captured a larger share of the market. The statistics of Gross Domestic Product (GDP) for 1977 are very revealing; GDP is the cash value of a country's total output from all types of

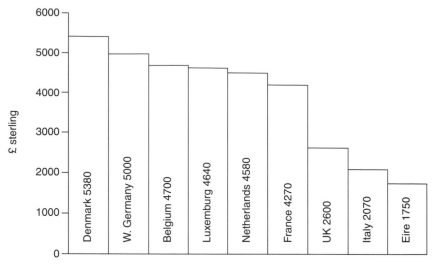

GDP per head of the population in 1977, shown in £ sterling

Figure 10.1

Source: based on statistics in Jack B. Watson, *Success in World History Since 1945* (John Murray, 1989), p. 150

production. To find out how efficient a country is, economists divide the GDP by the population of the country, which shows how much is being produced per head of the population. Fig 10.1 shows that Britain was economically one of the least efficient nations in the EC, while Denmark and West Germany were top of the league.

A major crisis erupted in 1980 when Britain discovered that her budget contribution for that year was to be £1209 million, whereas West Germany's was £699 million and France only had to pay £13 million. Britain protested that her contribution was ridiculously high, given the general state of her economy. The difference was so great because of the way the budget contribution was worked out: this took into consideration the amount of import duties received by each government from goods coming into that country from outside the EC; a proportion of those duties received had to be handed over as part of the annual budget contribution. Unfortunately for the British, they imported far more goods from the outside world than any of the other members, and this was why their payment was so high. After some ruthless bargaining by Britain's Prime Minister, Margaret Thatcher, a compromise was reached: Britain's contribution was reduced to a total of £1346 million over the next three years.

(f) *The 1986 changes*

Encouraging developments occurred in 1986 when all twelve members, working closely together, negotiated some important changes which, it was hoped, would improve the EC. They included:

● a move to a completely free and common market (no restrictions of any kind on internal trade and movement of goods) by 1992;
● more EC control over health, safety, protection of the environment and protection for consumers;
● more encouragement for scientific research and technology;
● more help for backward regions;

- the introduction of majority voting on many issues in the Council of Ministers; this would prevent a measure from being vetoed just by one state which felt that its national interests might be threatened by that measure;
- more powers for the European parliament so that measures could be passed with less delay. This meant that the domestic parliaments of the member states were gradually losing some control over their own internal affairs.

Those people who favoured a federal United States of Europe were pleased by the last two points, but in some of the member states, especially Britain and Denmark, they stirred up the old controversy about national sovereignty. Mrs Thatcher upset some of the other European leaders when she spoke out against any movement towards a politically united Europe: 'a centralized federal government in Europe would be a nightmare; co-operation with the other European countries must not be at the expense of individuality, the national customs and traditions which made Europe great in the past'.

(g) *The Common Agricultural Policy (CAP)*

One of the most controversial aspects of the EC was its Common Agricultural Policy (CAP). In order to help farmers and encourage them to stay in business, so that the Community could continue to produce much of its own food, it was decided to pay them subsidies (extra cash to top up their profits). This would ensure them worthwhile profits and at the same time would keep prices at reasonable levels for the consumers. This was such a good deal for the farmers that they were encouraged to produce far more than could be sold. Yet the policy was continued until by 1980 about three-quarters of the entire EC budget was being paid out each year in subsidies to farmers. Britain, the Netherlands and West Germany pressed for a limit to be placed on subsidies, but the French government was reluctant to agree to this because it did not want to upset French farmers, who were doing very well out of the subsidies.

In 1984 maximum production quotas were introduced for the first time, but this did not solve the problem. By 1987 the stockpiling of produce had reached ludicrous proportions. There was a vast wine 'lake' and a butter 'mountain' of one and a half million tonnes – enough to supply the entire EC for a year. There was enough milk powder to last five years, and storage fees alone were costing a million pounds a day. Efforts to get rid of the surplus included selling it off cheaply to the USSR, India, Pakistan and Bangladesh, distributing butter free of charge to the poor within the Community, and using it to make animal feed. Some of the oldest butter was burnt in boilers.

All this helped to cause a massive budget crisis in 1987: the Community was £3 billion in the red and had debts of £10 billion. In a determined effort to solve the problem, the EC introduced a harsh programme of production curbs and a price freeze to put a general squeeze on Europe's farmers. This naturally caused an outcry among farmers, but by the end of 1988 it was having some success and the surpluses were shrinking steadily. Member states were now begining to concentrate on preparing for 1992 when the introduction of the single European market would bring the removal of all internal trading barriers, and, many people hoped, much greater monetary integration.

(h) *Greater integration: the Maastricht Treaty (1991)*

A summit meeting of all the heads of the member states was held in Maastricht (Netherlands) in December 1991, and an agreement was drawn up for 'a new stage in the process of creating an even closer union among the peoples of Europe'. *Some of the points agreed were:*

- more powers for the European parliament;

- greater economic and monetary union – this should culminate in the adoption of a common currency (the ecu) shared by all the member states, around the end of the century;
- a common foreign and security policy;
- a detailed timetable was drawn up of the stages by which all this would be achieved.

Britain objected very strongly to the ideas of a federal Europe and monetary union, and to a whole section of the Treaty known as the *Social Chapter*, which was a list of regulations designed to protect people at work. There were rules about:

- safe and healthy working conditions;
- equality at work between men and women;
- consulting workers and keeping them informed about what was going on;
- protection of workers made redundant.

Britain argued that these would increase production costs and therefore cause unemployment. The other members seemed to think that proper treatment of workers was more important. In the end, because of British objections, *the Social Chapter was removed from the Treaty* and it was left to individual governments to decide whether or not to carry them out. The rest of the Maastricht Treaty without the Social Chapter had to be ratified (approved) by the national parliaments of the twelve members, and this had been achieved by October 1993.

The French, Dutch and Belgian governments supported the Treaty strongly because they thought it was the best way to make sure that the power of the reunified Germany was contained and controlled within the Community. The ordinary people of the Community were not as enthusiastic about the Treaty as their leaders. The people of Denmark at first voted against it, and it took determined campaigning by the government before it was approved by a narrow majority in a second referendum (May 1993). The Swiss people voted not to join the Community (December 1992), and so did the Norwegians, and even in the French referendum the majority in favour of Maastricht was tiny. In Britain, where the government would not allow a referendum, the Conservatives were split over Europe and the treaty was approved only by the narrowest of majorities in parliament.

By the mid-1990s, after almost forty years of existence, the European Community (known since 1992 as the European Union) had been a great success economically and had fostered good relations between the member states, but there were vital issues to be faced:

- How much closer could economic and political co-operation become? The goal of European monetary union (EMU) and a single currency (the euro) by 1 January 1999 caused problems for all the member states. The requirement for joining the single currency was that a country's budget deficit must be less than 3 per cent of its GDP. In September 1992 a currency crisis caused both Britain and Italy to withdraw from the ERM. By the end of 1996, governments were reducing spending and cutting welfare benefits in the struggle to keep their deficits low, and this provoked criticism and ill-feeling.
- What should the Union's attitude to the states of Eastern Europe be? There was some talk that they might be able to join the Union soon after the year 2000. In April 1994 Poland and Hungary formally applied for membership.

10.6 Communist unity in Eastern Europe

The communist countries of Eastern Europe were joined in a kind of unity under the leadership of the USSR. The main difference between the unity in Eastern Europe and that in the west was that the countries of Eastern Europe were forced into it by the USSR (see Section 7.2(d,e,g)) whereas the members of the EC joined voluntarily. By the end of 1948 there were nine states in the communist bloc: the USSR itself, Albania, Bulgaria, Czechoslovakia, East Germany, Hungary, Poland, Romania and Yugoslavia.

(a) *Organization of the communist bloc*

Stalin set about making all the states into carbon copies of the USSR with the same political, economic and educational systems, and the same Five Year Plans. All had to carry out the bulk of their trade with Russia and their foreign policies and armed forces were controlled from Moscow.

1 The Molotov Plan

This was the first Russian-sponsored step towards an economically united Eastern bloc. The idea of the Russian Foreign Minister, Molotov, it was a response to the American offer of Marshall Aid (see Section 7.2(e)). Since the Russians refused to allow any of their satellites to accept American aid, Molotov felt they had to be offered an alternative. The Plan was basically a set of trade agreements between the USSR and its satellites negotiated during the summer of 1947; it was designed to boost the trade of eastern Europe.

2 The Communist Information Bureau (Cominform)

This was set up by the USSR at the same time as the Molotov Plan. All the communist states had to become members and its aim was political: to make sure that all the governments followed the same line as the government of the USSR in Moscow. To be communist was not enough; it had to be Russian-style communism.

3 The Council for Mutual Economic Assistance (COMECON)

COMECON was set up by the USSR in 1949. The aim was to help plan the economies of the individual states. All industry was nationalized (taken over by the state), and agriculture was collectivized (organized into a system of large, state-owned farms). Later, Nikita Khrushchev (Russian leader 1956–64) tried to use COMECON to organize the communist bloc into a single integrated economy; he wanted East Germany and Czechoslovakia to develop as the main industrial areas, and Hungary and Romania to concentrate on agriculture. However, this provoked hostile reactions in many of the states and Khrushchev had to change his plans to allow more variations within the economies of the different countries. The Eastern bloc enjoyed some success economically, with steadily increasing production. However, their average GDP (see Section 10.5(e) for an explanation of GDP) and general efficiency were below those of the EC. Albania had the doubtful distinction of being the most backward country in Europe. In the 1980s the economies of the Eastern bloc states experienced difficulties, with shortages, inflation and a fall in the standard of living.

Even so the communist bloc had a good record in social services; in some Eastern European countries, health services were as good as, if not better than, those in some

EC countries. For example, in Britain in 1980 there was, on average, one doctor for every 618 people; in the USSR there was one doctor for every 258 people, and in Czechoslovakia the figure was 293. Only Albania, Yugoslavia and Romania had a worse ratio than Britain's.

4 The Warsaw Pact (1955)

This was signed by the USSR and all the satellite states except Yugoslavia. They promised to defend each other against any attack from outside; the armies of the member states came under overall Russian control from Moscow. Ironically, the only time Warsaw Pact troops took part in joint action was against one of their own members – Czechoslovakia – when the USSR disapproved of Czech internal policies (1968).

(b) *Tensions in the Eastern bloc*

Although there were some disagreements in the EC about problems like the Common Agricultural Policy and the sovereignty of the individual states, these were not as serious as the tensions which occurred between the USSR and some of her satellite states. In the early years of the Cominform, Moscow felt that it had to clamp down on any leader or movement which seemed to threaten the solidarity of the communist bloc. Sometimes the Russians did not hesitate to use force.

1 Yugoslavia was the first state to stand up against Moscow

Here, the communist leader, Tito, owed much of his popularity to his successful resistance against the Nazi forces occupying Yugoslavia during the Second World War. In 1945 he was legally elected as leader of the new Yugoslav republic and so he did not owe his position to the Russians. By 1948 he had fallen out with Stalin. *He was determined to follow his own brand of communism, not Stalin's.* He was against over-centralization (everything being controlled and organized from the centre by the government). He objected to Stalin's plan for the Yugoslav economy and to the constant Russian attempts to interfere in Yugoslavia's affairs. He wanted to be free to trade with the west as well as with the USSR. Stalin therefore expelled Yugoslavia from the Cominform and cut off economic aid, expecting that the country would soon be ruined economically and that Tito would be forced to resign. However, Stalin had miscalculated: Tito was much too popular to be toppled by outside pressures, and so Stalin decided it would be too risky to invade Yugoslavia. Tito was able to remain in power and *he continued to operate communism in his own way*. This included full contact and trade with the west and acceptance of aid from the International Monetary Fund (IMF).

The Yugoslavs began to reverse the process of centralization: industries were denationalized, and instead of being state-owned, they became public property, managed by workers' representatives through councils and assemblies. The same applied in agriculture: the communes were the most important unit in the state. These were groups of families each containing between 5000 and 100 000 people. The elected Commune Assembly organized matters to do with the economy, education, health, culture and welfare. The system was a remarkable example of ordinary people playing a part in making the decisions which closely affected their own lives, both at work and in the community. It achieved much because workers had a personal stake in the success of their firm and their commune. Many Marxists thought this was the way a genuine communist state should be run, rather than the over-centralization of the USSR.

There were some weaknesses, however. One was workers' unwillingness to sack col-

Illus. 10.5 Marshal Tito (left) and Mr Khrushchev (centre) bury their differences, 1955

leagues; another was a tendency to pay themselves too much. These led to over-employment and high costs and prices. Nevertheless, with its capitalist elements (like wage differentials and a free market) this was an alternative Marxist system which many developing African states, especially Tanzania, found attractive.

Khrushchev decided that his wisest course of action was to improve relations with Tito. In 1955 he visited Belgrade, the Yugoslav capital, and apologized for Stalin's actions (Illus. 10.5). The breach was fully healed the following year when Khrushchev gave his formal approval to Tito's successful brand of communism.

2   Stalin acts against other leaders

As the rift with Yugoslavia widened, Stalin arranged for the arrest of any communist leaders in the other states who attempted to follow independent policies. He was able to do this because most of these other leaders lacked Tito's popularity and owed their positions to Russian support in the first place.

- *In Hungary* the Foreign Minister Laszlo Rajk and Interior Minister Janos Kadar, both anti-Stalin communists, were arrested. Rajk was hanged, Kadar was put in gaol and tortured, and about 200 000 people were expelled from the party (1949).
- *In Bulgaria* the Prime Minister, Traichko Koslov, was arrested and executed (1949).
- *In Czechoslovakia* the Communist party general secretary, Rudolph Slansky, and ten other cabinet ministers were executed (1952).

- *In Poland* Communist party leader and Vice-President Wladislaw Gomulka was imprisoned because he had spoken out in support of Tito.
- *In Albania* communist premier Koze Xoxe was removed and executed because he sympathised with Tito.

3 Khrushchev: 'different roads to socialism'

After Stalin's death in 1953 there were signs that the satellite states might be given more freedom. In 1956 Khrushchev made a famous speech at the Twentieth Communist Party Congress in which he criticized many of Stalin's policies and seemed prepared to concede that there were 'different roads to socialism' (see Section 16.5(a)). He soon healed the rift with Yugoslavia and in April 1956 he abolished Cominform, which had been annoying Russia's partners ever since it was set up in 1947. However, it was not long before events in Poland and Hungary showed that there were sharp limits to Khrushchev's new toleration.

(c) *Crisis in Poland*

There was a general strike and a massive anti-government and anti-soviet demonstration in Posen (Poznan) in June 1956. The banners demanded 'bread and freedom' and the workers were protesting against poor living standards, wage reductions and high taxes. Although they were dispersed by Polish troops, tension remained high throughout the summer. In October, Russian tanks surrounded Warsaw, the Polish capital, though as yet they took no action. *In the end the Russians decided to compromise:* Gomulka, who had earlier been imprisoned on Stalin's orders, was allowed to be reappointed as First Secretary of the Communist Party. It was accepted that Polish communism could develop in its own way provided that the Poles went along with Russia in foreign affairs.The Russians obviously felt that Gomulka could be trusted not to stray too far. Relations between the two states continued reasonably smoothly, although the Polish version of communism would definitely not have been acceptable to Stalin. For example they introduced the collectivization of agriculture only very slowly, and probably only about 10 per cent of farmland was ever collectivized. Poland also traded with countries outside the communist bloc. Gomulka remained in power until he resigned in 1970.

(d) *The Hungarian Revolution (1956)*

The situation in Hungary ended very differently from the one in Poland. After Stalin's death (1953), the pro-Stalin leader, Rakosi, was replaced by a more moderate communist, Imry Nagy. However, Rakosi continued to interfere and overthrew Nagy (1955). From then on resentment steadily built up against the government until it exploded in a full-scale rising (October 1956). *Its causes were many:*

- hatred of Rakosi's brutal and repressive regime under which at least 2000 people had been executed and 200 000 others had been put in prisons and concentration camps;
- living standards of ordinary people were getting worse while hated Communist party leaders were living comfortable lives;
- intense anti-Russian feeling;
- Khrushchev's speech at the Twentieth Congress and Gomulka's return to power in Poland encouraged the Hungarians to resist their government.

Rakosi was overthrown, Nagy became Prime Minister, and the popular Roman

Catholic Cardinal Mindszenty, who had been in prison for six years for anti-communist views, was released. Until this point the Russians seemed prepared to compromise as they had done in Poland. *But then Nagy went too far: he announced plans for a government including members of other political parties and talked of withdrawing Hungary from the Warsaw Pact.* This was too much for the Russians: if Nagy had his way, Hungary might become a non-communist state and would cease to be an ally of the USSR. It would encourage people in other Eastern bloc states to do the same. Russian tanks moved in, surrounded Budapest, the Hungarian capital, and opened fire (3 November). The Hungarians resisted bravely and fighting lasted two weeks before the Russians brought the country under control. About 20 000 people were killed and another 20 000 imprisoned. Nagy was executed although he had been promised a safe-conduct, and perhaps as many as 200 000 fled the country and went to the west. The Russians installed Janos Kadar as the new Hungarian leader. Although he had once been imprisoned on Stalin's orders, he was now a reliable ally of Moscow, and he stayed in power until 1988. (See also question 1 at the end of Chapter 9.)

(e) *The crisis in Czechoslovakia (1968)*

After their military intervention in Hungary, the Russians did not interfere so directly anywhere until 1968 when they felt that the Czechs were straying too far from the accepted communist line. In the meantime they had allowed considerable variations within the states, and sometimes did not press unpopular plans. For example, Yugoslavia, Albania and Romania continued with their own version of communism. In 1962 when Khrushchev suggested that each satellite state should concentrate on producing one particular product, the Hungarians, Romanians and Poles, who wanted to develop an all-round economy, protested strongly and the idea was quietly dropped. Provided no policies were introduced which threatened communist party domination, the Russians seemed reluctant to interfere. In the mid-1960s it was the turn of the Czechs to see how far they could go before the Russians called a halt. Their government was run by the pro-Moscow communist, Antonin Novotny, and *opposition gradually escalated, for several reasons.*

- The Czechs were industrially and culturally the most advanced of the Eastern bloc peoples, and *they objected to the over-centralized Russian control of their economy*. It seemed senseless, for example, that they should have to put up with poor quality iron-ore from Siberia when they could have been using high-grade ore from Sweden.
- Between 1918 and 1938, When Czechoslovakia was an independent state, the Czechs had enjoyed great freedom, but now *they resented all the restrictions on personal liberty:* newspapers, books and magazines were heavily censored (that is, they could only print what the government allowed), and there was no freedom of speech; anybody who criticized the government could be arrested.
- When people tried to hold protest marches, they were dispersed by the police, whose methods were violent and brutal.

Matters came to a head in January 1968 when Novotny was forced to resign and Alexander Dubček became First Secretary of the communist party. *Dubček and his supporters had a completely new programme:*

- the communist party would no longer dictate policy;
- industry would be de-centralized; this meant that factories would be run by works councils instead of being controlled from the capital by party officials;
- instead of farms being collectivized (owned and run by the state), they would become independent co-operatives;

- there would be wider powers for trades unions;
- there would be more trade with the west and freedom to travel abroad; the frontier with West Germany, which had been closed since 1948, was immediately thrown open;
- there was to be freedom of speech and freedom for the press; criticism of the government was encouraged. Dubček believed that although the country would remain communist, the government should earn the right to be in power by responding to people's wishes. He called it 'socialism with a human face';
- he was very careful to assure the Russians that Czechoslovakia would stay in the Warsaw Pact and remain a reliable ally.

During the spring and summer of 1968 this programme was carried into operation. The Russians became more and more worried by it, and in August a massive invasion of Czechoslovakia took place by Russian, Polish, Bulgarian, Hungarian and East German troops. The Czech government decided not to resist so as to avoid the sort of bloodshed which had occurred in Hungary in 1956. The Czech people tried to resist passively for a time by going on strike and holding peaceful anti-Russian demonstrations, but in the end the government was forced to abandon its new programme. The following year *Dubček* was replaced by Gustav Husak, a communist leader who did as Moscow told him and who therefore managed to stay in power until 1987.

The Russians intervened because Dubček was going to allow freedom of speech and freedom for the press, which was bound to lead to similar demands throughout the soviet bloc. The Russians dared not risk this happening in case it led to mass protests and uprisings in the USSR itself. There was pressure for Russian action from some other communist leaders, especially those in East Germany, who were afraid that protests might spread over the frontier into Germany from Czechoslovakia. Soon afterwards, Brezhnev, the Russian leader who had ordered the invasion, announced what he called the *Brezhnev Doctrine*: this said that intervention in the internal affairs of any communist country was justified if socialism (by which he meant communism) was threatened.

(f) *The communist bloc moves towards collapse*

Although the states of Eastern Europe seemed on the surface to be firmly under Russian control, resentment against Moscow's hard line simmered on, especially in Poland and Czechoslovakia

- *In Poland, Gomulka was forced to resign after riots (1970)* and his replacement, Gierek, also resigned (1980) following industrial unrest, food shortages and strikes in the port of Gdansk and other cities. The new government was forced to allow the formation of an independent trade union movement known as Solidarity. The Russians moved troops up to the Polish frontier, but no invasion took place this time, perhaps because they had just sent troops into Afghanistan and were unwilling to risk another military involvement so soon.
- *The Helsinki Agreements (1975) caused problems in the communist bloc.* These were signed at a conference in Helsinki (the capital of Finland) by every nation in Europe (except Albania and Andorra) and also by Canada, the USA and Cyprus. They promised to work for increased co-operation in economic affairs and peacekeeping, and to protect human rights. Before very long people in the USSR and other communist states were accusing their governments of failing to allow basic human rights.
- *In Czechoslovakia a human rights group calling itself Charter 77 was formed (in 1977)*, and during the 1980s it became more outspoken in its criticisms of the Husak government. In December 1986 a spokesman for the group said: 'while Husak lives,

political stagnation will reign supreme; once he has gone, the party will explode'.

• *By this time all the communist states were suffering serious economic problems*, much worse than those in the EC. Although not many people in the west realized it at the time, communism and the communist bloc were fast approaching collapse and disintegration.

10.7 Why and how did communism collapse in Eastern Europe?

In the short period August 1988 to December 1991 communism in Eastern Europe was swept away. Poland was the first to reject communism, closely followed by Hungary and East Germany and the rest, until by the end of 1991 even Russia had ceased to be communist after seventy-four years. *Why did this dramatic collapse take place?*

(a) *Economic failure*

Communism as it existed in Eastern Europe was a failure economically. It simply did not produce the standard of living which should have been possible, given the vast resources available. The economic systems were inefficient, over-centralized and subject to too many restrictions; all the states, for example, were expected to do most of their trading within the communist bloc. By the mid-1980s there were problems everywhere. According to Misha Glenny, a BBC correspondent in Eastern Europe, 'the communist party leaderships refused to admit that the working class lived in more squalid conditions, breathing in more damaged air and drinking more toxic water, than western working classes ... the communist record on health, education, housing, and a range of other social services has been atrocious'. Increasing contact with the West in the 1980s showed people how backward the East was in comparison with the West, and suggested that their living standards were falling even further. It showed also that it must be their own leaders and the communist system which were the cause of all their problems.

(b) *Mikhail Gorbachev*

Mikhail Gorbachev, who became leader of the USSR in March 1985, started the protest which led to the collapse. He recognized the failings of the system and he admitted that it was 'an absurd situation' that the USSR, the world's biggest producer of steel, fuel and energy, should be suffering shortages because of waste and inefficiency (see Section 16.7 for the situation in the USSR). He hoped to save communism by revitalizing and modernizing it. He introduced new policies of *glasnost* (openness) and *perestroika* (economic and social reform). Criticism of the system was encouraged in the drive for improvement, provided nobody criticized the communist party. He also helped to engineer the overthrow of the old-fashioned, hard-line communist leaders in Czechoslovakia, and he was probably involved in plotting the overthrow of the East German, Romanian and Bulgarian leaders. His hope was that more progressive leaders would increase the chances of saving communism in Russia's satellite states.

Unfortunately for Gorbachev, once the process of reform began, it proved impossible to control it. The most dangerous time for any repressive regime is when it begins to try to reform itself by making concessions. These are never enough to satisfy the critics, and in Russia, criticism inevitably turned against the communist party itself and demanded more. Public opinion even turned against Gorbachev because many people felt he was not moving fast enough.

The same happened in the satellite states: the communist leaderships found it difficult to adapt to the new situation of having a leader in Moscow who was more progressive than they were. *The critics became more daring as they realized that Gorbachev would not send soviet troops in to fire on them.* With no help to be expected from Moscow, when it came to the crisis, none of the communist governments was prepared to use sufficient force against the demonstrators (except in Romania). When they came, the rebellions were too widespread, and it would have needed a huge commitment of tanks and troops to hold down the whole of Eastern Europe simultaneously. Having only just succeeded in withdrawing from Afghanistan, Gorbachev had no desire for an even greater involvement. In the end it was a triumph of 'people power': demonstrators deliberately defied the threat of violence in such huge numbers that troops would have had to shoot a large proportion of the population in the big cities to keep control.

(c) *Poland leads the way*

General Jaruzelski, who became leader in 1981, was prepared to take a tough line: when Solidarity (the new trades union movement) demanded a referendum to demonstrate the strength of its support, Jaruzelski declared martial law (that is, the army took over control), banned Solidarity and arrested thousands of activists. The army obeyed his orders because everybody was still afraid of Russian military intervention. By July 1983 the government was in firm control: Jaruzelski felt it safe to lift martial law and Solidarity members were gradually released. But the underlying problem was still there: all attempts to improve the economy failed. In 1988 when Jaruzelski tried to economize by cutting government subsidies, protest strikes broke out because the changes sent food prices up. This time Jaruzelski decided not to risk using force; he knew that there would be no backing from Moscow, and realized that he needed opposition support to deal with the economic crisis. Talks opened in February 1989 between the communist government, and Solidarity and other opposition groups (the Roman Catholic Church had been loud in its criticisms). *By April 1989 sensational changes in the constitution had been agreed:*

- Solidarity was allowed to become a political party;
- there were to be two houses of parliament, a lower house and a senate;
- in the lower house, 65 per cent of the seats had to be communist;
- the senate was to be freely elected – no guaranteed communist seats;
- the two houses voting together would elect a President, who would then choose a Prime Minister.

In the elections of June 1989 Solidarity won 92 out of the 100 seats in the senate and 160 out of the 161 seats which they could fight in the lower house. A compromise deal was worked out when it came to forming a government: Jaruzelski was narrowly elected President, thanks to all the guaranteed communist seats in the lower house, but he chose a Solidarity supporter, *Tadeusz Mazowiecki*, as Prime Minister, the first non-communist leader in the Eastern bloc (August). Mazowiecki chose a mixed government of communists and Solidarity supporters.

The new constitution proved to be only transitional. After the collapse of communism in the other East European states, further changes in Poland removed the guaranteed communist seats, and in the elections of December 1990, *Lech Walesa*, the Solidarity leader, was elected President. The peaceful revolution in Poland was complete.

(d) *The peaceful revolution spreads to Hungary*

Once the Poles had thrown off communism without interference from the USSR, it was only a matter of time before the rest of Eastern Europe tried to follow suit. In Hungary even Kadar himself admitted in 1985 that living standards had fallen over the previous five years, and he blamed poor management, poor organization and outdated machinery and equipment in the state sector of industry. He announced new measures of decentralization – company councils and elected works managers. By 1987 there was conflict in the communist party between those who wanted more reform and those who wanted a return to strict central control. This reached a climax in May 1988 when, amid dramatic scenes at the party conference, Kadar and eight of his supporters were voted off the Politburo, leaving the progressives in control.

But as in the USSR, progress was not drastic enough for many people. Two large opposition parties became increasingly active. These were the liberal Alliance of Free Democrats, and the Democratic Forum, which stood for the interests of farmers and peasants. The Hungarian communist leadership, following the example of the Poles, decided to go peacefully. Free elections were held in March 1990, and in spite of a change of name to the Hungarian Socialist Party, the communists suffered a crushing defeat.The election was won by the Democratic Forum, whose leader, *Jozsef Antall*, became Prime Minister.

(e) *Germany reunited*

In East Germany, *Erich Honecker*, who had been communist leader since 1971, refused all reform and intended to stand firm, along with Czechoslovakia, Romania and the rest, to keep communism in place. However, *Honecker was soon overtaken by events:*

- Gorbachev, desperate to get financial help for the USSR from West Germany, paid a visit to Chancellor Kohl in Bonn, and promised to help bring an end to the divided Europe, in return for German economic aid. In effect he was secretly promising freedom for East Germany (June 1989).
- During August and September 1989 thousands of East Germans began to escape to the west via Poland, Czechoslovakia and Hungary, when Hungary opened its frontier with Austria.
- The Protestant Church in East Germany became the focus of an opposition party called New Forum which campaigned to bring an end to the repressive and atheistic communist regime. In October 1989 there was a wave of demonstrations all over East Germany demanding freedom and an end to communism.

Honecker wanted to order the army to open fire on the demonstrators, but other leading communists were not prepared to cause widespread bloodshed. *They dropped Honecker, and his successor, Egon Krenz, made concessions.* The Berlin Wall was opened (9 November 1989) and free elections promised.

When the great powers began to drop hints that they would not stand in the way of a reunited Germany, the West German political parties moved into the East. Chancellor Kohl staged an election tour, and the East German version of his party (CDU) won an overwhelming victory (March 1990). The East German CDU leader, *Lothar de Maiziere*, became Prime Minister. He was hoping for gradual moves towards reunification, but again the pressure of 'people power' carried all before it. Nearly everybody in East Germany seemed to want immediate union.

The USSR and the USA agreed that reunification could take place; Gorbachev promised that all Russian troops would be withdrawn from East Germany by 1994. France and Britain, who were less happy about German reunification, felt bound to go along with the flow. *Germany was formally reunited at midnight on 3 October 1990* In elections for the whole of Germany (December 1990) the conservative CDU/CSU alliance, together with their liberal FDP supporters, won a comfortable majority over the socialist SPD. The communists (renamed the Party of Democratic Socialism – PDS) won only 17 of the 662 seats in the Bundestag (lower house of parliament). Helmut Kohl became the first Chancellor of all Germany since the Second World War.

(f) *Czechoslovakia*

Czechoslovakia had one of the most successful economies of Eastern Europe. She traded extensively with the west and her industry and commerce remained buoyant throughout the 1970s. But during the early 1980s the economy ran into trouble, mainly because there had been very little attempt to modernize industry. Husak, who had been in power since 1968, resigned (1987), but his successor, Milos Jakes, did not have a reputation as a reformer. Then things changed suddenly in a matter of days, in what became known as the *Velvet Revolution*. On 17 November 1989 there was a huge demonstration in Prague at which many people were injured by police brutality. Charter 77, now led by the famous playwright, Václav Havel, organized further opposition, and after Alexander Dubček had spoken at a public rally for the first time since 1968, a national strike was declared. This was enough to topple the communist regime: Jakes resigned and Havel was elected President (29 December 1989).

(g) *The rest of Eastern Europe*

The end of communism in the remaining states of Eastern Europe was less clearcut.

1 Romania

In Romania the communist regime of *Nicolae Ceauşescu* (leader since 1965) was one of the most brutal and repressive anywhere in the world. His secret police, the Securitate, were responsible for many deaths. When the revolution came, it was short and bloody: it began in Timisoara, a town in western Romania, with a demonstration in support of a popular priest who was being harassed by the Securitate. This was brutally put down and many people were killed (17 December 1989). This caused outrage throughout the country, and when, four days later Ceauşescu and his wife appeared on the balcony of Communist Party Headquarters in Bucharest to address a massed rally, they were greeted with boos and shouts of 'murderers of Timisoara'. TV coverage was abruptly halted and Ceauşescu abandoned his speech. It seemed as though the entire population of Bucharest now streamed out on to the streets. At first the army fired on the crowds and many were killed and wounded. The following day the crowds came out again; but by now the army was refusing to continue the killing, and the Ceauşescus had lost control. They were arrested, tried by a military tribunal and shot (25 December 1989).

The hated Ceauşescus had gone, but many elements of communism remained in Romania. The country had never had democratic government and opposition had been so ruthlessly crushed that there was no equivalent of the Polish Solidarity and Czech Charter 77. When a committee calling itself the National Salvation Front was formed, it was full of former communists, though admittedly they were communists who wanted reform. Ion Iliescu, who had been a member of Ceauşescu's government until 1984, was chosen as President. He won the presidential election of May 1990, and the NSF won the elections for a new parliament. They strongly denied that the new government was really a communist one under a different name and they stayed in control until November 1996, when new elections brought Emil Constantinescu, a Christian Democrat, to power at the head of a non-communist coalition.

2 Bulgaria

In Bulgaria the communist leader *Todor Zhivkov* had been in power since 1954. He had stubbornly refused all reforms, even when pressurized by Gorbachev. The progressive communists decided to get rid of him. The Politburo voted to remove him (December 1989) and *in June 1990 free elections were held*. The communists, now calling themselves the Bulgarian Socialist Party, won a comfortable victory over the main opposition party, the Union of Democratic Forces, probably because their propaganda machine told people that the introduction of capitalism would bring economic disaster.

3 Albania

Albania had been communist since 1945 when the communist resistance movement seized power and set up a republic; so, as with Yugoslavia, the Russians were not responsible for the introduction of communism. Since 1946 until his death in 1985 the leader had been *Enver Hoxha*, who was a great admirer of Stalin and copied his system faithfully. Under its new leader, *Ramiz Alia*, Albania was still the poorest and most backward country in Europe. During the winter of 1991 many young Albanians tried to escape from their poverty by crossing the Adriatic Sea to Italy, but most of them were sent back. By this time student demonstrations were breaking out, and statues of Hoxha and Lenin were overturned. Eventually the communist leadership bowed to the inevitable and allowed free elections. *In 1992 the first non-communist president, Sali Berisla, was elected.*

4 Yugoslavia

Yugoslavia saw the most tragic events, when the end of communism led to civil war (see Section 10.8).

(h) *After communism*

The states of Eastern Europe faced broadly similar problems: how to change from a planned or 'command' economy to a free economy where 'market forces' ruled. Heavy industry, which in theory should have been privatized, was mostly old-fashioned and uncompetitive; it had now lost its guaranteed markets within the communist bloc, and so nobody wanted to buy shares in it. Although shops were better stocked than before, prices of consumer goods soared and very few people could afford to buy them. The standard of living was even lower than under the final years of communism, and very little help was forthcoming from the West. Many people had expected a miraculous improvement, and, not making allowances for the seriousness of the problems, they soon grew disillusioned with their new governments.

- *The East Germans* were the most fortunate, having the wealth of the former West Germany to help them. But there were tensions even here: many west Germans resented the vast amounts of 'their' money being poured into the east, and they had to pay higher taxes and suffer higher interest rates. The easterners resented the large numbers of westerners who now moved in and took the best jobs.
- *In Poland* the first four years of non-communist rule were hard for ordinary people

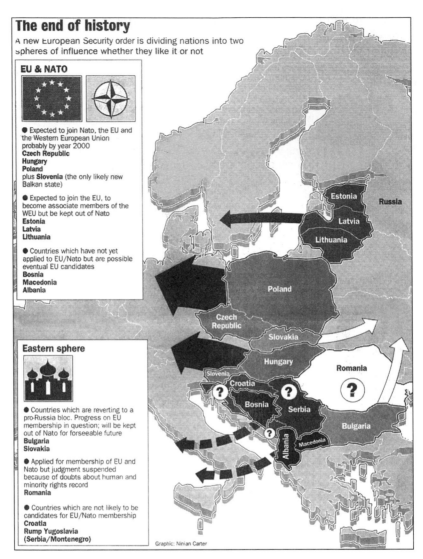

The end of history

A new European Security order is dividing nations into two spheres of influence whether they like it or not

EU & NATO

● Expected to join Nato, the EU and the Western European Union probably by year 2000
Czech Republic
Hungary
Poland
plus **Slovenia** (the only likely new Balkan state)

● Expected to join the EU, to become associate members of the WEU but be kept out of Nato
Estonia
Latvia
Lithuania

● Countries which have not yet applied to EU/Nato but are possible eventual EU candidates
Bosnia
Macedonia
Albania

Eastern sphere

● Countries which are reverting to a pro-Russia bloc. Progress on EU membership in question; will be kept out of Nato for forseeable future
Bulgaria
Slovakia

● Applied for membership of EU and Nato but judgment suspended because of doubts about human and minority rights record
Romania

● Countries which are not likely to be candidates for EU/Nato membership
Croatia
Rump Yugoslavia
(Serbia/Montenegro)

Graphic: Ninian Carter

Map 10.3   Eastern Europe: What does the future hold?

Source: *Observer*, 21 April 1996

as the government pushed ahead with its reorganization of the economy. By 1994 there were clear signs of recovery, but many people were bitterly disappointed with their new democratic government. In the presidential election of December 1995, Lech Walesa was defeated by a former communist party member, Aleksander Kwasniewski.

● *In Czechoslovakia* there were problems of a different kind: Slovakia, the eastern half of the country, demanded independence, and for a time civil war seemed a strong possibility. Fortunately a peaceful settlement was worked out and the country split into two – the Czech republic and Slovakia (1992) (see Map 10.3).

● Predictably the slowest economic progress was made in *Romania, Bulgaria and Albania*, where the first half of the 1990s was beset by falling output and inflation.

10.8 Civil war in Yugoslavia

Yugoslavia was formed after the First World War, and consisted of the pre-First World War state of Serbia, plus territory gained by Serbia from Turkey in 1913 (containing many Muslims), and territory taken from the defeated Habsburg Empire. It included people of many different nationalities, and the state was organized on federal lines. It consisted of six republics – Serbia, Croatia, Montenegro, Slovenia, Bosnia-Herzegovina and Macedonia. There were also two provinces – Vojvodina and Kosovo – which were associated with Serbia. Under communism and the leadership of Tito, the nationalist feelings of the different peoples were kept strictly under control, and people were encouraged to think of themselves primarily as Yugoslavs rather than as Serbs or Croats. The different nationalities lived peacefully together, and had apparently succeeded in putting behind them memories of the atrocities committed during the Second World War. One such atrocity was when Croat and Muslim supporters of the fascist regime set up by the Italians to rule Croatia and Bosnia during the war were responsible for the murder of some 700 000 Serbs.

However, there was still a Croat nationalist movement and some Croat nationalist leaders, such as *Franjo Tudjman*, were given spells in gaol. Tito (who died in 1980) had left careful plans for the country to be ruled by a collective presidency after his death. This would consist of one representative from each of the six republics and one from each of the two provinces; a different president of this council would be elected each year.

(a) *Things begin to go wrong*

Although the collective leadership seemed to work well at first, in the mid-1980s things began to go wrong.

- *The economy was in trouble*, with inflation running at 90 per cent in 1986 and unemployment standing at over 1 million – 13 per cent of the working population. There were differences between areas: for example, Slovenia was reasonably prosperous while parts of Serbia were poverty-stricken.
- *Slobodan Milošević, who became President of Serbia in 1988, bears much of the responsibility for the tragedy which followed.* He deliberately stirred up Serbian nationalist feelings to increase his own popularity, using the situation in Kosovo. He claimed that the Serbian minority in Kosovo were being terrorized by the Albanian majority, though there was no definite evidence of this. The Serbian government's hard-line treatment of the Albanians led to protest demonstrations and the first outbreaks of violence. Milošević remained in power after the first free elections in Serbia in 1990, having successfully convinced the voters that he was now a nationalist and not a communist. He wanted to preserve the united federal state of Yugoslavia, but intended that Serbia should be the dominant republic.
- *By the end of 1990 free elections had also been held in the other republics, and new non-communist governments had taken over.* They resented Serbia's attitude, none more so than the new president of Croatia, Franjo Tudjman, former communist and now leader of the right-wing Croatian Democratic Union. He did all he could to stir up Croatian nationalism and wanted an independent state of Croatia.
- *Slovenia also wanted to become independent, and so the future looked bleak for the united Yugoslavia.* Only Milošević opposed the breakup of the state, but he wanted it kept on Serbian terms and refused to make any concessions to the other nationalities. He refused to accept a Croat as president of Yugoslavia (1991) and used Yugoslav federal cash to help the Serb economy.

- *The situation was complicated because each republic had ethnic minorities:* there were about 600 000 Serbs living in Croatia – about 15 per cent of the population – and about 1.3 million Serbs in Bosnia-Herzegovina – roughly a third of the population. Tudjman would give no guarantees to the Serbs of Croatia, and this gave Serbia the excuse to announce that she would defend all Serbs forced to live under Croatian rule. War was not inevitable: with statesmanlike leaders prepared to make sensible concessions, peaceful solutions could have been found. But clearly, if Yugoslavia broke up, with men like Milošević and Tudjman in power, there was little chance of a peaceful future.

(b) *The move to war: the Serb–Croat War*

Crisis-point was reached in June 1991 when Slovenia and Croatia declared themselves independent, against the wishes of Serbia. Fighting seemed likely between troops of the Yugoslav federal army (mainly Serbian) stationed in those countries, and the new Croatian and Slovenian militia armies which had just been formed. *Civil war was avoided in Slovenia mainly because there were very few Serbs living there.* The EC was able to act as mediator, and secured the withdrawal of Yugoslav troops from Slovenia.

However, it was a different story in Croatia, with its large Serbian minority. Serbian troops invaded the eastern area of Croatia (eastern Slavonia) where many Serbs lived, and other towns and cities, including Dubrovnik on the Dalmatian coast, were shelled. By the end of August 1991 they had captured about one-third of the country. Only then, having captured all the territory he wanted, did Milošević agree to a ceasefire. A UN force of 13 000 troops – UNPROFOR – was sent to police it (February 1992). By this time the international community had recognized the independence of Slovenia, Croatia and Bosnia-Herzegovina.

(c) *The war in Bosnia-Herzegovina*

Just as hostilities between Croatia and Serbia were dying down, an even more bloody struggle was about to break out in Bosnia, which contained a mixed population – 44 per cent Muslim, 33 per cent Serb and 17 per cent Croat. Bosnia declared itself independent under the presidency of the Muslim *Alia Izetbegović* (March 1992). The EC recognized its independence, making the same mistake as it had done with Croatia – it failed to make sure that the new government guaranteed fair treatment for its minorities. The Bosnian Serbs rejected the new constitution and objected to a Muslim president. *Fighting soon broke out between Bosnian Serbs, who received help and encouragement from Serbia, and Bosnian Muslims.* The Serbs hoped that the large strip of land in the east of Bosnia, which bordered onto Serbia, could break away from the Muslim-dominated Bosnia and become part of Serbia. At the same time Croatia attacked and occupied areas in the north of Bosnia where most of the Bosnian Croats lived (see Map 10.3).

Atrocities were committed by all sides, but it seemed that the Bosnian Serbs were the most guilty. They carried out '*ethnic cleansing*', which meant driving out the Muslim civilian population from Serb majority areas, putting them into camps, and in some cases murdering all the men. Such barbarism had not been seen in Europe since the Nazi treatment of the Jews during the Second World War. Sarajevo, the capital of Bosnia, was besieged and shelled by the Serbs, and throughout the country there was chaos: 2 million refugees had been driven out of their homes by 'ethnic cleansing' and not enough food and medical supplies were available.

The UN force, UNPROFOR, did its best to distribute aid, but its job was very difficult because it had no supporting artillery or aircraft. Later the UN tried to protect the Muslims by declaring Srebrenica, Zepa and Gorazde, three mainly Muslim towns in the

Serb majority region, as 'safe areas'; but not enough troops were provided to defend them if the Serbs decided to attack. The EC was reluctant to send any troops and the Americans felt that Europe should be able to sort its own problems out. However, they did all agree to put economic sanctions on Serbia to force Milošević to stop helping the Bosnian Serbs. The war dragged on into 1995; there were endless talks, threats of NATO action, and attempts to get a cease-fire, but no progress could be made.

During 1995 crucial changes took place which enabled a peace agreement to be signed in November. *Serb behaviour eventually proved too much for the international community:*

- Serb forces again bombarded Sarajevo, killing a number of people, after they had promised to withdraw their heavy weapons (May);
- Serbs seized UN peacekeepers as hostages to deter NATO airstrikes;
- they attacked and captured Srebrenica and Zepa, two of the UN 'safe areas', and at Srebrenica they committed the ultimate act of barbarism, killing perhaps as many as 8000 Muslims in a terrible final burst of 'ethnic cleansing' (July).

After this, things moved more quickly:

1   The Croats and Muslims (who had signed a ceasefire in 1994) agreed to fight together against the Serbs. The areas of western Slavonia (May) and the Krajina (August) were recaptured from the Serbs;
2   At a conference in London attended by the Americans, it was agreed to use NATO airstrikes and to deploy a 'rapid reaction force' against the Bosnian Serbs if they continued their aggression;
3   The Bosnian Serbs ignored this and continued to shell Sarajevo. 27 people were killed by a single mortar shell on 28 August. This was followed by a massive NATO bombing of Bosnian Serb positions, which continued until they agreed to move their weapons away from Sarajevo. More UN troops were sent, though in fact the UN position was weakened because NATO was now running the operation. By this time the Bosnian Serb leaders, Radovan Karadžić and General Mladić, had been indicted by the European Court for war crimes;
4   President Milošević of Serbia had now had enough of the war and wanted to get the economic sanctions on his country lifted. With the Bosnian Serb leaders now discredited in international eyes as war criminals, he was able to represent them at the conference table;
5   With the Americans now taking the lead, a cease-fire was arranged, and Presidents Clinton and Yeltsin agreed to co-operate on peace arrangements. *A peace conference met in the USA at Dayton (Ohio) in November and a treaty was formally signed in Paris in December 1995* (see Map 10.4):

  - Bosnia was to remain one state, with a single elected parliament and president, and a unified Sarajevo as its capital;
  - the state would consist of two sections: the Bosnian Muslim/Croat federation and the Bosnian Serb republic;
  - Gorazde, the surviving 'safe area', was to remain in Muslim hands, linked to Sarajevo by a corridor through Serb territory;
  - all indicted war criminals were banned from public life;
  - all Bosnian refugees, over 2 million of them, had the right to return, and there was to be freedom of movement throughout the new state;
  - 60 000 NATO troops were to police the settlement;
  - it was understood that the UN would lift the economic sanctions on Serbia.

There was general relief at the peace, though there were no real winners, and the set-

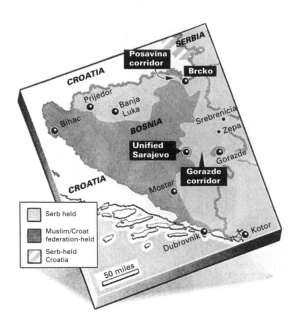

Map 10.4 The Bosnian Peace Settlement

Source: *The Guardian*, 22 November 1995

tlement was full of problems. Only time would tell whether it was possible to maintain the new state or whether the Bosnian Serb republic would eventually try to break away and join Serbia.

Questions

1 Using the information from this chapter:
   (a) Make a list of the differences you have noticed between the kind of unity which existed in Western Europe and the unity which existed in Eastern Europe.   1.4c–5c
   (b) Explain why the Russians intervened with force in some Eastern bloc countries (Poland and Hungary in 1956), but not in others (for example, Yugoslavia).   1.4b–9a, 6c–7c
   (c) Explain why the unity in Eastern Europe collapsed in 1989. Do you think that the economic and political causes of the collapse were equally important?
                                                                                       1.4b–9a, 6c–9b

2 *President de Gaulle prevents Britain from entering the EEC (1963)*   Britain applied for membership of the EEC, and in October 1961 talks began in Brussels to work out the terms for Britain's entry. However, in January 1963 President de Gaulle of France broke off the talks, saying that he did not think Britain was ready for EEC membership. Study Sources A to E and then answer the questions which follow.

A British cartoon of 1963 showing Macmillan (the British Prime Minister) bowling to de Gaulle in a cricket match (Figure 10.2)

"VOILA, THIS IS WHAT YOU CALL 'HIT FOR SIX, NON' . . ."

Source: *Daily Mirror*

Source B

Statement by de Gaulle at a press conference, 14 January 1963

Britain presented her application to the EEC after having earlier refused to take part and she is not prepared to accept all the terms of the Treaty of Rome. England is insular and maritime, linked through its trade to very diverse and different countries. In short, the nature and structure of England differ profoundly from those of the continentals. The question is to know if Britain can give up all preference with regard to the Commonwealth and stop claiming that its agriculture be privileged. The entry of Britain would completely change the Common Market which would become a colossal Atlantic grouping under American domination and control.

Source C

Speech by Macmillan at Liverpool, 21 January 1963

We made it clear that we accepted the Treaty of Rome, including the Common Agricultural Policy and the common tariff – we have reached solutions over a very large part of the field. It was known right from the beginning that there would be special problems affecting the Commonwealth; if there was an objection in principle to our retaining links with the Commonwealth, we should surely have been told so from the start.

Statement by Paul-Henri Spaak, Foreign Minister of Belgium, 15 January 1963

As far as the Belgian government is concerned, the approach of Britain at the Brussels negotiations is altogether different from the picture of it which the President of France has given. Some of the differences mentioned by de Gaulle have already been overcome, and although some problems remain, they are no more difficult to overcome than the rest.

Sources: Sources B, C and D are taken from *Keesing's Contemporary Archives for 1963*

Source E

The view of two British historians

The decision to 'enter Europe' had been taken slowly, and in fact, dishonestly, as far as Britain was concerned. The motives behind the application were not those of European unity, and Macmillan had no intention of making Britain a European power. The real reason behind the British application was the need to find somewhere for Britain to act a leading role and improve her international reputation. Once inside the Common Market, Macmillan planned to organize it into a sort of 'second pillar' of western defence, and to lead it in co-operation with America, as part of an extended Atlantic partnership.

Source: A. Sked and C. Cook, *Post-War Britain* (Penguin, 1979)

(a) Do you think the cartoonist in Source A is sympathetic to de Gaulle or to Macmillan? Explain your answer. 1.6c–7c 5 marks

(b) In what ways does Source C seem to disagree with Source B? 1.6c, 3.4 6 marks

(c) Mr Spaak, the Belgian Foreign Minister (Source D), says that 'some of the difficulties mentioned by de Gaulle had already been overcome'. Do you think that the evidence in Sources B and C supports this statement? Explain your answer. 1.6c, 3.4 4 marks

(d) What reasons can you suggest for the differences of attitude and the contradictions shown in these sources? 1.6c–10 5 marks

(e) How reliable do you think each of these sources is? 3.7 5 marks

(f) How useful is each one of these sources in trying to decide why de Gaulle prevented Britain from joining the EEC in 1963? 3.5–10 10 marks

Total: 35 marks

3 *Czechoslovakia and the unity of the communist bloc, 1968* In 1968 armed forces from the USSR and other Warsaw Pact countries invaded Czechoslovakia to put a stop to a programme of important changes being introduced by Alexander Dubček, the new Czech communist leader. The Russians felt that this programme threatened communism and the unity of the communist bloc. The Russians forced Dubček to abandon his programme, and he later had to resign. Study Sources A and B and then answer the questions which follow.

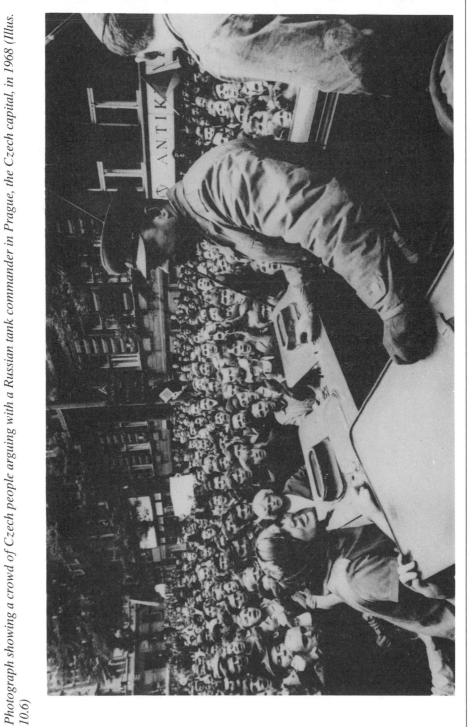

Photograph showing a crowd of Czech people arguing with a Russian tank commander in Prague, the Czech capital, in 1968 (Illus. 10.6)

Extract from the memoirs of Andrei Gromyko, Foreign Minister of the USSR in 1968

The people of Czechoslovakia were happy at the collapse of the anti-communist forces. They knew now that they would continue along the sure path of socialism (communism) with the firm friendship of the USSR and the other socialist countries.

Source: A. Gromyko, *Memories* (Hutchinson, 1989)

(a) Mr Gromyko in Source B tells us that 'the people of Czechoslovakia were happy at the collapse of the anti-communist forces'. Does Source A prove that he was wrong? Explain your answer. 1.6c–8c, 3.5–8 5 marks

(b) Using information from Section 10.6(e), explain the political and economic causes which prompted Alexander Dubček to introduce a programme of change in 1968. 1.4b–5b 5 marks

(c) What political and economic changes did Dubček introduce? 1.4a–5a 5 marks

(d) Why did most Czechs look on these changes as progress, whereas the Russian government objected to them? 1.6a, 5c–8c 5 marks

Total: 20 marks

Conflict in the Middle East

Summary of events

The area known as the Middle East has been one of the world's most troubled regions, especially since 1945. Wars and civil wars have raged almost non-stop, and there has hardly been a time when the whole region was at peace. Strictly speaking, the Middle East consists of Egypt, the Sudan, Jordan, Syria, Lebanon, Iraq, Saudi Arabia, Kuwait, Iran, Turkey, the Yemen republics, the United Arab Emirates and Oman (see Map 11.1). Most of these states, except Turkey and Iran, are peopled by Arabs; Iran, though not an Arab state, contains many Arabs living in the area around the northern end of the Persian Gulf. The Middle East also contains the small Jewish state of Israel which was set up by the United Nations in 1948 in Palestine. The creation of Israel in Palestine, an area belonging to the Palestinian Arabs, outraged Arab opinion through-out the world (other Arab states outside the Middle East are Morocco, Algeria, Tunisia and Libya). The Arabs especially blamed Britain who, they felt, had been more sympathetic to the Jews than to the Arabs; most of all they blamed the USA which had supported the idea of a Jewish state very strongly. The Arab states refused to recognize Israel as a legal state and they vowed to destroy it. Although there were four short wars between Israel and the various Arab states (1948–9, 1956, 1967 and 1973), Arab attacks failed, and Israel survived.

The Arab desire to destroy Israel tended for much of the time to overshadow all other concerns. However, two other themes which ran through Middle East affairs got mixed up with the anti-Israel struggle:

- the desire of some Arabs to achieve political and economic unity among the Arab states.
- the desire of many Arabs to put an end to foreign intervention in their countries.
The Middle East attracted a lot of attention from both Western and communist powers, because of its strategic position and rich oil resources.

Interpretations of the Middle East situation vary depending on whose viewpoint one looks at. For example, many British politicians and journalists regarded Colonel Nasser (Egyptian leader 1954–70) as some kind of dangerous fanatic who was almost as bad as Hitler. On the other hand, most Arabs thought he was a hero, the symbol of the Arab people's move towards unity and freedom.

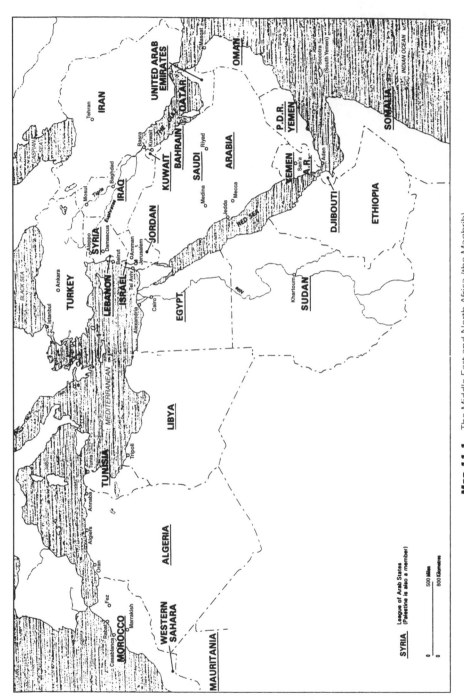

Map 11.1 The Middle East and North Africa (the Maghrib)

Source: A. Hourani, *A History of the Arab Peoples* (Faber & Faber, 1991) pp. 478–9

11.1 Arab unity and interference from the outside world

(a) *Arabs have several things in common*

They all speak the Arabic language, they are all Muslims (followers of the religion known as Islam), except for about half the population of Lebanon who are Christian; and most of them wanted to see the destruction of Israel so that the Palestinian Arabs could have back the land which they feel is rightfully theirs. Many Arabs wanted to see the unity carried much further into some sort of political and economic union, like the European Community. As early as 1931 an Islamic conference in Jerusalem put out this announcement: 'The Arab lands are a complete and indivisible whole ... all efforts are to be directed towards their complete independence, in their entirety and unified'.

Several attempts were made to increase unity among the Arab states.

- *The Arab League, founded in 1945*, included Egypt, Syria, Jordan, Iraq, Lebanon, Saudi Arabia and Yemen; membership later expanded to include twenty states in 1980. However, it achieved very little politically and was constantly hampered by internal squabbles.
- In the mid-1950s Arab unity (sometimes known as pan-Arabism, 'pan' meaning 'all') received a boost with *the energetic leadership of Colonel Gamal Abdel Nasser of Egypt*, who gained enormous prestige in the Arab world after the 1956 Suez Crisis (see Section 11.3). In 1958 Syria joined Egypt to form the *United Arab Republic* with Nasser as President. However, this only lasted until 1961, when Syria withdrew because of resentment at Nasser's attempts to dominate the union.
- After Nasser's death in 1970, his successor, President Sadat, organized a loose union between Egypt, Libya and Syria, known as the *Federation of Arab Republics*; but it never amounted to much.

In spite of their similarities, there were too many points on which the Arab states disagreed for unity ever to be really close. For example:

- Jordan and Saudi Arabia were ruled (and still are) by fairly conservative royal families who were often criticized for being too pro-British by the governments of Egypt and Syria, which were pro-Arab nationalist as well as socialist.
- The other Arab states fell out with Egypt in 1979 because Egypt signed a separate peace treaty with Israel (see Section 11.6). This caused Egypt to be expelled from the Arab League.

(b) *Interference in the Middle East by other countries*

This took place for several reasons.

- *Britain and France had been involved in the Middle East for many years.* Britain ruled Egypt from 1882 (when British troops invaded it) until 1922 when the country was given semi-independence under its own king. However, British troops still remained in Egypt and the Egyptians had to continue doing what Britain wanted. By the Versailles Settlement at the end of the First World War, Britain and France were given large areas of the Middle East taken from the defeated Turks, to look after as mandates. Map 11.2 shows which areas were involved. Although Britain gave independence to Iraq (1932) and to Jordan (1946), both remained pro-British. France gave independence to Syria and Lebanon (1945) but hoped to maintain some influence in the Middle East.

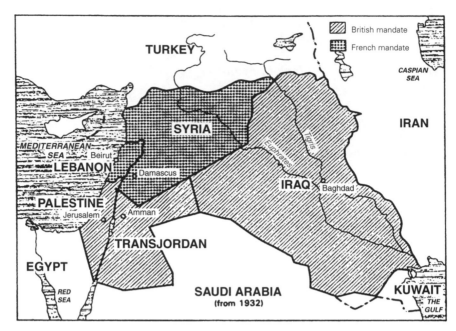

Map 11.2   Areas given to Britain and France to be 'looked after' at the end of the First World War (mandated territories)

Source: A. Hourani, *A History of the Arab Peoples* (Faber & Faber, 1991) p. 476

- *The Middle East held a very important strategic position in the world* – it acted as a sort of crossroads between the Western nations, the communist bloc and the Third World countries of Africa and Asia.
- *At one time the Middle East produced over a third of the world's oil supplies*, the main producers being Iran, Iraq, Saudi Arabia and Kuwait. In the days before North Sea oil was available, and before nuclear power, the European nations were heavily dependent on oil supplies from the Middle East and wanted to make sure that the oil-producing states had friendly governments which would sell them oil cheaply.
- *The lack of unity among the Arab states* encouraged other countries to intervene in the Middle East.

Most of the Arab states had nationalist governments which bitterly resented Western influence. *One by one, governments which were thought to be too pro-West were swept away and replaced by regimes which wanted to be non-aligned*; this meant being free to act independently of both East (communist bloc) and West.

1   Egypt

At the end of the Second World War, British troops stayed on in the canal zone (the area around the Suez Canal). This was to enable Britain to control the canal, in which over half the shares were owned by the British and French. In 1952 a group of Egyptian army officers, tired of waiting for the British to leave, overthrew Farouk, the king of Egypt (who they thought was not firm enough with the British), and seized power themselves. *By 1954 Colonel Nasser had become President* and his policy of standing up to Britain soon led to the Suez War of 1956 (see Section 11.3 for full details). This brought complete humiliation for Britain and was the end of British influence in Egypt.

2 Jordan

King Abdullah had been given his throne by the British in 1946. He was assassinated in 1951 by nationalists who felt that he was too much under Britain's thumb. His successor, King Hussein, had to tread very carefully to survive. He ended the treaty which allowed British troops to use bases in Jordan (1957) and all British troops were withdrawn.

3 Iraq

King Faisal and his Prime Minister, Nuri-es-Said, were pro-British; in 1955 they signed an agreement with Turkey (the *Baghdad Pact*) to set up a joint defence and economic policy. Pakistan, Iran and Britain also joined, Britain promising to help Iraq if she was attacked. The British humiliation in the 1956 Suez War encouraged the anti-British movement in Iraq to act: Faisal and Nuri-es-Said were murdered and Iraq became a republic (1958). The new government was sympathetic towards Egypt and it withdrew Iraq from the Baghdad Pact. This marked the end of Britain's attempt to play a major role in Arab affairs.

4 Iran

In Iran important changes were taking place. Iran was the only Middle East state which had a frontier with the USSR. In 1945 the Russians tried to set up a communist government in northern Iran, the part which bordered on the USSR and which had a large and active communist party. The Western-educated Shah (ruler) of Iran, Reza Pahlevi, resisted the Russians and signed a defence treaty with the USA (1950); they provided him with economic and military aid, including tanks and jet fighters. The Americans saw the situation as part of the Cold War – Iran was yet another front on which the communists must be prevented from advancing. However, there was a strong nationalist movement in Iran which resented all foreign influence. This soon began to turn against the USA and against Britain too. This was because Britain held a majority of the shares in the *Anglo-Iranian Oil Company* and its refinery at Abadan. It was widely felt that the British were taking too much of the profits, and in 1951 the Premier of Iran, *Dr Mussadiq*, nationalized the company (took it under the control of the Iranian government). However, most of the world, encouraged by Britain, boycotted Iran's oil exports and Mussadiq was forced to resign. In 1954 a compromise was reached in which British Petroleum was allowed 40 per cent of the shares. Iran now took 50 per cent of the profits, which the Shah was able to use for a cautious modernization and land reform programme.

This was not enough for the left and for the devout Muslims. They resented the Shah's close ties with the USA which they considered to be an immoral influence on their country; they also suspected that a large slice of the country's wealth was finding its way into his private fortune. In January 1979 he was forced to leave the country, and *an Islamic republic was set up* under a religious leader, the Ayatollah (a sort of High Priest) *Khomeini*. Like Nasser, he wanted his country to be non-aligned.

11.2 The creation of Israel and the Arab–Israeli war 1948–9

(a) Why did the creation of the state of Israel lead to war?

1   The origin of the problem went back almost 2000 years to the year AD 71, *when most of the Jews were driven out of Palestine, which was then their homeland, by the Romans.* In fact, small communities of Jews stayed behind in Palestine, and over the following 1700 years there was a gradual trickle of Jews returning from exile. Until the end of the nineteenth century though, there were never enough Jews to make the Arabs, who now looked on Palestine as their homeland, feel threatened.

2   In 1897 some Jews living in Europe founded the *World Zionist Organization* at Basle in Switzerland. Zionists were people who believed that Jews ought to be able to go back to Palestine and have what they called 'a national homeland'; in other words, a Jewish state. Jews had recently suffered persecution in Russia, France and Germany, and a Jewish state would provide a safe refuge for Jews from all over the world. The problem was that *Palestine was inhabited by Arabs*, who were alarmed at the prospect of losing their land to the Jews.

3   Britain became involved in 1917 when the Foreign Minister, *Arthur Balfour, announced that Britain supported the idea of a Jewish national home in Palestine.* After 1919, when Palestine became a British mandate, large numbers of Jews began to arrive in Palestine, and the Arabs protested bitterly to the British that they wanted:

- an independent Palestine for the Arabs;
- an end to the immigration of Jews.

The British government stated (1922) that there was no intention that the Jews should occupy the whole of Palestine and that there would be no interference with the rights of the Palestinian Arabs. The British hoped to persuade Jews and Arabs to live together peacefully in the same state; they failed to understand the deep religious gulf between the two.

4   Nazi persecution of Jews in Germany after 1933 caused a flood of refugees, and by 1940 about half the population of Palestine was Jewish. *In 1937 the British Peel Commission proposed dividing Palestine into two separate states*, one Arab and one Jewish, but the Arabs rejected the idea. The British tried again in 1939, offering an independent Arab state within ten years, and Jewish immigration limited to 10 000 a year; this time the Jews rejected the proposal.

5   *The Second World War made the situation much worse:* there were hundreds of thousands of Jewish refugees from Hitler's Europe desperately looking for somewhere to go. In 1945 the USA pressed Britain to allow 100 000 Jews into Palestine; this demand was echoed by David Ben Gurion, one of the Jewish leaders, but the British, not wanting to offend the Arabs, refused.

6   *The Jews, after all that their race had suffered at the hands of the Nazis, were determined to fight for their 'national home'.* They began a terrorist campaign against both Arabs and British; one of the most spectacular incidents was the blowing up of the King David Hotel in Jerusalem, which the British were using as their headquarters; 91 people were killed and many more injured. The British responded by arresting Jewish leaders and by turning back ships such as the *Exodus*, crammed with Jews intending to enter Palestine.

7   *The British, weakened by the strain of the Second World War, felt unable to cope.* Ernest Bevin, the Labour Foreign Secretary, asked the United Nations to deal with the problem, and *in November 1947 the UN voted to divide Palestine*, setting

aside roughly half of it to form an independent Jewish state. Early in 1948 the British decided to come out altogether and let the UN carry out its own plan. Although fighting was already going on between Jews and Arabs (who bitterly resented the loss of half of Palestine), the British withdrew all their troops. *In May 1948 Ben Gurion declared the independence of the new state of Israel.* It was immediately attacked by Egypt, Syria, Jordan, Iraq and Lebanon.

(b) *Who was to blame for the tragedy?*

● *Most of the rest of the world seemed to blame Britain for the chaos in Palestine:* many British newspapers which supported the Conservative party also criticized Bevin and Britain's Labour government for its handling of the situation. It was said that British troops should have stayed on to ensure that the partition of Palestine was carried out smoothly. The Arabs accused the British of being pro-Jewish for letting far too many Jews into Palestine in the first place and for causing them to lose half their homeland. The Jews accused the British of being pro-Arab for trying to limit Jewish immigration.

● *Bevin blamed the USA for the chaos*, and there is some evidence to support his case. It was US President Truman who pressurized Britain to allow 100 000 extra Jews to go to Palestine in April 1946. Although this was bound to upset the Arabs even more, Truman refused to provide any American troops to help keep order in Palestine, and refused to allow any more Jews to enter the USA. It was Truman who rejected the British *Morrison Plan (July 1946)* which would have set up separate Arab and Jewish provinces under British supervision. It was the Americans who pushed the plan for partition through the UN, even though all the Arab nations voted against it; this was bound to cause more violence in Palestine.

● *Some historians have defended the British*, pointing out that they were trying to be fair to both sides, and that in the end, it was impossible to persuade both Arabs and Jews to accept a peaceful solution. The British withdrawal was understandable: it would force the Americans and the UN to take more responsibility for the situation they had helped create. It would save the British a lot of expense: since 1945 they had already spent over £100 million trying to keep the peace, and they could not afford to continue.

(c) *The war and its outcome*

Most people expected the Arabs to win easily, but against seemingly overwhelming odds, *the Israelis defeated them and even captured more of Palestine than the UN partition had given them*. They ended up with about three-quarters of Palestine plus the Egyptian port of Eilat on the Red Sea. The Israelis won partly because they fought desperately, and partly because the Arab states were divided among themselves and poorly equipped; King Abdullah of Jordan was more interested in seizing the area of Palestine west of the River Jordan (known as the West Bank) so that he could make it part of his own state, than in giving it to the Palestinian Arabs. The most tragic outcome of the war was that the Palestinian Arabs became the innocent victims who found themselves without a state or a homeland. Some were in the new Jewish state of Israel, others who lived in the area seized by King Abdullah, found themselves living in Jordan. After some Jews had slaughtered the entire population of an Arab village in Israel, nearly a million Arabs fled into Egypt, Lebanon, Jordan and Syria where they had to live in miserable refugee camps. Jerusalem was divided between Israel and Jordan. The USA, Britain and France guaranteed Israel's frontiers, but the Arab states did not regard the ceasefire as permanent. They would not recognize the legality of

Israel, and they regarded this war as only the first round in the struggle to destroy Israel and liberate Palestine. (For a map showing the situation at the end of the war, see Source D in question 2 at the end of the chapter.)

11.3 The Suez War of 1956

(a) *Who was to blame for the war?*

It is possible to blame different countries depending on one's point of view:

- the Arabs blamed the Israelis, who actually began hostilities by invading Egypt;
- the communist bloc and many Arab states blamed Britain and France, accusing them of imperialist tactics (trying to keep control in the Middle East against the wishes of the Arab nations) by attacking Egypt. They accused the Americans of encouraging Britain to attack;
- the British, French and Israelis blamed Colonel Nasser of Egypt for being anti-Western. However, even the Americans thought that Britain and France had overreacted by using force, and most British historians agree.

1   *Colonel Nasser, the new ruler of Egypt, was aggressively in favour of Arab unity and independence*, including the liberation of Palestine from the Jews; almost everything he did irritated the British, Americans or French:

   - He organized guerrilla fighters known as *fedayeen* (self-sacrificers) to carry out sabotage and murder inside Israel, and Egyptian ships blockaded the Gulf of Aqaba leading to the Israeli port of Eilat.
   - In 1936 Britain had signed an agreement with Egypt which allowed the British to keep troops at Suez. This treaty was due to expire in 1956, and Britain wanted it renewed. Nasser refused and insisted that all British troops should withdraw immediately the treaty ended.
   - He sent help to the Algerian Arabs in their struggle against France (see Section 21.5(c)), prodded the other Arab states into opposing the British-sponsored Baghdad Pact, and forced King Hussein of Jordan to dismiss his British army chief-of-staff.
   - He signed an arms deal with Czechoslovakia (September 1955) for Russian fighters, bombers and tanks, and Russian military experts went to train the Egyptian army.

2   *The Americans were outraged at this*, since it meant that the West no longer controlled arms supplies to Egypt. Egypt now became part of the Cold War: any country which was not part of the Western alliance and which bought arms from Eastern Europe was, in American eyes, just as bad as a communist country. It was seen as a sinister plot by the Russians to 'move into' the Middle East. The Americans therefore cancelled a promised grant of 46 million dollars towards the building of a dam as Aswan (July 1956); their intention was to force Nasser to abandon his new links with the communists.

3   *Crisis point was reached when Nasser immediately retaliated by nationalizing the Suez Canal*, intending to use the income from it to finance the dam (Illus. 11.1). Shareholders in the canal, the majority of whom were British and French, were promised compensation.

4   *Anthony Eden, the British Conservative Prime Minister, took the lead at this point.* He believed that Nasser was on the way to forming a united Arabia under

Illus. 11.1   President Nasser of Egypt acclaimed by wildly cheering crowds in Cairo, after proclaiming the nationalisation of the Suez Canal, 1956

Egyptian control and communist influence, which could cut off Europe's oil supplies at will. He viewed Nasser as another Hitler or Mussolini, and according to historian Hugh Thomas, 'saw Egypt through a forest of Flanders poppies and gleaming jackboots'. He was not alone in this: Churchill remarked: 'We can't have this malicious swine sitting across our communications', and the new Labour leader, Hugh Gaitskell, agreed that Nasser must not be appeased in the way that Hitler and Mussolini had been appeased in the 1930s. Everybody in Britain ignored the fact that Nasser had offered compensation to the shareholders and had promised that the ships of all nations (except Israel) would be able to use the canal.

5   Secret talks took place between the British, French and Israelis and a plan was hatched: Israel would invade Egypt across the Sinai peninsula, whereupon British and French troops would occupy the canal zone on the pretext that they were protecting it from damage in the fighting. Anglo-French control of the canal would be restored, and the defeat, it was hoped, would topple Nasser from power.

Recent research has shown that the war could easily have been avoided and that Eden was more in favour of getting rid of Nasser by peaceful means. In fact there was a secret Anglo-American plan (*Omega*) to overthrow Nasser using political and economic pressures. In mid-October 1956 Eden was still willing to continue talks with Egypt; he had called off the military operation, and there seemed a good chance of compromise being reached over control of the Suez Canal. However, Eden was under pressure from several directions to use force. MI6 (the British intelligence service) and some members of the British government, including Harold Macmillan (Chancellor of the Exchequer), urged military action. Macmillan assured Eden that the USA would not oppose a British use of force. In the end, it was probably pressure from the French government which caused Eden to opt for a joint military operation with France and Israel.

(b) *The war*

The war began with the planned *Israeli invasion of Egypt (29 October)*. This was a brilliant success, and within a week the Israelis had captured the entire Sinai peninsula. Meanwhile the British and French bombed Egyptian airfields and landed troops at Port Said at the northern end of the canal. *The attacks caused an outcry from the rest of the world*, and the Americans, who were afraid of upsetting all the Arabs and forcing them into closer ties with the USSR, refused to support Britain, although they had earlier hinted that support would be forthcoming. At the United Nations, Americans and Russians for once agreed: they demanded an immediate ceasefire, and prepared to send a UN force. With the pressure of world opinion against them, *Britain, France and Israel agreed to withdraw*, while UN troops moved in to police the frontier between Egypt and Israel.

(c) *The outcome of the war*

This was a complete humiliation for Britain and France, who achieved none of their aims, and *it was a triumph for Nasser*.

● The war failed to overthrow Nasser, and his prestige as leader of Arab nationalism against interfering Europeans was greatly increased; for the ordinary Arab people, he was a hero.
● The Egyptians blocked the canal, the Arabs reduced oil supplies to western Europe where petrol rationing was introduced for a time, and Russian aid replaced that from the USA (Illus. 11.2).
● The British action soon lost them an ally in Iraq, where premier Nuri-es-Said came under increasing attack from other Arabs for his pro-British attitude; he was murdered in 1958.
● Britain was now weak and unable to follow a foreign policy independently of the USA.
● The Algerians were encouraged in their struggle for independence from France which they achieved in 1962.

The war was not without success for Israel: although she had been compelled to hand back all territory captured from Egypt, she had inflicted heavy losses on the Egyptians in men and equipment, which would take years to make good. For the time being the *fedayeen* raids ceased and Israel had a breathing space in which to consolidate.

Illus. 11.2   Sunken ships block the Suez Canal after the 1956 war

11.4 The Six-Day War of 1967

The Arab states had not signed a peace treaty at the end of the 1948–9 war and were still refusing to give Israel official recognition. In 1967 they joined together again in a determined attempt to destroy Israel. The lead was taken by Iraq, Syria and Egypt.

(a) *The build-up to war*

1   *In Iraq* a new government came to power in 1963 which was influenced by the ideas of the *Ba'ath party* in neighbouring Syria. Supporters of the Ba'ath (meaning 'resurrection') believed in Arab independence and unity and were left-wing in outlook, wanting social reform and better treatment for ordinary people. They were prepared to co-operate with Egypt, and in June 1967 their president, Aref, announced: 'Our goal is clear – to wipe Israel off the map'.

2   *In Syria* political upheavels brought the Ba'ath party to power in 1966. It supported *El Fatah, the Palestinian Liberation Movement*, a more effective guerrilla force than the *fedayeen*. The Syrians also began to bombard Jewish settlements from the Golan Heights which overlooked the frontier.

3   *In Egypt* Colonel Nasser was immensely popular because of his leadership of the Arab world and his attempts to improve conditions in Egypt with his socialist policies. These included limiting the size of farms to 100 acres and redistributing surplus land to peasants. Attempts were made to industrialize the country, and over 1000 new factories were built, almost all under government control. *The Aswan Dam project* was vitally important, providing electricity, and water for irrigating an extra million acres of land. After early delays at the time of the Suez War in 1956, work on the dam eventually got under way and the project was completed in 1971. With all going well at home and the prospect of effective help from Iraq and Syria, Nasser decided that the time was ripe for another attack on Israel. He began to move troops up to the frontier in Sinai and closed the Gulf of Aqaba.

4   *The Russians encouraged Egypt and Syria* and kept up a flow of anti-Israeli propaganda (because Israel was being supported by the USA). Their aim was to increase their influence in the Middle East at the expense of the Americans and Israelis. They hinted that they would send help if war came.

5   *Syria, Jordan and Lebanon* also massed troops along their frontiers with Israel, while contingents from Iraq, Saudi Arabia and Algeria joined them. Israel's situation seemed hopeless.

6   *The Israelis decided that the best policy was to attack first rather than wait to be defeated.* They launched a series of devastating air strikes which destroyed most of the Egyptian air force on the ground (5 June). Israeli troops moved with remarkable speed, capturing the Gaza Strip and the whole of Sinai from Egypt, the rest of Jerusalem and the West Bank from Jordan, and the Golan Heights from Syria. The Arabs had no choice but to accept a UN ceasefire order (10 June), and it was all over in less than a week. *Reasons for the spectacular Israeli success were:*
   ● the slow and ponderous Arab troop build-up which gave the Israelis plenty of warning;
   ● Israeli superiority in the air;
   ● inadequate Arab preparations and communications.

(b) *Results of the war*

1   *For the Israelis it was a great success:* this time they had ignored a UN order to return the captured territory; this acted as a series of buffer zones between Israel and the Arab states, and meant that it would be much easier to defend Israel (see Map 11.3). However, it did bring a new problem – how to deal with about a million extra Arabs who now found themselves under Israeli rule. Many of these were living in the refugee camps set up in 1948 on the West Bank and in the Gaza Strip.

2   *It was a humiliation for the Arab states*, and especially for Nasser, who now realized that the Arabs needed outside help if they were ever to free Palestine. The Russians had been a disappointment to Nasser and had sent no help. To try to improve their relations with Egypt and Syria, the Russians began to supply them with modern weapons. Sooner or later the Arabs would try again to destroy Israel and liberate Palestine. The next attempt came in 1973 with the Yom Kippur War.

11.5 The Yom Kippur War of 1973

(a) *Events leading up to the war*

Several things combined to cause the renewed conflict:

1   *Pressure was brought to bear on the Arab states by the Palestine Liberation Organization (PLO)* under its leader Yasser Arafat, for some further action. When very little happened, a more extreme group within the PLO, called the Popular Front for the Liberation of Palestine, embarked on a series of terrorist attacks to draw world attention to the grave injustice being done to the Arabs of Palestine. They hi-jacked airliners and flew three of them to Amman, the capital of Jordan, where they were blown up (1970). This was embarassing for King Hussein of Jordan, who now favoured a negotiated peace, and in September 1970 he expelled all PLO members based in Jordan. However, terrorist attacks continued, reaching a horrifying climax when some members of the Israeli team were murdered at the 1972 Munich Olympics.

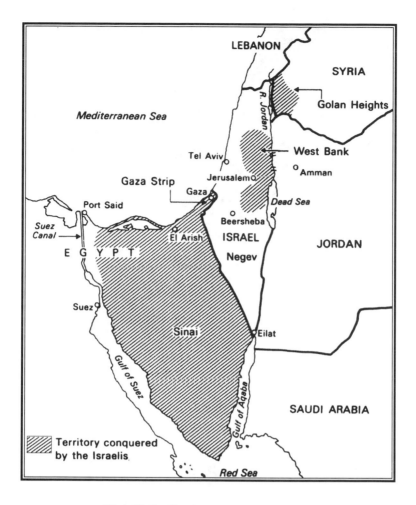

Map 11.3 The situation after the 1967 war

2 *Anwar Sadat, the President of Egypt since Nasser's death in 1970, was becoming increasingly convinced of the need for a negotiated peace settlement with Israel,* before PLO terrorism turned world opinion against them. He was prepared to work either with the USA or the USSR, but he hoped to win American support for the Arabs, so that the Americans would persuade the Israelis to agree to a peace settlement. However, the Americans refused to get involved.

3 *Sadat, together with Syria, decided to attack Israel again, hoping that this would force the Americans to act as mediators.* The Egyptians were feeling more confident because they now had modern Russian weapons and their army had been trained by Russian experts.

(b) *The war began on 6 October 1973*

Egyptian and Syrian forces attacked early on the feast of Yom Kippur, a Jewish religious festival, hoping to catch the Israelis off guard. After some early Arab successes,

Illus. 11.3 *The child soldiers of the Palestine refugee camps; trained from the age of 7, these boys and girls would be ready for front-line service by the age of 15*

the Israelis, using mainly American weapons, were able to turn the tables. They succeeded in hanging on to all the territory they had captured in 1967 and even crossed the Suez Canal into Egypt. In one sense Sadat's plan had been successful – both the USA and the USSR decided it was time to intervene to try to bring about a peace settlement. Acting with UN co-operation, they organized a ceasefire which both sides accepted.

(c) *The outcome of the war*

The end of the war brought a glimmer of hope for some sort of permanent peace. Egyptian and Israeli leaders came together (though not in the same room) in Geneva.

The Israelis agreed to move their troops back from the Suez Canal (which had been closed since the 1967 war) enabling the Egyptians to clear and open the canal in 1975 (but not to Israeli ships).

An important development during the war was that the Arab oil-producing states tried to bring pressure to bear on the USA and on Western European states which were friendly to Israel, by reducing oil supplies. This caused serious oil shortages, especially in Europe. At the same time producers, well aware that oil supplies were not unlimited, looked on their action as a way of preserving resources. With this in mind, the *Organization of Petroleum Exporting Countries (OPEC)* began to raise oil prices substantially. This contributed to inflation and caused an energy crisis in the world's industrial nations.

11.6 Camp David and the Egyptian–Israeli peace, 1978–9

(a) *Why did the two sides begin to talk to each other?*

1   President Sadat had become convinced that *Israel could not be destroyed by force*, and that it was foolish to keep on wasting Egypt's resources in fruitless wars. But it took great courage to be the first Arab leader to meet the Israelis face to face. Even to talk with Israeli leaders meant conceding that Egypt recognized the lawful existence of the state of Israel. He knew that the PLO and the more aggressive Arab states, Iraq and Syria, would bitterly resent any approach. In spite of all the dangers, Sadat offered to go to Israel and talk to the Knesset (the Israeli parliament).

2   *The Israelis were suffering economic problems*, partly because of their enormous defence expenditure, and partly because of a world recession. The USA was pressing them to settle their differences with at least some of the Arabs. They accepted Sadat's offer; he visited Israel in November 1977, and Menahem Begin, the Israeli Prime Minister, visited Egypt the following month.

3   *President Carter of the USA played a vital role* in setting up formal negotiations between the two sides at Camp David (near Washington) which began in September 1978.

(b) *The Peace Treaty and its aftermath*

With Carter acting as intermediary, the talks led to a peace treaty being signed in Washington (March 1979) (Illus. 11.4). *The main points agreed were:*

● the state of war which had existed between Egypt and Israel since 1948 was now ended;
● Israel promised to withdraw its troops from Sinai;
● Egypt promised not to attack Israel again and guaranteed to supply her with oil from the recently opened wells in southern Sinai;
● Israeli ships could use the Suez Canal.

The treaty was condemned by the PLO and most other Arab states (except Sudan and Morocco) and there was clearly a long way to go before similar treaties could be signed by Israel with Syria and Jordan. World opinion began to move against Israel and to accept that the PLO had a good case; but when the USA tried to bring the PLO and

Illus. 11.4 Egypt and Israel sign a peace treaty: (left to right) Anwar Sadat (Egypt), Jimmy Carter (USA) and Menachem Begin (Israel) at the White House

Israel together in an international conference, the Israelis would not co-operate. In November 1980 Begin announced that:

● Israel would never return the Golan Heights to Syria, not even in exchange for a peace treaty; and
● they would never allow the West Bank to become part of an independent Palestinian state; that would be a mortal threat to Israel's existence.

At the same time resentment among West Bank Arabs mounted at the Israeli policy of establishing Jewish settlements on land owned by Arabs. Many observers feared fresh violence unless Begin's government adopted a more moderate approach.

The peace also seemed threatened for a time when *President Sadat was assassinated* by some extremist Muslim soldiers while he was watching a military parade (October 1981). They believed that he had betrayed the Arab and Muslim cause by doing a deal with the Israelis. However, Sadat's successor, *Hosni Mubarak*, bravely announced that he would continue the Camp David agreement.

For most of the 1980s the Arab–Israeli feud was overshadowed by the Iran–Iraq War (see Section 11.9) which occupied much of the Arab world's attention. But in 1987 there were massive demonstrations by Palestinians living in the refugee camps of the Gaza Strip and the West Bank. They were protesting against Israeli repressive policies and the brutal behaviour of Israeli troops in the camps and in the occupied territories. An Israeli clampdown failed to quell the unrest, and the Israelis' tough methods earned them UN and worldwide condemnation.

11.7 Peace between Israel and the PLO

The election of a less aggressive government (Labour) in Israel in June 1992 raised hopes for better relations with the Palestinians. Prime Minister Yitzak Rabin and Foreign Minister Shimon Peres both believed in negotiation, and were prepared to make concessions in order to achieve a lasting peace. Yasser Arafat, the PLO leader, responded and talks opened. But there was so much mutual suspicion and distrust after all the years of hostility that progress was difficult. However, both sides persevered and by early 1996, remarkable changes had taken place.

(a) *The peace accord of September 1993*

This was the first major breakthrough. *It was agreed that:*

- Israel formally recognized the PLO;
- the PLO recognized Israel's right to exist and promised to give up terrorism;
- the Palestinians were to be given limited self-rule in Jericho (on the West Bank)
and in part of the Gaza Strip, areas occupied by Israel since the 1967 war. Israeli troops would be withdrawn from these areas.

Extremist groups on both sides opposed the agreement. The Popular Front for the Liberation of Palestine still wanted a completely independent Palestinian state. Israeli settlers on the West Bank were against all concessions to the PLO. However, the moderate leaders on both sides showed great courage and determination, and two years later they took an even more momentous step forward.

(b) *Self-rule for the Palestinians (September 1995)*

- Israel agreed to withdraw its troops from most of the West Bank (except Hebron) in stages over several years, handing over both civil and security powers to the PLO. This would end Israeli control of the areas which they had held since 1967 (see Map 11.4).
- The areas would be ruled by a parliament or Palestinian Council of 88 members to be elected early in 1996 by all West Bankers and Arab residents of Jerusalem aged over 18.
- All Palestinian prisoners held by Israel (about 6000) would be released, in three phases.

Most of the world's leaders welcomed this brave attempt to bring peace to the troubled region. But once again extremists on both sides claimed that their leaders were guilty of 'shameful surrender'. Tragically *Prime Minister Yitzak Rabin was assassinated by an Israeli right-winger* shortly after addressing a peace rally (4 November 1995). Peres became Prime Minister; the murder caused a revulsion of feeling against the extremists and the agreement was gradually put into operation. In January 1996 King Hussein of Jordan paid an official public visit to Israel for the first time, 1200 Palestinian prisoners were released and talks opened between Israel and Syria. The promised elections were held; although the extremists urged people to boycott them, there was an encouragingly large turnout of over 80 per cent. As expected, Yasser Arafat became the new Palestinian President and his supporters were in a large majority in the newly elected parliament. This was expected to hold office until 1999, when, it was hoped, a permanent peace agreement would have been reached.

However, the situation changed rapidly during the spring of 1996: four suicide bombings carried out by the militant Palestinian group, Hamas, claimed 63 lives; the

Map 11.4 The Israeli–Palestinian Agreement, 1995

Source: *The Guardian*, 25 September 1995

militant Shiite Islamic group, Hizbollah, shelled villages in northern Israel from southern Lebanon. All this enabled the hard-line Likud leader, Binyamin Netanyahu, who denounced Labour policy as 'too soft' towards the Palestinians, to win a narrow victory in the election of May 1996. This dismayed much of the outside world and threw the whole peace process into doubt.

11.8 Conflict in the Lebanon

Originally part of the Ottoman (Turkish) Empire, Lebanon (see Map 11.5) was made a French mandate at the end of the First World War and became fully independent in 1945. It soon became a prosperous state, making money from banking and from serving as an important outlet for the exports of Syria, Jordan and Iraq. However, in 1975 civil war broke out, and although all-out war ended in 1976, chaos and disorder continued right through the 1980s as different factions struggled to gain influence.

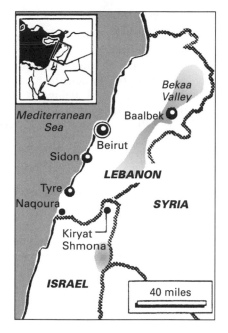

Map 11.5 The Lebanon

Source: *The Guardian*, May 1996

(a) *What caused civil war to break out in 1975?*

1 Religious differences

The potential for trouble was there from the beginning, since the country was a bewildering mixture of different religious groups, some Muslim, some Christian, which had developed independently, separated from each other by mountain ranges.

There were four main Christian groups:

- Maronites (the wealthiest and most conservative);
- Greek Orthodox;
- Roman Catholic;
- Armenians.

There were three Muslim groups:

- Shia – the largest group, mainly poor working class;
- Sunni – a smaller group, but wealthier and with more political influence than the Shia;
- Druze – a small group living in the centre of the country, mainly peasants.

There was a long history of hatred between Maronites and Druzes, but this seemed to be kept in check by the carefully framed constitution which tried to give fair representation to all groups. The President was always a Maronite, the Prime Minister a Sunni, the Speaker (chairman of parliament) a Shia, and the army chief of staff a Druze. Of the 44 seats in parliament, the Maronites were allowed 13, Sunni 9, Shia 8, Greek Orthodox 5, Druze 3, Roman Catholics 3 and Armenians 2.

2   The presence of Palestinian refugees from Israel

This complicated the situation even more. By 1975 there were at least half a million of them living in squalid camps away from the main centres of population. The Palestinians were not popular in Lebanon because they were continually involved in frontier incidents with Israel, provoking the Israelis to hit back at the Palestinians in southern Lebanon. In particular the Palestinians, being left-wing and Muslim, alarmed conservative and Christian Maronites who looked on the Palestinians as a dangerous destabilising influence. By 1975 the PLO had its headquarters in Lebanon, and this meant that Syria, the chief supporter of the PLO, was constantly interfering in Lebanon's affairs.

3   A dispute between Muslims and Christians over fishing rights (1975)

This upset the delicate balance. It began as an apparently minor incident, but it escalated when some Palestinians sided with the Muslims, and a group of right-wing Christians known as the *Phalange* began to attack Palestinians. Soon a full-scale civil war developed: the Maronites saw it as a chance to expel the Palestinians who had formed an alliance with the Druze (long-term enemies of the Maronites).

It is probably impossible to discover with complete certainty which side was responsible for the escalation of the war. Both sides claimed that the original fishing dispute could have been settled easily, and each blamed the other for escalating the violence. Either way, the PLO were certainly involved: the Phalangists claimed that PLO guerrillas fired on a church where some party leaders were attending Mass; the PLO claimed that the Phalangists started it by attacking a bus carrying Palestinians (see question 3 at the end of the chapter).

For a time it looked as though the Druze would win, but this alarmed Israel, which threatened to invade Lebanon. The Syrians did not want this to happen, and so in 1976 President Assad of Syria sent troops into the Lebanon to keep the PLO under some sort of control. Order was restored and it was a setback for the Druze and the PLO. It was the Syrians who now controlled Lebanon; Yasser Arafat, the PLO leader, had to agree to withdraw his troops from the area around Beirut (the capital of Lebanon).

(b) *Chaos continued*

It was over ten years before something approaching peace was restored in Lebanon, as *different conflicts raged in different places.*

1   *In the south, bordering on Israel, fighting soon broke out between Palestinians and Christians*; the Israelis seized this opportunity to send troops in to help the Christians. A small semi-independent Christian state of Free Lebanon was declared under Major Haddad. The Israelis supported this because it acted as a buffer zone to protect them from further Palestinian attacks. The Palestinians and Muslims counter-attacked, and although by 1982 there were 7000 UNIFIL (United Nations Interim Force in the Lebanon) troops in the area, it was a constant struggle to keep the peace.

2   *In 1980* there was a short struggle between supporters of *the two main Maronite groups* (the Gemayel and Chamoun families) which was won by the Gemayels.

3   *In 1982, in reprisal for a Palestinian attack on Israel, Israeli troops invaded Lebanon and penetrated as far as Beirut.* For a time the Gemayels, supported by the Israelis, were in control of Beirut. During this period the Palestinians were expelled from Beirut, and from then on the PLO was divided. The hard-liners went to Iraq and

the rest dispersed into different Arab countries where they were, on the whole, not welcome. The Israelis withdrew and a multi-national force (made up of troops from the USA, France, Italy and Britain) took their place to maintain the peace. However, a spate of attacks and suicide bombings forced them to withdraw.

4   *In 1984 an alliance of Shia militia (known as Amal) and Druze militia backed by Syria, drove President Gemayel out of Beirut.* Then the Shia and Druze themselves came to blows in a struggle for control of West Beirut. Yasser Arafat used the general confusion to rearm his Palestinians in the refugee camps.

At the end of 1986 the situation was extremely complex

●   Shiite Amal militia, backed by Syria, alarmed at the renewed strength of the PLO which seemed likely to set up a state within a state, were besieging the refugee camps, hoping to starve them into surrender.

●   At the same time an alliance of Druze, Sunni and communists was trying to drive Amal out of West Beirut. Another more extreme Shia group known as Hizbollah (Party of God), which was backed by Iran, was also involved in the struggle.

●   Early in 1987 fierce fighting again erupted between Shia and Druze militia for control of West Beirut. Several European and American hostages were seized, including Terry Waite, the Archbishop of Canterbury's special envoy, who had gone to West Beirut to try to negotiate the release of some earlier hostages.

●   With the country seeming to be in a state of total disintegration, President Assad of Syria, responding to a request from the Lebanese government, again sent his troops and tanks into West Beirut (February 1987). Within a week calm had been restored.

(c) *Peace at last*

Although assassinations of leading figures continued, the situation gradually stabilised. *In September 1990 important changes were introduced in the country's constitution, giving the Muslims fairer representation.* The membership of the National Assembly was increased to 108, equally divided between Christians and Muslims. The government, with Syrian help, gradually restored its authority over more and more of the country and managed to get most of the militia armies disbanded. The government also succeeded in getting all the Western hostages released, the last of them in June 1992. All this was very much because of the Syrian presence; in May 1991 the two states signed a treaty of 'brotherhood and co-ordination'. However, this was strongly criticized by the Israelis, who claimed that the treaty marked the 'virtual annexation of Lebanon by Syria'.

11.9 The Iran–Iraq War 1980–8

The Middle East and the Arab world were thrown into fresh confusion in September 1980 when Iraqi troops invaded Iran.

(a) *Iraq's motives*

President Saddam Hussein of Iraq had several motives for launching the attack.

●   *He was afraid of militant Islam spreading across the border into Iraq from Iran.* Iran had become an Islamic republic in 1979 under the leadership of the Ayatollah

Khomeini and his fundamentalist Shiite Muslim supporters. They believed that the country should be run according to the Islamic religion, with a strict moral code enforced by severe punishments. According to Khomeini, 'in Islam the legislative power to establish laws belongs to God Almighty'. The population of Iraq was mainly Sunni Muslim, but there was a large Shia minority. Saddam, whose government was non-religious, was afraid that the Shias might rise up against him, and he had some of their leaders executed early in 1980. The Iranians retaliated by launching raids across the frontier.

- *The Iraqis claimed that the Iranian border province of Khuzestan should rightfully belong to them.* This was an area peopled largely by Arabs, and Saddam hoped that they would rally to support Iraq (most Iranians were Persians, not Arabs).
- *There was a long-standing dispute over the Shatt-el-Arab waterway.* This was an important outlet for the oil exports of both countries, and it formed part of the frontier between the two states. The Shatt-el-Arab had once been completely under Iraqi control, but five years earlier the Iranian government had forced Iraq to share control of it with Iran.
- *Saddam thought that the Iranian forces would be weak and demoralized so soon after the fundamentalist takeover*, so he expected a quick victory.

It soon became clear that he had miscalculated badly.

(b) *The war drags on*

The Iranians quickly organized themselves to deal with the invasion, which began with the Iraqi seizure of the disputed waterway. The Iranians replied with mass infantry attacks against heavily fortified Iraqi positions. On paper Iraq seemed much the stronger, being well supplied with Soviet tanks, helicopter gunships and missiles, and some British and American weapons as well. However, the Iranian revolutionary guards, inspired by their religion, and ready to become martyrs, fought with fanatical determination; eventually they too began to get modern equipment (anti-aircraft and anti-tank missiles) from China and North Korea (and secretly from the USA). As the war dragged on, Iraq concentrated on strangling Iranian oil exports, which paid for their arms supplies; Iran meanwhile captured Iraqi territory, and early in 1987 their troops were only ten miles from Basra, Iraq's second most important city, which had to be evacuated. By this time the territorial dispute had been lost in the deeper racial and religious conflict: Khomeini had sworn never to stop fighting until his Shia Muslim fundamentalists had destroyed the 'godless' Saddam regime.

The war had important international repercussions.

- *The stability of the entire Arab world was threatened:* the more conservative states – Saudi Arabia, Jordan and Kuwait – gave cautious support to Iraq; but Syria, Libya, Algeria, South Yemen and the PLO were critical of Iraq for starting the war at a time when, they believed, all Arab states should have been concentrating on the destruction of Israel. The Saudis and the other Gulf states, suspicious of Khomeini's extreme brand of Islam, wanted to see Iran's ability to dominate the Persian Gulf controlled. As early as November 1980 an Arab summit conference in Amman (Jordan) to draw up new plans for dealing with Israel, failed to get off the ground because the anti-Iraq states, led by Syria, refused to attend.
- *The attacks on Iran's oil exports threatened the energy supplies of the West*, and at various times brought American, Russian, British and French warships into the region, raising the international temperature. In 1987 the situation took a more dangerous turn as oil-tankers, whatever their nationality, were threatened by mines; which side was responsible for laying them was open to debate.

- *The success of Iran's Shia fundamentalist troops, especially the threat to Basra, alarmed the non-religious Arab governments*, and many Arabs were afraid of what might happen if Iraq was defeated. Even President Assad of Syria, at first a strong supporter of Iran, was worried in case Iraq split up and became another Lebanon; this could well destabilize Syria itself. An Islamic conference held in Kuwait (January 1987) was attended by representatives of forty-four nations, but Iran's leaders refused to attend, and no agreement could be reached on how to bring the war to an end.
- The war entered a new and even more terrible phase towards the end of 1987 when both sides began to bombard each other's capital cities, Tehran (Iran) and Baghdad (Iraq), causing thousands of deaths.

(c) *The end of the war, 1988*

Although neither side had achieved its aims, the cost of the war, both economically and in human lives, was telling heavily. Both sides began to look for a way to end the fighting, though for a time they continued to pour out propaganda; Saddam talked about 'total victory' and the Iranians demanded 'total surrender'. The UN became involved, did some straight talking to both sides, and succeeded in arranging a ceasefire (August 1988). This was monitored by UN troops, and against all expectations, the truce lasted. Peace negotiations opened in October 1988 and terms were finally agreed in 1990.

11.10 The Gulf War, 1990–1

Even before he had accepted the peace terms at the end of the Iran–Iraq War, Saddam Hussein began his next act of aggression. His forces invaded and quickly occupied the small neighbouring state of Kuwait (August 1990).

(a) *Saddam Hussein's motives*

- His real motive was probably to get his hands on the wealth of Kuwait, since he was seriously short of cash after the long war with Iran. Kuwait, though small, had valuable oil-wells which he would now be able to control.
- He claimed that Kuwait was historically part of Iraq, though in fact Kuwait had existed as a separate territory – a British protectorate – since 1899, whereas Iraq had not been created until after the First World War.
- He did not expect any action from the outside world now that his troops were firmly entrenched in Kuwait, and he had the strongest army in the region. He thought Europe and the USA were reasonably amenable to him since they had supplied him with arms during his war with Iran. Nor had anybody interfered when he brutally crushed the Kurds (who were demanding an independent state) in the north of Iraq.

(b) *The world unites against Saddam Hussein*

Once again, as in the case of Iran, Saddam had miscalculated. President Bush of the USA took the lead in pressing for action to remove the Iraqis from Kuwait.The UN placed trade sanctions on Iraq, cutting off her oil exports, her main source of income. Saddam was ordered to remove his troops by 15 January 1991, after which the UN would use 'all necessary means' to clear them out. Saddam hoped that this was all bluff and talked of 'the mother of all wars' if they tried to throw him out. But Bush and Margaret Thatcher had decided that Saddam's power must be curbed; he controlled too much of the oil that the industrial West needed. Fortunately for Britain and the USA, Saudi Arabia, Syria and Egypt were also nervous about what Saddam might do next, so they supported the UN action.

In spite of frantic diplomatic efforts, *Saddam Hussein felt that he could not lose face by withdrawing from Kuwait*, though he knew that an international force of over 600 000 had been assembled in Saudi Arabia. More than thirty nations contributed with troops, armaments or cash; for example the USA, Britain, France, Italy, Egypt, Syria and Saudi Arabia provided troops; Germany and Japan donated cash. When the 15 January deadline passed, operation *Desert Storm* was launched against the Iraqis.

The campaign, in two parts, was quickly successful. First came a series of bombing attacks on Baghdad (the Iraqi capital), whose unfortunate citizens again suffered heavy casualties, and on military targets such as roads and bridges. The second phase, the attack on the Iraqi army itself, began on 24 February. *Within four days the Iraqis had been driven out of Kuwait and routed.* Kuwait was liberated and Saddam Hussein accepted defeat. However, although Iraq lost many troops (some estimates put Iraqi dead at 90 000 compared with less than 400 for the allies), Saddam was allowed to withdraw with much of his army intact. The retreating Iraqis were at the mercy of the allies, but Bush called a ceasefire, afraid that if the slaughter continued, the allies would lose the support of the other Arab nations.

(c) *The aftermath of the war – Saddam Hussein survives*

The war had unfortunate consequences for many of the Iraqi people. It was widely expected outside Iraq that after this humiliating defeat, Saddam Hussein would soon be overthrown. There were uprisings of Kurds in the north and Shia Muslims in the south, and it seemed as though Iraq was breaking up. However, the allies had left Saddam enough troops, tanks and aircraft to deal with the situation, and both rebellions were ruthlessly crushed. At first nobody intervened: Russia, Syria and Turkey had Kurdish minorities of their own and did not want the rebellion spreading over from Iraq. Similarly a Shiite victory in southern Iraq would probably increase the power of Iran in that region, and the USA did not want that. But eventually world opinion became so outraged at Saddam's continued ruthless bombings of his people that the USA and Britain, with UN backing, declared the areas 'no-fly zones', and used their air power to keep Saddam's aircraft out. And so Saddam Hussein remained in power.

The war and its aftermath were very revealing about the motives of the West and the great powers. Their primary concern was not with international justice and moral questions of right and wrong, but with their own self-interest. They only took action against Saddam in the first place because they felt he was threatening their oil supplies. Often in the past when other small nations had been invaded, no international action had been taken. For example, when East Timor was occupied by neighbouring Indonesia in 1975, the rest of the world ignored it, because their interests were not threatened. After the Gulf War, Saddam, who on any assessment must rank as one of the most brutal dictators of the century, was allowed to remain in power because the West thought that his survival was the best way of keeping Iraq united and the region stable.

Questions

1. (a) Using the summary of events and Section 11.1, make a list of the important changes which took place in the Middle East between 1945 and 1980. Arrange them under headings: political, economic, military, religious.
   (b) What things in the Middle East stayed more or less the same during this period?

   1.4a–7a

(c) Explain the different reasons why other countries were constantly interfering in the Middle East.   1.4b–7b

(d) Do you think that foreign interference was the main reason why the Middle East has been so unstable since 1945?   1.6b–9a

2 *Palestine and the creation of Israel, 1946–9* Study Sources A to F and then answer the questions which follow.

Source A

A statement to the House of Commons by Ernest Bevin, the British Foreign Minister, 25 February 1947

It has been the objective of the British government to lay the foundations for an independent Palestinian state in which Arabs and Jews would enjoy equal rights. But for the Jews the essential point is the creation of a Jewish state; for the Arabs the essential point is to resist a Jewish state. So what the UN now has to decide is this:

(1) Shall the claims of the Jews be allowed that Palestine is to be a Jewish state?
(2) Shall the claims of the Arabs be allowed that it is to be an Arab state with safeguards for the Jews?
(3) Shall it be a Palestinian state in which the interests of both communities are as carefully balanced and protected as possible?

Source B

Telegram from President Truman of the USA to Clement Attlee, the British Prime Minister, 4 October 1946

I cannot give my support to your Morrison Plan for provincial self-government in Palestine. I believe the best solution is the creation of a viable Jewish state. I urge that steps be taken at the earliest possible moment to admit 100 000 Jewish refugees to Palestine.

Source C

A statement from the Arab Higher Council in Jerusalem, 5 October 1946

Increasing American interests in all Arab and Muslim countries will be jeopardised by the President's ill-considered statements on Jewish immigration and a Jewish state in Palestine. His real motive is his need of Jewish votes in the USA. The Arabs of Palestine and their neighbours are resolved to oppose President Truman's hostile policy by all means at their disposal.

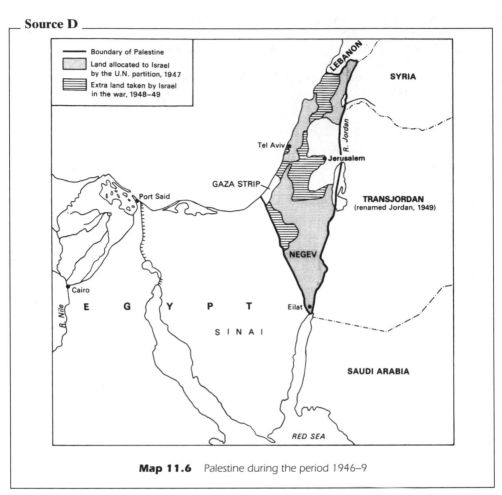

Map 11.6 Palestine during the period 1946–9

Source: D. Heater, *Our World This Century* (Oxford, 1987)

Source E

Announcement by Faris el-Khoury Bey, leader of the Syrian delegation to the Conference on Palestine, 4 February 1947

Speaking on behalf of all the Arab states and the Arabs of Palestine, I have to tell you that we can enter no discussions involving any scheme for the partitioning of Palestine or providing for the setting up in that country of a Jewish state.

Sources A, B, C and E are all taken from *Keesing's Contemporary Archives for 1946 and 1947*

Source F

The view of two British historians

Bevin had done his best, in his opinion, to sort the situation out, and if his efforts had ended in failure, the fault was certainly not his and the British government's. The only policy left to Britain was to get out. He expected the Arabs to win the war which everyone knew was close, but his main concern was that Britain should not become involved.

Source: A. Sked and C. Cook, *Post-War Britain* (Penguin, 1979)

(a) In Source A, Bevin gives three possible alternatives which the UN could choose for the future of Palestine. From the evidence in the source, which alternative do you think Bevin and the British government wanted? Explain your answer.   1.6c–7c, 3.3   3 marks
(b) Source B shows that Truman wanted a Jewish state in Palestine. Do Sources C and E prove that he was wrong to want a Jewish state?   1.4c–8c, 3.4   4 marks
(c) 'Sources A, B, C and E were all written during the crisis over the future of Palestine; therefore they are all very reliable and useful as evidence'. Explain whether you agree or disagree with this statement.   3.5–10   4 marks
(d) Source D tells us that 'Bevin expected the Arabs to win the war'. Does Source D (the map) show that Bevin was right in his expectations?   3.3.   3 marks
(e) Source F says that Bevin thought that it was not his fault or the fault of the British government if he had failed to sort out the problems of Palestine. Does the evidence of the other Sources support Bevin's claim or not?
1.4b–6b, 4c–8c, 3.4   11 marks

Total: 25 marks

3   *Civil war in the Lebanon, 1975*   In 1975 civil war developed between Muslims, supported by Palestinians, on one side, and various Christian groups, including the Phalangists, on the other side. Both sides blamed each other for the escalating violence.

Study Sources A and B and then answer the questions which follow.

__ **Source A** _____

Statement by Yasser Arafat, leader of the Palestinian Liberation Organization (PLO), 1975

Phalangists seized a Palestinian vehicle in the Beirut suburb of Ain Rumaneh [a Christian area] and killed the driver. Then armed Phalangists on April 13th ambushed a bus returning a group of Palestinians to Tal Zataar camp as it passed through Ain Rumaneh. 27 men, women and children were martyred, and a large number wounded. This bloody massacre against an unarmed people is a plot carried out in co-ordination with Jewish supporters.

__ **Source B** _____

Statement by a Phalangist spokesman, 1975

Fighting started when Palestinian guerrillas opened fire from a car on a church in Ain Rumaneh in which Mr Gemayel [a Christian leader] was attending Mass. Three people were killed. Then Palestinian reinforcements arrived by bus and there was a shoot-out between the guerrillas and the [Christian] population of the area.

Sources A and B are from *Keesing's Contemporary Archives for 1975*

(a) In what ways do Sources A and B disagree with each other?   3.4   4 marks
(b) How can you explain these differences?   1.6c–8c   3 marks

(c) 'Sources which contradict each other, like Sources A and B, can be of no value to the historian'. Explain whether you agree or disagree with this statement.

3.5–9   4 marks

(d) 'The presence of the Palestinians in the Lebanon inflamed an already delicate situation'.

    (i)   Using information from Sections 11.2(c) and 11.8, explain why the Palestinians were in the Lebanon in the first place.

1.4b–5b, 4c–5c   4 marks

    (ii)   Using evidence from Section 11.8(a) and the sources, explain whether you agree or disagree with the statement.   1.4b–7b, 4c–7c, 3.4   4 marks

(e) What political changes and developments took place which enabled law and order to be gradually restored in the Lebanon in the early 1990s?

1.4a–5a, 4c–5c   6 marks

Total: 25 marks

PART II

The rise of fascism and governments of the right

12 Italy 1918–45: the first appearance of fascism

Summary of events

The unification of Italy was only completed in 1870, and the new state suffered from economic and political weaknesses. The First World War was a great strain on her economy, and there was bitter disappointment at her treatment by the Versailles settlement. Between 1919 and 1922 there were five different governments, all of which were incapable of taking the decisive action that the situation demanded. In 1919 *Benito Mussolini founded the Italian fascist party*, which won 35 seats in the 1921 elections. At the same time there seemed to be a real danger of a left-wing revolution; in an atmosphere of strikes and riots, the fascists staged a 'march on Rome' which culminated in King Victor Emmanuel inviting Mussolini to form a government (October 1922); he remained in power until July 1943. Gradually Mussolini took on the powers of a dictator and attempted to control the entire way of life of the Italian people. At first it seemed as though his authoritarian regime might bring lasting benefits to Italy, and he won popularity with his adventurous and successful foreign policy (see Section 5.2). Later he made the fatal mistake of entering the Second World War on the side of Germany (June 1940) even though he knew Italy could not afford involvement in another war. After the Italians suffered defeats by the British, who captured her African possessions and occupied Sicily, they turned against Mussolini. He was deposed and arrested (July 1943), but was rescued by the Germans (September) and set up as ruler in northern Italy, backed by German troops. In April 1945, as British and American troops advanced northwards through Italy towards Milan, Mussolini tried to escape to Switzerland but was captured and shot dead by his Italian enemies (known as partisans).

12.1 Why was Mussolini able to come to power?

(a) *Disillusionment and frustration*

There was a general atmosphere of disillusionment and frustration in Italy by the summer of 1919, caused by a combination of factors.

1 Disappointment at Italy's gains from the peace settlement

When she entered the war the Allies had promised her Trentino, the south Tyrol, Istria, Trieste, part of Dalmatia, Adalia, some Aegean islands, and a protectorate over Albania. Although she was given the first four areas, the rest were awarded to other states, mainly Yugoslavia; Albania was to be independent. The Italians felt cheated in view of their valiant efforts during the war and the loss of close on 700 000 men. Particularly irritating was their failure to get Fiume (given to Yugoslavia), though in fact this was not one of the areas which had been promised to them. Gabriele D'Annunzio, a famous romantic poet, marched with a few hundred supporters and occupied Fiume before the Yugoslavs had time to take it. Some army units deserted and supported D'Annunzio, providing him with arms and ammunition, and he began to have hopes of overthrowing the government. However, in June 1920, after D'Annunzio had held out in Fiume for 15 months, the new Prime Minister, Giovanni Giolitti, decided that the government's authority must be restored. He ordered the army to remove D'Annunzio from Fiume – a risky move since he was viewed as a national hero. The army obeyed orders and D'Annunzio surrendered without a fight, but it left the government highly unpopular.

2 The economic effects of the war

The effects of the war on the economy and the standard of living were disastrous. The government had borrowed heavily, especially from the USA, and these debts now had to be repaid. As the lira declined in value (from 5 lire to the dollar in 1914 to 28 lire to the dollar in 1921) the cost of living increased accordingly by at least five times. There was massive unemployment as heavy industry cut back its wartime production levels, and 2.5 million ex-servicemen had difficulty finding jobs.

3 Growing contempt for the parliamentary system

Votes for all men and proportional representation were introduced for the 1919 elections. Although this gave a fairer representation than under the previous system, it meant that there was a large number of parties in parliament. After the election of May 1921, for example, there were at least nine parties represented, including liberals, nationalists, socialists, communists, Catholic popular party and fascists (see question 3 at the end of the chapter). This made it difficult for any one party to gain an overall majority, and coalition governments were inevitable. No consistent policy was possible as five different cabinets with shaky majorities came and went. There was growing impatience with a system which seemed designed to prevent decisive government.

(b) *A wave of strikes, 1919 and 1920*

These were accompanied by rioting, looting of shops and occupation of factories by workers. In Turin, factory councils reminiscent of the Russian soviets (see Section 15.2(c)(ii)) were appearing. In the south, socialist leagues of farm workers seized land from wealthy landowners and set up co-operatives. The government's prestige sank even lower because of its failure to protect property; many property-owners were convinced that a left-wing revolution was at hand, especially when the Italian communist party was formed in January 1921. But in fact the chances of revolution were receding by then: the strikes and factory occupations were fizzling out, because although workers tried to maintain production, claiming control of the factories, it proved impossible (suppliers refused them raw materials and they needed engineers and managers).

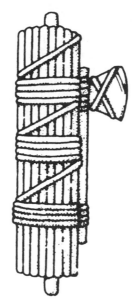

Figure 12.1 The Fascist Symbol

Source: Christopher Culpin, *Making History* (Collins Educational) p. 50

Although the formation of the communist party made a revolution less likely (because it split the forces of the left), the fear of a revolution remained strong.

(c) *Mussolini attracted widespread support*

Mussolini and the fascist party were attractive to many sections of society because, as he himself said, he aimed to rescue Italy from feeble government. Mussolini (born 1883), the son of a blacksmith in the Romagna, had a varied early career, working for a time as a stonemason's mate and then as a primary school teacher. Politically he was a socialist and began to make a name for himself as a journalist, becoming editor of the socialist newspaper *Avanti*. He fell out with the socialists because they were against Italian intervention in the war, and started his own paper, *Il Popolo d'Italia*. In 1919 he founded the fascist party with a socialist and republican programme, and he showed sympathy with the factory occupations of 1919–20. The local party branches were known as *fasci di combattimento* (fighting groups) – the word *fasces* meant the bundle of rods with protruding axe which used to symbolize the authority and power of the ancient Roman consuls (see Figure 12.1).

As the factory occupations began to fail, Mussolini altered course and came out as the defender of private enterprise and property, thus attracting much needed financial support from wealthy business interests. Beginning in late 1920 black-shirted squads of fascists regularly attacked and burned down local socialist headquarters and newspaper offices and beat up socialist councillors. By the end of 1921, even though his political programme was vague in the extreme, he had gained the support of property-owners in general, because they saw him as a guarantee of law and order (especially after the formation of the communist party in January 1921). Having won over big business, Mussolini began to make conciliatory speeches about the Roman Catholic Church (which he had earlier criticized); Pope Pius XI swung the Church into line behind Mussolini, seeing him as a good anti-communist weapon. When Mussolini announced that he had dropped the republican part of his programme (September 1922), even the king began to look more favourably on the fascists.

(d) *Lack of effective opposition*

The anti-fascist groups failed to co-operate with each other and made no determined efforts to keep the fascists out. The communists refused to co-operate with the socialists, and Giolitti (Prime Minister from June 1920 to July 1921) held the elections of May 1921 so that the fascists, still unrepresented in parliament, could win some seats and then support his government. He was willing to overlook their violence in the hope that they would become more responsible once they were in parliament. However, they won only 35 seats whereas the socialists had 123, so there should have been no question of a fascist takeover, though the number of fascist squads throughout the country was increasing rapidly. The socialists must take much of the blame for refusing to work with the government to curb fascist violence; a coalition of Giolitti's nationalist bloc and the socialists could have made a reasonably stable government, thus keeping the fascists out. But the socialists would not co-operate and this caused Giolitti to resign in despair. The socialists tried to use the situation to their own advantage by calling a general strike in the summer of 1922.

(e) *The attempted general strike, summer 1922*

This played into the hands of the fascists, who were able to use it to their advantage by announcing that if the government failed to quell the strike, they would crush it themselves. When the strike failed through lack of support, Mussolini was able to pose as *the saviour of the nation from communism*, and by October 1922 the fascists felt confident enough to stage their 'march on Rome'. As about 50 000 blackshirts converged on the capital, while others occupied important towns in the north, the Prime Minister, Luigi Facta, was prepared to resist. But King Victor Emmanuel III refused to declare a state of emergency and instead, invited Mussolini, who had remained nervously in Milan, to come to Rome and form a new government, which he obligingly did, arriving by train. Afterwards the fascists fostered the myth that they had seized power heroically, but it had been achieved legally by the mere threat of force, while the army and the police stood aside (Illus. 12.1).

The role of the king was important: he made the crucial decision not to use the army to stop the blackshirts, though many historians believe that the regular army would have had little difficulty in dispersing the disorderly and poorly armed squads, many of which arrived by train. The march was an enormous bluff which came off. The reasons why the king decided against armed resistance remain something of a mystery, since he was apparently reluctant to discuss them. Suggestions include:

- lack of confidence in Facta;
- doubts about whether the army with its fascist sympathies could be relied on to obey orders; and
- fears of a long civil war if it failed to crush the fascists quickly.

There is no doubt that he had a certain amount of sympathy with the fascist aim of providing strong government and was also afraid that some of the generals might force him to abdicate in favour of his cousin, the Duke of Aosta, who openly supported the fascists. Whatever the king's motives, the outcome was clear: Mussolini became the first ever fascist premier in history.

Illus. 12.1   Mussolini and supporters soon after the March on Rome

12.2 What did the term 'fascism' stand for?

It is important to try to define what the term 'fascist' stood for, because it was later applied to other regimes and rulers such as Hitler, Franco (Spain), Salazar (Portugal) and Peron (Argentina) which were sometimes quite different from the Italian version of fascism. Nowadays there is a tendency among the left to label as 'fascist' anybody who holds right-wing views. The fact that fascism never produced a great theoretical writer who could explain its philosophies clearly in the way that Marx did for communism makes it difficult to pin down exactly what was involved. Mussolini's constantly changing aims before 1923 suggest that his main concern was simply to acquire power; after that he seems to have improvised his ideas as he went along. After a few years it emerged that fascism as Mussolini tried to put it into practice did involve certain basic principles:

● *Extreme nationalism:* an emphasis on the rebirth of the nation after a period of decline; building up the greatness and prestige of the state, with the implication that one's own nation is superior to all others.
● A *totalitarian system of government* – that is, a complete way of life in which the government attempted to arouse and mobilize the great mass of ordinary people, to control and organize, with strong discipline, as many aspects of people's lives as possible. This was necessary to promote the greatness of the state, which was more important than the interests of the individual.
● A *one-party state was essential:* there was no place for democracy. Fascism was especially hostile to communism, which explains much of its popularity. The fascist party members were the élite of the nation, and great emphasis was placed on the cult of the leader/hero who would win mass support with thrilling speeches and skilful propaganda.
● *Economic self-sufficiency (autarchy)* was vitally important in developing the

greatness of the state; the government must therefore direct the economic life of the nation (though not in the Marxist sense of the state owning factories and land).

- *Military strength and violence* were an integral part of the way of life. Mussolini himself remarked, 'Peace is absurd: fascism does not believe in it'. Hence they fostered the myth that they had seized power by force, they allowed the violent treatment of opponents and critics, and they pursued an aggressive foreign policy.

12.3 Mussolini introduces the fascist state

There was no sudden change in the system of government and state institutions; Mussolini was merely the Prime Minister of a coalition cabinet in which only four out of twelve ministers were fascists, and he had to move cautiously. However, the king had given him special powers to last until the end of 1923 to deal with the crisis. *The Acerbo Law (November 1923)* changed the rules of general elections. From now on the party which got most votes in a general election would automatically be given two-thirds of the seats in parliament. As a result of the next election (April 1924) the fascists and their supporters came out with 404 seats while the opposition parties could manage only 107. The right-wing success can be explained by the general desire for a strong government which would put the country back on its feet again, after the weak minority governments of the preceding years. Beginning in the summer of 1924, by a mixture of violence and intimidation, and helped by divisions among his opponents, Mussolini gradually developed Italian government and society along fascist lines. At the same time he consolidated his own hold over the country, which was largely complete by 1930.

(a) *All parties except the fascists were suppressed*

Persistent opponents of the regime were either exiled or murdered, the most notorious cases being those of the socialists Giacomo Matteotti and Giovanni Amendola, both of whom were beaten to death by fascist thugs. However, the Italian system was never as brutal as the Nazi regime in Germany, and after 1926 when Mussolini felt more secure, violence was much reduced. *Further changes in the constitution included:*

- the Prime Minister (Mussolini) was responsible only to the king, not to parliament (1925);
- the Prime Minister could rule by decree, which meant that new laws did not need to be discussed by parliament (1926);
- the electorate was reduced from about 10 million to 3 million (the wealthiest).

Although parliament still met, all important decisions were taken by the Fascist Grand Council which always did as Mussolini told it. In effect Mussolini, who adopted the title *Il Duce* (the leader), was a dictator.

(b) *Changes in local government*

Elected town councils and mayors were abolished and towns were run by officials appointed from Rome. In practice the local fascist party bosses (known as *ras*) often had as much power as the government officials.

(c) Censorship

A strict press censorship was enforced in which anti-fascist newspapers and magazines were either banned or their editors replaced by fascist supporters. Radio, films and the theatre were controlled in the same way.

(d) Education supervised

Education in schools and universities was closely supervised. Teachers had to wear uniforms, and new textbooks were written to glorify the fascist system. Children were encouraged to criticize teachers who seemed to lack enthusiasm for the party. Children and young people were forced to join the government youth organizations which indoctrinated them with the brilliance of the *Duce* and the glories of war. The other main message was total obedience to authority, which was necessary because everything was seen in terms of struggle – 'Believe, Obey, Fight!'.

(e) Employment policies

The government tried to promote co-operation between employers and workers and to end class warfare in what was known as the *Corporate State*. Fascist-controlled unions had the sole right to negotiate for the workers, and both unions and employers' associations were organized into corporations, and were expected to work together to settle disputes over pay and working conditions. Strikes and lockouts were not allowed. By 1934 there were twenty-two corporations each dealing with a separate industry, and in this way Mussolini hoped to control workers and direct production and the economy. To compensate for their loss of freedom, workers were assured of such benefits as free Sundays, annual holidays with pay, social security, sports and theatre facilities and cheap tours and holidays.

(f) An understanding was reached with the Pope

The Papacy had been hostile to the Italian government since 1870, when all the territory belonging to the Papacy (Papal States) had been incorporated in the new kingdom of Italy. Though he had been sympathetic towards Mussolini in 1922, Pope Pius XI disapproved of the increasing totalitarianism of fascist government (the fascist youth organizations, for example, clashed with the Catholic scouts). Mussolini, who was probably an atheist himself, was nevertheless well aware of the power of the Roman Catholic Church, and he put himself out to win over Pius who, as the Duce well knew, was obsessed with the fear of communism. The result was the *Lateran Treaty (1929)*, by which Italy recognized the Vatican City as a sovereign state, paid the Pope a large sum of money as compensation for all his losses, accepted the Catholic faith as the official state religion, and made religious instruction compulsory in all schools. In return the Papacy recognized the kingdom of Italy. *Some historians see the ending of the long breach between church and state as Mussolini's most lasting and worthwhile achievement.*

> **How totalitarian was Mussolini's system?**
>
> It seems clear that in spite of his efforts Mussolini did not succeed in creating a completely totalitarian system in the fascist sense of there being 'no individuals or groups not controlled by the state', nor like the Nazis did in Germany. He

> never completely eliminated the influence of the king or the
> Pope, and the latter became highly critical of Mussolini when
> he began to persecute Jews in the later 1930s. The historian
> and philosopher Benedetto Croce and other university pro-
> fessors were constant critics of fascism and yet they survived,
> apparently because Mussolini was afraid of hostile foreign
> reaction if he had them arrested. Even fascist sympathizers
> admitted that the corporative system was not a success in
> controlling production. According to historian Elizabeth
> Wiskemann, 'on the whole the big industrialists only made
> gestures of submission and in fact bought their freedom from
> the fascist state by generous subscriptions to fascist party
> funds'. As far as the mass of the population was concerned, it
> seems that they were prepared to tolerate fascism while it
> appeared to bring benefits, but soon grew tired of it when its

12.4 What benefits did fascism bring for the Italians?

What really mattered to ordinary people was whether the regime's policies were effective or not. Did Mussolini rescue Italy from weak government as he had promised, or
was he, as some of his critics alleged at the time, just a windbag whose government was
just as corrupt and inefficient as previous ones?

(a) *A promising beginning*

Much of fascist policy was concerned with the economy, though Mussolini knew very
little about economics. The big drive was for self-sufficiency, which was thought to be
essential for a 'warrior-nation'. The early years seemed to be successful, or so the
government propaganda told people.

1   *Industry was encouraged* with government subsidies where necessary, so that iron
    and steel production doubled by 1930 and artificial silk production increased
    tenfold. By 1937 production of hydro-electric power had doubled.
2   The '*Battle of Wheat*' encouraged farmers to concentrate on wheat production as
    part of the drive for self-sufficiency; by 1935 wheat imports had been cut by 75 per
    cent.
3   *A programme of land reclamation was launched*, involving draining marshes,
    irrigating, and planting forests in mountainous areas, again as part of the drive to
    improve and increase agricultural yield. The great showpiece was the reclaimed
    Pontine Marshes near Rome.
4   *An impressive public works programme* was designed, among other things to
    reduce unemployment. It included the building of motorways, bridges, blocks of
    flats, railway stations, sports stadiums, schools, and new towns on reclaimed land; a
    start was made on electrifying main railway lines, and the great fascist boast was
    that Mussolini had made the trains run on time. Even sportsmen did well under
    fascism – the Italian soccer team won the World Cup twice – in 1934 and 1938!

5	*The 'after-work'* (Dopolavoro) *organization* provided the Italian people with things to do in their leisure time. There were cheap holidays, tours and cruises, and *Dopolavoro* also controlled theatres, dramatic societies, libraries, orchestras, brass bands and sporting organizations.
6	To promote the image of Italy as a great power, a virile foreign policy was carried out (see Section 5.2).

However, the promise of the early years of Mussolini's rule was in many ways never fulfilled.

(b) *Unsolved problems*

Even before Italy became involved in the Second World War, it was clear that fascism had not solved many of her problems.

1	*Little had been done to remedy her basic shortage of raw materials* – coal and oil – and much more effort could have been made to develop hydro-electric power. As an iron and steel producer Italy could not even match a small state like Belgium (see Table 12.1).

Table 12.1	Iron and steel output (in million tons)

	Iron			*Steel*		
	1918	1930	1940	1918	1930	1940
Italy	0.3	0.5	1.0	0.3	0.5	1.0
Belgium	—	3.4	1.8	—	3.4	1.9
Germany	11.9	9.7	13.9	15.0	11.5	19.0
USA	39.7	32.3	43.0	45.2	41.4	60.8

2	*Although the 'Battle of Wheat' was a victory, it was achieved only at the expense of dairy and arable farming*, whose output fell; the climate in the south is much better suited to grazing and orchards than growing wheat and this would have been much more lucrative for the farmers. As a result, agriculture remained inefficient and farm labourers the poorest class in the country. Their wages fell by between 20 and 40 per cent during the 1930s. Italy still had what is known as a 'dualist economy' – the north was industrial and reasonably prosperous, while the south was largely agricultural, backward and poverty-stricken. The attempt at self-sufficiency had been a dismal failure.
3	*Mussolini revalued the lira far too high* at 90 to the pound instead of 150 (1926), in an attempt to show that Italy had a strong currency. Unfortunately this made Italian exports more expensive on the world market and led to reduced orders, especially in the cotton industry. Many factories were on a three-day week and workers suffered wage reductions of between 10 and 20 per cent – *before* the world economic crisis which started in 1929.
4	*The great depression which began in 1929 with the Wall Street Crash in the USA (see Section 19.4) made matters worse.* Exports fell further, unemployment rose to 1.1 million, yet the Duce refused to devalue the lira until 1936. Instead wages and salaries were cut, and although the cost of living was falling because of the

depression, wages fell more than prices, so that workers suffered a fall of over 10 per cent in real wages. Particularly annoying for industrial workers was that they had no way of protesting, since strikes were illegal and the unions weak.

5 *Another failing of the regime was in social services*, where there was nothing approaching a 'welfare state'. There was no official government health insurance until 1943, and only an inadequate unemployment insurance scheme, which was not improved even during the depression.

6 *The regime was inefficient and corrupt*, so that many of its policies were not carried out. For example, in spite of all the publicity about the land reclamation, only about one-tenth of the programme had been carried out by 1939 and work was at a standstill even before the war began. Immense sums of money disappeared into the pockets of corrupt officials. Part of the problem was that Mussolini tried increasingly to do everything himself; he refused to delegate because he wanted total control. But it was impossible for one man to do so much, and it placed an intolerable burden on him. According to his biographer, Dennis Mack Smith:

> by trying to control everything, he ended by controlling very little ... although he gave out a constant stream of orders, he had no way of checking that they were carried out. As officials knew this, they often only pretended to obey, and took no action at all.

12.5 Opposition and downfall

The conclusion probably has to be that after the first flush of enthusiasm for Mussolini and his new ideas, the average Italian can have felt little benefit from the regime, and disenchantment had probably set in long before the Second World War started. And yet there was not a great deal of serious opposition to him. This was partly because it was difficult to have an organized opposition in parliament, and there were heavy punishments for opponents and critics; and partly because the Italians have a tradition of accepting whatever happens politically with a minimum of fuss and lots of resignation. The government continued to control the media which kept on telling people that Mussolini was a hero (Illus. 12.2).

(a) *So why was Mussolini eventually overthrown?*

• *Entry into the war was a disastrous mistake.* The majority of Italians were against it: they already disapproved when Mussolini began to sack Jews from important jobs (1938) and felt that Italy was becoming a German satellite. Economically Italy was incapable of waging a major war; the army was equipped with obsolete rifles and artillery; there were only a thousand planes and no heavy tanks. His declaration of war on the USA (December 1941) horrified many of his right-wing supporters (such as industrialists and bankers), who resented the closer economic controls which wartime brought.

• *The general public suffered hardships.* Taxes were increased to pay for the war, there was food rationing, massive inflation and a 30 per cent fall in real wages. After November 1942 there were British bombing raids on major cities. By March 1943 unrest showed itself in strikes in Milan and Turin, the first since 1922.

• After a few early successes, *the Italians suffered a string of defeats* culminating in the surrender of all Italian troops in North Africa (May 1943).

• *Mussolini seemed to have lost his touch.* He was suffering from a stomach ulcer and nervous strain, and all he could think of was to sack some of the ministers who had

Illus. 12.2   Mussolini addressing a crowd

criticized him. Breaking point came with the Allied capture of Sicily (July 1943). Many of the fascist leaders themselves realized the lunacy of trying to continue the war, but Mussolini refused to make peace because that would mean deserting Hitler. The Fascist Grand Council turned against Mussolini and the king dismissed him. Nobody lifted a finger to save him, and fascism disappeared.

(b) *Verdict on Italian fascism*

This is still a very controversial topic in Italy where memories of personal experiences are strong. Broadly speaking *there are two interpretations of the fascist era:*

1   it was a temporary aberration (a departure from normal development) in Italian history, the work solely of Mussolini; historian A. Cassels calls it 'a gigantic confidence trick perpetrated on the Italian nation by Benito Mussolini – an artificial creation of Mussolini';
2   fascism grew naturally from Italian history; the environment and the circumstances shaped the rise and success of fascism, not the reverse.

Most historians now accept the second theory, that the roots of fascism lay in traditional Italian society and the movement grew to fruition in the circumstances after the Second World War. The Italian historian Renzo de Felice argues that fascism was primarily a movement of 'an emerging middle class' which was keen to challenge the traditional, liberal, ruling class for power. He claims that the movement achieved a great deal – especially the modernizing of Italy's economy, which was very backward in 1918. On the other hand, British historian Martin Blinkhorn does not accept this claim about the economy and argues that de Felice has not paid enough attention to 'the negative and brutal side of fascism'. Another historian, Elizabeth Wiskemann, claims that the only achievements of fascism remaining at the end of the war were the agreements with the Pope and the public works, and even they could have been achieved just as well by a democratic government.

Questions

1   Section 12.1 looked at the various causes of Mussolini's rise to power in Italy.

   (a)   Divide the causes up into different types – political, economic, religious, social.

                                                    1.4b–5b

   (b)   Describe what connections you have noticed between the various causes.   1.7b

   (c)   Arrange the causes in a list, putting the most important ones at the top and the least important at the bottom.   1.6b–8a

2   *Mussolini and fascism*   Study Sources A to G and then answer the questions which follow.

Source A

Extract from Mussolini's Autobiography, published in 1928

Instead of the old trade unions we substituted Fascist corporations ... We have solved a series of problems of no little importance: we have abolished all the perennial troubles and disorder and doubt that poisoned our national soul. We have given a rhythm, a law and a protection to work: we have found in the collaboration of classes the reason for our possibilities, for our future power. We do not lose time in troubles, in strikes, which, while they vex the spirit, imperil our own strength and the solidarity of our economy.

Source B

Extract from Mussolini's book The Doctrine of Fascism *(1941)*

Fascism stands for liberty and for the only liberty worth having, the liberty of the State and of the individual within the State. The Fascist conception of the State is all-embracing: outside it no human or spiritual values may exist, much less have any value. Fascism is totalitarian and the Fascist state interprets, develops and lends additional power to the whole life of the people.

   Fascism, in short, is not only a law-giver and a founder of institutions, but is an educator and a promoter of spiritual life. It does not merely aim at remoulding the forms of life, but also their content, man, his character and his faith. To achieve this purpose it enforces discipline and makes use of authority, entering into the mind and ruling with undisputed sway.

Sources: A and B are quoted in D. Gregory, *Mussolini and the Fascist Era* (Arnold, 1968)

A British cartoon in Punch, *January 1925 (Figure 12.2)*

PUNCH. OR THE LONDON CHARIVARI.—JANUARY 14, 1925.

A "SIEGE PERILOUS."

THE VOLCANO (*to Signor MUSSOLINI, who is trying to suppress its activities*). "THIS WILL HURT YOU MORE THAN IT HURTS ME

Extract from a letter written by Pope Pius XI, to be read in all Roman Catholic churches (29 June 1931)

A conception of the State which makes the rising generations belong to it entirely, without any exception, from the tenderest years up to adult life, cannot be reconciled by a Catholic either with Catholic doctrine or with the natural rights of the family. It is not possible for a Catholic to accept the claim that the Church and the Pope must limit themselves to the external practices of religion (such as Mass and the Sacraments) and that all the rest of education belongs to the State ...

Source: quoted in D. Gregory, *Mussolini and the Fascist Era* (Arnold, 1968)

Source E

British historian Dennis Mack Smith writes about the murder of Matteotti, the socialist leader

Matteotti was killed because he tried to have the election (of 1924) declared invalid. He made a short but courageous speech that was noisily interrupted a hundred times in a concerted attempt to silence him. Mussolini could not contain his anger as the socialist leader spelt out in detail how the election had only been won by fraud and violence, and how only a minority of electors had been able to vote freely. Mussolini was provoked to reply that he would have taken no account of the vote if it had gone against him.

Source: D. Mack Smith, *Mussolini* (Paladin Books, 1983)

Source F

Italian historian and liberal politician, Benedetto Croce (who became a member of the government in 1944 after the overthrow of Mussolini) gives his view of fascism (in 1944)

Fascism was an interruption in Italy's achievement of ever greater 'freedom', a short-term moral infection. Since the turn of the century, the liberal 'sense of freedom' was debased by materialism, nationalism and a growing admiration for 'heroic' figures. The masses and the liberal politicians were easily manipulated by a minority of fascist hooligans.

Source G

Italian historian Renzo de Felice gives his view of fascism (1977)

The fascist movement was mainly one of an emerging middle class eager to challenge the traditional, liberal political class for power. The spirit of this new middle class was vital, optimistic and creative; it was, in fact, a revolutionary phenomenon. However, the only way Mussolini was able to get to power was with help from the conservatives, and he was unfortunately always dependent on them afterwards. He was therefore never able to achieve the full aims of Fascism – to revolutionise Italy by transforming it into a totalitarian, corporative society.

Sources: Sources F and G are summarized briefly in M. Blinkhorn, *Mussolini and Fascist Italy* (Methuen, 1984)

(a) (i)   Sources A and B were both written by Mussolini. What contradictions
          can you find in the two sets of writings?   1.4c–6c   3 marks
    (ii) What explanations can you suggest as to why Mussolini might be
          thought to be contradicting himself?   1.7c–8c   3 marks

(b) In Source B Mussolini writes: 'Fascism stands for liberty . . . of the individual
    within the state'. How useful are Sources C, D and E in helping the historian
    to decide whether or not this was true?   3.4–6   7 marks

(c) Sources F and G give the views of two Italian historians about Fascism in Italy.
    What reasons can you suggest for such widely differing views of the same
    system?   1.6c–7c, 9b; 2.4–6, 9   5 marks

(d) Using the evidence in Sources E to G and Chapter 12, explain which of the
    two interpretations of fascism you find the more convincing.
                                                    2.6–10, 3.7, 10   12 marks

Total: 30 marks

3   Study the election statistics below carefully, together with the information in
    Section 12.1(d), and then answer the questions which follow.

Results of the general election held on 15 May 1921

Extreme Nationalists	10		
Fascists	35	184	Government bloc (right wing)
National Bloc (Giolitti)	139		
Radicals (Liberal Democrats)	68	175	Possible opposition group
Popolari (Catholic party)	107		from parties in the centre
Reformists	29		
Socialists	123		
Communists	15	176	Left-wing opposition
National minorities	9		

(a) What evidence do these statistics give you about how strong and how
    influential the fascists were in the parliament which met after the election?
                                                           1.4c–5c   5 marks

(b) After the election, Giovanni Giolitti served as Prime Minister of the right-
    wing coalition government from May to July 1921. From the evidence of these
    statistics and Section 12.1(d), explain what some his difficulties would have
    been.   1.4c–5c   5 marks

(c) Explain how it happened that Mussolini and the fascists, in spite of having
    only 35 seats in parliament, were able to come to power in October 1922.
                                                           1.4b–9a   10 marks

Total: 20 marks

Germany 1918–45: the Weimar Republic and Hitler

Summary of events

As Germany moved towards defeat in 1918, public opinion turned against the government, and in October, the *Kaiser*, in a desperate bid to hang on to power, appointed Prince Max of Baden as Chancellor. He was known to be in favour of a more democratic form of government in which parliament had more power. But it was too late: in November revolution broke out, the *Kaiser* escaped to Holland and abdicated, and Prince Max resigned. Friedrich Ebert, leader of the left-wing Social Democrat party, became head of the government. In January 1919 a general election was held, the first completely democratic one ever to take place in Germany. The Social Democrats emerged as the largest single party and Ebert became first President of the Republic. They had some Marxist ideas but believed that the way to achieve socialism was through parliamentary democracy.

The new government was by no means popular with all Germans: even before the elections the communists had attempted to seize power in the *Spartacist Rising (January 1919)*. In 1920 right-wing enemies of the republic occupied Berlin (the *Kapp Putsch*). The government managed to survive these threats and several later ones, including *Hitler's Munich Beer Hall Putsch (1923)*.

By the end of 1919 a new constitution had been agreed by the National Assembly (parliament), which was meeting at Weimar because Berlin was still torn by political unrest. This Weimar constitution (sometimes called the most perfect democratic constitution of modern times, at least on paper), gave its name to the *Weimar Republic* and lasted until 1933, when it was destroyed by Hitler. It passed through three phases:

1 *1919 to the end of 1923* – a period of instability when the republic was struggling to survive;
2 *from the end of 1923 to the end of 1929*, when Gustav Stresemann was the leading politician. Thanks to the *Dawes Plan of 1924*, by which the USA provided huge loans, Germany seemed to be recovering from her defeat and was enjoying an industrial boom;
3 *October 1929 to January 1933* – instability again; the world economic crisis, beginning with the Wall Street Crash in October 1929, soon had disastrous effects on Germany, producing 6.5 million unemployed. The government was unable to cope with the situation and by the end of 1932 the Weimar Republic seemed on the verge of collapse.

Meanwhile Adolf Hitler and his National Socialists (Nazis) had been carrying out a great propaganda campaign blaming the government for all the ills of Germany, and setting out Nazi solutions to the problems. In January 1933 President Hindenburg appointed Hitler as Chancellor, and soon afterwards Hitler saw to it that democracy ceased to exist; the Weimar Republic was at an end, and from then until April 1945, Hitler was the dictator of Germany. Only defeat in the Second World War and the death of Hitler (30 April 1945) freed the German people from the Nazi tyranny.

13.1 Why did the Weimar Republic collapse?

(a) *It had a number of disadvantages*

These hampered it from the beginning.

1   *It had accepted the humiliating and unpopular Versailles Treaty* (see Section 2.8), with its arms limitations, reparations and war guilt clause, and was therefore always associated with defeat and dishonour. German nationalists could never forgive it for that.

2   *There was a traditional lack of respect for democratic government* and a great admiration for the army and the 'officer class' as the rightful leaders of Germany. In 1919 the view was widespread that the army had not been defeated: it had been betrayed – 'stabbed in the back' – by the democrats who had needlessly agreed to the Versailles Treaty. What most Germans did not realize was that it was General Ludendorff who had asked for an armistice while the *Kaiser* was still in power (see Section 2.6(b)). However, the 'stab in the back' legend was eagerly fostered by all enemies of the republic.

3   *The parliamentary system introduced in the new Weimar constitution had weaknesses*, the most serious of which was that it was based on a system of proportional representation, so that all political groups would have a fair representation. Unfortunately there were so many different groups that no party could ever win an overall majority. For example, in 1928 the *Reichstag* (lower house of parliament) contained at least eight groups of which the largest were the Social Democrats (153), nationalists (conservatives – 78) and the Catholic Centre Party (62). The communists had 54 seats, while the smallest groups were the Bavarian People's Party (16) and the National Socialists (12). A succession of coalition governments was inevitable, with the Social Democrats having to rely on co-operation from left-wing liberals and the Catholic Centre. No party was able to carry out its programme.

4   *The political parties had very little experience of how to operate a democratic parliamentary system*, because before 1919 the *Reichstag* had not controlled policy; the Chancellor had the final authority and was the one who really ruled the country. Under the Weimar constitution it was the other way round – the Chancellor was responsible to the *Reichstag*, which had the final say. However, the *Reichstag* usually failed to give a clear lead because the parties refused to compromise. The communists and nationalists did not believe in the republic anyway and refused to support the Social Democrats. Disagreements became so bitter that some of the parties organized their own private armies, for self-defence to begin with, but this increased the threat of civil war. The combination of these weaknesses led to more outbreaks of violence and attempts to overthrow the republic.

(b) *Outbreaks of violence*

The government seemed incapable of preventing these.

1   The Spartacist Rising

In January 1919 the Spartacist Rising occurred (Spartacus was a Roman who led a revolt of slaves in 71 BC), in which the communists, inspired by the success of the Russian Revolution and led by Karl Liebknecht and Rosa Luxemburg, occupied almost every major city in Germany. In Berlin, President Ebert found himself beseiged in the Chancellery. The government managed to defeat the communists only because it accepted the help of the *Freikorps* (independent volunteer regiments raised by anti-communist ex-army officers). It was a sign of the government's weakness that it had to depend on private forces which it did not itself control. The two communist leaders did not receive a fair trial – they were simply clubbed to death by *Freikorps* members.

2   The Kapp Putsch (March 1920)

This was an attempt by right-wing groups to seize power. It was sparked off when the government tried to disband the *Freikorps*. They refused to disband and declared Dr Wolfgang Kapp Chancellor. Berlin was occupied by a *Freikorps* regiment and the cabinet fled to Dresden. The German army (*Reichswehr*) took no action against the *Putsch* (coup or rising) because the generals were in sympathy with the right. In the end the workers of Berlin came to the aid of the Social Democrat government by calling a general strike which paralysed the capital. Kapp resigned and the government regained control. However, it was so weak that nobody was punished except Kapp, who was imprisoned, and it took two months to get the *Freikorps* disbanded. Even then the ex-members remained hostile to the republic and many later joined Hitler's private armies.

3   A series of political assassinations took place

These were mainly carried out by ex-*Freikorps* members. Victims included Walter Rathenau (the Jewish Foreign Minister) and Gustav Erzberger (leader of the armistice delegation). When the government sought strong measures against such acts of terrorism, there was great opposition from the right-wing parties, who sympathized with the criminals. Whereas the communist leaders had been brutally murdered, the courts allowed right-wing offenders off lightly and the government was unable to intervene. In fact throughout Germany the legal and teaching professions, the civil service and the *Reichswehr* tended to be anti-Weimar, which was a crippling handicap for the republic.

4   The Beer Hall Putsch

Another threat to the government occurred in November 1923 in Bavaria, at a time when there was much public annoyance at the French occupation of the Ruhr (see Section 4.2(a)) and the disastrous fall in the value of the mark (see below). Hitler, helped by General Ludendorff, aimed to take control of the Bavarian state government in Munich, and then lead a national revolution to overthrow the government in Berlin. However, the police easily broke up Hitler's march, and the Beer Hall Putsch (so called because the march set out from the Munich beer hall in which Hitler had announced his 'national revolution' the previous evening) soon fizzled out. Hitler was sentenced to five years' imprisonment but served only nine months (because the Bavarian authorities had a lot of sympathy with his aims).

5 The private armies expanded

The violence died down during the years 1924 to 1929 as the republic became more stable, but when unemployment grew in the early 1930s, the private armies expanded and regular street fights occurred between Nazis and communists. All parties had their meetings broken up by rival armies and the police seemed powerless to prevent it happening.

> All this showed that the government was incapable of keeping law and order, and respect for it dwindled. An increasing number of people began to favour a return to strong, authoritarian government, which would maintain strict public order.
>
> Probably the crucial cause of the collapse of the republic was the economy and its weaknesses.

(c) *Economic problems*

The Weimar Republic was constantly plagued by economic problems which the government failed to solve permanently.

1 *In 1919 Germany was close to bankruptcy* because of the enormous expense of the war, which had lasted much longer than most people expected.
2 *Her attempts to pay reparations instalments made matters worse.* In August 1921, after paying the £50 million due, Germany requested permission to suspend payments until her economy recovered. France refused, and in 1922 the Germans claimed they were unable to make the full annual payment.
3 *In January 1923 French troops occupied the Ruhr* (an important German industrial area) in an attempt to seize goods from factories and mines. The German government ordered the workers to follow a policy of passive resistance, and German industry in the Ruhr was paralysed. The French had failed in their aim, but the effect on the German economy was catastrophic – galloping inflation and the collapse of the mark. (See Table 13.1 on p. 270)

The economic situation improved dramatically in the years after 1924, largely thanks to the *Dawes Plan* of that year, which provided an immediate loan from the USA equivalent to £40 million, relaxed the fixed reparations payments and in effect allowed Germany to pay what she could afford. French troops withdrew from the Ruhr. The currency was stabilized, there was a boom in such industries as iron, steel, coal, chemicals and electricals, and wealthy landowners and industrialists were quite happy with the republic, since they were doing well out of it. Germany was even able to pay her reparations instalments under the Dawes Plan.

The work of the Dawes Plan was carried a stage further by the *Young Plan agreed in October 1929*. This reduced the reparations total from £6600 million to £2000 million, to be paid in annual instalments over fifty-nine years. There were other successes for the republic in foreign affairs, thanks to the work of Stresemann (see Section 4.1), and it seemed stable and well-established. But behind this success there was a fatal weakness.

The collapse of the mark

The rate of exchange at the end of the war was 20 marks to the dollar, but even before the Ruhr occupation, reparations difficulties had caused the mark to fall in value. Table 13.1 shows the disastrous decline in the mark:

Table 13.1   The collapse of the mark, 1918–23

Date		Marks required in exchange for £1
November	1918	20
February	1922	1000
June	1922	1500
December	1922	50 000
February	1923	100 000
November	1923	21 000 000 00

Illus. 13.1   Hyper-inflation. Boys making kites out of worthless banknotes in the early 1920s

By November 1923 the value of the mark was falling so rapidly that a worker paid in mark notes had to spend them immediately: if he waited until the following day, his notes would be worthless (Illus. 13.1). It was only when the new Chancellor, Gustav Stresemann, introduced a new currency known as the Rentenmark, in 1924, that the financial situation finally stabilized.

This financial disaster had profound effects on German society: the working classes were badly hit – wages failed to keep pace with inflation and trades union funds were wiped out. Worst affected were the middle classes and small capitalists who lost their savings; many began to look towards the Nazis for improvement. On the other hand landowners and industrialists came out of the crisis well, because they still owned their material wealth – rich farming land, mines and factories. This strengthened the control of big business over the German economy. Some historians have even suggested that the inflation was deliberately engineered by wealthy industrialists with this aim in mind. The accusation is impossible to prove one way or the other, though the currency and the economy did recover remarkably quickly.

4   *The prosperity was much more dependent on the American loans than most people realized.* If the USA were to find herself in financial difficulties so that she stopped the loans, or worse still, wanted them paid back quickly, the German economy would be shaken again. Unfortunately this is exactly what happened in 1929.

5   Following the Wall Street Crash (October 1929), the world economic crisis developed (see Section 19.4). *The USA stopped any further loans and began to call in many of the short-term loans already made to Germany.* This caused a crisis of confidence in the currency and led to a run on the banks, many of which had to close. The industrial boom had led to world-wide over-production, and German exports, along with those of other countries, were severely reduced. Factories had to close, and by the middle of 1931 unemployment was approaching 4 million. Sadly for Germany, Gustav Stresemann, the politician best equipped to deal with the crisis, died of a heart attack in October 1929 at the early age of 51.

6   *To deal with the crisis* the government of Chancellor Brüning (Catholic Centre Party) reduced social services, unemployment benefit, and salaries and pensions of government officials, and stopped reparations payments. High tariffs were introduced to keep out foreign foodstuffs and thus help German farmers, while the government bought shares in factories hit by the slump. However, these measures did not produce quick results, though they did help after a time; unemployment continued to rise and by the spring of 1932 it stood at over 6 million. The government came under criticism from almost all groups in society, especially industrialists and the working class who demanded more decisive action. The loss of much working-class support because of increasing unemployment and the reduction in unemployment benefit, was a serious blow to the republic. *By the end of 1932 the Weimar Republic had thus been brought to the verge of collapse. Even so, it might still have survived if there had been no other alternative.*

(d) *The alternative – Hitler and the Nazis*

Hitler and the Nazi party offered what seemed to be an attractive alternative just when the republic was at its most ineffective. The fortunes of the Nazi party were linked closely to the economic situation: the more unstable the economy, the more seats the Nazis won in the *Reichstag* – see Table 13.2.

Table 13.2 Nazi electoral success and the state of the economy, 1924–32

	Date	Seats	State of the economy
March	1924	32	still unstable after 1923 inflation
December	1924	14	recovering after Dawes Plan
	1928	12	prosperity and stability
	1930	107	unemployment mounting – Nazis second largest party
July	1932	230	massive unemployment – Nazis largest single party
November	1932	196	first signs of economic recovery

There is no doubt that the rise of Hitler and the Nazis, fostered by the economic crisis, was one of the most important causes of the downfall of the republic. (Note that the same causes to some extent explain both the rise of Hitler and the downfall of the republic.)

(e) *What made the Nazis so popular?*

1 *They offered national unity, prosperity and full employment* by ridding Germany of what they claimed were the real causes of the troubles – Marxists, the 'November criminals' (the people who had agreed to the armistice in November 1918 and later the Versailles Treaty), Jesuits, Freemasons and Jews. Great play was made in Nazi propaganda with the 'stab in the back' myth.

2 *They promised to overthrow the Versailles Settlement*, which was so unpopular with most Germans, and to build Germany into a great power again. This would include bringing all Germans (in Austria, Czechoslovakia and Poland) into the *Reich*.

3 *The Nazi private army, the SA (Sturmabteilung – Storm Troopers) was attractive* to young people out of work; it gave them a small wage and a uniform.

4 *Wealthy landowners and industrialists encouraged the Nazis because they feared a communist revolution* and they approved of the Nazi policy of hostility to communists. There is some controversy among historians about how far this support went. Some German Marxist historians claim that from the early 1920s the Nazis were financed by industrialists as an anti-communist force, that Hitler was, in effect, 'a tool of the capitalists'. But historian Joachim Fest believes that the amounts of money involved have been greatly exaggerated, and that though some industrialists were quietly in favour of Hitler becoming Chancellor, it was only *after* he came to power that funds began to flow into the party coffers from big business.

5 *Hitler himself had extraordinary political abilities.* He possessed tremendous energy and will-power and a remarkable gift for public speaking which enabled him to put forward his ideas with great emotional force. Many Germans began to look towards him as some sort of Messiah (saviour) figure (Illus. 13.2). A full version of his views and aims was set out in his book *Mein Kampf* (My Struggle) which he wrote in prison after the *Beer Hall Putsch*.

6 *The striking contrast between the governments of the Weimar Republic and the Nazi party impressed people:* the former were respectable, dull and unable to maintain law and order, the latter promised strong, decisive government and the restoration of national pride – an irresistible combination.

Illus. 13.2 Hitler with a crowd of young admirers

7 *Without the economic crisis though, it is doubtful whether Hitler would have had much chance of attaining power.* It was the widespread unemployment and social misery, together with the fear of communism and socialism, which gained the Nazis mass support, not only among the working class (recent research suggests that between 1928 and 1932 the Nazis attracted over 2 million voters away from the socialist SPD), but also among the lower middle classes – office-workers, shopkeepers, civil servants, teachers and small-scale farmers.

In July 1932 then, the Nazis were the largest single party, but Hitler failed to become Chancellor, partly because the Nazis still lacked an overall majority (they had 230 seats out of 608 in the *Reichstag*), and because he was not yet quite 'respectable' – conservative President Hindenburg viewed him as an upstart and refused to have him as Chancellor. Given these circumstances, *was it inevitable that Hitler would come to power?* This is still a matter for disagreement among historians. Some feel that by the autumn of 1932 nothing could have saved the Weimar Republic, and that consequently nothing could have kept Hitler out. Others believe that the first signs of economic improvement could be seen, and that it should have been possible to block Hitler's progress. In fact Brüning's policies seem to have started to pay off, though he himself had been replaced as Chancellor by Franz von Papen (conservative/nationalist) in May 1932. This theory seems to be supported by the election results of November 1932 when the Nazis lost 34 seats and about 2 million votes, which was a serious setback for them. Perhaps the republic was weathering the storm and the Nazi challenge would fade out. However, at this point a further influence came into play, which killed off the republic by letting Hitler into power legally.

(f) *Hitler becomes Chancellor*

A small clique of right-wing politicians with support from the *Reichswehr* decided to bring Hitler into a coalition government with the nationalists. The main conspirators were Franz von Papen and General Kurt von Schleicher. Their reasons for this momentous decision were:

- they were afraid of the Nazis attempting to seize power by a *Putsch*;
- they believed they could control Hitler better *inside* the government than if he remained outside it, and that a taste of power would make the Nazis modify their extremism;
- the Nationalists only had 37 seats in the *Reichstag* (July 1932), but the Nazi votes would go a long way towards giving them a majority which might make possible a restoration of the monarchy, and a return to the system which had existed under Bismarck (Chancellor 1870–90), in which the *Reichstag* had much less power. Though this would destroy the Weimar Republic, these right-wing politicians were prepared to go ahead because it would give them a better chance of controlling the communists (who had had their best result so far in the July 1932 election, winning 89 seats).

There was some complicated manoeuvring involving Papen, Schleicher and a group of wealthy businessmen; President Hindenburg was persuaded to dismiss Brüning and appoint Papen as Chancellor. They hoped to bring Hitler in as Vice-Chancellor, but he would settle for nothing less than himself as Chancellor. In January 1933 therefore they persuaded Hindenburg to invite Hitler to become Chancellor with Papen as Vice-Chancellor, even though the Nazis had by then lost ground in the elections of November 1932. Papen still believed Hitler could be controlled and remarked to a friend: 'In two months we'll have pushed Hitler into a corner so hard that he'll be squeaking'.

Hitler was able to come to power legally therefore, because all the other parties, including the *Reichswehr*, failed to recognize the danger from the Nazis, and so failed to unite in opposition to them. It ought to have been possible to keep the Nazis out – they were losing ground and had nowhere near an overall majority. But instead of uniting with the other parties to exclude them, the nationalists made the fatal mistake of *inviting* Hitler into power.

> In conclusion, according to historian J.W. Hiden: though there were signs of economic improvement by the late summer of 1932, it was perhaps inevitable that the Weimar Republic would collapse, since the powerful conservative groups and the army were prepared to abandon it, and replace it with a conservative, nationalist and anti-democratic state similar to the one which had existed before 1914. In fact it is possible to argue that the Weimar Republic had

> already ceased to exist in May 1932 when Hindenburg
> appointed Papen as Chancellor with responsibility to him,
> not to the *Reichstag.*
>
> *It was not inevitable that Hitler would take its place:* that
> need not have happened; Papen, Schleicher, Hindenburg and
> the others must take the blame for being prepared to invite
> him into power, and then failing to control him.

13.2 What did National Socialism stand for?

What it did *not* mean was nationalization and the redistribution of wealth. The word
'socialism' was included only to attract the support of the German workers, though it
has to be admitted that Hitler did promise a better deal for workers. In fact it bore
many similarities to Mussolini's fascism (see Section 12.2).

The movement's general principles were:

1   It was more than just one political party among many. *It was a way of life dedicated
    to the rebirth of the nation.* All classes in society must be united to make Germany
    a great nation again and restore national pride. Since the Nazis had the only
    correct way to achieve this, it followed that all other parties, especially
    communists, must be eliminated.
2   Great emphasis was laid on *the ruthlessly efficient organization of all aspects of the
    lives of the masses* under the central government, in order to achieve greatness,
    with violence and terror if necessary. The state was supreme; the interests of the
    individual always came second to the interests of the state, that is a totalitarian
    state in which propaganda had a vital role to play.
3   Since it was likely that greatness could only be achieved by war, *the entire state
    must be organized on a military footing.*
4   *The race theory was vitally important* – this was that mankind could be divided into
    two groups, Aryans and non-Aryans. The Aryans were the Germans, ideally tall,
    blond, blue-eyed and handsome; they were the master race, destined to rule the
    world. All the rest, such as Slavs, coloured peoples and particularly Jews were
    inferior and were destined to become the slave races of the Germans.

All the various facets and details of the Nazi system sprang from these four basic concepts. There has been great debate among historians about whether National Socialism
was a natural development of German history, or whether it was a one-off, a distortion
of normal development. Many British and American historians argued that it was a
natural extension of earlier Prussian militarism and German traditions. Marxist historians believed that National Socialism and fascism in general were the final stage of
Western capitalism which was bound to collapse because of its fatal flaws. But German
historians like Gerhard Ritter and K.D. Bracher stressed the personal contribution of
Hitler, arguing that Hitler was striving to break away from the past and introduce
something completely new, and that National Socialism was a grotesque departure
from the normal and logical historical development. This is probably the majority view
at the moment (see question 2 at the end of the chapter).

13.3 Hitler consolidates his power

Hitler was an Austrian, the son of a customs official in Braunau-am-Inn on the border with Germany. He had hoped to become an artist but failed to gain admittance to the Vienna Academy of Fine Arts, and afterwards spent six down-and-out years living in Vienna dosshouses and developing his hatred of Jews. In Munich Hitler had joined Anton Drexler's tiny German Workers' party (1919) which he soon took over and transformed into the National Socialist German Workers' Party (NSDAP). Now, in January 1933, he was Chancellor of a coalition government of National Socialists and nationalists, but he was not yet satisfied with the amount of power he possessed: Nazis held only three out of eleven cabinet posts. He therefore insisted on a general election in the hope of winning an overall majority for the Nazis.

(a) *The election of 5 March 1933*

The election campaign was an extremely violent one. The Nazis, now in power, were able to use all the apparatus of state, including press and radio, to try to whip up a majority. Senior police officers were replaced with reliable Nazis, and 50 000 auxiliary policemen were called up, most of them from the SA and the SS (*Schutzstaffeln* – Hitler's second private army, formed originally to be his personal bodyguard). They had orders to avoid hostility to the SA and SS but to show no mercy to communists and other 'enemies of the state'. Meetings of all parties except Nazis and nationalists were wrecked and speakers beaten up, while police looked the other way.

(b) *The Reichstag fire*

The climax of the election campaign came on the night of 27 February when the *Reichstag* was badly damaged by a fire apparently started by a young half-witted Dutch anarchist called van der Lubbe, who was arrested, tried and executed for his pains. It has been suggested that the SA knew about van der Lubbe's plans, but allowed him to go ahead and even started fires of their own elsewhere in the building with the intention of blaming it on the communists. There is no conclusive evidence of this, but what is certain is that *Hitler used the fire to stir up fear of communism and as a pretext for the banning of the party*. However, in spite of all their efforts, the Nazis still failed to win an overall majority. With almost 90 per cent of the electorate voting, the Nazis won 288 out of the 647 seats, 36 short of the magic figure (324) needed for an overall majority. The nationalists again won 52 seats. Hitler was still dependent on the support of Papen and Hugenberg (leader of the nationalists). This turned out to be the Nazis' best performance in a 'free' election, and they never won an overall majority. It is worth remembering that even at the height of their electoral triumph the Nazis were supported by only 44 per cent of the voting electorate.

13.4 How was Hitler able to stay in power?

(a) *The Enabling Law, 23 March 1933*

The legal basis of his power was the Enabling Law which was forced through the *Reichstag* on 23 March 1933. This stated that the government could introduce laws without the approval of the *Reichstag* for the next four years, could ignore the constitution and sign agreements with foreign countries. All laws would be drafted by the

Chancellor and come into operation the day they were published. This meant that Hitler was to be the complete dictator for the next four years, but since his will was now law, he would be able to extend the four-year period indefinitely. He no longer needed the support of Papen and Hugenberg; the Weimar constitution had been abandoned. Such a major constitutional change needed approval by a two-thirds majority, yet the Nazis did not have even a simple majority.

How did they get the Enabling Law through the Reichstag?

The method was typical of the Nazis. The Kroll Opera House (where the *Reichstag* had been meeting since the fire) was surrounded by Hitler's private armies, and MPs had to push their way through solid ranks of SS troops to get into the building. The 81 communist MPs were simply not allowed to pass (many were in jail already). Inside the building, rows of brown-shirted SA troops lined the walls, and the SS could be heard chanting outside: 'We want the bill, or fire and murder'. It took courage to vote against the Enabling bill in such surroundings. When the Catholic Centre Party decided to vote in favour of the bill, the result was a foregone conclusion. Only the Social Democrats spoke against it and it passed by 441 votes to 94 (all Social Democrats).

(b) *Gleichschaltung*

Hitler followed a policy known as *Gleichschaltung* (forcible co-ordination) which turned Germany into a totalitarian or fascist state. The government tried to control as many aspects of life as possible, using a huge police force and the notorious State Secret Police, the *Gestapo (Geheime Staatspolizei)*. It became dangerous to oppose or criticize the government in any way. *The main features of the Nazi totalitarian state were as follows.*

1   All political parties except the National Socialists were banned so that Germany became *a one-party state* like Italy and the USSR.
2   The separate state parliaments (*Lander*) still existed but lost all power. Most of their functions were taken over by *a Nazi Special Commissioner* appointed in each state by the Berlin government, who had complete power over all officials and affairs within his state. There were no more state, provincial or municipal elections.
3   *The civil service was purged:* all Jews and other suspected 'enemies of the state' were removed until it was fully reliable.
4   *Trades unions, a likely source of resistance, were abolished*, their funds confiscated and their leaders arrested. They were replaced by the *German Labour Front* to which all workers had to belong. The government dealt with all grievances, and strikes were not allowed.
5   *The education system was closely controlled* so that children could be indoctrinated with Nazi opinions. School textbooks were often rewritten to fit in with Nazi theory, the most obvious examples being in history and biology. History was distorted to fit in with Hitler's view that great things could only be achieved by force. Human biology was dominated by the Nazi race theory. Teachers, lecturers and professors were closely watched to make sure they did not express opinions which strayed from the party line, and many lived in fear in case they were reported to the *Gestapo* by children of convinced Nazis.
     The system was supplemented by the *Hitler Youth*, which all boys had to join at 14; girls joined the *League of German Maidens*. They all learned that their first duty was to obey Hitler, who took on the title *Führer* (leader or guide); the

favourite slogan was 'the Führer is always right'. Children were even encouraged to betray their parents to the *Gestapo*, and many did so.

6   *All communications and the media were controlled by the Minister of Propaganda, Dr Joseph Goebbels.* Radio, newspapers, magazines, books, theatre, films, music and art were all supervised. By the end of 1934 about 4000 books were on the forbidden list because they were 'un-German'. It was impossible to perform the plays of Bertholt Brecht (a communist) or the music of Felix Mendelssohn and Gustav Mahler (they were Jewish). Writers, artists and scholars were harassed until it became impossible to express any opinion which did not fit in with the Nazi system. By these methods public opinion could be moulded and mass support assured.

7   *The economic life of the country was closely organized.* Although the Nazis (unlike the communists) had no special ideas about the economy, they did have two main aims: *to remove unemployment and to make Germany self-sufficient by boosting exports and reducing imports (known as autarky).* Nazi policies involved:

- telling industrialists what to produce, depending on what the country needed at that moment; closing factories down if their products were not required;
- moving workers around the country to places where jobs existed;
- controlling food prices and rents;
- manipulating foreign exchange rates to avoid inflation;
- introducing vast schemes of public works – slum clearance, land drainage, and *autobahn* (motorway) building;
- forcing foreign countries to buy German goods either by refusing to pay cash for goods bought from those countries, so that they had to accept German goods instead (often armaments), or by refusing permission to foreigners with bank accounts in Germany to withdraw their cash, so that they had to spend it in Germany on German goods;
- manufacturing synthetic rubber and wool and experimenting to produce petrol from coal in order to reduce dependence on foreign countries.

8   *Religion was brought under state control,* since the churches were a possible source of opposition. At first Hitler moved cautiously with both Roman Catholics and Protestants.

- **The Roman Catholic Church**
  In 1933 Hitler signed an agreement (known as the *Concordat*) with the Pope in which he promised not to interfere with German Catholics in any way; in return they agreed to dissolve the Catholic Centre Party and take no further part in politics. But relations soon became strained when the government broke the Concordat by dissolving the Catholic Youth League because it rivalled the Hitler Youth. When the Catholics protested, their schools were closed down. By 1937 Catholics were completely disillusioned with the Nazis, and Pope Pius XI issued an Encyclical (a letter to be read out in all Roman Catholic churches in Germany) in which he condemned the Nazi movement for being 'hostile to Christ and his Church'. Hitler was unimpressed, however, and thousands of priests and nuns were arrested and sent to concentration camps.

- **The Protestant Churches**
  Since a majority of Germans belonged to one or other of the various Protestant groups, Hitler tried to organize them into a '*Reich* Church' with a Nazi as the first *Reich* bishop. But many pastors (priests) objected and a group of them, led by *Martin Niemoller*, protested to Hitler about government

interference and about his treatment of the Jews. Once again the Nazis were completely ruthless – Niemoller and over 800 other pastors were sent to concentration camps. (Niemoller himself managed to survive for eight years until he was liberated in 1945.) Hundreds more were arrested later and the rest were forced to swear an oath of obedience to the Fuhrer.

Eventually the persecutions appeared to bring the churches under control, but resistance continued, and the churches were the only organizations to keep up a quiet protest campaign against the Nazi system. For example, in 1941 some Catholic bishops protested against the Nazi policy of killing mentally handicapped and mentally ill people in German asylums. Over 70 000 people were murdered in this 'euthanasia' campaign. Hitler publicly ordered the mass killings to be stopped, but evidence suggests that they still continued.

9   *Above all, Germany was a police state.* The police, helped by the SS and the *Gestapo*, tried to prevent all open opposition to the regime. The lawcourts were not impartial: 'enemies of the state' rarely received a fair trial, and the *concentration camps* introduced by Hitler in 1933 were full. The main ones before 1939 were Dachau near Munich, Buchenwald near Weimar, and Sachsenhausen near Berlin. They contained 'political' prisoners – communists, Social Democrats, Catholic priests, Protestant pastors and, above all, Jews.

However, recent research in Germany has shown that the police state was not as efficient as used to be thought. The Gestapo was understaffed; for example, there were only 43 officials to police Essen, a city with a population of 650 000. They had to rely heavily on ordinary people coming forward with information to denounce others. After 1943, as people became more disillusioned with the war, they were less willing to help the authorities, and the Gestapo's job became more difficult.

10   *The worst aspect of the Nazi system was Hitler's anti-Semitic (anti-Jewish) policy.* There were only just over half a million Jews in Germany, a tiny proportion of the population, but Hitler decided to use them as scapegoats for everything – the humiliation at Versailles, the depression, unemployment and communism – and claimed that there was a world Jewish plot. Lots of Germans were in such a desperate situation that they were prepared to accept the propaganda about the Jews and were not sorry to see thousands of them removed from their jobs as lawyers, doctors, teachers and journalists. The campaign was given legal status by the *Nuremberg Laws (1935)*, which deprived Jews of their German citizenship, forbade them to marry non-Jews (to preserve the purity of the Aryan race) and ruled that even a person with only one Jewish grandparent must be classed as a Jew.

Later the policy became more extreme. Jews were harassed in every possible way; their property was attacked and burnt, shops looted, synagogues destroyed, and Jews themselves herded into concentration camps (Illus. 13.3). Eventually the terrible nature of what Hitler called his 'final solution' of the Jewish problem became clear: *he intended to exterminate the entire Jewish race.* During the war, as the Germans occupied such countries as Czechoslovakia, Poland and western Russia, he was able to lay his hands on non-German Jews as well. It is believed that by 1945, out of a total of 9 million Jews living in Europe at the outbreak of the Second World War, well over 5 million had been murdered, most of them in the gas chambers of the Nazi extermination camps. The *Holocaust*, as it became known, was probably the worst and most shocking of the many crimes against humanity committed by the Nazi regime.

Illus. 13.3 Jewish people being taken to a concentration camp

> It would be wrong though to give the impression that Hitler
> hung on to power just by terrorising the entire nation. If you
> were a Jew, a communist or a socialist, or if you persisted in
> protesting and criticizing the Nazis, you would run into trou-
> ble; but many people who had no great interest in politics
> could usually live quite happily under the Nazis. This was
> because *Hitler took care to please many important groups in
> society*.

(c) *Hitler's policies were popular with many sections of the German people*

1   *His arrival in power in January 1933 caused a great wave of enthusiasm and
anticipation* after the weak and indecisive governments of the Weimar Republic.
Hitler seemed to be offering action and a great new Germany. He was careful to
foster this enthusiasm by military parades, torchlight processions and firework
displays, the most famous of which were the huge rallies held every year in
Nuremberg which seemed to appeal to the masses (Illus. 13.4).

2   *Hitler was successful in eliminating unemployment.* This was probably the most
important reason for his popularity with ordinary people. When he came to power
the unemployment figure still stood at over 6 million, but as early as July 1935 it
had dropped to under 2 million, and by 1939 it had disappeared completely. *How
was this achieved?* The public works schemes provided thousands of extra jobs. A
large party bureaucracy was set up now that the party was expanding so rapidly,
and this provided thousands of extra office and administrative posts. There were
purges of Jews and anti-Nazis from the civil service and from many other jobs

Illus. 13.4 Hitler about to address a Nazi rally at Nuremberg

connected with law, education, journalism, broadcasting, the theatre and music, leaving large numbers of vacancies. Conscription was reintroduced in 1935. Rearmament was started in 1934 and gradually speeded up. Thus Hitler had provided what the unemployed had been demanding in their marches in 1932: work and bread (*Arbeit und Brot*).

3   *Care was taken to keep the support of the workers* once it had been gained by the provision of jobs. This was important because the abolition of trade unions still rankled with many of them. The Strength through Joy Organization (*Kraft durch Freude*) provided benefits such as subsidized holidays in Germany and abroad, cruises, ski-ing holidays, cheap theatre and concert tickets and convalescent homes. Other benefits were holidays with pay and control of rents.

4   *Wealthy industrialists and businessmen were delighted with the Nazis* in spite of the government's interference with their industries. This was partly because they now felt safe from a communist revolution, and because they were glad to be rid of trades unions which had constantly pestered them with demands for shorter working hours and increased wages. In addition they were able to buy back at low prices the shares which they had sold to the state during the crisis of 1929–32, and there was promise of great profits from the public works schemes, rearmament and other orders which the government placed with them.

5   Farmers, though doubtful about Hitler at first, gradually warmed towards the Nazis as soon as it became clear that farmers were in a specially favoured position in the state because of the declared Nazi aim of self-sufficiency in food production. Prices of agricultural produce were fixed so that they were assured of a reasonable profit. Farms were declared to be hereditary estates, and on the death of the owner, had to be passed on to his next-of-kin. This meant that a farmer could not be forced to sell or mortgage his farm to pay off his debts, and was welcomed by many farmers who were heavily in debt as a result of the financial crisis.

6   Hitler gained the support of the *Reichswehr* (army), which was crucial if he was to feel secure in power. The *Reichswehr* was the one organization which could have removed him by force. Yet by the summer of 1934, Hitler had won it over:
   • the officer class was well-disposed towards Hitler because of his much publicized aim of setting aside the restrictions of the Versailles Treaty by rearmament and expansion of the army to its full strength;

Illus. 13.5   Hitler and the Sturmabteilung (SA) at the 1938 Nuremberg Rally

- there had been a steady infiltration of National Socialists into the lower ranks and this was beginning to work through to the lower officer classes;
- the army leaders were much impressed by Hitler's handling of the troublesome SA in the notorious *Röhm Purge* (also known as *'the Night of the Long Knives'*) of 30 June 1934.

The background to this was that the SA, under their leader, Ernst Röhm, a personal friend of Hitler from the early days of the movement, was becoming an embarrassment to the new Chancellor. Röhm wanted his brownshirts to be merged with the *Reichswehr* and himself made a general. Hitler knew that the aristocratic *Reichswehr* generals would not hear of either; they considered the SA to be little more than a bunch of gangsters, while Röhm himself was known to be a homosexual (which was frowned on in army circles) and had criticized the generals in public for their stiff-necked conservatism. Röhm persisted in his demands, forcing Hitler to choose between the SA and the *Reichswehr*.

Hitler's solution to the dilemma was typical of Nazi methods – ruthless but efficient; he used one of his private armies to deal with the other. Röhm and most of the SA leaders were murdered by SS troops, and Hitler seized the opportunity to have murdered a number of other enemies and critics who had nothing to do with the SA. For example, two of Papen's advisers were shot dead by the SS because ten days earlier Papen had made a speech at Marburg criticizing Hitler. Papen himself was probably saved only by the fact that he was a close friend of President Hindenburg. It is thought that at least 400 people were murdered during that one night or soon afterwards. Hitler justified his actions on the grounds that they were all plotting against the state.

The purge had important results: the *Reichswehr* were relieved to be rid of the SA and impressed by Hitler's decisive handling of the problem. When President Hindenburg died only a month later, the *Reichswehr* agreed that Hitler should become President as well as Chancellor (though he preferred to be known as the *Führer*). The *Reichswehr* took an oath of allegiance to the *Führer*.

8   *Finally, Hitler's foreign policy was a brilliant success.* With each successive triumph, more and more Germans began to think of him as infallible (see Section 5.3).

13.5 Nazism and fascism

(a) *Similarities*

Hitler's Nazi state was in many ways similar to Mussolini's fascist system (see Section 12.3). Both:

● were intensely anti-communist and because of this drew a solid basis of support from all classes;
● attempted to organize a totalitarian state, controlling industry, agriculture, and the way of life of the people, so that personal freedom was limited;
● attempted to make the country self-sufficient;
● emphasized the close unity of all classes working together to achieve these ends;
● emphasized the supremacy of the state, were intensely nationalistic, and glorified war and the cult of the leader who would guide the rebirth of the nation from its troubles.

(b) *But there were some important differences*

● Fascism never seemed to take root in Italy as deeply as it did in Germany.
● The Italian system was not as efficient as that in Germany. The Italians never came anywhere near achieving self-sufficiency and never eliminated unemployment; in fact unemployment rose.
● The Italian system was not as ruthless and brutal as that in Germany and there were no mass atrocities, though there were unpleasant incidents like the murders of Matteotti and Amendola.
● Italian fascism was not particularly anti-Jewish or racist until 1938 when Mussolini adopted the policy to emulate Hitler.
● Mussolini was more successful than Hitler with his religious policy after his agreement with the Pope in 1929.
● Finally, their constitutional positions were different: the monarchy still remained in Italy, and though Mussolini normally ignored Victor Emmanuel, the king played a vital role in 1943 when Mussolini's critics were able to turn to him as head of state. He was able to announce Mussolini's dismissal and order his arrest. Unfortunately there was nobody in Germany who could dismiss Hitler.

13.6 How successful was Hitler in domestic affairs up to 1939?

There are conflicting views about this.

(a) *He was successful*

One school of thought claims that the Nazis were extremely successful because they provided many benefits of the sort mentioned above in Section 13.4(c), and developed a flourishing economy. If only Hitler had managed to keep Germany out of war, so the theory goes, all would have been well, and his Third *Reich* might well have lasted a thousand years (as he boasted it would).

(b) *He was superficially successful*

The other view is that Hitler's policies were only superficially successful and could not stand the test of time. The so-called 'economic miracle' was an illusion; there was a huge budget deficit and the country was, technically, bankrupt. Even the superficial success was achieved by methods unacceptable in a modern civilized society:

● full employment was achieved only at the cost of a brutal anti-Jewish campaign and a massive rearmament programme;
● self-sufficiency was not possible unless Germany was able to take over and exploit large areas of eastern Europe belonging to Poland, Czechoslovakia and Russia;
● permanent success therefore depended on success in war, thus there was no possibility of Hitler keeping out of war (see also Section 5.3(a)).

The conclusion must therefore be, as Alan Bullock wrote in his biography of Hitler:

> Recognition of the benefits which Hitler's rule brought to Germany needs to be tempered by the realisation that for the Führer – and for a considerable section of the German people – these were by-products of his true purpose, the creation of an instrument of power with which to realize a policy of expansion that in the end was to admit no limits.

Questions

1 (a) After reading Chapter 13, make a list of the main changes that took place in Germany after Hitler became Chancellor in January 1933.   1.4a, 7a
   (b) Say what type of change each one is, for example, political, economic, social, religious, or any other types you can think of.   1.5a
   (c) Why did some people think these changes were a sign of progress, but others disagreed?   1.6a, 1.6c–9b
2 *The nature of National Socialism in Germany*   Study Sources A to F and then answer the questions which follow.

Source A

From The Roots of National Socialism, 1783–1933, *a book by British historian R. Butler, first published in 1942*

National Socialism is the inevitable reappearance of Prussian militarism and terror, as seen during the 18th century. The Nazis combined two strands of nationalist thinking: a revival of former imperialism together with a social, economic and

---

spiritual national revolution. They were able to manipulate the emotions of the German people at a time of anxiety and deep resentment towards the Weimar system. Anti-Semitic tendencies can also be traced back to earlier days.

Source: adapted from a summary in David Smith, 'Origins of National Socialism', in *Modern History Review* (September 1995)

Source B

The view of Sir Lewis Namier, a Polish Jew who settled in Britain and became a historian. This article was published in 1948

To what extent is the average German responsible for the misdeeds of his rulers? ... Attempts to absolve the German people of responsibility even for the Second Reich [the regime of Kaiser Wilhelm II] are unconvincing. And as for Hitler and his Third Reich, these arose from the people, indeed from the lower depths of the people, and the unmeasured adulation of which the Fuhrer became the object was as spontaneous as the man was self-made. Friends of the Germans must ask themselves why individual Germans in non-German surroundings become useful, decent citizens, but in groups, both at home and abroad, are apt to develop tendencies that make them a menace to their fellow-men?

Source: Sir Lewis Namier, 'German Unity and the German Wars', in *Avenues of History* (Hamish Hamilton, 1952)

Source C

From National Socialism and the German Past, *a book by German historian Gerhard Ritter, published in 1955*

Nazi propaganda was not a repetition of the deeds of German forefathers, but an unquenchable will for success in the future. Hitler wanted his state to be something completely new, breaking out of the mould of the past. It is an illusion to see Frederick the Great and Kaiser Wilhelm II as forerunners of Hitler. He may have stressed the traditional linkage in public, but in private he was sharply critical of the old archaic institutions associated with hereditary monarchy. He wished himself to be seen not as above the people, but more the people's inspiration, the *Volksfuhrer* (people's guide).

Source D

The view of another German historian, Karl Dietrich Bracher, writing in 1970

Without Hitler, German history would probably have taken a completely different path; rarely in history has there been such a close interdependence of general and personal factors and the indispensable role of the individual as in the period 1919 and 1945. The National Socialist road to power was never inevitable; this completely destroys the argument of historical continuity.

Sources: C and D are adapted from a summary in David Smith, 'Origins of National Socialism', in *Modern History Review* (September 1995)

The view of a British historian and biographer of Hitler, Alan Bullock, writing in 1993

I do not believe that Hitler created the historical circumstances of which he was able to take advantage. Nor was there anything inevitable about his rise. He would not have succeeded had it not been for a stroke of luck – the unexpected chance offered by the economic depression which hit Germany with such force that it allowed him to convert the Nazi vote of 800 000 in the election of 1928 to more than 13 million in 1932. And I do not believe that if Hitler had not seized the opportunity, then someone else would have done, and the result would have been much the same.

Source: Alan Bullock, 'Personality in History: Hitler and Stalin', in *Modern History Review* (November 1993)

Source F

Recent information from a British historian, Jeremy Noakes

According to recent research, the [Nazi] party succeeded in winning a significant amount of working class support among blue collar workers engaged in handicrafts and small-scale manufacturing . . . in March 1933, 33% of workers entitled to vote supported the Nazis . . . between 1928 and 1933 the Nazi party had won over 2 million SPD [socialist] voters . . . It is important to emphasise how unstable support for the Nazi party was. As far as membership was concerned, the party was like a revolving door with people joining and leaving all the time. After the November 1932 election, in which the Nazis lost support, there were good grounds for thinking that it might disintegrate. In local elections in Thuringia and Saxony in December 1932, the Nazis lost heavily – in its previous stronghold of Thuringia it was 40% down on its already reduced vote of November. The party's propaganda headquarters summed up the situation by stressing 'it must not come to another election. The results could not be imagined'. What would have happened if Hitler had continued to be denied office will remain one of the big ifs of history, but at the time, the party's prospects appeared bleak.

Source: Jeremy Noakes, 'Who Supported Hitler?', in *Modern History Review*, April 1995

(a) Make a list of points on which there seems to be some agreement among the writers.   1.6c, 3.4   3 marks

(b) What differences can you find between these interpretations of National Socialism?   1.6c, 3.4   5 marks

(c) What do you think are the strengths and weaknesses of each of these interpretations?   2.7   10 marks

(d) What explanations can you suggest for the differences of interpretation?   2.4–6, 2.8–10   12 marks

Total: 30 marks

⟨14⟩ Japan and Spain

Summary of events

During the twenty years after Mussolini's March on Rome (1922), many other countries, faced with severe economic problems, followed the examples of Italy and Germany and turned to fascism or right-wing nationalism.

In Japan the democratically elected government, increasingly embarrassed by economic, financial and political problems, fell under the influence of the army in the early 1930s. The military soon involved Japan in war with China, and later took the country into the Second World War with its attack on Pearl Harbor (1941). After a brilliant start, the Japanese eventually suffered defeat and devastation when the two atomic bombs were dropped. After the war Japan returned to democracy and made a remarkable recovery, soon becoming one of the world's most powerful states economically.

In Spain an incompetent parliamentary government was replaced by General Primo de Rivera, who ruled from 1923 until 1930 as a sort of benevolent dictator. The world economic crisis brought him down, and in an atmosphere of growing republicanism, King Alfonso XIII abdicated, hoping to avoid bloodshed (1931). Various republican governments failed to solve the many problems facing them, and the situation deteriorated into civil war (1936–9) with the forces of the right fighting the left-wing republic. The war was won by the right-wing nationalists, whose leader, General Franco, became head of the government. He kept Spain neutral during the Second World War, and stayed in power until his death in 1975, after which the monarchy was restored and the country gradually returned to democracy.

Portugal also had a right-wing dictatorship – Antonio Salazar ruled from 1932 until he had a stroke in 1968. His *Estado Novo* (New State) was sustained by the army and the secret police. In 1974 his successor was overthrown and democracy returned to Portugal. Although all three regimes – in Japan, Spain and Portugal – had many features similar to the regimes of Mussolini and Hitler, such as a one-party totalitarian state, death or imprisonment of opponents, secret police and brutal repression, they were not, strictly speaking, fascist states: they lacked the vital element of mass mobilization in pursuit of the rebirth of the nation which was such a striking feature in Italy and Germany.

Many South American politicians were influenced by fascism. Juan Peron, leader of **Argentina** from 1943 until 1955 and again in 1973–4, and Getulio Vargas, who led *Estado Novo* (New State) in **Brazil** from 1939 until 1945, were two of those who were impressed by the apparent success of Fascist Italy and Nazi Germany. They adopted some of the European fascist ideas, especially the mobilization of mass support. They won huge support from the poor working classes in the mass union movement. But they were not really like Mussolini and Hitler either. Their governments can best by summed up as a combination of nationalism and social reform. As historian Eric Hobsbawm puts it: 'European fascist movements destroyed labour movements, the Latin American leaders they inspired, created them'.

14.1 Japan between the wars

(a) *In 1918 Japan was in a strong position in the Far East*

She had a powerful navy, a great deal of influence in China, and had benefited economically from the First World War, while the states of Europe were busy fighting each other. Japan took advantage of the situation both by providing the Allies with shipping and other goods, and by stepping in to supply orders, especially in Asia, which the Europeans could not fulfil. During the war years, her export of cotton cloth almost trebled, while her merchant fleet doubled in tonnage. Politically the course seemed set fair for democracy when in 1925 all adult males were given the vote. Hopes were soon dashed: at the beginning of the 1930s the army assumed control of the government.

(b) *Why did Japan become a military dictatorship?*

During the 1920s problems developed, as they did in Italy and Germany, which democratically elected governments seemed incapable of solving.

1 Influential groups opposed democracy

From the beginning, democracy was not popular with many influential groups in Japanese society, such as the army and the conservatives, who were strongly entrenched in the upper house of parliament (the Peers) and in the Privy Council. They seized every opportunity to discredit the government. For example, they criticized Baron Shidehara Kijuro (Foreign Minister 1924–7) for his conciliatory approach to China, which he thought was the best way to strengthen Japan's economic hold over that country. The army was itching to interfere in China, which was torn by civil war, and considered Shidehara's policy to be 'soft'. They were strong enough to bring the government down in 1927 and reverse his policy.

2 Corruption

Many politicians were corrupt and regularly accepted bribes from big business; sometimes fighting broke out in the lower house (the Diet) as charges and counter-charges of corruption were flung about. The system was not one to inspire respect, and the prestige of parliament suffered.

Neither (i) nor (ii) made military dictatorship inevitable, but when economic problems were added to the political ones, the situation became serious.

3 The trade boom ended

The great trading boom of the war years lasted only until the middle of 1921, when Europe began to revive and recover lost markets. In Japan unemployment and industrial unrest developed, and at the same time farmers were hit by the rapidly falling price of rice caused by a series of bumper harvests. When farmers and industrial workers tried to organize themselves into a political party, they were ruthlessly suppressed by the police. Thus the workers, as well as the army and the right, gradually became hostile to a parliament which posed as democratic, but allowed the left to be suppressed and accepted bribes from big business.

4 The world economic crisis

Beginning in 1929 (see Section 19.4), this affected Japan severely. Her exports shrank disastrously and other countries introduced or raised tariffs against her to safeguard their own industries. One of the worst affected trades was the export of raw silk, which went mostly to the USA. The period after the Wall Street Crash was no time for luxuries, and the Americans drastically reduced their imports of raw silk, so that by 1932 the price had fallen to less than one-fifth of the 1923 figure. This was a further blow for Japanese farmers, since about half of them relied for their livelihood on the production of raw silk as well as rice. There was desperate poverty, especially in the north, for which factory workers and peasants blamed the government and big business. Most of the army recruits were peasants; consequently the rank and file as well as the officer class were disgusted with what they took to be weak parliamentary government. As early as 1927, many officers, attracted by fascism, were planning to seize power and introduce a strong nationalist government.

5 The situation in Manchuria

Matters were brought to a head in 1931 by the situation in Manchuria, a large province of China, with a population of 30 million, where Japan had valuable investment and trade. The Chinese were trying to squeeze out Japanese trade and business, which would have been a severe blow to a Japanese economy already hard hit by the depression. To preserve their economic advantages, Japanese army units invaded and occupied Manchuria (September 1931) without permission from the government (Illus. 14.1). When Prime Minister Inukai criticized extremist action, he was assassinated by a group of army officers (May 1932); his successor felt he had to support the army's actions.

For the next thirteen years the army more or less ran the country, introducing similar methods to those adopted in Italy and Germany: ruthless suppression of communists, assassination of opponents, tight control of education, a build-up of armaments and an aggressive foreign policy which aimed to capture territory in Asia as markets for Japanese exports. This led to an attack on China (1937) and participation in the Second World War in the Pacific (see Section 6.2(c), Maps 6.4 and 5.1 for Japanese conquests). Some historians blame the Emperor Hirohito, who, though he deplored the attack on Manchuria, refused to become involved in political controversy, afraid to risk his orders for a withdrawal being ignored. Historian Richard Storry claims that 'it would have been better for Japan and for the world if the risk had been taken'. He believes that Hirohito's prestige was so great that the majority of officers would have obeyed him if he had tried to restrain the attacks on Manchuria and China.

14.2 Japan recovers

At the end of the Second World War Japan was defeated; her economy was in ruins with a large proportion of her factories and a quarter of her housing destroyed by

Illus. 14.1 *Japanese troops invade Manchuria, 1931*

bombing (see Sections 6.5 and 6.6(d)). Until 1952 she was occupied by allied troops, mostly American, under the command of General MacArthur. For the first three years the Americans aimed to make sure that Japan could never again start a war – she was forbidden to have armed forces and was given a democratic constitution under which ministers had to be members of the Diet (parliament). The Americans did not at this stage seem concerned to restore the Japanese economy. During 1948 the American attitude gradually changed: as the Cold War developed in Europe and the Kuomintang crumbled in China, they felt the need for a strong ally in South East Asia and began to encourage Japanese economic recovery. From 1950 industry recovered rapidly and by 1953 production had reached the 1937 levels. American occupying forces were withdrawn in April 1952 (as had been agreed by the *Treaty of San Francisco* the previous September) though some American troops remained for defence purposes.

(a) *How was Japan's rapid recovery possible?*

1   *American help was vital:* Japanese goods were allowed into American markets on favourable terms and the USA supplied aid and new equipment: an economically healthy Japan meant a strong bulwark against communism in South East Asia.
2   *The Korean War (1950–3)* brought orders for military equipment and supplies, and American firms began to co-operate with the Japanese in the development of new industries.
3   The alliance with the USA meant that *Japan felt well protected* and was therefore able to invest in industry money that would otherwise have gone on armaments.
4   *Profits from exports were ruthlessly ploughed back into industry*, and this was helped by keeping wages and government expenditure low. Japanese goods (motorcycles, cars, television and hi-fi equipment, textiles and ships) were therefore highly competitive on world markets.
5   *Recovery was helped by a series of stable governments*, mostly conservative in character, which had the solid support of the farmers who benefited from the land reform carried through by the Americans. Enjoying plots of their own for the first time, they were afraid that their land would be nationalized if the socialists came to power.

(b) *Japanese recovery was not without its problems*

1   *There was a good deal of anti-American feeling in some quarters:*

- many Japanese felt inhibited by their close ties with the USA;
- they felt that the Americans exaggerated the threat from communist China; they wanted good relations with China and the USSR but this was difficult with Japan in the American camp;
- the renewal of the defence treaty with the USA in 1960 caused strikes and demonstrations.

The Japanese gradually restored good relations with Russia and in the early 1970s reached an understanding with their old enemy China.
2   *Another problem was working class unrest* at low wages and overcrowded living-conditions. Stability depended on economic prosperity, but as the Japanese economy remained buoyant throughout the 1970s, the situation gradually improved. During the world recession of the 1980s, Japan coped better than any of the other industrialized countries, and 1984 saw a record 11 per cent growth in industrial production. Exports continued to increase, particularly to the USA, Canada and the EC. Inflation was well under control at below 3 per cent and unemployment was relatively low at less than 3 per cent of the working population (1.6 million in 1984).
3   *Japan's prosperity caused some problems:* there were constant protests from the USA, Canada and western Europe that the Japanese were flooding foreign markets with their exports while refusing to buy a comparable amount of imports from their customers. In response Japan abolished or reduced import duties on

almost 200 commodities (1982–3) and agreed to limit car exports to the USA (November 1983); France herself restricted imports of cars, TVs and radios from Japan. To compensate for these setbacks the Japanese managed to achieve a 20 per cent increase in exports to the European Community between January and May 1986.

The Japanese success story was symbolized by a remarkable engineering feat – a tunnel 54 kilometres long linking Honshu (the largest island) with Hokkaido to the north. Completed in 1985, it had taken twenty-one years to build and was the world's longest tunnel. Another new development which continued into the 1990s was that Japanese manufacturers were beginning to set up car, electronics and textile factories in the USA, Britain and western Europe; her economic success and power seemed without limit.

14.3 Spain

(a) *Spain in the 1920s and 1930s*

The constitutional monarchy under Alfonso XIII (king since 1885) was never very efficient and reached rock bottom in 1921 when a Spanish army sent to put down a revolt led by Abd-el-Krim in Spanish Morocco, was massacred by the Moors. In 1923 General Primo de Rivera seized power in a bloodless coup, with Alfonso's approval, and ruled for the next seven years. The king called him 'my Mussolini', but though Primo was a military dictator, he was not a fascist. He was responsible for a number of public works – railways, roads and irrigation schemes; industrial production developed at three times the rate before 1923; most impressive of all, he managed to end the war in Morocco (1925). When the world economic crisis reached Spain in 1930, unemployment rose, Primo and his advisers bungled the finances, causing depreciation of the peseta, and the army withdrew its support, whereupon Primo resigned. In April 1931 municipal elections were held in which the republicans won control of all the large cities. As huge crowds gathered on the streets of Madrid, Alfonso decided to abdicate to avoid bloodshed, and a republic was proclaimed. The monarchy had been overthrown without bloodshed, but unfortunately the slaughter had merely been postponed until 1936.

(b) *Why did civil war break out in Spain in 1936?*

1 The new republic faced some serious problems

- Catalonia and the Basque provinces (see Map 14.1) wanted independence;
- the Roman Catholic Church was bitterly hostile to the republic, which in return disliked the Church and was determined to reduce its power;
- it was felt that the army had too much influence in politics and might attempt another coup;
- there were additional problems caused by the depression: agricultural prices were falling, wine and olive exports declined, land went out of cultivation and peasant unemployment rose. In industry iron production fell by a third and steel production by almost half. It was a time of falling wages, unemployment and falling standards of living. Unless it could make some headway with this final problem, the republic was likely to lose the support of the workers.

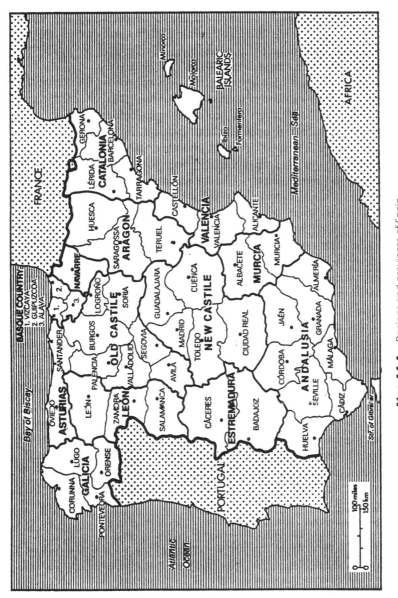

Map 14.1 Regions and provinces of Spain

Source: Hugh Thomas, *The Spanish Civil War* (Penguin, 1977 edn) p. 15

2 Right-wing opposition

The left's solutions to these problems were not acceptable to the right, which became increasingly alarmed at the prospect of social revolution. The dominant grouping in the *Cortes* (parliament), the socialists and middle class radicals, began energetically:

- Catalonia was allowed some self-government;
- an attack was made on the Church (Church and state were separated, priests would no longer be paid by the government, Jesuits were expelled, other orders could be dissolved, and religious education ceased);
- a large number of army officers were compulsorily retired;
- a start was made on the nationalization of large estates; and
- attempts were made to raise wages of industrial workers.

Each of these measures infuriated one or other of the right-wing groups (Church, army, landowners and industrialists). In 1932 some army officers tried to overthrow the Prime Minister, Manuel Azana, but the rising was easily suppressed, as the majority of the army remained loyal at this stage. A new right-wing party, the *Ceda*, was formed to defend the Church and the landlords.

3 Left-wing opposition

The republic was further weakened by opposition from two powerul left-wing groups, the *anarchists* and the *syndicalists* (certain powerful trades unions) who favoured a general strike and the overthrow of the capitalist system. They despised the socialists for co-operating with the middle-class groups. They organized strikes, riots and assassinations. Matters came to a head in January 1933 when some government guards set fire to houses in the village of Casas Viejas near Cadiz, to smoke out some anarchists. Twenty-five people were killed, which lost the government much working-class support, and caused even the socialists to withdraw support from Azana, who resigned. In the following elections (November 1933) the right-wing parties won a majority, the largest group being the new Catholic *Ceda* under its leader Gil Robles.

4 The actions of the new right-wing government

The new government aroused the left to fury. They

- cancelled most of Azana's reforms
- interfered with the working of the new Catalan government and
- refused to allow the Basques self-government.

This was a serious error, since the Basques had supported the right in the elections, but now switched to the left.

As the government moved further right, the left-wing groups (socialists, anarchists, syndicalists and now communists) drew closer together to form a *Popular Front*. Revolutionary violence grew: anarchists derailed the Barcelona-Seville express, killing nineteen people; there was a general strike in 1934 and there were rebellions in Catalonia and Asturias. The miners of Asturias fought bravely but were crushed ruthlessly by troops under the command of General Franco. In the words of historian Hugh Thomas, 'after the manner in which the revolution had been quelled, it would have required a superhuman effort to avoid the culminating disaster of civil war. But no such effort was forthcoming'. Instead, as the financial, as well as the political situation deteriorated, the right fell apart, and in the elections of February 1936 the *Popular Front* emerged victorious.

5 The new government turned out to be ineffective

The socialists decided not to support it, hoping to seize power when the middle-class republican government failed. The government seemed incapable of keeping order, and crisis point came in July 1936 when Calvo Sotelo, the leading right-wing politician, was murdered by police. This terrified the right and convinced them that *the only way to restore order was by a military dictatorship*. A group of generals, conspiring with the right, especially with the new fascist *Falange* party of José Antonio de Rivera (Primo's son), had already planned a military takeover. Using Calvo Sotelo's murder as an excuse, they began a revolt in Morocco, where General Franco soon assumed the leadership. The civil war had begun.

(c) *The civil war 1936–9*

By the end of July 1936, the right, calling themselves *nationalists*, controlled much of the north and the area around Cadiz and Seville in the south; the *republicans* controlled the centre and north-east, including the major cities of Madrid and Barcelona. The struggle was a bitter one in which both sides committed terrible atrocities. The Church suffered horrifying losses at the hands of the republicans, with over 6000 priests and nuns murdered. The nationalists were helped by Italy and Germany, who sent arms and men, together with food supplies and raw materials. The republicans received some help from Russia, but France and Britain refused to intervene, merely allowing volunteers to fight in Spain. The nationalists captured Barcelona and the whole of Catalonia in January 1939, and the war ended in March 1939 when they captured Madrid (Map 14.2).

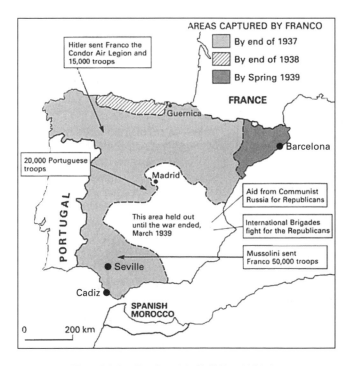

Map 14.2   The Spanish Civil War, 1936–9

Source: B. Catchpole, *A Map History of the Modern World* (Heinemann, 1974)

Reasons for the nationalist victory

- Franco was extremely skilful in holding together the various right-wing groups (army, Church, monarchists and Falangists);
- The republicans were much less united, and anarchists and communists actually fought each other for a time in Barcelona;
- The extent of foreign help for the nationalists was probably decisive: this included 50 000 Italian and 20 000 Portuguese troops, a large Italian airforce, and hundreds of German planes and tanks. One of the most notorious actions was the German bombing of the defenceless Basque town of *Guernica*, in which over 1600 people were killed (see question 2 at the end of the chapter).

(d) *Franco in power*

Franco, taking the title *Caudillo* (leader), set up a government which was similar in many ways to those of Mussolini and Hitler. It was marked by repression, military courts and mass executions. But in other ways it was not fascist: for example, the regime supported the Church, which was given back its control over education. That would never have happened in a true fascist state. Franco was also shrewd enough to keep Spain out the Second World War, though Hitler expected Spanish help and tried to persuade Franco to get involved. When Hitler and Mussolini were defeated, Franco survived and ruled Spain until his death in 1975. During the 1960s he gradually relaxed the repressiveness of his regime: military courts were abolished, workers were allowed a limited right to strike, and elections were introduced for some members of parliament (though political parties were still banned). Much was done to modernize Spanish agriculture and industry and the economy was helped by Spain's growing tourist industry. Eventually Franco came to be regarded as standing above politics. He was preparing Alfonso XIII's grandson, *Juan Carlos*, to succeed him, believing that a conservative monarchy was the best way of keeping Spain stable. When Franco died in 1975, Juan Carlos became king, and soon showed that he was in favour of a return to all-party democracy. The first free elections were held in 1977. Later, under the leadership of socialist Prime Minister *Felipe Gonzalez*, Spain joined the European Community (January 1986).

Questions

1 Section 14.1 described what happened in Japan between the wars.

  (a) Make a list of things which you have noticed which changed during this period, and say what type of change each one was – political, economic, social.
  1.4a, 5a, 7a
  (b) What things stayed the same?
  1.4a
  (c) Why did some people welcome the changes while others saw them as a disaster?
  1.6a, 6c–8c
  (d) Do you think the world economic crisis was the most important reason for Japan becoming a military dictatorship?
  1.4b–9a

2 *The bombing of Guernica, 26 April 1937* Study Sources A to D and then answer the questions which follow.

Source A

Extracts from an eye-witness account of the bombing

Until the past week, thought IGNACIA OZAMIZ, with the exception of food shortages and the dead being brought from the front for burial, the war had hardly

---

affected Guernica. Lying to the north-east of Bilbao, Guernica, a town of 6000 inhabitants, was a symbol of liberty and tradition for the Basques. In a few hours it became the universal symbol of fascist terror. They hadn't taken adequate precautions against air-raids, though there were some crude shelters. First a solitary Heinkel flew over and dropped half a dozen bombs. Then she saw another nine planes appear, flying low, and she threw herself on the ground as the first bombs fell. Some crashed on the nearby hospital. Then fighters dived down and machine-gunned people trying to flee. After the high explosive bombs, successive waves of planes dropped incendiaries. The town was beginning to burn, the wooden rafters catching alight and a pall of smoke was rising into the sky ... when we left the shelter we saw that our house and everything in sight was burning. . . How could they say the Reds had done it when they hardly had a single plane, poor souls?

Source: Ronald Fraser, *Blood of Spain* (Penguin, 1979)

Source B

The Nationalists maintained that Guernica had been blown up by Basques themselves, in order to discredit the blameless Nationalists. A later version said that Republican planes dropped bombs to detonate charges of dynamite placed in the sewers. Twenty years later it was still a crime in Franco's Spain to say that Guernica had been destroyed by the Nationalists.

Source: David Mitchell, *The Spanish Civil War* (Granada, 1971)

Source C

A statement by Juan Sangroniz, a Nationalist

Our consciences were uneasy about it. After living through the raid we knew only too well that the destruction had come from the air. The Reds had hardly any planes, we knew that too. Amongst our own, we'd admit the truth: our side had bombed the town and it was a bad thing. 'But what can we do about it now?' we'd say. It was better simply to keep quiet.

Source: quoted in Ronald Fraser, *Blood of Spain* (Penguin, 1979)

Source D

A Nationalist officer admitted to a reporter from *the Sunday Times* in August [1937] that Guernica had been bombed by his side ... Years later, the German air ace, Adolph Galland, admitted that the Germans were responsible. He argued that the attack was an error, caused by bad bomb sights and lack of experience. The Germans, he said, were trying for the bridge over the river, missed it completely, and by mistake, destroyed the town. The Germans said the wind caused the bombs to drift westwards. In fact Guernica was a military target, being a communications centre close to the battle line. Retreating republican soldiers could only escape with any ease through Guernica because the bridge over the river was the last one before the sea. But if the aim of the [German] Condor Legion was to destroy the bridge why did they not use their supremely accurate Stuka bombers? At least part of the aim must have been to cause maximum panic and confusion among civilians as well as soldiers. The use of incendiary bombs proves that some destruction of buildings and people other than the bridge must have been intended.

Source: Hugh Thomas, *The Spanish Civil War* (Penguin, 1977, 3rd edn)

(a) Using all the sources, make a list of the various suggestions made about who was responsible for, and what methods were used in, the attack on Guernica.

3.4   8 marks

(b) Why do you think there are so many different interpretations of what happened?   1.6c–9c, 2.4–10   5 marks

(c) What are the strengths and weaknesses of each of these sources? Which one do you think is most useful for the historian trying to get at the truth?

3.5–10   12 marks

Total: 25 marks

PART III

Communism – rise and decline

15 Russia and the Revolutions, 1900–24

Summary of events

In the early years of the twentieth century, Russia was in a troubled state. The tsar (emperor) Nicholas II insisted on ruling as an autocrat (someone who rules a country as he or she sees fit, without being responsible to a parliament), but had failed to deal adequately with the country's many problems. Unrest and criticism of the government reached a climax in 1905 with the Russian defeats in the war with Japan (1904–5), leading to a general strike and an attempted revolution, which forced Nicholas to make concessions (the October Manifesto). These included the granting of *an elected parliament (the Duma)*. When it became clear that the *Duma* was ineffective, unrest increased and culminated, after disastrous Russian defeats in the First World War, in two revolutions, both in 1917. The first revolution (March) overthrew the tsar and set up a moderate *provisional government*. When this coped no better than the tsar, it was itself overthrown by the *Bolshevik revolution* (November). The new Bolshevik government was shaky at first, and its opponents (known as the Whites) tried to destroy it, causing a bitter civil war (1918–20). Thanks to the leadership of Lenin and Trotsky, the Bolsheviks (Reds) won the civil war, and, now calling themselves communists, were able to consolidate their power. Lenin was able to begin the task of leading Russia to recovery (until his premature death in 1924).

15.1 After 1905: were the 1917 Revolutions inevitable?

Nicholas survived the 1905 revolution because:

- his opponents were not united;
- there was no central leadership (the whole thing having flared up spontaneously);
- he had been willing to compromise at the critical moment; and
- most of the army remained loyal.

Tsarism now had a breathing space in which Nicholas had a chance to make a constitutional monarchy work, and to throw himself in with people demanding moderate reforms:

- improvements in industrial working conditions and pay;
- cancellation of redemption payments (annual payments to the government by

peasants in return for their freedom and some land, following the abolition of serfdom in 1861), which had reduced over half the rural population to dire poverty;
- more freedom for the press; and
- genuine democracy in which the *Duma* would play an important part in running the country.

Unfortunately Nicholas seems to have had very little intention of keeping to the spirit of the October Manifesto, having agreed to it only because he had no choice.

1   *The First Duma (1906)* was not democratically elected, for although all classes were allowed to vote, the system was rigged so that landowners and middle classes would be in the majority. Even so, it put forward far-reaching demands such as confiscation of large estates, a genuinely democratic electoral system and the right of the *Duma* to approve the tsar's ministers, the right to strike and abolition of the death penalty. This was far too drastic for Nicholas who had the *Duma* dispersed by troops after only ten weeks.
2   *The Second Duma (1907)* suffered the same fate, after which Nicholas changed the voting system, depriving peasants and urban workers of the vote.
3   *The Third Duma (1907–12) and the Fourth Duma (1912–17)* were much more conservative and therefore lasted longer. Though on occasion they criticized the government, they had no power, because the tsar controlled the ministers and the secret police.

Some foreign observers were surprised at the ease with which Nicholas ignored his promises and was able to dismiss the first two *Dumas* without provoking another general strike. The fact was that the revolutionary impetus had subsided for the time being, and many leaders were either in prison or in exile.

This, together with the improvement in the economy beginning after 1906, has given rise to some controversy about whether or not the 1917 revolutions were inevitable. We shall look at each theory in turn.

(a) *The 1917 revolutions were not inevitable*

This theory is that given time, plus gradually improving living standards, the chances of revolution would fade, and that if Russia had not become disastrously involved in the First World War, the monarchy might have survived. Three areas of evidence support this view.

1   Peter Stolypin, Prime Minister from 1906 to 1911, made *determined efforts to win over the peasants*, believing that, given twenty years of peace, there would be no question of revolution. Redemption payments were abolished and peasants encouraged to buy their own land (about 2 million had done so by 1916 and another 3.5 million had emigrated to Siberia where they had their own farms). As a result, there emerged a class of comfortably-off peasants (*kulaks*) on whom the government could rely for support against revolution (or so Stolypin hoped).
2   As more factories came under the control of inspectors, there were signs of *improving working conditions*; as industrial profits increased, the first signs of a more prosperous workforce could be detected. In 1912 a workers' sickness and accident insurance scheme was introduced.
3   At the same time *the revolutionary parties seemed to have lost heart*; they were short of money, torn by disagreements, and their leaders were still in exile.

(b) *The 1917 revolutions were inevitable*

The other view is that, given the tsar's deliberate flouting of his 1905 promises, there was bound to be a revolution sooner or later, and the situation was deteriorating again long before the First World War. The evidence to support this view seems more convincing.

1 The land reforms failed

By 1911 it was becoming clear that Stolypin's land reforms would not have the desired effect, partly because the peasant population was growing too rapidly (at the rate of 1.5 million a year) for his schemes to cope with, and because farming methods were too inefficient to support the growing population adequately. The assassination of Stolypin in 1911 removed one of the few really able tsarist ministers and perhaps the only man who could have saved the monarchy.

2 Industrial unrest

There was a wave of industrial strikes set off by the shooting of 270 striking goldminers in the Lena goldfields (April 1912). In all there were over 2000 separate strikes in that year, 2400 in 1913, and over 4000 in the first seven months of 1914, *before* war broke out. Whatever improvements had taken place, they were obviously not enough to remove all the pre-1905 grievances.

3 Government repression

There was little relaxation of the government's repressive policy, as the secret police rooted out revolutionaries among university students and lecturers and deported masses of Jews, thereby ensuring that both groups were firmly anti-tsarist. The situation was particularly dangerous because the government had made the mistake of alienating three of the most important sections in society – peasants, industrial workers and intelligentsia (educated classes).

4 The revolutionary parties revived

As 1912 progressed, the fortunes of the various revolutionary parties, especially the *Bolsheviks* and *Mensheviks*, revived. Both groups had developed from an earlier movement, the Social Democrat Labour Party, which was Marxist in outlook. Karl Marx (1818–83) was a German Jew whose political ideas were set out in the *Communist Manifesto (1848)* and *Das Kapital [Capital] (1867)*. He believed that economic factors are the real cause of historical change, and that workers (proletariat) are everywhere exploited by capitalists (middle-class bourgeoisie); this means that when a society becomes fully industrialized, the workers will inevitably rise up against their exploiters and take control themselves, running the country in their interests. Marx called this 'the dictatorship of the proletariat'.

One of the Social Democrat leaders was *Vladimir Lenin*, who helped to edit the revolutionary newspaper *Iskra* (The Spark). It was over an election to the editorial board of *Iskra* in 1903 that the party had split into Lenin supporters, the *Bolsheviks* (the Russian word for 'majority') and the rest, the *Mensheviks* (minority).

- *Lenin and the Bolsheviks* wanted a small, disciplined party of professional revolutionaries who would work full-time to bring about revolution; because the industrial workers were in a minority, Lenin believed they must work with the peasants as well, and get them involved in revolutionary activity.

- *The Mensheviks*, on the other hand, were happy to have party membership open to anybody who cared to join; they believed that a revolution could not take place in Russia until the country was fully industrialized, and industrial workers were in a big majority over peasants; they had very little faith in co-operation from peasants who were actually one of the most conservative groups in society.

The Mensheviks were the strict Marxists, believing in a proletarian revolution, whereas Lenin was the one moving away from Marxism. In 1912 appeared the new Bolshevik newspaper *Pravda* (Truth), which was extremely important as a means of publicizing Bolshevik ideas and giving political direction to the already developing strike wave.

The Social Revolutionaries were another revolutionary party; they were not Marxists – they did not approve of increasing industrialization and did not think in terms of a proletarian revolution. After the overthrow of the tsarist regime, they wanted a mainly agrarian society based on peasant communities operating collectively.

5 The royal family was discredited

The royal family was discredited by a number of scandals. It was widely suspected that Nicholas himself was a party to the murder of Stolypin, who was shot by a member of the secret police in the tsar's presence during a gala performance at the Kiev opera. Nothing was ever proved, but Nicholas and his right-wing supporters were probably not sorry to see the back of Stolypin, who was becoming too liberal for their comfort.

More serious was the royal family's association with *Rasputin*, a self-professed 'holy man', who made himself indispensable to the Empress Alexandra by his ability to help the ailing heir to the throne, Alexei. This unfortunate child had inherited haemophilia from his mother's family, and Rasputin was able, on occasion, apparently through hypnosis, to stop the bleeding when Alexei suffered a haemorrhage. Eventually Rasputin became a real power behind the throne, but attracted public criticism by his drunkenness and his numerous affairs with court ladies. Alexandra preferred to ignore the scandals and the *Duma*'s request that Rasputin be sent away from the court (1912).

> The weight of evidence seems to suggest therefore that events were moving towards some sort of upheaval before the First World War broke out. There was a general strike organized by the Bolsheviks in St Petersburg (the capital) in July 1914, with street demonstrations, shootings and barricades. The strike ended on 15 July, a few days before the war began; the government still controlled the army and the police at this point and may well have been able to hold on to power, but historians like George Kennan believe that the tsarist regime would have collapsed sooner or later even without the First World War to finish it off.

(c) *War failures made revolution certain*

Historians agree that Russian failures in the war made revolution certain, and caused troops and police to mutiny, so that there was nobody left to defend the autocracy. The war revealed the incompetent and corrupt organization and the shortage of equipment.

Poor transport organization and distribution meant that arms and ammunition were slow to reach the front. Although there was plenty of food in the country, it did not get to the big cities in sufficient quantities, because most of the trains were being monopolized by the military. Bread was scarce and very expensive.

Norman Stone has shown that the Russian army acquitted itself reasonably well, and Brusilov's 1916 offensive was an impressive success (see Section 2.3(c)). However, Nicholas made the fatal mistake of appointing himself supreme commander (August 1915); his tactical blunders threw away all the advantages won by Brusilov's offensive, and drew on himself the blame for later defeats, and for the high death rate.

By January 1917 most groups in society were disillusioned with the incompetent way the tsar was running the war. The aristocracy, the *Duma*, many industrialists and the army were beginning to turn against Nicholas, feeling that it would be better to sacrifice him to avoid a much worse revolution that might sweep away the whole social structure. General Krimov told a secret meeting of *Duma* members at the end of 1916:

> We would welcome the news of a *coup d'état*. A revolution is imminent and we at the front feel it to be so. If you decide on such an extreme step, we will support you. Clearly there is no other way.

15.2 The two Revolutions: March and November 1917

The revolutions are still known in Russia as the February and October Revolutions. This is because the Russians were still using the old Julian calendar which was 13 days behind the Gregorian calendar used by the rest of Europe. Russia adopted the Gregorian calendar in 1918.

(a) *The March Revolution*

The first revolution began on 8 March when bread riots broke out in Petrograd (St Petersburg). The rioters were quickly joined by thousands of strikers from a nearby armaments factory. The tsar sent orders for the troops to use force to end the demonstrations and forty people were killed. Soon though, some of the troops began to refuse to fire at the unarmed crowds and the whole Petrograd garrison mutinied. Mobs seized public buildings, released prisoners from jails and took over police stations and arsenals. The *Duma* advised Nicholas to set up a constitutional monarchy, but he refused and sent more troops to Petrograd to try to restore order. This convinced the *Duma* and the generals that Nicholas, who was on his way back to Petrograd, would have to go. Some of his senior generals told Nicholas that the only way to save the monarchy was for him to renounce the throne. On 15 March, in the imperial train standing in a siding near Pskov, the tsar abdicated in favour of his brother, the Grand Duke Michael. Unfortunately nobody had made sure that Michael would accept the throne, so when he refused, the Russian monarchy came to an end. It is probably true to say that nobody actually organized this first revolution, although the Bolsheviks claimed that revolutionary agitators were at work in the factories. It was a spontaneous outburst of popular unrest at the chaotic situation which the imperial government had allowed to develop. Faced with this, the privileged classes – aristocracy, army, *Duma* and industrialists – turned against Nicholas in the hope of saving their own skins.

(b) *The provisional government*

Most people expected the autocracy of the tsarist system to be replaced by a democratic republic with an elected parliament. The *Duma*, struggling to take control, set up
a mainly liberal *provisional government* with Prince George Lvov as prime minister. In
July he was replaced by Alexander Kerensky, a moderate socialist. But the new
government was just as perplexed by the enormous problems facing it as the tsar had
been. In November a second revolution took place which overthrew the provisional
government and brought the Bolsheviks to power.

(c) *Why did the provisional government fall from power so soon?*

1   It took the unpopular decision to continue the war, but *the June offensive,
     Kerensky's idea, was another disastrous failure.* It caused the collapse of army
     morale and discipline, and sent hundreds of thousands of deserting troops
     streaming home.

2   *The government had to share power with the Petrograd soviet,* an elected committee
     of soldiers' and workers' representatives, which tried to govern the city. Other
     soviets appeared in Moscow and all the provincial cities. When the Petrograd
     soviet ordered all soldiers to obey only the soviet, it meant that in the last resort,
     the provisional government could not rely on the support of the army.

3   *The government lost support because it delayed elections,* which it had promised, for
     a Constituent Assembly (parliament), arguing that these were not possible in the
     middle of a war when several million troops were away fighting. Another promise
     not kept was for land reform – the redistribution of land from large estates among
     peasants. Tired of waiting, some peasants started to seize land from landlords. The
     Bolsheviks were able to use peasant discontent to win support.

4   Meanwhile, thanks to the new political amnesty, *Lenin was able to return from
     exile in Switzerland* (April). The Germans allowed him to travel through to
     Petrograd in a special 'sealed' train, in the hope that he would cause further chaos
     in Russia. After a rapturous welcome, he urged (in his *April Theses*) that the
     Bolsheviks should cease to support the provisional government, that all power
     should be taken by the soviets, and that Russia should withdraw from the war.

5   *There was growing economic chaos,* with inflation, rising bread prices, lagging
     wages, and shortages of raw materials and fuel. In the midst of all this, Lenin and
     the Bolsheviks put forward what seemed to be a realistic and attractive policy: a
     separate peace with Germany to get Russia out of the war, all land to be given to
     the peasants, and more food at cheaper prices.

6   *The Kornilov affair* embarrassed the government and increased the popularity of
     the Bolsheviks. General Kornilov, the army commander-in-chief, viewed the
     Bolsheviks as traitors, decided it was time to move against the soviet, and brought
     troops towards Petrograd (August). However, many of his soldiers mutinied and
     Kornilov was arrested. Army discipline seemed on the verge of collapse; public
     opinion swung against the war and in favour of the Bolsheviks, who were still the
     only party to talk openly about making a separate peace. By October they had won
     a majority over the Mensheviks and Social Revolutionaries in both the Petrograd
     and Moscow soviets, though they were in a minority in the country as a whole.
     Leon Trotsky (who had just become a Bolshevik) was elected Chairman of the
     Petrograd soviet.

7   On 20 October, urged on by Lenin, *the Petrograd soviet took the crucial decision to
     attempt to seize power.* Trotsky made most of the plans, which went off without a
     hitch. During the night of 6–7 November, Bolshevik Red Guards occupied all key

Illus. 15.1 Street fighting in Petrograd, 1917

points and later arrested the provisional government ministers except Kerensky, who managed to escape. It was almost a bloodless coup, enabling Lenin to set up a new soviet government with himself in charge.

The coup was successful because Lenin had judged to perfection the moment of maximum hostility towards the Kerensky government. The Bolsheviks knew exactly what they were aiming for, and were well-disciplined and organized, whereas the other revolutionary groups were in disarray. The Mensheviks, for example, thought that the next revolution should not take place until the industrial workers were in a majority in the country.

(d) *Lenin and the Bolsheviks consolidate their control*

The Bolsheviks were in control in Petrograd as a result of their coup, but elsewhere the takeover was not so smooth. Fighting lasted a week in Moscow before the soviet won control, and it was the end of November before other cities were brought to heel. Country areas were more difficult to deal with, and at first the peasants were only lukewarm towards the new government. They preferred the Social Revolutionaries, who also promised them land and who saw the peasants as the backbone of the nation, whereas the Bolsheviks seemed to favour industrial workers. Very few people expected the Bolshevik government to last long because of the complexity of the problems fac-

Illus. 15.2 Lenin addressing a crowd while Trotsky stands listening (left foreground)

ing it. As soon as the other political groups recovered from the shock of the Bolshevik coup, there was bound to be some determined opposition. At the same time they had somehow to extricate Russia from the war and then set about repairing the shattered economy, while at the same time keeping their promises about land and food for the peasants and workers.

15.3 How successfully did Lenin and the Bolsheviks deal with their problems (1917–24)?

(a) *Lack of majority support*

The Bolsheviks had nothing like majority support in the country as a whole. One problem therefore was how to keep themselves in power and yet allow free elections. One of Lenin's first decrees nationalized all land so that it could be redistributed among the peasants and, so he hoped, win their support. Lenin knew that he would have to allow elections, since he had criticized Kerensky so bitterly for postponing them; but he realized that a Bolshevik majority in the Constituent Assembly was highly unlikely. Kerensky had arranged elections for mid-November, and they went ahead as planned. Lenin's worst fears were realized: the Bolsheviks won 175 seats out of about 700, but the Social Revolutionaries won 370; the Mensheviks won only 15, left-wing Social Revolutionaries 40, various nationality groups 80, and Cadets (Constitutional Democrats who wanted genuine democracy) 17.

Under a genuine democratic system, the Social Revolutionaries, who had an over-all majority, would have formed a government. However, Lenin was determined that the Bolsheviks were going to stay in power; there was no way in which he was going to hand it over to the Social Revolutionaries, or even share it, after the Bolsheviks had done all the hard work of getting rid of the provisional government. After some anti-Bolshevik speeches at the first meeting of the Constituent Assembly (January 1918), it was dispersed by Bolshevik Red Guards and not allowed to meet again. Lenin's justifi-cation for this undemocratic action was that it was really the highest form of democ-racy: since the Bolsheviks knew what the workers wanted, they had no need of an elected parliament to tell them. Armed force had triumphed for the time being, but opposition was to lead to civil war later in the year.

(b) *The war with Germany*

The next pressing problem was how to withdraw from the war. An armistice between Russia and the Central Powers had been agreed in December 1917, but long negotia-tions followed during which Trotsky tried, without success, to persuade the Germans to moderate their demands. *The Treaty of Brest-Litovsk (March 1918)* was cruel: Russia lost Poland, Estonia, Latvia and Lithuania, the Ukraine, Georgia and Finland; this included a third of Russia's farming land, a third of her population, two-thirds of her coalmines and half her heavy industry (Map 15.1). This was a high price to pay, but Lenin insisted that it was worth it, pointing out that Russia needed to sacrifice space in

Map 15.1 Russian losses by the Treaty of Brest-Litovsk, 1918

Source: J. Brooman, Russia in War and Revolution, 1900–24 (Longman) p. 28

order to gain time to recover. He probably expected Russia to get the land back anyway when, as he hoped, the revolution spread to Germany and other countries.

(c) Civil war

By April 1918 armed opposition to the Bolsheviks was breaking out in many areas, leading to civil war. The opposition (known as the Whites) was a mixed bag, consisting of Social Revolutionaries, Mensheviks, ex-tsarist officers and any other groups which did not like what they had seen of the Bolsheviks. There was great discontent, even among soldiers and workers who had supported the Bolsheviks in 1917, at the high-handed way in which the Bolsheviks treated the soviets (elected councils) all over Russia. People expected that every town would have its own soviet which would run the town's affairs and local industry. Instead, officials (known as *commissars*) appointed by the government arrived, supported by Red Guards; they threw Social Revolutionary and Menshevik members out of the soviets, leaving Bolshevik members in control. It turned into dictatorship from the centre instead of local control. The slogan of the government's opponents became 'LONG LIVE THE SOVIETS AND DOWN WITH THE COMMISSARS'. Their general aim was not to restore the tsar, but simply to set up a democratic government on Western lines.

In Siberia, Admiral Kolchak, former Black Sea Fleet commander, set up a White government; General Denikin was in the Caucasus with a large White army. Most bizarre of all, the Czechoslovak Legion of about 40 000 men had seized long stretches of the Trans-Siberian Railway in the region of Omsk. These troops were originally prisoners taken by the Russians from the Austro-Hungarian army, who had then changed sides after the March revolution and fought for the Kerensky government against the Germans. After Brest-Litovsk the Bolsheviks gave them permission to leave Russia via the Trans-Siberian Railway to Vladivostock, but then decided to disarm them in case they co-operated with the Allies, who were already showing interest in the destruction of the new Bolshevik government. The Czechs resisted with great spirit and their control of the railway was a serious embarassment to the government. After an assassination attempt on Lenin in August 1918, the Bolsheviks launched what became known as the *Red Terror*, during which thousands of Social Revolutionaries and other opponents were rounded up and shot.

The situation was complicated by foreign intervention to help the Whites, with the excuse that they wanted a government which would continue the war against Germany. When intervention continued even after the defeat of Germany, it became clear that their aim was to destroy the Bolshevik government, which was now advocating world revolution. The USA, Japan, France and Britain sent troops, with landings at Murmansk, Archangel and Vladivostock (see Map 15.2). The situation seemed grim for the Bolsheviks when early in 1919 Kolchak (whom the Allies intended to head the next government) advanced towards Moscow, the new capital. However, Trotsky, now Commissar for War, had done a magnificent job creating the well-disciplined Red Army, based on conscription and including thousands of experienced officers from the old tsarist armies (Illus. 15.3). Kolchak was forced back and later captured and executed by the Reds. The Czech Legion was defeated, and Denikin, advancing from the south to within 250 miles of Moscow, was forced to retreat; he later escaped with British help.

By the end of 1919 it was clear that the Bolsheviks (now calling themselves communists) would survive, though in 1920 there was an invasion of the Ukraine by Polish and French troops which forced the Russians to hand over part of the Ukraine and White Russia (*Treaty of Riga, 1921*). From the communist point of view, the important thing

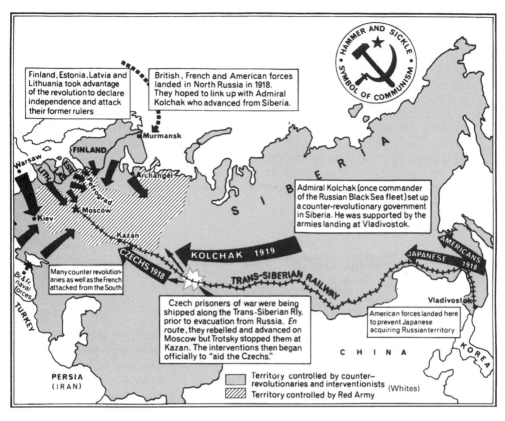

Finland, Estonia, Latvia and Lithuania took advantage of the revolution to declare independence and attack their former rulers

British, French and American forces landed in North Russia in 1918. They hoped to link up with Admiral Kolchak who advanced from Siberia.

HAMMER AND SICKLE · SYMBOL OF COMMUNISM

Murmansk

FINLAND

Warsaw

Archangel

Petrograd

Moscow

Kiev

Kazan

S I B E R I A

Admiral Kolchak (once commander of the Russian Black Sea fleet) set up a counter-revolutionary government in Siberia. He was supported by the armies landing at Vladivostok.

CZECHS 1918

KOLCHAK 1919

AMERICANS 1918

JAPANESE 1918

TRANS-SIBERIAN RAILWAY

Br. & Fr. naval forces

TURKEY

Many counter revolutionaries as well as the French attacked from the South

Czech prisoners of war were being shipped along the Trans-Siberian Rly. prior to evacuation from Russia. *En route*, they rebelled and advanced on Moscow but Trotsky stopped them at Kazan. The interventions then began officially to "aid the Czechs."

Vladivostok

American forces landed here to prevent Japanese acquiring Russian territory

C H I N A

K O R E A

PERSIA (IRAN)

Territory controlled by counter-revolutionaries and interventionists (Whites)

Territory controlled by Red Army

Map 15.2   Civil war and interventions in Russia, 1918–22

Source: B. Catchpole, *A Map History of the Modern World* (Heinemann, 1974) p. 37

Illus. 15.3   The Red Army in the Crimea during the civil war, 1918

was that they had won the civil war. There were a number of reasons for the communist victory.

1   *The Whites were not centrally organized.* Kolchak and Denikin failed to link up, and the nearer they drew to Moscow, the more they strained their lines of communication. They lost the support of many peasants by their brutal behaviour, and because peasants feared that a White victory would mean the loss of their newly acquired land.
2   *The Red Armies had more troops*, probably outnumbering the Whites by about ten to one. They controlled most of the modern industry and so were better supplied with armaments, and had the inspired leadership of Trotsky.
3   Lenin took decisive measures, known as *war communism*, to control the economic resources of the state. All factories of any size were nationalized, all private trade

Illus. 15.4   Starving victims of the civil war

banned, and food and grain seized from peasants to feed town workers and troops. This was successful at first since it enabled the government to survive the civil war, but it had disastrous results later.

4   Lenin was able to present the Bolsheviks as *a nationalist government fighting against foreigners*; and even though war communism was unpopular with the peasants, the Whites became even more unpopular because of their foreign connections.

(d) *Economic problems*

From early 1921 Lenin had the formidable task of rebuilding an economy shattered by the First World War and then by civil war. War communism had been unpopular with the peasants who, seeing no point in working hard to produce food which was taken away from them without compensation, simply produced enough for their own needs. This caused severe food shortages aggravated by droughts in 1920–1 (Illus. 15.4). In addition industry was almost at a standstill. *In March 1921 a serious naval mutiny occurred at Kronstadt*, the island naval base in the Gulf of Finland, just off St Petersburg. This was suppressed only through prompt action by Trotsky, who sent troops across the ice on the Gulf of Finland.

The mutiny seems to have convinced Lenin that a new approach was needed to win back the faltering support of the peasants; this was vitally important since peasants formed a large majority of the population. He put into operation what became known as the *New Economic Policy (NEP)*. Peasants were now allowed to keep surplus produce after payment of a tax representing a certain proportion of the surplus. This, plus the reintroduction of private trade, revived incentive, and food production increased. Small industries and trade in their products were also restored to private ownership, though heavy industry such as coal, iron and steel, together with power, transport and banking, remained under state control. Lenin also found that often the old managers had to be brought back, as well as such capitalist incentives as bonuses and piece-rates.

Some of the other communist leaders, especially Kamenev and Zinoviev, disapproved of NEP because they thought it encouraged the development of *kulaks* (wealthy peasants) who would turn out to be the enemies of communism. *Lenin saw NEP as a temporary compromise* – a return to a certain amount of private enterprise until recovery was assured. His long-term aim was probably full state control of agriculture through the introduction of collective farms. He hoped it would be possible, given time, to persuade the peasants of the advantages of collective farms, so that force would not be necessary.

NEP was moderately successful: the economy began to recover, and great progress was made with the electrification of industry (one of Lenin's pet schemes). Towards the end of 1927, when NEP began to be abandoned, the ordinary Russian was probably better off than at any time since 1914, though there were continuing food shortages.

(e) *Political problems were solved decisively*

Russia was now the world's first communist state, the Union of Soviet Socialist Republics (USSR); power was held by the communist party, and no other parties were allowed. *The main political problem now for Lenin was disagreement and criticism inside the communist party.* In March 1921 Lenin banned 'factionalism' within the party. This meant that discussion would be allowed, but once a decision had been taken, all sections of the party had to stick to it. Anybody who persisted in holding a different view from the official party line would be expelled from the party. During the rest of 1921 about one-third of the party members were 'purged' (expelled) with the help of the ruthless secret police (*Cheka*); many more resigned, mainly because they were against NEP. Lenin also rejected the claim of the trades unions that they should run industry. Trades unions had to do as the government told them, and their main function was to increase production. Control by Lenin and the communist party was now complete. (For his successes in foreign affairs see Section 4.3(a) and (b)).

In May 1922 Lenin suffered a stroke; after this he gradually grew weaker, suffering two more strokes, until he died in January 1924 at the early age of 53. His work of completing the revolution by introducing a fully communist state was not finished, and the successful communist revolutions which Lenin had predicted in other countries had not taken place. This left the USSR isolated and facing an uncertain future. Although his health had been failing for some time, Lenin had made no clear plans about how the government was to be organized after his death, and this meant that a power struggle was inevitable.

Lenin remains a controversial figure

Some historians admire him: A.J.P. Taylor had this to say:

> Lenin did more than any other political figure to change the face of the twentieth century world. The creation of Soviet Russia and its survival were due to him. He was a very great man and even, despite his faults, a very good man.

But others see him as a ruthless dictator who paved the way for the even more ruthless and brutal dictatorship of Stalin. He rejected genuine democracy when he used force to disperse the Constituent Assembly in 1918. He was convinced that the Bolshevik party had a historic mission: to lead the working-class revolution; since the working class were small in number and needed to be led and guided, it followed, as he himself put it, that 'the will of a class is sometimes fulfilled by a dictator'. The killing of thousands of opponents during the Red Terror was also justified, in Lenin's eyes, by the need to fulfil his mission. When he died, Lenin left in place the weapons which Stalin was able to use for his tyranny – a one-party state, a ban on 'factionalism', the use of secret police, and the removal of most of the powers of the trades unions.

His defenders argue that had Lenin lived another twenty years (to the same age as Stalin), Russia would have developed quite differently. For example, the unofficial Soviet historian, Roy Medvedev, believes that Lenin intended to continue NEP for perhaps another twenty-five years, and to launch a campaign among the peasants to develop literacy, to teach them how to produce and use agricultural machinery and tractors and to show them the benefits of agrarian co-operatives. This was how socialism (communism) would triumph in the end, not through the Stalin method of brute force.

Questions

1 *The fall of Tsarism*

Source A

From a Petrograd police report, October 1916

Military defeats brought the masses a clearer understanding of the problems of war
– unfair distribution of foodstuffs, an immense and rapid increase in the cost of
living, and inadequacy in sources of supply. These factors show that neglect of the
home front is the prime cause of the disorganization of the huge machine of state,
and that a terrible crisis is on the way. Everywhere there are exceptionally strong
feelings of hostility and opposition to the government because of the unbearable
burden of the war and the impossible conditions of everyday life. The situation is
serious enough to deserve immediate attention.

Source: quoted in R. Brown and C. Daniels (eds), *Twentieth-Century Europe* (Macmillan, 1981,
adapted)

  (a) Using the information in Sections 15.1 and 2(a), and Source A, make a list of
causes of the downfall of the tsar Nicholas II, indicating what type of cause
each one was (political, economic, military). Point out any connections you
can see between the causes.   1.4b, 5b, 7b   15 marks

  (b) How far would you agree that Russian failures in the First World War were
the main cause of the tsar's downfall?   1.6b–9a, 6c–8c   15 marks

  (c) What are the uses and weaknesses of Source A for the historian?
    3.5, 7, 8   5 marks

(d) Historian John Laver wrote: 'When revolution came to Petrograd in March
1917 . . . most of Russia was taken by surprise'. Do you think the evidence of
Sections 15.1 and 2(a) and Source A support this view or not?
    2.4–8, 3.4   15 marks

Total: 50 marks

2 *Russia under Lenin and the Bolsheviks*   Study Sources A to G and then answer the
questions which follow.

Source A

*From Lenin's instructions for Harvesting Grain and for Grain Requisitioning
Detachments (War Communism), August 1918*

1. All Soviets of Workers' and Peasants' Deputies, all committees of the poor and
trade unions are to form detachments.
2. The tasks of the detachments are:

  (a) Harvest winter grain in former landlord-owned estates.
  (b) Harvest grain in front line areas.
  (c) Harvest grain on the land of kulaks or rich people.
  (d) Help in harvest everywhere.

3. Grain for the poor must be stored locally, the rest must be sent to grain
collection centres.
4. Every food requisition detachment is to consist of not fewer than 75 men and
two or three machine guns.

From an article by Lenin in The Red Sword, *a weekly magazine of the Cheka (secret police), 1919*

For us there do not, and cannot, exist the old systems of morality and 'humanity' invented by the bourgeoisie for the purpose of exploiting and oppressing the 'lower classes'. Our morality is new, for it rests on the bright idea of destroying all oppression and coercion. To us, everything is permitted, for we are the first in the world to raise the sword in the name of freeing everybody from bondage. Blood? Let there be blood if it alone will save us from the return of the old jackals.

— **Source C** —

Reports from British refugees on conditions in Russia, October 1918

These people are unanimous in describing conditions as unbearable, owing to the rule of the Bolsheviks, as well as to the appalling economic conditions brought about by Lenin's regime.

The Russian nation is groaning under the tyranny of the Bolsheviks. Workers and peasants are compelled to work under threat of death. Since only the Red Guards have weapons, a rising of the people is not possible.

Famine is widespread. The peasants refuse to sell food but will only barter it. Unless people have about 1000 roubles (£100) a month, they have to starve. It is possible to buy food from the Red Guards who are well fed. Lenin and his colleagues are living in luxury.

— **Source D** —

From the decree introducing Lenin's New Economic Policy (NEP), March 1921

In order to ensure an efficient and untroubled economic life on the basis of a freer use by the farmer of the products of his labour, in order to strengthen the peasant economy and raise its productivity, requisitioning as a means of state collection of food supplies and raw material, is to be replaced by a tax in kind. It will be in the form of a percentage or partial deduction from the products raised by the peasant. All the reserves of food, raw material and fodder which remain with the peasants after the tax has been paid may be used by them as they wish – for improving their holdings, for increasing personal consumption and for exchange for products of factory and hand-industry.

Source: quoted in W.H. Chamberlin, *The Russian Revolution 1917–1921* (Macmillan, 1935)

Source E

Table 15.1 *Russian production statistics, compiled from various Soviet sources*

	1913	1920	1921	1922	1923	1924	1925	1926
Factory production (m. roubles)	10 251	1 401	2 004	2 619	4 005	4 660	7 739	11 083
Coal (m. tons)	29	8.7	8.9	9.5	13.7	16.1	18.1	27.6
Electricity (m. Kwhs)	1 945	—	520	775	1 146	1 562	2 925	3 508
Pig iron (000 tons)	4 216	—	116	188	309	755	1 535	2 441
Steel (000 tons)	4 231	—	183	392	709	1 140	2 135	3 141
Sown area (m. hectares)	105	—	90.3	77.7	91.7	98.1	104.3	110.3
Grain harvest (m. tons)	80.1	46.1	37.6	50.3	56.6	51.4	72.5	76.8

Source: quoted in John Laver, *Russia 1914–41* (Hodder & Stoughton, 1991)

Source F

Maxim Gorky, Russian writer and friend of Lenin, writing about Lenin soon after his death

I have never met anyone in Russia, nor do I know of anyone, who hated, loathed and despised all unhappiness, grief and suffering as Lenin did. [Lenin had once said to him] 'our ideal is not to use force against anyone'.

Source G

Statements made by Lenin

(i) November 1917, a few days after the revolution
We do not use the sort of terror as was used by the French revolutionaries who guillotined unarmed people, and I hope we shall not have to use it. When we have made arrests we have said 'We will let you go if you sign a piece of paper promising not to commit acts of sabotage'. And such signatures are given.

(ii) April 1918
There will be no famine in Russia if stocks are controlled, and any breach of the rules laid down is followed by the harshest punishment – the arrest and shooting of takers of bribes and swindlers.

(iii) November 1918
Is it possible to act humanely in a struggle of such unprecedented ferocity? We are being blockaded by Europe, we are deprived of the help of the European proletariat, counter-revolution is creeping like a bear on us from every side. Are we not to fight? Ought we not to struggle and resist ... There is only one way to free the masses and that is to crush the exploiters. This is the task of the Cheka, and for this it deserves the gratitude of the proletariat.

Sources: Sources A, B, C, F and G are quoted in R.W. Clark, *Lenin* (Faber, 1988)

(a) Using information from Sections 15.2 and 3 and the sources, explain the reasons why the Russian economy was in such a poor state in 1921 compared with 1913.　　　　　　　　　　　　　　　　1.4b–9a, 3.4   5 marks

(b) Using information from Chapter 15 and Sources A, C and D, make a list of the differences that you can find between war communism and the New Economic Policy (NEP). Why were some people not happy about NEP?

1.4a–6a, 1.6c–7c, 3.4   8 marks

(c) From the evidence of the statistics in Source E, how successful do you think NEP was?   1.4c–5c   6 marks

(d) What similarities and contradictions can you find in the various statements by Lenin in Sources B, F and G?
     What reasons can you suggest for what seem to be contradictions in Lenin's ideas?   1.6c–8c, 3.4   10 marks

(e) What uses and limitations do Sources C, E and F have for the historian?

3.5–9   6 marks

(f) A.J.P. Taylor wrote that Lenin was 'a very great man and even, despite his faults, a very good man'. How far does the evidence of the sources support this verdict on Lenin?   2.4–8, 3.5–10   15 marks

Total: 50 marks

Communist rule in the USSR, 1924–91

Summary of events

This period in the history of the USSR falls into four phases.

1 1924–53

Joseph Stalin was the dominant figure, in effect a dictator from late 1928 until his death in 1953 at the age of 73. When Lenin died in January 1924, it was widely expected that Trotsky would take over as leader, but a complex power struggle developed from which Stalin had emerged triumphant by the end of 1929. Immense problems faced communist Russia, which was still only a few years old. Industry and agriculture were backward and inefficient, there were constant food shortages, pressing social and political problems, and – many Russians thought – the danger of another attempt by foreign capitalist powers to destroy the new communist state. Stalin made determined efforts to overcome all these problems. There were the:

- Five Year Plans to revolutionize industry;
- collectivization of agriculture; and
- introduction of a totalitarian regime which was, if anything, more ruthless than Hitler's system in Germany.

Yet brutal though Stalin's methods were, they seem to have been successful, at least to the extent that when the dreaded attack from the west eventually came, in the form of a massive German invasion in June 1941, the Russians were able to hold out, and eventually end up on the winning side, though at a terrible cost.

2 1953–64

Nikita Khrushchev gradually emerged as the dominant leader during this period. He began a de-Stalinisation policy and made some progress in improving living standards.

3 1964–85

This was a period of stagnation and decline; the leading figure was *Leonid Brezhnev*.

4 1985–91

Mikhail Gorbachev tried to reform and modernize Russian communism and to encourage the same thing in the satellite states of Eastern Europe. However, he proved unable to control the rising tide of criticism of communism, and in 1989–90, non-communist governments were established in most of the states of Eastern Europe (see Section 10.7). When Gorbachev failed to keep his promises of economic reform and higher living standards, the people of the USSR turned against communism and he lost power to *Boris Yeltsin*. The communist party was declared illegal, the USSR broke up into fifteen separate states, and Gorbachev resigned as President of the USSR (December 1991).

16.1 How did Stalin manage to get to supreme power?

Joseph Djugashvili (he took the name 'Stalin' – man of steel – some time after joining the Bolsheviks in 1904) was born in 1879 in the small town of Gori in the province of Georgia. His parents were poor peasants; his father, a shoemaker, had been born a serf. Joseph's mother wanted him to become a priest and he was educated for four years at Tiflis Theological Seminary, but he hated its repressive atmosphere and was expelled in 1899 for spreading socialist ideas. After 1917, thanks to his outstanding ability as an administrator, he was quietly able to build up his own position under Lenin. When Lenin died in 1924, Stalin was Secretary-General of the communist party and a member of the seven-man Politburo, the committee which decided government policy. At first it seemed unlikely that Stalin would become the dominant figure; Trotsky called him 'the party's most eminent mediocrity ... a man destined to play second or third fiddle'. Lenin thought him stubborn and rude, and suggested in his will that Stalin should be removed from his post. The most obvious successor to Lenin was Trotsky, an inspired orator, an intellectual and a man of action – the organizer of the Red Armies. However, circumstances arose which Stalin was able to use to eliminate his rivals.

(a) *Trotsky's brilliance worked against him*

It aroused envy and resentment among the other Politburo members. He was arrogant and condescending and many resented the fact that he had only joined the Bolsheviks shortly before the November revolution. The other Politburo members therefore decided to run the country jointly: collective action was better than a one-man show. They worked together, doing all they could to prevent Trotsky from becoming leader.

(b) *The other Politburo members underestimated Stalin*

They saw him as nothing more than a competent administrator; they ignored Lenin's advice about removing him.

(c) *Stalin used his position*

As Secretary-General of the party, Stalin had full powers of *appointment and promotion*. He used these to place his own supporters in key positions, while at the same time removing the supporters of others to distant parts of the country.

(d) *Stalin used disagreements to his own advantage*

Disagreements in the Politburo over policy arose partly because Marx had never described in detail exactly how the new communist society should be organized. Even Lenin was vague about it, except that 'the dictatorship of the proletariat' would be established – that is, workers would run the state and the economy in their own interests. When all opposition had been crushed, the ultimate goal of a classless society would be achieved, in which, according to Marx, the ruling principle would be: 'from each according to his ability, to each according to his needs'. With NEP (see Section 15.3(d)) Lenin had departed from socialist principles, though he probably intended this to be only a temporary measure until the crisis passed. Now the right wing of the party, led by Bukharin, and the left, whose views were most strongly put by Trotsky, Kamenev and Zinoviev, fell out about what to do next:

1 *Bukharin wanted to continue NEP*, even though it was causing an increase in the numbers of *kulaks* (wealthy peasants), who were thought to be the enemies of communism. His opponents wanted to abandon NEP and concentrate on rapid industrialization at the expense of the peasants.
2 Bukharin thought it important to consolidate soviet power in Russia, based on a prosperous peasantry and with a very gradual industrialization; this policy became known as '*socialism in one country*'. Trotsky believed that they must work for revolution outside Russia – '*permanent revolution*'. When this was achieved, the industrialized states of Western Europe would help Russia with her industrialization.

Illus. 16.1   Joseph Stalin

Stalin, quietly ambitious, seemed to have no strong views either way at first, but he supported the right simply to isolate Trotsky. Later, when a split occurred between Bukharin on the one hand, and Kamenev and Zinoviev, who were feeling unhappy about NEP, on the other, Stalin supported Bukharin. One by one, Trotsky, Kamenev and Zinoviev were voted off the Politburo, replaced by Stalin's yes-men, and expelled from the party (1927). The following year Stalin decided that NEP must go – the *kulaks* were holding up agricultural progress. When Bukharin protested, he too was expelled (1929) and Stalin was left supreme (Illus. 16.1). Having reached the pinnacle, Stalin attacked the many problems facing Russia, which fell into three categories:

- economic;
- political and social; and
- foreign (see Section 4.3).

16.2 How successful was Stalin in solving Russia's economic problems?

(a) *What were Russia's economic problems?*

1   Although Russian industry was recovering from the effects of the First World War, *production from heavy industry was still surprisingly low*. In 1929 for example, France, which did not rank as a leading industrial power, produced more coal and steel than Russia, while Germany, Britain and especially the USA were streets ahead. Stalin believed that a rapid expansion of heavy industry was essential to enable Russia to deal with the attack which he was convinced would come sooner or later from the Western capitalist powers who hated communism. Industrialization would have the added advantage of increasing support for the government, because *it was the industrial workers who were the communists' greatest allies:* the more industrial workers there were in relation to peasants (whom Stalin saw as the enemies of socialism), the more secure the communist state would be. One serious obstacle to overcome though, was *lack of capital to finance expansion*, since foreigners were unwilling to invest in a communist state.

2   *More food would have to be produced*, both to feed the growing industrial population and to provide a surplus for export, which would bring in foreign capital and profits for investment in industry. Yet the primitive agricultural system which was allowed to continue under NEP was incapable of providing such resources.

(b) *The approach: the Five Year Plans and collectivization*

Although he had no economic experience whatsoever, Stalin seems to have had no hesitation in plunging the country into a series of dramatic changes designed to overcome the problems in the shortest possible time. In a speech in February 1931 he explained why: 'We are 50 or 100 years behind the advanced countries. We must make good this distance in 10 years. Either we do it or we shall be crushed'. NEP had been permissible as a temporary measure, but must now be abandoned: both industry and agriculture must be taken firmly under government control.

1 The Five Year Plans

Industrial expansion was tackled by a series of Five Year Plans, the first two of which (1928–32 and 1933–7) were said to have been completed a year ahead of schedule, although in fact neither of them reached the full target. The first plan concentrated on heavy industry – coal, iron, steel, oil and machinery (including tractors), which were scheduled to triple output. The two later plans provided for some increases in consumer goods as well as in heavy industry. It has to be said that in spite of all kinds of mistakes and some exaggeration of the official Soviet figures, the plans were a remarkable success: by 1940 the USSR had overtaken Britain in iron and steel production, though not yet in coal, and she was within reach of Germany (see Tables 16.1 and 16.2).

Table 16.1   Industrial expansion in the USSR: production in millions of tons

	1900	*1913*	*1929*	*1938*	*1940*
Coal	16.0	36.0	40.1	132.9	164.9
Pig iron	2.7	4.8	8.0	26.3	14.9
Steel	2.5	5.2	4.9	18.0	18.4

Table 16.2   Industrial production in the USSR compared with other great powers in 1940 (in millions of tons)

	Pig Iron	*Steel*	*Coal*	*Electricity (in bn kw.)*
USSR	14.9	18.4	164.6	39.6
USA	31.9	47.2	395.0	115.9
Britain	6.7	10.3	227.0	30.7
Germany	18.3	22.7	186.0	55.2
France	6.0	16.1	45.5	19.3

Hundreds of factories were built, many of them in new towns east of the Ural Mountains where they would be safer from invasion. Well-known examples are the iron and steel works at Magnitogorsk, tractor works at Kharkov and Gorki, a hydro-electric dam at Dnepropetrovsk and the oil refineries in the Caucasus.

How was all this achieved?
The cash was provided almost entirely by the Russians themselves, with no foreign investment. Some came from grain exports, some from charging peasants heavily for use of government equipment, and the ruthless ploughing back of all profits and surpluses. Hundreds of foreign technicians were brought in and great emphasis was placed on expanding education in colleges and universities, and even in factory schools, to provide a whole new generation of skilled workers. In the factories, the old capitalist methods of piecework and pay differentials between skilled and unskilled workers were used to encourage production. Medals were given to workers who achieved record output; these were known as *Stakhanovites*, after Alexei Stakhanov, a champion miner who, in August 1935, supported by a well-organized team, managed to cut 102 tons of coal in a single shift (by ordinary methods even the highly efficient miners of the Ruhr in Germany were cutting only 10 tons per shift).

Ordinary workers were ruthlessly disciplined: there were severe punishments for bad workmanship, people were accused of being 'saboteurs' when targets were not met, and given spells in forced labour camps. Primitive housing conditions and a severe shortage of consumer goods (because of the concentration on heavy industry) on top of all the regimentation must have made life grim for most workers. As historian Richard Freeborn points out:

> It is probably no exaggeration to claim that the First Five Year Plan represented a declaration of war by the state machine against the workers and peasants of the USSR who were subjected to a greater exploitation than any they had known under capitalism.

However, by the mid-1930s things were improving as benefits such as medical care, education and holidays with pay became available.

2 Collectivization

This process dealt with the problems of agriculture. The idea was that small farms and holdings belonging to the peasants should be merged to form large collective farms (*kolkhoz*) jointly owned by the peasants. There were two main reasons for Stalin's decision to collectivize:

- the existing system of small farms was inefficient, whereas large farms, under state direction, and using tractors and combine harvesters, would vastly increase grain production (Illus. 16.2);
- he wanted to eliminate the class of prosperous peasants (*kulaks* or nepmen) which NEP had encouraged because, he claimed, they were standing in the way of progress. The real reason was probably political: Stalin saw the *kulaks* as the enemy of communism. 'We must smash the *kulaks* so hard that they will never rise to their feet again'.

Illus. 16.2 Russian peasants admire the first tractor in their village, 1926

The policy was launched in earnest in 1929, and had to be carried through by sheer brute force, so determined was the resistance in the countryside. *It proved to be a disaster from which, it is perhaps no exaggeration to claim, Russia has not fully recovered even today.*

There was no problem in collectivizing landless labourers, but all peasants who owned any property at all, whether they were *kulaks* or not, were hostile to the plan, and had to be forced to join by armies of party members who urged poorer peasants to seize cattle and machinery from the *kulaks* to be handed over to the collectives. *Kulaks* often reacted by slaughtering cattle and burning crops rather than allow the state to take them. Peasants who refused to join collective farms were arrested and taken to labour camps, or shot. When newly collectivized peasants tried to sabotage the system by producing only enough for their own needs, local officials insisted on seizing the required quotas.

Total grain production did not increase at all (except for 1930) – in fact it was less in 1934 than it had been in 1928. This led to famine in many areas during 1932–3, especially in the Ukraine. Yet one and three-quarter million tons of grain were exported during that same period while over 5 million peasants died of starvation. Some historians have even claimed that Stalin welcomed the famine, since, along with the 10 million *kulaks* who were removed or executed, it helped to break peasant resistance. In this way, well over 90 per cent of all farmland had been collectivized by 1937.

In one sense Stalin could claim that collectivization was a success: it allowed greater mechanization, which did achieve a substantial increase in production in 1937. On the other hand, so many animals had been slaughtered that it was 1953 before livestock production recovered to the 1928 figure, and the cost in human life and suffering was enormous. The statistics in Table 16.3 give some idea of the scale of the problems created.

Table 16.3 Grain and livestock statistics in the USSR

Actual grain harvest (in m. tons)

1913	1928	1929	1930	1931	1932	1933	1934	1936	1937
80.1	73.3	71.7	83.5	69.5	69.6	68.4	67.6	56.1	97.4

Grain taken by the state (in m. tons)

1928	1929	1930	1931	1932	1933
10.8	16.1	22.1	22.8	18.5	22.6

Grain exported (in m. tons)

1927–8	1929	1930	1931	1932	1933
0.029	0.18	4.76	5.06	1.73	1.69

Livestock in the the USSR (millions)

	1928	1929	1930	1931	1932	1933	1934	1935
Cattle	70.5	67.1	52.5	47.9	40.7	38.4	42.2	49.3
Pigs	26.0	20.4	13.6	14.4	11.6	12.1	17.4	22.6
Sheep and goats	146.7	147.0	108.8	77.7	52.1	50.2	51.9	61.1

16.3 Political and social problems and Stalin's solutions

(a) *The problems*

These were to some extent of Stalin's own making. He felt that under his totalitarian regime, political and social activities must be controlled just as much as economic life. He aimed at complete and unchallenged power for himself and became increasingly suspicious and intolerant of criticism.

1   Starting in 1930, there was growing opposition in the party; the *Ryutin platform* (1932) aimed to slow down industrialization, allow peasants to leave collective farms, and remove Stalin (described as 'the evil genius of the Revolution') from the leadership if necessary. However, Stalin was equally determined that political opponents and critics must be eliminated once and for all.
2   A new constitution was needed to consolidate the hold of Stalin and the communist party over the whole country.
3   Social and cultural aspects of life needed to be brought into line and harnessed to the service of the state.
4   The non-Russian parts of the country wanted to become independent, but Stalin, although he was non-Russian himself (he was born in Georgia), had no sympathy with nationalist ambitions and was determined to hold the union together.

(b) *Stalin's methods were typically dramatic*

1   The purges

Using the murder of Sergei Kirov, one of his supporters on the Politburo (December 1934), as an excuse, Stalin launched what became known as *the purges*. It seems fairly certain that Stalin himself organized Kirov's murder, 'the crime of the century', as historian Robert Conquest calls it, 'the keystone of the entire edifice of terror and suffering by which Stalin secured his grip on the soviet peoples'; but it was blamed on Stalin's critics.

Over the next four years hundreds of important officials were arrested, tortured, made to confess to all sorts of crimes of which they were largely innocent (such as plotting with the exiled Trotsky or with capitalist governments to overthrow the soviet state) and forced to appear in a series of 'show trials' at which they were invariably found guilty and sentenced to death or labour camp. Those executed included M.N. Ryutin (author of the Ryutin platform), all the 'Old Bolsheviks' – Zinoviev, Kamenev, Bukharin and Radek – who had helped to make the 1917 revolution, the Commander-in-Chief of the Red Army, Tukhachevsky, thirteen other generals and about two-thirds of the top officers. Millions of innocent people ended up in labour camps (some estimates put the figure at about 8 million). Even Trotsky was sought out and murdered in exile in Mexico City (1940).

The purges were successful in eliminating possible alternative leaders and in terrorizing the masses into obedience; but the consequences were serious: many of the best brains in the government, in the army and in industry had disappeared. In a country where numbers of highly educated people were still relatively small, this was bound to hinder progress.

2   A new constitution

In 1936, after much discussion, a new and apparently more democratic constitution was introduced in which everyone was allowed to vote by secret ballot to choose members of a national assembly known as the *Supreme Soviet*. However, this met for only about two weeks in the year, when it elected a smaller body, the *Praesidium*, to act on its behalf. The Supreme Soviet also chose the *Union Soviet of Commissars*, a small group of ministers of which Stalin was the secretary, and which wielded the real power.

In fact the democracy was an illusion: the constitution merely underlined the fact that Stalin and the party ran things, and though there was mention of freedom of speech, anybody who ventured to criticize Stalin was quickly 'purged'.

3 Social and cultural policies

- *Writers, artists and musicians* were expected to produce works of realism glorifying soviet achievements; anyone who did not conform was persecuted, and even those who tried, often fell foul of Stalin. The young composer Dmitri Shostakovich was condemned when his new opera, *Lady Macbeth of Mtsensk*, failed to please Stalin, even though the music critics had at first praised it. Further performances were banned, and the American ambassador noted that 'half the artists and musicians in Moscow are having nervous prostration and the others are trying to imagine how to write and compose in a manner to please Stalin'.
- *Education*, like everything else, was closely watched by the secret police, and although it was compulsory and free, it tended to deteriorate into indoctrination; but at least literacy increased, which along with the improvement in social services, was an unprecedented achievement.
- Finally, *an attempt was made to clamp down on the Orthodox Church*. Churches were closed and clergy persecuted; but this was one of Stalin's failures: in 1940 probably half the population were still convinced believers, and during the war the persecution was relaxed to help maintain morale.

4 Holding the union together

In 1914, before the First World War, the tsarist empire included many non-Russian areas – Poland, Finland, the Ukraine, Belorussia (White Russia), Georgia, Armenia, Azerbaijan, Kazakhstan, Kirghizia, Uzbekistan, Turkmenistan, Tajikistan, and the three Baltic states of Estonia, Latvia and Lithuania (see Map 16.1). Poland and the three Baltic republics were given independence by the Treaty of Brest-Litovsk (March 1918). Many of the others wanted independence too, and at first the new Bolshevik government was sympathetic to these different nationalities. Lenin gave Finland independence in November 1917.

However, some of the others were not prepared to wait: by March 1918 the Ukraine, Georgia, Armenia and Azerbaijan had declared themselves independent and soon showed themselves to be anti-Bolshevik. Stalin, who was appointed Commissar (Minister) for Nationalities by Lenin, decided that these hostile states surrounding Russia were too much of a threat; during the civil war they were all forced to become part of Russia again. By 1925 there were six soviet republics – Russia itself, Transcaucasia (consisting of Georgia, Armenia and Azerbaijan), the Ukraine, Belorussia, Uzbekistan and Turkmenistan.

The problem for the communist government was that 47 per cent of the population of the USSR were non-Russian, and it would be difficult to hold them all together if they were bitterly resentful of rule from Moscow. Stalin adopted a two-handed approach which worked successfully until Gorbachev came to power in 1985:

- on the one hand, national cultures and languages were encouraged and the republics had a certain amount of independence;

- on the other hand, it had to be clearly understood that Moscow had the final say in all important decisions. If necessary, force would be used to preserve control by Moscow.

When the Ukraine communist party stepped out of line in 1932 by admitting that collectivization had been a failure, Moscow carried out a ruthless purge of what Stalin called 'bourgeois nationalist deviationists'. Similar campaigns followed in Belorussia, Trancaucasia and Central Asia. Later, in 1951, when the Georgian communist leaders tried to take Georgia out of the USSR, Stalin had them removed and shot.

(c) *1945–53*

After the war, Stalin continued to rule the USSR for a further eight years until his death in 1953. The western half of European Russia was devastated by the war: roads, railways and industries were shattered and 25 million people were homeless. Stalin was determined that there should be no relaxation of government controls: the economy must be reconstructed. *The Fourth Five Year Plan* was started in 1946, and, incredibly in the circumstances, succeeded in restoring industrial production to its 1940 levels. Just as he was about to launch another set of purges, Stalin died, to the immense relief of his close associates.

16.4 Was the Stalin approach necessary?

Historians have failed to agree about the extent of Stalin's achievement, or indeed whether he achieved any more with his brutality than he could have done using less drastic methods.

- Stalin's defenders, who included many Soviet historians, argued that *the situation was so desperate that only the pressures of brute force could have produced such a rapid industrialization, together with the necessary food.* For them, the supreme justification is that thanks to Stalin, Russia was strong enough to defeat the Germans.
- The opposing view is that *Stalin's policies, though superficially successful, actually weakened Russia:* ridiculously high targets for industrial production placed unnecessary pressure on the workers and led to slipshod work and poor quality products; the brutal enforcement of collectivization vastly reduced the amount of meat available and made peasants so bitter that in the Ukraine the German invaders were welcomed. The purges slowed economic progress by removing many of the most experienced men, and almost caused military defeat during the first few months of the war by depriving the army of all its experienced generals. In fact Russia won the war *in spite of Stalin*, not because of him.

Whichever view one accepts, a final point to bear in mind is that many Marxists, both inside and outside Russia, feel that Stalin betrayed the idealism of Marx and Lenin. Russian historian Roy Medvedev thinks that Stalin deserves no credit at all. Instead of a new classless society in which everybody was free and equal, ordinary workers and peasants were just as exploited as they had been under the tsars. The party had taken the place of the capitalists, and enjoyed all the privileges – the best houses, country retreats and cars. Instead of Marxism, socialism and the 'dictatorship of the proletariat', there was merely Stalinism and the dictatorship of Stalin.

16.5 The Khrushchev era – 1953–64

(a) *The rise of Khrushchev 1953–7*

With the death of Stalin, the situation was similar to that after Lenin's death in 1924: there was no obvious candidate to take over the reins. Stalin had allowed no one to show any initiative in case he developed into a dangerous rival. The leading members of the Politburo or Praesidium as it was now called, decided to share power and rule as a group. Malenkov became Chairman of the Council of Ministers, Khrushchev Party Secretary, and Voroshilov Chairman of the Praesidium. Also involved were Beria, the Chief of the Secret Police, Bulganin and Molotov.

Gradually Nikita Khrushchev began to emerge as the dominant personality. The son of a peasant farmer, he had worked as a farm labourer and then as a mechanic in a coalmine before going to technical college and joining the communist party. Beria, who had an atrocious record of cruelty as chief of police, was executed, probably because the others were nervous in case he turned against them. Malenkov resigned in 1955 after disagreeing with Khrushchev about industrial policies, but it was significant that in the new relaxed atmosphere, he was not executed or imprisoned.

Khrushchev's position was further strengthened by an amazing speech which he delivered at the Twentieth Communist Party Congress (1956) strongly criticizing various aspects of Stalin's policies. He:

- condemned Stalin for encouraging the cult of his own personality instead of allowing the party to rule;
- revealed details about Stalin's purges of the 1930s and criticized his conduct of the war;
- claimed that socialism could be achieved in ways other than those insisted on by Stalin;
- suggested that peaceful co-existence with the West was not only possible but essential if nuclear war were to be avoided.

Khrushchev was not quite supreme yet; Molotov and Malenkov believed his speech was too drastic and would encourage unrest (they blamed him for the Hungarian revolution of October 1956), and they tried to force him out of office. However, as Party Secretary, Khrushchev, like Stalin before him, had been quietly filling key positions with his own supporters, and since he could rely on the army, it was Molotov and Malenkov who found themselves compulsorily retired (June 1957). After that, Khrushchev was fully responsible for all Russian policy until 1964. But he never wielded as much power as Stalin; the Central Committee of the party was ultimately in charge, and it was the party which voted him out in 1964.

(b) *Khrushchev's problems and policies*

In spite of Russia's recovery during Stalin's last years, there were a number of serious problems: the low standard of living among industrial and agricultural workers, and the inefficiency of agriculture, which was still a long way from providing all Russia's needs. Khrushchev was fully aware of the problems both at home and abroad and was keen to introduce important changes as part of *a general de-Stalinization policy*.

1 Industrial policy

Industry continued to be organized under the Five Year Plans, but for the first time these concentrated more on light industries producing consumer goods (radios, TV sets, washing machines and sewing machines) in an attempt to raise living standards. To reduce over centralization and encourage efficiency, a hundred Regional Economic Councils were set up to make decisions about and organize their local industries. Managers were encouraged to make profits instead of just meeting quotas, and wages depended on output.

All this certainly led to an improvement in living standards: a vast housing programme was started in 1958; between 1955 and 1966 the number of radios per thousand of the population increased from 66 to 171, TV sets from 4 to 82, refrigerators from 4 to 40, and washing machines from 1 to 77.

However, this was way behind the USA, which in 1966 could boast per thousand of the population no fewer than 1300 radios, 376 TV sets, 293 refrigerators, and 259 washing machines. Of course, much depends on how one measures progress, but it was Khrushchev himself who had rashly claimed that the gap between Russia and America would be closed within a few years. Another more spectacular piece of technological progress was the first manned orbit of the earth by Uri Gagarin (1961).

2 Agricultural policy

In agriculture there was a drive to increase food production. Khrushchev's special brainchild was *the virgin lands scheme (started 1954)*, which involved cultivating for the first time huge areas of land in Siberia and Kazakhstan. Peasants on collective farms were allowed to keep or sell crops grown on their private plots, and the government increased its payments for crops from the collectives, thus providing incentives to produce more.

By 1958 total farm output had risen by 56 per cent; between 1953 and 1962 grain production rose from 82 million tons to 147 million. But then things began to go wrong; the 1963 grain output was down to 110 million tons, mainly because of the failure of the virgin lands scheme. The trouble was that much of the land was of poor quality, not enough fertilizers were used, and the exhausted soil began to blow away in dust storms. In general there was still too much interference in agriculture from local party officials, and it remained the least efficient sector of the economy. The Russians had to rely on grain imports, often from the USA.

3 Political changes

The thaw included the return to party control instead of Stalin's personality cult, a reduction in secret police activities (sacked politicians and officials retired into obscurity instead of being tortured and executed), more freedom for ordinary people, more tourism, and a slight relaxation of press controls.

4 Foreign affairs

Following his Twentieth Congress speech, Khrushchev aimed for *peaceful co-existence and a thaw in the Cold War* (see Section 7.3), and seemed prepared to allow different 'roads to socialism' among the satellites. However, these departures from strict Marxist–Leninist ideas (including his encouragement of profit and wage incentives) laid him open to Chinese accusations of '*revisionism*' (see Section 8.5(d)). In addition, encouraged by his speech, Poland and Hungary tried to break Moscow's grip. Khrushchev's reaction to the developments in Hungary showed how limited his toleration was (see Sections 9.3(e) and 10.6(c–d)).

(c) *Khrushchev's fall*

In October 1964 the Central Committee of the party voted Khrushchev into retirement on the grounds of ill-health; in fact, although he was seventy, his health was perfectly good. The real reasons were probably the failure of his agricultural policy (though he had been no less successful than previous governments in this), his loss of prestige over the Cuban missiles crisis (see Section 7.4(b)), and the widening breach with China, which he made no attempt to heal. Perhaps his colleagues were tired of his extrovert personality (once in a heated moment at the United Nations, he took off his shoe and hammered the table with it) and felt he was taking too much on himself. Without consulting them he had just tried to win the friendship of President Nasser of Egypt by awarding him the Order of Lenin at a time when he was busy arresting Egyptian communists. Khrushchev was a man of outstanding personality: a tough politician and yet at the same time impulsive and full of warmth and humour. He deserves to be remembered for his foreign policy innovations, for the return to comparatively civilized politics (at least inside Russia), and for the improved living standards of the masses.

16.6 The USSR stagnates

(a) *The Brezhnev era*

After Khrushchev's departure, three men, Kosygin, Brezhnev and Podgorny, seemed to be sharing power. At first Kosygin was the leading figure and the chief spokesman on foreign affairs, while Brezhnev and Podgorny looked after home affairs. In the early 1970s Kosygin was eclipsed by Brezhnev after a disagreement over economic policies. Kosygin pressed for more economic decentralization, but this was unpopular with the other leaders, who claimed that it encouraged too much independence of thought in the satellite states, especially Czechoslovakia. Brezhnev established firm personal control by 1977, and he remained leader until his death in November 1982. Broadly speaking, his policies were similar to those of the Khrushchev period.

1 Economic policies

Economic policies maintained wage differentials and profit incentives, and some growth took place, but the rate was slow. The system remained strongly centralized, and Brezhnev was reluctant to take any major initiatives. By 1982 therefore, much of Russian industry was old-fashioned and in need of new production and processing technology. There was concern about the failure of the coal and oil industries to increase output, and the building industry was notorious for slowness and poor quality. Low agricultural yield was still a major problem – not once in the period 1980–4 did grain production come anywhere near the targets set. The 1981 harvest was disastrous and 1982 was only slightly better, throwing Russia into an uncomfortable dependency on American wheat. It was calculated that in the USA in 1980 one agricultural worker produced enough to feed seventy-five people, while his counterpart in Russia could manage only enough to feed ten.

2 The Eastern Bloc

The Eastern Bloc states were expected to obey Moscow's wishes and to maintain their existing structure. When liberal trends developed in Czechoslovakia (especially abolition of press censorship), a massive invasion took place by Russian and other Warsaw

Pact troops. The reforming government of Dubček was replaced by a strongly centralized, pro-Moscow regime (1968) (see Section 10.6(e)).

Soon afterwards Brezhnev declared the so-called *Brezhnev Doctrine*: according to this, intervention in the internal affairs of any communist country was justified *if socialism in that country was considered to be threatened*. This caused some friction with Romania, which had always tried to maintain some independence, refusing to send troops into Czechoslovakia and keeping on good terms with China. The Russian invasion of Afghanistan (1979) was the most blatant application of the doctrine, while more subtle pressures were brought to bear on Poland (1981) to control the independent trade union movement, Solidarity (see Section 10.6(f)).

3 Human rights

Brezhnev's record on human rights was not impressive; though he claimed to be in favour of the Helsinki Agreement (see Section 10.6(f)), and appeared to make important concessions about human rights in the USSR, in fact little progress was made. Groups were set up to check whether the terms of the agreement were being kept, but the authorities put them under intense pressure. Their members were arrested, imprisoned, exiled or deported, and finally the groups were dissolved altogether (September 1982).

4 Foreign policy

The Russians worked towards détente, but after 1979 relations with the West deteriorated sharply as a result of the invasion of Afghanistan. Brezhnev continued to advocate disarmament but presided over a rapid increase in Soviet armed forces, particularly the navy and the new SS-20 missiles (see Section 7.4(c)). He stepped up Soviet aid to Cuba and offered aid to Angola, Mozambique and Ethiopia.

(b) *Andropov and Chernenko*

After Brezhnev's death Russia was ruled for a short period by two elderly and ailing politicians – Andropov (November 1982–February 1984) and then Chernenko (February 1984–March 1985).

Head of the KGB until May 1982, Andropov immediately launched a vigorous campaign to modernize and streamline the soviet system. He began an anti-corruption drive and introduced a programme of economic reform, hoping to increase production by encouraging decentralization. Some of the older party officials were replaced with younger, more go-ahead men. Unfortunately he was dogged by ill-health and died after little more than a year in office.

The 72-year-old Chernenko was a more conventional type of Soviet politician. There was no relaxation in the treatment of human rights activists. Dr Andrei Sakharov, the famous nuclear physicist, was still kept in exile in Siberia (where he had been since 1980), in spite of appeals by Western leaders for his release. Members of an unofficial trade union, supporters of a group 'for the establishment of trust between the USSR and the USA', and members of unofficial religious groups were all arrested.

16.7 Gorbachev and the end of communist rule

Mikhail Gorbachev, who came to power in March 1985, was, at fifty-four, the most gifted and dynamic leader Russia had seen for many years. He was determined to transform and revitalize the country after the sterile years following Khrushchev's fall. He intended to achieve this by *modernizing and streamlining the communist party* with new policies of *glasnost* (openness) and *perestroika* (restructuring – which meant economic and social reform).

The new thinking soon made an impact on foreign affairs, with initiatives on détente, relations with China, a withdrawal from Afghanistan, and ultimately the ending of the Cold War in late 1990 (see Section 8.5).

Gorbachev outlined what was wrong at home in a speech to the Party Conference in 1988: the system was too centralized, leaving no room for local individual initiative. It was based almost completely on state ownership and control, and weighted strongly towards defence and heavy industry, leaving consumer goods for ordinary people in short supply (Illus. 16.3).

*Gorbachev did **not** want to end communism; he wanted to replace the existing system, which was still basically Stalinist, with a socialist system which was humane and democratic.* He did not have the same success at home as abroad. His policies failed to provide results quickly enough, and led to the collapse of communism, the breakup of the USSR, and the end of his own political career.

(a) *Gorbachev's new policies*

1 Glasnost

This was soon seen in areas such as *human rights and cultural affairs*. Several well-known dissidents were released, and the Sakharovs were allowed to return to Moscow

Illus. 16.3 Mikhail Gorbachev tries to persuade Russian workers of the benefits of *glasnost* and *perestroika*

from internal exile in Gorky (December 1986). Leaders like Bukharin who had been disgraced and executed during Stalin's purges of the 1930s were declared innocent of all crimes. *Pravda* was allowed to print an article criticizing Brezhnev for overreacting against dissidents, and a new law was introduced to prevent dissidents from being sent to mental institutions (January 1988). Important political events like the Nineteenth Party Conference in 1988 and the first session of the new Congress of People's Deputies (May1989) were televised.

In cultural matters and the media generally, there were some startling developments. In May 1986 both the Union of Soviet Film-makers and the Union of Writers were allowed to sack their reactionary heads and elect more independent-minded leaders. Long-banned anti-Stalin films and novels were shown and published, and preparations were made to publish works by the great poet Osip Mandelstam, who died in a labour camp in 1938.

There was a new freedom in news reporting: in April 1986, for example, when a nuclear reactor at Chernobyl in the Ukraine exploded, killing hundreds of people and releasing a massive radioactive cloud which drifted across most of Europe, the disaster was discussed with unprecedented frankness. The aims of this new approach were to:

- use the media to publicize the inefficiency and corruption which the government was so anxious to stamp out;
- educate public opinion; and
- mobilize support for the new policies.

Glasnost was encouraged provided nobody criticized the party itself.

2 Economic affairs

Important changes were soon afoot. In November 1986 Gorbachev announced that '1987 will be the year for broad applications of the new methods of economic management'. Small-scale private enterprise such as family restaurants, family businesses making clothes or handicrafts or providing services such as car or TV repairs, painting and decorating and private tuition, was to be allowed, and so were workers' co-operatives up to a maximum of fifty workers. One motive behind this reform was to provide competition for the slow and inefficient services provided by the state, in the hope of stimulating a rapid improvement. Another was the need to provide alternative employment as patterns of employment changed over the following decade: as more automation and computerization are introduced into factories and offices, the need for manual and clerical workers declines.

Another important change was that responsibility for quality control throughout industry as a whole was to be taken over by independent state bodies rather than factory management.

The most important part of the reforms was the *Law on State Enterprises (June 1987)*. This removed the central planners' total control over raw materials, production quotas and trade, and made factories work to orders from customers.

3 Political changes

These began in January 1987 when Gorbachev announced moves towards democracy within the party. Instead of members of local soviets being *appointed* by the local communist party, they were to be *elected by the people*, and there was to be a choice of candidates (though not of parties). There were to be secret elections for top party positions, and elections in factories to choose managers.

During 1988 dramatic changes in central government were achieved. The old parliament (Supreme Soviet) of about 1450 deputies only met for about two weeks each year. Its function was to elect two smaller bodies – the Praesidium (33 members) and the Council of Ministers (71 members). It was these two committees which took all important decisions and saw that policies were carried out. Now the Supreme Soviet was to be replaced by a Congress of People's Deputies (2250 members) whose main function was to elect a new and much smaller Supreme Soviet (450 representatives) which would be a proper working parliament, sitting for about eight months a year. The chairman of the Supreme Soviet would be head of state.

Elections went ahead, and the first Congress of People's Deputies met in May 1989. During the second session (December 1989) it was decided that reserved seats for the communist party should be abolished. Gorbachev was elected President of the Soviet Union (March 1990), with two councils to advise and help him: one contained his own personal advisers, the other contained representatives from the 15 republics. These new bodies completely sidelined the old system, and it meant that the communist party was on the verge of losing its privileged position.

(b) *What went wrong with Gorbachev's policies?*

1 Opposition from radicals and conservatives

As the reforms got under way, Gorbachev ran into problems. Some party members, such as *Boris Yeltsin*, the Moscow party leader, were more radical than Gorbachev, and felt that the reforms were not drastic enough. They wanted a change to a Western-style market economy as quickly as possible, though they knew this would cause great short-term hardship for the Russian people. On the other hand, the traditional (conservative) communists like *Yegor Ligachev*, felt that the changes were too drastic and that the party was in danger of losing control. This caused a dangerous split in the party and made it difficult for Gorbachev to satisfy either group.

The conservatives were in a large majority, and when the Congress of People's Deputies elected the new Supreme Soviet (May 1989), it was packed with conservatives; Yeltsin and many other radicals were not elected. This led to massive protest demonstrations in Moscow, where Yeltsin was a popular figure since he had cleaned up the corrupt Moscow communist party organization. Demonstrations would not have been allowed before Gorbachev's time, but *glasnost* – encouraging people to voice their criticisms – was now in full flow, and was beginning to turn against the communist party.

2 The economic reforms did not produce results quickly enough

The rate of economic growth in 1988 and 1989 stayed exactly the same as it had been in previous years. In 1990 national income actually fell and continued to fall – by about 15 per cent – in 1991. Some economists think that the USSR was going through an economic crisis as serious as the one in the USA in the early 1930s.

A major cause of the crisis was the disastrous results of the Law on State Enterprises. The problem was that wages were now dependent on output, but since output was measured by its value in roubles, factories were tempted not to increase overall output, but to concentrate on more expensive goods and reduce output of cheaper goods. This led to higher wages, forcing the government to print more money to pay them with. Inflation soared and so did the government's budget deficit. Basic goods such as soap, washing-powder, razor-blades, cups and saucers, TV sets and food were in very short supply, and the queues in the towns got longer.

Disillusion with Gorbachev and his reforms rapidly set in, and, having had their expectations raised by his promises, people became outraged at the shortages. In July 1989 some coalminers in Siberia found there was no soap to wash themselves with at the end of their shift. 'What kind of a regime is it', they asked, 'if we can't even get washed?' After staging a sit-in, they decided to go on strike; they were quickly joined by other miners in Siberia, in Kazakhstan and in the Donbass (Ukraine), the biggest coalmining area in the USSR, until half a million miners were on strike. *It was the first major strike since 1917.* The miners were well-disciplined and organized, holding mass meetings outside party headquarters in the main towns. They put forward detailed demands, forty-two in all. These included better living and working conditions, better supplies of food, a share in the profits, and more local control over the mines. Later, influenced by what was happening in Poland (where a non-communist prime minister had just been elected – see Section 10.7(c)), they called for independent trade unions like Poland's Solidarity, and in some areas they demanded an end to the privileged position of the communist party. The government soon gave way and granted many of the demands, promising a complete reorganization of the industry and full local control.

By the end of July the strike was over, but the general economic situation did not improve. Early in 1990 it was calculated that about a quarter of the population was living below the poverty line; worst affected were those with large families, the unemployed and pensioners. *Gorbachev was fast losing control of the reform movement which he had started*, and the success of the miners was bound to encourage the radicals to press for even more far-reaching changes.

3 Nationalist pressures

These also contributed towards Gorbachev's failure and led to the breakup of the USSR. The Soviet Union was a federal state consisting of fifteen separate republics each with its own parliament (Map 16.1). The Russian republic was just one of the fifteen, with its parliament in Moscow. (Moscow was also the meeting-place for the *federal* Supreme Soviet and Congress of People's Deputies.) The republics had been kept under tight control since Stalin's time, but *glasnost* and *perestroika* encouraged them to hope for more powers for their parliaments and more independence from Moscow. Gorbachev himself seemed sympathetic, provided that the Communist Party of the Soviet Union (CPSU) remained in overall control. However, once started, demands got out of hand.

● *Trouble began in Nagorno-Karabakh*, a small Christian autonomous republic within the Soviet republic of Azerbaijan, which was Muslim. The parliament of Nagorno-Karabakh requested to become part of neighbouring Christian Armenia (February 1988), but Gorbachev refused. He was afraid that if he agreed, this would upset the conservatives (who opposed internal frontier changes) and turn them against his entire reform programme. Fighting broke out between Azerbaijan and Armenia, and Moscow had clearly lost control.

● *Worse was to follow in the three Baltic Soviet republics of Lithuania, Latvia and Estonia*, which had been taken over against their will by the Russians in 1940. Independence movements denounced by Gorbachev as 'national excesses' had been growing in strength. In March 1990, encouraged by what was happening in the satellite states of Eastern Europe, Lithuania took the lead by declaring itself independent. The other two soon followed, though they voted to proceed more gradually. Moscow refused to recognize their independence.

● Boris Yeltsin, who had been excluded from the new Supreme Soviet by the conservatives, made a dramatic comeback when he was elected president of the parliament of the *Russian republic* (Russian Federation) in May 1990.

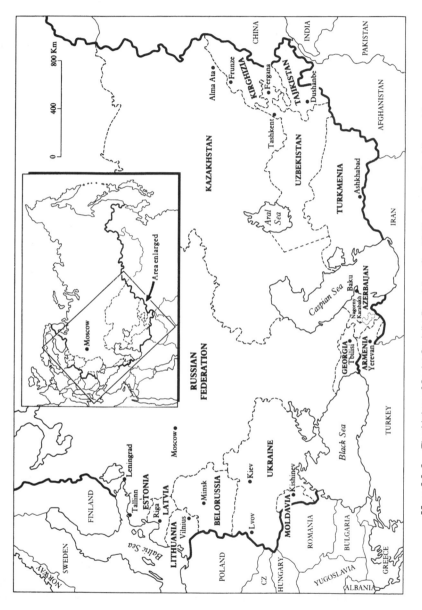

Map 16.1 The Union of Soviet Socialist Republics after 1945, showing the 15 republics

Source: Angus Roxburgh, *The Second Russian Revolution* (BBC Books, 1991) p. 1

4   Gorbachev and Yeltsin were now bitter rivals

They disagreed on many fundamental issues.

* *Yeltsin believed that the union should be voluntary:* each republic should be independent but also have joint responsibilities to the Soviet Union as well. If any republic wanted to opt out, as Lithuania did, it should be allowed to do so. However, Gorbachev thought that a purely voluntary union would lead to disintegration.
* *Yeltsin was now completely disillusioned with the communist party* and the way the traditionalists had treated him. He thought the party no longer deserved its privileged position in the state. Gorbachev was still a convinced communist and thought the only way forward was through a humane and democratic communist party.
* On the economy *Yeltsin thought the answer was a rapid changeover to a market economy*, though he knew that this would be painful for the Russian people. Gorbachev was much more cautious, realizing that Yeltsin's plans would cause massive unemployment and even higher prices. He was fully aware of how unpopular he was already; if things got even worse, he might well be overthrown.

(c) *The coup of August 1991*

As the crisis deepened, Gorbachev and Yeltsin tried to work together, and Gorbachev found himself being pushed towards free multi-party elections. This brought bitter attacks from Ligachev and the conservatives, and Yeltsin resigned from the communist party (July 1990). *Gorbachev was now losing control:* many of the republics were demanding independence, and when Soviet troops were used against nationalists in Lithuania and Latvia, the people organized massive demonstrations. In April 1991 Georgia declared independence: it seemed that the USSR was falling apart. However, the following month Gorbachev held a conference with the leaders of the fifteen republics and persuaded them to form a new voluntary union in which they would be largely independent of Moscow. The agreement was to be formally signed on 20 August 1991.

At this point a group of hardline communists, including Gorbachev's vice-president, Gennady Yanayev, decided they had had enough, and launched a coup to remove Gorbachev and reverse his reforms. *On 18 August Gorbachev, who was on holiday in the Crimea, was arrested and told to hand over power to Yanayev.* When he refused, he was kept under house arrest while the coup went ahead in Moscow. The public was told that Gorbachev was ill and that an eight-member committee was now in charge. They declared a state of emergency, banned demonstrations, and brought in tanks and troops to surround public buildings in Moscow, including the White House (the parliament of the Russian Federation) which they intended to seize. Gorbachev's new union treaty, which was due to be signed the following day, was cancelled.

However, *the coup was poorly organized and the leaders failed to have Yeltsin arrested.* He rushed to the White House, and, standing on a tank outside, he condemned the coup and called on the people of Moscow to rally round in support. The troops were confused, not knowing which side to support, but none of them would make a move against the popular Yeltsin. It soon became clear that some sections of the army were sympathetic to the reformers. By the evening of 20 August, thousands of people were on the streets, barricades were built against the tanks, and the army hesitated to cause heavy casualties by attacking the White House. *On 21 August the coup leaders admitted defeat and were eventually arrested.* Yeltsin had triumphed and Gorbachev was able to return to Moscow. But things could never be the same again, and the failed coup had important consequences:

- the communist party was disgraced and discredited by the actions of the hardliners. Gorbachev soon resigned as party general secretary and the party was banned in the Russian Federation;
- Yeltsin was seen as the hero and Gorbachev was increasingly sidelined. Yeltsin ruled the Russian Federation as a separate republic, introducing a drastic programme to move to a free-market economy. When the Ukraine, the second largest soviet republic, voted to become independent (1 December 1991), it was clear that the old USSR was finished;
- Yeltsin was already negotiating for a new union of the republics. This was joined first by the Russian Federation, the Ukraine, and Belorussia (8 December 1991), and eight other republics joined later. The new union was known as the Commonwealth of Independent States (CIS). Although the member states were fully independent, they agreed to work together on economic matters and defence;
- these developments meant that Gorbachev's role as president of the USSR had ceased to exist, and he resigned on Christmas Day 1991.

(d) *Verdict on Gorbachev*

There can be no question that Gorbachev, in spite of his failures, was one of the outstanding leaders of the twentieth century. His achievement, especially in foreign affairs, was enormous. His policies of *glasnost* and *perestroika* restored freedom to the people of the USSR. His policies of reducing military expenditure, détente, and withdrawal from Afghanistan and Eastern Europe, made a vital contribution to the ending of the Cold War. It has been suggested that Gorbachev was the real successor of Lenin, and that he was trying to get communism back on the track intended for it by Lenin before it was hi-jacked by Stalin, who twisted and perverted it.

> **Could Gorbachev have succeeded and preserved a modernized, humane communism, if he had tackled the problems differently?**
>
> Much has already been written about this, and comparisons made with communist China. Why did communism survive there but not in the USSR? One explanation goes as follows:
>
>> Both the USSR and China needed reform in two areas – the communist party and government **and** the economy. Gorbachev believed these could only be achieved one at a time, and chose to introduce the political reforms first, without any really fundamental economic innovations. The Chinese did it the other way round, introducing economic reform first (see Section 18.3) and leaving the power of the communist party unchanged. This meant that although the people suffered economic hardship, the government retained tight control over them, and in the last resort was prepared to use force against them, unlike Gorbachev.

One final point which needs to be emphasized is that 1991 did not mean the end of communism, in Russia or Eastern Europe. Reformed communist parties re-emerged, sometimes under different names, in a multi-party setting, in Lithuania, Bulgaria, Poland and Russia (see below). What really ended in 1991 was not communism but Stalinism.

(e) *Russia after Gorbachev*

Yeltsin was faced with the same problem as Gorbachev: how to transform Russia into a market economy by privatizing the inefficient, subsidized state industries and agriculture. Yeltsin was hugely popular, but this would only last if he could improve the people's living standards. Through 1992 and 1993 the economy continued to decline as output fell even more steeply than under Gorbachev. Living standards declined and many people were worse off than before *glasnost* and *perestroika*.

The government was also embarrassed by armed conflict within the Russian Federation: rebel forces in the small republic of Chechenia declared independence, and Yeltsin sent troops and heavy artillery against the Chechens. Although TV viewers worldwide saw pictures of the Chechen capital, Grozny, reduced to rubble, the Russian army seemed unable to defeat the rebels. As the elections for the Duma (the lower house of the Russian Federation parliament) approached (December 1995), Yeltsin's popularity was waning and support for the reformed communist party under their leader, Gennady Zyuganov, was reviving. The communists scored something of a triumph in the elections, winning 23 per cent of the votes and becoming the largest party in the Duma.

During the first half of 1996 the economy began to show signs of recovery: the budget deficit and inflation were both coming down steadily, and production was increasing. Elections for a new president were due in June, and Western governments, worried about the prospect of a Zyuganov victory, were clearly hoping that Yeltsin would be re-elected. The International Monetary Fund was persuaded to give Russia a $10.2 billion loan (March). The leaders of the former Soviet republics (members of the Commonwealth of Independent States) also backed Yeltsin, because they were afraid that a communist president might try to end their independence. Yeltsin's chances received a boost when he succeeded in negotiating a ceasefire in Chechenia (May), and *he eventually won a comfortable victory, taking almost 35 per cent of the votes* against 32 per cent for Zyuganov. However, this showed that communism (new-style) was far from dead, and there were fears that Yeltsin's failing health (he underwent major heart surgery in November 1996) might prevent him from completing his full term in office.

Questions

1   *Communism in Russia*   Study Sources A to E and then answer the questions which follow.

*A Russian poster of 1952 (Illus. 16.4). The writing tells us that the children are
thanking Stalin (who was 72-years-old in 1952) for a happy childhood. Stalin was
Russian leader from 1929 until his death in 1953.*

Extract from a book by Lenin, the first Russian communist leader from 1917 until 1924

In capitalist society we have a democracy that is false, a democracy only for the rich, for the minority. The dictatorship of the proletariat will for the first time create democracy for the people, for the majority. Communism alone is capable of providing really complete democracy.

Source: V.I. Lenin, *The State and Revolution*, September 1917; quoted in Robert C. Tucker, *The Lenin Anthology* (Norton, 1975)

Source C

Communism does not accept the possibility of improving capitalism, that evil system dominated by the selfish few. Communist society will be free and will remove the barriers between man and man, rich and poor, professional and labourer, between town and country; a vision of men striding together in harmony towards the enrichment and fulfilment of all.

Source: D. Harkness, *The Post-War World* (Macmillan, 1974)

Source D

Information from a recent work by historian Alan Bullock

Lenin did not want to be a dictator, and while he was in charge, the system was run by a group of party leaders. But Stalin was determined to replace this with his own personal rule. Under Stalin there was an unrestricted and ruthless exercise of power, including terrorism and the repression of all other parties. The Stalinist repression was responsible for a greater number of deaths – on some calculations up to double the number put to death by the Nazis. After his death, the system reverted to its original group leadership.

Source: A. Bullock, *Hitler and Stalin, Parallel Lives* (HarperCollins, 1991)

Source E

Gorbachev is probably like Lenin was, and he seems to hope that rule by the communist party alone can ultimately be strengthened and maintained through reforms, 'glasnost'. He deserves respect because he has attacked a whole series of problems, and he desires to renew his country.

Source: Heinz Brahm, 'A Portrait of Gorbachev', in *The Soviet Union 1987–89* (Longman 1990)

(a) Source A is a propaganda poster designed to flatter Stalin. Do you think the designer of the poster has succeeded in his aim? Explain your answer fully.
2.4–6   4 marks

(b) What use is Source A for the historian?   3.5–8   4 marks

(c) What evidence is there in Source D to suggest why it was thought necessary to produce the poster?   3.4   3 marks

(d) How does Source D conflict with Sources B and C in the information it gives about life in the USSR under communist rule?   1.6c–8c, 3.4   6 marks

(e) From the evidence of the sources, what reasons can you suggest for the differences between Source D and the other sources? 2.4–9 8 marks

Total: 25 marks

2 *Mikhail Gorbachev* Study Sources A to E and then answer the questions which follow.

Source A

The view of Vladimir Bukovsky, a reformer, in 1992

Gorbachev and his Politburo weren't thinkers or philosophers ... in the early 1920s Lenin had already faced the failure of communism and started NEP. Gorbachev's intention was to return to this example. This had the further advantage of allowing him to claim that Stalinism had been a distortion, a historic mistake, and the regime was now returning to the path it should never have left.... Gorbachev's trouble was that he weakened his own system; his only instrument of power was the communist party, but his reforms weakened precisely that instrument. He was like the proverbial man sawing off the branch on which he was sitting.... The whole enterprise was senseless, doomed through its inherent lack of productivity. No enterprise, including gas, oil and other primary products, was profitable.

Source B

The view of Valentin Falin, a communist hardliner

Had Gorbachev in 1985 or 1986 proposed clear and practical aims, nine-tenths of the population, including a majority of the party, would have been behind him, such was the confidence in him ... But he had no idea what he hoped to achieve ideologically, socially, economically or in terms of human rights. Instead he took to improvisations and meaningless slogans. I could never have imagined that a General Secretary could have had a mind so devoid of substance.

Source C

The view of General Leonid Shebarshin, one of the Directors of the KGB, 1989–91

It should have been possible to jettison totalitarianism over a period of time through careful consideration. I do not believe Gorbachev thought his reforms were going to destroy communism. I accept that he was trying to resurrect it ... Anyone could see that things were not moving in the right direction. Receiving vital information from the KGB, Gorbachev did not study it and draw conclusions. I don't think he took an overview ... his education was defective. Nationalism was the danger in 1989 and I warned him of it. I thought bloodshed would start in Georgia, but before that came Karabakh.

Sources: Sources A, B and C are quoted in D. Pryce-Jones, *The War that Never Was: The Fall of the Soviet Empire 1985–91* (Weidenfeld & Nicolson, 1995)

Information from David Pryce-Jones, writer and expert on Soviet affairs

Gorbachev's vision of détente appeared to be the kind of normalisation for which the west had hoped for so long. His standing in the west soared – he was the politician of the year in Germany, and Man of the Decade for *Time* magazine, recipient of many honours including the Nobel Prize for Peace ... In the USA a Harris opinion poll in mid-1986 showed that over half those questioned had a favourable impression of Gorbachev, a proportion which had risen to three-quarters two years later. By that time less than a third of those questioned held the view that the Soviet Union was an enemy ... [When Gorbachev visited East Germany] about 40 000 people marched past the rostrum chanting 'Gorbi'.

Source: D. Pryce-Jones, *The War that Never Was: The Fall of the Soviet Empire 1985–91* (Weidenfeld & Nicolson, 1995)

Source E

The view of the ordinary Russian woman-in-the-street, interviewed in April 1990

Talking is the only thing we're free to do now. In every other way it's a disaster. Gorbachev does it too: yak-yak-yak ... We used to be a country, but now we're a big debating society. And no-one does anything. There's no food, no cars, nothing in the shops. What's the point of having money when there's nothing to buy? I tell you honestly, I've come to hate Gorbachev. Sasha [her husband] still supports him, but for me he's worse than useless. And I'll tell you something else ... I hate the bloody communists as well. They've wrecked this country and they don't have the faintest idea how to put things right.

Source: quoted in John Simpson, *Despatches from the Barricades* (Hutchinson, 1990)

(a) What differences in attitude and interpretation can you find in these views about Mikhail Gorbachev in Sources A to E?   1.4c–6c, 8c, 9c, 2.7–10   8 marks

(b) What reasons can you suggest for the differences?   1.7c–9b, 2.8–10   8 marks

(c) What do you think are the uses and weaknesses of each of these sources for the historian?   3.5–10   10 marks

(d) Using the sources and information from Section 15.7, explain whether or not you would agree with the statement that 'the most important cause of Gorbachev's failure was his problems with the nationalities'.

1.4b–9a   14 marks

Total: 40 marks

Summary of events

China had a long history of national unity and since the mid-seventeenth century had been ruled by the Manchu or Ch'ing dynasty. However, during the 1840s, the country moved into a troubled period of foreign interference, civil war and disintegration, which lasted until the communist victory in 1949.

The last emperor was overthrown in 1911 and a republic proclaimed. The period 1916 to 1928, known as the *Warlord Era*, was one of great chaos, as a number of generals seized control of different provinces. A party known as the *Kuomintang (KMT)* or Nationalists was trying to govern China and control the generals who were busy fighting each other. The KMT leaders were Dr Sun Yat-sen and, after his death in 1925, General Chiang Kai-shek. *The Chinese Communist Party (CCP)* was founded in 1921, and at first it co-operated with the KMT in its struggle against the warlords. As the KMT gradually established control over more and more of China, it felt strong enough to do without the help of the communists, and it tried to destroy them. The communists, under their leader Mao Zedong (Mao Tse-tung), reacted vigorously, and after escaping from surrounding KMT forces, embarked on the 6000 mile Long March (1934–5) to form a new power base in northern China.

Civil war dragged on, complicated by Japanese interference which culminated in a full-scale invasion in 1937. When the Second World War ended with defeat for Japan and their withdrawal from China, the KMT and the CCP continued to fight it out. Chiang Kai-shek had help from the USA, but in 1949 it was Mao and the communists who finally triumphed. Chiang and his supporters fled to the island of Taiwan (Formosa). Mao Zedong quickly established control over the whole of China, and he remained leader until his death in 1976.

17.1 Revolution and the warlord era

(a) *Background to the revolution of 1911*

In the early part of the nineteenth century China kept itself very much separate from the rest of the world; life went on quietly and peacefully with no great changes, as it had done since the Manchus took over in the 1640s. In the mid-nineteenth century China found itself faced by a number of crises. To begin with *Europeans started to force their way into China* to take advantage of trading possibilities. The British were first on the scene, fighting and defeating the Chinese in the Opium Wars (1839–42). They forced China to hand over Hong Kong and to allow them to trade at certain ports. Other Western nations followed, and eventually these 'barbarians' as the Chinese regarded them, had rights and concessions in about eighty ports and other towns.

Next came the *Taiping Rebellion (1850–64)*, which spread all over southern China. It was partly a religious movement and partly a political reform movement, which aimed to set up a 'Heavenly Kingdom of Great Peace' (*Taiping tianguo*). The movement was eventually defeated, not by the government, but by regional armies. This began the process in which provinces began to assert their independence from the central government, culminating in the Warlord Era (1916–28).

China was defeated in a war with Japan (1894–5) and forced to hand over territory. A Chinese uprising – *the Boxer Rising* – against foreign influence took place in 1898–1900, but it was defeated by an international army, and the Empress Tz'u-hsi was forced to pay massive compensation for damage done to foreign property in China. More territory was lost to Japan as a result of the Japanese victory in the Russo-Japanese War (1904–5), and China was clearly in a sorry state.

In the early years of the twentieth century thousands of young Chinese travelled abroad and were educated abroad. They returned with radical, revolutionary ideas of overthrowing the Manchu dynasty and westernizing China. Some revolutionaries, like Dr Sun Yat-sen, wanted a democratic state modelled on the USA.

(b) *The 1911 revolution*

The government tried to respond to the new radical ideas by introducing reforms, promising democracy and setting up elected provincial assemblies. However, this only encouraged the provinces to distance themselves still further from the central government, which was now extremely unpopular. *The revolution began among soldiers in Wuchang in October 1911 and most provinces quickly declared themselves independent of Beijing (the capital).*

The government, ruling on behalf of the child emperor Pu Yi (who was only five years old), in desperation sought help from a retired general, *Yuan Shih-kai*, who had been commander of the Chinese Northern Army, and still had a lot of influence with the generals. However, the plan backfired: Yuan, who was still only in his early fifties, turned out to have ambitions of his own. He did a deal with the revolutionaries – they agreed to his becoming first president of the Chinese republic in return for the abdication of Pu Yi and the end of the Manchu dynasty. With the support of the army, Yuan ruled as a military dictator from 1912 until 1915, but he made the mistake of proclaiming himself emperor (1915). This lost him the support of the army, which forced him to abdicate. He died in 1916.

(c) *The Warlord Era (1916–28)*

The abdication and death of Yuan Shi-Kai removed the last person who seemed capable of maintaining some sort of unity in China. The country now disintegrated into literally hundreds of states of varying sizes, each controlled by a warlord and his private army. As they fought each other, it was the ordinary Chinese peasants who suffered untold hardships (Illus. 17.1). However, *two important positive developments took place during this period:*

● the May the Fourth Movement began in 1919 with a huge student demonstration in Beijing, protesting against the warlords and against traditional Chinese culture. The movement was also anti-Japanese, especially when the 1919 Versailles Settlement gave Japan the right to take over Germany's concessions in Shantung province.

Illus. 17.1 A street execution in China in 1927, towards the end of the Warlord Era

- The Kuomintang or Nationalist party grew gradually stronger and succeeded in bringing the warlords under control by 1928.

17.2 The Kuomintang, Dr Sun Yat-sen and Chiang Kai-shek

(a) *The Kuomintang*

The main hope for the survival of a united China lay with the Kuomintang or National People's Party formed in 1912 by Dr Sun Yat-sen. He had trained as a doctor in Hawaii and Hong Kong and lived abroad until the 1911 revolution. He was dismayed by the disintegration of China and wanted to create a modern, united, democratic state. Returning to China after the revolution, he succeeded in setting up a government at Canton in southern China (1917). His ideas were influential but he had very little power outside the Canton area. The KMT was not a communist party, though it was prepared to co-operate with the communists, and developed its own party organization along communist lines, as well as building up its own army. Sun himself summarized his aims as the *Three Principles*:

nationalism – to rid China of foreign influence and build her into a strong and united power, respected abroad;

democracy – China should not be ruled by warlords, but by the people themselves, after they had been educated to equip them for democratic self-government;

land reform – sometimes known as 'the people's livelihood'; this was vague – although Sun announced a long-term policy of economic development and redistribution of land to the peasants and was in favour of rent restraint, he was opposed to the confiscation of landlords' property.

Sun gained enormous respect as an intellectual statesman and revolutionary leader, but when he died in 1925 little progress had been made towards achieving the three principles, mainly because he was not himself a general. Until the KMT armies were built up, he had to rely on alliances with sympathetic warlords, and he had difficulty exercising any authority outside the south.

(b) *Chiang Kai-shek*

General Chiang Kai-shek became leader of the KMT after Sun's death. He had received his military training in Japan before the First World War, and being a strong nationalist, joined the KMT (Illus. 17.2). At this stage the new Soviet Russian government was providing help and guidance to the KMT in the hope that nationalist China would be friendly towards Russia. In 1923 Chiang spent some time in Moscow studying the organization of the communist party and the Red Army. The following year he became head of the Whampoa Military Academy (near Canton) which was set up with Russian cash, arms and advisers to train officers for the KMT army. However, in spite of his Russian contacts, Chiang was not a communist. In fact he was more right-wing than Sun Yat-sen and became increasingly anti-communist, his sympathies lying with businessmen and landowners. Soon after becoming party leader, he removed all left-wingers from leading positions in the party, though for the time being he continued the KMT alliance with the communists.

In 1926 he set out on the *Northern March* to destroy the warlords of central and northern China. Starting from Canton, the KMT and the communists had captured Hankow, Shanghai and Nanking by 1927. Beijing (Peking) was taken in 1928. Much of Chiang's success sprang from massive local support among the peasants attracted by communist promises of land. The capture of Shanghai was helped by a rising of industrial workers organized by *Zhou Enlai*, a member of the KMT and also a communist.

During 1927 Chiang decided that the communists were becoming too powerful – in areas where communists were strong, landlords were being attacked and land seized; it was time to destroy an embarrassing ally. All communists were expelled from the KMT and a terrible 'purification movement' was launched in which thousands of communists, trade union and peasant leaders were massacred; some estimates put the total murdered as high as 250 000. The communists had been checked, the warlords were under control and Chiang was the military and political leader of China.

The Kuomintang government proved to be a great disappointment for the majority of Chinese. Chiang could claim to have achieved Sun's first principle, nationalism, but relying as he did on the support of wealthy landowners, no moves were made towards democracy or land reform, though there was some limited progress with the building of more schools and roads.

17.3 Mao Zedong and the communists

(a) *Mao Zedong and the Chinese Communist Party*

The party had been officially founded in 1921; at first it consisted mostly of intellectuals and had very little military strength, which explains why it was willing to work with the KMT.

Illus. 17.2 General Chiang Kai-shek

Mao, who was present at the founding meeting, was born in Hunan province (1893) in south-east China, the son of a prosperous peasant farmer. After spending some time working on the land, Mao trained as a teacher, and then moved northwards to Beijing where he worked as a library assistant at the university, a centre of Marxist studies. Later he moved back to Hunan and built up a reputation as a skilful trade union and peasant association organizer. After the communist breach with the KMT Mao was responsible for changing the party's strategy: they would concentrate on winning mass support among the peasants rather than trying to capture industrial towns where several communist insurrections had already failed because of the strength of the KMT. In 1931 Mao was elected chairman of the Central Executive Committee of the party, and from then on, he gradually consolidated his position as the real leader of Chinese communism.

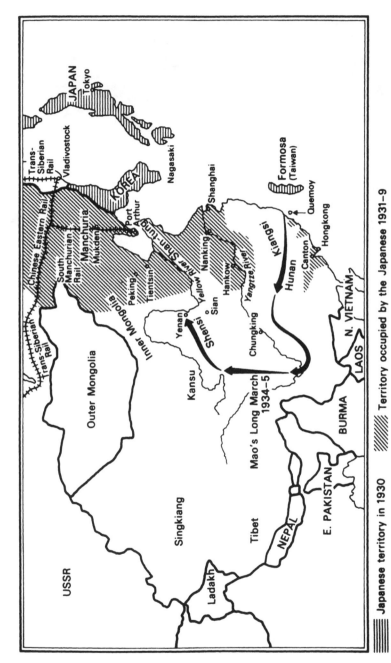

Map 17.1 China after the First World War

|||| Japanese territory in 1930   ▨ Territory occupied by the Japanese 1931–9

Mao and his supporters concentrated on survival as Chiang carried out five 'extermination campaigns' against them between 1930 and 1934. They took to the mountains between Hunan and Kiangsi provinces and concentrated on building up the Red Army. However, early in 1934 Mao's base area was surrounded by KMT armies poised for the final destruction of Chinese communism. Mao decided that the only chance of survival was to break through Chiang's lines and set up another power base somewhere else. In October 1934 the breakthrough was achieved and almost 100 000 communists set out on the remarkable *Long March* which was to become part of Chinese legend. They covered about 6000 miles in 368 days and, in the words of American journalist, Edgar Snow,

> crossed 18 mountain ranges, 5 of which were snow-capped, and 24 rivers. They passed through 12 different provinces, occupied 62 cities, and broke through enveloping armies of 10 different provincial warlords, besides defeating, eluding, or out-manoeuvring the various forces of government troops sent against them.

Eventually the 20 000 survivors found refuge at Yenan in Shensi province, where a new base was organized. Mao was able to control the provinces of Shensi and Kansu. *During the next ten years the communists continued to gain support, while Chiang and the KMT steadily lost popularity.*

(b) *Why did Mao and the communists gain support?*

1 The inefficiency and corruption of the KMT in government

They had little to offer in the way of reform, spent too much time looking after the interests of industrialists, bankers and landowners, and made no effective attempts to organize mass support. This provided the main opportunity for Mao and the communists to win support.

2 There was little improvement in factory conditions

This was in spite of laws designed to remove the worst abuses, such as child labour in textile mills. Often these laws were not applied: there was widespread bribery of inspectors and Chiang himself was not prepared to offend his industrial supporters.

3 There was no improvement in peasant poverty

In the early 1930s there was a series of droughts and bad harvests which caused widespread famine in rural areas. At the same time there was usually plenty of rice and wheat being hoarded in the cities by profiteering merchants. In addition there were high taxes and forced labour.

In contrast, *the land policy followed in areas controlled by the communists was much more attractive*: at first in the south, they seized the estates of rich landlords and redistributed them among the peasants. After the temporary truce with the KMT during the war with Japan, the communists compromised, and confined themselves to a policy of restricting rents and making sure that even the poorest labourers got a small piece of land. This less drastic policy had the advantage of winning the support of the smaller landowners as well as the peasants.

4   The KMT put up no effective resistance to the Japanese

This was the crucial factor. The Japanese occupied Manchuria in 1931 and were obviously preparing to bring the neighbouring provinces of northern China under their control. Chiang seemed to think it was more important to destroy the communists than to resist the Japanese, and moved into south Shensi to attack Mao (1936). *Here a remarkable incident took place:* Chiang was taken prisoner by some of his own troops, mostly Manchurians, who were incensed at the Japanese invasion. They demanded that Chiang should turn against the Japanese, but at first he was unwilling. Only after the prominent communist Zhou Enlai came to see him at Sian did he agree to a fresh alliance with the CCP and a national front against the Japanese.

The new alliance brought great advantages for the communists: the KMT extermination campaigns ceased for the time being and consequently the CCP was secure in its Shensi base. When full-scale war broke out with Japan in 1937, the KMT forces were quickly defeated and most of eastern China was occupied by the Japanese as Chiang retreated westwards. This enabled the communists, undefeated in Shensi, to present themselves as patriotic nationalists, leading an effective guerrilla campaign against the Japanese in the north. This won them massive support among the peasants and middle classes, who were appalled at Japanese arrogance and brutality. Whereas in 1937 the CCP had five base areas controlling 12 million people, by 1945 this had grown to nineteen base areas controlling 100 million people.

17.4   The communist victory, 1949

(a)   *Victory for the communists was still not inevitable*

When the Japanese were defeated in 1945, the KMT and the CCP became locked in the final struggle for power. Many observers, especially in the USA, hoped and expected that Chiang would be victorious. The Americans helped the KMT to take over all areas previously occupied by the Japanese – except Manchuria, which had been captured by the Russians a few days before the war ended. Here the Russians obstructed the KMT and allowed CCP guerrillas to move in. *In fact the apparent strength of the KMT was deceptive:* in 1948 the ever-increasing communist armies were large enough to abandon their guerrilla campaign and challenge Chiang's armies directly. As soon as they came under direct pressure, the KMT armies began to disintegrate. In January 1949 the communists took Beijing, and later in the year, Chiang and what remained of his forces fled to the island of Taiwan, leaving Mao Zedong in command of mainland China (Illus. 17.3).

(b)   *There were several reasons for the CCP triumph*

The communists continued to win popular support by their restrained land policy, which varied according to the needs of particular areas: some or all of a landlord's estate might be confiscated and redistributed among the peasants, or there might simply be rent restriction; communist armies were well-disciplined and communist administration was honest and fair.

On the other hand the KMT administration was inefficient and corrupt, much of its American aid finding its way into the pockets of officials. Its policy of paying for the wars by printing extra money resulted in galloping inflation, which caused hardship for the masses and ruined many of the middle class. Its armies were poorly paid and were allowed to loot the countryside; subjected to communist propaganda, the troops gradu-

Illus. 17.3 Mao Zedong proclaims the new Chinese Republic in 1949

ally became disillusioned with Chiang and began to desert to the communists. The KMT tried to terrorize the local populations into submission, but this only alienated more areas. Chiang also made some tactical blunders: like Hitler, he could not bear to order retreats and consequently his scattered armies were surrounded, and often, as happened at Beijing and Shanghai, surrendered without resistance, totally disillusioned.

Finally, the CCP leaders, Mao Zedong and Zhou Enlai, were shrewd enough to take advantage of KMT weaknesses and were completely dedicated. The communist generals, Lin Biao, Chu Teh and Ch-en Yi, had prepared their armies carefully and were more competent tactically than their KMT counterparts.

Questions

1   *The communist victory in China*   Study Sources A to E and then answer the
questions which follow.

Source A

*Extracts from the writings of Edgar Snow, an American journalist who lived in
China for many years from 1928 onwards. He got to know all the leading figures
during this period, and his book* Red Star Over China, *describing his experiences,
was published in 1937*

I had to admit that most of the peasants to whom I talked seemed to support the
communists and the Red Army. Many of them were very free with their criticisms
and complaints, but when asked whether they preferred it to the old days, the
answer was nearly always an emphatic yes. I noticed also that most of them talked
about the soviets as 'our government'. To understand peasant support for the
communist movement, it is necessary to keep in mind the burden borne by the
peasantry under the former regime [the Kuomintang]. Now, wherever the Reds
went, there was no doubt that they radically changed the situation for the tenant
farmer, the poor farmer, and all the 'have-not' elements. All forms of taxation
were abolished in the new districts for the first year, to give the farmers a
breathing-space. Second, the Reds gave land to the land-hungry peasants, and
began a reclamation of great areas of 'wasteland' – mostly the land of absentee or
fleeing landlords. Thirdly, they took land and livestock from the wealthy classes
and redistributed them among the poor ... However, both the landlord and the
rich peasant were allowed as much land as they could till with their own labour.

Source B

The eight rules of the Red Army (1928), quoted by Edgar Snow

1.   Return and roll up the straw matting on which you sleep.
2.   Be courteous and polite to the people and help them when you can.
3.   Return all borrowed articles.
4.   Replace all damaged articles.
5.   Be honest in all transactions with the peasants.
6.   Pay for all articles purchased.
7.   Don't take liberties with women.
8.   Be sanitary, and, especially, establish latrines a safe distance from people's
      houses.

Edgar Snow adds: These eight points were enforced with better and better success,
and today [1937] are still the code of the Red Soldier, memorised and frequently
repeated by him.

Source C

Statement by a Red general, Peng Dehuai, in 1936

I remember the winter of 1928 when my forces in Hunan were encircled. The KMT
troops burned down all the houses in the surrounding area, seized all the food
there and then blockaded us. We had no cloth, we used bark to make short tunics,
we had no quarters, no lights, no salt. We were sick and half-starved. The peasants

were no better off, and we would not touch what little they had. But the peasants encouraged us. They dug up from the ground the grain which they had hidden from the KMT troops and gave it to us, and they ate potatoes and wild roots. Even before we arrived they had fought the landlords and tax-collectors, so they welcomed us. Many joined us, and nearly all helped us in some way. They wanted us to win. Tactics are important, but we could not exist if the majority of the people did not support us. We are nothing but the fist of the people beating their oppressors.

Sources: Sources A, B and C are from Edgar Snow, *Red Star Over China* (Penguin, 1938 edition)

Source D

Report by an American official to the US State Department, November 1944

Relying on his dispirited troops, on his decadent and corrupt bureaucracy, and whatever nervous foreign support he can muster, Chiang Kai-shek may plunge China into civil war. He cannot succeed. The Communists are already too strong for him. Chiang's feudal China cannot long exist alongside a dynamic popular government in North China. The Communists are in China to stay. And China's destiny is not Chiang's but theirs.

Source E

Extracts from a speech by John F. Kennedy to Congress on the Communist capture of Peking (Beijing), January 1949

Over this weekend we have learned the extent of the disaster that has befallen China and the United States. The responsibility for the failure of our foreign policy in the Far East rests squarely with the White House ... So concerned were our diplomats and their advisers with the imperfection of the democratic system in China after 20 years of war and the tales of corruption in high places, that they lost sight of our tremendous stake in a non-Communist China. This house must now take up the responsibility of preventing the onrushing tide of Communism from engulfing all of Asia.

Sources: Sources D and E are quoted in Howard Zinn, *A People's History of the United States* (Longman, 1980)

(a) According to Source A, how did things change in the areas controlled by the communists? Were these changes thought to be progress or not?

1.4a–6a 5 marks

(b) Sources A, D and E were all written by Americans.

(i) What similarities and differences can you find in the attitudes of these three Americans towards the Chinese communists? 1.4c–6c 5 marks

(ii) What reasons can you suggest to explain the differences of opinion among the three Americans? 1.7c–9b 5 marks

(c) What are the strengths and weaknesses of these five sources for the historian?

3.5–9 10 marks

(d) Using the evidence from the sources and from Section 17.4(b), make a list of reasons for the communist victory in China, placing what you think are the most important reasons at the top. 1.4b–9a 15 marks

Total: 40 marks

⬡18 China since 1949: the communists in control

Summary of events

After the communist victory over the Kuomintang in 1949, Mao Zedong (Mao Tse-tung) set about rebuilding a shattered China. At first there was Russian advice and aid, but in the late 1950s relations cooled and Russian economic aid was reduced. In 1958 Mao introduced the *Great Leap Forward*, in which communism was adapted – not altogether successfully – to meet the Chinese situation, with the emphasis on decentralisation, agriculture, communes and contact with the masses. Mao became highly critical of the Russians who, in his view, were straying from strict Marxist–Leninist principles and following the 'capitalist road' in both foreign and domestic affairs. During the 1960s these disagreements caused a serious rift in world communism, which was only healed after Gorbachev became Russian leader in 1985. With the *Cultural Revolution (1966–9)* Mao tried successfully to crush opposition within the party and to keep China developing along Marxist–Leninist lines.

After Mao's death in 1976, there was a power struggle from which Deng Xiaoping emerged as undisputed leader (1981). Much less conservative than Mao, Deng was reponsible for some important policy changes, moderating Mao's hard-line communism and looking towards Japan and the capitalist West for ideas and help. This aroused resentment among the Maoist supporters, who accused Deng of straying along the 'capitalist road'; in 1987 they forced him to slow down the pace of his reforms.

Encouraged by Gorbachev's *glasnost* policy in the USSR, student protests began in Tiananmen Square in Beijing, in April 1989, continuing through into June. They demanded democracy and an end to corruption in the communist party. On 3–4 June the army moved in, attacked the students, killing hundreds, and restored order. The communists remained in firm control. The economic reforms continued with some success, but there was no political reform. Deng Xiaoping continued as supreme leader until his death (at the age of 92) in 1997.

Illus. 18.1 China – building a canal by mass labour

18.1 How successful was Mao Zedong in dealing with China's problems?

(a) *What were the problems facing Mao Zedong?*

The problems facing the People's Republic in 1949 were complex to say the least. The country was devastated after the long civil war and the war with Japan: railways, roads, canals and dykes had been destroyed and there were chronic food shortages. Industry was backward, agriculture was inefficient and incapable of feeding the poverty-stricken masses, and inflation seemed out of control. Mao had the support of the peasants and many of the middle class who were disgusted by the miserable performance of the KMT, but it was essential for him to improve conditions if he were to hold on to their support. To control and organize such a vast country with a population of at least 600 million must have been a superhuman task. Yet Mao managed it, and China today, whatever its faults, is still very much his creation (Illus. 18.1). He began by looking closely at Stalin's methods and experimented, by a process of trial and error, to find which would work in China and where a special Chinese approach was necessary.

(b) *The constitution of 1950 (officially adopted 1954)*

This included the National People's Congress (the final authority for legislation), whose members were elected for four years by people over eighteen, the State Council and the Chairman of the Republic (both elected by the Congress), whose function was to make sure that laws were carried out and the administration of the country went ahead. The State Council chose the Political Bureau (Politburo) which took all the main decisions. The whole system was, of course, dominated by the communist party, and only party members could stand for election. The constitution was important because it provided China with a strong central government for the first time for many years, and it has remained largely unchanged (see Figure 18.1).

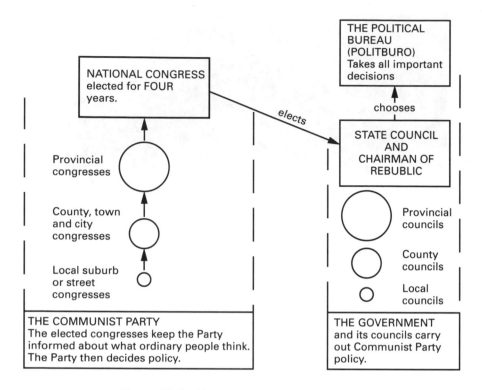

Figure 18.1   How the government of China works

(c) *Agricultural changes*

These transformed China from a country of small, inefficient private farms into one of large co-operative farms like those in Russia (1950–6). In the first stage, land was taken from large landowners and redistributed among the peasants, no doubt with violence in places. Some sources mention as many as 2 million people killed, though historian Jack Gray believes that 'the redistribution of China's land was carried out with a remarkable degree of attention to legality and the minimum of physical violence against landlords'. The next step was achieved without violence: peasants were persuaded (not forced as they were in Russia) to join together in co-operative (collective) farms in order to increase food production. By 1956 about 95 per cent of all peasants were in co-operatives (consisting of between 100 and 300 families) with joint ownership of the farm and its equipment.

(d) *Industrial changes*

These began with the government nationalizing most businesses. In 1953 it embarked on a Five Year Plan concentrating on the development of heavy industry (iron, steel, chemicals and coal). The Russians helped with cash, equipment and advisers, and the plan had some success. Before it was complete, however, Mao began to have grave doubts as to whether China was suited to this sort of heavy industrialization. On the other hand he could claim that under his leadership the country had recovered from the ravages of the wars: full communications had been restored, inflation was under control and the economy was looking much healthier.

(e) *The Hundred Flowers Campaign (1957)*

This seems to some extent to have developed out of industrialization which produced a vast new class of technicians and engineers. The party *cadres* (groups who organized the masses politically and economically – the collectivization of the farms, for example, was carried out by the cadres) believed that this new class of experts would threaten their authority. The government, feeling pleased with its progress so far, decided that open discussion of the problems might improve relations between cadres and experts or intellectuals. 'Let a hundred flowers bloom and a hundred schools of thought contend', said Mao, calling for constructive criticism. Unfortunately he got more than he had anticipated – critics attacked:

- the cadres for incompetence and over-enthusiasm;
- the government for over-centralization;
- the communist party for being undemocratic; some suggested that opposition parties should be allowed.

Mao hurriedly called off the campaign and clamped down on his critics, insisting that his policies were right. The campaign showed how much opposition there still was to communism and to the uneducated cadres, and it convinced Mao that a drive was needed *to consolidate the advance of socialism* – so in 1958 he called for the '*Great Leap Forward*'.

(f) *The Great Leap Forward*

This was a policy designed to meet the Chinese situation and was not based on Russian experience. It involved further important developments in both industry and agriculture, in order to increase output (agriculture in particular was not providing the required food) and to adapt industry to Chinese conditions. Its most important features were:

1 *The introduction of communes*, units larger than collective farms, containing up to 75 000 people, divided into brigades and work teams with an elected council. They ran their own collective farms and factories, carried out most of the functions of local government within the commune and undertook special local projects. One typical commune in 1965, for example, contained 30 000 people, of which a third were children at school or in crèches, a third were housewives or elderly, and the rest were the workforce. This included a science team of 32 graduates and 43 technicians. Each family received a shareout of profits and also had a small private plot of land.
2 *A complete change of emphasis in industry:* instead of aiming for large-scale works of the type seen in the USSR and the West, much smaller factories were set up in the countryside to provide machinery for agriculture. Mao talked of 600 000 'backyard steel furnaces' springing up, organized and managed by the communes, which also undertook to build roads, canals, dams, reservoirs and irrigation channels.

At first it looked as though the Great Leap might be a failure: there was some opposition to the communes, a series of bad harvests (1959–61) and the withdrawal of all Russian aid following the breach between the two. All this, coupled with the lack of experience among the cadres, caused hardship in the years 1959–63; statistics which emerged later suggested that some 20 million people may have died prematurely as a result of hardships caused by the Great Leap. Even Mao's prestige suffered and he was forced to resign as Chairman of the People's Congress (to be succeeded by Liu Shaoqui), though he remained chairman of the communist party.

However, in the long term *the importance of the Great Leap became clear:* eventually both agricultural and industrial production increased substantially, and China was at least managing to feed its massive population without famine (which had rarely happened under the KMT). The communes proved to be a successful innovation. They were much more than merely collective farms – they were an efficient unit of local government and they enabled the central government in Beijing to keep in touch with local opinion. They seemed to be the ideal solution to the problem of running a vast country while at the same time avoiding the over-centralization that stifles initiative. The crucial decision had been taken that China would remain predominantly an agricultural country with small-scale industry scattered around the countryside. The economy would be labour-intensive (relying on massive numbers of workers instead of using labour-saving machines). Given the country's enormous population, this was the best way of making sure that everybody had a job, and it enabled China to avoid the growing unemployment problems of the highly industrialized Western nations. Other benefits were the spread of education and welfare services, and an improvement in the position of women in society.

(g) *The Cultural Revolution (1966–9)*

This was Mao's attempt to keep the revolution and the Great Leap on a pure Marxist–Leninist course. In the early 1960s, when the success of the Great Leap was by no means certain, opposition to Mao grew. Right-wing members of the party believed that incentives (piecework, greater wage differentials and larger private plots, which had been creeping in in some areas) were necessary if the communes were to function efficiently. They also felt that there should be an expert managerial class to push forward with industrialization on the Russian model, instead of relying on the cadres. But to the Maoists, this was totally unacceptable; it was exactly what Mao was condemning among the Russians, whom he dismissed as 'revisionists' taking the capitalist road. The party must avoid the emergence of a privileged class who would exploit the workers; it was vital to keep in touch with the masses.

Between 1963 and 1966 there was a great public debate about which course to follow, between the rightists (who included Liu Shaoqui and Deng Xiaoping) and the Maoists. Mao, using his position as chairman of the party to rouse the young people, launched a desperate campaign to 'save' the revolution. In this Great Proletarian Cultural Revolution, as he called it, Mao appealed to the masses. His supporters, the Red Guards (mostly students), toured the country arguing Mao's case, while schools, and later factories, were closed down. It was an incredible propaganda exercise in which Mao was trying to renew revolutionary fervour (Illus. 18.2).

Unfortunately it brought chaos and something close to civil war. Once the student masses had been roused, they denounced and physically attacked anybody in authority, not just critics of Mao. Teachers, professionals, local party officials, all were

Illus. 18.2 A group of young Red Guards demonstrating in Tiananmen Square, Beijing, in praise of Mao, during the Cultural Revolution

targets; millions of people were disgraced and ruined. Life in China during the Cultural Revolution is vividly described in the book *Wild Swans* by Jung Chang (see Source C in question 1 at the end of the chapter). By 1967 the extremists among the Red Guards were almost out of control, and Mao had to call in the army commanded by Lin Biao to restore order. Mao, privately admitting that he had made mistakes, in public blamed his advisers and the Red Guard leaders. Many were arrested and executed for 'committing excesses'. At the party conference in April 1969 the Cultural Revolution was formally ended, and Mao was declared free of all blame for what had happened. Later, Mao blamed Defence Minister Lin Biao (his chosen successor), who had always been one of his most reliable supporters, for the over-enthusiasm of the Red Guards. Some sources claim that Mao decided to make Lin Biao the scapegoat because he was trying to manoeuvre Mao into retiring. He was accused of plotting to assassinate Mao (which was highly unlikely), and was killed in an air crash in 1971 while trying to escape to the USSR, or so the official reports claimed.

The Cultural Revolution caused great disruption, ruined millions of lives, and probably held up China's economic development by ten years. And yet in spite of that, there was some economic recovery in the mid-1970s and China had made great strides since 1949. John Gittings, a journalist and expert on Chinese affairs, writing in 1989, had this to say about China at the time of Mao's death in 1976:

> A healthier, better educated, better organized population lived, still mostly in rural areas, on land which had been considerably improved. Grain production had at least kept pace with the rapid increase in population. Industrial development had tripled steel production, laid the foundation for a significant petroleum industry, created a machine-building industry virtually from scratch, and provided the base for China to become a nuclear power. Light industry provided a reasonable flow of consumer goods by comparison with the Soviet Union.

Source: John Gittings, 'The Rise and Fall of China', in *Modern History Review*, November 1989

The most surprising development in Mao's policies during his last years was in foreign affairs, when Mao and Zhou Enlai decided it was time to improve relations with the USA (see Section 8.5 (a) and (c)).

18.2 Life after Mao

(a) *A power struggle followed the death of Mao in 1976*

There were three main contestants: *Hua Guofeng*, named by Mao himself as his successor, *Deng Xiaoping*, who had been sacked from his position as general secretary of the party during the Cultural Revolution for allegedly being too liberal, and a group known as the *Gang of Four*, led by Jiang Quing, Mao's widow, who were extremely militant Mao supporters, more Maoist than Mao himself. At first Hua seemed to be the dominant figure, having the Gang of Four arrested and keeping Deng in the background; but Deng soon reasserted himself and for a time seemed to be sharing the leadership with Hua. From the middle of 1978 Deng gradually gained the ascendancy and Hua was forced to resign as party chairman, leaving Deng as undisputed leader (June 1981). As a gesture of open criticism of Mao and his policies, the Gang of Four were put on trial for 'evil, monstrous and unpardonable crimes' committed during the Cultural Revolution.

(b) *There was a period of dramatic policy changes*

This began in June 1978 as Deng Xiaoping gained the ascendancy.

1   *Many changes introduced during the Cultural Revolution were reversed:* the revolutionary committees set up to run local government were abolished and replaced by more democratically elected groups. Property confiscated from former capitalists was returned to survivors, and there was more religious freedom and greater freedom for intellectuals to express themselves in literature and the arts.

2   In economic matters Deng and his protégé, *Hu Yaobang*, wanted technical and financial help from the West in order to modernize industry, agriculture, science and technology. Loans were accepted from foreign governments and banks, and contracts signed with foreign companies for the supply of modern equipment. In 1980 China joined the IMF and the World Bank. On the home front, state farms

were given more control over planning, financing and profits; bonuses, piece-rates and profit-sharing schemes were encouraged, and the state paid higher prices to the communes for their produce and reduced taxes in order to stimulate efficiency and output. These measures had some success – grain output reached a record level in 1979, and many peasants became prosperous.

As so often happens, this reform programme led to demands for more radical reform.

(c) *Demands for more radical reform: the Democracy Wall*

In November 1978 there was a poster campaign in Beijing and other cities, often in sup-port of Deng Xiaoping. Soon there were massive demonstrations demanding more drastic changes, and early in 1978 the government felt obliged to ban marches and poster campaigns. However, there still remained what was called the 'Democracy Wall' in Beijing, where the public could express itself with huge wall posters (Illus. 18.3). During 1979 the posters displayed there became progressively more daring, attacking Chairman Mao and demanding a wide range of human rights:

● the right to criticize the government openly;
● representation for non-communist parties in the National People's Congress;
● freedom to change jobs and to travel abroad;
● abolition of the communes.

This infuriated Deng, who had approved the Democracy Wall in the first place only because most of the posters were criticizing the Gang of Four. Now he launched a fierce attack on the leading dissidents, accusing them of trying to destroy the socialist system. Several were arrested and given prison sentences of up to fifteen years. In November 1979 the Democracy Wall was abolished altogether. Law and order and party discipline were restored. 'Without the party', Deng remarked, 'China will ret-rogress into divisions and confusions'.

Illus. 18.3   Dazibao in Beijing. When Chinese people want to express their opinions publicly, they write in large letters on posters (known as Dazibao) which they paste on walls. These 'big-character' posters became a feature of the Cultural Revolution and continued afterwards

(d) Modernization and its problems

Following the first flush of reforming zeal and the embarrassment of the Democracy Wall, the pace slowed considerably. But Deng, together with his two protégés, *Hu Yaobang* (Party General Secretary) and *Zhao Ziyang* (Prime Minister), was determined to press ahead with modernisation as soon as possible.

Zhao Ziyang had won a reputation as a brilliant administrator in Sichuan province where he was responsible for an 80 per cent increase in industrial production in 1979. He also began experiments, later extended to the whole country, to break up the communes so as to give peasants control of individual plots. The land, although still officially owned by the state, was divided up and allocated to individual peasant households, which would be allowed to keep most of the profits. This was successful in raising agricultural production, and the standard of living for many people improved. In December 1984 Zhao announced that compulsory state purchase of crops was to be abandoned; the state would continue to buy staple products, but in much smaller quantities than before. Prices of surplus grain, pork, cotton and vegetables would be allowed to fluctuate on the open market.

By this time, however, modernization, and what Deng called the move to 'market socialism', were having some unfortunate side-effects. Although exports increased by 10 per cent during 1984, imports increased by 38 per cent, leaving a record trade deficit of 1100 million dollars, and causing a sharp fall in China's foreign exchange reserves. The government tried with some success to control imports by placing heavy duties on all imported goods except vital raw materials and microchip equipment (80 per cent on cars and 70 per cent on colour TVs and videos). Another unwelcome development was that the annual rate of inflation began to rise, reaching 22 per cent in 1986.

(e) The thoughts of Deng Xiaoping

Apparently not unduly worried by these trends, the 82-year-old Deng explained his ideas for the future, in a magazine article of November 1986. His main aim was to enable his people to get richer. By the year 2000, if all went well, the average annual income per head should have risen from the equivalent of £280 to somewhere near £700, and China's production should have doubled. 'To get rich is not a crime', he added. He was happy with way agricultural reform was going, but emphasized that in industry, sweeping decentralization was still needed. The party must withdraw from administrative tasks, issue fewer instructions, and allow more initiative at the lower levels. Only capitalist investment could create the conditions in which China could become a prosperous, modernized state. His other main theme was China's international role: to lead a peace alliance of the rest of the world against the dangerous ambitions of the USA and the USSR. Nothing, he said, could possibly alter the course he had set for his country (Illus. 18.4).

18.3 Tiananmen Square, 1989, and the crisis of communism

(a) The crisis of 1987

In spite of his radical words, Deng always had to keep an eye on the traditional, conservative or Maoist members of the Politburo, who were still powerful and might be able to get rid of him if his economic reforms failed or if party control seemed to be slipping.

Illus. 18.4 Deng Xiaoping

Deng was doing a clever balancing act between the reformers like Zhao Ziyang and Hu Yaobang on the one hand, and the hardliners like Li Peng on the other. Deng's tactics were to encourage criticism from students and intellectuals, but only up to a point: enough to enable him to drop some of the oldest and most inefficient party bureaucrats. If the criticism looked like getting out of hand, it had to be stopped (as had happened in 1979) for fear of antagonizing the hardliners.

In December 1986 there was a series of student demonstrations supporting Deng Xiaoping and the 'Four Modernizations' (agriculture, industry, science and defence), but urging a much quicker pace and, ominously, more democracy. After the students ignored a new ban on wall posters and a new rule requiring five days' notice for demonstrations, Deng decided that this challenge to party control and discipline had gone far enough, and the demonstrators were dispersed. However, it had been enough to alarm the hardliners, who forced the resignation of the reformer, Hu Yaobang as Party General Secretary. He was accused of being too liberal in his political outlook, encouraging intellectuals to demand greater democracy and even some sort of opposition party. Although this was a serious blow to Deng, it was not a complete disaster since his place was taken by Zhao Ziyang, another economic reformer, but one who had so far kept clear of controversial political ideas; however, Li Peng, a hardliner, took Zhao's place as Prime Minister.

Zhao soon announced that the government had no intention of abandoning its economic reform programme, and promised new measures to speed up financial reform, and at the same time, a clampdown on 'bourgeois intellectuals' who threatened party control. This highlighted *the dilemma facing Deng and Zhao:* was it possible to offer people a choice in buying and selling and yet deny them any choice in other areas such as policies and political parties? Many Western observers thought it was impossible to have one without the other (and so did Gorbachev in the USSR), and by the end of January 1987 there were signs that they could be right. On the other hand, if the economic reforms proved successful, Deng and Zhao could turn out to be right.

(b) *Tiananmen Square, 1989*

Unfortunately for Deng and Zhao, the economic reforms ran into problems during 1988 and 1989. Inflation went up to 30 per cent, and wages, especially of state employees (such as civil servants, party officials, police and soldiers), lagged well behind prices. Probably encouraged by Gorbachev's political reforms, and the knowledge that he was to pay a visit to Beijing in mid May 1989, *student demonstrations began again in Tiananmen Square on 17 April*; they were demanding political reform, democracy and an end to communist party corruption. On 4 May Zhao Ziyang said that the students' 'just demands would be met', and allowed the press to report the demands; but this outraged Deng. The demonstrations continued throughout Gorbachev's visit (15–18 May, to mark the formal reconciliation between China and the USSR) and into June, with sometimes as many as 250 000 people occupying the square and surrounding streets. The scene was vividly described by John Simpson, the Foreign Affairs editor of the BBC, who was there for much of the time:

> There was a new spirit of courage and daring ... There was a sense of liberation, that just to be in the Square was a statement in itself. People smiled and shook my hand ... everyone, it seemed, listened to the BBC's Chinese language service. The gentleness, the smiles and the headbands were irresistibly reminiscent of the big rock concerts and the anti-Vietnam demonstrations in the 1960s. There was the same certainty that because the protesters were young and peaceful the government must capitulate ... Food was delivered on a regular basis. Ordinary people responded with generosity to requests for bottled water ... Hundreds of thousands of people had decided to join in on the side which seemed certain to win. The major avenues of Peking were blocked with bicycles, cars, lorries, buses and flatbed trucks all heading for the Square, filled with people cheering, singing, playing musical instruments, waving flags, enjoying themselves. The racket of it all could be heard streets away ... Victory seemed a foregone conclusion; how could any government resist a popular uprising of this magnitude?

Source: John Simpson, *Despatches from the Barricades* (Hutchinson, 1990)

It certainly began to look very much as though the government had lost control and might soon give way to the demands. Behind the scenes, however, a power struggle was going on in the Politburo between Zhao Ziyang and the hardline Li Peng, the Prime Minister. Li Peng, with the support of Deng Xiaoping, eventually won. *Thousands of*

Illus. 18.5 Tanks advance in Tiananmen Square, Beijing, June 1989. The man was pulled away by bystanders

troops were brought in, and on 3–4 June, the army, using paratroopers, tanks and infantry, attacked the students, killing between 1500 and 3000 of them (Illus. 18.5). Tiananmen Square was under government control again, and demonstrations in other large cities were also dispersed, though with less bloodshed. The hardliners were triumphant: Zhao Ziyang was removed from his position as party chief and replaced by Jiang Zemin, a more 'middle of the road' politician. Prime Minister Li Peng became the leading figure. Many student leaders were arrested, tried and executed.

There was worldwide condemnation of the massacres, but Deng and the hardliners were convinced that they had taken the right decision. They felt that to have given way to the students' demands for democracy would have caused too much disruption and confusion; one-party control was needed to supervise the transition to a 'socialist market economy'. Later, events in the USSR seemed to prove them right: when Gorbachev tried to introduce economic and political reforms *both at the same time,* he failed; the communist party lost control, the economic reforms were a disaster, and the USSR broke up into fifteen separate states (see Section 16.7). Whatever the rest of the world thought about the Tiananmen Square massacres, the Chinese leadership could congratulate itself on avoiding Gorbachev's mistakes and preserving communism in China at a time when it was being swept away in Eastern Europe.

(c) *China since 1989*

Although they had clamped down on any political changes, China's leaders, Deng Xiaoping, Li Peng and Jiang Zemin, were still committed to progressive 'open door' economic policies. They hoped that a successful economy which enabled more and more people to become prosperous would make people forget their desire for 'democracy'.

During the 1990s the economy was booming; from 1991 to 1996 China led the world with average GDP increases of 11.4 per cent, and living standards were rising fast. Eastern China was especially prosperous with lots of foreign investment and plenty of consumer goods for sale. On the other hand, some of the remote western provinces were not sharing in the prosperity.

A new Five Year Plan, unveiled in March 1996, aimed to keep the economic boom on course by increasing grain production, keeping average GDP growth at 8 per cent, and spreading wealth more evenly among the regions. Although Deng Xiaoping died in February 1997, Li Peng and Jiang Zemin seemed set to lead China into the twenty-first century. Internal criticism had disappeared, partly because of China's economic success, and there was no more mention of political reform. As Li Peng told parliament in March 1996, 'maintenance of political and social stability is the basic prerequisite of economic reform and development; stability in turn is realized through the deepening of reform'.

Questions

1 *The Cultural Revolution* Study Sources A to E and then answer the questions which follow.

___ **Source A** ___

The view of the Central Committee of the Chinese Communist Party about the Cultural Revolution

Although the bourgeoisie has been overthrown, it is still trying to use the old ideas, culture, customs and habits of the exploiting classes to corrupt the masses, capture their minds and endeavour to stage a come-back. The Proletariat must be the exact opposite: it must meet head-on every challenge of the bourgeoisie in the ideological field and use new ideas, culture, customs and habits of the proletariat to change the mental outlook of the whole of society. Since the Cultural Revolution is a revolution, it inevitably meets with resistance. This resistance comes chiefly from those in authority who have wormed their way into the Party and are taking the Capitalist road. It also comes from the force of habits from the old society. What the Central Committee demands of the Party Committee at all levels is to boldly arouse the masses, encourage those comrades who have made mistakes but are willing to correct them, to cast off their burdens and join in the struggle.
A most important task is to transform the old education system.

Source: quoted in *Peking Review*, August 1966

*The Red Guards and their Little Red Books (*The Thoughts of Chairman Mao*)*
(Illus 18.6)

Source: Camera Press

Source C

The experiences of a young girl, Jung Chang, who was a teenager during the
Cultural Revolution

When Lin Biao called for everything that represented the old culture to be
destroyed, some pupils in my school started to smash things up. Being more than
2000 years old, the school had a lot of antiques ... the school gateway had an old
tiled roof with carved eaves. These were hammered to pieces ... All the things I
loved were disappearing. The saddest thing of all for me was the ransacking of the
library ... Books were major targets of Mao's order to destroy ... books were
burning all across China ... Like everyone else, I was supposed to join in the
'revolutionary actions'. But I, like most pupils, was able to avoid them, because no-
one made sure we took part. I could see that many pupils hated the whole thing,
but nobody tried to stop it ... 'denunciation meetings' were becoming a major
feature of the Cultural Revolution. They involved a hysterical crowd and were
seldom without physical brutality. Peking University had taken the lead, under the
personal supervision of Mao. At its first denunciation meeting over 60 professors
were beaten, kicked and forced to kneel for hours.

Source: Jung Chang, *Wild Swans* (HarperCollins, 1991)

Statement by a Chinese embassy official following the news of the death of Lin Biao in an air crash in 1971

Lin Biao repeatedly committed errors; and Mao Zedong had waged many struggles against him. Sometimes Lin Biao was obliged to quell his arrogance and then was able to accomplish some useful work. But he was not able to give up his underhand nature and during the Cultural Revolution he appeared to support the thought of Mao Zedong. He was thus able to hoodwink the masses to become in their eyes the successor to Mao Zedong. But he was a double-faced man who was in reality opposed to the revolutionary line of Mao Zedong. He undertook anti-party activities in a planned way with the aim of taking over power. Mao Zedong unmasked his plot and made efforts to recover him but Lin Biao attempted a coup d'etat and tried to assassinate Mao Zedong.

Source: quoted in *China Now*, March 1973

Source E

Comments by a British reporter based in Singapore

The power game in China is being played out between not only the moderates and the Maoists, the army and the leftists, but also between Peking [Beijing] and the provinces.

And the military commander is very much master of the provinces. In almost all the provincial revolutionary committees that now run China, the soldiers take the decisions.

Broadly speaking it can be said that seven military regions out of eleven are in the hands of men who disapproved of the Cultural Revolution and distrusted Mao's impatience for a classless Communist Utopia.

Source: Dennis Bloodworth, *Observer* Foreign News Service, November 1971

(a) From the evidence of Sources A, B and C, what changes took place in China during the Cultural Revolution?   1.4a–7a   5 marks

(b) (i) What different attitudes towards the Cultural Revolution can you find in Sources A, B and C?   1.4c–6c   4 marks

    (ii) What reasons can you suggest for these different attitudes?   1.7c–9b   4 marks

(c) Can you suggest any ways in which the photograph in Source B could be used as political propaganda?   3.5, 7   3 marks

(d) (i) From the evidence of Sources C and D and Section 18.1(g), what part did Lin Biao play in the Cultural Revolution?   3.4   5 marks

    (ii) What problems does the historian come across when investigating the role of Lin Biao in the Cultural Revolution?   2.4–8, 3.4–5, 7, 8   9 marks

(e) From the evidence of the sources and Section 18.1(g), how successful do you think the Cultural Revolution was in achieving its aims?   10 marks

Total: 40 marks

PART IV

The United States of America

The USA before the Second World War

Summary of events

During the second half of the nineteenth century, the USA experienced remarkable social and economic changes:

● *large numbers of immigrants* began to arrive from Europe, and this continued into the twentieth century. Between 1860 and 1930 over 30 million people arrived in the USA from abroad.

● *there was a vast and successful industrial revolution*, mainly in the last quarter of the nineteenth century. The USA entered the twentieth century on a wave of business prosperity. By 1914 she had easily surpassed Britain and Germany, the leading industrial nations of Europe, in output of coal, iron and steel, and was clearly a rival economic force to be reckoned with.

During the First World War the Americans played an important part in the defeat of Germany and her allies; Democrat President Woodrow Wilson (1913–21) was a leading figure at the Versailles Conference, and the USA was now one of the world's great powers. However, after the war the Americans decided not to play an active role in world affairs, a policy known as *isolationism*. It was a bitter disappointment for Wilson when the Senate rejected both the Versailles Settlement and the League of Nations (1920).

After Wilson came three Republican Presidents: Warren Harding (1921–3), who died in office; Calvin Coolidge (1923–9) and Herbert C. Hoover (1929–33). Until 1929 the country enjoyed a period of great prosperity, though not everybody shared in it. The boom ended suddenly with the *Wall Street Crash* (October 1929), which led to the great depression, or world economic crisis, only six months after the unfortunate Hoover's inauguration. The effects on the USA were catastrophic: by 1933 almost 14 million people were out of work and Hoover's efforts failed to make any impression on the crisis. Nobody was surprised when the Republicans lost the presidential election of November 1932. The new Democrat President, Franklin D. Roosevelt, introduced policies known as the *New Deal* to try and put the country on the road to recovery. Though it was not entirely successful, the New Deal achieved enough, together with the circumstances of the Second World War, to keep Roosevelt in the White House (the official residence of the President in Washington) until his death in April 1945. He was the only President to be elected for a fourth term.

19.1 The American system of government

The American constitution (the set of rules by which the country is governed) was first drawn up in 1787. Since then, twenty-six extra points (amendments) have been added; the last one, which lowered the voting age to 18, was added in 1971.

The USA has a federal system of government

This is a system in which a country is divided up into a number of states. There were originally thirteen states in the USA; by 1900 the number had grown to forty-five as the frontier was extended. Later, five more states were formed and added to the union; these were Oklahoma (1907), Arizona and New Mexico (1912) and Alaska and Hawaii (1959) (Map 19.1). Each of these states has its own state capital and government and they share power with the federal (central or national) government in the federal capital, Washington. Figure 19.1 shows how the power is shared out.

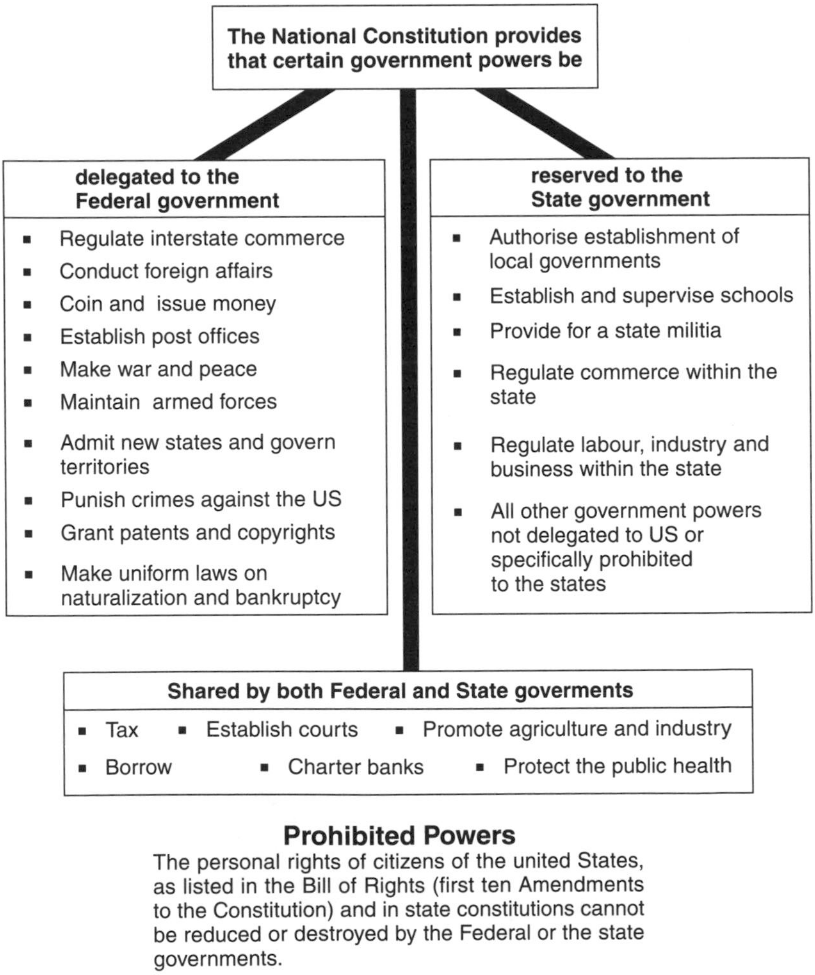

The National Constitution provides that certain government powers be

delegated to the Federal government	reserved to the State government
■ Regulate interstate commerce	■ Authorise establishment of local governments
■ Conduct foreign affairs	
■ Coin and issue money	■ Establish and supervise schools
■ Establish post offices	■ Provide for a state militia
■ Make war and peace	■ Regulate commerce within the state
■ Maintain armed forces	
■ Admit new states and govern territories	■ Regulate labour, industry and business within the state
■ Punish crimes against the US	■ All other government powers not delegated to US or specifically prohibited to the states
■ Grant patents and copyrights	
■ Make uniform laws on naturalization and bankruptcy	

Shared by both Federal and State goverments

- ■ Tax ■ Establish courts ■ Promote agriculture and industry
- ■ Borrow ■ Charter banks ■ Protect the public health

Prohibited Powers

The personal rights of citizens of the united States, as listed in the Bill of Rights (first ten Amendments to the Constitution) and in state constitutions cannot be reduced or destroyed by the Federal or the state governments.

Figure 19.1 How Federal Government and States divide powers

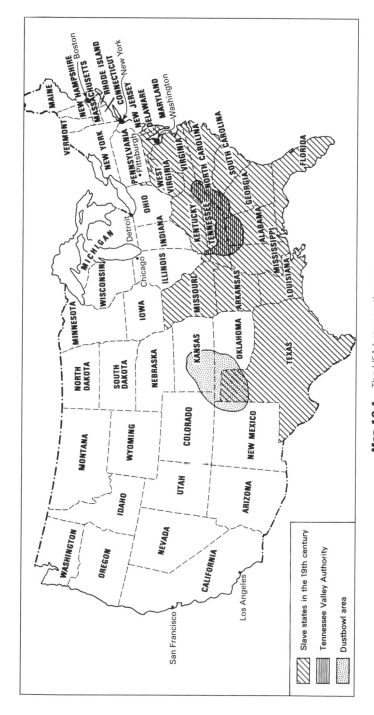

Map 19.1 The USA between the wars

Source: D. Heater, *Our World This Century* (Oxford 1992) p. 97

THE USA BEFORE THE SECOND WORLD WAR   375

The federal government consists of three main parts:

Congress: known as the legislative part, which makes the laws;
President: known as the executive part; he carries out the laws;
Judiciary: the legal system, of which the most important part is the *Supreme Court.*

(a) *Congress*

(i) *The federal parliament, known as Congress, meets in Washington and consists of two houses:*

- the House of Representatives
- the Senate.

Members of both houses are elected by universal suffrage. The House of Representatives (usually referred to simply as 'the House') contains 435 members, elected for two years, who represent districts of roughly equal population. Senators are elected for six years, one-third retiring every two years; there are two from each state, irrespective of the population of the state, making a total of 100.

(ii) *The main job of Congress is to legislate (make the laws)* All new laws have to be passed by a simple majority in both houses; treaties with foreign countries need a two-thirds vote in the Senate. If there is a disagreement between the two houses, a joint conference is held which usually succeeds in producing a compromise proposal which is then voted on by both houses. Congress can make laws about taxation, currency, postage, foreign trade, and the army and navy. It also has the power to declare war. In 1917, for example, when Woodrow Wilson decided it was time for the USA to go to war with Germany, he had to ask Congress to declare war.

(iii) *There are two main parties represented in Congress:*

- Republicans
- Democrats

Both parties contain people of widely differing views.

The Republicans have traditionally been the party which has a lot of support in the North, particularly among businessmen and industrialists. The more conservative of the two parties, they believed in:

- *keeping high tariffs* (import duties) to protect American industry from foreign imports:
- *a* laissez-faire *approach to government:* they wanted to leave businessmen alone to run industry and the economy with as little interference from the government as possible. Republican Presidents Coolidge (1923–9) and Hoover (1929–33), for example, both favoured non-intervention and felt that it was not the government's job to sort out economic and social problems.

The Democrats have drawn much of their support from the South, and from immigrants in the large cities of the North. They have been the more progressive of the two parties: Democrat Presidents such as Franklin D. Roosevelt (1933–45), Harry S. Truman (1945–53) and John F. Kennedy (1961–3) wanted the government to take a more active role in dealing with social and economic problems.

However, the parties are not as united or as tightly organized as political parties in Britain, where all the MPs belonging to the government party are expected to support the government all the time. In the USA party discipline is much weaker, and votes in Congress often cut across party lines. There are left and right-wingers in both parties. Some right-wing Democrats voted against

Roosevelt's New Deal even though he was a Democrat, while some left-wing Republicans voted for it. But they did not change parties, and their party did not throw them out.

(b) *The President*

The President is elected for a four-year term. Each party chooses its candidate for the presidency and the election always takes place in November. The successful candidate (referred to as the 'President elect') is sworn in as President the following January. The powers of the President appear to be very wide: he or she is Commander-in-Chief of the armed forces, controls the civil service, runs foreign affairs, makes treaties with foreign states, and appoints judges, ambassadors and the members of the cabinet. With the help of supporters among the Congressmen, the President can introduce laws into Congress and can veto laws passed by Congress if he or she does not approve of them.

(c) *The Supreme Court*

This consists of nine judges appointed by the President, with the approval of the Senate. Once a Supreme Court judge is appointed, he or she can remain in office for life, unless forced to resign through ill-health or scandal. The court acts as adjudicator in disputes between President and Congress, between the federal and state governments, between states, and in any problems which arise from the constitution.

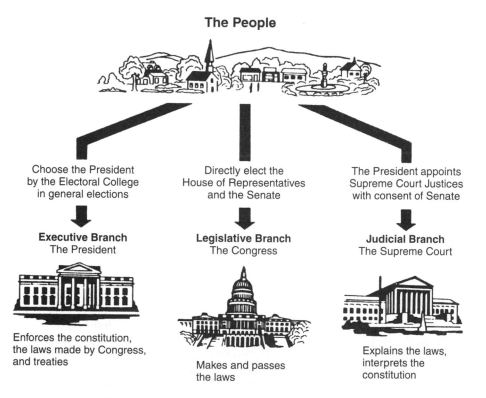

The People

Choose the President by the Electoral College in general elections

Directly elect the House of Representatives and the Senate

The President appoints Supreme Court Justices with consent of Senate

Executive Branch
The President

Legislative Branch
The Congress

Judicial Branch
The Supreme Court

Enforces the constitution, the laws made by Congress, and treaties

Makes and passes the laws

Explains the laws, interprets the constitution

Figure 19.2   The three separate branches of the Federal government

Sources: both from D. Harkness, *The Post-war World* (Macmillan, 1974) pp. 232 and 231

(d) *The separation of powers*

When the Founding Fathers of the USA (among whom were George Washington, Benjamin Franklin, Alexander Hamilton and James Madison) met in Philadelphia in 1787 to draw up the new constitution, one of their main concerns was to make sure that none of the three parts of government – Congress, President and Supreme Court – became too powerful. *They deliberately devised a system of 'checks and balances' in which the three branches of government work separately from each other* (see Figure 19.2). The President and his or her cabinet, for example, are not members of Congress, unlike the British Prime Minister and cabinet, who are all members of parliament. Each branch acts as a check on the power of the others. This means that the President is not as powerful as it might appear: since elections for the House are held every two years and a third of the Senate is elected every two years, a President's party can lose its majority in one or both houses after he or she has been in office only two years. Although the President can veto laws, Congress can overrule this veto if it can raise a two-thirds majority in both houses. Nor can the President dissolve Congress; it is just a question of hoping things will change for the better at the next set of elections. On the other hand, Congress cannot get rid of the President unless it can be shown that he or she has committed treason or some other serious crime. In that case a President can be threatened with *impeachment* (a formal accusation of crimes before the Senate which it would then try). It was to avoid impeachment that Richard Nixon resigned in disgrace (August 1974) because of his involvement in the Watergate Scandal (see Section 20. 4). A President's success has usually depended on how skilful he is at persuading Congress to approve his programme of changes. The Supreme Court keeps a watchful eye on both President and Congress, and can make life difficult for both of them by declaring a law 'unconstitutional', which means that it is illegal and has to be changed.

19.2 Into the melting pot – the era of immigration

(a) *A huge wave of immigration*

During the second half of the nineteenth century there was a huge wave of immigration into the USA. People had been crossing the Atlantic to settle in America since the seventeenth century, but in relatively small numbers. During the entire eighteenth century the total immigration into North America was probably no more than half a million. *Between 1860 and 1930 the total was over 30 million.* Between 1840 and 1870 the Irish were the predominant immigrant group. After 1850 Germans and Swedes arrived in vast numbers, and by 1910 there were at least eight million Germans in the USA. Between 1890 and 1920 it was the turn of Russians, Poles and Italians to come flooding in. Table 19.1 shows in detail the numbers of immigrants into the USA and where they came from.

Peoples' motives for leaving their home countries were mixed. Some were attracted by the prospect of jobs and a better life, and they were keen to escape from poverty. This was the case with the Irish, Swedes, Norwegians and Italians. Persecution drove many people to emigrate; this was especially true of the Jews who left Russia and other eastern European states in their millions after 1880 to escape pogroms (organized massacres). Immigration was much reduced after 1924 when the US government introduced annual quotas. Exceptions were still made, however, and during the 30 years following the end of the Second World War, a further seven million people arrived.

Illus. 19.1   Immigrants arriving in the USA

Table 19.1   US population and immigration, 1851–1950 (Figures in thousands to nearest thousand)

	1851–60	1861–70	1871–80	1881–90	1891–1900	1901–10	1911–20	1921–30	1931–40	1941–50	Quota per annum (1951)
Total Population (census year 1860, 1870, etc.)	31 443	39 818	50 156	62 948	75 995	91 972	105 711	122 775	131 669	150 697	
Total Immigration	2 598	2 315	2 812	5 247	3 688	8 795	5 736	2 478	528	1 035	154
Selected Countries of Origin:											
Ireland (N & S)	914	436	437	655	388	339	146	221	13	28[b]	18[b]
Germany	952	787	718	1 453	505	341	144	412	118[c]	227	26
Austria		8	73	354	593	2 145	454	33		25	1
Hungary							443	31	8	3	1
England	247	222	438	645	217	388	250	157	22	112	66[UK]
Italy	9	12	56	307	652	2 046	1 110	455	68	58	6
Sweden	21[a]	38	116	392	226	250	95	97	4	11	3
Poland	1	2	13	52	97		5	228	17	8	7
Russia		3	39	213	505	1 597	921	62	1	1	3
China	41	64	123	62	15	21	21	30	5	17	0

[a]   Includes Norway for this decade
[b]   Eire only
[c]   Includes Austria
Source: Roger Thompson, *The Golden Door* (Allman & Son, 1969) p. 309

Having arrived in the USA, many immigrants soon took part in a second migration, moving from their ports of arrival on the east coast into the mid-west. Germans, Norwegians and Swedes tended to move westwards, settling in such states as Nebraska, Wisconsin, Missouri, Minnesota, Iowa and Illinois. This was all part of a general American move westwards: the US population west of the Mississippi grew from only about five million in 1860 to around 30 million in 1910.

(b) *What were the consequences of immigration?*

● The most obvious consequence was the increase in population. It has been calculated that if there had been no mass movement of people to the USA between 1880 and the 1920s, the population would have been 12 per cent lower than it actually was in 1930.

● Immigrants helped to speed up economic development. Economic historian William Ashworth calculated that without immigration, the labour force of the USA would have been 14 per cent lower than it actually was in 1920, and 'with fewer people, much of the natural wealth of the country would have waited longer for effective use'.

● The movement of people from countryside to town resulted in the growth of huge urban areas known as conurbations. In 1880 only New York had over a million inhabitants; by 1910 Philadelphia and Chicago had passed that figure too.

● The movement to take jobs in industry, mining, engineering and building meant that the proportion of the population working in agriculture declined steadily. In the USA in 1870 about 58 per cent of all Americans worked in agriculture; by 1914 this had fallen to 14 per cent, and to only six per cent in 1965.

● The USA acquired the most remarkable mixture of nationalities, cultures and religions in the world (Illus. 19.1). Immigrants tended to concentrate in the cities, though many Germans, Swedes and Norwegians moved westwards in order to farm. In 1914 immigrants made up over half the population of every large American city, and there were some thirty different nationalities. This led idealistic Americans to claim with pride that the USA was a *'melting-pot'* into which all nationalities were thrown and melted down, to emerge as a single, unified American nation. In fact this seems to have been something of a myth, certainly until well after the First World War. Immigrants would congregate in national groups living in city ghettoes. Each new wave of immigrants was treated with contempt and hostility by earlier immigrants who feared for their jobs. The Irish, for example, would often refuse to work with Poles and Italians. Later the Poles and Italians were equally hostile to Mexicans. Some writers have said that the USA was not really a 'melting-pot' at all; as historian Roger Thompson puts it, the country was 'more like a salad-bowl, where, although a dressing is poured over the ingredients, they nonetheless remain separate'.

● There was growing agitation against allowing too many foreigners into the USA. The movement was racial in character, claiming that America's continuing greatness depended on preserving the purity of its Anglo-Saxon stock. This, it was felt, would be weakened by allowing the entry of unlimited numbers of Jews and southern and eastern Europeans. From 1921 the US government gradually restricted entry, until it was fixed at 150 000 a year in 1924. This was applied strictly during the depression years of the 1930s when unemployment was high. After the Second World War restrictions were gradually relaxed; the USA took in some 700 000 refugees escaping from Castro's Cuba between 1959 and 1975 and over 100 000 refugees from Vietnam after the communists took over South Vietnam in 1975.

19.3 The USA becomes economic leader of the world

(a) *Economic expansion and the rise of big business*

In the half century before the First World War, a vast industrial expansion took the USA to the top of the league table of world industrial producers. The statistics in Table 19.2 show that already in 1900 she had overtaken most of her nearest rivals.

Table 19.2 America and her chief rivals, 1900

	USA	Nearest rival
Coal production (tons)	262 m.	219 m. (Britain)
Exports (£)	311 m.	390 m. (Britain)
Pig-iron (tons)	16 m.	8 m. (Britain)
Steel (tons)	13 m.	6 m. (Germany)
Railways (miles)	183 000	28 000 (Germany)
Silver (fine oz)	55 m.	57 m. (Mexico)
Gold (fine oz)	3.8 m.	3.3 m. (Australia)
Cotton production (bales)	10.6 m.	3 m. (India)
Petroleum (metric tons)	9.5 m.	11.5 m. (Russia)
Wheat (bushels)	638 m.	552 m. (Russia)

Source: J. Nichol and S. Lang, *Work Out Modern World History* (Macmillan, 1990)

It was made possible by the rich supplies of raw materials – coal, iron-ore and oil – and by the spread of railways. The rapidly increasing population, much of it from immigration (see Section 19.1), provided the workforce and the markets. Import duties (tariffs) protected US industry from foreign competition, and it was a time of opportunity and enterprise. As American historian John A. Garraty puts it: 'the dominant spirit of the time encouraged businessmen to maximum effort by emphasising progress, glorifying material wealth and justifying aggressiveness'. The most successful businessmen like Andrew Carnegie (steel), John D. Rockefeller (oil), Cornelius Vanderbilt (shipping and railways), J. Pierpoint Morgan (banking) and P.D. Armour (meat), made vast fortunes and built up huge industrial empires which gave them power over both politicians and ordinary people.

(b) *The great boom of the 1920s*

After a slow start, as the country returned to normal after the First World War, the economy began to expand again: industrial production reached levels which had hardly been thought possible, doubling between 1921 and 1929 without any great increase in the numbers of workers. Sales, profits and wages also reached new heights, and the '*Roaring Twenties*' as they became known, saw a great variety of new things to be bought – radio sets, refrigerators, washing machines, vacuum cleaners, smart new clothes, motor-cycles, and above all, motor-cars. At the end of the war there were already 7 million cars in the USA, but by 1929 there were close on 24 million; Henry Ford led the field with his Model T. Perhaps the most famous of all the new commodities on offer was the Hollywood film industry which made huge profits and exported its products all over the world. *What caused the boom?*

1   *It was the climax of the great industrial expansion of the late nineteenth century*, when the USA had overtaken her two greatest rivals, Britain and Germany. The war gave American industry an enormous boost: countries whose industries and imports from Europe had been disrupted bought American goods, and continued to do so when the war was over. The USA was therefore the real economic victor of the war.

2   *The Republican governments' economic policies contributed to the prosperity in the short term.* Their approach was one of *laissez-faire*, but they did take two significant actions:

   - the Fordney–McCumber tariff (1922) raised import duties on goods coming into America to the highest level ever, thus protecting American industry and encouraging Americans to buy home-produced goods;
   - a general lowering of income tax in 1926 and 1928 left people with more cash to spend on American goods.

3   *American industry was becoming increasingly efficient*, as more mechanization was introduced. More and more factories were adopting the moving production line methods first used by Henry Ford in 1915, which speeded up production and reduced costs. Management also began to apply F.W. Taylor's 'time and motion' studies, which saved more time and increased productivity.

4   *As profits increased, so did wages* (though not as much as profits). Between 1923 and 1929 the average wage for industrial workers rose by 8 per cent. Though this was not spectacular, it was enough to enable some workers to buy the new consumer luxuries, often on credit.

5   *Advertising helped the boom and itself became big business during the 1920s.* Newspapers and magazines carried more advertising than ever before, radio commercials became commonplace and cinemas showed filmed advertisements.

6   *The motor-car industry stimulated expansion* in a number of allied industries – tyres, batteries, petroleum for petrol, garages and tourism.

7   *Many new roads were built* and mileage almost doubled between 1919 and 1929. It was now more feasible to transport goods by road, and the numbers of trucks registered increased fourfold during the same period. Prices were competitive and this meant that railways and canals had lost their monopoly.

8   *Giant corporations* with their methods of mass production played an important part in the boom by keeping costs down. Another technique, encouraged by the government, was the trade association. This helped to standardize methods, tools and prices in smaller firms making the same product. In this way the American economy became dominated by giant corporations and trade associations, using mass production methods for the mass consumer.

(c) *Free and equal?*

Although lots of people were doing well during the 'Roaring Twenties', the wealth was not shared out equally; there were some unfortunate groups of people who must have felt that their freedom did not extend very far.

1   Farmers were not sharing in the general prosperity

They had done well during the war, but during the 1920s prices of farm produce gradually fell. Farmers' profits dwindled and farm labourers' wages in the mid-west and the agricultural south were often less than half those of industrial workers in the north-east. The cause of the trouble was simple – farmers, with their new combine-harvesters and chemical fertilizers, were producing too much food for the home market to absorb. This was at a time when European agriculture was recovering from the war and when there was strong competition from Canada, Russia and Argentina on the world market. It meant that not enough of the surplus food could be exported. The government with its *laissez-faire* attitude did hardly anything to help. Even when Congress passed the McNary–Haugen Bill designed to allow the government to buy up farmers' surplus crops, Coolidge twice vetoed it (1927 and 1928) on the grounds that it would make the problem worse by encouraging farmers to produce even more.

2 Not all industries were prosperous

Coalmining, for example, was suffering competition from oil, and many workers were laid off.

3 The black population was left out of the prosperity

In the south where the majority of black people lived, white farmers always laid off black labourers first. About three-quarters of a million moved north during the 1920s looking for jobs in industry, but they almost always had to make do with the lowest paid jobs, the worst conditions at work and the worst slum housing. Black people also had to suffer the persecutions of the *Ku Klux Klan*, the notorious white-hooded anti-black organization which had about 5 million members in 1924. Assaults, whippings and lynchings were common, and although the Klan gradually declined after 1925, prejudice and discrimination against black people and against other coloured and minority groups continued (see Section 20.2).

4 Hostility to immigrants

Immigrants, especially those from eastern Europe, were treated with hostility. It was thought that, being non-Anglo-Saxon, they were threatening the greatness of the American nation.

5 Super-corporations

Industry became increasingly monopolized by large trusts or super-corporations. By 1929 the wealthiest 5 per cent of corporations took over 84 per cent of the total income of all corporations. Although trusts increased efficiency, there is no doubt that they kept prices higher, and wages lower than was necessary. They were able to keep trades unions weak by forbidding workers to join. The Republicans, who were pro-business, did nothing to limit the growth of the super-corporations because the system seemed to be working well.

6 Wealth was concentrated at the top

Between 1922 and 1929 real wages of industrial workers increased by only 1.4 per cent a year; 6 million families (42 per cent of the total) had an income of less than $1000 a year. Working conditions were still appalling – about 25 000 workers were killed at work every year and 100 000 were disabled. After touring working-class areas of New York in 1928, Congressman La Guardia remarked: ' I confess I was not prepared for what I actually saw. It seemed almost unbelievable that such conditions of poverty could really exist'. In New York City alone there were 2 million families, many of them immigrants, living in slum tenements which had been condemned as firetraps.

7   The freedom of workers to protest was extremely limited

Strikes were crushed by force, militant trades unions had been destroyed and the more moderate unions were weak. Although there was a Socialist party, there was no hope of it ever forming a government. After a bomb exploded in Washington in 1919, the authorities whipped up a '*Red Scare*'; they arrested and deported over 4000 citizens of foreign origin, many of them Russians, who were suspected of being communists or anarchists. Most of them were, in fact, completely innocent.

8   Prohibition was introduced in 1919

This was the banning of the manufacture, import and sale of all alcoholic liquor. It was the result of the efforts of a well-meaning pressure group during the First World War, which believed that a 'dry' America would mean a more efficient and moral America. But it proved impossible to eliminate bootleggers (manufacturers of illegal liquor), who protected their premises from rivals with hired gangs who shot each other up in gun-fights. Gang violence became part of the American scene, especially in Chicago where Al Capone made himself a fortune, much of it from bootlegging. The row over Prohibition was one aspect of a traditional American conflict: *between the countryside and the city*. Many country people believed that city life was sinful and unhealthy, while life in the country was pure, noble and moral.

9   Women still not treated equally

Many women felt that they were still treated as second-class citizens. Some progress had been made towards equal rights for women: they had been given the vote in 1920, the birth control movement was spreading, and more women were able to take jobs. On the other hand, these were usually jobs men did not want; women were paid lower wages than men for the same job, and education for women was still heavily slanted towards preparing them to be wives and mothers rather than professional career women.

19.4   The Great Depression arrives: October 1929

(a) *The Wall Street Crash, October 1929*

As 1929 opened, most Americans seemed blissfully unaware that anything serious was wrong with the economy. In 1928 President Coolidge told Congress: 'The country can regard the present with satisfaction, and anticipate the future with optimism'. Prosperity seemed permanent. The Republican Herbert C. Hoover won an overwhelming victory in the 1928 presidential election. Sadly the prosperity was built on suspect foundations and it could not last. 'America the Golden' was about to suffer a profound shock. In September 1929 the buying of shares at the New York stock exchange in Wall Street, began to slow down. Rumours spread that the boom might be over, and so people rushed to sell their shares before prices fell too far. By 24 October the rush had turned into a panic and share prices fell dramatically. Thousands of people who had bought their shares when prices were high were ruined.

This disaster is always remembered as the Wall Street Crash. Its effects spread rapidly: so many people in financial difficulties rushed to the banks to draw out their savings that thousands of banks had to close. As the demand for goods fell, factories closed down, and unemployment rose alarmingly. The great boom had suddenly turned into the great depression. It rapidly affected not only the USA, but other countries as well, and so it became known as *the world economic crisis*. The Wall Street Crash did not cause the depression; it was just a symptom of a problem of which the real causes lay much deeper.

(b) *What caused the Great Depression?*

1 Domestic over-production

American industrialists, encouraged by high profits and helped by increased mechanization, were *producing too many goods for the home market to absorb* (in the same

Illus. 19.2 A soup kitchen for down-and-outs

Illus. 19.3   A breadline in New York in 1933

way as the farmers). This was not apparent in the early 1920s, but as the 1930s approached, unsold stocks of goods began to build up, and manufacturers produced less. Since fewer workers were required, men were laid off; and as there was no unemployment benefit, these men and their families bought less. And so the vicious circle continued.

2   There was a maldistribution of income

This means that the enormous profits being made by industrialists were not being shared evenly enough among the workers. The average wage for industrial workers rose by about 8 per cent between 1923 and 1929, but during the same period, industrial profits increased by 72 per cent. An 8 per cent increase in wages meant that there was not enough buying power in the hands of the general public to sustain the boom; they could manage to absorb goods produced for a limited time, with the help of credit, but by 1929 they were fast approaching the limit. Unfortunately manufacturers, usually super-corporations, were not prepared to reduce prices or to increase wages substantially, and so a glut of consumer goods built up. This refusal by the manufacturers to make some compromise was shortsighted to say the least; at the beginning of 1929 there were still millions of Americans who had no radio, no electric washer and no car because they could not afford them. If employers had allowed larger wage increases and been content with less profit, there is no reason why the boom could not have continued for several more years, while its benefits were more widely shared. Even so, a slump was still not inevitable, provided the Americans could export their surplus products.

3 Exports began to fall away

This was partly because foreign countries were reluctant to buy American goods when the Americans themselves put up tariff barriers to protect their industries from foreign imports. Although the Fordney–McCumber tariff (1922) helped to keep foreign goods out, at the same time it prevented foreign states, especially those in Europe, from making much-needed profits from trade with the USA. Without those profits, the nations of Europe would be unable to afford American goods, and they would be struggling to pay their war debts to the USA. To make matters worse, many states retaliated by introducing tariffs against American goods. A slump of some sort was clearly on the way.

4 Speculation

The situation was worsened by a great rush of *speculation* on the New York stock market, which began to gather momentum about 1926. Speculation is the buying of shares in companies; people with cash to spare like to do this for two possible motives:

- to get the dividend – this is the annual sharing-out of a company's profits among its shareholders;
- to make a quick profit by selling the shares for more than they originally paid for them.

In the mid-1920s it was the second motive which most attracted investors: as company profits increased, more people wanted to buy shares; this forced share prices up and there were plenty of chances of quick profits from buying and selling shares. The average value of a share rose from $9 in 1924 to $26 in 1929. Share prices of some companies rose spectacularly: the stock of the Radio Corporation of America, for example, stood at $85 a share early in 1928 and had risen to $505 in September 1929, and that was a company which did not pay dividends.

Promise of quick profits encouraged all sorts of rash moves: ordinary people spent their savings or borrowed money to buy a few shares. Stockbrokers sold shares on credit; banks speculated in shares using the cash deposited with them. It was all something of a gamble; but there was enormous confidence that prosperity would continue indefinitely.

This confidence lasted well on into 1929, but when the first signs appeared that sales of goods were beginning to slow down, some better-informed investors decided to sell their shares while prices were still high. This caused suspicion to spread – more people than usual were trying to sell shares – something must be wrong! Confidence in the future began to waver for the first time and more people decided to sell their shares while the going was good. And so a process of what economists call *self-fulfilling expectation* developed. This means that by their own actions, investors actually caused the dramatic collapse of share prices which they were afraid of.

By October 1929 there was a flood of people rushing to sell shares, but because confidence had been shaken, there were far fewer people wanting to buy. Share prices tumbled and unfortunate investors had to accept whatever they could get. One especially bad day was 24 October – Black Thursday – when nearly 13 million shares were 'dumped' on the stock market at very low prices. By mid-1930 share prices were on average about 25 per cent of their peak level the previous year, but they were still falling. Rock bottom was reached in 1932, and by then the whole of the USA was in the grip of depression.

(c) *How did the Depression affect people?*

1   To begin with, *the stock market crash ruined millions of investors* who had paid high prices for their shares. If investors had bought shares on credit or with borrowed money, their creditors lost heavily too, since they had no hope of receiving payment.

2   *Banks were in a shaky position*, having themselves speculated unsuccessfully. When, added to this, millions of people rushed to withdraw their savings in the belief that their cash would be safer at home, many banks were overwhelmed, did not have enough cash to pay everybody, and closed down for good. There were over 25 000 banks in the country in 1929, but by 1933 there were fewer than 15 000. This meant that millions of ordinary people who had had nothing to do with the speculation were ruined as their life savings disappeared.

3   As the demand for all types of goods fell, *workers were laid off and factories closed*. Industrial production in 1933 was only half the 1929 total, while unemployment stood at around 14 million. About a quarter of the total labour force was without jobs, and one in eight farmers lost all their property. *There was a drop in living standards*, with bread lines (queues), charity soup kitchens, evictions of tenants who could not afford the rent, and near starvation for many people (Illus. 19.2 and 19.3). The 'great American dream' of prosperity for everybody had turned into a nightmare. In the words of historian Donald McCoy: 'the American people were affected as though a war had been fought from coast to coast'. And there were no unemployment and sickness benefits to help out. Outside every large city, homeless people lived in camps nicknamed 'Hoovervilles' after the President who was blamed for the depression.

4   *Many other countries, especially Germany, were affected* because their prosperity depended to a large extent on loans from the USA. As soon as the crash came, the loans stopped, and the Americans called in the short-term loans they had already made. By 1931 most of Europe was in a similar plight. The depression had political results too; in many states – Germany, Austria, Japan and Britain – right-wing governments came to power when the existing regimes failed to cope with the situation.

(d) *Who was to blame for the disaster?*

At the time it was fashionable to blame the unfortunate President Hoover, but this is unfair. The origins of the trouble go much further back, and the Republican party as a whole must share the blame. There were several measures the government could have taken to control the situation: they could have encouraged overseas countries to buy more American goods by lowering American tariffs instead of raising them. Decisive action could have been taken in 1928 and 1929 to limit the amount of credit which the stock market was allowing speculators. But their *laissez-faire* attitude would not allow such interference in private affairs.

(e) *What did Hoover's government do to ease the depression?*

Hoover tried to solve the problem by encouraging employers not to reduce wages and not to lay workers off. The government lent money to banks, industrialists and farmers to save them from bankruptcy, and began work schemes to relieve unemployment. In 1931 Hoover declared a one-year moratorium on war debts. This meant that foreign governments could miss one instalment of their debts to the USA in the hope that they would use the money saved to buy more American goods. But it made little difference

– American exports in 1932 were less than a third of the 1929 total. Hoover's policies made very little impact on the depression. Even in a crisis as serious as this, he was against relief payments to individuals because he believed in self-reliance and 'rugged individualism'. It was no surprise when the Democrat candidate, Franklin D. Roosevelt, easily beat Hoover in the presidential election of November 1932 (Illus. 19.4).

19.5 Roosevelt and the New Deal

The 51-year-old Roosevelt came from a wealthy New York family; educated at Harvard, he entered politics in 1910 and was Assistant Secretary to the Navy during the First World War. It seemed as though his career might be over when, at the age of forty, he was stricken with polio (1921), which left his legs completely paralysed. With tremendous determination he overcame his disability, though he was never able to walk unaided. He now brought the same determination to bear in his attempts to drag America out of the depression. He was dynamic, full of vitality and brimming with new ideas. He was a brilliant communicator – his radio talks (which he called his fireside chats) inspired confidence and won him great popularity. During the election campaign

Illus. 19.4 The winner and the loser. Franklin D. Roosevelt (right) waves acknowledgement to the cheering crowds, while defeated President Herbert Hoover looks downcast during their ride through Washington in March 1933

he had said: 'I pledge you, I pledge myself, to a new deal for the American people'. The phrase stuck, and his policies have always been remembered as the New Deal. Right from the beginning he brought new hope when he said in his inauguration speech: 'Let me assert my firm belief that the only thing we have to fear is fear itself. This nation asks for action, and action now ... I shall ask Congress for the power to wage war against the emergency'.

(a) What were the aims of the New Deal?

Basically Roosevelt had three aims:

relief: to give direct help to the poverty-stricken millions who were without food and homes;

recovery: to reduce unemployment, stimulate the demand for goods, and get the economy moving again;

reform: to take whatever measures were necessary to prevent a repeat of the economic disaster.

It was obvious that drastic measures were needed, and Roosevelt's methods were a complete change from those of the *laissez-faire* Republicans. He was prepared to intervene in economic and social affairs as much as possible and to spend government cash to pull the country out of depression. The Republicans were always reluctant to take steps of this sort.

(b) What did the New Deal involve?

The measures which go to make up the New Deal were introduced over the years 1933 to 1940.

1 Banking and financial systems

It was important to get the banking and financial systems working properly again. This was achieved by the government taking over the banks temporarily and guaranteeing that depositors would not lose their cash if there was another financial crisis. This restored confidence and money began to flow into the banks again. The *Securities Exchange Commission (1934)* reformed the stock exchange; among other things, it insisted that people buying shares on credit must make a down-payment of at least 50 per cent instead of only 10 per cent.

2 The Farmers' Relief Act (1933)

This tried to help farmers, whose main problem was that they were still producing too much, which kept prices and profits low. Under the Act, the government paid compensation to farmers who reduced output, thereby raising prices. This had some success – by 1937 the average income of farmers had almost doubled.

3 The Civilian Conservation Corps (CCC)

This was a popular Roosevelt idea to provide jobs for young men in conservation projects in the countryside. By 1940 about 2.5 million had 'enjoyed' a six-month spell in the CCC, which gave them a small wage ($30 a month of which $25 had to be sent home to the family), as well as food, clothing and shelter.

4 The National Industrial Recovery Act (1933)

This was the most important part of the programme. It tried to get people back to work permanently, so that they would then be able to buy more. This would stimulate industry and help the economy to function normally. The Act introduced the *Public Works Administration (PWA)*, which organized and provided cash for the building of useful works – dams, bridges, roads, hospitals, schools, airports and government buildings – creating several million extra jobs. Another section of the Act set up the *National Recovery Administration (NRA)* which abolished child labour, introduced a maximum eight-hour working day and a minimum wage, and thus helped to create more employment. Although these rules were not compulsory, employers were pressured to accept them; those who did were privileged to use an official sticker on their goods showing a blue eagle and the letters NRA. The public was encouraged to boycott firms which refused to co-operate. The response was tremendous, with well over 2 million employers accepting the new standards.

5 The Federal Emergency Relief Administration

This provided further relief and recovery. It provided $500 million for dole money and soup kitchens. The *Works Progress Administration (WPA)*, founded in 1935, funded a variety of projects such as roads, schools and hospitals (similar to the PWA but smaller-scale projects), and the Federal Theatre Project created jobs for playwrights, artists, actors, musicians and circus performers, as well as increasing public appreciation of the arts.

6 The Social Security Act (1935)

This introduced old age pensions and unemployment insurance schemes, to be jointly financed by federal and state governments, employers and workers. However, this was not a great success at the time, because payments were usually not very generous; nor was there any provision made for sickness insurance. The USA was lagging well behind countries such as Germany and Britain in social welfare.

7 Working conditions

Two acts encouraged trades unions and helped improve working conditions.

The *Wagner Act (1935)*, the work of Senator Robert F. Wagner of New York, gave unions a proper legal foundation and the right to bargain for their members in any dispute with management. It also set up the National Labour Relations Board to which workers could appeal against unfair practices by management.

The *Fair Labour Standards Act (1938)* introduced a maximum 45-hour working week as well as a minimum wage in certain low-paid trades, and made most child labour illegal.

8 Other measures

Also included in the New Deal were such measures as the *Tennessee Valley Authority (TVA)*, which revitalized a huge area of rural America which had been ruined by soil erosion and careless farming (see Map 19.2). The new authority built dams to provide cheap electricity, and organized conservation, irrigation and afforestation to prevent soil erosion. There were loans for householders in danger of losing their homes

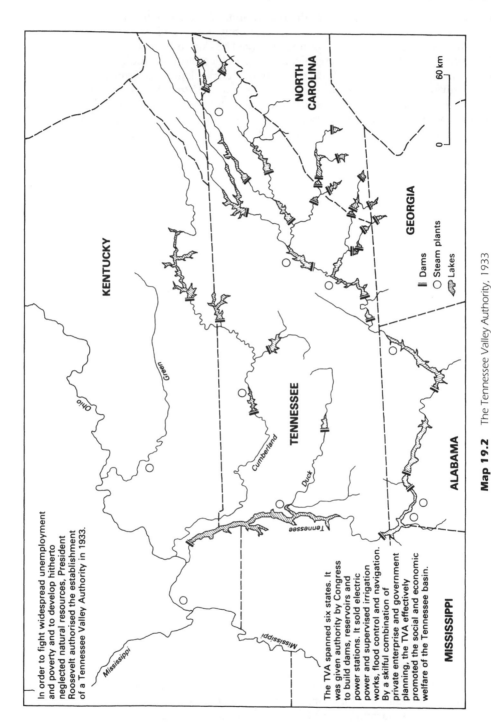

In order to fight widespread unemployment and poverty and to develop hitherto neglected natural resources, President Roosevelt authorised the establishment of a Tennessee Valley Authority in 1933.

The TVA spanned six states. It was given authority by Congress to build dams, reservoirs and power stations. It sold electric power and supervised irrigation works, flood control and navigation. By a skilful combination of private enterprise and government planning, the TVA effectively promoted the social and economic welfare of the Tennessee basin.

Dams
Steam plants
Lakes

0   60 km

NORTH CAROLINA

GEORGIA

KENTUCKY

TENNESSEE

ALABAMA

MISSISSIPPI

Green

Ohio

Cumberland

Duck

Tennessee

Mississippi

Map 19.2 The Tennessee Valley Authority, 1933

Source: Martin Gilbert, *American History Atlas* (Weidenfeld & Nicolson) p. 82

because they could not afford mortgage repayments; slum clearance and building of new houses and flats; increased taxes on the incomes of the wealthy; and trade agreements which at last reduced American tariffs in return for tariff reductions by the other party to the treaty (in the hope of increasing American exports). One of the very first New Deal measures was the end of Prohibition; as 'FDR' himself remarked, 'I think this would be a good time for beer'.

(c) *Opposition to the New Deal*

It was inevitable that such a far-reaching programme would arouse opposition.

- *Businessmen* objected strongly to the growth of trades unions, the regulation of hours and wages, and increased taxation.
- Some of the *state governments* resented the extent to which the federal government was interfering in what they considered to be internal state affairs.
- *The Supreme Court* claimed that the President was taking on too much power; they ruled several measures (including NRA) as unconstitutional, and this held up their operation. However, the Supreme Court became more amenable during Roosevelt's second term after he had appointed five more co-operative judges to replace those who had died or resigned.
- There was also opposition from *socialists* who felt that the New Deal was not drastic enough and still left too much power in the hands of big business.
- Some people poured scorn on the wide variety of new organizations, known by

Illus. 19.5   President F.D. Roosevelt

their initials. Ex-president Hoover remarked: 'There are only four letters of the alphabet not now in use by the administration. When we establish the Quick Loan Corporation for Xylophones, Yachts and Zithers, the alphabet of our fathers will be exhausted'. From then on the term '*Alphabet Agencies*' stuck.

But Roosevelt was tremendously popular with the millions of ordinary Americans, the 'forgotten men' as he called them, who had benefited from his policies. He had won the support of trades unions and of many farmers and black people. Although the forces of the right did their best to remove him in 1936 and 1940, Roosevelt won a crushing victory in 1936 and a another comfortable one in 1940 (Illus. 19.5).

(d) *What did the New Deal achieve?*

It has to be said that *it did not achieve all that FDR had hoped*. Some of the measures failed completely or were only partly successful. The Farmers' Relief Act, for example, certainly helped farmers, but it threw many farm labourers out of work. Nor did it do much to help farmers living in parts of Kansas, Oklahoma and Texas; in the mid-1930s these areas were badly hit by drought and soil erosion, which turned them into a huge 'dustbowl' (see Map 19.1). Although unemployment was reduced to less than eight million by 1937, it was still a serious problem. Part of the failure was due to the Supreme Court's opposition. Another reason was that although he was bold in many ways, Roosevelt was too cautious in the amounts of money he was prepared to spend to stimulate industry. In 1938 he reduced government spending, causing another recession (a period when sales of industrial products fall) which sent unemployment up to 10.5 million. *The New Deal therefore did not rescue the USA from the depression*; it was only the war effort which brought unemployment below the million mark in 1943.

  Still, in spite of this, Roosevelt's first eight years in office were a remarkable period. Never before had an American government intervened so directly in the lives of ordinary people; never before had so much attention been focused on an American President. *And much was achieved:*

* in the early days the chief success of the New Deal was in providing relief for the destitute and jobless, and in the creation of millions of extra jobs;
* confidence was restored in the government, and some historians think it may even have prevented a violent revolution;
* the public works schemes and the Tennessee Valley Authority provided services of lasting value;
* welfare benefits such as the 1935 Social Security Act were an important step towards a welfare state. Although 'rugged individualism' was still a vital ingredient in American society, the American government had accepted that it had a duty to help those in need;
* many of the other innovations were continued – national direction of resources and collective bargaining between workers and management became accepted as normal;
* some historians believe that Roosevelt's greatest achievement was to preserve what might be called the American middle way – democracy and free enterprise – at a time when other states like Germany and Italy had responded to similar crises by turning to fascism.

(e) *The Second World War and the American economy*

It was the war which finally put an end to the Depression. The USA entered the war in December 1941 after the Japanese had bombed the American naval base at Pearl Harbor in the Hawaiian Islands. However, the Americans had begun to supply Britain and France with aircraft, tanks and other armaments as soon as war broke out in Europe in September 1939. 'We have the men, the skills, and above all the will', said Roosevelt. 'We must be the arsenal of democracy'. Between June 1940 and December 1941 the USA provided 23 000 aircraft.

After Pearl Harbor, production of armaments soared: in 1943, 86 000 aircraft were built, while in 1944 the figure was over 96 000. It was the same with ships: in 1939 American shipyards turned out 237 000 tons of shipping; in 1943 this had risen to 10 million tons. In fact the Gross National Product (GNP) of the USA almost doubled between 1939 and 1945. In June 1940 there were still eight million people out of work, but by the end of 1942 there was almost full employment. It was calculated that by 1945 the war effort had created seven million extra jobs in the USA. In addition, about 15 million Americans served in the armed forces. *Economically therefore, the USA did well out of the Second World War* – there were plenty of jobs, wages rose steadily, and there was no decline in the standard of living as there was in Europe.

Questions

1   *The Great Depression*   Study Sources A to I and then answer the questions which follow.

Source A

Speech by President Hoover in 1928

We in America today are nearer to the financial triumph over poverty than ever before in the history of our land. The poor man is vanishing from us. Under the Republican system, our industrial output has increased as never before, and our wages have grown steadily in buying power.

Source: quoted in J. Nichol and S. Lang, *Work Out Modern World History* (Macmillan, 1990)

Source B

President Harding talking to one of his secretaries (1922)

John, I can't make a damn thing out of this tax problem. I listen to one side and they seem right and then I talk to the other side and they seem just as right. I know somewhere there is an economist who will give me the truth but I don't know where to find him. God! what a job!

Source: quoted in Samuel E. Morison, *The Oxford History of the American People* (Oxford University Press, 1965)

An American historian's view

In the USA too much wealth had fallen into too few hands, with the result that consumers were unable to buy all the goods produced. The trouble came to a head mainly because of the easy credit policies of the Federal Reserve Board, which favoured the rich. Its effects were so profound and so prolonged because the government did not fully understand what was happening or what to do about it. The chronic problem of under-consumption operated to speed the downward spiral, and manufacturers closed plants and laid off workers, thereby causing demand to shrink further.

Source: John A. Garraty, *The American Nation* (Harper & Row, 1979 edition)

Source D

Arthur A. Robertson talks to Studs Terkel about his experiences

In 1929 it was strictly a gambling casino with loaded dice. I saw shoeshine boys buying 50 000 dollars worth of stock with 500 dollars down payment. A cigar stock at the time was selling for 114 dollars a share. The market collapsed. The 114 dollar stock dropped to two dollars, and the company president jumped out of the window of his Wall Street office.

Source: quoted in Studs Terkel, *Hard Times* (Pantheon, 1970)

Source E

Table 19.3   *Share prices of some leading US companies (in $)*

	US Steel	General Electric	Radio Corporation of America
1928	138	128	94
3.9.29	279	296	505
24.10.29 am	205	315	68
24.10.29 noon	193	283	44
1930	182	75	48
1931	145	50	24
1932	48	21	9
1933	24	12	4

Source: J. Nichol and S. Lang, *Work Out Modern World History* (Macmillan, 1990)

Source F

Two newspaper reports

(i) Indiana Harbor, Indiana, 5 August 1931
Fifteen hundred jobless men stormed the plant of the Fruit Growers' Express Company demanding that they be given jobs to keep them from starving. The Company's answer was to call the city police, who routed the jobless with menacing clubs.

(ii) New York, 3 June 1932
Several hundred jobless surrounded a restaurant just off Union Square today demanding they be fed without charge.

Source: quoted in H. Zinn, *A People's History of the United States* (Longman, 1980)

Yip Harburg, a songwriter, talks to Studs Terkel

I was walking along the street at that time [1932] and you'd see the bread lines [queues]. The biggest one in New York City was owned by William Randolph Hearst. He had a big truck with several people on it, and big cauldrons of hot soup, bread. I wrote a song about it called 'Brother, Can You Spare a Dime'. In the song the man is really saying: I made an investment in this country. Where the hell are my dividends?

Source: quoted in Studs Terkel, *Hard Times* (Pantheon, 1970)

Source H

Extract from The Grapes of Wrath, *a novel by John Steinbeck, which tells the story of a poor Oklahoma farmer who is trying to get to California in search of a better life. It was first published in 1939*

He drove his car into a town and scoured the farms for work. Where can we sleep the night? Well, there's Hooverville on the edge of the river. The rag town lay close to the water; and the houses were tents, and weed-thatched enclosures, paper houses, a great junk pile. The man drove his family in and became a citizen of Hooverville.

Source: John Steinbeck, *The Grapes of Wrath* (Penguin edition, 1951)

Source I

A scene from the Great Depression (Illus. 19.6)

Source: Topham Picture Library

(a) Do you think Sources A to E give a full explanation of the causes of the depression, bearing in mind the information given in Section 19.4(a–b)?

1.4b–6b, 3.4   10 marks

(b) Using Section 19.4(a–b) and Sources A to E, show how the causes of the depression, the motives of people involved, and the consequences of their actions were interlinked.

1.4b–9a   10 marks

(c) Using Sources C to I, make a list of some of the consequences of the great depression for the American people.

1.4b–5b, 4c–7c, 3.4   10 marks

(d) Look at each of these sources again and explain:

   (i)   how reliable

   (ii) how useful each one is for a historian studying the great depression.

3.5–9   20 marks

Total: 50 marks

2   *Roosevelt and the New Deal*   Study Sources A to E about the New Deal and then answer the questions which follow.

Source A

Cartoon published in March 1933 (Figure 19.3)

Source: J. Nichol and S. Lang, *Work Out Modern World History* (Macmillan, 1990)

Cartoon published in 1935 (Figure 19.4)

___

Source C

A biographer of Roosevelt writing about events in 1936

Unemployment had dropped from 12 to 4 million. Real estate was up. In New York City an office building had rented every office before completion, and there were traffic jams again. The cash income of farmers had almost doubled. A vast number of people were being helped and everywhere you went you could see it.

Source: Ted Morgan, *FDR* (Grafton, 1986)

Source D

The view of a British journalist and historian living in the USA

Roosevelt came in on a promise to guarantee full employment in peacetime. He didn't make it. In 1938 there were still ten million unemployed. In the next four years the number did indeed shrink – it went out of sight – but this was not Roosevelt's doing but Hitler's. The stacks of the steel mills barely began to belch smoke again until the first war orders came in from the British and the French.

Source: Alistair Cooke, *America* (BBC, 1973)

Table 19.4 *Numbers of unemployed at the beginning of each year (in millions)*

Year	millions unemployed	Year	millions unemployed
1926	0.9	1936	9.0
1930	4.3	1937	7.7
1931	8.0	1938	10.4
1932	12.0	1939	9.5
1933	12.8	1940	8.1
1934	11.3	1941	5.3
1935	10.6	1944	0.75

Source: J. Nichol and S. Lang, *Work Out Modern World History* (Macmillan, 1990)

(a) Using the information from Section 19.5(b), make a list of the changes introduced by the New Deal, classifying them into social and economic changes.   1.4a–5a   7 marks

(b) Explain in your own words how the two cartoons in Sources A and B give conflicting views of Roosevelt's New Deal.   1.4c–6c   7 marks

(c) How do you explain these different interpretations of the New Deal? See Section 19.5(c–e) for information.   1.8c–9b   6 marks

(d) To what extent do you think Sources C and D contradict each other?   2.5–6, 3.4   5 marks

(e) How useful is each one of these sources for the historian trying to decide whether or not the New Deal was a success?   2.6, 3.4–10   10 marks

Total: 35 marks

20 The USA since 1945

Summary of events

When the war ended in 1945, the economic boom continued as factories switched from producing armaments to producing consumer goods. Lots of new goods had appeared by this time – TV sets, dishwashers, modern record-players and tape-recorders – and many ordinary working people could afford to buy these luxury goods for the first time. This was the big difference between the 1950s and the 1920s, when too many people had been too poor to keep the boom going. The 1950s was the time of the *affluent society*, and in the twenty years following the end of the war, GNP increased by almost eight times. The USA continued to be the world's largest industrial power and the world's richest nation.

In spite of the general affluence, *there were still serious problems in American society*. There was a great deal of poverty and constant unemployment; black people, on the whole, were still not getting their fair share of the prosperity and did not have equal rights with whites. The Cold War caused some problems for Americans at home and led to another outbreak of anti-communist feeling, like the one after the First World War. There were unhappy experiences such as the assassinations of President Kennedy in Dallas, Texas, allegedly by Lee Harvey Oswald (1963), and of Dr Martin Luther King (1968); there was the failure of American policy in Vietnam, and the forced resignation of President Nixon (1974) as a result of the Watergate scandal, all of which shook confidence in American society and values, and in the American system. Both political parties took turns in power; the Presidents were:

1945–53	Harry S Truman	Democrat
1953–61	Dwight D. Eisenhower	Republican
1961–3	John F. Kennedy	Democrat
1963–9	Lyndon B. Johnson	Democrat
1969–74	Richard M. Nixon	Republican
1974–7	Gerald R. Ford	Republican
1977–81	Jimmy Carter	Democrat
1981–9	Ronald Reagan	Republican
1989–93	George Bush	Republican
1993–	Bill Clinton	Democrat

20.1 Poverty and social policies

Ironically in the world's richest country, poverty remained a problem. Although the economy was on the whole a spectacular success story, with industry flourishing and exports booming, there was constant unemployment which crept steadily up to 5.5 million (about 7 per cent of the labour force) in 1960. In spite of all the New Deal improvements, social welfare and pensions were still limited, and there was no national health system. It was calculated that in 1966 some 30 million Americans were living below the poverty line, and many of them were aged over 65.

(a) *Truman (1945–53)*

Truman, a man of great courage and common sense, once compared by a reporter to a bantam-weight prize fighter, had to face the special problem of returning the country to normal after the war. This was achieved, though not without difficulties: removal of wartime price controls caused inflation and strikes, and the Republicans won control of Congress in 1946. In the fight against poverty he had a programme known as the *Fair Deal*, which he hoped would continue Roosevelt's New Deal. It included:

- a national health scheme;
- a higher minimum wage;
- slum clearance; and
- full employment.

However, the Republican majority in Congress threw out his proposals, and even passed over his veto the Taft–Hartley Act (1947) which reduced trade union powers. The attitude of Congress gained Truman working-class support and enabled him to win the 1948 Presidential election, together with a Democrat majority in Congress. Some of the Fair Deal then became law (extension of social security benefits and an increase in the minimum wage), but Congress still refused to pass his national health and old age pensions schemes, which was a bitter disappointment for him. Many southern Democrats voted against Truman because they disapproved of his support for black civil rights.

(b) *Eisenhower (1953–61)*

Eisenhower had no programme for dealing with poverty, though he did not try to reverse the New Deal and the Fair Deal. Some improvements were made:

- insurance for the long-term disabled;
- financial help towards medical bills for people over 65;
- federal cash for housing; and
- more spending on education to encourage study in science and mathematics (it was feared that the Americans were falling behind the Russians, who in 1957 launched the first space satellite – Sputnik).

Farmers faced problems in the 1950s because increased production kept prices and incomes low. The government spent massive sums paying farmers to take land out of cultivation, but this was not a success: farm incomes did not rise rapidly and poorer farmers hardly benefited at all. Many of them sold up and moved into the cities.

Much remained to be done but the Republicans were totally against national schemes such as Truman's health service, because they thought they were too much like socialism.

(c) *Kennedy (1961–3)*

By the time Kennedy became President in 1961, the problems were more serious, with over 4.5 million unemployed. He won the election partly because the Republicans were blamed for inflation and unemployment, and because he ran a brilliant campaign, accusing them of neglecting education and social services. He came over as elegant, articulate, witty and dynamic, and his election seemed to many people to be the beginning of a new era. He had a detailed programme:

- medical payments for the poor and aged;
- more federal aid for education and housing; and
- increased unemployment and social security benefits.

'We stand today on the edge of a New Frontier', he said, and implied that only when these reforms were introduced would the frontier be crossed and poverty eliminated.

Unfortunately for Kennedy, he had to face strong opposition from Congress, where many right-wing Democrats as well as Republicans viewed his proposals as 'creeping socialism'. Hardly a single one was passed without some watering down, and many were rejected completely. Congress would allow no extra federal cash for education and rejected his scheme to pay hospital bills for elderly people. His successes were:

- an extension of social security benefits to each child whose father was unemployed;
- raising of the minimum wage from a dollar to 1.25 an hour;
- federal loans to enable people to buy houses;
- federal grants to the states enabling them to extend the period covered by unemployment benefit.

Kennedy's overall achievement was limited: unemployment benefit was only enough for subsistence and even that was only for a limited period. Unemployment still stood at 4.5 million in 1962, and soup kitchens had to be set up to feed poor families.

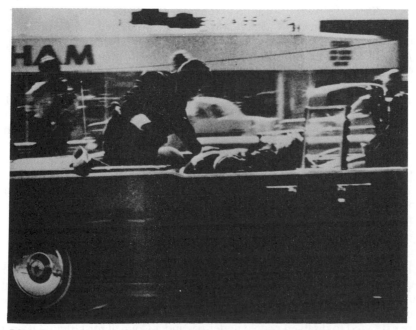

Illus. 20.1 The assassination of John F. Kennedy, 1963. Here the President slumps forward, seconds after having been shot

(d) *Johnson (1963–9)*

Kennedy's Vice-President, Johnson became President when Kennedy was assassinated (Illus. 20.1). Coming from a humble background in Texas, he was just as committed as Kennedy to social reform, and achieved enough in his first year to enable him to win a landslide victory in the 1964 election. In 1964 Johnson's economic advisers fixed an annual income of $3000 for a family of two or more as the poverty line, and they estimated that over 9 million families (30 million people, nearly 20 per cent of the population) were on or below the line. Many of them were black people, Puerto Ricans, native Americans and Mexicans. Johnson announced that he wanted to move America towards the *Great Society* where there would be an end to poverty and racial injustice and 'abundance and liberty for all'.

Many of his measures became law partly because after the 1964 elections the Democrats had a huge majority in Congress, and partly because Johnson was more skilful and persuasive in handling Congress than Kennedy had been.

● The *Economic Opportunity Act (1964)* provided a number of schemes under which young people from poor homes could receive job training and higher education.
● Other measures were the provision of federal money for special education schemes in slum areas, including help in paying for books and transport; financial aid for clearing slums and rebuilding city areas; and the *Appalachian Regional Development Act (1965)* which created new jobs in one of the poorest regions.
● Perhaps his most important innovation was *the Social Security Amendment Act (1965)*, also known as *Medicare*: this was a partial national health scheme, though it applied only to people over 65.

This is an impressive list, and yet the overall results were not as successful as Johnson would have hoped, for a number of reasons: it has been suggested that the entire programme was under-financed because of the enormous expenditure on the war in Vietnam. On the other hand, there was a lack of public support because of *the strong American tradition of self-help:* it was up to the poor to help themselves and wrong to use taxpayers' money on schemes which, it was thought, would only make the poor more lazy. Thus many state governments failed to take advantage of federal offers of help.

In the mid-1960s violence increased and seemed to be getting out of hand; there were riots in black ghettos where the sense of injustice was strongest; there were student riots in the universities in protest against the Vietnam war (Illus. 20.2). There were a number of political assassinations – President Kennedy in 1963, Martin Luther King and Senator Robert Kennedy in 1968. Between 1960 and 1967 the number of violent crimes rose by 90 per cent. Johnson could only hope that his 'war on poverty' would gradually remove the causes of discontent; beyond that he had no answer to the problem. The general discontent and especially the student protests about Vietnam ('LBJ, LBJ, how many kids have you burnt today?') caused Johnson not to stand for re-election in November 1968, and it helps to explain why the Republicans won, on a platform of restoring law and order.

(f) *Nixon (1969–74)*

Unemployment was soon rising again, with over 4 million out of work in 1971; their plight was worsened by rapidly rising prices. The Republicans were anxious to cut public expenditure and Nixon reduced spending on Johnson's poverty programme, and introduced a wages and prices freeze. However, social security benefits were increased, Medicare extended to disabled people under 65, and a Council for Urban Affairs set up to try to deal with the problems of slums and ghettos. Violence was less of a problem

Illus. 20.2 An anti-Vietnam War demonstration in San Francisco

under Nixon, partly because protestors could now see the approaching end of America's controversial involvement in Vietnam, and because students were allowed some say in running their colleges and universities.

During the last quarter of the century, in spite of some economic success under Reagan, the underlying problem of poverty and deprivation is still there. In the world's richest country there is a permanent underclass of unemployed, poor and deprived people, the inner cities need re-vitalising, and yet federal spending on welfare, although it has increased since 1981, is well below the level of government welfare funding in Western European states like Germany, France and Britain (see Section 20.5(c) for later developments).

20.2 Racial problems and civil rights

(a) *Racial discrimination*

When slavery was abolished in the USA (1863), black people expected to have the same rights as whites: the right to own land, to receive a good education and to vote. However, in the southern states in particular, where slavery had existed for over 200 years, many white people, who had grown up thinking of black people as slaves, and therefore inferior, found it difficult to treat them as equals. Almost immediately, black people found that they were discriminated against in all sorts of ways:

- prevented from voting;
- forced to attend separate schools which provided poorer quality education than that enjoyed by whites;
- segregated in places like restaurants, and on buses, coaches and trains; and
- they usually found themselves doing the most unpleasant and worst paid jobs. Most trades unions, which were meant to protect the interests of workers, refused to allow black people to join.

The first organized attempt to campaign for black people's rights began in 1910 with the formation of the *National Association for the Advancement of Colored People (NAACP)*. But very little progress was made and black people were still being treated as second-class citizens during the Second World War. Even when American troops were travelling on the *Queen Mary* to fight in Europe, blacks had to travel in the depths of the ship near the engine room, well away from the fresh air.

(b) *The government's attitude changes*

In 1946 President Truman appointed a committee to investigate civil rights. It recommended that Congress should pass laws to stop racial discrimination in jobs and to allow blacks to vote. *What caused this change of heart?*

The committee itself gave several reasons:

1   some politicians were worried by their consciences – they felt that it was not morally right to treat fellow human beings in such an unfair way;

2   excluding blacks from top jobs was a waste of talent and expertise;

3   it was important to do something to calm the black population, who were becoming more outspoken in their demands for civil rights;

4   the USA could not claim to be a genuinely democratic country when 10 per cent of its population were denied voting and other rights. This gave the USSR a chance to condemn the USA as 'a consistent oppressor of under-privileged peoples'. The US government wanted that excuse removed;

5   nationalism was growing rapidly in Asia and Africa. Non-white people in India and Indonesia were on the point of gaining independence. These new states might turn against the USA and towards communism if American whites continued their unfair treatment of blacks.

Over the next few years the government and the Supreme Court introduced *new laws to bring about racial equality*.

●   Separate schools for blacks and whites were illegal, and some black people had to be included on all juries (1954).

●   Schools must be desegregated; this meant that black children had to attend white schools and vice versa.

●   The 1957 Civil Rights Act set up a commission to investigate the denial of voting rights to black people.

●   The 1960 Civil Rights Act provided help for blacks to register as voters, but it was not very effective; many were afraid to register for fear of being harassed by whites.

Unfortunately laws and regulations were not always carried out. For example, whites in some southern states refused to carry out the schools desegregation order. President Eisenhower sent federal troops to escort black children into the high school at *Little Rock, Arkansas*, where the governor had defied a Supreme Court order (1957) (see Question 1, Source A, at the end of the chapter). This was a symbolic victory, but southern whites continued to defy the law, and by 1961 only 25 per cent of schools and colleges in the south were desegregated.

(c) *The campaign for equal rights*

In the mid-1950s a mass civil rights movement developed. *This happened for a number of reasons.*

●   By 1955 a larger proportion of black people lived in the north than was the case

Illus. 20.3   Dr Martin Luther King

earlier. In 1900 almost 90 per cent of all black people lived in the southern states, working on the plantations. By 1955 almost 50 per cent lived in northern industrial cities where they became more aware of political issues. A black middle class developed which produced talented leaders.

● As Asian and African states such as India and Ghana gained their independence, black Americans resented their own unfair treatment more than ever.

● Black people, whose hopes had been raised by Truman's committee, grew increasingly impatient at the slow pace and the small amount of change. Even the small advances they made aroused intense hostility among many southern whites; the Ku Klux Klan revived and some southern state governments banned the NAACP. It was obvious that only a nationwide mass movement would have any effect.

The campaign took off in 1955 when *Dr Martin Luther King*, a Baptist minister, emerged as the outstanding leader of the non-violent civil rights movement (Illus. 20.3). After a black lady, Rosa Parks, had been arrested for sitting in a seat reserved for whites on a bus in Montgomery, Alabama, he organized a boycott of all Montgomery buses. King insisted that the campaign must be peaceful:

> Love must be our regulating ideal. If you will protest courageously, and yet with dignity and Christian love, when the history books are written in future generations, historians will have to say 'there lived a great people – a black people – who injected new dignity into the veins of civilization'.

His campaign was successful, and segregated seating was stopped on Montgomery buses. This was just a beginning: King's campaigns of sit-ins and peaceful disobedience reached a climax in 1963 with a massive rally in Washington attended by a quarter of a million people. He made a speech in which he talked about his dream of a future America in which everybody would be equal:

> I have a dream that my four little children will one day live in a nation where they will not be judged by the colour of their skin, but by the content of their character.

In 1967 King was awarded the Nobel Prize for Peace, but tragically, in April 1968 he was assassinated in Memphis, Tennessee.

Progress was slow, however, and some blacks broke away from King's non-violent movement and began to form more militant organizations such as *the Black Panthers and the Black Power movement*. They used the same methods against the whites as the Ku Klux Klan had used for years – arson, beatings and murders. In 1964 there were race riots in Harlem (New York) and in 1965 the most severe race riots in American history took place in the Watts district of Los Angeles; thirty-five people were killed and over 1000 injured (see Question 1 at the end of the chapter). Some black people became Muslims, arguing that Christianity was the religion of the racist whites. The most famous of these was the world heavyweight boxing champion, Cassius Clay, who changed his name to Muhammed Ali.

Democrat Presidents Kennedy (1961–3) and Johnson (1963–9) were both sympathetic to the demands of black people. Kennedy admitted in 1963 that a black American had

> half as much chance of completing high school as a white, one-third as much chance of completing college, twice as much chance of becoming unemployed, one-seventh as much chance of earning $10 000 dollars a year, and a life expectancy which is seven times less.

Kennedy showed his good intentions by appointing the USA's first black ambassador and by presenting a Civil Rights Bill to Congress. This was delayed at first by the conservative Congress but passed in 1964 after a debate lasting 736 hours. It was a far-reaching measure: it guaranteed the vote for blacks and made racial discrimination in public facilities (such as hotels, restaurants and stores) and in jobs illegal. Again the Act was not always carried out, especially in the south, where black people were still afraid to vote.

Johnson introduced the *Voting Rights Act (1965)* to try to make sure that blacks exercised their right to vote. He followed it up with another *Civil Rights Act (1968)* which made it illegal to discriminate in selling property or letting accommodation. Again there was bitter white hostility to these reforms, and the problem was to make sure that the Acts were carried out.

During the 1970s much progress was made, especially in voting: by 1975 there were 18 black members of Congress, 278 black members of state governments, and 120 black mayors had been elected. However, there could never be full equality until black poverty and discrimination in jobs and housing were removed. Unemployment was always higher among black people; in the big northern cities they were still living in overcrowded slum areas known as *ghettos*, from which the whites had moved out. *In the early 1990s, most black Americans were worse off economically than they had been twenty years earlier.* The underlying tensions broke out in the spring of 1992 in Los Angeles: after four white policemen were acquitted of beating up a black motorist (in spite of the incident having been videotaped), crowds of black people rioted. Many were killed, thousands were injured, and millions of dollars worth of damage was done to property.

20.3 Anti-communism and McCarthy

(a) Anti-communist feeling

After the Second World War the USA took upon itself the world role of preventing the spread of communism, causing her to become deeply involved in Europe, Korea, Vietnam, Latin America and Cuba (see Chapters 7 and 8). There had been a strong anti-communist movement in the USA ever since the communists came to power in Russia in 1917. In a way this is surprising, because the American Communist Party (formed in 1919) never attracted much support. Even during the Depression of the 1930s, when a mass swing to the left might have been expected, party membership was never more than 100 000, and there was never a real communist threat.

Some US historians argue that Senator Joseph McCarthy and other right-wingers who whipped up anti-communist feelings were trying to protect what they saw as the traditional American way of life, with its emphasis on 'self-help' and 'rugged individualism'. They thought that this was being threatened by the rapid changes in society, and by developments like the New Deal and the Fair Deal which they disliked because they were financed by higher taxation. Many were deeply religious people, some of them fundamentalists, who wanted to get back to what they called 'true Christianity'. It was difficult for them to pinpoint exactly who was responsible for this American 'decline', and so they focused on communism as the source of all evil. The spread of communism in Eastern Europe, the beginning of the Cold War, the communist victory in China (1949) and the attack on South Korea by communist North Korea (June 1950) threw the 'radical right' into a panic.

1 Troop demobilization

The rapid demobilization of American troops at the end of the war worried some people. The general wish was to 'bring the boys home' as soon as possible, and the army planned to have 5.5 million soldiers back home by July 1946. However, Congress insisted that it should be done much more quickly: by 1950 the army was down to only 600 000 men, none of them fully prepared for service. This thoroughly alarmed the people who thought that the USA should be ready to take deterrent action against communist expansion.

2 Fear of espionage

Reports of espionage (spying) prompted Truman to set up a *Loyalty Review Board* to investigate people working in the government, civil service, atomic research and armaments (1947). During the next five years, over 6 million people were investigated; no cases of espionage were discovered, though about 500 people were sacked because it was decided that their loyalty to the USA was 'questionable'.

3 Alger Hiss and the Rosenbergs

Much more sensational were the cases of Alger Hiss and Julius and Ethel Rosenberg. Hiss, a former top official in the State Department (the equivalent of the British Foreign Office), was accused of being a communist and of passing secret documents to Moscow. He was eventually found guilty of perjury and given a five-year jail sentence (1950). The Rosenbergs were convicted of passing secret information about the atomic bomb to the Russians, though much of the evidence was doubtful. They were sentenced to death in the electric chair. They were eventually executed in 1953, in spite of world-wide appeals for mercy.

These cases helped to intensify the anti-communist feeling sweeping America, and led Congress to pass the *McCarran Act*, which required organizations suspected of being communist to supply lists of members. Many of these people were later sacked from their jobs, although they had committed no offence. Truman, who felt that things were going too far, vetoed this Act, but Congress passed it over his veto. *The climax of this wave of hysteria came with McCarthyism.*

4 McCarthyism

Senator Joseph McCarthy was a right-wing Republican who hit the headlines in 1950 when he claimed (in a speech at Wheeling, West Virginia on 9 February) that the State Department was 'infested' with communists. He claimed to have a list of 205 people who were members of the party and who were 'still working and shaping policy'. Although he could produce no evidence to support his claims, many people believed him, and he launched a campaign to root out the communists. All sorts of people were accused of being communists; socialists, liberals, intellectuals, artists, pacifists, and anyone whose views did not appear orthodox were attacked and hounded out of their jobs for 'un-American activities' (Illus. 20.4).

McCarthy became the most feared man in the country, and was supported by many national newspapers. McCarthyism reached its climax soon after Eisenhower's election. McCarthy won many votes for the Republicans among those who took his accusations seriously, but he went too far when he began to accuse leading generals of having communist sympathies. Some of the hearings were televised and many people were shocked at the brutal way in which he banged the table with rage and abused and bul-

Illus. 20.4 Senator Joseph McCarthy testifying before the Senate Foreign Relations Committee, March 1951

lied witnesses. Even Republican Senators felt he was going too far, and the Senate condemned him by 67 votes to 22. McCarthy foolishly attacked the President for supporting the Senate, but this finally ruined his reputation and McCarthyism was finished. But it had been an unpleasant experience for many Americans: at least 9 million people had been 'investigated', thousands of innocent people had lost their jobs, and an atmosphere of suspicion and insecurity had been created (see Question 2 at the end of the chapter).

5 After McCarthy

Right-wing extremism continued even after the disgrace of McCarthy. Public opinion had turned against him not because he was attacking communists, but because of his brutal methods and because he had overstepped the mark by criticizing generals. Anticommunist feeling was still strong and Congress passed an Act making the Communist Party illegal (1954). There were also worries in case communism gained a foothold in the countries of Latin America, especially after Fidel Castro came to power in Cuba in 1959, and began nationalizing American-owned estates and factories. In response, Kennedy launched the *Alliance for Progress (1961)* which aimed to pump billions of dollars of aid into Latin America to enable economic and social reform to be carried out. Kennedy did genuinely want to help the poor nations of Latin America, and US aid was put to good use. But other motives were important too:

- By helping to solve economic problems, the US hoped to reduce unrest, making it less likely that communist governments would come to power in these states;
- US industry would benefit, because it was understood that much of the cash would be spent buying American goods.

(b) *The military–industrial complex*

Another by-product of the Cold War was what President Eisenhower called the *'military–industrial complex'*. This was the situation in which the US military leaders and armaments manufacturers worked together in a partnership. The army chiefs decided what was needed, and as the arms race developed, more and more orders were placed – atomic bombs, then hydrogen bombs, and later many different types of missile (see Section 7.4). Armaments manufacturers made huge profits, though nobody was quite sure just how much, because all the dealings were secret. *It was in their interests to keep the Cold War going* – the more it intensified, the greater their profits. When the Russians launched the first space satellite (Sputnik) in 1957, Eisenhower set up the *National Aeronautics and Space Administration (NASA)*, and even more expensive orders were placed.

At any sign of a possible improvement in East–West relations, for example when Khrushchev talked about 'peaceful co-existence', the armaments manufacturers were far from happy. Some historians have suggested that the American U2 spy plane which was shot down over Russia in 1960 was sent deliberately in order to ruin the summit conference which was about to begin in Paris (see Section 7.3(c)). If true, this would mean that the military–industrial partnership was even more powerful than the super-corporations, so powerful that it was able to influence American foreign policy. *The amounts of cash involved were staggering:* in 1950 the total budget was around $40 billion, of which $12 billion was military spending. By 1960 the military budget was almost $46 billion, and that was half the country's total budget. By 1970 military spending had reached $80 billion. A Senate report found that over 2000 former top officers were employed by defence contractors, who were all making fortunes.

20.4 Nixon and Watergate

Richard M. Nixon (1969–74) was Eisenhower's Vice-President from 1956, and had narrowly lost to Kennedy in the 1960 election. On his election in 1969 he faced an unenviable task – what to do about Vietnam, poverty, unemployment, violence and the general crisis of confidence that was afflicting America (see Section 20.1(f) for his social policies).

(a) *Foreign policy*

Overseas problems, especially Vietnam, dominated his presidency (at least until 1973, when Watergate took over). After the Democrat majority in Congress refused to vote any further cash for the war, *Nixon extricated the USA from Vietnam with a negotiated peace signed in 1973* (see Section 8.3(c)), to the vast relief of most of the American people, who celebrated 'peace with honour'. Yet in April 1975 South Vietnam fell to the communists; the American struggle to prevent the spread of communism in south-east Asia had ended in failure, and her world reputation was somewhat tattered.

However, *Nixon was responsible for a radical and constructive change in foreign policy* when he sought, with some success, to improve the USA's relations with the USSR and China (see Section 8.5(a–c)). His visit to meet Chairman Mao in Beijing in February 1972 was a brilliant success; in May 1972 he was in Moscow for the signing of an arms limitation treaty.

By the end of his first term in office, Nixon's achievements seemed full of promise: he had brought the American people within sight of peace, he was following sensible policies of *détente* with the communist world, and law and order had returned. The Americans had enjoyed a moment of glory by putting the first men on the moon (Neil Armstrong and Ed Aldrin, 20 July 1969). Nixon won the election of November 1972 overwhelmingly, and in January 1973 was inaugurated for a second term. However, his second term was ruined by a new crisis.

(b) *The Watergate scandal*

This *broke in January 1973* when a number of men were charged with having broken into the Democratic Party offices in the Watergate Building, Washington, in June 1972 during the presidential election campaign. They had planted listening devices and photocopied important documents. It turned out that the burglary had been organized by leading members of Nixon's staff who were sent to jail. Nixon insisted that he knew nothing about the affair, but suspicions mounted when he consistently refused to hand over tapes of discussions in the White House which, it was thought, would settle matters one way or the other. The President was widely accused of having deliberately 'covered up' for the culprits. He received a further blow when his Vice-President, *Spiro Agnew, was forced to resign* (December 1973) after facing charges of bribery and corruption. He was replaced by *Gerald Ford*, a little-known politician, but one with an unblemished record.

Nixon was called on to resign, but refused even when it was discovered that he had been guilty of tax evasion. He was threatened with *impeachment* (a formal accusation of his crimes before the Senate, which would then try him for the offences). To avoid this, Nixon resigned (August 1974) and Ford became President. It was a tragic end to a presidency which had shown positive achievements, especially in foreign affairs, but the scandal shook people's faith in politicians and in a system which could allow such things to happen.

Ford won admiration for the way in which he restored dignity to American politics, but given the recession, unemployment and inflation, it was no surprise when he lost the 1976 election to the Democrat James Earl Carter.

20.5 The USA since 1977

(a) *Jimmy Carter (1977–81)*

Carter's presidency was something of a disappointment. He was elected as an outsider – ex-naval officer, peanut farmer, ex-Governor of Georgia, and a man of deep religious convictions; he was the newcomer to Washington who would restore the public's faith in politicians. *He managed some significant achievements. He*

- stopped giving US aid to authoritarian right-wing governments merely to keep communism out;
- co-operated with Britain to bring about black majority rule in Zimbabwe (see Section 21.4(c));
- signed a second Strategic Arms Limitation Treaty (SALT II) with the USSR (1979); and
- played a vital role in the Camp David talks, bringing peace between Egypt and Israel (see Section 11.6).

Unfortunately Carter's lack of experience of handling Congress meant that he had the same difficulties as Kennedy, and he *failed to pilot the majority of his reforming programme into law*. By 1980 the world recession was biting deeply, bringing factory closures, unemployment and oil shortages. Apart from Camp David, Democratic foreign policy seemed unimpressive; even an achievement like SALT II was unpopular with the military leaders and the arms manufacturers. There was the American inability to take effective action against the Russian occupation of Afghanistan (1979). Just as frustrating was their failure to free a number of *American hostages seized in Teheran* by Iranian students (November 1979) and held for over a year. The Iranians were trying to force the American government to return the exiled Shah and his fortune, but stalemate persisted even after the Shah's death. A combination of these problems and frustrations resulted in a decisive Republican victory in the election of November 1980. Ironically the hostages were set free minutes after the inauguration of Carter's successor (January 1981).

(b) *Ronald Reagan (1981–9)*

Reagan, a former film star, quickly became the most popular President since the Second World War. He was a reassuring father-figure who won a reputation as 'The Great Communicator' because of his straightforward and simple way of addressing the US public. *Americans particularly admired his determination to stand no nonsense from the Evil Empire* (as he called the USSR); he wanted to work for peaceful relations with them, but from a position of strength. He persuaded Congress to vote extra cash to build MX intercontinental ballistic missiles (May 1983) and deployed Cruise and Pershing missiles in Europe (December 1983). He intervened in *Central America*, sending financial and military aid to rebels in Nicaragua against the left-wing Sandinista government. He continued friendly relations with China, visiting Beijing in April 1984, but he did not meet any top Russian politicians until shortly before the presidential election of November 1984.

On the home front there was a marked economic recovery, America enjoying the most sustained period of economic growth since 1945. Those in work were highly prosperous, but 'Reaganomics', as the President's policies became known, had similarities with Margaret Thatcher's monetarist policies in Britain – they benefited the wealthy but increased the tax burden on the poor, and at the same time reduced social programmes to help them. According to Congressional investigations, taxes took only 4 per cent of the income of the poorest families in 1978, but over 10 per cent in 1984. In April 1984 it was calculated that, thanks to successive Reagan budgets since 1981, the poorest families had gained an average of $20 a year from tax cuts, but had lost $410 a year in benefits. On the other hand, households with the highest incomes (over $80 000 a year) had gained an average of $8400 from tax cuts and lost $130 in benefits.

Reagan nevertheless retained his popularity with the vast majority of Americans and *won a sweeping victory in the presidential election (November 1984)* over his Democratic rival, Walter Mondale, who was portrayed by the media, probably unfairly, as an unexciting and old-fashioned politician with nothing new to offer. Reagan took 59 per cent of the popular vote; at 73, he was the oldest person ever to be President.

During his second term in office, everything seemed to go wrong for him. He was dogged by economic problems, disasters, scandals and controversies.

1 Economic problems

● *Congress became increasingly worried by the rapidly growing federal budget deficit:* the Senate rejected Reagan's 1987 budget for increased defence spending at a time when they felt it was vital to reduce the deficit. Senators also complained that the cash allowed for Medicare would be five per cent short of the amount needed to cover rising medical costs. In the end Reagan was forced to accept a cut in defence spending of around 8 per cent and to spend more than he wanted on social services (February 1986).
● *There was a serious depression in the agricultural mid-west* which brought falling prices, falling government subsidies and rising unemployment.

2 Disasters in the space programme

1986 was a disastrous year for America's space programme. The space shuttle, *Challenger*, exploded only seconds after lift-off, killing all seven crew members (January). A Titan rocket carrying secret military equipment exploded immediately after lift-off (April), and in May a Delta rocket failed, the third successive failure of a major space launch. This seemed likely to delay for many years Reagan's plans to develop a permanent orbital space station.

3 Foreign policy problems

● *The bombing of Libya (April 1986) provoked a mixed reaction.* Reagan was convinced that Libyan-backed terrorists were responsible for numerous outrages, including bomb attacks at Rome and Vienna airports in December 1985. After Libyan missile attacks on American aircraft, American F-111 bombers attacked the Libyan cities of Tripoli and Benghazi, killing 100 civilians. While the attack was widely applauded in most circles in the USA, world opinion on the whole condemned it as an over-reaction.
● *American policy towards South Africa caused a row between President and Congress.* Reagan wanted only limited sanctions but Congress was in favour of a much

stronger package to try to bring an end to apartheid, and they managed to overturn the President's veto (September 1986).

• *The Reykjavik meeting with Gorbachev (October 1986)* left the feeling that Reagan had been outmanoeuvred by the Soviet leader. However, failure turned to success in October 1987 with the signing of the INF Treaty (see Section 8.5(b)).

The growing dissatisfaction was reflected in the mid-term Congressional elections (November 1986) when the Republicans lost many seats, leaving the Democrats with an even larger majority in the House of Representatives (260–175), and more important, now in control of the Senate (54–45). With two years of his second term still to go, Reagan was a 'lame-duck' President – a Republican faced with a Democrat Congress. He would have the utmost difficulty persuading Congress to vote him cash for policies such as Star Wars (which most Democrats thought impossible) and aid for the Contra rebels in Nicaragua; and under the constitution, a two-thirds majority in both houses could over-rule the President's veto.

4   The Irangate scandal

This was the most damaging blow to the President. Towards the end of 1986, it emerged that *the US had been supplying arms secretly to Iran in return for the release of hostages*. However, Reagan had always insisted publicly that the USA would never negotiate with governments which condoned terrorism and the taking of hostages. Worse still, it emerged that profits from the Iranian arms sales were being used to supply military aid to the Contra rebels in Nicaragua; this was illegal since Congress had banned all military aid to the Contras from October 1984.

A congressional investigation found that a group of Reagan's advisers, including his National Security Chief, Donald Regan, Lieutenant-Colonel Oliver North and Rear Admiral John Poindexter had been responsible and had all broken the law. Reagan accepted responsibility for the arms sales to Iran but not for sending funds to the Contras. It seems that he was only dimly aware of what was going on, and was probably no longer in touch with affairs. 'Irangate', as it was dubbed, did not destroy Reagan, as Watergate did Nixon, but it certainly tarnished the administration's record in its last two years.

5   A severe stock market crash (October 1987)

This was brought on by the fact that the American economy was in serious trouble. There was a huge budget deficit, mainly because Reagan had more than doubled defence spending since 1981, while at the same time cutting taxes. *During the period 1981–7, the national debt had more than doubled* – to $2400 billion, and borrowing had to be stepped up simply to pay off the massive annual interest of $192 billion. At the same time the USA had the largest trading deficit of any leading industrialized country, and the economy was beginning to slow down as industry moved into recession.

In spite of all this, Reagan somehow managed to retain his personal popularity. During 1988 the economy and the balance of payments improved and unemployment fell. This enabled the Republican George Bush to win a comfortable victory in the election of November 1988.

(c) George Bush (1989–93)

George Bush, who had been Reagan's Vice-President, scored a big foreign policy success with his *decisive leadership against Saddam Hussein*, after the Iraqi invasion of Kuwait (August 1990). When the Gulf War ended in the defeat of Saddam, Bush's reputation stood high (see Section 11.10). However, as time passed, he was increasingly criticized for not having pressed home the advantage and for allowing the brutal Saddam to remain in power.

Meanwhile all was not well at home: a recession began in 1990, the budget deficit was still growing, and unemployment increased again. During the election campaign Bush had promised, in a famous reply to the Democrat candidate, Michael Dukakis, not to raise taxes: 'Read my lips, no new taxes'. But now he found himself forced to raise indirect taxes and reduce the number of wealthy people exempt from tax. Although people with jobs were comfortably off materially, the middle classes felt insecure in the face of the general trend towards fewer jobs. Among the working classes there was a permanent 'underclass' of unemployed people, both black and white, living in decaying inner city ghettos, with a high potential for crime, drugs and violence. Many of these people were completely alienated from politics and politicians, seeing little chance of help from either party. It was in this atmosphere that the election of November 1992 brought a narrow victory for the Democrat Bill Clinton.

(d) Bill Clinton (1993–)

Bill Clinton, like John F. Kennedy thirty years earlier and Franklin D. Roosevelt sixty years earlier, came into the White House like a breath of fresh air. He had been a Rhodes scholar at Oxford, and the youngest ever Governor of Arkansas, elected in 1978 at the age of thirty-two. He had campaigned on a programme of welfare reform and a change in direction – away from 'Reaganomics'. Unfortunately he experienced the same problems as Kennedy – how to persuade or manoeuvre the Republicans in Congress into approving his reforms, and his task became even more difficult after big Republican gains in the Congressional elections of 1994. However, he did have *some successes*, including the introduction of a minimum wage of $4.75 an hour (May 1996), to increase to $5.15 in May 1997.

Clinton could also point to some solid achievements in foreign affairs – his positive contributions to peace in the Middle East, Bosnia and Northern Ireland. At the same time his presidency was dogged by rumours of shady business deals which he and his wife, Hillary, were said to have been involved in while he was Governor of Arkansas – the so-called '*Whitewater scandal*'. When two of his former business associates and the current Governor of Arkansas were convicted of multiple fraud (May 1996), the Republicans hoped that Whitewater would do to Clinton what Watergate did to Nixon – drive him from office, or at least help to bring about his defeat in the election of November 1996.

Peace and prosperity were enough, however, to help Clinton win a comfortable victory over his Republican challenger, Bob Dole; but disappointingly for the Democrats, they failed to win back control of the Senate and the House of Representatives. As he moved into his second term, there seemed a good chance of compromise between Democrat President Clinton and the Republican-controlled Congress, because Clinton's policies had moved so much closer to those of the Republicans.

Questions

1   *The Struggle for Civil Rights in the USA*   Study Sources A to F and then answer the questions which follow.

Desegregation – a group of black students leaves the high school at Little Rock, Arkansas, under military protection, 1957 (Illus. 20.5)

Extract from a book by the black civil rights leader, Martin Luther King, published in 1959

We are too often loud and boisterous, and spend far too much on drink. Even the most poverty-stricken among us can purchase a ten-cent bar of soap; even the most uneducated among us can have high morals. By improving our standards, we will go a long way towards breaking down the arguments of those who argue in favour of segregation.

The other part of our programme must be non-violent resistance to all forms of racial injustice, even when this means going to jail; and bold action to end the demoralisation caused by the legacy of slavery and segregation, inferior schools, slums and second-class citizenship. A new frontal assault on the poverty, disease and ignorance of a people too long ignored by America's conscience will make victory more certain.

Source: Martin Luther King, *Stride towards Freedom* (Harper & Row, 1979 edn)

Extracts from a later book by Martin Luther King published in 1967

There is a remarkable record of achievements that have already come through non-violent action. The 1960 sit-ins desegregated lunch-counters in more than 150 cities within a year. The 1961 'freedom rides' put an end to segregation in inter-state travel. The 1956 bus boycott in Montgomery, Alabama, ended segregation on the buses not only of that city but in practically every city of the South. Most significant is that this progress occurred with minimum loss of life. Fewer people have been killed in 10 years of non-violent demonstrations across the South than were killed in one day of rioting in Watts [the black area of Los Angeles where there were race riots in 1965].

Source: Martin Luther King, *Chaos or Community* (Penguin, 1967)

Source D

Speech by Malcolm X, a black Muslim civil rights leader, 1964

There's no such thing as a non-violent revolution; revolution is bloody, revolution is hostile, revolution knows no compromise; revolution overturns and destroys anything that gets in its way. I don't see any American dream; I see an American nightmare. Our goal is complete freedom, complete justice, complete equality, by any means necessary.

Source: quoted in George Breitmann, *Malcolm X Speaks* (Grove Press, New York, 1966)

Source E

Statement by Mayor Daley of Chicago, January 1966, in reply to a request from Martin Luther King for an end to segregation in Chicago

You [King] say there is segregation.
We believe that we do not have segregation in Chicago. Here we recognise every man regardless of race, national origin or creed, and they are entitled to their equal rights such as in housing and education, as provided in the US constitution. Our goals are yours. By the end of this decade [1970] slums will have been eliminated in Chicago.

Source F

The National Advisory Committee Report on Urban Disorders: the Committee was appointed by President Johnson, and reported in 1968

The urban riots in 1967 in the black ghettoes of the country involved Negroes acting against local symbols of white American society. The overwhelming majority of people killed and injured were Negro civilians. They are extremely proud of their race and extremely hostile to both whites and middle-class Negroes. White racism is to blame for the explosive mixture which has been accumulating in our cities since the end of World War II; for generations the nation has perpetuated a system of racial injustice: discrimination in education, employment and housing. White Americans are deeply implicated in it. White institutions created it, whites maintain it and condone it. It is now time to end the destruction and the violence.

Source: Sources E and F are quoted in James A. Colaiaco, *Martin Luther King* (Macmillan, 1988)

(a) The photograph in Source A shows black students protected by federal troops leaving a school which had previously been reserved for whites (1957). Yet Martin Luther King, writing two years later (Source B), talks of racial injustice continuing. Does the photograph suggest that King was exaggerating the difficulties faced by black people in the USA?   3.3–6   4 marks

(b) How do Sources B, C, D and F show that there were different methods of carrying out the civil rights campaign and different attitudes to the problem?
                                                                        3.4, 1.6c, 8c   6 marks

(c) 'The evidence in Source F proves that Martin Luther King's claims of success in Source C were false'. Do you agree or disagree with this statement?
                                                                        1.6c–9b, 3.4–6   5 marks

(d) Do you think the evidence in Source F supports Mayor Daley's claim in Source E that 'we do not have segregation in Chicago'?
                                                                        1.6c–9b, 3.4–6   5 marks

(e) Look again at Sources B, C, D, E and F, and then put them into a league table with the one you think is most reliable at the top and the least reliable at the bottom. Explain why you have placed them in this order.   3.7–8   15 marks

Total: 35 marks

2 *Anti-communism and Senator McCarthy*   Study Sources A to E and then answer the questions which follow.

__ **Source A** _____

Speech by Republican Senator Joseph McCarthy to the Women's Republican Club of West Virginia, 9 February 1950

The reason we find ourselves in a position of impotency is not because our only powerful potential enemy has sent men to invade our shores, but rather because of the traitorous actions of those who have been treated so well by this nation. The State Department is infested with communists; I have here in my hand a list of 205 – a list of names that were known to the Secretary of State as being members of the Communist party, and who are still nevertheless working and shaping policy.

Source: quoted in John A. Garraty, *The American Nation* (Harper & Row, 1979 edition)

__ **Source B** _____

Mike Hammer, the hero of Micky Spillane's novel One Lonely Night, *first published in 1951*

I killed more people tonight than I have fingers on my hands. I shot them in cold blood and enjoyed every minute of it. They were Commies ... red sons-of-bitches who should have died long ago.

__ **Source C** _____

Report by Democratic Senator Millard Tydings of his investigation into McCarthy's charges, July 1950

McCarthy's charges are a fraud and a hoax perpetrated on the American people and on the Senate of the United States. They represent the most dishonest campaign of half-truths and untruths in the history of the Republic.

Source: quoted in Samuel E. Morison, *The Oxford History of the American People* (Oxford University Press, 1965)

President Truman talking about the McCarran Act which Congress passed over his veto

The great bulk of them [terms of the Act] are not directed towards the real and present danger that exists from communism. Instead of striking blows at communism, they would strike blows at our own liberties and at our position in the forefront of those working for freedom in the world.

Source: quoted in Jack B. Watson, *Success in Modern World History Since 1945* (John Murray, 1989)

Source E

Comments from an American historian, Samuel Eliot Morison, in 1965

The theory that there was a communist conspiracy would never have been so widely received but for the diabolical cunning of Senator Joseph R. McCarthy of Wisconsin. Estimates of him and his objectives vary from pure white to deepest black. He was probably simply a plain rogue who wanted power to make Presidents and officials jump while he cracked the whip. In the opinion of many, he aimed at the Presidency. He was cruel and greedy and did nothing for the people of his native state. He was also one of the most colossal liars in our history.

Source: S.E. Morison, *The Oxford History of the American People* (Oxford University Press, 1965)

(a) From the evidence of the sources, what different motives may have been behind Senator McCarthy's actions? 1.4b–5b 4 marks
(b) Which motive do you think was most important? 1.6b 2 marks
(c) Source E says that McCarthy was 'one of the most colossal liars in our history'. Explain why, if this is true, so many Americans seemed to believe him. Use the sources and the information in Section 20.3 to help you. 1.4c–10 8 marks
(d) From the evidence of the sources and Section 20.3, why did the American people eventually turn against McCarthy? 1.4b–5b, 6c–9b 6 marks
(e) What do you think are the strengths and weaknesses of these sources for the historian? 2.6–9, 3.5–9 10 marks

Total: 30 marks

PART V

Decolonization and after

The end of the European empires

Summary of events

At the end of the Second World War in 1945, the nations of Europe still claimed ownership of vast areas of the rest of the world, particularly in Asia and Africa.

- *Britain's empire was the largest in area*, consisting of India, Burma, Ceylon, Malaya, enormous tracts of Africa, and many assorted islands and other territories such as Cyprus, Hong Kong, the West Indies, the Falklands and Gibraltar.
- *France had the second largest empire*, with territories in Africa, Indo-China and the West Indies. In addition, Britain and France still held land in the Middle East taken from Turkey at the end of the First World War. Britain held Transjordan and Palestine, and France held Syria. They were known as *'mandated' territories*, which meant that Britain and France were intended to 'look after' them and prepare them for independence.
- *Other important empires* were those of Holland (Dutch East Indies), Belgium (Congo and Ruanda Urundi), Portugal (Angola, Mozambique and Guinea), Spain (Spanish Sahara, Ifni, Spanish Morocco and Spanish Guinea) and Italy (Libya, Somalia and Eritrea).

Over the next 30 years, remarkable changes took place: by 1975 most of these colonial territories had gained their independence. Sometimes, as in the Dutch and French colonies, they had to fight for it against determined European resistance. The problems involved were often complex; in India there were bitter religious differences to resolve. In some areas – Algeria, Kenya, Tanganyika, Uganda and Rhodesia – large numbers of whites had settled, and they were relentlessly hostile to independence which would place them under black rule. Britain was prepared to grant independence when it was felt that individual territories were ready for it, and most of the new states retained a link with Britain by remaining in the *British Commonwealth* (a group of former British-controlled nations which agreed to continue associating together, mainly because there were certain advantages to be gained from doing so). The main British territories which gained independence, sometimes changing their names (new names in brackets), were:

India and Pakistan – 1947
Burma and Ceylon (Sri Lanka) – 1948
Transjordan (Jordan) – 1946 and Palestine – 1948 (see Sections 11.1–2)

Malaysia and Gold Coast (Ghana) – 1957
Nigeria, Somaliland (became part of Somalia) and Cyprus –
1960
Tanganyika and Zanzibar (together forming Tanzania) –
1961
Jamaica, Trinidad and Tobago, Uganda – 1962
Kenya – 1963
Nyasaland (Malawi), Northern Rhodesia (Zambia) and
Malta – 1964
British Guiana (Guyana), Barbados, and Bechuanaland
(Botswana) – 1966
Aden (South Yemen) – 1967
Southern Rhodesia (Zimbabwe) – 1980
British Honduras (Belize) – 1981

The other colonial powers were at first determined to hold on to their empires by military force. But they all gave way in the end. The main territories gaining independence were:

French
Syria – 1946
Indo-China – 1954
Morocco and Tunisia – 1956
Guinea – 1958;   Senegal, Ivory Coast, Mauretania, Niger, Upper Volta (later Burkina-Faso), Chad, Madagascar (Malagasey), Gabon, Sudan (Mali), Cameroun, Congo, Oubangui-Shari (Central Africa), Togo and Dahomey (Benin from 1975) – 1960

Dutch
East Indies (Indonesia) – 1949
Surinam – 1975

Belgian
Congo (Zaire since 1971) – 1960
Ruanda-Urundi (became two separate states: Rwanda and Burundi) – 1962

Spanish
Spanish Morocco – 1956
Guinea (Equatorial Guinea) – 1968
Ifni (became part of Morocco) – 1969
Spanish Sahara (divided between Morocco and Mauretania) – 1975

Portuguese
Guinea (Guinea-Bissau) – 1974
Angola and Mozambique – 1975
East Timor (seized by Indonesia later in 1975) – 1975

21.1 Why did the European powers give up their empires?

(a) *Nationalist movements*

These had been in existence in many of Europe's overseas colonies, especially those in Asia, for many years before the Second World War. *Nationalists* were people who had a natural desire to get rid of their foreign rulers so that they could have a government run by people of their own nationality. Although the European powers claimed to have brought the benefits of western civilization to their colonies, there was a general feeling among colonial peoples that they were being exploited by the Europeans, who took most of the profits from their partnership. The development and prosperity of the colonies were being held back in the interests of Europe, and most of the colonial peoples continued to live in poverty. In India, the *Indian National Congress Party* had been agitating against British rule since 1885, and in south-east Asia, Vietnamese nationalists began to campaign against French rule during the 1920s. However, nationalism was not so strong in other areas, and progress towards independence would have been much more slow without the boost of the Second World War.

(b) *The effects of the Second World War*

The Second World War gave a great stimulus to nationalist movements in a number of ways:

- *Before the war, colonial peoples believed it would be impossible to defeat the militarily superior Europeans by force of arms.* Japanese successes in the early part of the war showed that it was possible for non-Europeans to defeat European armies. Japanese forces captured the British territories of Malaya, Singapore, Hong Kong and Burma, the Dutch East Indies and French Indo-China. Although the Japanese were eventually defeated, the nationalists, many of whom had fought against the Japanese, had no intention of tamely accepting European rule again. If necessary they would continue to fight against the Europeans, using the guerrilla tactics they had learned fighting the Japanese. This is exactly what happened in Indo-China, the Dutch East Indies, Malaya and Burma.
- *Asians and Africans became more aware of social and political matters as a result of their involvement in the war.* Many Africans, who had left their homeland for the first time to fight in the Allied armies, were appalled at the contrast between the primitive conditions in Africa and the relatively comfortable conditions they experienced even as members of the armed forces. Some Asian nationalist leaders worked with the Japanese, thinking that after the war there would be more chance of independence being granted by the Japanese than by the Europeans. Many of them, like Dr Sukarno in the Dutch East Indies, gained experience helping to govern the occupied areas. Sukarno later became the first President of Indonesia (1949).
- *Some European policies during the war encouraged colonial peoples to expect*

independence as soon as the war was over. The Dutch government, shocked that people were so ready to co-operate with the Japanese in the East Indies, offered them some degree of independence as soon as the Japanese were defeated. The *1941 Atlantic Charter* set out joint Anglo-American thinking about how the world should be organized after the war. *Two of the points mentioned were:*

—Nations should not expand by taking territory from other nations
—All peoples should have the right to choose their own form of government.

Though Churchill later said that this only applied to victims of Hitler's aggression, the hopes of Asian and African peoples had been raised.

● *The war weakened the European states,* so that in the end, they were not militarily strong enough to hold on to their empires in the face of really determined campaigns for independence. The British were the first to recognize this, and they responded by giving independence to India (1947). After that, *British policy was to delay independence as long as possible, but to give way when the pressure became irresistible.* It was a further ten years before the Gold Coast became the first British territory in Africa to win independence. As Iain Macleod (British Colonial Secretary) later put it: 'we could not possibly have held by force our territories in Africa; the march of men towards freedom cannot be halted; it can only be guided'. The French, Dutch, Spanish and Portuguese reacted differently and seemed determined to hold on to their empires. But this involved them in costly military campaigns, and eventually they all had to admit defeat.

(c) *Outside pressures*

There were outside pressures on the colonial powers to give up their empires. *The USA,* no doubt remembering that it had been the earliest part of the British Empire to declare independence (1776), was hostile to imperialism (building up empires and owning colonies). During the war, President Roosevelt made it clear that he took the Atlantic Charter to apply to all peoples, not just those taken over by the Germans. He and his successor, Truman, pressurized the British government to speed up independence for India. One reason given by the USA for wanting to see the end of the European empires was that delays in granting independence to European colonies in Asia and Africa would encourage the development of communism in those areas. Also important was the fact that the Americans looked on the newly-independent nations as potential markets into which they could step and establish both economic and political influence.

The United Nations Organization, under US influence, came out firmly against imperialism and demanded a step-by-step programme for decolonization. *The USSR* also added its voice to the chorus and constantly denounced imperialism. As well as putting the European states under pressure, this encouraged nationalists all over the world to intensify their campaigns.

Almost every case was different; the following sections will look at some of the different ways in which colonies and territories gained their independence.

21.2 Indian independence and partition

The British had promised the Indians 'dominion status' as soon as the war was over. This meant becoming more or less completely independent, though still acknowledging the British monarch as head of state, like Australia. The Labour government, newly elected in 1945, wanted to show that it disapproved of exploiting the Indians and was anxious to press ahead with independence. *Ernest Bevin*, the Foreign Secretary, had earlier toyed with the idea of delaying independence for a few years to cnable Britain to finance a development programme for India. This idea was dropped because the Indians would be suspicious of any delay, and because Britain could not afford the expense, given her own economic difficulties. Bevin and *Clement Attlee*, the Prime Minister, therefore decided to give India full independence, allowing the Indians to work out the details for themselves. Sadly this turned out to be far more difficult than had been expected: the problems were so complex that the country ended up having to be divided into two states – India and Pakistan.

(a) *Why was the partition of India necessary?*

1 Religious hostilities between Hindus and Muslims

This was the main problem. Hindus made up about two-thirds of the 400 million population, and the rest were mostly Muslims. After their victories in the 1937 elections when they won eight out of the eleven states, the *Hindu National Congress Party* unwisely called on the *Muslim League* to merge with Congress. This alarmed the Muslim League, who were afraid that an independent India would be dominated by Hindus. The Muslim leader, *M.A. Jinnah*, demanded *a separate Muslim state of Pakistan*, and adopted as his slogan 'Pakistan or Perish'.

2 Compromise attempts failed

Attempts to draw up a compromise solution acceptable to both Hindus and Muslims failed. The British proposed a federal scheme in which the central government would have only limited powers, while those of the provincial governments would be much greater. This would enable provinces with a Muslim majority to control their own affairs and there would be no need for a separate state. Both sides accepted the idea in principle but failed to agree on the details.

3 Violence broke out in August 1946

This happened when the Viceroy (the king's representative in India), Lord Wavell, invited the Congress leader, *Jawaharlal Nehru*, to form an interim government, still hoping that details could be worked out later. Nehru formed a cabinet which included two Muslims, but Jinnah was convinced that the Hindus could not be trusted to treat the Muslims fairly. He called for a day of 'direct action' in support of a separate Pakistan. Fierce rioting followed in Calcutta, where 5000 people were killed, and it soon spread to Bengal where Muslims set about slaughtering Hindus. As Hindus retaliated, *the country seemed on the verge of civil war.*

4 Mountbatten decides on partition

The British government, realizing that they lacked the military strength to control the situation, announced early in 1947 that *they would leave India no later than June 1948.* The idea was to try to shock the Indians into adopting a more responsible attitude. *Lord Louis Mountbatten* was sent as the new Viceroy, and he soon decided that partition was the only way to avoid civil war. He realized that there would probably be bloodshed whatever solution was tried, but felt that partition would produce less violence than if Britain tried to insist on the Muslims remaining part of India. Within a short time Mountbatten had worked out a plan for dividing the country up and for the

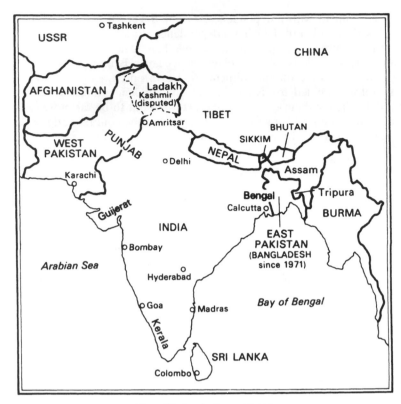

Map 21.1 India and Pakistan

British withdrawal. This was accepted by Nehru and Jinnah, although *M.K. Gandhi*, known as the *Mahatma* ('Great Soul'), the other highly respected Congress leader, who believed in non-violence, was still hoping for a united India. Afraid that delay would cause more violence, Mountbatten brought the date for British withdrawal forward to August 1947.

(b) *How was partition carried out?*

The Indian Independence Act was rushed through the British parliament (August 1947), separating the Muslim majority areas in the north-west and north-east from the rest of India to become the independent state of Pakistan. The new Pakistan unfortunately consisted of two separate areas over a thousand miles apart (see Map 21.1). Independence day for both India and Pakistan was 15 August 1947. Problems followed immediately.

1 *It had been necessary to split the provinces of the Punjab and Bengal which had mixed Hindu and Muslim populations.* This meant that millions of people found themselves on the wrong side of the new frontiers – Muslims in India and Hindus in Pakistan.

2 *Afraid of being attacked, millions of people headed for the frontiers,* Muslims trying to get into Pakistan and Hindus into India. Clashes occurred which developed into near-hysterical mob violence, especially in the Punjab, where about 250 000 people were murdered (Illus. 21.1). Violence was not quite so widespread in Bengal where Gandhi, still preaching non-violence and toleration, managed to calm the situation.

Illus. 21.1 New Delhi, 1947. During a lull in the rioting, victims of the many clashes are removed from the streets

3 *Violence began to die down before the end of 1947, but in January 1948 Gandhi was shot dead by a Hindu fanatic* who detested his tolerance towards Muslims. It was a tragic end to a disastrous set of circumstances, but the shock somehow seemed to bring people to their senses, so that the new governments of India and Pakistan could begin to think about their other problems.

From the British point of view, the government could claim that although so many deaths were regrettable, the granting of independence to India and Pakistan was an act of far-sighted statesmanship. Attlee argued, with some justification, that Britain could not be blamed for the violence; this was due, he said, 'to the failure of the Indians to agree among themselves'. V.P. Menon, a distinguished Indian political observer, believed that Britain's decision to leave India 'not only touched the hearts and stirred the emotions of India . . . it earned for Britain universal respect and goodwill'.

4 In the longer term, *Pakistan did not work well as a divided state*, and in 1971 East Pakistan broke away and became the independent state of Bangladesh.

21.3 The West Indies, Malaya and Cyprus

As these three territories moved towards independence, interesting experiments in setting up federations of states were tried, with varying degrees of success. A federation is when a number of states join together under a central or federal government which has overall authority; each of the states has its own separate parliament which deals with internal affairs. This is the type of system which works well in the USA, Canada and

Australia, and many people thought it would be suitable for the British West Indies and for Malaya and neighbouring British territories.

- *The West Indies Federation was the first one to be tried*, but it proved to be a failure: set up in 1958, it only survived until 1962.
- *The Federation of Malaysia*, set up in 1963, was much more successful.
- *The British handling of independence for Cyprus* unfortunately was not a success story and the island had a troubled history after the Second World War.

(a) *The West Indies*

Britain's West Indian possessions consisted of a large assortment of islands in the Caribbean Sea (see Map 21.2); the largest were Jamaica and Trinidad, and others included Grenada, St Vincent, Barbados, St Lucia, Antigua, the Seychelles and the Bahamas. There were also British Honduras on the mainland of Central America and British Guiana on the north-east coast of South America. Together these territories had a population of around 6 million. Britain was prepared in principle to give them all independence, but there were problems:

- *Some of the islands were very small, and there were doubts about whether they were viable as independent states.* Grenada, St Vincent and Antigua, for example, had populations of only about 100 000 each, while some were even smaller: the twin islands of St Kitts and Nevis had only about 60 000 between them.
- *The British Labour government felt that a federation could be the ideal way of uniting such small and widely scattered territories, but many of the territories themselves objected.* Some, like Honduras and Guiana, wanted nothing to do with a federation, prefering completely separate independence. This left Jamaica and Trinidad worried about whether they would be able to cope with the problems of the smaller islands. Some islands did not like the prospect of being dominated by Jamaica and Trinidad, and some of the smallest were not even sure they wanted independence at all, prefering to remain under British guidance and protection.

Britain went ahead in spite of the difficulties and established the West Indies Federation in 1958 (excluding British Honduras and British Guiana). But it never really functioned successfully. The one thing they all had in common – a passionate commitment to cricket – was not enough to hold them together, and there were constant squabbles about how much each island should pay into the federal budget and how many representatives they should each have in the federal parliament. When Jamaica and Trinidad withdrew in 1961, the federation no longer seemed viable.

In 1962 Britain decided to abandon the federation and grant independence separately to all those that wanted it. *By 1983 all parts of the British West Indies, except a few tiny islands, had become independent.* Jamaica and Trinidad and Tobago were first in 1962, and the islands of St Kitts and Nevis were last in 1983. British Guiana became known as Guyana (1966) and British Honduras took the name Belize (1981). All of them became members of the British Commonwealth.

Ironically, having rejected the idea of a fully-fledged federation, they soon found that there were economic benefits to be had from co-operation. The Caribbean Free Trade Association was set up in 1968, and this soon developed into the *Caribbean Community and Common Market (CARICOM) in 1973*, which all the former British West Indies territories (including Guyana and Belize) joined.

(b) *Malaya*

Malaya was liberated from Japanese occupation in 1945, but there were two difficult problems to be faced before the British were prepared to withdraw.

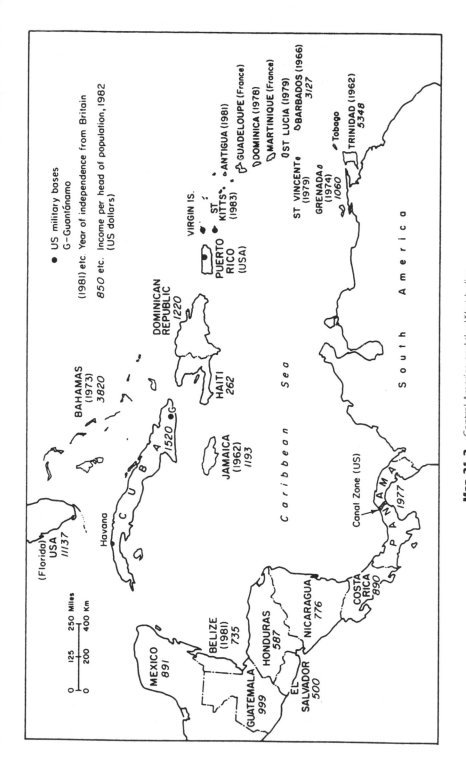

Map 21.2 Central America and the West Indies

Source: Jack B. Watson, *Success in World History since 1945* (John Murray, 1989) p. 207

1   *It was a complex area which would be difficult to organize.* It consisted of nine
    states each ruled by a sultan, two British settlements, Malacca and Penang, and
    Singapore, a small island less than a mile from the mainland. The population was
    multi-racial: mostly Malays and Chinese, but with some Indians and Europeans as
    well. In preparation for independence it was decided to group the states and the
    settlements into the *Federation of Malaya (1948),* while Singapore remained a
    separate colony. Each state had its own legislature for local affairs; the sultans
    retained some power, but the central government had firm overall control. All
    adults had the vote and this meant that the Malays, the largest group, usually
    dominated affairs.
2   *Chinese communist guerrillas led by Chin Peng, who had played a leading role in
    the resistance to the Japanese, now began to stir up strikes and violence against the
    British*, in support of an independent communist state. The British decided to
    declare a state of emergency in 1948, and in the end they dealt with the
    communists successfully, though it took time, and the state of emergency remained
    in force until 1960. Their tactics were to re-settle all Chinese suspected of helping
    the guerrillas, into specially guarded villages. It was made clear that independence
    would follow as soon as the country was ready for it; this ensured that the Malays
    remained firmly pro-British and gave very little help to the communists, who were
    Chinese.

The move towards independence was accelerated when the Malay party, under their
able leader *Tunku Abdul Rahman*, joined forces with the main Chinese and Indian
groups to form the *Alliance Party,* which won 51 out of the 52 seats in the 1955 elections. This seemed to suggest stability and the British were persuaded to grant full
independence in 1957 when Malaya was admitted to the Commonwealth.

The Federation of Malaysia was set up in 1963. Malaya was running well under the
leadership of Tunku Abdul Rahman, and its economy, based on exports of rubber and
tin, was the most prosperous in south-east Asia. In 1961 when the Tunku proposed that
Singapore and three other British colonies, North Borneo (Sabah), Brunei and
Sarawak, should join Malaya to form the Federation of Malaysia, Britain agreed (see
Map 21.3). After a United Nations investigation team reported that a large majority of
the populations concerned was in favour of the union, the Federation of Malaysia was
officially proclaimed (September 1963). Brunei decided not to join, and eventually
became an independent state within the Commonwealth (1984). Although Singapore
decided to leave the federation to become an independent republic in 1965, the rest of
the federation continued successfully.

(c) *Cyprus*

The British Labour government (1945–51) considered giving Cyprus independence, but
progress was delayed by complications, the most serious of which was the mixed population – about 80 per cent were Greek-speaking Christians of the Orthodox Church,
while the rest were Muslims of Turkish origin. The Greek Cypriots wanted the island
to unite with Greece (*enosis*), but the Turks were strongly opposed to this. Churchill's
government (1951–5) inflamed the situation in 1954 when their plans for self-
government allowed the Cypriots far less power than Labour had had in mind. There
were hostile demonstrations which were dispersed by British troops.

Sir Anthony Eden, Churchill's successor, decided to drop the idea of independence
for Cyprus, believing that Britain needed the island as a military base to protect her
interests in the Middle East. He announced that Cyprus must remain permanently
British, though the Greek government promised that Britain could retain her military
bases even if *enosis* took place.

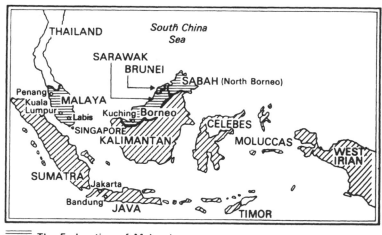

▤ The Federation of Malaysia

▨ Indonesia (formerly Dutch East Indies)

Map 21.3 Malaysia and Indonesia

The Greek Cypriots, led by *Archbishop Makarios*, pressed their demands, while a guerrilla organization called *Eoka*, led by General Grivas, waged a terrorist campaign against the British, who declared a state of emergency (1955) and deployed about 35 000 troops to try to keep order. British policy also involved deporting Makarios and executing terrorists (see Question 3 at the end of the chapter). The situation became even more difficult in 1958 when the Turks set up a rival organization in support of dividing the island.

Eventually, to avoid possible civil war between the two groups, Harold Macmillan, Eden's successor, decided to compromise. He appointed the sympathetic and tactful Hugh Foot as governor and he negotiated a deal with Makarios:

● the Archbishop dropped *enosis* and in return Cyprus was granted full independence;
● Turkish interests were safeguarded, Britain retained two military bases, and, along with Greece and Turkey, guaranteed the independence of Cyprus;
● Makarios became the first President with a Turkish Cypriot, Fazil Kutchuk, as Vice-President (1960). It seemed the perfect solution.

Unfortunately it only lasted until 1963 when civil war broke out between Greeks and Turks. In 1974 Turkey sent troops to help establish a separate Turkish state in the north, and the island has remained divided since then. Turks occupy the north (roughly one-third of the island's area), Greeks the south, with UN troops keeping the peace between the two (see Map 21.4). Many attempts were made to find agreement, but all failed. In the mid-1980s the UN began to press the idea of a federation as the most likely way of reconciling the two states. Though this solution was at first rejected by the Greeks (1987), they later seemed to show more interest, and federation may yet turn out to be the way to reconciliation.

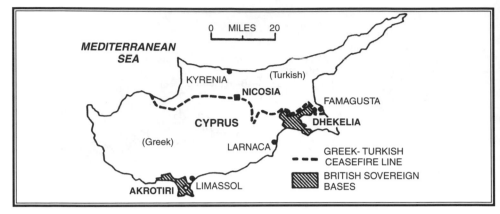

Map 21.4 Cyprus divided

21.4 The British leave Africa

African nationalism spread rapidly after 1945; this was because more and more Africans were being educated in Britain and the USA, where they were made aware of racial discrimination. Colonialism was seen as the humiliation and exploitation of blacks by whites, and working-class Africans in the new towns were particularly receptive to nationalist ideas. The British, especially the Labour governments of 1945–51, were quite willing to allow independence, and were confident that they would still be able to exercise influence through trade links, which they hoped to preserve by including the new states as members of the Commonwealth. This practice of exercising influence over former colonies after independence by economic means is known as *neo-colonialism*; it became widespread in most of the new states of the Third World. Even so, the British intended to move the colonies towards independence very gradually, and the African nationalists had to campaign vigorously and often violently to make them act more quickly.

The British colonies in Africa fell into three distinct groups which had important differences in character which were to affect progress towards independence.

> **West Africa: Gold Coast, Nigeria, Sierra Leone and the Gambia**
>
> Here there were relatively few Europeans, and they tended to be administrators rather than permanent settlers with profitable estates to defend. This made the move to independence comparatively straightforward.
>
> **East Africa: Kenya, Uganda and Tanganyika**
>
> Here, especially in Kenya, things were complicated by the 'settler-factor' – the presence of European and Asian settlers who feared for their future under black governments.

(a) *West Africa*

1 The Gold Coast

The Gold Coast was the first black African state south of the Sahara to win independence after the Second World War, taking the name *Ghana (1957)*. It was achieved fairly smoothly, though not without some incident. The nationalist leader, *Kwame Nkrumah*, educated in London and the USA and since 1949 leader of the *Convention People's Party (CPP)*, organized the campaign for independence. There were boycotts of European goods, violent demonstrations and a general strike (1950), and Nkrumah and other leaders were imprisoned for a time. But the British, realizing that he had mass support, soon released him and agreed to allow a new constitution which included:

- the vote for all adults;
- an elected assembly;
- an eleven-person Executive Council of which eight were chosen by the assembly.

In the 1951 elections, the first under the new constitution, the CPP won 34 seats out of 38. Nkrumah was released from prison, invited to form a government and became Prime Minister in 1952. This was self-government but not yet full independence. The Gold Coast had a small but well-educated group of politicians and other professionals, who, for the next five years, gained experience of government under British supervision. In 1957 Ghana, as it became known, received full independence.

2 Nigeria

Nigeria was easily the largest of Britain's African colonies, with a population of over 60 million. It was a more difficult proposition than Ghana because of its great size, and because of its regional differences between the vast Muslim north, dominated by the Hausa and Fulani tribes, the western region (Yorubas) and the eastern region (Ibos). The leading nationalist was *Nnamdi Azikiwe*, popularly known to his supporters as 'Zik'. After his return to Nigeria in 1937 he soon gained enormous prestige. In 1945 he showed he meant business by organizing an impressive general strike, which was enough to prompt the British to begin preparing Nigeria for independence. It was decided that a federal system would be most suitable; in 1954 a new constitution introduced local assemblies for the three regions with a central (federal) government in Lagos, the capital. The regions assumed self-government first and the country as a whole became independent in 1960. Sadly, in spite of the careful preparations for independence, tribal differences caused civil war to break out in 1967 (see Section 22.3).

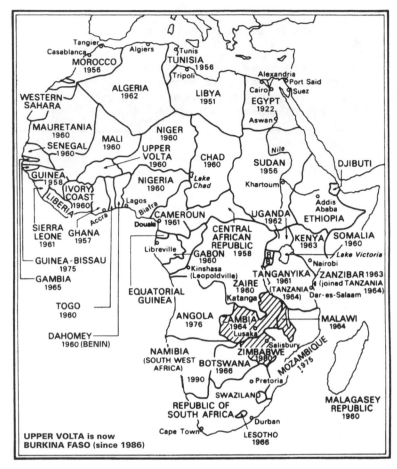

//// The Central African Federation 1953–63
//// Northern Rhodesia (Zambia) Southern Rhodesia (Zimbabwe)
Nyasland (Malawi)

R Rwanda 1962
B Burundi 1962

Map 21.5 *Africa becomes independent*

3 Sierra Leone and the Gambia

These, the other two British colonies in West Africa, achieved independence without serious incident – Sierra Leone in 1961 and the Gambia in 1965.

(b) *East Africa*

The British thought that independence for the colonies of East Africa was not so necessary as for West Africa, and that when independence did come, it would be in the form of multi-racial governments, in which the European and Asian settlers would play a significant part. But during Harold Macmillan's government (1957–63) *an important change took place in British policy towards both East and Central Africa.* Macmillan had come to realize the strength of black African nationalist feeling; in a famous speech in Cape Town in 1960, he talked of

> the wind of change blowing through the continent. Whether we like it or not, this growth of national consciousness is a political fact, and our national policies must take account of it.

1 Tanganyika

In Tanganyika the nationalist campaign was conducted by the *Tanganyika African National Union (TANU)* led by Dr Julius Nycrere, who had been educated at Edinburgh University. He insisted that the government must be African, but he also made it clear that whites had nothing to fear from black rule. Macmillan's government, impressed by Nyerere's ability and sincerity, conceded independence with black majority rule (1961). The island of Zanzibar was later united with Tanganyika, and the country took the name *Tanzania* (1964). Nyerere was President until his retirement in 1985.

2 Uganda

In Uganda independence was delayed for a time by tribal squabbles; the ruler (known as the Kabaka) of the Buganda area objected to the introduction of democracy. Eventually a solution was found in a federal constitution which allowed the Kabaka to retain some powers in Buganda. Uganda itself became independent in 1962 with *Dr Milton Obote* as Prime Minister.

3 Kenya

Kenya was the most difficult area to deal with because *the 66 000 white settlers were violently opposed to black majority rule*. They refused to negotiate with the African nationalist leader *Jomo Kenyatta* and his *Kenya African Unity Party (KAU)* and were determined to prolong white settler rule. They provoked a confrontation, hoping that violence would destroy the African party. The British government was under pressure from both sides, and the white settlers were supported by certain big business interests in Britain; even so, it did not handle the situation with much imagination. KAU was able to make little progress, the only British concession being to allow six Africans to join the Legislative Council of fifty-four members.

African impatience burst out in a campaign of terrorist attacks on European-owned farms and on black workers. It was organized by the *Mau Mau* secret society, whose members were mainly from the Kikuyu tribe, who had been deprived of much of their best land by the white settlers. A state of emergency was declared (1952) and Kenyatta and other nationalist leaders were arrested (Illus. 21.2). Kenyatta was kept in gaol for six years (1953–9) although he had publicly condemned terrorism. The British committed 100 000 troops to flush out the terrorists, and over the next eight years some 10 000 people (mostly Africans) were killed, and about 90 000 Kikuyu imprisoned in conditions little better than concentration camps.

The terrorists had been defeated by 1960, but by then, ironically, the British, encouraged by the 'wind of change' and by the expense of the anti-terrorist campaign, had had their change of heart. They realized that Kenyatta was, after all, a moderate, and allowed him to become Prime Minister when Kenya became independent in 1963. In spite of his treatment by the British, Kenyatta favoured reconciliation; whites who decided to stay on after independence were fairly treated provided they took Kenyan citizenship (Illus. 21.3).

Illus. 21.2   Mau Mau suspects are rounded up in Kenya

Illus. 21.3   New President Jomo Kenyatta celebrates as Kenya becomes a republic, 1964

(c) Central Africa

This was the most troublesome area for Britain to deal with because this was where the settlers were most numerous and most deeply entrenched, particularly in Southern Rhodesia. Another problem was that numbers of well-educated Africans were much smaller than in West Africa because the settlers had made sure that there was very little money spent on further and higher education for black Africans. Alarmed at the spread of nationalism, the whites decided that their best policy was to combine resources. They persuaded Churchill's government (1953) to allow them to set up a union of the three colonies – Nyasaland and Northern and Southern Rhodesia, to be known as the *Central African Federation*. Their aim was to preserve the supremacy of the white minority (about 300 000 Europeans out of a total population of about 8.5 million). The federal parliament in Salisbury (the capital of Southern Rhodesia) was heavily weighted to favour the whites, who hoped that the federation would soon gain full independence from Britain, with dominion status.

The Africans watched with growing distrust, and their leaders, Dr Hastings Banda (Nyasaland), Kenneth Kaunda (Northern Rhodesia) and Joshua Nkomo (Southern Rhodesia) began to campaign for black majority rule. As violence developed, a state of emergency was declared in Nyasaland and Southern Rhodesia, with mass arrests of Africans (1959).

However, there was much support for the Africans in Britain, especially in the Labour party, and the Conservative Colonial Secretary, Iain Macleod, was sympathetic. *The Monckton Commission (1960) recommended:*

- votes for Africans;
- an end to racial discrimination;
- the right of territories to leave the Federation.

1 Nyasaland and Northern Rhodesia

The British introduced new constitutions in Nyasaland and Northern Rhodesia which in effect allowed the Africans their own parliaments (1961–2). Both wanted to leave the Federation, which was therefore terminated in December 1963, signalling defeat for the settlers. *The following year Nyasaland and Northern Rhodesia became fully independent, taking the names Malawi and Zambia.*

2 Southern Rhodesia

Southern Rhodesia took much longer to deal with, and it was 1980 before the colony achieved independence with black majority rule. *It was in Rhodesia, as it was now known, that the white settlers fought most fiercely to preserve their privileged position.* There were just over 200 000 whites, about 20 000 Asians, and four million black Africans, but the *Rhodesia Front*, a right-wing white racist party, was determined never to surrender control of the country to black African rule. The black African parties were banned.

When Zambia and Malawi were given independence, the whites assumed that Rhodesia would get the same treatment and put in a formal request for independence. The British Conservative government refused and made it clear that independence would be granted *only if the constitution was changed to allow black Africans at least a third of the seats in parliament.* Ian Smith (who became Prime Minister of Rhodesia in April 1964) rejected this idea and refused to make any concessions. He argued that continued white rule was essential in view of the problems being faced by the new black governments in other African states, and because the Zimbabwe nationalists seemed bitterly divided. Harold Wilson, the new British Labour Prime Minister (1964–70), continued to refuse independence unless the constitution was changed to prepare for black majority rule. Since no compromise seemed possible, Smith declared Rhodesia independent, against the wishes of Britain (a unilateral declaration of independence or UDI), in November 1965.

There were mixed reactions to UDI:

- *At first there seemed very little Britain could do about it*, once the government had decided not to use force against the illegal Smith regime. It was hoped to bring the country to its knees by *economic sanctions*, and Britain stopped buying sugar and tobacco from Rhodesia.
- *The UN condemned UDI* and called on all member states to place a complete trade embargo on Rhodesia.
- *South Africa, also ruled by a white minority government, and Portugal, which still owned neighbouring Mozambique, were sympathetic to the Smith regime* and refused to obey the Security Council resolution. This meant that Rhodesia was able to continue trading through these countries. Many other countries, while publicly condemning UDI, privately evaded the embargo; the USA, for example, bought Rhodesian chrome because it was the cheapest available. Companies and businesspeople in many countries, including British oil companies, continued to break sanctions, and although the Rhodesian economy suffered to some extent, it was not serious enough to topple the Smith regime.
- *The Commonwealth was seriously shaken.* Ghana and Nigeria wanted Britain to use force, and offered to supply troops. Zambia and Tanzania hoped that economic sanctions would suffice; relations with Britain became extremely cool when it seemed that she was deliberately soft-pedalling sanctions, especially as Zambia was suffering more from them than Rhodesia. When Wilson twice met Smith (aboard HMS *Tiger* in 1966 and HMS *Fearless* in 1968) to put new proposals, there was a howl of protest in case he betrayed the black Rhodesians. Perhaps fortunately for the future of the Commonwealth, Smith rejected both sets of proposals.

In 1970 Rhodesia declared itself a republic, and the rights of black citizens were gradually whittled away until they were suffering similar treatment to that experienced by blacks in South Africa (see Section 22.8). In 1976 the first signs began to appear that the whites would have to compromise.

Why did the whites give way?

1 *Mozambique's independence from Portugal (June 1975)* was a serious blow to Rhodesia. The new President of Mozambique, Samora Machel, applied economic sanctions and allowed Zimbabwean guerrillas to operate from Mozambique. Thousands of black guerrillas were soon active in Rhodesia, straining the white security forces to their limits and forcing Smith to hire foreign mercenaries.
2 *The South Africans became less inclined to support Rhodesia* after their invasion of Angola (October 1975) had been called off on American orders. The Americans and South Africans were helping the rebel FNLA which was trying to overthrow the ruling MPLA party, which had Russian and Cuban backing. The Americans were afraid that the USSR and Cuba might become involved in Rhodesia unless some compromise could be found; together with South Africa, they urged Smith to make concessions to the blacks before it was too late.
3 *By 1978 nationalist guerrillas controlled large areas* of Rhodesia and the whites were on the verge of defeat.

Smith still tried everything he knew to delay black majority rule as long as possible. He was able to present the divisions between the nationalist leaders as his excuse for the lack of progress, and this was a genuine problem:

- **ZAPU** (Zimbabwe African People's Union) was the party of the veteran nationalist Joshua Nkomo;
- **ZANU** (Zimbabwe African National Union) was the party of the Reverend Ndabaningi Sithole;

These two, representing different tribes, seemed to be bitter enemies.

- **UANC** (United African National Council) was the party of Bishop Abel Muzorewa;
- **Robert Mugabe**, leader of the guerrilla wing of ZANU, was another powerful figure.

Smith tried to compromise by introducing his own scheme, a joint government of whites and UANC, the most moderate of the nationalist parties, with Bishop Muzorewa as Prime Minister (April 1979). However, it was ZANU and ZAPU which had mass support and they continued the guerrilla war. Smith soon had to admit defeat and the British called the *Lancaster House Conference* in London (September–December 1979), which agreed that:

- there should be a new constitution which would allow the black majority to rule;
- in the new republic of Zimbabwe, there would be a 100-seat parliament in which 80 seats were reserved for black Africans;
- Muzorewa would step down as Prime Ministe;
- the guerrilla war would end.

In the elections which followed, Mugabe's ZANU won a sweeping victory, taking 57 out of the 80 black African seats. This gave him a comfortable overall majority, enabling him to become Prime Minister when Zimbabwe officially became independent in April 1980. The transference to black majority rule was welcomed by all African and Commonwealth leaders as a triumph of common sense and moderation. Civil war between ZAPU and ZANU, which many had feared, did not materialize; the two parties merged in 1987, when Mugabe became the country's first President. He was re-elected for a further term in March 1996.

21.5 The end of the French Empire

The main French possessions at the end of the Second World War were

- Syria in the Middle East, from which they withdrew in 1946
- Guadaloupe and Martinique (islands in the West Indies)
- French Guiana (on the mainland of South America)

and huge areas of north and west Africa:

- Tunisia, Morocco and Algeria (together known as the Maghrib)
- French West Africa
- French Equatorial Africa and
- the large island of Madagascar off the south-east coast of Africa.

The French began by trying to suppress all nationalist agitation, regarding it as high treason. *As the 1944 Brazzaville Declaration put it:*

> The colonising work of France makes it impossible to accept any idea of autonomy for the colonies or any possibility of development outside the French Empire. Even at a distant date, there will be no self-government in the colonies.

But gradually the French were influenced by Britain's moves towards decolonization, and after their defeat in Indo-China in 1954, they too were forced to bow to the 'wind of change'.

(a) *Indo-China*

Before the war, the French had exercised direct rule over the area around Saigon and had protectorates over Annam, Tonkin, Cambodia and Laos. A protectorate was a country which was officially independent with its own ruler, but which was under the 'protection' or guardianship of the mother country. It usually meant in practice that the mother country, in this case France, controlled affairs in the protectorate just as it did in a colony.

During the war, the whole area was occupied by the Japanese, and resistance was organized by the communist *Ho Chi Minh* and the *League for Vietnamese Independence (Vietminh)*. When the Japanese withdrew in 1945, Ho Chi Minh declared Vietnam independent. This was unacceptable to the French, and an eight-year armed struggle began which culminated in the *French defeat at Dien Bien Phu in May 1954* (see Section 8.3(a)). The defeat was a humiliating blow for the French and it caused a political crisis. The government resigned and the new and more liberal premier Pierre Mèndes-France, realizing that public opinion was turning against the war, decided to withdraw.

At the Geneva Conference (July 1954) it was agreed that Vietnam, Laos and Cambodia should become independent. Unfortunately this was not the end of the troubles. Although the French had withdrawn, the Americans were unwilling to allow the whole of Vietnam to come under the rule of the communist Ho Chi Minh, and an even more bloody struggle developed (see Section 8.3(b–e)); there were also problems in Cambodia (see Section 9.3(j)).

(b) *Tunisia and Morocco*

Both these areas were protectorates – Tunisia had a ruler known as the Bey, and Morocco had a Muslim king, Muhamed V. But nationalists resented French control and had been campaigning for real independence since before the Second World War. The situation was complicated by the presence of large numbers of European settlers who were more numerous than in Kenya and Rhodesia. Tunisia had about 250 000 and Morocco about 300 000 in 1945, and they were committed to maintaining the connection with France which guaranteed their privileged position.

1 Tunisia

In Tunisia the main nationalist group was the *New Destour led by Habib Bourghiba*. They had widespread support among both rural and townspeople who believed independence would improve their living standards. A guerrilla campaign was launched against the French, who responded by banning New Destour and imprisoning Bourghiba (1952). 70 000 French troops were deployed against the guerrillas, but failed to crush them. The French became aware of a disturbing trend: with Bourghiba and other moderate leaders in gaol, the guerrilla movement was becoming more left-wing and less willing to negotiate. Under pressure at the same time in Indo-China and Morocco, the French realized that they would have to give way.With a moderate like Bourghiba at the head of the country, there would be more chance of maintaining French influence after independence. He was released from gaol and Mèndes-France allowed him to form a government. *In March 1956 Tunisia became fully independent under Bourghiba's leadership.*

2 Morocco

The pattern of events in Morocco was remarkably similar. There was a nationalist party calling itself *Istiqlal (Independence)*, and King Muhamed himself seemed to be in the forefront of opposition to the French. The new trade unions also played an important role. The French deposed the king (1953), provoking violent demonstrations and a guerrilla campaign. Faced with the prospect of yet another long and expensive anti-guerrilla war, the French decided to give way. The king was allowed to return and *Morocco became independent in 1956.*

(c) *Algeria*

It was here that the 'settler factor' had the most serious consequences. There were over a million French settlers (known as *colons*) who controlled something like one-third of all the most fertile land in Algeria, taken from the original Algerian owners during the century before 1940. The whites exported most of the crops they produced and also used some of the land to grow vines for wine-making; this made less food available for the growing African population whose standard of living was clearly falling. There was an active, though peaceful, nationalist movement led by Messali Hadj, but after almost ten years of campaigning following the end of the Second World War, they had achieved absolutely nothing:

- the French settlers would make no concessions whatsoever;
- Algerians were allowed no say in the government of their country;
- Algeria continued to be treated not as a colony or a protectorate, but as an extension or province of France itself;
- in spite of what had happened in Indo-China, Tunisia and Morocco, no French government dared consider independence for Algeria, since this would incur the wrath of the settlers and their supporters in France.

Encouraged by the French defeat in Indo-China, a more militant nationalist group was formed – *the National Liberation Front (FLN), led by Ben Bella*, which launched a guerrilla war towards the end of 1954. The war gradually escalated as the French sent more troops. By 1960 they had 700 000 troops engaged in a massive anti-terrorist operation. *The war was having profound effects in France itself.*

- Many French politicians realized that even if the army won the military struggle, the FLN still had the support of most of the Algerian people, and while this lasted, *French control of Algeria could never be secure.*
- *The war split public opinion in France* between those who wanted to continue supporting the white settlers and those who thought the struggle was hopeless. At times feelings ran so high that France itself seemed on the verge of civil war.
- *The French army*, after its defeats in the Second World War and Indo-China, saw the Algerian war as a chance to restore its reputation and refused to contemplate

surrender. Some generals were even prepared to stage a military coup to remove any French government which was willing to give Algeria independence.

- *In 1958 the war caused the downfall of the French government* and brought an end to the Fourth Republic which had been in existence since France was liberated in 1944. Suspecting that the government was about to give way as it had in Tunisia and Morocco, some army officers organized demonstrations in Algiers and demanded that General de Gaulle should be called in to head a new government. They were convinced that the general, a great patriot, would never agree to Algerian independence. *Civil war seemed imminent*; the government could see no way out of the deadlock and consequently resigned. President Coty called upon de Gaulle, who agreed to become Prime Minister on condition that he could draw up a new constitution. This turned out to be *the end of the Fourth Republic*.
- De Gaulle soon produced his new constitution giving the President much more power, and was elected President of the Fifth Republic (December 1958), a position which he held until his resignation in April 1969.

Meanwhile vicious fighting continued, with both sides committing atrocities, and it was not long before de Gaulle decided that outright military victory was out of the question. When he showed a willingness to negotiate with the FLN, the army and the settlers were incensed; this was not what they had expected from him. Led by General Salan, they set up *l'Organisation de l'Armée Secrète (OAS) (1961)*, which began a terrorist campaign, blowing up buildings and murdering critics both in Algeria and in France. They even attempted to assassinate de Gaulle and seized power in Algeria. This was going too far for most French people and for many of the army too. When de Gaulle appeared on TV dressed in his full general's uniform and denounced the OAS, the rebellion collapsed. The French public was sick of the war and there was widespread approval when Ben Bella, who had been in prison since 1956, was released to attend peace talks at Evian. *It was agreed that Algeria should become independent in July 1962*, and Ben Bella was elected first President the following year. About 800 000 settlers left the country and the new government took over most of their land and businesses.

(d) *The rest of the French Empire*

The French possessions in Africa south of the Sahara were:

- **French West Africa** consisting of *eight* colonies: Dahomey, Guinea, Ivory Coast, Mauretania, Niger, Senegal, Sudan and Upper Volta;
- **French Equatorial Africa** consisting of *four* colonies: Chad, Gabon, Middle Congo and Oubangui-Shari;
- A third group consisted of **Cameroun and Togo** (former German colonies given to France to be looked after as mandates in 1919), and the island of **Madagascar**.

French policy after 1945 was to treat these territories as if they were part of France, and any moves towards more privileges for the Africans were opposed by the French settlers. In 1949 the French government decided to clamp down on all nationalist movements, and many nationalist leaders and trade unionists were arrested. Often they were denounced as communist agitators, though without much evidence to support the accusations.

Gradually the French were forced by events in Indo-China and the Maghrib, together with the fact that Britain was preparing the Gold Coast and Nigeria for independence, to change their policy. *In 1956 the twelve colonies of West and Equatorial Africa were each given self-government for internal affairs, but they continued to press for full independence.*

When de Gaulle came to power in 1958 he proposed a new plan, hoping to keep as much control over the colonies as possible:

- the twelve colonies would continue to have self-government, each with its own parliament for local affairs;
- they would all be members of a new union, *the French Community*, and France would take all important decisions about taxation and foreign affairs;
- all members of the community would receive economic aid from France;
- there would be a referendum in each colony to decide whether the plan should be accepted or not;
- colonies which opted for full independence could have it, but would receive no French aid.

De Gaulle was confident that none of them would dare face the future without French help. He was almost right: eleven colonies voted in favour of his plan, but one, *Guinea, under the leadership of Sekou Touré, returned a 95 per cent vote against the plan.* Guinea was given independence immediately (1958) but all French aid was stopped. However, Guinea's brave stand encouraged the other eleven, as well as Togo, Cameroun and Madagascar: they all demanded full independence and de Gaulle agreed. They all became independent republics during 1960. However, this new independence was not quite so complete as the new states had hoped: *de Gaulle was intent on neo-colonialism* – all the states except Guinea found that France still influenced their economic and foreign policies, and any independent action was almost out of the question.

Three French possessions outside Africa – Martinique, Guadaloupe and French Guiana – were not given independence. They continued to be treated as extensions of the mother country and their official status was 'overseas *départements*' (a *département* is a sort of county or province). Their peoples voted in French elections and their representatives sat in the French National Assembly in Paris.

21.6 Holland, Belgium, Spain, Portugal and Italy

All these colonial powers, with the exception of Italy, were, if anything, even more determined than France to hold on to their overseas possessions. This was probably because, being less wealthy than Britain and France, they lacked the resources to sustain neo-colonialism. There was no way that they would be able to maintain the equivalent of the British Commonwealth or the French influence over their former colonies, against competition from foreign capital.

(a) *Holland*

Before the war Holland had a huge empire in the East Indies including the large islands of Sumatra, Java and Celebes, West Irian (part of the island of New Guinea) and about two-thirds of the island of Borneo (see Map 21.3). They also owned some islands in the West Indies, and Surinam on the mainland of South America, between British and French Guiana.

It was in the valuable East Indies that the first challenge came to Dutch control even before the war. The Dutch operated in a way similar to the French in Algeria – they grew crops for export and did very little to improve the living standards of the East Indians. Nationalist groups campaigned throughout the 1930s, and many leaders, including *Ahmed Sukarno*, were arrested.

When the Japanese invaded in 1942, they released Sukarno and others and allowed them to play a part in the administration of the country, promising independence when the war was over. With the Japanese defeat in 1945, *Sukarno declared an independent republic of Indonesia*, not expecting any resistance from the Dutch, who had been defeated and their country occupied by the Germans. However, Dutch troops soon arrived and made determined efforts to regain control. Although the Dutch had some success, the war dragged on, and they were still a long way from complete victory in 1949, when they at last decided to negotiate. *Reasons for their decision were:*

- the expense of the campaign was crippling for a small country like Holland to sustain;
- outright victory still seemed a long way off;
- they were under strong pressure from the UN to reach agreement;
- other countries, including the USA and Australia, were pressing Holland to grant independence so that they could exert their influence in the area, once exclusive Dutch control ended;
- the Dutch hoped that by making concessions, they would be able to preserve the link between Holland and Indonesia and maintain some influence.

Holland agreed to recognize the independence of the United States of Indonesia (1949) with Sukarno as president, but not including West Irian. Sukarno agreed to a Netherlands–Indonesia Union under the Dutch crown, and Dutch troops were withdrawn. However, the following year Sukarno broke away from the Union and began to pressurize the Dutch to hand over West Irian, seizing Dutch-owned property and expelling Europeans. Eventually in 1963 Holland gave way and allowed West Irian to become part of Indonesia.

Important developments took place in 1965 when Sukarno was overthrown in a right-wing military coup, apparently because he was thought to be too much under the influence of communist China and the Indonesian communist party. The USA was involved in the coup, and welcomed Sukarno's successor, *General Suharto*. He introduced what he called his 'New Order'. This involved a purge of communists during which at least half a million people were murdered. The regime had all the hallmarks of a brutal military dictatorship, but there were few protests from the West because Suharto was anti-communist.

Of the other Dutch possessions, Surinam was allowed to become an independent republic in 1975; the West Indian islands were treated as part of Holland, though allowed some control over their internal affairs.

(b) *Belgium*

Belgian control of their African possessions, the Belgian Congo and Ruanda-Urundi, ended in chaos, violence and civil war. *The Belgians thought that the best way to preserve their control was by:*

- *denying the Africans any advanced education* – this would prevent them from coming into contact with nationalist ideas and deprive them of an educated professional class who could lead them to independence;
- *using tribal rivalries to their advantage* by playing off different tribes against each other. This worked well in the huge Congo which contained about 150 tribes; men from

one tribe would be used to keep order in another tribal area. In Ruanda-Urundi the Belgians used the Tutsi tribe to help them control the other main tribal group, the Hutu.

In spite of all these efforts, nationalist ideas still began to filter in from neighbouring French and British colonies.

1 The Belgian Congo

The Belgians seemed taken by surprise when widespread rioting broke out (January 1959) in the capital of the Congo, Leopoldville. The crowds were protesting against unemployment and declining living standards, and disorders soon spread throughout the whole country.

The Belgians suddenly changed their policy and announced that the Congo could become independent in six months. This was inviting disaster: the Belgians' own policies meant that there was no experienced group of Africans to which power could be handed over; the Congolese had not been educated for professional jobs – there were only seventeen graduates in the entire country, and there were no African doctors, lawyers, engineers or officers in the army. *The Congolese National Movement (MNC), led by Patrice Lumumba*, had been in existence less than a year. The huge size of the country and the large number of tribes would make it difficult to govern. Six months was far too short a time to prepare for independence.

Why did the Belgians take this extraordinary decision?

• They were afraid of further bloodshed if they hesitated; there were over 100 000 Belgians in the country who could be at risk.

• They did not want to face the expense of a long anti-guerrilla campaign like the one dragging on in Algeria.

• They hoped that granting independence immediately while the Congo was weak and divided would leave the new state completely helpless; it would be dependent on Belgium for support and advice, and so Belgian influence could be preserved.

The Congo became independent on 30 June 1960 with Lumumba as Prime Minister and Joseph Kasavubu, the leader of a rival nationalist group, as President. Unfortunately everything went wrong shortly after independence and the country was plunged into a disastrous civil war (see Section 22.5). Order was not restored until 1964.

2 Ruanda-Urundi

The other Belgian territory of Ruanda-Urundi was given independence in 1962 and divided into two states – Rwanda and Burundi, both governed by members of the Tutsi tribe, as they had been throughout the colonial period. Neither of the states had been properly prepared, and after independence, both had a very unsettled history of bitter rivalry and violence between the Tutsis and the Hutus (see Section 22.7).

(c) *Spain*

Spain owned some areas in Africa: the largest was Spanish Sahara, and there were also the small colonies of Spanish Morocco, Ifni and Spanish Guinea. General Franco, the right-wing dictator who ruled Spain from 1939 until 1975, showed little interest in the colonies.

• When nationalist movements developed, he did not resist long in the case of *Spanish Morocco:* when the French gave independence to French Morocco (1956),

Franco followed suit and Spanish Morocco became part of Morocco. The other two small colonies had to wait much longer:

- *Ifni* was allowed to join Morocco, but not until 1969; and
- *Guinea* became independent as Equatorial Guinea in 1968.

Spanish Sahara

Here Franco resisted even longer, because it was a valuable source of phosphates. Only after Franco's death in 1975 did the new Spanish government agree to release Sahara. Unfortunately the process was badly bungled: instead of making it into an independent state ruled by its nationalist party, the *Polisario Front*, it was decided to divide it between its two neighbouring states, Morocco and Mauretania. The Polisario Front, under its leader, *Mohamed Abdelazia*, declared the Democratic Arab Republic of Sahara (1976) which was recognized by Algeria, Libya, the communist states and India. Algeria and Libya sent help and in 1979 Mauretania decided to withdraw, making it easier for Sahara to struggle on against Morocco. However, the fact that Sahara had been officially recognized by the USSR was enough to arouse American suspicions. Just when it seemed that the Moroccans too were prepared to negotiate peace, the new American president, Ronald Reagan, encouraged them to continue the fight, stepping up aid to Morocco. The war dragged on through the 1980s; yet another new Third World country had become a victim of super-power self-interest. In 1990 the UN proposed that a referendum should be held so that the people of Sahara could choose whether to be independent or become part of Morocco, but progress towards organizing this was painfully slow.

(d) *Portugal*

The main Portuguese possessions were in Africa: the two large areas of *Angola* and *Mozambique*, and the small West African colony of *Portuguese Guinea*. They also still owned the eastern half of the island of Timor in the East Indies. The right-wing Portuguese government of Dr Salazar blithely ignored nationalist developments in the rest of Africa, and for many years after 1945 the Portuguese colonies seemed quiet and resigned to their position. They were mainly agricultural; there were few industrial workers and the black populations were almost entirely illiterate. In 1956 there were only fifty Africans in the whole of Mozambique who had received any secondary education. Though nationalist groups were formed in all three colonies in 1956, they remained insignificant. *Several factors changed the situation.*

- By 1960 the nationalists were greatly encouraged by the large number of other African states winning independence.
- The Salazar regime, having learned nothing from the experiences of the other colonial powers, stepped up its repressive policies, but this only made the nationalists more resolute.
- Fighting broke out first in Angola (1961) where Agostinho Neto's MPLA (*People's Movement for Angolan Liberation*) was the main nationalist movement. Violence soon spread to Guinea where Amilcar Cabral led the resistance, and to Mozambique, where the FRELIMO guerrillas were organized by Eduardo Mondlane.
- The nationalists, who all had strong Marxist connections, received economic and military aid from the communist bloc.
- The Portuguese army found it impossible to suppress the nationalist guerrillas; the troops became demoralized and the cost escalated until by 1973 the government was spending 40 per cent of its budget fighting three colonial wars at once.

- Still the Portuguese government refused to abandon its policy; but public opinion and many army officers were sick of the wars, and in 1974 the Salazar dictatorship was overthrown by a military coup.

Soon all three colonies were granted independence: Guinea took the name Guinea-Bissau (September 1974), and Mozambique and Angola became independent the following year. This caused a serious crisis for Rhodesia and South Africa; they were now the only states left in Africa ruled by white minorities, and their governments felt increasingly threatened.

Angola

Now it was the turn of Angola to become a victim of outside interference and the Cold War. South African troops immediately invaded the country in support of UNITA (*National Union for the Total Independence of Angola*), while General Mobutu of Zaire, with American backing, launched another invasion in support of the FNLA (*National Front for the Liberation of Angola*). The Americans thought that a joint Angolan government of these two groups would be more amenable and open to western influence than the Marxist MPLA. The MPLA received aid in the form of Russian weapons and a Cuban army; this enabled them to defeat both invasion forces by March 1976, and Neto was accepted as president of the new state. This proved to be only a temporary respite – further invasions followed and Angola was torn by civil war right through into the 1990s (see Section 22.6). The South Africans also interfered in Mozambique, sending raiding parties over the border and doing their best to destabilize the FRELIMO government. Again the country was torn by civil war for many years (see Section 9.3(j)).

East Timor

One other Portuguese territory deserves mention: East Timor was half of the small island in the East Indies; the western half belonged to Holland and became part of Indonesia in 1949 (see Map 21.6). East Timor's nationalist movement (FRETILIN) won a short civil war against the ruling group, which wanted to stay with Portugal (September 1975). The USA denounced the new government as Marxist, which was not entirely accurate; after only a few weeks, Indonesian troops invaded, overthrew the government and incorporated East Timor into Indonesia, a sequence of events vividly described in Timothy Mo's novel *The Redundancy of Courage*. The USA continued to supply military goods to the Indonesians, who were guilty of appalling atrocities both during and after the war. It is estimated that about 100 000 people were killed (one-sixth of the population) while another 300 000 were put into detention camps. Resistance was still continuing in the early 1990s, but although the UN condemned Indonesia's action, East Timor was too small and, unlike Kuwait, too unimportant to warrant any sanctions being applied against Indonesia.

(e) *Italy*

It was officially decided in 1947 that Italy, having supported Hitler and suffered defeat in the Second World War, must lose her overseas empire. Her African possessions were to be administered by France and Britain until the UN decided what to do with them. The UN followed a policy of placing the territories under governments which would be sympathetic to Western interests.

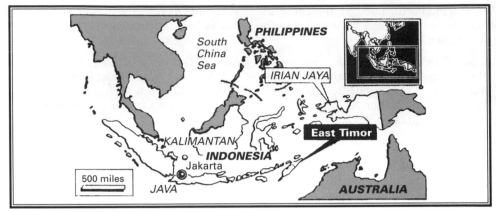

Map 21.6 Indonesia and East Timo

Source: *The Guardian*, 20.4.96

- *Ethiopia* was handed back to the rule of the Emperor Haile Selassie, who had been forced into exile when the Italians invaded Ethiopia (Abyssinia) in 1935.
- *Libya* was given independence under King Idris (1951).
- *Eritrea* was made part of Ethiopia (1952) but it was to have a large measure of self-government within a federal system.
- *Italian Somaliland* was merged with British Somaliland to form the independent state of Somalia (1960).

Some of these arrangements did not prove to be very successful. Both Idris and Haile Selassie became unpopular with their peoples, Idris because he was thought to be too pro-West, and Haile Selassie because he made no attempt to modernize Ethiopia and did little to improve the living standards of his people. He also made the mistake of cancelling Eritrea's rights of self-government (1962), which prompted the Eritreans into launching a war for independence. King Idris was overthrown in 1969 by a socialist revolutionary movement which nationalized the oil industry and began to modernize the country. Haile Selassie was overthrown in 1974. New leaders soon emerged – Colonel Gaddafi in Libya and Colonel Mengistu in Ethiopia, both of whom turned to the USSR for economic aid. Mengistu seemed to have the more serious problems. He made the mistake of refusing to come to terms with the Eritreans and was faced with other provinces – Tigre and Ogaden – also wanting independence. As he struggled to suppress all these breakaway movements, military expenditure soared and his country sank into even deeper poverty and famine.

21.7 Verdict on decolonization

Although some states, particularly Britain, handled decolonization better than others, in general it was not a pleasant experience for the colonies, and there was no simple happy ending. There were some gains for the new states, which now had much more control over what went on inside their frontiers; and there were some gains for ordinary people, such as advances in education and social services. On the other hand *there were new problems to be faced:*

- *Neo-colonialism* meant that Western European countries and the USA still exerted a great deal of control over the new states, which continued to need the markets and the investment that the west could provide.

- *Many new states, especially in Africa, had been badly prepared or not prepared at all for independence.* Their frontiers were often artificial ones forced on them by the Europeans and there was little incentive for different tribes to stay together. In Nigeria and the Belgian Congo tribal differences helped to cause civil war. When the British withdrew from Nyasaland (Malawi) there were only three secondary schools for 3 million Africans, and not one single industrial factory. When the Portuguese were forced to withdraw from Mozambique, they deliberately destroyed installations and machinery in revenge.
- *In most cases, the governments which took over were run by the local political élite groups:* there was no social revolution and no guarantee that ordinary people would be any better off. In countries where new governments were prepared to introduce socialist policies (nationalizing resources or foreign businesses), or where governments showed any sign of being pro-communist, the Western countries disapproved. They often responded by cutting off aid or helping to destabilize the government. This happened in Indo-China, Indonesia, East Timor, Chad, Angola, Mozambique, Zaire and Jamaica.
- *All the Third World states faced the problem of intense poverty.* They were eonomically underdeveloped and often relied on exports of one or two commodities; a fall in the world price of their product was a major disaster. Loans from abroad left them heavily in debt (see Section 23.2). As usual, Africa was worst hit: it was the only area of the world where in 1987, incomes were, on average, lower than in 1972.

Questions

1   *The USA and decolonization*   You will have noticed while reading this chapter that the USA often became involved in the decolonization programme.

   (a)   Make a list of all the occasions between 1941 and 1990 when the USA played a part, and explain what that part was.   1.4c–5c   10 marks
   (b)   What were the different motives behind American intervention?
                                                                        1.4b–5b, 6c–8c   10 marks
   (c)   In what ways did the former colonial peoples benefit from independence? In what ways might they have been disappointed by the changes?   10 marks

Total: 30 marks

2   *The decolonization of Africa*   Study Sources A to E and then answer the questions which follow.

Source A

Table 21.1   *The growth in the European settler population in Africa*

	1935–6	1953
Southern Rhodesia	55 419	160 000
Angola	30 000	78 000
Belgian Congo	18 680	76 764
French West Africa	19 061	62 236
Northern Rhodesia	9 913	50 000
Mozambique	10 000	48 813
Kenya	17 997	42 000
Algeria	720 000	1 200 000
Morocco	98 000	300 000

Source: based on statistics in Bill Freund, *The Making of Contemporary Africa* (Macmillan, 1984)

Report of a Belgian government enquiry into conditions in the Belgian Congo, 1947

There can be no doubt that it is the forced labour on roads which is the most unpopular, either because it means long journeys to work, or else because it means painful toil, often even for mothers of young children and for pregnant women.

_ Source C _

Report of the British government Royal Commission on conditions in African towns, 1955

The wages of the majority of African workers are too low to enable them to obtain housing in Nairobi (Kenya). The high cost of housing relative to wages causes over-crowding, because housing is shared to lighten the cost. This, with the high cost of food in towns, makes family life impossible for the majority.

_ Source D _

Some information from a Canadian historian

By the end of the 1940s there were only 32 journalists, 38 medical doctors, 114 lawyers and 435 clergy in the Gold Coast out of a total population of 4.5 million. Although all the western powers cultivated their reputations for providing education to Third World peoples, the idea that they introduced programmes of mass education is simply untrue.

Source: T.E. Vadney, *The World Since 1945* (Penguin, 1987)

_ Source E _

Comments by Sir James Robertson, former Governor-General of Nigeria, in 1979

When we came to Africa there were no railways, telegraphs, schools, hospitals, no proper government at all. When we left, there were railways, there was a system of roads, there was a police force, there was an Army, there were hospitals, schools and even universities. All this was done in about 50 years. We had set up a civilisation which had not existed before.

Source: Sources B, C and E are quoted in Basil Davidson, *Modern Africa, a Social and Political History* (Longman, 1989 edition)

(a) Using information from Sections 21.4–5 and the statistics in Source A, what conclusions can you draw about some of the problems involved in the decolonization of Africa?   1.4c–8c, 3.4   6 marks

(b) Why do you think Source E seems to disagree with Sources B, C and D?
        1.6c–8c   5 marks

(c) 'Source E was written thirty-two years after Source B and 24 years after Source C. Therefore Source E is more reliable than the other two'.
Explain fully whether you agree or disagree with this statement.   3.7   5 marks

(d) How useful are these sources to a historian trying to explain why the

European colonies in Africa wanted independence after the Second World
War?   3.5–6, 8–9   14 marks

3   *The Crisis in Cyprus 1955–6*   The crisis in Cyprus was difficult for the British
    government to deal with. It was also a complex one for historians to interpret, as
    the following sources show. Study Sources A to I carefully and then answer the
    questions which follow.

Source A

*Dr Kutchuk, leader of the Turkish community in Cyprus, gave this statement to the
press on 6 August, 1955*

A handful of ambitious adventurers using Hitlerite methods of propaganda have
concocted a so-called 'Cyprus question'. Unless Greek ambitions are stopped, they
could bring about a Third World War. Cyprus was never Greek: historically it is
Turkish, and geographically it is part of Turkey. Britain has neither the legal nor
moral right to hand over Cyprus to any other nation except Turkey, should she
decide to leave the island. The terrorist activities in Cyprus are carried out by a
handful of people egged on by Greece. It is the duty of Britain to stamp out this
terrorism.

Source B

*Statement by the Turkish Prime Minister, Mr Adnam Menderes, in Istanbul, 24
August, 1955*

If a change occurs in the status of the island, it should revert to Turkey. [It had
been given to Britain by Turkey in 1878.] The pressure exerted by the
irresponsible people in the Greek government has been going on for months, but
there are limits. We cannot understand how a government can treat a provincial
cleric [Archbishop Makarios] like an independent state and bow to his wishes.

Source C

Statement by the British government, 9 March 1956

He [Makarios] has remained silent while policemen and soldiers have been
murdered in cold blood, while women and children have been maimed by bombs.
He has referred in sermons to convicted terrorists as patriots, and he has urged his
fellow-countrymen to take the law into their own hands. This has been accepted as
not merely condoning, but approving assassination and bomb-throwing.

Source D

News report in Keesing's Contemporary Archives, *17 March 1956*

On the orders of Sir John Harding [Governor of Cyprus], Archbishop Makarios
and three other leaders of the *enosis* movement were arrested on March 9th and
deported on the same day to the Seychelles in the Indian Ocean. This was
regarded by the Turkish press and by Turkish public opinion generally as fully
justified in view of the Archbishop's proved involvement in terrorist activities.
Articles welcoming the British government's action and expressing full support for
it were published in nearly all Turkish newspapers.

Lord Hailsham, a Conservative peer, speaking in the House of Lords, 14 March 1956

Our duty to world peace is to remain in Cyprus at the present moment. Are we for that to be accused of being oppressors and tyrants and to have our soldiers and policemen murdered?

Source F

Statement on the radio by King Paul of Greece, 20 December 1954

Our Cypriot brethren demand their freedom through the right of self-determination for which two great wars have been fought. Greece, faced with the British refusal to discuss the case directly, was bound to bring the issue before the UN. As long as the Cypriots proclaim their indomitable will to decide their own destiny, no power on earth can prevent the natural evolution of that desire.

Source G

Statement by Sir Paul Pavlides, 19 September 1955

Sir Paul Pavlides, a prominent merchant of Limassol, said that he had resigned from the Cyprus executive council in view of Britain's failure to recognize the rights of the Cypriot people to determine their future.

Source H

Speech by Aneurin Bevan, a Labour MP, in the House of Commons, 14 March 1956

It is hard to discover whether the government wants Cyprus as a base, or whether they want a base in Cyprus. If the former is the case, then the discussions with Archbishop Makarios have been dishonest from the beginning. I can see no real conflict between Britain's strategic interests and the Cypriot desire for self-government. There is no justification for the Archbishop's deportation; it is essential to remember that persons whom we look on here as terrorists are looked on by their fellow nationals as patriots. Why does the Tory party keep deceiving itself? It is no use refusing to negotiate because they have been associated with violence – it is absurd when we consider the history of Ireland, Gold Coast and India.

Source I

Speech by Dr Bell, Bishop of Chichester, and a member of the World Council of Churches, in the House of Lords, 14 March 1956

I believe that the Archbishop's deportation is a blunder which strikes a blow at British prestige and reduces Britain's capacity for world leadership. The British government has offered Cyprus neither self-government nor self-determination, but a limited form of self-government with large areas reserved to British rule. There is no democratic constitution and it is artificial, no solution at all.

Sources: All these sources are taken from *Keesing's Contemporary Archives for 1956*

(a) Show how a historian could present two completely different interpretations
     of the crisis in Cyprus, depending on which of the nine sources he chose.

                                                      2.4–6, 3.4   20 marks
(b) Explain how such widely differing sources could have been written. Comment
     on each source.   1.6c–9b   18 marks
(c) Comment on the reliability and value of each source.   3.5–10   27 marks

                                                         Total: 65 marks

⬡22 Problems in Africa

Summary of events

After achieving independence, the new African nations faced similar problems. It is not possible in the limited space available to look at events in every state in Africa. The following sections examine the problems common to all the states, and show what happened in some of the countries which experienced one or more of these problems.

- *Ghana* suffered economic problems, the failure of democracy and several coups;
- *Nigeria* experienced civil war, a succession of military coups and brutal military dictatorship;
- *Tanzania* – extreme poverty;
- *the Congo* – civil war and military dictatorship;
- *Angola* – civil war prolonged by outside interference;
- *Burundi and Rwanda* – civil war and horrifying tribal slaughter;
- *South Africa* was a special case: after 1980, when Rhodesia (Zimbabwe) gained its independence, it was the last bastion of white rule on the continent of Africa, and the white minority was determined to hold out to the bitter end against black nationalism. Gradually the pressures became too much for the white minority, and in May 1994 Nelson Mandela became the first black president of South Africa.

22.1 Problems common to the African states

(a) *Tribal differences*

They each contained a number of different tribes which had only been held together by the foreign colonial rulers and which had united in the nationalist struggle for freedom from the foreigners. As soon as the Europeans withdrew, there was little incentive to stay together, and they tended to regard loyalty to the tribe as more important than loyalty to their new nation. In Nigeria, the Congo (Zaire), Burundi and Rwanda, tribal differences became so intense that they led to civil war.

(b) *They were economically under-developed*

In this they were like many other Third World states. They often relied on one or two commodities for export, so that a fall in the world price of their products was a major disaster. Nigeria, for example, relied heavily on its oil exports which produced about 80

456 *DECOLONIZATION AND AFTER*

per cent of its annual income. There was a shortage of capital and skills of all kinds, and the population was growing at a rate of over two per cent a year. Loans from abroad left them heavily in debt, and as they concentrated on increasing exports to pay for the loans, food for home consumption became more scarce. All this left the African nations heavily dependent on Western European countries and the USA both for markets and investment and enabled those countries to exert some control over African governments (neo-colonialism).

Some states suffered direct military intervention from countries which did not like their government, usually because they were thought to be too left-wing. This happened to Angola, which found itself invaded by troops from South Africa and Zaire because those countries disapproved of Angola's Marxist-style government.

(c) *Political problems*

African politicians lacked experience of how to work the systems of parliamentary democracy left behind by the Europeans. Faced with difficult problems, they often failed to cope, and governments became corrupt. This led to the creation of one-party states as the only way to achieve progress. In many states such as Kenya and Tanzania this worked well, providing stable and effective government. On the other hand, since it was impossible to oppose such governments by legal means, violence was the only answer. Military coups to remove unpopular rulers became common. President Nkrumah of Ghana, for example, was removed by the army in 1966 after two assassination attempts had failed.

(d) *Economic and natural disasters*

In the 1980s the whole of Africa was beset by economic and natural disasters. The world recession reduced demand for African exports such as oil, copper and cobalt, and there was a severe drought (1982–5) which caused crop failures, deaths of livestock, famine and starvation. The drought ended in 1986 and much of the continent had record harvests that year. However, by this time, Africa, like the rest of the world, was suffering from a severe debt crisis, and at the same time had been forced by the International Monetary Fund to economise drastically in return for further loans. This often meant that countries had to devalue their currency, and reduce food price subsidies, leading to increased food prices at a time when unemployment was rising, wages falling, and social services being cut as part of the austerity programme. Table 23.1 in the next chapter shows how poor most of the African states were in comparison with the rest of the world.

22.2 Ghana

Kwame Nkrumah ruled Ghana from independence in 1957 until his removal by the army in 1966 (Illus. 22.1).

(a) *His initial achievements were impressive*

He was a socialist in outlook and wanted his people to enjoy a higher standard of living that would come from efficient organization and industrialization. Production of cocoa (Ghana's main export) doubled, forestry, fishing and cattle-breeding expanded, and the

Illus. 22.1 Kwame Nkrumah

country's modest deposits of gold and bauxite were more effectively exploited. The building of a dam on the Volta River (begun 1961) provided water for irrigation and hydro-electric power, producing enough electricity for the towns as well as for a new aluminium smelting plant. Government money was provided for village projects in which local people built roads and schools.

Nkrumah also gained prestige internationally: he strongly supported the *pan-African movement*, believing that only through a federation of the whole continent could African power make itself felt. As a start, an economic union was formed with Guinea and Mali, though nothing much came of it. He supported the *Organization of African Unity* (set up in 1963), and usually played a responsible role in world affairs, keeping Ghana in the Commonwealth while at the same time forging links with the USSR and China.

(b) *Why was Nkrumah overthrown?*

He tried to introduce industrialization too quickly and borrowed vast amounts of capital from abroad, hoping to balance the budget from increased exports. Unfortunately Ghana was still uncomfortably dependent on cocoa exports, and a steep fall in the world price of cocoa left her with a huge balance of payments deficit. There was criticism that too much money was being wasted on unnecessary projects, like the ten-mile stretch of motorway from Accra (the capital) to Tema.

Probably the most important reason for his downfall was that he gradually began to abandon parliamentary government in favour of a one-party state and personal dictator-

ship. He justified this on the grounds that the opposition parties, which were based on tribal differences, were not constructive and merely wanted more power in their own areas. They had no experience of working a parliamentary system, and as Nkrumah himself wrote: 'Even a system based on a democratic constitution may need backing up in the period following independence by emergency measures of a totalitarian kind'.

From 1959 onwards, opponents could be deported or imprisoned for up to five years without trial. Even the respected opposition leader, J.B. Danqua, was arrested in 1961 and died in prison. In 1964 all parties except Nkrumah's were banned, and even within his own party no criticism was allowed. He began to build up the image of himself as the 'father of the nation'. Slogans such as 'Nkrumah is our Messiah, Nkrumah never dies' were circulated, and numerous statues of the saviour were erected. This struck many people as absurd, but Nkrumah justified it on the grounds that the population could identify itself better with a single personality as leader than with vague notions of the state. All this, plus the fact that he was believed to have amassed a personal fortune through corruption, was too much for the army, which seized control when Nkrumah was on a visit to China (1966).

The military government promised a return to democracy as soon as a new constitution could be drawn up, complete with safeguards against a return to dictatorship. The constitution was ready in 1969 and the elections returned *Dr Kofi Busia*, leader of the Progressive Party, as the new Prime Minister (October 1969).

(c) *Kofi Busia*

Dr Busia only lasted until January 1972 when he too was overthrown by the army. An academic who had studied economics at Oxford, *Busia illustrates perfectly the difficulties of democratically elected politicians in the African situation*. In power in the first place only by permission of the army, he had to produce quick results. Yet the problems were enormous – rising unemployment, rising prices and massive debts to be repaid. Canada and the USA were prepared to wait for repayment, but other countries, including Britain, were not so sympathetic. Busia, who had a reputation for honesty, genuinely tried to keep up payments, but these were using up about 40 per cent of Ghana's export profits. In 1971 imports were limited and the currency devalued by nearly 50 per cent. Busia was hampered by the tribal squabbles which re-emerged under conditions of democracy, and the economic situation deteriorated so rapidly that in January 1972 he was removed from power, without resistance, by *Colonel Ignatius Acheampong*, who headed a military government until July 1978.

(d) *J.J. Rawlings*

As Ghana continued to flounder amid her economic problems, Acheampong was himself removed from power by General Fred Akuffo, for alleged corruption. In June 1979 a group of junior officers led by 32-year old Jerry J. Rawlings, a charismatic airforce officer of mixed Ghanaian and Scottish parentage, seized power on the grounds that corrupt soldiers and politicians needed to be weeded out before a return to democracy. They launched what was described as a 'house-cleaning' exercise in which Acheampong and Akuffo were executed after secret trials. In July, elections were held as a result of which Rawlings returned Ghana to civilian rule with *Dr Hilla Limann* as President (September 1979).

Limann was no more successful than previous leaders in halting Ghana's economic decline. Corruption was still rife at all levels, and smuggling and hoarding of basic goods were commonplace. During 1981 inflation was running at 125 per cent, and there

Illus. 22.2 Jerry Rawlings – Ghanaian leader

was widespread labour unrest as wages remained low. Limann was removed in a military coup (December 1981), and *Flight-Lieutenant Rawlings became chairman of a Provisional National Defence Council.* He was rare among military leaders: the army did not want power, he said, but simply to be 'part of the decision-making process' which would change Ghana's whole economic and social system (Illus. 22.2). Though Rawlings remained leader, the PNDC appointed a civilian government of well-known figures from political and academic circles. Ghana suffered badly from the drought in 1983, but there was ample rainfall in 1984, bringing a good maize harvest. The new recovery programme seemed to be working, production rose by 7 per cent, and early in 1985 inflation was down to 40 per cent. As Ghana celebrated 30 years of independence (March 1987), she was still on course for recovery, and Rawlings and the PNDC, evoking memories of Nkrumah, were running an apparently successful campaign to unite the 12 million Ghanaians solidly behind them. Yet for many people there remained one big criticism: there was no progress towards representative democracy. *Rawlings responded in 1991 by calling an assembly to draw up a new constitution, and promised democratic elections in 1992.* These duly went ahead (November) and Rawlings himself was elected President for a four-year term, with over 58 per cent of the votes. He was both Head of State and Commander-in-Chief of the Armed Forces.

22.3 Nigeria

Superficially Nigeria, which gained independence in 1960, seemed to have advantages over Ghana; it was potentially a wealthy state, extensive oil resources having been discovered in the eastern coastal area. The Prime Minister was the capable and moderate *Sir Abubakar Tafawa Balewa*, assisted by the veteran nationalist leader Azikiwe, who was made President when Nigeria became a republic in 1963. However, in 1966 the government was overthrown by a military coup, and the following year civil war broke out which lasted until 1970.

(a) *What caused the civil war?*

Λ combination of the problems mentioned in Section 22.1 led to the outbreak.

- *Nigeria's tribal differences were more serious than Ghana's*, and although the constitution was a federal one in which each of the three regions (north, east and west) had its own local government, the regions felt that the central government in Lagos did not safeguard their interests sufficiently. Balewa came from the Muslim north where the Hausa and Fulani tribes were powerful; the Yorubas of the west and the Ibos of the east were constantly complaining about northern domination, even though Azikiwe was an Ibo.
- *To make matters worse, there was an economic recession.* By 1964 prices had risen 15 per cent, unemployment was rising and wages were, on average, well below what had been calculated as the minimum living wage. Criticism of the government mounted and Balewa replied by arresting Chief Awolowo, Prime Minister of the western region, which for a time seemed likely to break away from the federation. The central government was also accused of corruption after blatantly trying to 'fix' the results of the 1964 elections.
- *In January 1966 there was a military coup carried out by mainly Ibo officers, in which Balewa and some other leading politicians were killed.* After this the situation deteriorated steadily: in the north there were savage massacres of Ibos who had moved into the region for better jobs. The new leader, General Ironsi, himself an Ibo, was murdered by northern soldiers. When a northerner, *Colonel Yakubu Gowon*, emerged supreme, almost all the Ibos fled from other parts of Nigeria back to the east, whose leader, Colonel Ojukwu, announced that the eastern region had seceded (withdrawn) from Nigeria to become the independent state of Biafra (May 1967). Gowon launched what he described as a 'short surgical police action' to bring the east back into Nigeria.

(b) *The civil war*

It took more than a short police action, as the Biafrans fought back vigorously. It was a bitter and terrible war in which Biafra lost more civilians from disease and starvation than troops killed in the fighting (Illus. 22.3). Neither the UN nor the Commonwealth was able to mediate, and the Biafrans hung on to the bitter end as Nigerian troops closed in on all sides. The final surrender came in January 1970. Nigerian unity had been preserved.

(c) *Recovery after the war was remarkably swift*

There were pressing problems: famine in Biafra, inter-tribal bitterness, unemployment, and economic resources strained by the war. Gowon showed considerable statesmanship in this difficult situation. There was no revenge-taking, as the Ibos had feared, and Gowon made every effort to reconcile them and persuaded them to return to their jobs in other parts of the country. He introduced a new federal system of twelve states, later

Illus. 22.3 Biafra – a 15-year-old victim of the civil war and famine

increased to nineteen, to give more recognition of local tribal differences. Nigeria was able to take advantage of rising oil prices in the mid-1970s, which gave her a healthy balance of payments position. *In 1975 Gowon was removed by another army group, which probably thought he intended to return the country to civilian rule too early.* Nigeria continued to prosper and the army kept its promise of a return to democratic government in 1979. Elections were held, resulting in *President Shagari* becoming head of a civilian government. With Nigeria's oil much in demand abroad, prosperity seemed assured and prospects for a stable government bright.

(d) *Unfulfilled promise*

Unfortunately disappointment was soon to follow: during 1981 the economy got into difficulties because of the fall in world oil prices, and the healthy trade balance of 1980 became a deficit in 1983. Although Shagari was elected for another four-year term (August 1983), he was removed by a military coup the following December. According to the new leader, *Major-General Bukhari*, the civilian government was guilty of mis-management of the economy, financial corruption and rigging of the election. Before long Bukhari became the victim of yet another coup carried out by a rival group of army officers who complained that he had not done enough to reverse the fall in living standards, rising prices, chronic shortages and unemployment.

The new president, *Major-General Babangida*, began energetically, introducing what he called a 'belt-tightening' campaign, and announcing plans to develop the non-oil side of the economy. He aimed to expand production of rice, maize, fish, vegetable oil and animal products, and to give special priority to steel manufacture and the assembly of motor vehicles. Following the example of Jerry Rawlings in Ghana, he declared that his military government would not remain in power 'a day longer than was absolutely necessary'. A committee of academics was set to work to produce a new constitution which could 'guarantee an acceptable and painless succession mechanism'; October 1990 was fixed as the date for a return to civilian rule. Another blow came in 1986 with a further dramatic fall in oil prices which in June reached a record low of only 10 dollars a barrel. This was a disaster for the government, which had based its 1986 budget calculations on a price of 23.50 dollars a barrel. It was forced to accept a loan from the World Bank to enable the recovery programme to go ahead.

In spite of the economic problems, local and state elections were held as promised in 1990 and 1991 and there seemed a good chance of a return to democratic civilian rule. However, in 1993, *General Sani Abacha seized power in a bloodless coup*, claiming that the elections had been rigged. His rule soon developed into a repressive military dictatorship with the imprisonment and execution of opposition leaders, which brought worldwide condemnation (November 1995). Nigeria was suspended from the Commonwealth and the UN applied economic sanctions; most countries stopped buying Nigerian oil and aid was suspended, which were further blows to the economy. Abacha meanwhile continued apparently unmoved, maintaining that he would hand power to a democratically elected president in 1998, or when he felt ready.

22.4 Tanzania

Tanzania became independent in 1961 and was joined in 1964 by the island of Zanzibar to form Tanzania. It was ruled by *Dr Julius Nyerere*, leader of the Tanzanian African Nationalist Union (TANU), who had to deal with formidable problems:

- Tanzania was one of the poorest states in the whole of Africa;
- there was very little industry, few mineral resources, and a heavy dependence on coffee production;
- later came Tanzania's expensive involvement in military operations to overthrow President Idi Amin of Uganda.
- on the other hand, tribal problems were not as serious as elsewhere, and the Swahili language provided a common bond.

Nyerere retired as President in 1985 (aged 63) though he remained chairman of the party until 1990. He was succeeded as President by *Ali Hassan Mwinyi*, who had been Vice-President.

(a) *Nyerere's approach and achievements*

His approach was different from that of any other African ruler. He began conventionally enough by expanding the economy: during the first ten years of independence, production of coffee and cotton doubled and sugar production trebled, while health services and education expanded. But Nyerere was not happy that Tanzania seemed to be developing along the same lines as Kenya, with an ever-widening gulf between the wealthy élite and the resentful masses. His proposed solution to the problem was set out in a remarkable document known as the *Arusha Declaration*, published in 1967. The country was to be run on socialist lines.

- All human beings should be treated as equal.
- The state must have effective control over the means of production and must intervene in economic life to make sure that people were not exploited, and that poverty and disease were eliminated.
- There must be no great accumulations of wealth, or society would no longer be classless.
- Bribery and corruption must be eliminated.
- According to Nyerere, Tanzania was at war, and the enemy was poverty and oppression. The way to victory was not through money and foreign aid, but through hard work and self-reliance. The first priority was to improve agriculture so that the country could be self-sufficient in food production.

Nyerere strove hard to put these aims into practice: all important enterprises, including those owned by foreigners, were nationalized; five-year development plans were introduced. Village projects were encouraged and given aid by the government; these involved *ujamaa* ('familyhood' or self-help): families in each village pooled resources and farmed collectively, using more modern techniques. Foreign loans and investments as well as imports were reduced to a minimum to avoid running into debt. Politically, Nyerere's brand of socialism meant a one-party state run by TANU, but elections were still held. It seemed that some elements of genuine democracy existed, since voters in each constituency had a choice of two TANU candidates and every election resulted in a large proportion of MPs losing their seats. Nyerere himself provided dignified leadership, and with his simple life-style and complete indifference to wealth, he set the perfect example for the party and the country to follow. It was a fascinating experiment which tried to combine socialist direction from the centre with the African traditions of local decision-making. It tried to provide an alternative to Western capitalist society with its pursuit of profit, which most other African states seemed to be copying.

(b) *Success or failure?*

Despite Nyerere's achievements, it was clear when he retired in 1985 that his experiment had been, at best, only a limited success. At an international conference on the Arusha Declaration (held December 1986), President Mwinyi gave some impressive social statistics which few other African countries could match: 3.7 million children in primary school; two universities with over 4500 students; a literacy rate of 85 per cent; 150 hospitals and 2600 dispensaries; infant mortality down to 137 per thousand; life expectancy up to 52.

However, other parts of the Arusha Declaration were not achieved: corruption crept in because many officials were not as high-minded as Nyerere himself. There was insufficient investment in agriculture so that production was far below what was expected. The nationalization of the sisal estates carried out in the 1960s was a failure – Nyerere himself admitted that production had declined from 220 000 tonnes in 1970 to only 47 000 tonnes in 1984, and in May 1985 he reversed the nationalization. From the end of 1978 Tanzania was in difficulties because of the fall in world prices of coffee and tea (her main exports), rising oil prices (which used up almost half her earnings from exports) and the expense of the war against Amin in Uganda (at least £1000 million). Although oil prices began to fall during 1981, there was soon the problem of the near collapse of her other exports (cattle, cement and agricultural produce), which left her without foreign exchange. Loans from the International Monetary Fund only brought her the added problem of how to meet the interest repayments. Tanzania was nowhere near being a socialist state, nor was it self-sufficient – two major aims of the Declaration.

Nevertheless Nyerere was deservedly highly respected both as an African and world statesman, as an enemy of apartheid in South Africa, and as an outspoken critic of the world economy and the way it exploited poor countries. He played a vital role in the overthrow of Idi Amin, the brutal dictator who ruled Uganda from 1971 until 1979. Nyerere's prestige was at its height when he was chosen as chairman of the Organization of African Unity (OAU) for 1984–5.

Nyerere's successor, President Mwinyi, while keeping to the one-party system, began to move away from strict government control, allowing more private enterprise and a mixed economy. He was re-elected for further five-year terms in 1990 and again in 1995.

22.5 The Congo/Zaire

(a) *Why and how did civil war develop?*

Section 21.6(b) explained how the Belgians suddenly allowed the Congo to become independent in June 1960, with completely inadequate preparations. There was no experienced group of Africans to which power could be handed over. The Congolese had not been educated for professional jobs, very few had received any higher education and no political parties had been allowed. This did not mean that civil war was inevitable, but there were added complications.

1   *There were about 150 different tribes, which would have made the Congo difficult to hold together even with experienced administrators.* Violent and chaotic elections were held in which the Congolese National Movement (MNC) led by a former post office clerk, Patrice Lumumba, emerged as the dominant party; but there were over fifty different groups. Agreement of any sort was going to be difficult; nevertheless the Belgians handed power over to a coalition government with Lumumba as Prime Minister, and Joseph Kasavubu, the leader of another group, as President.

2   *A mutiny broke out in the Congolese army (July 1960) only a few days after independence.* This was in protest against the fact that all officers were Belgians, whereas the Africans expected instant promotion. Lumumba was deprived of the means of keeping law and order, and tribal violence began to spread.

3   *The south-eastern province of Katanga*, which had rich copper deposits, was encouraged by the Belgian company (*Union Minière*) which still controlled the copper-mining industry, to declare itself independent under *Moise Tshombe*. This

was the wealthiest part of the Congo which the new state could not afford to lose. Lumumba, unable to rely on his mutinous army, appealed to the United Nations to help him preserve Congolese unity, and a 3000-strong peace-keeping force soon arrived.

(b) *The civil war and the role of the UN*

Lumumba wanted to use UN troops to force Katanga back into the Congo, but the situation was complex. Many Belgians preferred an independent Katanga which would be easier for them to influence, and they wanted to continue their control of the copper-mining. With this in mind, the UN Secretary-General, Dag Hammarskjöld, refused to allow a UN attack on Katanga, though at the same time he refused to recognize Katangese independence. In disgust Lumumba appealed for help to the Russians, but this horrified Kasavubu, who, encouraged by the Americans and Belgians, had Lumumba arrested (he was later murdered). As the chaos continued, Hammarskjöld realized that more decisive UN action was needed, and although he was killed in an air crash while flying to Katanga to see Tshombe, his successor, U Thant, followed the same line. By mid-1961 there were 20 000 UN troops in the Congo; in September they invaded Katanga and in December 1962 the province admitted failure and ended its secession; Tshombe went into exile.

Though successful, UN operations had been expensive, and within a few months all their troops were withdrawn. Tribal rivalries aggravated by unemployment caused disorders to break out again almost immediately, and calm was not restored until 1965, when General Joseph Mobutu of the Congolese army, using white mercenaries and backed by the USA and Belgium, crushed all resistance and took over the government himself.

(c) *General Mobutu in power*

It was probably inevitable that if the Congo, with its many problems (an under-developed economy, tribal divisions and a shortage of educated people), was to stay united, a strong authoritarian government was required. Mobutu provided exactly that! There was a gradual improvement in conditions as the Congolese gained experience of administration, and the economy began to look healthier after most of the European-owned mines were nationalized.

However, in the late 1970s there were more troubles. In 1977 Katanga (now known as Shaba) was invaded by troops from Angola, apparently encouraged by the Angolan government, which resented Mobutu's earlier intervention in her affairs (see Section 21.6(d)), and by the USSR which resented American support for Mobutu. This was a way for the USSR to make a gesture against the Americans, and yet another extension of the Cold War.

Having survived that problem, Zaire found itself in economic difficulties, mainly because of declining world copper prices, and drought which made expensive food imports necessary. Mobutu came under increasing criticism outside Zaire for his authoritarian style of government and his huge personal fortune. In May 1980 Amnesty International claimed that at least a thousand political prisoners were being held without trial and that several hundred had died from torture or starvation during 1978–9. In 1990 he promised to allow a multi-party system, but with himself above politics as head of state; his rule became more and more corrupt and unpopular. During 1996 his health began to fail; he underwent surgery for prostate cancer and spent a long time convalescing in the south of France. Meanwhile rebel forces, led by Laurent Kabila and supported by the Rwandan government, gathered strength and by the end of the year they controlled much of eastern Zaire.

22.6 Angola

(a) *Civil war escalates*

Section 21.6(d) described how Angola was engulfed by civil war immediately after gaining independence from Portugal in 1975. Part of the problem was that there were three different liberation movements which started to fight each other almost as soon as independence was declared.

- The **MPLA** (Popular Movement for the Liberation of Angola) was a Marxist-style party which tried to appeal across tribal divisions to all Angolans. It was the MPLA which claimed to be the new government, with its leader, Agostinho Neto, as president.
- **UNITA** (National Union for the Total Independence of Angola) with its leader, Jonas Savimbi, drew much of its support from the Ovimbundu tribe in the south of the country.
- **FNLA** (National Liberation Front); much weaker than the other two, it drew much of its support from the Bakongo tribe in the northwest.

Alarm bells immediately rang in the USA, which did not like the look of the Marxist MPLA. The Americans therefore decided to back the FNLA (which was also supported by President Mobutu of Zaire) which was encouraged to attack the MPLA. UNITA also launched an offensive against the MPLA. Cuba sent troops to help the MPLA, while South African troops supporting the other two groups, invaded Angola via neighbouring Namibia in the south. General Mobutu also sent troops in from Zaire to the north-east of Angola. No doubt there would have been fighting and bloodshed anyway, but outside interference and the extension of the Cold War to Angola certainly made the conflict much worse.

(b) *Angola and Namibia*

The problem of Namibia also complicated the situation. Lying between Angola and South Africa, Namibia (formerly German South West Africa) had been handed to South Africa in 1919 at the end of the First World War, to be prepared for independence. The white South African government had ignored UN orders and delayed handing Namibia over to black majority rule as long as possible. The Namibian liberation movement, *SWAPO* (South West Africa People's Organization) and its leader, *Sam Nujoma*, began a guerrilla campaign against South Africa. After 1975 the MPLA allowed SWAPO to have bases in southern Angola, so it was not surprising that the South African government was so hostile to the MPLA.

(c) *The Lisbon Peace Accords (May 1991)*

The civil war dragged on right through the 1980s until changing international circumstances brought the possibility of peace. In December 1988 the UN managed to arrange a peace settlement in which South Africa agreed to withdraw from Namibia provided that the 50 000 Cuban troops left Angola. This agreement went ahead: *Namibia became independent under the leadership of Sam Nujoma (1990)*. The end of the Cold War and of communist rule in Eastern Europe meant that all communist support for the MPLA ceased, all Cuban troops had gone home by June 1991, and South Africa was ready to end her involvement. The UN, the Organization of African Unity (OAU), the USA and Russia all played a part in setting up peace talks between the MPLA government of Angola and UNITA in Lisbon (the capital of Portugal). It was agreed that there should be a ceasefire followed by elections, to be monitored by the UN.

(d) *The failure of the peace*

At first all seemed to go well: the ceasefire held and elections took place in September 1992. The MPLA won 58 per cent of the seats (129) in parliament, UNITA only 31 per cent (70 seats). Although the presidential election was much more close – MPLA president José Eduardo Dos Santos won 49.57 per cent of the votes, with Jonas Savimbi (UNITA) taking 40.07 per cent – it was still a clear and decisive victory for the MPLA.

However, Savimbi and UNITA refused to accept the result, claiming that there had been fraud, even though the elections had been monitored by 400 UN observers; the leader of the UN team reported that the election had been 'generally free and fair'. Tragically UNITA, instead of accepting defeat gracefully, renewed the civil war, which was fought with increasing bitterness. By the end of January 1994 the UN reported that there were 3.3 million refugees and that an average of a thousand people a day, mainly civilians, were dying. The UN had too few personnel in Angola to bring the fighting to an end. This time the outside world could not be blamed for the civil war: this was clearly the fault of UNITA. *However, many observers blamed the USA for encouraging UNITA:* shortly before the Lisbon agreement, President Reagan officially met Savimbi in the USA, which made him seem like an equal with the MPLA government instead of a rebel leader. At the same time the USA had not officially recognized the MPLA as the legal government of Angola, even after the elections; it was not until May 1993, six months after UNITA had resumed the war, that the USA finally gave recognition to the MPLA government.

A ceasefire was eventually negotiated in October 1994 and a peace agreement reached in November. UNITA, which was losing the war by that time, accepted the 1992 election result, and in return would be allowed to play a part in what would be, in effect, a coalition government. Early in 1995, 7000 UN troops arrived to help enforce the agreement and supervise the transition to peace.

22.7 Burundi and Rwanda

The Belgians left these two small states, like the Congo, completely unprepared for independence. In both states there was an explosive mixture of two tribes – the *Tutsi* and the *Hutu*. The Hutus were in a majority but the Tutsis were the élite ruling group. There was continuous tension and skirmishing between the two tribes right from independence day in 1962.

(a) *Burundi*

There was a mass rising of Hutus against the ruling Tutsis in 1972: this was savagely put down, and over 100 000 Hutus were killed. In 1988 Hutu soldiers in the Burundi army massacred thousands of Tutsis. In 1993 the country held its first democratic elections and for the first time a Hutu president was chosen. Tutsi soldiers soon murdered the new president, but other members of the Hutu government were able to escape. As Hutus carried out reprisal killings against Tutsis, massacre followed massacre, and *the country disintegrated into chaos*. Eventually the army imposed a power-sharing agreement on the country: the Prime Minister was to be a Tutsi, the President a Hutu, but most of the power was concentrated in the hands of the Tutsi Prime Minister.

Fighting continued into 1996, and the Organization of African Unity which sent a peacekeeping force (the first time it had ever taken such action) was unable to prevent the continuing massacres and ethnic cleansing. The economy was in ruins, agricultural production seriously reduced because much of the rural population had fled, and the government seemed to have no ideas about how to end the war. *The outside world and the great powers showed little concern* – their interests were not involved or threatened – and the conflict in Burundi was not given much coverage in the world's media. In July 1996, the army overthrew the divided government, and Major Pierre Buyoya (a Tutsi moderate) declared himself president. He claimed that this was not a normal coup – the army had seized power in order to save lives.

(b) *Rwanda*

Tribal warfare began in 1959 before independence, and reached its first big climax in 1963, when the Hutus, fearing a Tutsi invasion from Burundi, massacred thousands of Rwandan Tutsis and overthrew the Tutsi government. In 1990 fighting broke out between the Tutsi-dominated Rwandese Patriotic Front (RPF), which was based over the border in Uganda, and the official Rwandan army (Hutu-dominated). This lasted off and on until 1993 when the UN helped to negotiate a peace settlement between the Rwandan government (Hutu) and the RPF (Tutsi). 2500 UN troops were sent to monitor the transition to peace (October 1993).

For a few months all seemed to be going well, and then disaster struck. The aircraft bringing the Hutu President of Rwanda and the Burundian President back from talks in Tanzania was brought down by a missile as it approached Kigali (the capital of Rwanda), killing both presidents (April 1994). This sparked off the most horrifying tribal slaughter: Hutus murdered all Tutsis they could lay hands on, including women and children. The Tutsi RPF marched on the capital; UN observers reported that the streets of Kigali were literally running with blood and the corpses were piled high. The small UN force was not equipped to deal with violence on this scale, and it soon withdrew. The civil war and the genocide continued through into June, by which time something like half a million Tutsis had been murdered by Hutu government forces and Hutu militia. It seemed to be a deliberate and carefully planned attempt to wipe out the entire Tutsi population of Rwanda. In addition, about a million Tutsi refugees had fled into neighbouring Tanzania and Zaire.

Meanwhile the rest of the world, though outraged and horrified by the scale of the genocide, did nothing to stop it; only France mounted a small expedition which offered protection to civilians during August and September 1994. By this time the RPF were beginning to get the upper hand: the Hutu government was driven out and a Tutsi RPF government set up in Kigali. In 1996 this new government was still trying to make its authority felt over the whole country, but it was a slow process. No real peace agreement was reached. Tutsis were still being slaughtered; Hutu moderates who were prepared to work with the Tutsi government and were willing to give evidence against the Hutus responsible for the 1994 massacres,were being murdered by Hutu extremists. The prospects for reconciliation were not good in the immediate future.

Towards the end of 1996 fighting broke out in the refugee camps in eastern Zaire, which housed almost a million Hutus who had left Rwanda after the Tutsi victory in 1994. Zairean Tutsi rebels (who controlled the large areas of eastern Zaire), supported by the Rwandan government army (Tutsi), attacked the remnants of the Hutu army and the Hutu militias (*interahamwe*), which had fled from Rwanda after their defeat. This new conflict was really a continuation of the 1994 Rwandan civil war. The defeated Hutu army and militias were planning to invade Rwanda and overthrow the Tutsi RPF government, while the Tutsis were determined to do all in their power to wipe out the Hutu extremists.

The militias used the camps as bases – innocent refugees were caught up in the fighting, and the militias used them as hostages, preventing them from returning home to Rwanda and preventing food supplies reaching them. The problems seemed complex:

- to get enough food into the camps to feed about a million refugees, many of whom were on the verge of starvation;
- to separate the extremist militias from the innocent civilian refugees and return them to Rwanda to face trial for genocide. Many people thought that only a large international military force would be strong enough to achieve this;
- to organize the return of the Hutu civilian refugees to Rwanda.

Fighting reached a climax in November 1996: just as the international community was preparing to send a force of 15 000 troops to eastern Zaire, with UN authorization, Zairean rebel forces and Rwandan Tutsi troops defeated the Hutu militias and broke their control over the refugees. Many of the Hutu extremists fled into the hills and their future was uncertain. The refugees were now free to return home and most of them streamed back over the border into Rwanda. They were prepared to take their chance as Hutus in a Tutsi-controlled country rather than remain any longer in the miserable camps. But the violence was still not over: in January 1997 a new wave of killings began as Hutu extremists launched a campaign against Tutsis who survived the 1994 massacres. Foreign aid workers and UN staff accused by the Hutus of helping the Rwandan government also came under attack.

22.8 South Africa

(a) The formation of the Union of South Africa

South Africa has had a complicated history. The first Europeans to settle there permanently were members of the *Dutch East India Company* who founded a colony at the Cape of Good Hope in 1652. It remained a Dutch colony until 1795, and during that time, the Dutch, who were known as *Afrikaners* or *Boers* (a word meaning 'farmers'), took land away from the native Africans and forced them to work as labourers, treating them as little better than slaves. They also brought more labourers in from Asia, Mozambique and Madagascar.

In 1795 the Cape was captured by the British during the French Revolutionary Wars, and the 1814 peace settlement decided that it should remain British. Many British settlers went out to Cape Colony. The Dutch settlers became restless under British rule, especially when the British government made all slaves free throughout the British Empire (1838). The Boer farmers felt that this threatened their livelihood, and many of them decided to leave Cape Colony. They moved northwards (in what became known as the *Great Trek*) and set up their own independent republics of the Transvaal and Orange Free State (1835–40). Some also moved into the area east of Cape Colony known as Natal. In the *Boer War (1899–1902)* the British defeated the Transvaal and the Orange Free State, and in 1910 they joined up with Cape Colony and Natal to form *the Union of South Africa*.

The population of the new state was mixed. Approximately:

> 70 per cent were black Africans known as Bantus;
> 18 per cent were whites of European origin; of these about 60 per cent were Dutch, the rest British;
> 9 per cent were of mixed race, known as 'coloureds';
> 3 per cent were Asians.

Although they made up the vast majority of the population, black Africans suffered even worse discrimination than black people in the USA.

- The whites dominated politics and the economic life of the new state, and, with only a few exceptions, blacks were not allowed to vote.
- Black people had to do most of the manual work in factories and on farms and were expected to live in areas reserved for them away from white residential areas. These reserved areas made up only about 7 per cent of the total area of South Africa and were not large enough to enable the Africans to produce sufficient food for themselves and to pay all their taxes. Black Africans were forbidden to buy land outside the reserves.
- The government controlled the movement of blacks by a system of *pass laws*. For example, a black person could not live in a town unless he had a pass showing he was working in a white-owned business. An African could not leave the farm where he worked without a pass from his employer.
- Living and working conditions for blacks were primitive; for example, in the goldmining industry, Africans had to live in single-sex compounds with sometimes as many as 90 men sharing a dormitory.
- By a law of 1911 black workers were forbidden to strike and were barred from holding skilled jobs.

(b) *Dr Malan introduces apartheid*

After the Second World War there were important changes in the way black Africans were treated. Under Prime Minister Malan (1948–54) a new policy called *apartheid (separateness)* was introduced. This tightened up control over blacks still further. *Why was apartheid introduced?*

- When India and Pakistan were given independence in 1947, white South Africans became alarmed at the growing racial equality within the Commonwealth, and they were determined to preserve their supremacy.
- Most of the whites, especially those of Dutch origin, were against racial equality, but the most extreme were the Afrikaner Nationalist Party led by Dr Malan. They claimed that whites were a master race, and that non-whites were inferior beings. The Dutch Reformed Church (the official state church of South Africa) supported this view and quoted passages from the Bible which, they claimed, proved their theory. This was very much out of line with the rest of the Christian churches which believe in racial equality.
- The Nationalists won the 1948 elections with promises to rescue the whites from the 'black menace' and to preserve the racial purity of the whites. This would help to ensure continued white supremacy.

(c) *Apartheid developed further*

Apartheid was continued and developed further by the Prime Ministers who followed Malan: Strijdom (1954–8), Verwoerd (1958–66) and Vorster (1966–78).

The main features of apartheid

1 *There was complete separation of blacks and whites as far as possible at all levels.* In country areas blacks had to live in special reserves; in urban areas they had separate townships built at suitable distances from the white residential areas. If an existing black township was thought to be too close to a 'white' area, the whole

community was uprooted and 're-grouped' somewhere else to make separation as complete as possible. There were separate buses, coaches, trains, cafes, toilets, park benches, hospitals, beaches, picnic areas, sports and even churches. Black children went to separate schools and were given a much inferior education. But there was a flaw in the system: *complete separation was impossible because over half the non-white population worked in white-owned mines, factories and other businesses.* The economy would have collapsed if all non-whites had been moved to reserves.

2   *Every person was given a racial classification and an identity card.* There were strict pass laws which meant that black Africans had to stay in their reserves or in their townships unless they were travelling to a white area to work, in which case they would be issued with passes. Otherwise all travelling was forbidden without police permission.

3   *Marriage and sexual relations between whites and non-whites were forbidden*; this was to preserve the purity of the white race. Police spied shamelessly on anybody suspected of breaking the rules.

4   *The Bantu Self-Government Act (1959)* set up seven regions called *Bantustans*, based on the original African reserves. It was claimed that they would eventually move towards self-government. In 1969 it was announced that the first Bantustan, the *Transkei*, had become 'independent'. However, the outside world dismissed this with contempt since the South African government continued to control the Transkei's economy and foreign affairs. The whole policy was criticized because the Bantustan areas covered only about 13 per cent of the country's total area; over 8 million black people were crammed into these relatively small areas, which were vastly overcrowded and unable to support the black populations adequately. They became very little better than rural slums. But the government took no notice of the protests and continued its policy; by 1980 two more African 'homelands', *Bophuthatswana and Venda*, had received 'independence'.

5   *Africans lost all political rights*, and their representation in parliament, which had been by white MPs, was abolished.

(d) *Opposition to apartheid*

1   Inside South Africa

Inside South Africa, *opposition to the system was difficult.* Anyone who objected, including whites, or broke the apartheid laws, was accused of being a communist and was severely punished under the *Suppression of Communism Act.* Africans were forbidden to strike, and their political party, the African National Congress (ANC), was helpless. *In spite of this, protests did take place.*

●   *Chief Albert Luthuli*, the ANC leader, organized a protest campaign in which black Africans stopped work on certain days. In 1952 Africans attempted a systematic breach of the laws by entering shops and other places reserved for whites. Over 8000 blacks were arrested and many were flogged. Luthuli was deprived of his chieftaincy and put in jail for a time, and the campaign was called off.

●   *In 1955 the ANC formed a coalition with Asian and coloured groups*, and at a massive open-air meeting at Kliptown (near Johannesburg), they just had time to announce *a freedom charter* before police broke up the crowd. *The charter soon became the main ANC programme.* It began by declaring: 'South Africa belongs to all who live in it, black and white, and no government can claim authority unless it is based on the will of the people'. It went on to demand:

—equality before the law;
—freedom of assembly, movement, speech, religion and the press;
—the right to vote:
—the right to work, with equal pay for equal work;
—40-hour working week, minimum wage and unemployment benefits;
—free medical care;
—free, compulsory and equal education.

- *Church leaders and missionaries*, both black and white, spoke out against apartheid. They included people like Trevor Huddleston, a British missionary who had been working in South Africa since 1943.
- *Later the ANC organized other protests, including the 1957 bus boycott:* instead of paying a fare increase on the bus route from their township to Johannesburg ten miles away, thousands of Africans walked to work and back for three months until fares were reduced.
- *Protests reached a climax in 1960* when a huge demonstration took place against the pass laws at *Sharpeville*, an African township near Johannesburg. Police fired on the crowd, killing sixty-seven Africans and wounding many more (Illus. 22.4). After this, 15 000 Africans were arrested and the ANC banned. Hundreds of people were beaten by police. This was an important turning-point in the campaign: until then most of the protests had been non-violent; but this brutal treatment by the authorities convinced many black leaders that violence could only be met with violence. There was a spate of bomb attacks, but the police soon clamped down, arresting most of the black leaders, like *Nelson Mandela* (Illus. 22.5), who was sentenced to life imprisonment (see Question 2 at the end of the chapter). Chief Luthuli still persevered with non-violent protests and after publishing his moving autobiography *Let My People Go*, he was awarded the Nobel Peace Prize. He was killed in 1967, the authorities claiming that he had deliberately stepped in front of a train.
- *Discontent and protest increased again in the 1970s* because wages of Africans failed to keep pace with inflation. In 1976, when the Transvaal authorities announced that Afrikaans (the language spoken by whites of Dutch descent) was to be used in black

Illus. 22.4 Bodies litter the ground after the Sharpeville massacre, 1960

Illus. 22.5 Nelson Mandela in 1962, before his long imprisonment

African schools, massive demonstrations took place at *Soweto*, a black township near Johannesburg. Although there were many children and young people in the crowd, police opened fire, killing at least 200 black Africans. This time the protests did not die down; they spread over the whole country. Again the government responded with brutality: over the next six months a further 500 Africans were killed; among the victims was *Steve Biko*, a young African leader who had been urging people to be proud of their blackness. He was beaten to death by police (1976).

2   Outside South Africa

Outside South Africa there was *opposition to apartheid from the rest of the Commonwealth*. Early in 1960 the British Conservative Prime Minister, Harold Macmillan, had the courage to speak out against it in Cape Town; he spoke about the growing strength of African nationalism: 'the wind of change is blowing through the continent ... our national policies must take account of it'. His warnings were ignored, and shortly afterwards, the world was horrified by the Sharpeville massacre. At the 1961 Commonwealth Conference, criticism of South Africa was intense, and many thought she would be expelled. In the end Verwoerd withdrew South Africa's application for continued membership (in 1960 she had decided to become a republic instead of a dominion, thereby severing the connection with the British crown; because of this she had to apply for readmission to the Commonwealth), and she ceased to a member of the Commonwealth.

3 The UN and the OAU

The United Nations and the Organization of African Unity condemned apartheid and were particularly critical of the continued South African occupation of South West Africa (see above Section 22.6(b)). The UN voted to place an *economic boycott* on South Africa (1962), but this proved useless because not all member states supported it. Britain, the USA, France, West Germany and Italy condemned apartheid in public, but continued to trade with South Africa. Among other things, they sold South Africa massive arms supplies, apparently hoping she would prove to be a bastion against the spread of communism in Africa. Consequently Verwoerd (until his assassination in 1966) and his successor Vorster (1966–78) were able to ignore the protests from the outside world until well into the 1970s.

(e) *The end of apartheid*

The system of apartheid continued without any concessions being made to black people, until 1980.

1 P.W. Botha

The new Prime Minister, P.W. Botha (elected 1979), realized that all was not well with the system. He decided that he must reform apartheid, dropping some of the most unpopular aspects in an attempt to preserve white control. *What caused this change?*

● *Criticism from abroad* (from the Commonwealth, the United Nations and the Organization of African Unity) gradually gathered momentum. External pressures became much greater in 1975 when the white-ruled Portuguese colonies of Angola and Mozambique achieved independence after a long struggle (see Section 21.6(d)). The African takeover of Zimbabwe (1980) removed the last of the white-ruled states which had been sympathetic to the South African government and apartheid. Now she was surrounded by hostile black states, and many Africans in these new states had sworn never to rest until their fellow-Africans in South Africa had been liberated.
● *There were economic problems* – South Africa was hit by recession in the late 1970s, and many white people were worse off. Whites began to emigrate in large numbers, but the black population was increasing. In 1980 whites were only 16 per cent of the population, whereas between the two world wars they had formed 21 per cent.
● *The African homelands were a failure:* they were poverty-stricken, their rulers were corrupt and no foreign government recognized them as genuinely independent states.
● *The USA*, which was treating its own black people better during the 1970s, began to criticize the South African government's racist policy.

In a speech in September 1979 which astonished many of his Nationalist supporters, the newly elected Prime Minister Botha said:

> A revolution in South Africa is no longer just a remote possibility. Either we adapt or we perish. White domination and legally enforced apartheid are a recipe for permanent conflict.

He went on to suggest that the black homelands must be made viable and that unnecessary discrimination must be abolished. *Gradually he introduced some important changes which he hoped would be enough to silence the critics both inside and outside South Africa:*

- blacks were allowed to join trades unions and to go on strike (1979);
- blacks were allowed to elect their own local township councils (but not to vote in national elections) (1981);
- a new constitution was introduced setting up two new houses of parliament, one for coloureds and one for Asians (but not for Africans). The new system was weighted so that the whites kept overall control. It came into force in 1984;
- sexual relations and marriage were allowed between people of different races (1985);
- the hated pass laws for non-whites were abolished (1986).

This was as far as Botha was prepared to go. He would not even consider the ANC's main demands (the right to vote and to play a full part in ruling the country). Far from being won over by these concessions, black Africans were incensed that the new constitution made no provision for them, and were determined to settle for nothing less than full political rights.

Violence escalated, with both sides guilty of excesses. The ANC used the 'necklace', a tyre placed round the victim's neck and set on fire, to murder black councillors and black police, who were regarded as collaborators with apartheid. On the twenty-fifth anniversary of Sharpeville, police opened fire on a procession of black mourners going to a funeral near Uitenhage (Port Elizabeth), killing over forty people (March 1985). In July a state of emergency was declared in the worst affected areas, and it was extended to the whole country in June 1986. This gave the police the power to arrest people without warrants and freedom from all criminal proceedings; thousands of people were arrested, and newspapers, radio and TV were banned from reporting demonstrations and strikes.

However, as so often happens when an authoritarian regime tries to reform itself, it proved impossible to stop the process of change (the same happened in the USSR when Gorbachev tried to reform communism). *By the late 1980s international pressure on South Africa was having more effect, and internal attitudes had changed.*

- *In August 1986 the Commonwealth (except Britain) agreed on a strong package of sanctions* (no further loans, no sales of oil, computer equipment or nuclear goods to South Africa, and no cultural and scientific contacts). British Prime Minister Margaret Thatcher would commit Britain only to a voluntary ban on investment in South Africa. Her argument was that severe economic sanctions would worsen the plight of black Africans, who would be thrown out of their jobs. This caused the rest of the Commonwealth to feel bitter against Britain; Rajiv Gandhi, the Indian Prime Minister, accused Mrs Thatcher of 'compromising on basic principles and values for economic ends'.
- *In September 1986 the USA joined the fray* when Congress voted (over President Reagan's veto) to stop American loans to South Africa, to cut airlinks and to ban imports of iron, steel, coal, textiles and uranium from South Africa.
- *The black population was no longer just a mass of uneducated and unskilled labourers:* there was a steadily growing number of well-educated, professional, middle-class black people, some of them holding important positions, like *Desmond Tutu*, who was awarded the Nobel Peace Prize in 1984 and became Anglican Archbishop of Cape Town in 1986.
- The Dutch Reformed Church, which had once supported apartheid, now

condemned it as incompatible with Christianity. *A majority of white South Africans* now recognized that it was difficult to defend the total exclusion of blacks from the country's political life. So although they were nervous about what might happen, they were resigned to the idea of black majority rule at some time in the future. White moderates were therefore prepared to make the best of the situation and get the best deal possible.

2 F.W. de Klerk

The new President, F.W. de Klerk (elected 1989), had a reputation for caution, but privately he had decided that apartheid would have to go completely, and he accepted that black majority rule must come eventually. The problem was how to achieve it without further violence and possible civil war. With great courage and determination, and in the face of bitter opposition from right-wing Afrikaner groups, *de Klerk gradually moved the country towards black majority rule:*

* Nelson Mandela was released after 27 years in jail (1990) and became leader of the ANC, which was made legal;
* most of the remaining apartheid laws were dropped;
* Namibia, the neighbouring territory ruled by South Africa since 1919, was given independence under a black government (1990);
* talks began in 1991 between the government and the ANC to work out a new constitution which would allow blacks full political rights.

Meanwhile the ANC was doing its best to present itself as a moderate party which had no plans for wholesale nationalization, and to reassure whites that they would be safe and happy under black rule. Nelson Mandela condemned violence and called for reconciliation between blacks and whites. The negotiations were long and difficult; de Klerk had to face right-wing opposition from his own National Party and from various extreme white racialist groups who claimed that he had betrayed them. The ANC was involved in a power struggle with another black party, *the Natal-based Zulu Inkatha Freedom party led by Chief Buthelezi.*

3 Transition to black majority rule

In the spring of 1993 the talks were successful and agreement was reached about how to carry through the transition to black majority rule. A general election was held and the ANC won almost two-thirds of the votes. As had been agreed, a coalition government of the ANC, National Party and Inkatha took office with Nelson Mandela as the first black president of South Africa and F.W. de Klerk as the deputy president (May 1994). Although there had been violence and bloodshed, it was a remarkable achievement, for which both de Klerk and Mandela deserve the credit, that South Africa was able to move from apartheid to black majority rule without civil war (Illus. 22.6). A new constitution was agreed, to come into operation after the elections of 1999, which would not allow minority parties to take part in the government. When this was revealed (May 1996), the Nationalists immediately announced that they would withdraw from the government at the end of June. Many observers saw this as a crisis which Mandela could well do without. As the country moved towards the millenium, the main problems facing the president were how to maintain sound financial and economic policies, while at the same time bringing about the promised improvements in the living standards of black people. And now this had to be achieved by the ANC alone, without the expertise of the National Party.

Illus. 22.6 De Klerk and Mandela

Questions

1 *Civil war in the Congo* Study Sources A, B and C and answer the questions which follow.

___ Source A ___

A statement by Mr Eyskens, the Prime Minister of Belgium, in the Belgian Senate, 12 July 1960

Legally, Belgium cannot recognise the independence of Katanga in the present circumstances, but the Congo is independent and can obviously modify the Law which we gave her. It may develop towards a federal constitution. We cannot get ourselves involved in this. But here is a government – Mr Tshombe's government – which seems to be taking decisions in certain fields, has a parliamentary majority and is trying to re-establish order. I prefer the presence of such a government to the confusion and disorder which the Communists want so that they can increase their influence.

___ Source B ___

Telegram from Mr Lumumba, Prime Minister of the Congolese Republic, to Dag Hammarskjöld, Secretary-General of the UN, asking for UN military help in view of the Belgian action in sending more troops to the Congo, 13 July 1960

The Belgians have acted in violation of the Treaty of Friendship which said that Belgian troops can only intervene at the express request of the Congolese government. No such request has been made and the Belgian action therefore constitututes an act of aggression against the Congo. The real cause of most of the disorder lies in colonialist provocations. We accuse the Belgian government of having prepared the secession (withdrawal) of Katanga in order to preserve its power over our country. The overwhelming majority of the Katangese population is opposed to secession. Our request for military aid is aimed at the protection of the Congo against the present foreign aggression. We strongly emphasise the extreme urgency of sending UN troops to the Congo.

Source: Sources A and B are taken from *Keesing's Contemporary Archives, 1960*

Source C

The view of Basil Davidson, a modern expert on African affairs

Up till 1959 the Belgians believed that 'their' Congo would remain theirs for perhaps another hundred years, but *they suddenly changed their strategy*. Independence came in June 1960, with Lumumba as Prime Minister, but so did confusion and disaster. Most of the Belgian civil servants went home at once, soldiers mutinied, and Katanga lost no time in trying to form its own independent government. Foreign business interests saw that this separatism in Katanga could safeguard their interests, and so supported it.

Source: Basil Davidson, *Modern Africa, a Social and Political History* (Longman, 1989 edition)

(a)   Source C says that the Belgians 'suddenly changed their strategy' towards the Congo. Using information from Section 21.6(b)), explain why this sudden change took place.   1.4b, 4c, 6c; 3.4   7 marks
(b)   How do the three sources differ in their explanations of what was causing the disorder and chaos in the Congo?   1.4b–6b, 6c–8c; 3.4   9 marks
(c)   Comment on the reliability of each of the three sources.   3.7   6 marks
(d)   'The crisis in the Congo was effectively brought to an end by the intervention of the United Nations'. Using information from Section 22.5(b), explain whether you agree or disagree with this statement.   1.4c–5c   8 marks
                                                                                        Total: 30 marks

2   *Apartheid in South Africa*   These sources are about some of the things that happened in South Africa during the time apartheid was in operation. Sources B, C and D are about the demonstration at Sharpeville in 1960, when police opened fire on the crowd. Study the sources carefully and then answer the questions which follow.

Source A

An eye-witness account by Trevor Huddleston, a white British missionary, of what happened when the black township of Sophiatown, where he had been working, was removed – February 1955

On the broad belt of grass between the European suburb of Westdene (in Johannesburg) and Sophiatown, a whole fleet of army lorries was drawn up: a grim sight against the grey, watery sky. Lining the whole street were thousands of police, both white and black, the former armed with both rifles and revolvers, the latter with clubs. A few Sten guns were in position at various points. Military lorries were drawn up, already piled high with the pathetic possessions which had come from the row of rooms in the background. The first lorries began to move off to Meadowlands eight miles to the west.

Source: Trevor Huddleston, *Naught for your Comfort* (Collins, 1956); quoted in Trevor Huddleston, *Return to Africa* (HarperCollins, 1991)

___ Source B ___

The police report of what happened at Sharpeville

The crowd at Sharpeville police station was between 15 000 and 20 000. In view of the provocative attitude of the crowd who were armed with sticks, stones and pieces of iron, it was feared that they would burst through the fence. Stones were thrown and two shots were fired from the crowd. The police opened fire; the officers emphasised that they had been with their backs to the wall facing a frenzied mob of 20 000 natives. If they had not fired they would have been overwhelmed.

___ Source C ___

Evidence taken from 100 wounded Africans in hospital; they all agreed that . . .

There were not more than 5000 Africans present; they were not carrying sticks or other arms and they had no violent intentions. The leader of the crowd said in English several times: 'We have come here to talk, not to fight'. He was arrested by police. Then without giving any warning or order to disperse, the white police opened fire.

___ Source D ___

Report from a senior Johannesburg surgeon

The post-mortem examinations which I made on 52 of the Africans showed that 70 per cent of the bullets had entered from the back.

Sources: Sources B, C and D are taken from *Keesing's Contemporary Archives, 1960*

___ Source E ___

Speech by Nelson Mandela in 1964 during his trial for sabotage

We of the ANC had always stood for a non-racial democracy, and we shrank from any policy which might drive the races further apart. But the hard facts were that 50 years of non-violence had brought the African people nothing but more and more repressive laws, and fewer and fewer rights. It would be unrealistic and wrong for African leaders to continue preaching non-violence at a time when the government met our peaceful demands with force.

Source: quoted in L. Thompson, *A History of South Africa* (Yale University Press, 1990)

(a) From the evidence of Source A and Section 22.8(b–c), why were the Africans being moved from Sophiatown?   1.4b–5b, 3.4   4 marks
(b) What differences can you find in the two accounts of the Sharpeville shootings given in Sources B and C?   1.4c–6c   5 marks
(c) Taking into account the information from Section 22.8 and Source D, which of the two do you think is the more reliable account?   1.7c–8c, 3.5–7   10 marks
(d) From the evidence of these sources and Section 22.8(d), what change was Nelson Mandela suggesting in Source E, and for what reasons?1.3a–4a, 2b–7b   11 marks

Total: 30 marks

PART VI

Global problems

The changing world economy since 1900

Summary of events

For much of the nineteenth century Britain led the rest of the world in industrial production and trade. In the last quarter of the century Germany and the USA began to catch up, and by 1914 the USA was the world's leading industrial nation. The First and Second World Wars caused important changes in the world economy. The USA gained most economically from both wars, and it was the USA which became economically dominant as the world's richest nation. Meanwhile Britain's economy slowly declined and it was not improved by the fact that Britain stayed outside the European Community until 1973. In spite of slumps and depressions, the general trend was for the relatively wealthy industrialized countries to get wealthier, while the poorer nations of Africa and Asia (known as the Third World), most of which were once colonies of the European states, became even poorer. However, some Third World countries began to industrialize and get richer, and this caused a split in the Third World bloc.

23.1 Changes in the world economy since 1900

In one sense in 1900 there was already a single world economy. A few highly industrialized countries, mainly the USA, Britain and Germany, provided the world's manufactured goods, while the rest of the world provided raw materials and food (known as 'primary products'). The USA treated Latin America (especially Mexico) as an area of 'influence', in the same way that the European states treated their colonies in Africa and elsewhere. European nations usually decided what should be produced in their colonies: the British made sure that Uganda and the Sudan grew cotton for their textile industry; the Portuguese did the same in Mozambique. They fixed the prices at which colonial products were sold as low as possible, and also fixed the prices of manufactured goods exported to the colonies as high as possible. In other words, as historian Basil Davidson puts it: 'the Africans had to sell cheap and buy dear'. *The twentieth century brought some important changes.*

(a) *The USA became the dominant industrial power*

As a result the rest of the world became more dependent on the USA.

In 1880 Britain produced roughly twice as much coal and pig-iron as the USA, but by 1900 the roles had been reversed: the USA produced more coal than Britain and about twice as much pig-iron and steel. This growing domination continued right through the century: in 1945 for example, incomes in the USA were twice as high as in Britain and seven times higher than in the USSR; during the next thirty years American production almost doubled again. *What were the causes of the American success?*

1 The First World War and after

The First World War and its aftermath gave a big boost to the American economy (see Section 19.3). Many countries which had bought goods from Europe during the war (such as China and the states of Latin America) were unable to get hold of supplies because the war disrupted trade. This caused them to buy goods from the USA (and also Japan) instead, and after the war they continued to do so. *The USA was the economic winner of the First World War* and became even richer thanks to the interest on the war loans they had made to Britain and her allies (see Section 4.4). Only the USA was rich enough to provide loans to encourage German recovery during the 1920s, but this had the unfortunate effect of linking Europe too closely with the USA financially and economically. When the USA suffered its great slump (1930–5) (see Section 19.4), Europe and the rest of the world were also thrown into depression. In 1933, in the depth of the depression, about 25 million were out of work in the USA and as many as 50 million in the world as a whole.

2 The Second World War

The Second World War left the USA as the world's greatest industrial (and military) power. The Americans entered the war relatively late and their industry did well out of supplying war materials for Britain and her allies. At the end of the war, with Europe almost at a standstill economically, the USA was producing 43 per cent of the world's iron ore, 45 per cent of its crude steel, 60 per cent of its railway locomotives and 74 per cent of its motor vehicles (see also Section 19.5(e)). When the war was over, the industrial boom continued as industry switched to producing consumer goods which had been in short supply during the war. Once again, only the USA was rich enough to help Western Europe, which it did with *Marshall Aid* (see Section 7.2(e)). It was not just that the Americans wanted to be kind to Europe: *they had at least two other ulterior motives:*

- a prosperous Western Europe would be able to buy American goods and thus keep the great American war-time boom going;
- a prosperous Western Europe would be less likely to go communist.

(b) *After 1945 the world split into capitalist and communist blocs*

- *The capitalist bloc* consisted of the highly developed industrial nations – the USA, Canada, Western Europe, Japan, Australia and New Zealand. They believed in private enterprise and private ownership of wealth, with profit as the great motivating influence, and ideally, a minimum of state interference.
- *The communist bloc* consisted of the USSR, its satellite states in eastern Europe, and later, China, North Korea and North Vietnam. They believed in state controlled, centrally planned economies, which, they argued, would eliminate the worst aspects of capitalism – slumps, unemployment and the unequal distribution of wealth.

The next forty or so years seemed like a contest to find out which economic system was best. The collapse of communism in Eastern Europe at the end of the 1980s (see Sections 10.7 and 16.7) enabled the supporters of capitalism to claim the final victory. However, communism still continued in China, North Korea, Vietnam and Cuba. This big contest between the two rival economic and political systems was known as the *Cold War*; it had important economic consequences. It meant that both blocs spent enormous amounts of cash on building nuclear weapons and other armaments (see Section 7.4), and on even more expensive space programmes. Many people argued that much of this money could have been spent helping to solve the problems of the world's poorer nations.

(c) *1970s and 1980s: the USA had serious economic problems*

● *Defence costs and the war in Vietnam (1961–75)* (see Section 8.3) were a constant drain on the economy and the treasury.
● *There was a budget deficit every year in the late 1960s.* This means that the government was spending more money than it was collecting in taxes, and the difference had to be covered by selling gold reserves. By 1971 the dollar, which was once considered to be as good as gold, was weakening in value.
● President Nixon was forced to *devalue the dollar* by about 12 per cent and to put a 10 per cent duty on most imports (1971).
● *Rising oil prices* worsened America's balance of payments deficit, and led to the development of more nuclear power.
● President Reagan (1981–9) refused to cut defence spending and tried *new economic policies recommended by the American economist, Milton Friedman.* He argued that governments should abandon all attempts to plan their economies and concentrate on *monetarism*: this meant exercising a tight control on the money supply by keeping interest rates high. His theory was that this would force businesses to be more efficient. These were policies which Margaret Thatcher was already trying in Britain. At first the new ideas seemed to be working – in the mid-1980s unemployment fell and America was prosperous again. But the basic problem of the US economy – the huge budget deficit – refused to go away, mainly because of high defence spending. The Americans were even reduced to borrowing from Japan, whose economy was extremely successful at that time. The drain on American gold reserves weakened the dollar, and also weakened confidence in the economy. There was a sudden and dramatic fall in share prices (1987) which was followed by similar falls all over the world. In the late 1980s much of the world was suffering from a trade recession.

(d) *Japan's success*

Japan became economically one of the world's most successful states. At the end of the Second World War Japan was defeated and her economy was in ruins. She soon began to recover, and during the 1970s and 1980s, Japanese economic expansion was dramatic, as the following statistics of Gross National Product (GNP) per head show:

Year	$
1955	200
1978	7 300
1987	15 800
1990	27 000

(For full details see Section 14.2.)

23.2 The Third World and the North–South divide

During the 1950s the term *Third World* began to be used to describe countries which were not part of the First World (the industrialized capitalist nations) or the Second World (the industrialized communist states). The Third World states grew rapidly in number during the 1950s and 1960s as the European empires broke up and newly independent states emerged. By 1970 the Third World consisted of Africa, Asia (except the USSR and China), India, Pakistan, Bangladesh, Latin America and the Middle East. They were almost all once colonies or mandates of European powers, and were left in an undeveloped or under-developed state when they achieved independence.

(a) *The Third World and non-alignment*

The Third World states were in favour of non-alignment, which means that they did not want to get involved with either the capitalist or the communist bloc, and they were very suspicious of the motives of both of them. Prime Minister Nehru of India (1947–64) saw himself as a sort of unofficial leader of the Third World, which he thought could be a powerful force for world peace. Third World countries deeply resented the fact that both blocs continued to interfere in their internal affairs (neo-colonialism). The USA, for example, interfered unashamedly in the affairs of Central and South America, helping to overthrow governments which they did not approve of; this happened in Guatemala (1954), the Dominican Republic (1965) and Chile (1973). Britain, France and the USSR interfered in the Middle East. Frequent meetings of Third World leaders were held, and in 1979, ninety-two nations were represented at a 'non-aligned' conference in Havana (Cuba). By this time the Third World contained roughly 70 per cent of the world's population.

(b) *Third World poverty and the Brandt Report (1980)*

Economically the Third World was extremely poor. For example, although they contained 70 per cent of the world's population, Third World countries only consumed 30 per cent of the world's food, while the USA, with 10 per cent of the world's population, ate 40 per cent of the world's food. Third World people were often short of proteins and vitamins, and this caused poor health and a high death rate. In 1980 an international group of politicians under the chairmanship of Willi Brandt (who had been Chancellor of West Germany from 1967 until 1974), and including Edward Heath (Prime Minister of Britain 1970–4), produced a report (*the Brandt Report*) about the problems of the Third World. It said that the world could be roughly divided into two parts (see Map 23.1):

The North – the developed industrial nations of North America, Europe, the USSR, and Japan, plus Australia and New Zealand.
The South – most of the Third World countries.

The Report came to the conclusion that the North was getting richer and the South was getting poorer. This gap between the North and South is well illustrated by the statistics of calorie intake (Figure 23.1), and by the comparison of Gross National Product (GNP) of some typical North and South countries, or 'developed' and 'low and middle' economies (Table 23.1).

GNP is calculated by taking the total money value of a country's total output from

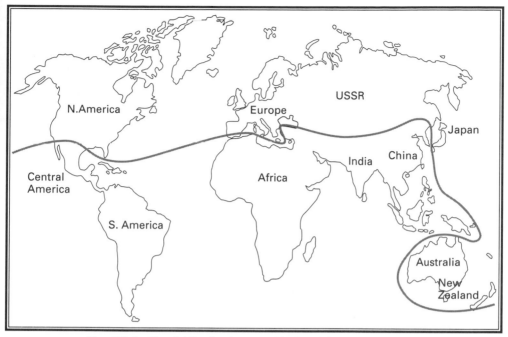

Map 23.1   The dividing line between North and South, rich and poor

Illus. 23.1   Scene in Lagos, the capital of Nigeria

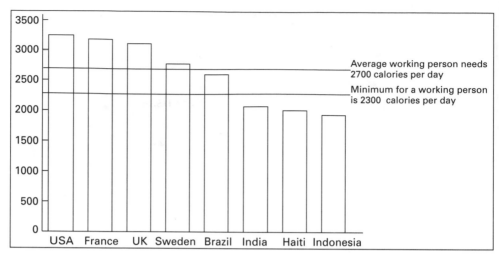

Figure 23.1 Calorie intake per person per day

all units of production, wherever production is situated; it includes interest, profits and dividends received from abroad. This total value is divided by the population, and this gives the amount of wealth produced per head of the population. In 1989–90 the GNP of the North averaged over 24 times that of the South. In 1992 a highly developed and efficient country like Japan could boast a GNP of over $28 000 per head of the population, and Norway $25 800. On the other hand, among poor African countries, Ethiopia could manage only $110 per head, the second lowest GNP in the world.

(c) *Why is the South so poor?*

● The South was and still is economically dependent on the North because of *neo-colonialism* (see Sections 21.4 and 21.7). The North expected the South to continue providing food and raw materials for them, and expected them to buy manufactured goods from the North. They did not encourage the South to develop their own industries.

● Many states found it difficult to break away from the *one-product economies* left behind from colonial days, because governments lacked the cash needed to diversify. Ghana (cocoa) and Zambia (copper) found themselves with this problem. In states like Ghana, which depended for its income on exporting crops, it meant that too little food would be left for the population. Governments then had to spend their scarce money on importing expensive food. A fall in the world price of their main product would be a major disaster. In the 1970s there was a dramatic fall in the world price of such products as cocoa, copper, coffee and cotton. Table 23.2 shows the disastrous effects on the incomes, and therefore the buying power of countries such as Ghana and Cameroon (cocoa), Zambia, Chile and Peru (copper), Mozambique, Egypt and the Sudan (cotton), and Ivory Coast, Zaire and Ethiopia (coffee).

● At the same time, *prices of manufactured goods continued to increase*. The South had to import these from the North. In spite of the efforts of the *United Nations Conference on Trade and Development (UNCTAD)*, which tried to negotiate fairer prices for the Third World, no real improvement was achieved.

● Although a great deal of financial aid was given by the North to the South, much of it was on a business basis – *the countries of the South had to pay interest*. Sometimes a condition of the deal was that countries of the South had to spend aid on goods from

Japan	28 220	Libya	5 310
Taiwan	10 202	Uganda	170
Hong Kong	15 380	Rwanda	250
Singapore	15 750	Tanzania	110
South Korea	6 790	Kenya	330
North Korea	943	Zaire	220
Thailand	1 840	Ethiopia	110
Vietnam	109	Sudan	400
China	380	Somalia	150
		Zimbabwe	570
		Zambia	290
Peru	950	Nigeria	320
Bolivia	680	Mozambique	60
Paraguay	1 340	South Africa	2 670
Brazil	2 770	Algeria	2 020
Argentina	2 780		
Colombia	1 290		
Chile	2 730	India	310
Venezuela	2 900	Pakistan	410
Uruguay	3 340	Bangladesh	220
		Sri Lanka	540
Germany	21 000	Russian Fed.	2 680
France	22 300	Poland	1 960
Britain	17 760	Romania	1 090
Italy	20 510	Czechoslovakia	2 440
Switzerland	36 230		
Greece	7 180		
Spain	14 020		
Portugal	7 450	USA	23 120
Norway	25 800	Canada	20 320
Sweden	26 780	Australia	17 070
Belgium	20 880	Haiti	380
		Dominican Rep	1 040
		Guyana	330
		Jamaica	1 340
		Trinidad & Tobago	3 940

Table 23.1   Gross National Product per head of the population in 1992 (in $US)
Source: World Bank statistics in *Europa World Year Book 1995*

the country which was making the loan. Some countries borrowed directly from banks in the USA and Western Europe, and by 1980 Third World countries owed the equivalent of 500 billion dollars; even the annual interest payable was about 50 billion dollars. Some countries were forced to borrow more cash just to pay the interest on the original loan.

● *Another problem for Third World countries was that their populations were increasing much faster than those in the North.* In 1975 the total world population stood at about 4000 million, and it was expected to reach 6000 million by 1997. Since the

Table 23.2 What commodities could buy in 1975 and 1980

	Barrels of oil	Capital (US$)
Copper		
(1 tonne could buy)		
1975	115	17 800
1980	58	9 500
Cocoa		
(1 tonne could buy)		
1975	148	23 400
1980	63	10 200
Coffee		
(1 tonne could buy)		
1975	148	22 800
1980	82	13 300
Cotton		
(1 tonne could buy)		
1975	119	18 400
1980	60	9 600

population of the South was growing so much faster, a larger proportion of the world's population than ever before would be poor (see Chapter 24).

● *Many Third World countries had suffered long and crippling wars and civil wars* which ravaged crops and ruined economies. Some of the worst wars were in Ethiopia, Nicaragua, Guatamala, Lebanon, the Congo/Zaire, Sudan, Somalia, Liberia, Mozambique and Angola.

● *Drought was sometimes a serious problem in Africa.* Niger in West Africa was badly affected: in 1974 it produced only half the food crops grown in 1970 (mainly millet and sorghum), and about 40 per cent of the cattle died (Illus. 23.2).

(d) *The Brandt Report was full of good ideas*

For example, it pointed out that it was in the North's interests to help the South to become more prosperous, because that would enable the South to buy more goods from the North. This would help to avoid unemployment and recession in the North. If just a fraction of the North's spending on armaments was switched to helping the South, vast improvements could be made. For example, for the price of one jet fighter (about 20 million dollars), 40 000 village pharmacies could be set up. The Report went on to make *some important recommendations* which, if carried out, would at least eliminate hunger from the world:

● the rich nations of the North should aim to be giving 0.7 per cent of their national income to poorer countries by 1985 and 1.0 per cent by the year 2000;
● a new World Development Fund should be set up in which decision-making would be more evenly shared between lenders and borrowers (not like the International Monetary Fund and the World Bank, which were dominated by the USA);
● an international energy plan should be drawn up;
● there should be a campaign to improve agricultural techniques in the South, and an international food programme should be drawn up.

Illus. 23.2 Drought in Africa

Did the Brandt Report change anything? Sadly there was no immediate improvement in the general economic situation of the South. By 1985 very few countries had reached the suggested 0.7 per cent giving target. Those that did were Norway, Sweden, Denmark, Netherlands and France; however, the USA gave only 0.24 per cent and Britain 0.11 per cent. There was a terrible famine in Africa, especially in Ethiopia and the Sudan in the mid-1980s, and the crisis in the poorer parts of the Third World seemed to be worsening.

23.3 The split in the Third World economy

During the 1970s some Third World states began to become more prosperous.

(a) *Oil*

Some Third World states were lucky enough to have oil resources. In 1973 the members of the Organization of Petroleum Exporting Countries (OPEC), partly in an attempt to conserve oil supplies, began to charge more for their oil. The Middle East oil-producing states made huge profits, as did Nigeria and Libya. This did not necessarily mean that their governments spent the money wisely or for the benefit of their populations. One African success story, however, was provided by Libya, the richest country in Africa, thanks to her oil resources and the shrewd policies of her leader, Colonel Gaddafi (who took power in 1969). He used much of the profits from oil on agricultural and industrial development, and to set up a welfare state. This was one country where ordinary people benefited from oil profits; with a GNP of £5460 in 1989, Libya could claim to be almost as economically successful as Greece and Portugal, the poorest members of the European Community.

(b) *Industrialization*

Some Third World states industrialized rapidly and with great success. These included Singapore, Taiwan, South Korea and Hong Kong (known as the four 'Pacific tiger' economies), and, among others, Thailand, Malaysia, Brazil and Mexico.

The GNPs of the four 'tiger' economies compared favourably with those of many European Community countries. The success of the newly industrialized countries in world export markets was made possible partly because they were able to attract firms from the North who were keen to take advantage of the much cheaper labour available in the Third World. Some firms even shifted all their production to newly industrialized countries, where low production costs enabled them to sell their goods at lower prices than goods produced in the North. This posed serious problems for the industrialized nations of the North, which were all suffering high unemployment during the 1990s. It seemed that the golden days of Western prosperity might have gone, at least for the foreseeable future, unless their workers were prepared to accept lower wages, or unless companies were prepared to make do with lower profits.

In the mid-1990s the world economy was moving into the next stage in which the Asian 'tigers' found themselves losing jobs to workers in countries such as *Malaysia* and *the Philippines*. Other Third World states in the process of industrializing were *Indonesia* and *China*, where wages were even lower and hours of work longer. Jacques Chirac, the French President, expressed the fears and concerns of many when he pointed out (April 1996) that developing countries should not compete with Europe by allowing miserable wages and working conditions; he called for a recognition that there are certain basic human rights which need to be encouraged and enforced:

- freedom to join trade unions and the freedom for these unions to bargain collectively, for the protection of workers against exploitation;
- abolition of forced labour and child labour.

In fact most developing countries accepted this when they joined the International Labour Organization (ILO) (see Section 9.4(b)), but accepting conditions and keeping to them are two different things.

23.4 The world economy and its effects on the environment

As the twentieth century wore on, and the North became more and more obsessed with industrialization, new methods and techniques were invented to help increase production and efficiency. The main motive was the creation of wealth and profit, and very little attention was paid to the side-effects all this was having. During the 1970s people became increasingly aware that all was not well with their environment. There were two main types of problem:

- industrialization was beginning to *exhaust the world's resources* of raw materials and fuel (oil, coal and gas);
- industrialization was causing massive pollution of the environment, and if this continued, *it was likely to severely damage the ecosystem*. This is the system by which living creatures, trees and plants function within the environment and are all interconnected. 'Ecology' is the study of the ecosystem.

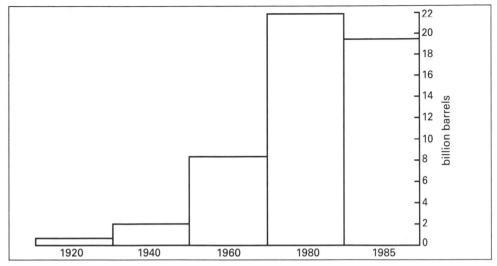

Figure 23.2 World oil production in billions of barrels per year

(a) *Exhaustion of the world's resources*

● *Fossil fuels* – coal, oil and natural gas – are the remains of plants and living creatures which died hundreds of millions of years ago. They cannot be replaced, and so are rapidly being used up. There is probably plenty of coal left, but nobody is quite sure just how much natural gas and oil are left. Oil production increased enormously during the century, as Figure 23.2 shows. Some experts believe that all the oil reserves will be used up early in the twenty-first century. This was one of the reasons why OPEC tried to conserve oil during the 1970s. The British responded by successfully drilling for oil in the North Sea, which made them less dependent on oil imports. Another response was to develop alternative sources of power, especially nuclear power.

● Other *raw materials* to be seriously depleted were tin, lead, copper, zinc and mercury. Experts think these may all be used up early in the twenty-first century, and again it is the Third World which is being stripped of the resources it needs to help it escape from poverty.

● Too much *timber* was being used. About half the world's tropical rain forest had been lost by 1987, and it was calculated that about 80 000 square kilometres, an area roughly the size of Austria, was being lost every year. A side-effect of this was the loss of many animal and insect species which had lived in the forests.

● Too many *fish* were being caught and too many *whales* killed.

● *The supply of phosphates (used for fertilizers) was being rapidly used up.* The more fertilizers farmers used to increase agricultural yields in an attempt to keep pace with the rising population, the more phosphate rock was quarried (an increase of 4 per cent a year since 1950). Supplies are expected to be exhausted by the middle of the twenty-first century.

● *There was a danger that supplies of fresh water might soon run out.* Most of the fresh water on the planet is tied up in the polar icecaps and glaciers, or deep in the ground. All living organisms – humans, animals, trees and plants – rely on rain to survive. With the world's population growing by 90 million a year, scientists at Stanford University (California) found that in 1995 humans and their farm animals, crops and forestry plantations were already using up one-fourth of all the water taken up by plants. This leaves less moisture to evaporate and therefore a likelihood of less rainfall.

● *The amount of land available for agriculture was dwindling.* This was partly because of spreading industrialization and the growth of cities, but also because of wasteful use of farmland. Badly designed irrigation schemes increased salt levels in the soil. Sometimes irrigation took too much water from lakes and rivers, and whole areas were turned into deserts. Soil erosion was another problem: scientists calculated that every year about 75 billion tons of soil were washed away by rain and floods or blown away by winds. Soil loss depends on how good farming practices are: in Western Europe and the USA (where methods were good), farmers lost on average 17 tons of topsoil every year from each hectare. In Africa, Asia and South America, the loss was 40 tons a year. On steep slopes in countries like Nigeria, 220 tons a year were being lost, while in some parts of Jamaica the figure reached 400 tons a year.

An encouraging sign was the setting up of the World Conservation Strategy (1980), which aimed to alert the world to all these problems.

(b) *Pollution of the environment – an ecological disaster?*

● *Discharges from heavy industry polluted the atmosphere, rivers, lakes and the sea.* In 1975 all five Great Lakes of North America were described as 'dead', meaning that they were so heavily polluted that no fish could live in them. About 10 per cent of the lakes in Sweden were in the same condition. Acid rain (rain polluted with sulphuric acid) caused extensive damage to trees in central Europe, especially in Germany and Czechoslovakia; Britain was blamed for producing the majority of the pollution causing the acid rain. The USSR and the communist states of Eastern Europe were guilty of the dirtiest industrialization: the whole region was badly polluted by years of poisonous emissions.

From about 1970 scientists were worried about what they called the 'greenhouse effect'; this was the uncontrollable warming of the earth's atmosphere (*global warming*) caused by the large amounts of human-produced gases emitted from industry. These acted like the glass roof of a greenhouse, trapping and magnifying the sun's heat. Opinions differed about exactly what its effects would be; one theory was that the ice-caps at the poles would melt, causing the level of the sea to rise, flooding large areas of land. Africa and large parts of Asia could become too hot for people to live in, and there could be violent storms and prolonged drought.

● *Getting rid of sewage from the world's great cities was a problem.* Some countries simply dumped sewage untreated or only partially treated straight into the sea. The sea around New York is badly polluted, and the Mediterranean is heavily polluted, mainly by human sewage.

● Farmers in the richer countries contributed to pollution by using *artificial fertilizers and pesticides* which drained off the land into streams and rivers.

● *Chemicals known as chlorofluorocarbons (CFCs)*, used in aerosol sprays, refrigerators and fire-extinguishers, were found to be harmful to the ozone layer which protects the earth from the sun's harmful ultra-violet radiation. In 1979 scientists discovered that there was a large hole in the ozone layer over the Antarctic; by 1989 the hole was much larger and another hole had been discovered over the Arctic. This meant that people were more likely to develop skin cancers because of the unfiltered radiation from the sun. Some progress was made towards dealing with this problem, and many countries banned the use of CFCs.

● *Nuclear power causes pollution when radioactivity leaks into the environment.* It is now known that this can cause cancer, particularly leukemia. It was shown that of all the people who worked at the Sellafield nuclear plant in Cumbria between 1947 and 1975, a quarter of those who have since died, died of cancer. There was a constant risk

Illus. 23.3   The Espenhain power station in former East Germany

of major accidents like the explosion at Three Mile Island in the USA in 1979, which contaminated a vast area around the power station. When leaks and accidents occurred, the authorities always assured the public that nobody had suffered harmful effects; however, nobody really knew how many people would die later from cancer caused by radiation.

The worst ever nuclear accident happened in 1986 at *Chernobyl* in the Ukraine (then part of the USSR). A nuclear reactor exploded, killing possibly hundreds of people and releasing a huge radioactive cloud which drifted across most of Europe. Ten years later it was reported that hundreds of cases of thyroid cancer were appearing in areas near Chernobyl. Even in Britain, a thousand miles away, hundreds of square miles of sheep pasture in Wales, Cumbria and Scotland were still contaminated and subject to restrictions. 300 000 sheep were affected and had to be checked for excessive radioactivity before they could be eaten.

Concern about the safety of nuclear power has led many countries to look towards alternative sources of power which were safer, particularly solar, wind and tide power.

One of the main difficulties to be faced is that *it would cost vast sums of money to put all these problems right*. Industrialists argue that to 'clean up' their factories and eliminate pollution would make their products more expensive. Governments and local authorities would have to spend extra cash to build better sewage works and to clean up rivers and beaches. In 1996 there were still twenty-seven power station reactors in operation in Eastern Europe of similar elderly design to the one which exploded at Chernobyl. These were all threatening further nuclear disasters, but governments claimed they could afford neither safety improvements nor closure. The following description of Chernobyl gives some idea of the seriousness of the problems involved.

At Chernobyl, the scene of the April 1986 explosion, just a few miles north of the Ukrainian capital Kiev, the prospect is bleak. Two of the station's remaining reactors are still in operation, surrounded by miles of heavily contaminated countryside. Radioactive elements slowly leach into the ground water – and hence into Kiev's drinking supply – from more than 800 pits where the most dangerous debris was buried ten year ago.

Source: article in the *Guardian* (13 April 1996)

Questions

1   *Causes of poverty in the South*   Section 23.2(c) gave seven suggested causes of why the South is so poor.

   (a)   Which are long-term and which are short-term causes?   1.4b–5b   7 marks

   (b)   Which of these causes could be said to be the South's own fault?
                                           1.4b–5b   4 marks

   (c)   'The main cause of the poverty of the South was the greed of the North'. Would you agree or disagree with this statement?   1.6b–9a   9 marks

                                                 Total: 20 marks

2   *Problems of world pollution*   Study Sources A and B and then answer the questions which follow.

Source A

Description of some of the pollution in East Germany in March 1990

An environmentalist stood in an open field and pointed to an evil green liquid bubbling up in the middle of a brackish pool of water. It was the chemical outflow from a fertilizer plant which had sprung a leak and was poisoning the entire area. In the Harz Mountains the trees had been so damaged by acid rain and other forms of pollution that the bird population had fallen drastically. The field-mice who were the natural prey of hawks, owls and eagles were living and breeding almost without hindrance. Now they were beginning to constitute a plague of biblical proportions. A gynaecologist explained why she had been unable to set up in private practice . . . the water supply in the town contained so much nitrate that it wasn't safe to treat patients there. The area around the town of Bitterfeld is perhaps the dirtiest in Europe . . . Five employees of the pesticide factory have died of cancer within four years. Carbon disulphide escaping from the machinery in a plant that spins cellulose fibres has been measured at concentrations 90 times the danger limit. It can cause brain damage. Farmers outside Bitterfeld find it difficult to get their animals to breed. Children in the town are more than twice as likely as children elsewhere to contract respiratory diseases. Their bone growth is retarded.

Source: John Simpson, *Despatches from the Barricades* (Hutchinson, 1990)

Source: Jack B. Watson, *Success in World History Since 1945* (John Murray, 1989)

(a) According to the sources, what are the main dangers threatening the world from pollution?   3.4   15 marks

(b) Source B says that 'other countries pressed on enthusiastically' with nuclear power. Do you think this means that the writer of Source B was wrong to be concerned about the dangers of nuclear power? Use the information in Section 23.4(b) to help you decide your answer.   1.3b–7b, 2.3–8   10 marks

(c) Using information from Section 23.3 and 23.4 and the sources, explain whether or not you think nuclear pollution is the worst ecological threat.
                                                                1.3b–7b   10 marks

(d) Since the 1970s, scientists have been aware of the damage being done to the world by pollution. Why therefore do you think so little has been done to control the damage?   1.6c–9b   15 marks

Total: 50 marks

⟨24⟩ The world's population

Summary of events

Before the seventeenth century the world's population increased very slowly. It has been estimated that by 1650 the population had doubled to about 500 million since the year 1 AD. Over the next 200 years the rate of increase was much faster, and by 1850 the population had more than doubled to 1200 million. After that, the population growth accelerated so rapidly that people talked about a population 'explosion'; it seems likely that by the year 2000 it will have passed the 6000 million mark. This chapter examines the causes of the population 'explosion', the regional variations and the consequences of all the changes.

24.1 The increasing world population since 1900

(a) *Statistics of population increase*

It is easy to see from the diagram in Figure 24.1 with its steeply climbing population total, why people talk about a population 'explosion' in the twentieth century. Between 1850 and 1900 the world's population was increasing, on average, by 0.6 per cent every year. During the next fifty years the rate of increase averaged 0.9 per cent a year; it was after 1960 that the full force of the 'explosion' was felt, with the total world population increasing at the rate of 1.9 per cent a year, on average. In 1990 the population was increasing by roughly one million every week, and the total had reached 5300 million. In 1994 there was an increase of 95 million, the biggest ever increase in a single year. In 1995 the record was broken again, as the total population grew by 100 million to 5750 million. According to the Population Institute in Washington, 90 per cent of the growth was in poor countries 'torn by civil strife and social unrest'. It was expected that during 1996 a further 90 million would be added to the population. However, there were important regional variations within the general population increase. Broadly speaking, the industrialized nations of Europe and North America had their most rapid increase before the First World War; after that their rate of increase slowed considerably. In the less developed, or Third World nations of Africa, Asia and Latin America, the rate of population increase accelerated after the Second World War, and it was in these areas that population growth caused the most serious problems. The growth rate began to

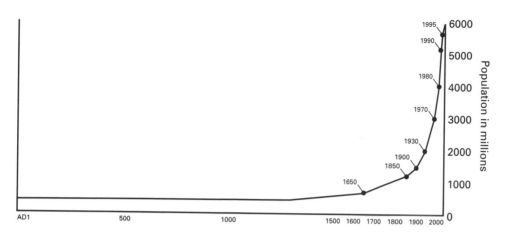

Figure 24.1 *World population increases AD 1–1995*

slow down in some Latin American countries after 1950, but in Asia and Africa the rate continued to increase. The diagram in Figure 24.2, which is based on statistics provided by the United Nations, shows:

1 the percentage rates at which the world's population grew between 1650 and 1959;
2 the percentage rates of population increase in the different continents during the periods 1900–50 and 1950–9.

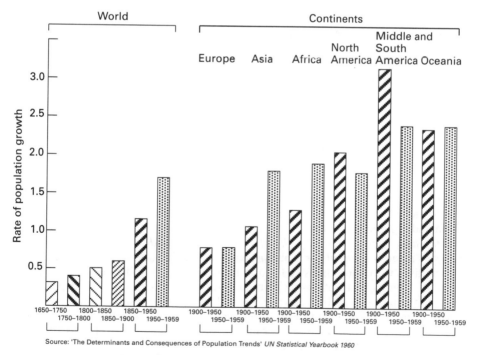

Source: 'The Determinants and Consequences of Population Trends' *UN Statistical Yearbook 1960*

Figure 24.2 *Rate of population growth by regions*

(b) *Reasons for the population increase*

The population increase in Europe and North America in the later part of the nine-teenth and the early twentieth centuries had several causes:

- Increasing industrialization, economic growth and prosperity meant that the necessary resources were there to sustain a larger population, and the two seemed to go hand-in-hand.
- There was a great improvement in public health, thanks to advances in medical science and sanitation. The work of Louis Pasteur and Joseph Lister in the 1860s on germs and antiseptic techniques helped to reduce the death rate. At the same time, the big industrial cities introduced piped water supplies and drainage schemes which all helped to reduce disease.
- There was a decline in infant mortality (the number of babies who died before the age of one). Again this was mainly thanks to medical improvements which helped to reduce deaths from diseases such as scarlet fever, diphtheria and whooping cough, which were so dangerous to young babies. The improvement in some countries can seen in Table 24.1, which shows how many babies per thousand born, died within their first year:

Table 24.1 Deaths within one year of birth, per thousand births

	England	Switzerland	France	Italy	Austria
1880–90	142	165	166	195	256
1931–38	52	43	65	104	80

- *Immigration* helped to swell the population of the USA and, to a lesser extent, some other countries on the continent of America, such as Canada, Argentina and Brazil. In the hundred years after 1820, some 35 million people entered the USA; in the last few years before 1914 they were arriving at a rate of a million a year (see Section 19.2).

After 1900 the growth rate in Europe began to slow down, mainly because more people were using modern contraceptive techniques. Later, the economic depression of the 1930s discouraged people from having as many children.

The rapid population growth after 1945 in Third World countries had three main causes:

- *Modern medical and hygiene techniques* began to make an impact for the first time; the child mortality rate fell and people lived longer, as killer diseases like smallpox, malaria and typhoid were gradually brought under control.
- *At the same time the vast majority of the population made no attempt to limit their families by using contraceptives.* This was partly through ignorance and the fact that contraceptives were too expensive for ordinary people to buy. The Roman Catholic Church said that contraception was forbidden for its members, on the grounds that it prevented the natural creation of new lives and was therefore sinful. Since the Roman Catholic Church was strong in Central and South America, its teaching had important effects. The population growth rate for many countries in these areas was over three per cent per annum. The average for the whole of Latin America was 2.4 per cent in 1960, whereas the average for Europe was only 0.75 per cent. *Any increase of over 2 per*

cent per annum means that the population of that country doubles in thirty years. This happened in Brazil and Mexico in the 30 years up to 1960.

● Many Third World countries had a long tradition of people *having as many children as possible to combat high infant mortality*; they wanted to make sure that their family continued. Muslims, for example, attach great value to having many sons. The same attitudes persisted in spite of the reduction in infant mortality.

24.2 Consequences of the population explosion

(a) *The industrializing nations of Europe and North America*

The population growth of the nineteenth century helped to stimulate further economic development. There was a plentiful workforce and more people to buy goods, and this encouraged more investment and enterprise. Nor were there any great problems about feeding and educating these growing numbers, because prosperity meant that the necessary resources were there.

Later on, there were unexpected effects on the age structure of the population in the developed nations. This was especially true in Europe where, because of the very low birth rates and longer life expectancy, a growing proportion of the population was over 65. By the 1970s, in countries such as Sweden, France and Britain, about 15 per cent of the population were over 65. In the early 1990s, with this proportion still increasing, questions were being asked about whether state welfare systems would be able to afford to pay pensions to all old people if this trend continued into the twenty-first century.

(b) *The Third World*

The rapid population growth caused serious problems: some countries like India, Pakistan and Bangladesh became overcrowded and there was not enough land to go round. This forced people to move into towns and cities, but these were already over-crowded and there were not enough houses or jobs for all the new arrivals. Many people were forced to live on the streets; some cities, especially those in Latin America, were surrounded by shanty-towns and slums which had no proper water supply, sanitation or lighting.

(c) *It became increasingly difficult to feed the population*

All areas of the world succeeded in increasing their food production during the late 1960s and 1970s, thanks to what became known as the 'green revolution'. Scientists developed new strains of heavy cropping rice and wheat on short, fast-growing stems, helped by fertilizers and irrigation schemes. For a time, food supplies seemed to be well ahead of population growth; even a densely populated country like India was able to export food, and China became self-sufficient. In the USA crop yields increased three-fold between 1945 and 1995, and the Americans were able to export surplus crops to over a hundred countries. However, in the mid-1980s, with the world's population growing faster than ever, the 'green revolution' was running into problems and scientists became concerned about the future:

● a point had been reached beyond which crop yields could not be increased any

further, and there was a limit to water supply, topsoil and phosphates for fertilizers (see Section 23.4(a));
- a survey carried out by scientists at Stanford University (California) in 1996 found that the amount of farmland available was dwindling because of industrialization, the spread of cities and soil erosion;
- they calculated that the number of mouths to feed in the USA would double by 2050.

There seemed no way in which food production could be doubled from less land. In 1996 on average there were 1.8 acres of cropland to each American and the US diet was made up of 31 per cent animal products. By 2050 there will probably only be 0.6 acres per head. The Stanford scientists came to the conclusion that the solution was for people everywhere to eat less meat; by 2050 the US diet will probably be about 85 per cent vegetarian.

Matters were made worse in parts of Africa (Ethiopia, Angola, Mozambique and Somalia) during the 1980s and 1990s by drought and civil wars which played a part in causing severe food shortages and tens of thousands of deaths from starvation.

(d) *Resource shortages in the Third World*

Third World governments were forced to spend their valuable cash to feed, house, and educate their growing populations. But this used up resources which they would have spent on industrializing and modernizing their countries, and so their economic development was delayed. The general shortage of resources meant that the poorest countries also lacked sufficient cash to spend on health care. Following a meningitis epidemic in the African state of Niger, Save the Children reported (April 1996) that one-sixth of the world's population – over 800 million people – had no access to health care. Health systems in many poorer countries were collapsing, and the situation was becoming worse because richer countries were reducing aid. The Report estimated that it cost at least $12 a person a year to provide basic health care. But sixteen African countries (including Niger, Uganda, Zaire, Tanzania, Mozambique and Liberia) plus Bangladesh, India, Pakistan, Nepal and Vietnam were spending much less than that. In comparison, Britain was spending the equivalent of $1039 (£723). In fact Zaire was spending only 40c per head a year, while Tanzania managed 70c. This meant that simple immunization against easily preventable diseases was not being carried out in these countries. Widespread epidemics could be expected before the end of the century, and a rise in the child mortality rate (*The Guardian*, 27 April 1996).

24.3 Attempts at population control

For many years people had been giving serious thought to the question of controlling the population before the world became too overcrowded and impossible to live in. Soon after the First World War scientists in a number of countries first began to be concerned at the population growth and felt that it was a problem that should be studied at international level. The first *World Population Congress* was held in Geneva in 1925, and the following year an *International Union for the Scientific Study of Population* was set up in Paris. As well as scientists, the organization also included statisticians and social scientists who were concerned about the economic and social effects if the world's population continued to grow. They did valuable work collecting statistics and encouraging governments to improve their data systems, so that accurate information about population trends could be collected.

(a) *The United Nations Population Commission*

When the United Nations Organization was set up in 1945, a Population Commission was included among its many agencies. When the Third World population began to 'explode' during the 1950s, it was the UN which took the lead in encouraging governments to introduce birth control programmes. India and Pakistan set up family planning clinics to advise people about the various methods of birth control available, and to provide them with cheap contraceptives. Huge publicity campaigns were launched with government posters recommending a maximum of three children per family (Figure 24.3). Many African governments recommended a maximum of three children, while the Chinese government went further and fixed the legal maximum at two children per family. But progress was very slow: ancient practices and attitudes were difficult to change, especially in countries like India and Pakistan. In the Roman Catholic countries of South America, the church continued to forbid artificial birth control.

(b) *How successful were the campaigns?*

The best that can be said is that in parts of Asia the population growth rate was beginning to fall slightly during the 1980s; but in many African and Latin American countries it was still rising. Table 24.2 shows what could be achieved with the spread of birth control:

Table 24.2 Use of contraceptives and the birth rate

	% of married women using contraceptives	*Fall in the % birth rate 1978–86*
India	35	4.5 > 3.2
China	74	3.2 > 2.1
Colombia (S. America)	65	4.3 > 2.6
South Korea	70	3.5 > 1.6
Kenya	under 20	4.6 constant
Pakistan	under 20	4.6 constant

Table 24.3 shows the 1986 populations and growth rates of the various regions, compared with the 1950–9 growth rates. The most rapid growth rate in 1986 was in Africa, where some countries had rates of over 3 per cent per year. The table also reveals how serious the problem of overcrowding was in some areas where there were on average over a hundred people to every square kilometre. This was not so serious in the developed nations of Europe which had the prosperity and resources to support their populations; but in the poorer nations of Asia, it meant grinding poverty. Bangladesh was probably the world's most crowded country, with an average of 700 people to every square kilometre. The population growth rates of Bangladesh and Britain provide a startling comparison: at the present growth rates, Bangladesh will double its population of 125 million in less than thirty years, but Britain's population of 58.6 million will take 385 years to double in size. The Population Institute predicted (December 1995) that, with effective birth control, the global population could stabilize by 2015 at about 8000 million. However, without effective promotion of family planning, the total could well have reached 14 000 million by 2050. With the population of Europe and North America growing so slowly, it meant that an ever-increasing proportion of the world's population would be poor.

Figure 24.3 Posters from the Indian government (left) and from the Africa branch of the International Planned Parenthood Association (right) encouraging people to use birth control and limit families to three children.

Table 24.3 Population growth rates and density

	1986 population (millions)	% growth rate 1950–9 (annual)	% growth rate 1980–5 (annual)	1986 population density per sq. km
N. America	266	1.75	0.9	12
Europe	493	0.75	0.3	100
USSR	281	1.4	1.0	13
Oceania	25	2.4	1.5	3
Africa	572	1.9	2.9	19
Latin America	414	2.4	2.3	20
E. Asia	1264	1.5	1.2	105
S. Asia	1601	2.2	2.2	101
World total	4917	1.7	1.7	36

On the other hand, some historians feel that the fears about the population explosion have been exaggerated. Paul Johnson, for example, believes that there is no need to panic; once Asia, Latin America and Africa become more successfully industrialized, living standards will rise, and this economic betterment, along with more effective use of contraception, will slow down the birth rate (see Source B in Question 2). According to Johnson, the example of China is most encouraging: 'The most important news during the 1980s, perhaps, was that the population of China appeared virtually to have stabilised'.

Questions

1 *Consequences of the population explosion*   Section 24.2 examined several consequences of the rapid population increase in the nineteenth and twentieth centuries. Explain which of these consequences you think

(a)   were economic
(b)   were social
(c)   could be described as beneficial or positive
(d)   could be described as unfortunate or negative.   1.5a–7a

2 *Population and poverty*   Study the statistics in Table 24.3, and the sources, and then answer the questions which follow.

Source A

Comments from Espiritu Santos Mendoza, a health official in Venezuela, a country in South America, in 1960

Our successful campaign to reduce infant mortality has given us more problems. If we do not have adequate food supplies at reasonable prices and an understanding of nutrition, the babies we have may sicken and die of malnutrition before they reach school age; when they reach school age there will not be enough schools unless we can greatly expand our educational facilities; if they lack schools they may become juvenile delinquents and present us with still other needs for services. If they reach working age without sufficient training, they will not earn enough to give their own children a good home – even if we manage to get enough housing

---

built. And whether they find jobs at all will depend on the rate at which we can expand our industry and improve our agriculture, and find the capital resources with which to do so. Unless we can move forward on all fronts at the same time, the saving of lives only puts us further behind.

Source: quoted in C. Ware (ed.), *The Twentieth Century* (Allen & Unwin, 1966)

Source B

The view of British historian, Paul Johnson, writing in 1991

By 1987 the world population was over 5 billion, and was increasing at the rate of 80 million a year or 150 a minute. One calculation put the estimated world population in the year 2000 at 6130 million, a five-fold increase during the century. How were these additional billions to be fed? Modern developing societies go through a cycle known as the 'demographic transition'. In the first phase, scientific medicine and public health reduce infant mortality and infectious diseases, thus cutting the death rate, while the birth-rate remains high. So population rises fast. In the second phase, rising living standards cause the birth-rate to fall. The rate of population increase slows down and eventually comes into balance. Between the first and second phases, however, population jumps alarmingly ... In Europe the transition was virtually complete by the 1970s, by which time the birth rate had fallen below the critical 20-per-thousand mark. Japan followed a similar pattern somewhat later than Europe. In the 1920s its birth-rate was still 34-per thousand, and its death-rate was falling steeply, from 30-per thousand at the beginning of the decade to 18 at the end, hence Japan's growing desperation. But even in the inter-war period, the second phase was beginning, and the birth-rate moved below the 20 mark in the second half of the1950s. Japan's population problem, once so threatening, was therefore 'solved' by the 1960s.

Source: Paul Johnson, *A History of the Modern World from 1917 to the 1990s* (Weidenfeld & Nicolson, 1991)

(a) From the evidence of the statistics in Table 24.3, which areas have had most success in limiting population growth since 1960 and which have had least success? 3.1–3 5 marks

(b) The statistics in Table 24.3 show that Europe is one of the most densely populated areas of the world. Source A is about a country in South America, which is below the world average in population density. Using the statistics and the information in Section 24.6, explain why the problem of poverty was less serious in Europe than in Latin America. 1.4b–5b, 3.4 10 marks

(c) To what extent do you think Source B proves that the fears of the writer in Source A were unfounded? 1.4c–9b, 2.4–8 15 marks

Total: 30 marks

Further reading

This list contains books suitable both for the general reader and for GCSE students. Those marked with an asterisk * are particularly suitable for GCSE students. Those marked ** are suitable for GCSE students and contain source material. 'Purnell' refers to *Purnell's History of the Twentieth Century* (10 volumes), BPC Publishing, 1969.

1 The world in 1914: outbreak of the First World War

** Brooman, J., *The End of Old Europe* (Longman, 1985)
Fischer, F., *Germany's Aims in the First World War* (Chatto & Windus, 1967)
** Harkness, J., D. Moore and H. Mcmillan, *Co-operation and Conflict: International Relations, 1890–1930* (Hodder & Stoughton, 1995)
Joll, J., *The Origins of the First World War* (Longman, 1992)
Turner, L.C.F., *Origins of the First World War* (Arnold, 1970)

2 The First World War and its aftermath

* Clark, A., *Suicide of the Empires* (Macdonald, 1970)
* Crinnion, V., *The Great War* (Macmillan, 1980)
** Evans, D., *The Great War 1914–18* (Arnold, 1987)
* Gibbons, S.R. and P. Morican, *World War One* (Longman, 1972)
* Horne, A., *Death of a Generation* (Macdonald, 1970)
Horne, A., *The Price of Glory* (Macmillan, 1962)
Liddell-Hart, Sir B., *The First World War* (Cassell, 1970)
** Lobban, R., *The First World War* (Oxford, 1991)
** Rees, R., *The Western Front* (Heinemann, 1996)
Sharp, A., *The Versailles Settlement: Peacemaking in Paris, 1919* (Macmillan, 1991)
Stone, N., *The Eastern Front* (Hodder & Stoughton, 1975)
* Taylor, A.A., *The First World War* (London University Tutorial Press, 1972)
Taylor, A.J.P., *The First World War* (Penguin, 1963)

3 The League of Nations

* Fitzsimmons, O., *Towards One World* (London University Tutorial Press, 1974)
* Gibbons, S.R. and P. Morican, *The League of Nations and UNO* (Longman, 1970)
Henig, R., *The League of Nations* (Edinburgh, 1976)

4 and 5 International relations 1919–39

* Allen, L., *Japan: The Years of Triumph* (Macdonald, 1971)
** Doig, R., *Co-operation and Conflict: International Affairs 1930–62* (Hodder & Stoughton, 1995)
** Fewster, S., *Japan 1850–1985* (Longman, 1988)
Beasley, W.E., *Japanese Imperialism 1894–1945* (Oxford, 1987)
Gilbert, M., *Appeasement in Action* (Purnell, vol. 4, ch. 57)
Gilbert, M. & R. Gott, *The Appeasers* (Weidenfeld & Nicolson, 1967 edn)
* Henig, R., *Versailles and After, 1919–33* (Methuen, 1984)
* Henig, R., *The Origins of the Second World War* (Methuen, 1985)

Martel, G., (ed.), *The Origins of the Second World War Reconsidered: The A.J.P. Taylor Debate after 25 Years* (Unwin Hyman, 1990 edn)

* Stone, R., *The Drift to War* (Heinemann, 1975)

Storry, R., *Japan and the Decline of the West in Asia 1894–1943* (Macmillan, 1979)

Taylor, A.J.P., *The Origins of the Second World War* (Penguin, 1964)

Thorne, C., *The Approach of War 1938–39* (Macmillan, 1967)

Watt, D.C., *How War Came* (Mandarin, 1990)

** Wolfson, R., *From Peace to War: European Relations 1919–39* (Arnold, 1985)

6 The Second World War, 1939–45

* Arnold-Forster, M., *The World at War* (Collins, 1973)

** Bayne-Jardine, C., *The Second World War and its Aftermath* (Longman, 1987)

Calvocoressi, P. and G. Wint, *Total War* (Penguin, 1974)

** Evans, D., *The Second World War* (Arnold, 1985)

Gilbert, M., *The Holocaust: The Jewish Tragedy* (Collins, 1987)

Gilbert, M., *Second World War* (Phoenix, 1995)

Liddell-Hart, Sir B., *History of the Second World War* (Cassell, 1970)

* Mortimore, M.J.A., *The Second World War* (London University Tutorial Press, 1974)

Parker, R.A.C., *Struggle for Survival: The History of the Second World War* (Oxford, 1990)

Taylor, A.J.P., *The Second World War* (Hamish Hamilton, 1975)

7 and 8 The Cold War, the spread of communism outside Europe and its effects on international relations

** Aylett, J.F., *The Cold War and After* (Hodder & Stoughton, 1996)

Bown, C. and P.J. Mooney, *Cold War to Détente 1945–83* (Heinemann, 1984)

Calvocoressi, P., *World Politics since 1945* (Longman, 1991 edn)

** Doig, R., *Co-operation and Conflict: International Affairs 1930–62* (Hodder & Stoughton, 1992)

Feis, H., *From Trust to Terror: The Onset of the Cold War* (Blond, 1970)

* Fitzgerald, C.P., *Communism takes China* (Macdonald, 1969)

Frankland, M., *Khrushchev* (Penguin, 1966)

** Hartley, L., *Superpower Relations since 1945* (Unwin Hyman, 1987)

Hastings, M., *The Korean War* (Pan, 1988)

* Heater, D., *The Cold War* (Oxford, 1970)

Higgins, H., *The Cold War* (Heinemann, 1984 edn)

Higgins, H., *Vietnam* (Heinemann, 1978)

Karnow, S., *Vietnam: A History* (Penguin, 1984)

Knapp, W., *A History of War and Peace 1939–1965* (Oxford, 1967)

Laqueur, W., *Europe in Our Time 1945–92* (Penguin, 1993)

Matthews, H.L., *Castro* (Allen Lane, 1969)

McCauley, M., *Origins of the Cold War* (Longman, 1983)

** Sayer, J., *Superpower Rivalry* (Arnold, 1987)

Thomas, H., *Cuba or the Pursuit of Freedom* (Harper & Row, 1971)

9 The United Nations Organization

Bailey, S., *The United Nations* (Macmillan, 1989)

* Fitzsimmons, O., *Towards One World* (London University Tutorial Press, 1974)

* Gibbons, S.R., and P. Morican, *The League of Nations and UNO* (Longman, 1970)

** Owens, R.J. and J., *The United Nations and its Agencies* (Pergamon Press, 1985)

Parsons, Anthony, *From Cold War to Hot Peace: UN Interventions 1947–1995* (Penguin, 1995)

10 The Two Europes, East and West since 1945

* Allan, P.D., *Russia and Eastern Europe* (Arnold, 1984)

** Hall, D., *Unity in Europe* (Unwin Hyman, 1986)

Lacouture, J., *De Gaulle: The Ruler, 1945–1970* (Harvill, 1991)

Laqueur, W., *Europe in Our Time 1945–92* (Penguin, 1993)

Morgan, R., *Tension in Eastern Europe* (Purnell, vol. 5, ch. 80)

Morgan, R., *Eastern Europe: Hopes and Realities* (Purnell, vol. 6, ch. 83)

Morgan, R., *The Czechoslovak Spring* (Purnell, vol. 6, ch. 94)

Pinder, J., *European Community: The Building of a Union* (Oxford, 1991)
Seaman, R.D.H., *Britain and Western Europe* (Arnold, 1984)

11   Conflict in the Middle East

Bullard, R., *The Persian Oil Crisis* (Purnell, vol. 5, ch. 80)
Dodd, C.H. and M. Sales, *Israel and the Arab World* (Routledge, 1973)
Hunter, R.E., *The Six Day War* (Purnell, vol. 6, ch. 94)
*   Jones, D., *The Arab World* (Hamish Hamilton, 1969)
Kyle, K., *Suez* (Weidenfeld & Nicolson, 1991)
**   Mandle, B., *Conflict in the Promised Land* (Heinemann, 1976)
Mansfield, P., *A History of the Middle East* (Penguin, 1992)
*   Nussbaum, E., *Israel* (Oxford, 1968)
*   Perkins, S.J., *The Arab–Israeli Conflict* (Macmillan, 1982)
**   Regan, G., *Israel and the Arabs* (Cambridge University Press, 1993 edn)
*   Scott-Bauman, M., *Israel and the Arabs* (Arnold, 1986)
Thomas, H., *The Suez Affair* (Weidenfeld & Nicolson, 1967)

12   Italy 1918–45: the first appearance of Fascism

Blinkhorn, M., *Mussolini and Fascist Italy* (Methuen, 1984)
Cassels, A., *Fascist Italy* (Routledge, 1969)
De Felice, R., *Interpretations of Fascism* (Harvard, 1977)
**   Gregory, D., *Mussolini and the Fascist Era* (Arnold, 1968)
Hibbert, C., *Benito Mussolini* (Penguin, 1965)
*   Rowlands, B.R., *Modern Italy* (London University Tutorial Press, 1970)
Smith, D.Mack, *Mussolini* (Paladin, 1983)
Tannenbaum, E., *Fascism in Italy* (Allen Lane, 1973)
Wiskemann, E., *Fascism in Italy; Its Development and Influence* (Macmillan, 1970)
**   Wolfson, R., *Benito Mussolini and Fascist Italy* (Arnold, 1986)

13   Germany 1918–45: the Weimar Republic and Hitler

**   Aylett, J.F., *Hitler's Germany* (Hodder & Stoughton, 1992)
Bracher, K.D., *The German Dictatorship* (Penguin, 1978)
Bullock, A., *Hitler: A Study in Tyranny* (Penguin, 1969)
Bullock, A., *Hitler and Stalin: Parallel Lives* (HarperCollins, 1991)
*   Bumstead, P.J., *Hitler* (London University Tutorial Press, 1977)
Carr, W., *A History of Germany 1815–1990* (Arnold, 4th edn, 1991)
*   Catchpole, B., *Twentieth Century Germany* (Oxford, 1970)
Craig, G.A., *Germany 1866–1945* (Oxford, 1978)
*   Delmer, S., *The Weimar Republic* (Macdonald, 1972)
Fest, J., *Hitler* (Weidenfeld & Nicolson, 1974)
Grey, Paul and R. Little, *Germany 1918–45* (Cambridge University Press, 1992)
Hiden, J.W., *The Weimar Republic* (Longman, 1974)
**   McKay, M., *Germany between the Wars 1919–45* (Longman, 1988)
**   Phillips, D.M., *Hitler and the Rise of the Nazis* (Arnold, 1968)
**   Rees, R., *Nazi Germany* (Heinemann, 1996)
**   Whittock, M., *Hitler and National Socialism* (Heinemann, 1996)

14   Japan and Spain

*   Allen, L., *Japan: The Years of Triumph* (Macdonald, 1971)
Beasley, W.E., *The Rise of Modern Japan* (Weidenfeld & Nicolson, 1990)
Beasley, W.E., *Japanese Imperialism 1894–1945* (Oxford, 1987)
**   Fewster, S., *Japan 1850–1985* (Longman, 1988)
Fraser, R., *Blood of Spain* (Penguin, 1979)
Horsley, W. and R. Buckley, *Nippon New Superpower: Japan since 1945* (BBC, 1990)
*   Mitchell, D., *The Spanish Civil War* (Granada, 1972)
Snellgrove, L.E., *Franco and the Spanish Civil War* (Longman, 1965)
Thomas, H., *The Spanish Civil War* (Penguin, 3rd edn, 1977)
*   Williams, B., *Modern Japan* (Longman, 1987)

15 and 16 Russia/the USSR since 1900

Acton, E., *Rethinking the Russian Revolution* (Arnold, 1990)

* Austin, M., *The Great Experiment: a Study of Russian Society* (English Universities Press, 1975)

** Aylett, J.F., *Russia in Revolution* (Hodder & Stoughton, 1992)

** Aylett, J.F., *Russia under Stalin* (Hodder & Stoughton, 1992)

** Bassett, J., *Socialism in One Country* (Heinemann, 1978)

Bullock, A., *Hitler and Stalin: Parallel Lives* (Harper Collins, 1991)

* Catchpole, B., *A Map History of Russia* (Heinemann, 1974)

Clark, R.W., *Lenin* (Faber & Faber, 1988)

Conquest, R., *The Great Terror* (Macmillan, 1968)

** Corfe, T., *Russia's Revolutions* (Cambridge University Press, 1994)

** Fiehn, T., *Russia and the USSR 1905–1941* (John Murray, 1996)

Frankland, M., *Khrushchev* (Penguin, 1966)

Freeborn, R., *A Short History of Modern Russia* (Hodder & Stoughton, 1966)

* Fry, D., *Russia: Lenin and Stalin* (Hamish Hamilton, 1966)

Grey, I., *Stalin* (Weidenfeld & Nicolson, 1979)

** Ingram, P., *The USSR 1905–1963* (Cambridge University Press, 1996)

** Kelly, N., *Russia 1905–56* (Heinemann, 1996)

Kochan, L., *The Making of Modern Russia* (Penguin, 1973)

** Laver, J., *Lenin: Liberator or Oppressor?* (Hodder & Stoughton, 1992)

** Laver, J., *Russia 1914–41* (Hodder & Stoughton, 1992)

** Laver, J., *Joseph Stalin: From Revolutionary to Despot* (Hodder & Stoughton, 1990)

** Laver, J., *The USSR 1945 to 1990* (Hodder & Stoughton, 1991)

** Laver, J., *Stagnation and Reform: the USSR 1964–1991* (Hodder & Stoughton, 1996)

** Lynch, M., *Stalin and Khrushchev* (Hodder & Stoughton, 1991)

Medvedev, R., *Let History Judge* (Spokesman, 1976)

Medvedev, R., *Khrushchev* (Anchor/Doubleday, 1983)

Montgomery-Hyde, H., *Stalin* (Hart-Davis, 1971)

* Pickering, S., *20th Century Russia* (Oxford, 1970)

* Pimlott, T., *The Russian Revolution* (Macmillan, 1984)

Roxburgh, A., *The Second Russian Revolution* (BBC, 1991)

Sakwa, R., *Gorbachev and his Reforms 1985–1990* (Philip Allan, 1990)

Taylor, A.J.P., *Lenin: October and After* (Purnell, vol. 3, ch. 37)

Westwood, J.N., *Endurance and Endeavour: Russian History 1812–1992* (Oxford, 1993)

** Willoughby, S., *The Russian Revolution* (Heinemann, 1996)

17 and 18 China since 1900

Bown, C., *China 1949–76* (Heinemann, 1978)

Chang, Jung, *Wild Swans* (HarperCollins, 1991)

Gray, J., *China under Mao* (Purnell, vol. 6, ch. 89)

* Fitzgerald, C.P., *Communism Takes China* (Macdonald, 1969)

Gittings, J., *China Changes Face: The Road From Revolution 1949–89* (Oxford, 1990)

Karnow, S., *Mao and China: Inside China's Cultural Revolution* (Penguin, 1985)

** Lynch, M., *China: From Empire to People's Republic* (Hodder & Stoughton, 1996)

* Mitchison, L., *China in the Twentieth Century* (Oxford, 1970)

** Morrison, D., *The Rise of Modern China* (Longman, 1988)

Moseley, G., *China: Empire to People's Republic* (Batsford, 1968)

** Roper, M, *China in Revolution 1911–1949* (Arnold, 1969) (documentary)

Spence, J., *The Search for Modern China* (Norton, 1990)

** Steele, P., *China Under Communism* (Arnold, 1987)

* Tarling, N., *Mao and the Transformation of China* (Heinemann, 1977)

** Williams, S., *China Since 1949* (Macmillan, 1986)

19 and 20 The USA since 1900

* Bassett, M., *The American Deal 1932–64* (Heinemann, 1977)

* Catchpole, B., *A Map History of the United States* (Heinemann, 1972)

** Campbell, Ian, *The USA 1917–1941* (Cambridge University Press, 1996)

Colaiaco, J., *Martin Luther King* (Macmillan, 1988)

Conkin, P.K., *The New Deal* (Routledge, 1968)
Galbraith, J.K., *The Great Crash* (Deutsch, 1980)
Garraty, J., *The American Nation* (Harper & Row, 7th edn 1990)
* Hill, C.P., *A History of the United States* (Arnold, 1974)
* Hill, C.P., *The USA Since the First World War* (Allen & Unwin, 1967)
McCoy, D.R., *Coming of Age: The United States During the 1920s and 1930s* (Penguin, 1973)
** Mills, R., M. Samuelson and C. White, *The USA Between the Wars* (John Murray, 1996)
Morgan, T., *FDR* (biography of F.D. Roosevelt) (Grafton/Collins, 1985)
Preston, S., *Twentieth Century US History* (Collins, 1992)
** Scott-Baumann, M., *The USA Between the Wars* (Hodder & Stoughton, 1992)
** Simkin, J., *USA Domestic Policies 1945–80* (Spartacus, 1986)
** Smith, N., *The USA 1917–1980* (Oxford, 1996)
Snowman, D., *America Since 1920* (Heinemann, 1978)
* Traynor, J., *Roosevelt's America 1932–41* (Macmillan, 1983)
* Triggs, T.D., *Boom and Slump in Inter-War America* (Macmillan, 1984)
Zinn, H., *A People's History of the United States* (Longman, 1980)

21 and 22   Decolonization and after
** Aylett, J.F., *South Africa* (Hodder & Stoughton, 1996)
Brown, J.M., *Modern India: The Origins of an Asian Democracy* (Oxford, 1985)
Courrière, Y., *The Algerian War* (Purnell, vol. 6, ch. 81)
Davenport, T.R.H., *South Africa: A Modern History* (Macmillan, 1987)
Davidson, B., *Africa in Modern History* (Macmillan, 1992)
Davidson, B., *Modern Africa: A Social and Political History* (Longman, 1989)
Freund, W., *The Making of Contemporary Africa* (Macmillan, 1984)
Hargreaves, J.D., *Decolonisation in Africa* (Longman, 1988)
* Hatch, J., *Africa – The Rebirth of Self-Rule* (Oxford, 1970)
Horne, A., *Dien Bien Phu* (Purnell, vol. 6, ch. 81)
Horne, A., *A Savage War of Peace* (Algeria) (Macmillan, 1972)
Huddleston, T., *Naught for Comfort* (Fount, 1977)
Huddleston, T., *Return to South Africa* (Harper Collins, 1991)
Hoskyns, C., *Two Tragedies: Congo and Biafra* (Purnell, vol. 6, ch. 85)
Jeffrey, R., *Asia: The Winning of Independence* (Macmillan, 1981)
* Le May, G.L., *Black and White in South Africa* (Macdonald, 1969)
Luthuli, A., *Let My People Go* (Fontana, 1963)
Mackic, J., *The Indonesian Confrontation* (Purnell, vol. 6, ch. 91)
Moon, P., *India: Independence and Partition* (Purnell, vol. 5, ch. 75)
Pandey, B.N., *The Rise of Modern India* (Hamish Hamilton, 1972)
Noman, O., *Pakistan: Political and Economic History Since 1947* (Kegan Paul, 1988)
Parsons, A., *From Cold War to Hot Peace: UN Interventions 1947–1995* (Penguin, 1995)
Phillips, D., *Cyprus: The Failure of Force* (Purnell, vol. 6, ch. 91)
** Roberts, M., *South Africa* (Longman, 1987)
** Simkin, J., *Africa Since 1945* (Spartacus, 1986)
Stephens, I., *The Pakistanis* (Oxford, 1968)
* Taylor, J.K.G., and J.A. Kohler, *Africa and the Middle East* (Arnold, 1984)
Thompson, L., *A History of South Africa* (Yale University Press, 1990)
Tutu, D., *Hope and Suffering* (Fount, 1984)
** Walker, A., *The Modern Commonwealth* (Longman, 1975)
* Watson, J.B., *Empire to Commonwealth* (Dent, 1971)
* Watson, J., *The West Indian Heritage* (John Murray, 1982 edn)

23 and 24   The world economy and population
Ashworth, W., *A Short History of the International Economy Since 1850* (Longman, 1987 edn)
Borthwick, M., *Pacific Century: The Emergence of Modern Pacific Asia* (Westview Press, 1972)
Brandt, W., *World Armament and World Hunger* (Gollancz, 1986)
The Brandt Report: North–South, a Programme for Survival (Pan, 1980)
Population Growth (VCOAD Publications)
van der Wee, H., *Prosperity and Upheaval: The World Economy 1945–1980* (Penguin, 1991)

Index